FOUNDATIONS OF DIGITAL EVIDENCE

George L. Paul

AMERICAN BAR ASSOCIATION
Defending Liberty
Pursuing Justice

Printed in the United States of America

12 11 10 09 08 5 4 3 2 1

Library of Congress Cataloging-in-Publication Data

Paul, George L.
    Foundations of digital evidence / George L. Paul.—1st ed.
      p. cm.
    Includes bibliographical references and index.
    ISBN 978-1-60442-104-0 (alk. paper)
    1. Electronic discovery (Law)—United States. 2. Discovery (Law)—United States.
  3. Electronic records—Law and legislation—United States. I. Title.

KF9650.P385 2008
347.73'64—dc22

2008022246

Discounts are available for books ordered in bulk. Special consideration is given to state bars, CLE programs, and other bar-related organizations. Inquire at Book Publishing, ABA Publishing, American Bar Association, 321 North Clark Street, Chicago, Illinois 60654-7598.

www.ababooks.org

Foreword

The common law tradition has always prided itself on its ability to respond to societal change in an incremental manner so that the change in the law is equal to but no greater than the change in society. The common law then becomes the perfect example of Burkean change: not the French Revolution, where the revolutionaries change everything including the names of the days of the week, but subtle change, where a tap on the accelerator is met by an equally slight application of the brake. Thus, when a person sold a horse to a neighbor, there was no need to inquire as to who first sold that horse that was again being sold. Who would care? But, when that person bought a Buick from a dealer, who bought it from the manufacturer, and the societal demands of an industrial economy required it (including the need to encourage more people to buy more Buicks), the law abolished the quaint notion of privity and permitted the car buyer's lawsuit against the car manufacturer, leaving for another day what would happen when the buyer tried to sue the company that made the brakes that the manufacturer had bought and placed in the Buick. This development was matched by interpreting the capacious due process clause to permit the buyer of the car to sue the manufacturer in the buyer's home state of New Jersey even though the manufacturer's factory was in Michigan, leaving for another day what would happen when the manufacturer's factory was in Tokyo.

It is impossible to exaggerate the changes in society that the computer has made. It is simply a fact that people remain tethered to electronic devices all day long and then go home to more electronic devices including a home computer that acts as a mailbox, jukebox, and movie theater. Yet, this nearly endless production and receipt of digital information has resulted in a remarkably slight change in the law. The slow and steady pace of common law development of case law seems to be continuing as courts use traditional concepts in new areas so that, for example, the ancient notion of "spoliation," i.e. destroying evidence to secure an advantage, as refined by the common law, is now applied in the digital world. Indeed, while they were not the product of case law, the new federal rules pertaining to electronic discovery made important changes in requiring the parties to discuss issues pertaining to electronic discovery, speaking to the form of production, the inadvertent production of privileged information and the good faith destruction of electronic information. But no one could accuse these new rules of being revolutionary, for they left to the development of the case law fundamental questions such as the correct balance between cost and value and the exact nature of the preservation obligation before and after litigation has begun.

Thus, some could look at the case law pertaining to electronic information and see a bucolic, Burkean landscape where there is perfect balance and peace; the changes being made in the fabric of the law by the revolutionary changes in the creation and receipt of digital information are subtle and no greater than absolutely necessary. If you picked up this book to consider an argument in favor of continuing this process of nearly imperceptible change, you picked up the wrong book. The thesis of this book is radical in the truest sense of that word: it demands that we look first at the roots of how information is now being created, and then demands that the legal rules pertaining to its acceptance in court be determined by a complete and thorough understanding of how the information is created, irrespective of the legal rules pertaining to information in old-fashioned books and other paper records. Paul's analysis is epistemological: how do we know that this information, in digital form, may be trusted and may be the empirical basis of knowledge as to how an event occurred?

He starts with authenticity and with the present rules that border on the tautological: we admit information when it appears to be what it purports to be or is the result of a process used to produce a result, if that process produces an "accurate" result. Instead, Paul insists that we first understand completely and thoroughly how this particular digital information came into existence and how different that process may have been from our traditional notions of how information comes into existence. He then demands that, once we are thoroughly grounded in the technology of the creation of digital information, we ask tough questions before we rely on it: (1) who created the system that generated the information and what were her intentions?; (2) what procedures and processes did she use and were they likely to produce the result she sought?; (3) what testing, if any, did she use as she proceeded to make sure that she was following the processes she had to in order to get the result she wanted?; (4) after she finished, what effort did she make to insure that the information that was created is the information that is before the court?; (5) is it possible that the information has been tampered with and is it not the information the system produced?; (6) if the information is purported to have been created at a certain time and on a certain computer, and those facts are significant in this lawsuit, how can we be certain that the computer correctly captured the time and place of creation?

Once the question of authenticity has been addressed, the court turns to admissibility and to the thickets of the hearsay rule. Paul's exploration of the hearsay rule as applied by the courts is not pleasant reading for a trial judge like me. The courts have not covered themselves with glory. Instead, as Paul convincingly shows, the courts have reached radically different and irreconcilable results in the application of what is supposed to be a relatively simple question: was this digital information a "business record" produced in the ordinary course of business? The problem is that the business record rule and digital information have little in common. The business record rule makes sense when Bob Cratchit methodically noted who owed Scrooge how much in Scrooge's book every day when Cratchit came to work. That rule has very little to do with a salesman in Arizona calling in an order to a computer using a voice recognition software system that generated, without human involvement, an invoice and an account receivable. As Paul shows, if the courts equate the two systems and find their products as equally reliable business records, they abnegate their responsibility to make any inquiry as to whether the system that produced the invoice was in fact designed to be as reliable as Cratchit's entries. Without such inquiry, all digital information will be admitted into evidence, no matter how error prone and corrupt the system that produced it.

Having examined the deficiencies in the present rules, Paul then creates a new paradigm of admissibility that focuses on system reliability: how can one ascertain whether the system that produced the information was reliable? He then produces a series of case studies by other authors that illustrate how the standards of system reliability can be addressed on a daily basis in specific industries. The case studies show how existing computer systems can be used to produce reliable digital information that should be admitted into evidence.

It may be odd to describe Paul, an obviously bookish Yalie who practices law, as a revolutionary but he has, like it or not, earned that title. He is, after all, suggesting an entirely new way of looking at how digital information should be considered by the court, and the consequential need to create new rules of evidence based not on tradition but on how digital information actually comes into creation.

Will George Paul prevail? Only time will tell but there are some powerful forces arrayed against his approach. First, to the extent that any change in the rules is implicated, there is inertia and the reality that any rule-making process will take several years. Second, there is the problem that the American courts, particularly federal ones, do not try many cases. This means that there are precious few lawyers who actually make a living trying cases. Those who do know that you learn the rules of evidence not in a classroom, but in a courtroom in the few seconds a lawyer has to say "objection." The absence of a true trial bar that knows the rules of evidence and will get excited about rule-change is a significant problem.

In the meanwhile, this book serves as a remarkable, albeit demanding, intellectual exercise. It does not apologize for the need of its reader to spend some time trying to understand how computers work and guides the reader through that process as it affects evidentiary problems. It makes a most compelling case for the need for that understanding and for awareness of the reality that digital information, far from being inherently reliable, can be manipulated, corrupted, and misused. The case it makes for rule changes based on that understanding and awareness is so well made that those who argue that no rule changes are needed will have to answer Paul's arguments if they expect to be taken seriously. In that sense, the book is a watershed and demands the attention of those who hope to understand how courts and lawyers will have to engage in the most revolutionary and creative thinking to forge rules of evidence that will make sense in a society utterly dependent on digital information.

John M. Facciola[1]

---

1. United States Magistrate Judge, United States District Court for the District of Columbia.

Contents

Preface

This is a practical book about the new world of digital information. It discusses how to approach such information with a new awareness, so that you can do your job more effectively.

Trial advocates—whether plaintiff, defense, big city or country lawyer—will benefit from the exploration of issues, case studies, witness examinations, and illustrations contained here. This book is immediately useful, today, probably in all your cases.

The book is divided into four parts.

Part I contains an introduction, entitled *New World of Evidence*, which gives historical background and an explanation of why we are at a tipping point. Part I also contains *Understanding the Digital Realm*, which explains the way our informational records have changed. How should we view and understand them, so that we thereafter ask the right questions in any search for truth? What are the key evidentiary concepts implicated by the new writing? This chapter explores issues both on the discrete level of individual records and on a systems-wide level—made relevant by the fact that the "reading and writing games" comprising systems now regularly make statements that turn up as evidence.

Part II covers the grand topic "Authenticity." This is the first and no doubt the greatest of all evidentiary concepts. Knowing whether a record is the true and accurate deed, contract, invoice, death warrant, photograph, or statement of account has long been of evidentiary concern. Chapter 3, *The Existing Scheme Regarding Authenticity*, explains where things stand concerning the issue of getting writings admitted into evidence, and covers the foundational burden, called *authentication*, that exists under the Federal Rules of Evidence. Understating the issues in this chapter will help you authenticate digital evidence, or contest its admission under the existing evidentiary scheme. This chapter gives all practitioners and judges immediately useful practical tools.

Chapter 4 is the first of three chapters discussing the three principal foundations that determine whether a digital writing is authentic. Chapter 4 discusses the evidentiary concept *integrity* of information. Here, "integrity" refers to whether a set of information, often called an "information object" in this book, has changed through time and space. How do we test whether information has changed in the digital age? If the concept of an original record has been shattered, what, if anything, has taken its place? Can we resurrect a new regime of authenticity in the digital age?

Chapter 5 concerns the various ways evidence of time appears in digital records. As a key component of authenticity, time evidence can be either weak and probabilistic, or strong and tied to a regime designed to allow more-certain knowledge than mere circumstances of probability. A fellow litigator and expert on trusted time systems, Steven Teppler, coauthored this chapter.

Chapter 6 discusses the thorny problem of identity. How do we know who is playing in our information systems? Is there a way to keep track? Who authored a digital record? Who signed it? Who sent it? Who modified it? Together with integrity, evidence of identity is perhaps the most philosophically difficult issue discussed here. Given that information systems are "complex," it is often difficult to determine who did what—just as it is difficult to determine causation in an economy or an ecosystem. Complex systems make it hard to test for cause and effect. They are characterized by "emergence," where lesser elements interact to form a larger whole that is far different than the sum of its parts. This leads to the next topic: the fact these emergent systems now regularly make statements appearing in court as evidence.

Part III thus covers hearsay, the other great evidentiary idea. This is the notion that the makers of statements need to be present in court and subject to cross examination—not have their statements come into evidence from others, repeating what was said. Information systems implicate the hearsay idea. They are, all the time, making statements memorialized in digital records. They make statements about events. They summarize information. They do computations and state results. Most often this information is inserted into records without any knowledge or action by human beings. Chapter 7 thus covers the hearsay rule and business records exception, and the cases grappling with whether information systems, when they generate information intended to be assertions, are covered by the hearsay rule and its great nineteenth-century exception. Chapter 8 then discusses the new, emerging norm of systems reliability. Under what circumstances should judges admit computer-generated information into evidence, and what factors should be used to test it, if we are to be intellectually honest and current about evidentiary concepts?

Part IV, written by expert contributors, contains case studies illustrating the points in the book. Three case studies illustrate the concept of *eunomia*. Ed Chase has written about the digital signature capabilities of the common file format PDF. Appendix A thus demonstrates there are already applications available that can be used to create informational records with testable integrity of information, and strong evidence about the identity of the entity originating the record. Indeed, there can be many variations on the theme, where many identities can work on a record and an application and its record can keep reliable track of who did what.

But *eunomic* regimes can also be custom-tailored by groups of players, where all agree on certain rules for a "game of information." Grace Powers's Appendix B discusses how players in the mortgage industry created a digital analogue for an artifact-based record—the unique promissory notes that have so long been used in lending. If players agree to abide by rules for certain *eunomic* techniques, then strong demonstrations of proof about ownership, possession, and origination of digital information can be accomplished. This has allowed the mortgage industry, using even the slippery soup of digital information, to empower players to buy and sell assets, all while complying with strict substantive legal requirements.

Rounding off the study of *eunomia* in Part IV, Timothy S. Reiniger explains how the venerable notary profession is adapting to the changes brought on by the digital age. The notarial process is used in the United States, but it is perhaps even more important in other nations. In the United States, the act of notarization gives important presumptions about the authenticity of records, and legal systems accordingly depend on notaries to lend authenticity to records and transactions. But what happens when notaries leave the world of pen and ink and physical objects, and try to provide their century-old function in electronic transactions? In Appendix C, Reiniger explains a new regime that provides authenticity, integrity, and identity, using both digital processes and real-world human actors.

Next, we get a taste of what is going on in other countries such as Argentina, France, Germany, Japan, and Russia in a case study called *Digital Evidence in Five Nations*. Stephen Mason of Great Britain has given us a sampling of how these nations have recognized the importance of digital evidence. They too have recognized that certain ordered regimes of information are preferable to depending on the chance existence of circumstantial evidence to establish the authenticity of records. As discussed in the *Introduction,* Mason's Appendix D shows that other nations are not strictly technologically neutral.

But what of the fact that digital evidence continues to be handled and processed after it gets taken up into the justice system? Does this not raise important issues given its highly malleable nature? Victor Limongelli has provided a case study, *The Role of the Vendor and Specialized Software in the Handling of Digital Evidence,* to discuss how vendors who handle digital information in its collection and processing need to be concerned with the very same issues as are implicated beforehand. How can participants in the justice system prove information has integrity after others have handled it? Or, if processing by a vendor's information system is involved, and a system purports to do certain things with the evidence, are there not towering *reliability* issues implicated?

Complementing the case studies on *eunomia* are a two illustrations of *dysnomia.*

Steve Teppler's real-world federal court case study *Will the Real "When" Please Stand Up?* addresses a company's poor handling of its own digital information. It illustrates the electronic files involved in the dispute, and a study of how the metadata involved betrayed an unreliable handling of information.

The final case study is *A Day in the Life of the Printed Electronic Document,* which also concerns an issue of evidence that arose in a federal court derivative action—litigation over the authenticity of a consulting agreement and board approval of that agreement. The case study examines how, without a *eunomic* scheme, it can be practically impossible to test a printout of an electronic record in the face of false testimony about its authenticity. In order to show that the risk of people "manufacturing" such business documents is not overblown, the study includes testimony and e-mail evidence of a participant in the scheme to backdate the document, which was a financial record of a publicly held company.

The book is written in nonlinear fashion. It attempts to be as practical as possible, and discusses as much as it can about admissibility and what practitioners need to understand about the weight of digital evidence. But some chapters are somewhat philosophical, because in order to truly understand, you need to go relentlessly to the heart of the matter. And some chapters are legalistic in that they discuss precedent and holdings in the fashion found in most law books. But it simply was not possible to include case law about all our topics, because the concepts implicated here have not yet percolated into the mindset of the profession, much less made their ways into courts and court decisions. Luckily, there are a few landmark cases that promote discussion.

Acknowledgments

The book was written under the auspices of the American Bar Association. The ABA has had a long involvement in the development of the law of evidence. This has ranged from Roscoe Pound's call for a new law of evidence, made at the ABA Annual Meeting in Minneapolis in 1906; to the ABA's "Committee on Improvements in the Law of Evidence," often just called the "Wigmore Committee;" to the famous and brutal debates between Professors Wigmore and Morgan of the early 1940s, published in the *ABA Journal,* about the American Law Institute's ill-fated "Model Code of Evidence;" to the activities of the ABA-affiliated National Conference of Commissioners on Uniform State Laws, which produced the Uniform Rules of Evidence, which had an impact on the federal rules we mostly use today.

Many leading experts have contributed to this book, which began as a series of conversations among friends, the members of the ABA's Information Security Committee. How can we know that information is authentic? How can we know "who" we are dealing with in the digital realm? The Information Security Committee, the author found, contained technologists and lawyers who knew more about such digital information issues than any other similar group. The members of that committee are invaluable resources, and many of its specialists have contributed.

Of special note, Bruce H. Nearon, the coauthor of a previous work, *The Discovery Revolution: E-Discovery Amendments to the Federal Rules of Civil Procedure,* gave life and impetus to the project for several years. Bruce is an inspiration and good friend.

Hoyt Kesterson II, one of the deans of Information Security in the United States and worldwide, spent hours speaking with the author about concepts and terminology, and even editing text. Mr. Kesterson is an expert on the asymmetric cryptography discussed here, and the leader of groups that have published international standards on the topic. Steve Teppler, a digital information expert and commercial litigator, took the lead as coauthor on Chapter 5's discussion of Time, as well as authoring a case study. A team of Randy Sabbett, Russell Shumway, and Sonya Sigler all contributed to the text and organization of the chapter on Identity.

Ben Wilson, a practitioner in Salt Lake City and longtime expert on digital evidence issues, supervised the peer review of the book, coordinating its review by technical experts. He also was greatly helpful in editing.

And other important contributors and thinkers were involved. Mark Brown, Kathryn Coburn, Paul F. Doyle, Todd Erb, Cece Gassner, Justin Henderson, Julie Knoop,

Jennifer Kurtz, Charles Merrill, John Messing, Marshall Ray, Gib Sorebo, Jon Stanley, Paul Starrett, Glenn Tenney, Lucy Thomson, John Tomaszewski, and Stephen Wu have all contributed ideas or text to the book.

Finally, there were distinguished members of the bench and bar who provided a final peer review of the book. These included Professor John Langbein, Sterling Professor of Law and Legal History of the Yale Law School, who reviewed the text on the history of the law of evidence and made suggestions about how to improve it; Jason Baron, Director of Litigation at the National Archives and Records Administration, College Park, Maryland, who supplied suggestions generally and about how to discuss the nature of scientific revolutions and the concept of "falsification"; and Ralph Losey, a partner at Akerman Senterfitt in Orlando, Florida, a national expert in e-discovery, who made general comments about hashing and other issues.

George L. Paul
Phoenix, Arizona
February 2008

About the Author

George L. Paul is a partner in the Business Litigation Section of Lewis and Roca LLP in Phoenix, Arizona. He has over 25 years of experience in business litigation and as a trial lawyer. He does both defense and plaintiff work.

He moved to Phoenix after graduating from Dartmouth College (B.A.) and Yale Law School (J.D.). The father of two teenagers, Mr. Paul enjoys fly-fishing, backpacking, hunting, and natural history study. Through the years he has seen, photographed, or made sound recordings of over 2000 bird species, many in the forests of Latin America. His intellectual interests include the study of complex systems, the philosophy of language, history, and the conservation of biodiversity.

Mr. Paul has written or co-authored several articles and a book on legal topics, including *The Authenticity Crisis, The Discovery Revolution,* and *Information Inflation: Can the Legal System Adapt?* He is currently active in the ABA's Section of Science and Technology (former Council Member), the ABA Section of Litigation, and the Law Practice Management Section. Mr. Paul is founder and past Chair of the Arizona State Bar's Section of Internet, E-Commerce & Technology Law.

Introduction

After digital information is obtained in discovery, how does one get such information admitted into evidence? Must one lay a foundation? If so, how and what are the governing rules? How might you keep digital information out of evidence? And is that realistic, given the existing scheme regarding admissibility? But if there is a way to do it, don't you want to know your best arguments?

And what if the digital information is hearsay? Did a "system" make a statement, without any person being involved? How does one address the hearsay rule in such a situation? How does one exclude such evidence as not fitting any hearsay exception? Are there legal arguments? Are there foundations that must first be laid? What is the developing law?

Accordingly, this book explores the admissibility of digital evidence.

THE WEIGHT OF THE EVIDENCE

But admissibility is not everything. There are other evidentiary concerns, indeed, which are probably far more important to the practitioner than admissibility. One of these is the *weight* of the evidence—the dynamic whereby the fact finder compares information to determine what fits into his mental construct, and what is rejected, and thus falls away.

Accordingly, this book is useful to litigators doing their jobs long before any trial process. A litigator must know how to ask questions of the information he receives in discovery. All the while, he analyzes the evidence because its authenticity and persuasiveness are his critical raw material—his force and power and the salvation of his client. It is this dynamic of *weight* that he uses to "build a case." Building a case is overwhelmingly fun—a creative process of the highest order. And the stakes are high: In our system, litigation lawyers not only build cases, they build *opposing* cases—antithetical mental constructs unleashed to annihilate one another. In our ancient ritual, litigation field marshals try to outflank each other. They unravel, unzip, disassemble, dissolve, and implode each other—quite suddenly, in many instances. The pop each other's conceptual bubbles. The way they do this is through the weight of the evidence. And in 98 percent of the cases, they do this long before any trial process.

Accordingly, litigators must know how to make digital evidence persuasive. Equally, if not more important, they must know how to *test* digital evidence when it threatens their case. If they know what they are doing, they can launch a crushing flank attack on the opponent. Such information is invaluable to an advocate.

NEW FOUNDATIONS

But in order to do any of this, we must ask, "What are the foundational bedrocks?" What are the new modes of reasoning, the new logic? How do we arrive at a trusted idea like "this is authentic," but with regard to new types of information that defy old paradigms? How do we either establish elements or point out they are missing?

Quite simply, how can lawyers of the new millennium do their jobs without understanding basic concepts about digital evidence? Without an understanding of how to test, prove, or attack the information of our new age, aren't lawyers mere ghosts of the past? Where should we test and probe, and where do we shore up? Do we understand the new information well enough to do these traditional jobs?

Digital evidence needs questioning like all evidence, but a new and different sort of questioning is in order, and this book points out where to begin one's thinking. This is a key part of our professional skill set from this point forward. If we abandon our role as society's experts in information, we loose our power and importance—our righteous calling as the high priests of information. This book is thus a call to a new professionalism.

JUDGES, PROFESSORS, AND STUDENTS OF THE LAW

But certain cases do go to trial, and it is those cases that become the showcases. It is those cases that make the law as it co-evolves with an ever-changing culture. In these cases, judges in the U.S. make rulings on admissibility. Decisions about admissibility have been trivialized of late, as judges were disempowered by the codification of evidence law and the strict rationality tests chosen to guide admissibility. But armed with a new awareness, thinking judges might now reconsider their habitual admissibility determinations—including the foundations necessary to properly authenticate digital information or qualify statements of information systems as reliable.

But in addition, increasingly in the United States and overwhelmingly throughout the world, judges and magistrates are the organs giving weight to evidence. Judges thus need to understand the new dynamics as well as any members of the profession. If they are considering digital information, they need to understand what they are weighing and how to weigh it.

Law students and their professors may read this book. They are the future of the profession, and in this instance we discuss nothing less than disputes being decided on true facts. And the book may be of interest to evidence scholars. It somewhat unabashedly throws down an intellectual gauntlet. It hints at a new scheme. Concepts underpinning many of the law's most basic assumptions are questioned. The book suggests some of these are now outdated, perhaps even the most important ones. And longstanding psychological constructs, adopted by our culture and legal system both, are implicated, and the book therefore tries to take its readers on a journey of sorts—outside their normal modes of thought.

In short, law is evolving at the start of the new millennium. We are at a crossroads—a change of phase. With our new information infrastructure, the concept of written evidence has reached a critical tipping point. Judges, professors, students, and thinkers must rewrite the rules. When something so important to civilization as writing suddenly morphs into a new system, the world's institutions, but particularly its legal systems, simply must adapt.

RELEVANCE TO BUSINESS AND INFORMATION GOVERNANCE

But foundations for digital information are essential to far more than litigation. Litigation is the resolution of unfortunate problems—an exception, one hopes, to the smooth operation of society. Businesses still need to think about these issues so they can properly create and handle the information of their enterprises. Unless business lawyers advise their clients how to handle information so as to establish proper foundations, a company's records will be suspect. They will be compromised, or become worthless through lack of provable authenticity. Increasingly, federal schemes mandating certain provable characteristics about information will require businesses, and their advisors, to understand digital information. We see such schemes arising in health care, the financial sector, and in publicly traded companies. Without an understanding of the new foundations, complying with rapidly evolving substantive law about digital information will not be possible.

For example, if a businessperson is required to prove that a digital file was not edited during the last five years, how does she know how to do that? Is she currently, given her setup, even capable of doing it? How can she test whether a certain person really "signed" something, if the information is digital? How can she know when something happened, and trust that it is an accurate time she is using? We provide case studies to demonstrate these challenges, and show how certain businesses have already met them successfully.

One function of this book, therefore, is that it provides a road map about how information's design and implementation by industry, government, and citizens must henceforth evolve so as to provide good "information governance." There can be no solid foundation underlying authentic informational records unless systems record enough data to allow testing for certain attributes. Overwhelmingly, our current systems lack good information governance, and we therefore cannot test for truth in relevant areas. We are relegated to consideration of the sloppy circumstances. Sometimes there is good information, but most of the time there is not. We are adrift.

But this book points out there are ways to design regimes of information that give "strong" knowledge, tantamount to a "demonstration," as the first evidence scholars called it. There are digital information schemes that allow one to have strong tests for authenticity, integrity, identity, and time. There are even ways, using such schemes, to recreate the concept of an original document. Accordingly, management of information needs to co-evolve in accordance with our new understanding of writing forms and the new-age written record. This is the coming revolution in the world of business records that will unfold over the next two decades. As explained in this book, we must evolve towards *eunomia*,[1] or good information governance in societal records.

RELEVANCE TO SOCIETY'S LARGER SEARCH FOR TRUTH

The book is also relevant to the larger society. The word "evidence" is a legal word, but at the same time it is also an everyday word used by laypeople. What is the evidence? What is the truth? Citizens will always ultimately demand an ability to learn the truth about the past—whether it be an historical event, a government scandal, or the facts of a personal matter. In the United States, we certainly assume a citizen's power to get at the truth is something our society values and will not lightly discard.

A presumption of this book is that the twenty-first century wants and deserves a skill set empowering the discovery of truth. Thus, the observations here are of value to an emerging intellectual fabric. Society must come to grips with whether it currently has an ability to learn the truth about everyday communications, agreements, transactions, and indeed all types of records of digital information. As explained below, we currently exist in a regime of *untestability*. Can society empower its citizens, historians, and auditors? Or must written assertions be taken on faith?

Society henceforward needs new skills, and a new understanding, for a new age of information.

THE CONSEQUENCES OF NEUTRALITY

In the 1990s certain states, most notably Utah and Washington, but also to some extent California, began legislating technological specifications for digital evidence records. But during 1999 and 2000, a strong movement of "technological neutrality" appeared in U.S. law. This started with the 1999 Uniform Electronic Transactions Act (UETA), published by the National Conference of Commissioners on Uniform State Laws (NCCUSL). The Act defined an "electronic signature" as "an electronic sound, symbol, or process attached to or logically associated with a record and executed or adopted by a person with the intent to sign the record." The UETA Comments made clear that anything electronic would suffice—from a mere "click" in a Web browser, to a recording of a voice on an answering machine, and so on. "Electronic records" were similarly technologically generic. Accordingly, generally under UETA as a matter of substantive law, any type of digital information could be either a signature or a record, with the totality of all the circumstantial evidence—digital and real world both—being relevant and necessary.

This neutrality policy was made a matter of preemptive federal law in the Electronic Signatures in Global and National Commerce Act of 2000 (E-SIGN").[2] Under Section

---

1. "Good order," after the Goddess of order and good governance in Greek mythology, Eunomia.

2. UETA and E-SIGN did create the potential for resurrecting the concept of a digital original. See, e.g., 15 U.S.C. § 7201, which sets forth definitions and requirements for such things as "control" and a "single authoritative copy" of transferable records. In her Case Study in Appendix B, Grace Powers illustrates how the mortgage industry worked with these E-SIGN and UETA concepts, which in turn correlate to certain requirements in the Uniform Commercial Code, to create digital "originals" that can be bought and sold on markets.

101 (a)(2)(A)(ii) of E-SIGN, 15 U.S.C. § 7002 (a)(2)(A)(ii), there is an exception to preemption by the technologically neutral E-SIGN "only if" a state statute, rule, or regulation does not specify procedures that require or accord greater legal status to specific technologies or technical specifications. The United States thus became substantively "technologically neutral" with regard to digital evidence on October 1, 2000, the effective date of E-SIGN. We are in a wide-open, "anything goes" world of digital information.

Accordingly, this book includes a discussion of digital evidence regimes in five other nations—Argentina, France, Germany, Japan, and the Russian Federation—not only to show the international relevance of these issues, but also to highlight how the United States is in the minority position worldwide. By contrast to the U.S. policy of technological neutrality, other countries have already embraced certain of the eunomic solutions we discuss here, as a matter of substantive law, and either mandate them or give them the benefit of presumptions in dispute resolution and commerce. In short, other nations have done what certain of the states in the United States started doing back in the mid-1990s until the neutrality policy was implemented in 2000.

Because our law does not legislate information regimes for interactions among citizens, but allows them to use any type of digital information and security procedures they choose, we in the United States must become expert in understanding the differences implicated by different information regimes. We therefore analyze information in its mode as evidence, and it is through the law and topic of evidence that we must address the issues in this book. Our policies mean we must understand the reality of the new information. Everyone here has a choice, and different schemes allowing different types of proof are used freely. It seems safe to say there will always be a need to get at the truth no matter what regime of information is involved.

PART I

Foundations

CHAPTER **1**

New World of Evidence

There has been a profound change in the world of law. After more than fifty centuries, civilization's system of writing changed suddenly. Indeed, within the course of merely twenty years, supporting technologies clustered into a completely new system of writing for our planet. The change has altered commerce, everyday communication, government, public discourse—indeed almost everything. Global human culture is forever different, and legal systems must now take this into account.

As a result, the *written record* was transformed. It is now fundamentally different than it was just a handful of years ago. And given the importance of written records to the law, a change in the nature of writing is perhaps the most significant thing that could happen in a legal system.

At issue is the digital information infrastructure that evolved at the end of the twentieth century. It has triggered a revolution in the world of evidence. Indeed, the legal profession is just now beginning to acknowledge, and with considerable confusion, what has happened.

From civilization's beginnings, writing was carried on physical material. One made a mark, and writing was thereafter enshrined on an artifact. Writing had a comfortable, static quality about it. Records were lifeless and lasting, except for a slow decay of inanimate matter. This quality was the records' beauty and usefulness, and at root, the foundation of both common-sense notions and legal systems of "evidence." Information was a collection of *things,* and it was in that physical aspect that we tested whether information had been altered. We celebrated the *original* artifact—the *thing* that gave birth to and thereafter carried the writing.

But lumps of matter do not make writing anymore. Written records are simply collections of information—information objects—that do not depend on matter for life. Beauty and usefulness are no longer immutability, but indeed precisely the opposite: editability. To read now, we of necessity see a presentation many levels abstracted. Before we view the presentation, the cards have been reshuffled below the table. But is there a record of any reshuffling? Is it possible to test if and how things were reshuffled? Given the evolution of information objects that now live apart from artifacts, the answer is a shocking and emphatic *no.*

No. It is not possible to conduct such a test unless special steps are taken in advance. And this marks an enormous change in civilization—the widespread inability to test whether informational records have changed through time. This book addresses this

3

authenticity crisis and what lawyers and others need to know to work through it if they want to engage in a "scientific" analysis of informational records.

The change from artifact to shape-shifting view results from the fact that recorded information now issues from complex systems. Indeed, such systems insert their own writing into records, and this too can be erased or edited. Even if such behavior were just one machine connected to one person, things would be complicated enough. But the new writing behavior, through the ability of many hundreds, thousands, and indeed millions of people to read and write to each another simultaneously, has resulted in new societal organs. These are networked, machine-human amalgamations—a mega-machine symbiosis that is *sui generis*.

Accordingly, the changes discussed in this book are more wonderful than if a new mountain had suddenly burst forth, to assume a shocking majesty in twenty brief years. This book discusses the emergence of an animate technology issuing from inanimate precursors. With the emergence of our new information ecosystems, we discuss a new form of life. The alien appears already to have captured civilization, and now coevolves with it.

Our legal and everyday political systems so far have few ideas about how to understand or tame the new life form. We now live in an age of information complexity, and that fact has largely destroyed our existing evidentiary scheme.

Let us examine the underpinnings of our current system, which is now beginning its next grand transition.

EMPIRICISM AND THE RISE OF THE LAW OF EVIDENCE

Lawyers go back to antiquity. During the early centuries of the profession, there was no formalized law of evidence as we know it. Indeed, as an example, until the beginning of the eighteenth century it was not permitted for accused felons even to call sworn witnesses in their defense. The system was markedly different then, and lawyers did not make a science out of collecting and testing information. Much stock was put in the power of the oath, and in turn, pains were taken to avoid conflicts of oaths by forbidding parties and witnesses with interest from testifying. The justice system was still moving out of the premodern era where it depended on religion—if not to resolve disputes, then at least to give legitimacy to the system and ensure acceptance of outcomes. For example, even in criminal trials deciding whether people should be put to death, it was not until 1696 that the system tolerated a conflict of oaths between testifying witnesses.[1]

---

1. During the seventeenth century the system of trials and evidence was still largely in a pre-modern era. Criminal defendants could not testify in their own defense, nor could they call sworn witnesses, although on occasion, people were allowed to talk, or affirm not upon oath, in their defense. George Fisher, in *The Jury's Rise of Lie Detector*, 107 YALE L. J. 575 (1997), discusses the highly charged political atmosphere of the 1680s, which saw many prominent citizens executed for treason upon oath of the infamous prosecution witness, Titus Oates, who told a tale of a Popish Plot to murder the king. During this period, the evidentiary rule still did not allow criminal defendants to call witnesses under oath in their defense. But the social standing of the potential targets of such treason prosecutions led to a major piece of legislation: the Treason Act of 1696. For the first time, the Act permitted accused traitors to call sworn witnesses. The new rule allowing sworn testimony on behalf of treason defendants was then extended to all accused felons six years later, with 1 Anne. Ch. 9 § 3 (1702). Accordingly, for the first time the criminal justice system fully embraced the possibility of conflicting oaths. *See* Fisher, *supra*, at 615–24.

Law, accordingly, is a product of its times. Each era has its peculiar consciousness. Each has its own *zeitgeist*. As a subset of a culture, a legal system thus incorporates a culture's common understandings, including both its technologies and philosophies.

In much of European culture of the 1600s the prevailing thought was that everyone was born with innate knowledge. The Continent's dominant philosopher, René Descartes, assumed, as did everyone else, that the human mind contained considerable innate knowledge and principles. Descartes concentrated on the flow of the mind—its reasoning and trajectories. Indeed, he almost made a religion out of it, postulating, *Cogito ergo sum*. The idea of innate knowledge went back to Aristotle; was confirmed by the Church; and was not questioned in serious fashion by Descartes or anyone else.

But a new philosophy exploded onto the scene in the 1690s. This was the writing of John Locke of England. He was a modest and practical man, himself the son of a lawyer who, when he had attended the University of Oxford in mid-century, had studied the reigning philosophy, that of medieval thinkers called scholastics. They merged Judeo-Christian beliefs with teachings of the ancients—primarily Aristotle but also to some extent Plato.

In his *Essay on Human Understanding* (1689), Locke produced what many consider the beginning of modern philosophy. And it took the world by storm. It was not some arcane, metaphysical tract read only by abstract thinkers. It was presented to and consumed by the public; simply devoured by members of the reading class. The work quickly went through several editions in England. It was gobbled up in Holland, where extracts were published even before the work went into print. The German thinker Thomasius absorbed it, after which the *Essay* launched a new intellectual trajectory in Germany. The publisher of the second French edition of the *Essay* (1729), Pierre Coste, summed up the European enthusiasm in his preface to that edition:

> It is a masterpiece of one of the finest geniuses which England produced in the last century. Four English editions appeared under the author's eye within the space of ten or a dozen years; and the French translation which I published in 1700, having made it known in Holland, France, Italy and Germany, it was, and still is, as highly esteemed in those countries as it is in England, and the breadth, the depth, the precision and the clarity which distinguish it from beginning to end are the subject of ceaseless admiration. Finally, as its crowning distinction, the book has been, so to speak, adopted both at Oxford and Cambridge, where it is read and expounded to the students as the book best fitted to form their minds and widen their knowledge. So Locke now fills the place which Aristotle and his principal commentators have occupied hitherto in both these famous universities.[2]

Clearly, the times were electrified. To displace Aristotle's twenty-century reign, and to be taken up as the state-of-the-art philosophy at Oxford and Cambridge in just a few years, is a significant achievement.

So what was Locke writing about? What was so important to the European mind at the turn of the eighteenth century?

The principle question Locke addressed was posed at the time as: *Quid est Veritas?* What is truth?[3] How should humanity approach this problem? How can we know we

---

2. Quotation from the Preface of the Second French Edition of Locke's *Essay* is taken from Paul Hazard, The European Mind; The Critical Years (1680–1715) 248 (Yale University Press 1953).

3. Hazard, *supra* note 2, at 242.

are not deluding ourselves? Of course, readers should realize the question "*Quid est Veritas?*" is also perhaps the key question for any modern legal system. Its embrace marked the beginning of modern law.

Locke's innovation was to look not in some faraway sphere, but inside the human mind. How is it we come to understand things? How should we classify our search for truth?

To answer those questions, Locke's *Essay on Human Understanding* made the first systematic study of how the human mind arrives at knowledge and understanding. Demolishing the long-accepted tenet of innate knowledge, Locke asserted that everything we know is in the form of "ideas" that come from either sensation or reflection on other ideas. When we use our senses our mind soaks things up like a sponge, or fills a blank piece of paper, and then combines and manipulates the ideas absorbed into more-complex ideas. As a consequence, said Locke, people have different mental abilities. They are subject to varying memories and subjectivities. The mind has a reality all its own, and the systematic study of its various inputs and processes allows the only surefire search to determine our understanding of *truth*. It all sounds self-evident today, but at the time it was groundbreaking.

The Modern Notion of "The Fact" Is Born as a Result of Empiricism

Locke's philosophy was called "empiricism." It marked a change in Western thought and deeply affected the West's legal systems. In the classic work *La Crise de la Conscience Européene* (Boivin: Paris 1935), intellectual historian Paul Hazard asserted that it was Locke who invested "the fact" with its "due status and sovereign dignity." Suddenly, people understood that facts were psychological entities—mental constructs—based on the absorption and consideration of data. Human understanding of knowledge and truth was conceived as the compilation of how all our ideas and impressions were juxtaposed within the mind:

> Since the mind, in all its thoughts and reasonings, hath no other immediate object but its own ideas, which it alone does or can contemplate, it is evident that our knowledge is only conversant about them . . . knowledge then seems to me to be nothing but the perception of the connexion and agreement, or disagreement and repugnancy, of any of our ideas.[4]

The interplay of how all our ideas either connect or repel each other results in a "fact." A fact emerges out of a milieu of circumstances.

Locke went further, and some of his writing seemed custom-designed for the legal profession. Book IV of the *Essay* was about "Knowledge and Probability," and included such chapters as "Of the Degrees of our Knowledge," "Of Judgment," "Of Probability," and "Of the Degrees of Assent."[5] Locke posited that some facts could be known with enough certainty to warrant the term "knowledge." A certain type of knowledge, akin almost to a mathematical proof, was called a "demonstration." One would use reasoning and new facts brought into a situation in order to achieve definite knowledge about it.

---

4. *See* JOHN LOCKE, AN ESSAY CONCERNING HUMAN UNDERSTANDING Book IV, ch. I, §§ 1–2.
5. *See* LOCKE, *supra*, chs. II, XIV, XV & XVI of Book IV.

Locke's example was that, through a demonstration, one could gain knowledge about whether the degrees in a triangle equaled the sum of the degrees in two right angles, something not immediately apparent by looking at a triangle and two right angles. Although his example was mathematical, Locke emphasized such demonstrations were not limited to the mathematical world and could exist elsewhere if one used reasoning, and extrinsic data, to clear up a situation in which the truth was not immediately apparent.

But there was also a level of understanding that fell short of knowledge. This was called "probability," and it had various degrees of likelihood. Locke's example, going back again to the triangle, was to assume a mathematician told someone that a triangle had the same number of degrees as two right angles, but the listener had not personally observed such a demonstration. The hearer's understanding would not be one of knowledge, but of mere probability. Indeed, the testimony of people about facts was considered a prime example of understanding in probability.[6]

The Law Absorbs Empiricism into a New Law of Evidence

Empiricism affected lawyers deeply. They were quick to acknowledge it was by operation of the mind that courts consider facts, even explicitly acknowledging that facts were mental constructs. Facts were pieced together by comparing the data taken in by the mind, and the mind contemplating which data agreed, or disagreed, with other data. The idea of "circumstantial evidence" was thus given life in the law, and we now often use the shorthand term "weight of the evidence" to refer to this empirical insight.

To their credit, lawyers concluded that if there were a new, systematic way to approach the discovery of truth, such advances should be incorporated into their profession. Soon after Locke's *Essay* was published, lawyers began devising more-elaborate rules governing the circumstances under which different kinds of evidence should be admitted; who had to produce what species of evidence to move forward in a suit; and, critically, how to rank evidence as to reliability, or weight. What gave knowledge? And what merely indicated probability? What was permanent? What was transient? What was akin to a scientific proof? What was a mere soup of circumstances, conflicting testimonies, and thus subjective? What was a demonstration?

A more systematized law of evidence thus evolved shortly after the beginning of the eighteenth century. Law no longer depended primarily on religion to achieve consensus in resolving disputes. It now depended on a professed, systematic search for truth. It is no accident that the first treatise on evidence, Lord Geoffrey Gilbert's *The Law of Evidence*, was introduced by a salutation to Locke and explicitly credited the empirical revolution for its insights into evidence. Gilbert's treatise, the most influential of the eighteenth century, was not published until 1754, long after his death in the year 1726.

---

6. In Book IV's Chapter XV, "Of Probability," Locke asserts that the grounds of probability were two: conformity with our own experience, and testimony of others' experience. If testimony of others was considered to determine the probability of facts, Locke noted that the number, integrity, and skill of the witnesses were relevant, as were the consistency of the parts and circumstances of the relation, together with contrary testimonies. Part IV, ch. XV, § 4.

The book went through seven editions.[7] Scholars estimate the book was written some time during the first two decades of the eighteenth century and agree it accurately sums up the law about evidence at the time of its publication.[8] Indeed, Gilbert's *Law of Evidence* dominated the subject for almost a century.

At the beginning of his treatise, indeed in its second paragraph, Gilbert introduced Locke's idea that there are degrees of knowledge and understanding about the world: "[I]t has been observed by a very learned man that there are several degrees from perfect Certainty and Demonstration, down to improbability and unlikeliness, even to the confines of impossiblility." Gilbert then took up the notion that these degrees of likelihood corresponded to a *psychological realm*, where varying "Acts of the Mind" corresponded to truth in reality. Quoting from Locke, Gilbert called the varying degrees of evidence "Degrees of Assent," which ranged from "full Assurance and Confidence, quite down to Conjecture, Doubt, Distrust, and Disbelief."[9]

The Law Understands Writings as "Demonstrations" and "Permanent Things"

Gilbert was probably concerned more in analyzing the weight and reliability of evidence than he was in discussing the concept of admissibility. Before ranking and classifying different types of evidence, Gilbert repeated the empirical insight that people are different, and that they come to facts by what they perceive, and that accordingly, the legal system needs to have a set of rules about the different types of evidence one must produce before going forward with a suit.

Gilbert's first and most critical ranking of evidence was made by differentiating written evidence from testimony. Critically, he classified writings as *permanent* forms of evidence, which were available at any time to be viewed. Writings were much more likely to allow a precise knowledge of a fact than was testimony. To the people of that century, writings were *qualitatively* more likely to allow knowledge than was testimony. Gilbert's example was that if two parties, J.S. and J.N., disputed who owned certain land, if we listened only to their testimony, we would have only the probability of knowing facts. We must choose between two outcomes, and if doing so is by means of their testimony, we are confined to the realm of probability.

But if one of these parties produced a written record about ownership, because it was a *permanent object* that could be viewed by the trier of fact, this third, intervening idea—the written deed—resolved the ambiguity of ownership in a formal way. It was a proof, or in the words of the empiricism of the day, a *demonstration*.[10] There had, in Locke's

---

7. John H. Langbein, *Historical Foundations of the Law of Evidence: A View from the Ryder Sources,* 96 COLUM. L. REV. 1168, 1172.

8. *See* Langbein, *supra* note 7. *See also* Thomas P. Gallanis, *The Rise of Modern Evidence Law,* 1999, 84 IOWA L. REV. 499, 515.

9. LORD GEOFFREY GILBERT, THE LAW OF EVIDENCE 1 (3rd ed. 1769).

10. If a "record be produced whereby the Land appears to be transferred from J.S. to J.N. now when we show any such third Perception, that doth necessarily infer the Relation in question, this is called Knowledge by Demonstration . . . This way of knowledge "is certainly the highest and clearest Knowledge that Mankind is capable of in his way of Reasoning, and therefore always to be sought when it may be had. . . . Demonstration is generally conversant about permanent Things, which being constantly obvious to our Senses, do afford to them a very clear and distinct Comparison, but transient Things that cannot always occur to our Senses are generally more obscure, because they have no constant Being, but must be retrieved by Memory and Recollection. *See* GILBERT, *supra* note 9, at 3.

methodology, been a demonstration of the facts, allowing knowledge rather than mere probability. This was because the consideration of written evidence allowed the fact finder to review permanent information himself, without the mediation of another person describing facts to him. Indeed, the law of evidence in its initial stages, roughly the eighteenth century and first couple of decades of the nineteenth century, was concerned primarily with how to treat and order written records.[11]

Thus, the "best evidence rule" was formally articulated: "The first therefore and most signal Rule, in Relation to Evidence, is this, That a Man must have the utmost Evidence, the Nature of the Fact is Capable of: For the Design of the Law is to come to rigid Demonstration in Maters of Right, and there can be no Demonstration of a Fact without the best Evidence that the Nature of the Thing is capable of . . ."[12] Many consider the best evidence rule to have addressed only the difference between originals and copies of written records. But the lawyers who originated our system of evidence in the eighteenth century considered that rule to prefer writings over testimony. As articulated, evidence should always strive towards achieving a *demonstration* of rights—knowledge of facts as opposed to mere probability.

Accordingly, from the beginning there has been an assumption in the law that writings concerned *permanent objects*. Gilbert arranged his treatise on the distinction between written and unwritten evidence, and "written evidence occupied virtually all the book."[13] One scholar has noted that "[t]he law of evidence in its infancy was concerned almost entirely with rules about the authenticity and the sufficiency of writings. What evidentiary practice there was in the civil trials that occurred [before the mid-eighteenth century] was mainly concerned with problems of written evidence."[14] Various types of writing were preferred over other types of writing. There was little effort spent analyzing evidentiary rules of oral testimony.

Scholars have confirmed that this concentration on writings, and their celebration as permanent forms of proof, was not a peculiarity in Gilbert's treatise. In fact, analysis of evidentiary decisions at the time reveals that most early decisions about evidence were about writings. This was because, as Gilbert put it, "the Design of the Law is to come to rigid Demonstration in Maters of Right."

THE NEXT GREAT FOUNDATION: THE HEARSAY RULE

Thus, the first great principle of evidence concerns objects—written artifacts. After the celebration of writings as permanent demonstrations, permitting knowledge of facts and not mere probabilistic understanding, the next "mega-rule" to evolve in the law of evidence was the rule against hearsay. This rule applied not to objects, but to statements. The rule certainly existed before Gilbert. But during Gilbert's day, neither judges nor lawyers made much use of it. Even well into the eighteenth century, the rule against

---

11. *See* Langbein, *supra* note 7, at 1168, 1173.
12. *See* GILBERT, *supra* note 9, at 4.
13. *See* Langbein, *supra* note 7, at 1173.
14. Langbein at 1181.

hearsay was only a fragment of what it was later to become.[15] This is largely because, as the evidence system evolved, the trial judge had a large amount of discretion. The hearsay rule was more like a principle, indicating that a speaker was not under oath when he had made a statement. It was not a rigid rule.

Recent scholarship suggests that by the late eighteenth and certainly early nineteenth century, the law of evidence entered a new phase in this area.[16] Judges lost some of their discretion, and what we now know as the "exclusionary rules" took a more modern form. There seems to have been a transition at the end of the eighteenth century. For example, the next major evidence treatise after Gilbert, written by a young University of Cambridge professor named Thomas Starkie, was the *Practical Treatise of the Law of Evidence*, which was published in 1824. It was much more modern in the way it viewed hearsay and other exclusionary rules, and in the far lesser discretion accorded to trial judges.[17]

But in addition, at this time another modern idea—that parties had a right to cross-examine witnesses with personal knowledge—appeared forcefully in the law. This was the idea that litigants had a right to "test" assertions through cross-examination.[18] Since the makers of out-of-court statements could not be cross-examined, it was not fair to allow their statements to be admitted as evidence. This ability to *test assertions* thereafter remained as one of the key policies of evidence law. Again, it is a common-sense notion. If a complex entity, such as a human being, makes statements, and those statements are used as proof in a trial, then that entity's perceptions, memory, motives, and biases should be subject to testing by the advocates. This rule became ever stronger throughout the nineteenth century as more and more classes of people, such as parties and people with interest, became eligible to testify. Indeed, it was not until after the Civil War, generally, that parties in the United States could even testify in their own civil suits.[19] Now a subtle, yet profound policy exists in the law of evidence that guarantees the testing of statements and assertions.

THE LONG MOVEMENT TO CODIFY THE LAW OF EVIDENCE

After the law of evidence solidified these two great rules, it went through a period of elaboration of many detailed, pedantic, and often conflicting minor rules that did not seem rational to lay observers. As discussed previously, many of these concerned the

---

15. The hearsay rule was a "curio" that rated only a passing mention for Gilbert, as well as for his followers, the treatise writers Bathurst and Buller. Examination of the legal decisions of the mid-eighteenth century confirm that the hearsay rule was not yet in place in a recognizably modern form: "It is hard to believe that the courts of the mid-eighteenth century enforced the hearsay rule or any of the other modern exclusionary rules that balance the potential prejudiciality of witness testimony against the supposed probative value. Counsel seem not to have objected to hearsay often, and the courts seem to have received it aplenty. I am inclined to think that the question of excluding hearsay and other suspect types of testimony may still have been remitted to judicial discretion, rather than being subject to firm rules of exclusion." *See* Langbein at 1189–90.

16. Gallanis, *supra* note 8, at 530.

17. For a discussion of Starkie's treatise, *see* Gallanis, *supra* note 8, at 516–30.

18. 5 John Henry Wigmore, Treatise, §§ 1365, 66 asserts that cross-examination "is beyond doubt the greatest legal engine ever invented for the discovery of truth."

19. Fisher notes that it was largely not until after the Civil War that criminal defendants and parties in civil cases were allowed to testify in most of the states. Fisher, *supra* note 1, at 668–72.

disqualification, from testimony, of the people who seemed to know the most about the issues at hand. As early as the 1820s, English philosopher Jeremy Bentham railed against evidence rules.[20] Picayune and often illogical evidence rules were so plentiful, and the entire mass considered so confusing, that there were recurring and increasingly urgent cries for reform of the law of evidence.

Historically, one of the most important of these calls for reform was made by Roscoe Pound, botanist-turned-law-school-professor-and-dean (Nebraska, then Harvard), in a speech entitled "The Causes of Popular Dissatisfaction with the Administration of Justice," made at an American Bar Association (ABA) meeting in St. Paul, Minnesota in 1906. This speech, described by Professor John Henry Wigmore as "The Spark that Kindled the White Flame of Progress,"[21] helped crystallize a twentieth-century movement to reform and codify the increasingly antiquated law of evidence. Almost from that time forward, some group or other in the United States was trying to systematize the law of evidence, reform it, and codify it.

The action picked up considerably in 1938, the year the U.S. Supreme Court promulgated the Federal Rules of Civil Procedure. That year the ABA's Committee on Improvements in the Law of Evidence, often simply called the Wigmore Committee, issued a report suggesting how to modernize the law of evidence, and unanimously urged the ABA to sponsor a competition to draft a "simplified code of evidence for use in jury trials."

Thereafter the American Law Institute (ALI) applied to the Carnegie Foundation for a study of the Law of Evidence with an eye to possible revisions and codification. It received a grant and began working in 1939. Professor Edmund Morgan of Harvard was named Reporter of the Project, and by 1942 the ALI had published a "Model Code of Evidence."

But Professor Wigmore attacked the Model Code in articles published in the *ABA Journal*.[22] He argued it gave back the trial judge too much discretion.[23] Professor Morgan and others fought back, but Wigmore was relentless in his opposition. Many people, particularly lawyers in California, opposed the Model Code.[24] Many considered the Code the product of effete, intellectual interests of the East. The ALI's Model Code failed as a vehicle to reform the law of evidence.

Shortly thereafter, the National Conference of Commissioners on Uniform State Laws, (NCCUSL), an arm of the ABA, began work on an evidence uniformity project of its own. The result was the Uniform Rules of Evidence, which was approved unanimously

---

20. Etienne Dumont, Bentham's Treatise on Judicial Evidence, 1825. Jeremy Bentham, Rationale of Judicial Evidence, 1827. *See* discussion in Charles A. Wright & Kenneth W. Graham, Jr., Federal Practice and Procedure: Evidence § 5001 (2d ed. 2005).

21. *See* John Henry Wigmore, *The Spark That Kindled the White Flame of Progress,* 20 J. Am. Jud. Soc'y 176 (1937).

22. John Henry Wigmore, *The American Law Institute Code of Evidence Rules: A Dissent,* 1942, 28 A.B.A.J., at 23.

23. Eleanor Swift, *One Hundred Years of Evidence Law Reform: Thayer's Triumph,* 88 Calif. L. Rev 2437, 2460 (2000).

24. Included in the opposition was the prominent California Bar Association Committee, which argued that the Code "seeks to destroy the foundation upon which our structure for the administration of justice is founded." *See* "Report of Committee on Administration of Justice on Model Code of Evidence," 19 Calif. St. B.J. 262, 281 (1944).

by the NCCUSL Conference in 1953. Considered less radical than the Model Code, the Uniform Rules comprised only 57 pages, as compared to the nearly 300 pages of the Model Code.[25]

However, the Uniform Rules were not adopted by many states. In 1958, the ABA House of Delegates urged the Judicial Conference of the United States to appoint a special committee to adopt the Uniform Rules. In 1961, the Judicial Conference decided that that an Advisory Committee on Rules of Evidence be established. The chairman of the Conference, Chief Justice Earl Warren, instead appointed a "Special Committee on Evidence," chaired by Professor James W. Moore of Yale Law School, which in turn recommended that federal courts adopt uniform evidence rules. And accordingly, in March of 1963, the Standing Committee on the Rules of Practice and Procedure recommended to the Judicial Conference that it appoint an Advisory Committee to draft rules of evidence.[26] An Advisory Committee was appointed, and work began in June of 1965. A draft was circulated in 1969. After the required participation by Congress, the Federal Rules of Evidence went into effect on July 1, 1975, almost fifteen years after they were first proposed.[27]

Accordingly, what we now study as the Federal Rules of Evidence is the result of several decades of tinkering with the contradictory set of state and federal precedents on evidentiary rules that existed at early and mid-twentieth century. The law of evidence became a code before the day of the personal computer. It is this codification, exemplified by the Federal Rules of Evidence and as adopted by many of the states, that is discussed in this book, which focuses primarily on the rules on authentication of evidence, the hearsay rule, and its codified exceptions.

THE "SCIENTIFIC METHOD" AND THE CONCEPT OF "TESTABILITY"

Perhaps the last great development in the law of evidence occurred in connection with a new policy, imposed by the Supreme Court, that federal courts should be gatekeepers, requiring foundations to be laid before specialized or scientific testimony can be admitted as evidence. This occurred in a line of decisions, starting with *Daubert v. Merrell Dow Pharmaceuticals,*[28] that generally requires the "scientific method" be followed when experts or specialists give specialized testimony and opinions.

In *Daubert* and these other decisions,[29] trial court judges were analogized to mandatory gatekeepers. This was not a new or radical concept but rather a return to the days of the eighteenth century when trial judges had much more discretion, but the Supreme Court apparently was rediscovering it in the context of perceived jury con-

---

25. Spencer A. Gard, *The New Uniform Rules of Evidence*, 2 KAN. L. REV. 333, 342 (1954).

26. Wright & Graham, *supra* note 20, § 5006, p. 180.

27. Pub. Law No. 93-595, 93d Cong., 2d Sess., 88 Stat., 1926, 1975.

28. 509 U.S. 579, 113 S. Ct 2786 (1993).

29. *Daubert* was followed by two other decisions that expanded the notion. General Electric Co. v. Joiner, 522 U.S. 136 (1997) clarified that it was the "abuse of discretion" standard that applied to the *Daubert* rule, even when the ruling was "outcome determinative." Kumho Tire Co. v. Carmichael, 118 S. Ct. 2339 (1998) expanded *Daubert* even more, clarifying that it covered not just scientific testimony but also "technical or other specialized knowledge," as described in Federal Rule of Evidence 702. *Kumho Tire* reiterated the requirement of "testability."

fusion. According to the Supreme Court, trial courts had not only the legal power to exclude unscientific testimony, they had the duty to exclude it. Otherwise, unscientific, unreliable evidence would be used by juries to decide disputes.

Henceforth, the law of evidence would contain an explicit policy of evidence being "scientific." No one rule or attribute was listed as to what made evidence scientific. To do so would not be possible, given the complexity of the concept. However, the Supreme Court listed as the first candidate factor the ability to *test an assertion.* Can a theory, or an assertion, be tested? Can it be verified, or falsified? The Court cited the philosopher Karl Popper and his writings for this idea.[30]

If an assertion or hypothesis cannot be tested, it likely would not be considered scientific, and an opinion or testimony based on such untestable thinking would possibly be excluded from evidence. Accordingly, we can say that a requirement that evidence be of a type generally subject to "testing" has joined the older policy that out-of-court statements be subject to cross-examination, also a species of testing. Our system does not expect, or allow, triers of fact to accept assertions blindly. Under the hearsay rule and the *Daubert* line of cases, if statements or assertions by their nature cannot be tested, they simply will not be considered as evidence. Not only is this right and ability to test a value inherent in the justice system, it is in conformance with modern notions about how we arrive at knowledge of the truth in the first place. Without an ability to falsify statements, or prove them wrong, we cannot know whether such statements are true or not. Assertions simply must be tested if we are to know if they are accurate. This holds true both for the assertions found in writings and the oral assertions of human beings.

THE NEW INFORMATION INFRASTRUCTURE UPSETS THE CURRENT EVIDENTIARY SYNTHESIS

The current evidentiary scheme comprises three main historical policies: (1) the notion of authentic writings, exemplified by the search for an "original" object tying certain people, acting at a certain time, to certain permanently recorded information; (2) the rule against hearsay, giving litigants the right to test factual statements through cross-examination, unless there was an accepted policy reason not to do so; and (3) the notion that evidence, particularly evidence implicating specialized knowledge, be generally scientific in that it be subject to a "test" of its hypotheses or methodologies.

These policies are all stressed by digital evidence.

For example, as we will discuss in the next chapter, when discussing digital evidence, it no longer makes sense to talk about an "original record." This is because many millions of identical records of pure information can now coexist; because all these records can be seamlessly edited; and thereafter, it is not possible to test those records of pure

---

30. *See* Karl Popper, Conjectures and Refutations: The Growth of Scientific Knowledge 37 (5th ed. 1989)("[T]he criterion of the scientific status of a theory is its falsifiability, or refutability, or testability"), cited in *Daubert,* 509 U.S. at 593, 113 S.Ct. at 2797. Of course, the citation to Popper does not itself acknowledge the academic debate that has been going on for the past 45 years or so, particularly after publication of Thomas Kuhn's *The Structure of Scientific Revolutions* (1962), on how scientists actually go about overturning their theories or "paradigms." For additional background, *see* Paul Hoyningen-Huene, Reconstructing Scientific Revolutions: Thomas S. Kuhn's Philosophy of Science 238–39 (U. Chicago 1993).

information for change. This gives rise to a new, societal authenticity problem discussed throughout this book. In fact, using our old rules in our new situation leads to results this book calls a regime of "trivial showings," discussed later in the book. Obviously, a new logic and system of proving and testing authenticity needs to be developed. Then, legal rules that allocate burdens and presumptions, and that determine accepted foundations, need to be fine-tuned.

Similarly, the law and concept of hearsay is stretched by information systems. As discussed in the next chapter and in Chapters 7 and 8, courts are currently befuddled by the fact that our information ecosystems, through their "reading and writing games,"[31] now regularly make out-of-court statements that would clearly be hearsay if coming from a person. Added to this is the fact that such statements, while they remain within an information ecosystem, can be edited just as can other digital information.

The law now routinely lets such statements into evidence, after defining them outside the hearsay rule simply because the assertions are "not made by people," or after utilizing a business-records exception that was never intended to apply to such statements in the first place. In fact, the nature of these assertions has yet to be fully explored by the law. New rules about the admissibility of such out-of-court statements are necessary. There is a need for a new doctrine, a twenty-first-century manifestation of the hearsay rule if you will, here called "systems reliability." It is discussed mainly in Chapters 7 and 8.

NEW FOUNDATIONS ARE NECESSARY

There is now a new world of evidence. New foundations are necessary.

Black's Law Dictionary defines "foundation" as "the basis on which something is supported; esp., evidence or testimony that establishes the admissibility of other evidence."[32] Courts have explained that "no rule of evidence requires a 'foundation'; 'foundation' is simply a loose term for preliminary questions designed to establish that evidence is admissible."[33] Others have explained that "foundational facts are those facts upon which the admissibility of evidence rests."[34] "Those facts include matters such as the genuineness of a document or statement, the maker's personal knowledge, and the like."[35] A "foundation" is the factual concrete that must be poured before the first brick in the evidentiary wall is laid.

This book seeks to establish new foundations for the digital world, but we discuss more than mere admissibility. We are talking about what we need to know about an information object, and what questions to ask it, to discover its attributes. What do we need to *prove*, to convincingly show that a digital information object is authentic? Put another way, how do we *test* whether a digital information object is authentic? What do we need to *prove* "who" did something in the digital realm? And conversely, how do we *test* that? What do we need in order to prove "when" something happened? And how do we test assertions that it happened at a particular time? How can we talk about the

---

31. *See* discussion of the reading and writing games in an information ecosystem in Chapter 2.
32. BLACK'S LAW DICTIONARY 682 (8th ed. 2004).
33. *See* A.I. Credit Corp. v. Legion Ins. Co., 265 F.3d 630, 637 (7th Cir. 2001).
34. Blake v. Pellegrino, 329 F.3d 43, 48 (1st Cir. 2003).
35. *Id.*

reliability of computer-generated information, the new protection against the "hearsay" now inundating our world of information?

In disusing these new foundations, understood in the broad sense of the term as building blocks going to weight, as well as admissibility of evidence, new concepts will necessarily be introduced. Among these is *eunomia*. This is an ancient Greek word, from the name of *Eunomia*, the Goddess of Good Order and Lawful Conduct, a word that also meant "good governance" with all components of a society in their proper places. In this book, *eunomia* is used to refer to good governance of information—information regimes that allow handlers of records the ability to test, verify, or disprove the authenticity of a record; its integrity; when it was created; who originated it; and so on, depending on the circumstances at play within a regime.

Eunomia allows us to conclude facts with strong inferences, after a sort of proof in a fashion. *Eunomia* thus allows us to get back to the idea of a demonstration, the concept Gilbert borrowed from Locke and that he posited applied to all writing, as a permanent form of evidence. As we will see, there is nothing permanent about writing anymore, and we need *eunomic* regimes to fill the voids created when writing suddenly changed from a permanent to a transient technology.

Indeed, *eunomia* must hereafter be a conscious destination of society, because one critical result of the fact that informational records have morphed into pure information objects is that there is a new dynamic of *untestability* in writing. Writing used to carry in its records the evidence of change. One could determine whether one had the right record by the fact that one could locate an artifact, and then inspect the object to determine if it had changed through time. But this is no longer possible, now that writing has broken free from the world of artifacts completely and morphed into pure information. Unless certain *eunomic* techniques are employed, it is not possible to test written records for change, other than fishing in a soup of circumstances to achieve probabilistic understanding. Untestability and transience are the new characteristics of writing, and they destroy the evidentiary foundations of the past, which were based on permanence and demonstration. They give rise to an authenticity crisis.

Accordingly, in order to prove facts in the digital world with some strong assurance, we must hereafter take steps in advance. We must be self-conscious in the creation of our records. We have lost the concept of original record, which formerly was the artifact that enshrined the authentic information.

But, it is possible to erect a new regime of authenticity. As described in Chapter 4, the concept of a *reference* has now replaced the concept of an original. How do we get references? We will see that we must *declare a reference*. How are we assured of authenticity? Quite simply this depends on the integrity of such references. They must be protected as immutable so that, in the future, they can be used as the standards against which one compares purported information objects—whether contracts, financial statements, or electronic love letters.

THE LAW'S NEW EMPIRICISM

Accordingly, the law of evidence is starting a second great celebration of empiricism. The legal profession appears to understand it has little organized concept of how the new writing system works, what is useful from the old ways of evidentiary analysis, what must be developed in the way of new methodologies and regimes, and how to search for the facts.

Certainly there are radically different structures, behaviors, and technologies supporting writing than there were when many of our profession studied the law for the first time. Quite simply, our old abstractions about documents no longer serve us. Society needs to put on new conceptual glasses, with different lenses and new frames, to now compose different shapes and forms so that we all can sense the new reality clearly. We cannot use our old concepts automatically. Old abstractions keep us captured in a bottle of outdated concepts.

CONCLUSION

Lawyers have a special role in society. When you really want to know what happened—in a dispute in business, or in a marriage, or in a government scandal—you call the lawyers, and they pore over information, including the writings involved. The New Empiricism means that lawyers must understand the workings of informational records better than any other social group. If not, they lose their effectiveness—their status and power in society. They simply cannot do their job—what people expect them to do—unless they have these core competencies.

This book seeks to lay a foundation for core competencies.

CHAPTER **2**

Understanding the Digital Realm

Fundamental to an understanding of the new, digital realm of information is the fact that writings are now produced by systems rather than people. Further, no longer must writing have a physical aspect. It can be a collection of pure information that can be freely rearranged. Unlike physical objects, which almost always contain information about their creation and modification, digital information objects do *not* necessarily contain information about previous states. Indeed, information about previous states can be destroyed, at will, by a person or program handling such records.

But notice the seeming paradox here. As products of systems, informational records often do reveal aspects about the system itself, or even about the outside world if the system is linked to it with sensors or other inputs. Such assertions can concern statements about the time something happened, who was involved, where something occurred, and attributes of any of a vast array of events (temperature, speed, blood alcohol level). These are inserted into digital records not by any humans, but instead by the system. This is new to the law, new to the concept of evidence even in its common sense and everyday connotation, and new to people trying to interpret what is reliable in written information.

Thus two monumental changes are brought on by digital technology, affecting the two most important concepts in the law of evidence. The first is related to the new type of writing that has evolved, viewed in its discrete manifestations. The "object" the law examines has changed radically. It is no longer physical matter. It is information itself. Indeed, writing's departure from the world of physical artifacts revolutionizes the concept of *authenticity*. The written record must now be analyzed differently than before.

The second change comes from our dealing with manifestations of unfolding information ecosystems. The fact that records increasingly contain factual assertions made not by humans but by systems means that an entirely new doctrine—something akin to a new hearsay rule—must evolve if we want to have rules about the reliability of digital writing. This is the new doctrine of *systems reliability*.

PHYSICAL RECORDS AND THE INSPECTION PARADIGM

Civilization's original writing technology employed the familiar physical realm. Information was stored on objects by manipulating templates of clay, sheets of papyrus, bark, copper, stone, parchment, and of course paper, among other variations. There was an alteration of molecules readable by the human eye. Matter was scratched, or stained, or moved, or overlaid by the displacement of an immeasurably large number of molecules. The records that resulted were "complex information objects," with huge numbers of molecules arranged in a unique way. The ability to store and transmit information depended on the human eye reading the artifact, and determining how its molecules had been visibly altered through script.[1]

The mode of authenticating such a physical record was physical *inspection*. First, on a global level, did the artifact look and feel like it was supposed to? Did it smell right? Critically, was it even the right artifact? Was it the right *object*? This *is* my beloved old diary, isn't it? This is a relation to a record on a gut level, a gestalt impression. Is it the right *thing*? Am I starting in the right place? Or am I not even holding the right record? Do I have the wrong object?

The traditional material used for writing resists reuse and modification. Accordingly, one could also examine whether the material carrying the writing had visibly, or perhaps even microscopically, been altered. Had someone changed things since the molecules were originally arranged, often having been *signed* by someone? Was there a smudge, or an erasure, or white-out, or perhaps an obvious discontinuity? Was the record written with pen, or with pencil?[2] Technologies such as seals made such physical inspection routines more efficient. A recognizable seal not only marked a record as having come from a certain source, but an unbroken seal was evidence the record had not been altered or modified since the seal had been affixed. Of course, a seal also was a complex object consisting of countless molecules whose integrity could be examined.

THE CONCEPT OF "ORIGINAL"

Because it was artifacts that originally gave life to the written record, the concept of "original" had rich meaning, and supported our longstanding notion of authenticity. Since written records contain so many molecules arranged in delicate, three-dimensional patterns, written records are unique. A traditional written record had a history. It had birth, when information was scratched out in a particular milieu, involving certain people at a certain time. And it had a subsequent life. An original thus signified (1) an author or originator; and (2) a set of information that would be enshrined as permanent in the artifact. Together they constituted an authentic written record.

---

1. Writing evolved at the dawn of civilization and indeed was one of the four or five technologies making civilization possible. Writing itself was the combination of two subtechnologies. The first was "script," an organized convention of signs, in its first manifestation called *cuneiform,* thought to have arrived at a relatively mature state in approximately 3200 B.C. as a Sumerian invention. Script continued to evolve until the Greeks took various elements and combined them into the modern *alphabet,* with one sign representing each sound of the language. The alphabet is considered the most efficient of scripts, with its few letters able to form any word in a language. It was invented only once but has been borrowed many times, including by the Romans. We use the Greek alphabet today. *See* David Diringer, The Alphabet: A Key to the History of Mankind, 3rd ed. rev., 2 vol. (1968); Walter Durfee, Alphabetics as a Science (1956).

The other constituent subtechnology of writing was the way script was carried through time. Without a way to record the script, writing is useless. The tablets of clay on which cuneiform was written marked the beginning of a physical technology for writing to be transmitted, but other physical substrates evolved over the ages, including ultimately the invention of carbon paper in the nineteenth century. *See* Roy Harris, *The Origin of Writing* (1986) and Albertine Gaur, *A History of Writing* (1984).

2. Some writing subtechnologies, such as pencil, facilitated the editing of physical records. Others, such as ink, made writings more permanent.

It would be expensive and probably unfeasible to try to exactly duplicate such an object. How to put all those quadrillions of molecules in their proper places? One could copy a record and record the same information it carried either accurately or inaccurately. In the twentieth century one could photograph it, of course, which led to a widespread use in the late twentieth century of photocopies. But one could not replicate the object identically. It was an original as much as each human being is an original. It had a creator, and a birth in time, and carried information through its unique arrangement of matter in its physical aspect.

A MORE ADVANCED FORM OF WRITING

Writings in the digital realm are different. They do not depend on the alteration of matter.[3] Such records are very close to "pure information," and exist by virtue of a mere succession of the differentiation of 1s and 0s, distinguished by electricity flowing in machine systems.[4] In writing today we deal in pure information objects, unfettered by matter. They can be whisked or shaken or rearranged in an instant.

Such records are actually layers of abstraction, one view stacked on top of another. At the deepest layer is the world of bits, 1s and 0s. As one builds on top of this, the bits of information can carry letters and numbers. This collection of letters and numbers may be partitioned into smaller collections to represent, for example, such categories as "name" and "date of birth." Then there are layers designed to be presentations of information to viewers of that data. Conjoined with this data is a collection of information about the other data, which collection is often called "metadata." This metadata is information that software developers have designed to be recorded in a record and that is inserted there by the system itself. For example, even without making any entry or modifying any data, each time one saves a document one is editing on a word-processing program that program, and the system that supports that program, will record the date and time of that "save" event in the data being "saved." This information then becomes a part of the record.

Such information can then be viewed by making certain commands to the program so as to view the "data about the data" contained in the record.

For example, one can pull up the "Properties Tab" of a Microsoft Word file and view a property that the publishers of Word have stated is the date and time this file was modified. Without any specific direction or intent on a human's part, the system is recording information into a record, which may also be viewed (see Figure 2-1).

There is also usually a top-layered presentation view that is normally viewed by the operator of the program in question. For example, in a word-processing application, such as Microsoft Word, one can view a page as it is being typed. This view contains what the layperson normally considers the data of a file. Interestingly, although the view now often looks very much like a page of paper, this is of course an illusion, something

---

3. Although digital information does need some sort of matter to carry the 0s and 1s through time, the nature of the material used allows alteration to the writing that leaves no traces whatsoever, so alteration is not really an issue. For example, the electrical charges on a hard drive can be changed repeatedly.

4. Hence the term "electronically stored information," recently adopted by the U.S. Federal Rules of Civil Procedure, Rules 16, 26–34 and 45. *See* GEORGE L. PAUL AND BRUCE H. NEARON, THE DISCOVERY REVOLUTION: E-DISCOVERY AMENDMENTS TO THE FEDERAL RULES OF CIVIL PROCEDURE (ABA 2006).

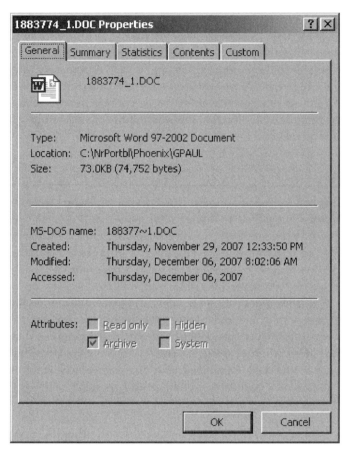

FIGURE 2.1
The System Inserts Information into Records without Human Intent

the application has designed so as to mimic old-style physical records. What we are viewing is simply the top-level view: the view of what the record normally shows to people who view it on a screen and also upon printing out the record onto paper.

Word processing and other programs take this concept of varying views one step further. Click a command such as "Track Changes," and there is a graphical view of how a document has been edited over time. Thus, even more data is available to be viewed upon command, under certain circumstances. This is a variable capability, and depends on the program being used.

The information in all of such views consists of data. Again, metadata is often called "data about data." One must remember, of course, that metadata is like other data, and like all data, can be edited and deleted. Thus, all this information the system is recording about its own processing, and inserting into records without human input, can be edited or deleted by human intervention or by systems. Accordingly, this self-insertion of statements, which the system makes about itself, cannot be reliably used to test the authenticity of a record.

Accordingly, a digital informational record is an object but is not a clump of molecules. It is a conceptual object. It is a collection of pure, freely editable information, with multiple views depending on choice of the operator. We normally think of a digital file as containing only the data one sees on a screen. However, such files usually contain much more information than what is viewed in the ordinary use of the application. This information can be viewed either using less-well-known commands of the application, or with a different application. What one might be able to view by poking around for other views will depend on the facts of the case and the type of records examined.

PURE INFORMATION OBJECTS AND THE AUTHENTICITY CRISIS

Because digital records do not depend on the alteration of matter, a process of inspecting them is not a reliable paradigm for testing authenticity. In an inspection one can only sense the information in the record in the *present*. Because what makes the record is only an *arrangement* of a manageable number of 1s and 0s,[5] and not untold numbers of molecules arranged in a three-dimensional space, millions and even billions of exactly identical digital records can coexist. This, indeed, is one of the hallmarks of digital technology. Millions of identical copies can spring from one record. They are merely pure records of information. They do not change depending on the material in which they are recorded, or whose electricity is giving them life.

Accordingly, one of the most important but least understood things about digital technology is that records can be changed without any ability to test for change by an inspection of the record itself. Conversely, the key to the inspection paradigm of traditional, physical records is that the ability to detect traces of change could be found from evidence in the record being inspected. Writing can be smeared or smudged, and that smear or smudge appears on the record because it is an artifact of three-dimensional matter that carries the information. A page can be torn out of a document, and be found to be missing upon inspection. One can sense a cut-and-paste job in a photograph. Magnetic clips can be heard in taped sound recordings, where a physical medium was altered.

Indeed, in all physical writings, it is possible to detect changes to the molecules comprising the original thing. Detecting evidence of change in the record itself was not guaranteed, of course, but at least there was a real possibility one could do so given the complex nature of real-world, physical objects. This technological fact of life was filed away both in the unspoken assumptions of the law, and in our common sense.

Now, one of the historical attributes of our new information complex is that software has generally evolved to facilitate undetectable or seamless editing of informational records. This is one of its main sources of power. The advantage of a word processor over a typewriter was the ability to easily modify the previous text, and yet leave no indication of that modification. The old information was lost—on purpose—and the new information was saved in an information object, often called a "file."

---

5. This could be hundreds of thousands, or millions, or even more bits. But in all instances, it is only a successive order of 1s and 0s, not their delicate arrangement in three-dimensional space that is involved. In all events the system involved can easily replicate the successive order exactly, identically, and in reliable succession.

Information was thus undetectably changed in the record as a result of the processing of information. The new arrangement of information was saved as the record. There was not, however, necessarily a record about a critical, second set of information: information *about the change that was made*. This history of what has been changed may or may not have been recorded. The ability to record such a history is dependent on the abilities of the program, and whether or not that function has been enabled by the user. Or, there may be an incomplete record of the history of any changes. Or, there may be no record of changes. Furthermore, whatever record there is can subsequently be destroyed.

Nearly every application in use today provides the ability to modify existing content in such a way that that modification would not be detectable unless a history of the change was being recorded. Thus, this seamless editing function is endemic. It evolved, historically, within the new information paradigm as a sort of dynamic, or attractor, in the evolution of software. It occurs with most business software such as word-processing applications, e-mail, spreadsheets, and graphics programs. But one also has the ability to seamlessly edit photos. Even a newbie user of Adobe Photoshop can make a dirty glass disappear off the table, or change the time on a clock, for example.

Seamless editing occurs in sound records as well. Words in sentences can be rearranged digitally, without any indication there has been a change. So, too, does it occur in digital video, as any viewer of modern commercial advertisements can attest.

THE PROBLEM OF THE UNTESTABILITY OF DIGITAL FILES

In short, almost everything that can be digitized can be modified, leaving no indication it has been changed. There may be no information in the file about the change. Who changed it? When? How was it changed? What was the information before it was changed?

Critically, it is most often impossible to answer these questions. There is simply not enough information available to allow a test for answers. The information about the smudge that appeared with the pencil, or the presence of white-out that appeared with the pen—the information about the change—is missing in the digital realm.

Accordingly, a profound authenticity crisis has come to affect society.[6] Our tried-and-true inspection paradigm, which was written into the law of evidence long ago, fails us with regard to digital records. No matter how carefully one studies things, one may only be able to discern the most recent version of a digital file, not its makeup seventeen versions ago much less its original composition. Indeed, there is now a panoply of products designed to erase any vestiges of the past history of files—to annihilate their metadata, and any vestigial changes or comments. Law firms frequently use these on, for example, Word files before they are sent outside the office.[7] This way, opposing firms can only know the current information in the file, the information of the present, and not

---

6. George L. Paul, *The Authenticity Crisis in Real Evidence*, first published in *Scientific Evidence Review*, Monograph No. 5, (ABA 2001), and then subsequently in *Law Practice Today*, 2006, available at http://www.abanet.org/lpm/lpt/articles/tch03065.shtml.

7. There are many such products on the market. The author's law firm uses Workshare Protect®. It will sanitize digital files of past changes, comments, and metadata.

discover the thinking of their opponents by looking at various other views that might be available.[8]

This endemic inability to test digital information about previous states—a combination of seamless editing with the fact that digital evidence consists of pure information objects, not complex three dimensional artifacts—is referred to here as *untestability*. This characteristic of untestability destroys the ancient regime of evidence that sprang up at the beginning of the eighteenth century and that reigns today. Untestability gives rise to our authenticity crisis.

We need to develop an entirely new regime of authenticity. How do we test whether pure information objects have changed through time, given that any single digital information object is untestable? How can we determine whether there is integrity of information? This issue is discussed in Chapter 4.

A PHILOSOPHICAL MODEL OF THE DIGITAL REALM

There is more to understanding the new information infrastructure than reflecting on the new qualities of the pure and radically simple information objects it contains. Is it possible to distill the situation into some basic metaphors understandable not only by lawyers, but by society at large? How should we conceive of the digital realm?

The Rise of the "Information Ecosystem"

First, one must recognize that the digital realm *evolved*. There were technological advances, which led to other advances in a cascading web of increasing complexity, which unfolded through time.[9] As the system evolved, it took on increasing characteristics of *connectivity* and something called *emergence*, meaning that the whole behaved quite differently than the sum of the parts.[10]

Although the following list makes certain simplifying assumptions and abstracts out certain developments that really were part of interrelated complexes, the key technological advances[11] occurred in the following order: (1) digitization and digital computers;[12]

---

8. Parties or their firms have been known to send out unscrubbed versions of files to opponents, who then learn unauthorized information. In *E-Discovery, Current Trends and Cases,* (ABA 2008), Ralph C. Losey tells the story of how the Office of the Director of National Intelligence bungled the release of classified information through leaving it in metadata, which it then left unscrubbed in a native-file PowerPoint presentation. It then compounded the error by posting the PowerPoint presentation in native format on a website, which made its classified metadata available to everyone on the Internet. Such mistakes are legion. Indeed, there is much discussion about the ethics of performing this technologically feasible task. Can lawyers look at attorney-client privileged metadata? The jurisdictions differ, but if done correctly, such information can easily be permanently eliminated from digital records.

9. Technologists speak of subsystems "clustering" or "bundling" together to form technologies, which emerge from constituent parts. *See* Arnulf Grütbler, Technology and Global Change 5, 19 (Cambridge University Press 1998). *See also* Lewis Mumford, *Technics and the Nature of Man, in* Knowledge Among Men (James Smithson, ed., 1966), *reprinted in* Carl Mitcham & Robert Mackey (eds.), Philosophy and Technology 77–85 (The Free Press 1972).

10. This also means that no one person or small group of people can explain how the system works.

11. These key technological advances were earlier discussed in George L. Paul & Jason R. Baron, *Information Inflation: Can The Legal System Adapt?* 13 Rich. J. L & Tech 10 (2007).

12. Digital computers were invented at the close of World War II and gradually diffused throughout society as the "mainframe" of the 1950s, 1960s, and 1970s.

(2) real time computing;[13] (3) the microprocessor;[14] (4) the personal computer;[15] (5) the evolution of software that "locked in" seamless editing as an almost universal function;[16] (6) local and wide-area networks leading to the Internet;[17] (7) e-mail;[18] and (8) the World Wide Web.[19]

Finally, there is the development of *technique* by people who now know how to function as a component of the technology.[20]

The result of this evolution is a new information infrastructure, which evolved quite suddenly. The new age of writing took about 20 years to evolve, or perhaps 25 at most, after it was jump-started by the invention and early diffusion of the personal computer in the late 1970s and early 1980s. When the author graduated from law school in 1982, he had long been writing on typewriters. White-out was in use, as was carbon paper. At the office in his early practice of law, some word processing occurred, but it was "batch

---

13. Although computers were used by institutions, governments, and large businesses in the 1950s, 1960s, and 1970s, these were primarily expensive mainframes that performed batch processing. Often, the results of the computation were not available for hours or the next day, because the process of computation was separate from the human user interface. The first commercial real-time computing system was American Airlines' SABRE reservations system, which was launched in 1964. Real-time computing didn't become widely available until the 1980s. Martin Campbell-Kelly & William Aspray, Computer: A History of the Information Machine 170–75 (1996).

14. At the time of this writing, three inventions lay claim to having been the first computer in a chip, or microprocessor: The Central Air Data Computer (CADC), the Intel® 4004, and the Texas Instruments TMS 1000. The CADC system was completed for the Navy's "TomCat" fighter jets in 1970. The TMS 1000 was first to market in calculator form. The first stand-alone microprocessor was the Intel 4004, which was introduced in November 1971. *See* IBM website on "Great Moments in Microprocessor History," http://www.128.ibm.com/developerworks/library/pa-microhist.html.

15. These machines used the newly invented microprocessor and spread after 1977, with leading products being the Apple II and Commodore PET. Such personal computers gained ascendancy in business in the mid-1980s. *See* Campbell-Kelly & Aspray, *supra* note 13, at 247–53.

16. One of the designs locked into most business productivity software is seamless editing. *See also* Thomas Friedman, *The World Is Flat* (discussing importance of workflow applications).

17. *See* Katie Hafner & Mathew Lyon, Where Wizards Stay Up Late: The Origins of the Internet (Simon & Schuster 1990) (describing growth of ARPANET). The networking dynamic is fundamental to the new writing paradigm. Corporate networks, using communication protocols, gained ascendancy in the 1980s and were fully deployed by the mid-1990s. *See* Campbell-Kelly & Aspray, *supra* note 13, at 247–53.

18. *See* Hafner & Lyon, *supra. See also* http://en.wikipedia.org/wiki/Ray_Tomlinson (first e-mail sent between users on different hosts connected on a network); George L. Paul and Bruce H. Nearon, *The Discovery Revolutions,* E-discovery Amendments to the Federal Rules of Civil Procedure (2006), p. 4.

19. The World Wide Web (the "Web"), a communications network that operates on the Internet, dates to *circa* 1990, when Tim Berners-Lee of CERN invented hypertext markup language (HTML). *See generally,* Tim Berners-Lee, Weaving The Web: The Original Design and Ultimate Destiny of the World Wide Web by Its Inventor (Harper San Francisco 1990). Mosaic Communications Corporation was the first company to attempt to capitalize on the web, when it released a "web browser" known as Mosaic Netscape 0.9, later renamed Netscape Navigator. On August 9, 1995, newly renamed Netscape went public, and the web caused the Internet to grow with inflationary force. *See* http://en.wikipedia.org/wiki/Netscape_CommunicationsCorporation. The web went from 20 host servers in 1992, to 50 as of January 1993, 200 as of August 1993, to (post-Netscape) 100,000 in January 1996, 650,000 in January 1997, and 4.3 million in 1999. *See* Berners-Lee, *supra,* at 67; http://vlib.org/admin/history. Now there are *tens of millions* of hosts and complete networks are added to the Internet daily. Romualdo Pastor-Satorras & Alessandro Vespignani, 7 Evolution and Structure of the Internet: A Statistical Physics Approach (Cambridge University Press 2005).

20. Technologists use the French word *technique* to refer to the disembodied nature of technology—the knowledge base of how to use technology hardware. *See* Grübler, *supra* note 9, at 20.

processing" handled by physically separate departments, not real-time processing by the authors of the documents themselves, who in any event were certainly not sending messages on information systems to and from others in their organization and around the globe.

Now, we have a different ballgame: People are able to work with the new writing in real time, as any user of instant messaging knows. They send huge amounts of information to each other, quite casually. The new form of writing has, among other things, caused an explosion of information as potential evidence.[21] Businesses now contain up to ten thousand times the amount of information they held when the physical information paradigm was still the way we communicated.[22]

The new information infrastructure was adopted by the business community, worldwide. Obviously, it also is revolutionizing social life and leisure activity. Information, if it is to be considered as evidence, now must be extracted from something akin to an ecosystem. These emergent organs now permeate the workplace, political campaigns, and various spaces such as the blogosphere, and various social networking sites. The degree and realness of the emergence can perhaps be measured by noting that some of these organs have been valued by the market at several billions to several tens of billions of dollars.

Reading and Writing Games and the Problem of Hearsay

The multifarious computer codes that allow all this to happen are complex and utilize many years of work, by many people, in thousands of different companies on many different types of software that coevolved to interconnect many objects. What has evolved is a complex system. Because this complex system does "decide" what information to insert into records, we simply must have a way to describe its actions.

Philosophers had a challenge similar to ours when trying to describe the functioning of human language. For many years, they tried to nail down the way language worked by postulating that each word represented an idea, or that a form of logic could be placed on top of human language systems. They tried to break down language, which is a complex system connecting objects in a network, into simple and discrete pieces.

In the end, such attempts to explain human language failed. Language was too complex and too subject to its environment. The same word could be a command, a statement, or a question, depending on the circumstances. Or the same word could have completely different meanings depending on the circumstances. What remained as a good, overarching metaphor for language is that it is a *game* engaged in by its participants.[23] As long as the participants use the same rules, or protocols, in the same context, they can communicate.

Much of the same can be said of the language that allows humans to speak to information systems, and information systems to speak to humans and to each other. There

---

21. Paul & Baron, *supra* note 11.

22. Paul & Nearon, *supra* note 18, at 4, 5. (Organizations now have thousands if not tens of thousands of times as much information within their boundaries as they did 20 years ago. Even the smallest of businesses may have the equivalent of 2000 four-drawer file cabinets of documents stored on its computer.).

23. *See* Ludwig Wittgenstein, Philosophical Investigations (1953).

are protocols to support communication—a universe of discourse[24] without which communication would not be possible. Many minds and machines are thus able to communicate with one another, worldwide, in a radically new sort of language game. Often, they combine into clusters, and groups of programs interact so that they can then interact with other groups of programs. Humans intervene by inserting information at various points along the way, but often it is very hard to determine where a human acted, where a group of programs acted, and where the result was a combination of everything.[25] This is one result of the complexity of such systems, which behave much like a larger organ of sorts.

In such an *oikos,* or household, there are untold numbers of reading and writing games occurring.[26] Conventions have been adopted in generations of coevolved computer programs that allow people or their machine agents to write information to machines, for machines to read the information, and for the machines to write back or write somewhere else. Because of the conventions involved, the information given in response to the received information can be a demand, a request, a question, or an answer, just like in human language.

Why are such reading and writing games relevant to those who want to understand digital evidence? It is because one of the main issues of the day is that the *oikos* itself is an emergent, behaving system, now regularly as a result of these reading and writing games making statements recorded in records read by people or programs. These statements are evidence. Traditionally, such assertions would have been considered hearsay. They are clearly out-of-court statements about facts, offered to prove the truth of the matter asserted. The maker of the statement, which is often a combination of the interactions of various programs and other ill-defined actors within an *oikos,* cannot be cross-examined in court. Often, it is not even possible to know who is doing the declaring. It is simply the information system taken in its totality.

In the jurisprudence that has tried to grapple with this over the last few years, judges have usually declared that because computers were not people, they could not make statements. Under the rules of evidence, written before assertions by such Borg-like amalgams had come to the fore, the conclusion was that nothing stated by a system is hearsay. Or if there was a conclusion that such statements might be hearsay, the statement almost always qualified as an exception to the hearsay rule. Accordingly, we are now close to having everything that computers create come into evidence. Every statement of the system is admissible, without a meaningful ability to cross-examine. This issue is covered in Part III.

---

24. There has been much work in the development of Open Systems Interconnection (OSI) concerning the nature of what an application process is actually doing and in the nature of the shared understanding between two communicating application processes.

25. Given such complexity, it is difficult if not impossible for one person or small group of people to understand the behavior of that complex system.

26. *Oikos* is ancient Greek for the word "home" or "household." It was the word used by German biologist Ernst Haekel (1843–1919) in 1873 to coin the term "ecology," or *okologie,* from Greek *oikos* + *logia,* "study of."

THE "EVENT"

The digital realm is a dynamic, interactive space. As we have discussed, it is a series of systems. Objects are connected and "communicate" with one another. Unlike the world of static informational records, the digital realm is constantly changing. For example, it is well known that each time a computer is turned on, a thousand or more files are changed merely from that act alone. Each keyboard action, click of the mouse, or other operation can set in motion a chain of events that affects many thousands and indeed millions of records. When something happens in the digital world, it can trigger the cascading knock-down of a row of digital dominos, leaving a wave of changed records in its wake.

In this digital realm, an "event" is the most basic phenomenon. It is a digital "happening," or a digital "occurrence."

Webopedia defines "event" as "an action or occurrence detected by a program. Events can be user actions . . . or system occurrences." Events are the actions taking place in the digital world. They are occurrences such as opening a file, saving a file, or printing a file—events like modifying, transmitting, receiving, archiving, restoring, or otherwise processing digital data. Some authors call this concept a "data-generating event,"[27] but this work prefers the more elementary word "event."

The world of events depends on the "reading and writing game" at issue in the particular circumstance. Events are incidents of importance that are recorded. Events are what create digital evidence.

Therefore, analyzing the event that caused the data to be recorded is an important task, because the occurrence of the event underpins several other evidentiary concerns. Critically, one usually begins by analyzing the event that caused the creation of a record. For example, an e-mail is either sent, or received, or forwarded. It can also be edited. An event can therefore be considered a "what" question. What happened? What unfolded? What changed? What occurred? What was the event in question? Accordingly, the "what" question is one of the new foundations of digital evidence. Many other foundational questions are related to the "what" of events, such as when?, who?, and where?

Unfolding of Events and the Concept of Time in the Digital Realm

The digital world therefore contains untold trillions of events each second, hour, day, and so on. These "whats" do not all happen simultaneously. Naturally, events precede or follow one another in time. One event may cause one or more subsequent events. The digital world, too, has a history that unfolds with passage of time.

Digital events occur at specific times. The value of this time can be correlated to the time we use to record physical or human events, in its atomic-clock-type manifestation. There is no necessity, however, that digital records contain any entry of information

---

27. *See also* the discussion of events in Bruce H. Nearon *et al.*, *The Merger of Information Security and Accountability*, 45 Jurimetrics J. 379, where the authors discuss what they called a "data-generating event." Not only is there an event, there are two other elements in a data-generating event: time data, and a record of the event.

about the time they occurred. One could have a rich informational record, still without any information whatsoever about the time of the event that created it.

Fortunately, digital records normally do contain records of time. At the time an event is occurring, a computer program reads the time on the computer's clock and then records that time somewhere in the record. Such time information, variously called a time stamp or time mark, is not necessarily viewable to the person who is typing or reading the document. For example, each time one modifies a file on a Word document, the time on the computer's clock is recorded in the Word file, but one must resort to a specific command in order to view it.

Questions concerning the reliability of time stamps are covered in Chapter 5. Suffice it to say that events do happen in time, and the time of certain events is often a critical evidentiary fact.

THE CONCEPT OF INTEGRITY OF INFORMATION

After a set of information originates, most often in association with an identity, there is an issue of whether that information has changed through time. Does it have what is called "integrity"? As discussed in the next chapters, without integrity we are at a loss to test for authenticity. Once information objects change, unless we have complete information about the changes, we lose track of the object. If there has been a change to the object without our knowledge, we will impute all sorts of false attributes to the object and draw false conclusions about it. Integrity of information is one, if not the key, new foundation of digital evidence.

THE CONCEPT OF "WHO" "ORIGINATED" THE EVENT

Sometimes events or information objects happen as a result of the instability of a system. For example, a computer may crash. Even then, some element of the overall system can be traced to be the initiator, or originator, of a cascade of events.

Usually, though, events and records are set in motion through the action of an entity, often indeed the *purposeful* action of an entity. The entity is sometimes a human being. For example, one can click "purchase" during a web-based credit card transaction, and purposely set in motion many events, such as the charge to a credit card, the purchase of a plane ticket, the making of a reservation on an international flight, even the initiation of a background check.

But the entity originating an event in the digital realm can also be a computer program, acting at the request or on behalf of a person, a group of people, or another computer program. Indeed, substantive law now allows contracts to be entered into by machines, or machine agents, through automated processes without any involvement of people whatsoever.[28] An example of a machine or computer program agent being the originator of an event is Word "autosaving" a file, which saves a snapshot of the state of a document without any human action.

---

28. The Arizona Electronic Transactions Act, A.R.S. § 44-7014, for example, provides that "[i]n any automated transaction, the parties may form a contract by the interaction of . . . electronic agents of the parties, even if no individual was aware of or reviewed the electronic agents' actions or the resulting terms and agreements."

Thus, we have foundational questions involving "who:" Who caused the event? Who sent the e-mail? Who signed the contract? Who edited the spreadsheet? Who saved the file?

This concept is unusually difficult, and is covered in Chapter 6. Because the word "who" usually connotes a person only, and our concept is broader than people, in this book we will use the term "identity." That identity may be of a person, or of a system, or of an element within a system. And this is one of the difficulties. Dealing with complex systems, the notion of identity becomes blurred. Smaller elements combine to create larger systems or behaviors, emerging to be something greater than the sum of the parts. Humans and their agents, the programs, work together to cause events to occur. Thus, the issue of who, and of identity, is one of the most perplexing in the new world of digital information. Who is responsible for what? What caused what?

There is also a concept of "origination" in the world of digital evidence. As noted above, this book submits that the hallowed evidentiary concept of "original" no longer has meaning in the digital realm. What *does* have meaning is the concept of "origination," because the digital realm comprises events, and events unfold through time, and there is a world of cause and effect in the digital realm. If one traces that cause and effect backwards through time (assuming one has enough information to do so), one can theoretically find an originating event. It may be important to determine where an event originated, as well as when it originated and who was associated with the origination.

Origination is particularly important when analyzing authenticity issues. What was the originating event? Who originated a record of information? How did they accomplish that task of origination?

One could find, for example, an e-mail that contained a unique Word attachment. The creation of the Word document could be considered the originating event. A few hours later, millions of identical Word attachments could exist the world over. Which is the *original* file of these many millions of precisely identical, pure collections of 0s and 1s? None is, as that question only has meaning when discussing artifacts, not pure information sets that are identical. But there could have been an originating event and an originating identity. Origination allows us to hold onto authenticity in the digital world, which concept is closely related to cause and effect.

This leads to yet another concept.

THE CONCEPT OF "WHERE"

Just as digital events unfold in time, they also unfold in space, even though informational records do not depend on physical matter to exist. The concept of space is necessitated by digital information residing in various types of physical devices. Records are found on hard drives, thumb drives, servers, microchips, and so on, as we all know.

Of course, the information must have a way to travel in and about its ecosystem. There are wires, and wireless broadcasting of information, and machines that direct traffic (called routers), and switches, and other physical devices that are found in various geographic locations but are linked together.

The totality of the various components, and the way they interact, combine to form networks. Networks exist in physical space as well as in virtual space. Thus, an originating event, such as the sending of an e-mail with an attachment, can occur in a specific place, such as a desktop machine that exists at a certain IP address and a certain physical location. The concept of "where" can be important in the collection of evidence. If we know where something happened, we can evaluate the competence of the process that created that record and determine our confidence in the accuracy of that record in recording that event. For example, the software version of the program operating in a specific computer where the record was generated may be shown to be flawed, thereby making suspect any record it creates. Digital records are products of their environment, and therefore, the "where" question allows us to evaluate the environment. It also tells us about the history of events as they unfolded, including what may have been the originating events. This history of events is often relevant in, for example, forensic investigations of security breaches.

REALM-SWITCHING AND THE PROBLEM OF PRINTOUTS OF FILES

Finally, complicating the authenticity problems discussed above is one last point: Digital records existing in the dynamic, untestable digital realm of pure information can be transmuted into more-traditional physical records through the act of printing them out on paper. These printouts can be extremely confusing. They mix the digital and physical realms together, even though the underpinnings of the operation of those realms are completely different, and indeed, diametrically opposed in many instances. Psychologically, such printouts mimic a traditional physical record, and people therefore often apply inappropriate mental frames or reliability to them that should properly be applied only to physical records.

A document typed on a typewriter is a world away from a printout of information contained in a digital record. The digital record can have changed many times since its origination, to be printed out long after the date it purports to have been written. One oftentimes sees parties and their counsel using such documents in court, or even photocopies of such documents, making the simpleminded assumption that the date on the document has some necessary connection to reality. This results from their being captives of inappropriate mental frameworks. The printout had a birth as a physical writing after a completely different life. A printout is a renaissance, or perhaps a reincarnation. The life story of the printout must not be confused with the life story of its parent electronic file. Thanks to this endemic printout problem, paper printouts of digital files are special cases and are inherently suspect as to authenticity.

CONCLUSION

Digital information objects are a species of pure information. Because they carry information only of the present, and are freely editable, they are not testable as to past states. This conflicts with how we have traditionally viewed written evidence, including our longstanding view that original documents give an assurance we are dealing with authentic records. The longstanding notion that writing is a permanent form of evidence has come to an end—unless we construct regimes that permit tests of information attributes.

In addition, digital information lives in and must be extracted from complex systems that are characterized by emergence, which indeed have become a new sort of entity on our planet—perhaps even a form of life. Such systems write statements into digital records that may or may not be reliable and accurate, depending on the circumstances. Given that these statements are also data, they too can be edited or deleted at will, and the problem of untestability therefore exists not only for human-entered data but also for system-generated data.

How anyone can test digital information for authenticity is not readily obvious. In many circumstances, it simply may not be possible to test information for its authenticity. Without a specific regime in place, only an understanding of the probability of facts going to authenticity might be possible.

PART II

Authenticity

Part II of this book examines issues relating to authenticity of digital information. Authenticity is a question that relates to objects, and here, to digital information objects. The questions usually asked to determine authenticity are either: "Is this object what people claim it to be?" or "Is this object what it purports to be on its face?" If the finder of fact, from all the evidence, concludes that the answer is *no,* the object is not authentic.

What type of facts does the authenticity issue implicate?

First, objects obviously carry information. A gun might carry fingerprints. A document carries text. But an issue going to authenticity does not inquire into the accuracy of such information per se. Indeed, a letter with a false assertion in it can be unquestionably authentic. The information can be innocently mistaken, or even a downright lie, and the information object still be authentic. Accuracy is not the issue.

Authenticity, instead, highlights that objects are themselves "facts," with attributes, or characteristics, tying them to the circumstances of a case in the form of explicit or implied statements. The statement could be, "This is John's gun," or, "This is a piece of Caesar's throne," or "Jane wrote this letter," or "This is the same letter Jane wrote and it has not been changed." Such statements made about an object's attributes come either from the object itself (such as, for example, a signature found on the object), or from sources extrinsic to the object (such as testimony or claims or assertions about the object). Accordingly, when we discuss objects, there is not only information carried by the object, but also a kind of "meta-information," or information *about* the object itself, which are the assertions about the object's attributes. Whether these assertions about the attributes of the object are true determines authenticity.

A gun, for example, might have a purported or claimed *owner.* This assertion about ownership is one way of characterizing the object as a fact. If the gun had owner A, the gun will be one type of fact that connects up to all the other evidence in the case with a certain force. If the gun had owner B, however, the gun might be a completely different type of fact, rearranging how all the other evidence in the case should rightly be viewed.

Accordingly an object's attributes affect how it connects with the other facts in the case. Thus, objects "connect up" to evidence differently, depending on their attributes. Or, such objects might not connect up at all. Proving the fingerprints on a gun do not match the defendant's fingerprints does not "connect up" to anything, really—if you used a gun at random taken from another city's crime lab, for example. But if you can prove the fingerprints are not the defendant's on what the prosecution asserts is the gun that committed the crime, you have proved something that has some force. This is why authenticity is a problem in the weight of the evidence, as we discuss in the next chapter.

REDISCOVERING AUTHENTICITY IN THE DIGITAL REALM

Digital information objects now compel us to rediscover the concept of authenticity. Formerly, authenticity applied almost overwhelmingly to physical objects. But how do you discuss or inquire into an object when there is no physical object there, but instead only pure information? Are there families of attributes a pure information object might have that will allow us to resurrect a theory of authenticity for the digital age? The answer is *yes*.

First, when we discuss the issue of "information," lying deep at the root of the issue is the idea of a singularity, or perhaps the coming to life of the information in the first place. For there to be organized information at all, some *identity* must have been involved in its birth or creation as its originator. Accordingly, a digital information object causes us to look for an entity that has an identity. Authorship is one sort of attribute for a digital information object, and it implicates an identity. Who authored the information?

Luckily, there are ways that identities can signify authorship of information. Identities do this in any number of ways by declaring they are the author(s). But "signing" is perhaps the classic paradigm. By signing information, the entity that authored it makes a record imbedded within the information object itself that associates that identity with the information.

But the act of signing, as a way of associating identities with information, can be used to do more than signify authorship. Signing is a more general act of associating an identity with information, and thus is enormously important in the law—indeed probably one of law's "top few inventions." The act of signature can mean many things depending on the facts: It can mean the signer authored the information. Or, it can mean the identity agreed with the information, or promised to abide by it, or transmitted it, or endorsed it, or saw it, or indeed, any of a number of acts, depending on the intent of the identity involved.

Given the fact that entities associate themselves with information objects for a variety of reasons, authenticity implicates the concept of identity broadly, as a family of attributes. Without knowing the entity associated with the information—whether it be as originator or signer or some other actor—it is hard if not impossible to talk about whether something is authentic.

For example, if some set of information is said to be a statute, but we cannot possibly know who promulgated or declared it or passed it, is it really the authentic law? Doesn't the fact that information purports to be the law necessarily implicate issues about identity of a promulgator?

Or, if we have a check, with an amount filled in, but the check is not signed, does the check have any meaning? Can we discuss whether the check is authentic? If we see information we are led to believe is a contract, but if there are no identities associated with it, can the information be a contract?

Information objects are used in reading and writing games—they are used to promulgate, promise, acknowledge, deed, convey, bequeath, record, declare, and so on. These games lose their meaning without the concept of *players*. Accordingly, authenticity implies an attribute of identity. This could be a single entity or a group. The identity need not be known for it to nevertheless exist as an important or relevant attribute. Certainly, when we discover that a twenty-first-century prankster in fact wrote the purportedly ancient but anonymous text, we have proved a document inauthentic by means of learning about an identity.

Indeed, the concept of identity is so fundamental, it is behind our everyday concept of authenticity in day-to-day parlance. If we wonder whether a person is "authentic," we assume there is a real person with a real identity in the equation. The mental question, "Is John really such a kind and caring person, or is his recent behavior towards his wealthy uncle James just a *show*?" implies there is a real John, a true John, that perhaps might be different than the apparent John. We search for identity when we question authenticity.

Next, for information objects, the idea of authenticity is bound up in the notion of the idea that records of information should be static—the idea the object of information will remain immutable after the object and its associated entity go their separate ways. If records could change through time in unpredictable, untestable ways after they became disassociated with their entities, the concept of authenticity would lose its meaning. Immutability, or at least the ability to know and track changes through time, is thus a key part of the concept of authenticity and an important attribute of information objects.

If the information contained in the law changes without the King's knowledge and consent, is it still really the law? If the details of my autobiography change after I write it, but without my knowledge, is it my autobiography? The information in a record must remain the same, so that we know it is still linked to the entity involved, in the way the record tacitly states and the entity intended.

Accordingly, given these philosophical underpinnings, a record can be inauthentic if some entity, other than the entity the record states is its author or signer, is the true author or signer. If someone authors a letter and signs it "Helen," but in fact it was Bill pretending to be Helen who authored it and signed it, the letter is not authentic. The purported attributes of the object are not true.

And, a record can also be inauthentic if the information in the record changes unknowably from its original state, when it was associated with the entity that gave it birth. Going back to our example, if Helen really did author or sign a letter, but Bill changed the information later without disclosing the change, the letter is not authentic. Authenticity is thus related to the concepts of identity and constancy of the information object associated with that identity.

The issue of time information is a little more complicated. Often, the time an entity associated itself with a certain set of defined information is not relevant. If for example, you are determining whether person B really is the authentic child of person A, it does not really matter exactly how old either of them are so long as the parental association is true. Or, if you want only authentic software on your computer, you don't care exactly when Apple published it, so long as it really came from Apple, had not changed since it came from Apple, and was going to work on your computer.

But time can enter into authenticity questions. Normally, what is implicated is the time of creation or signing of a record. If timing makes an information object a different kind of object depending on the time involved, then time may be relevant to authenticity.

Suppose a board of a corporation loses its authority, by statute, to grant bonuses after January 1. There is a board resolution dated December 19, giving a large bonus to the outgoing president. On January 10, the president presents it to the treasurer to collect his check. Suppose we know for certain that the board did sign the resolution. Suppose we know for sure that the information in the resolution has not changed since the signing. But suppose the truth of the matter is that the resolution, which was dated December 19, was never discussed before and was not created or signed until January 3.

In this case, time can be highly relevant to authenticity. The accurate information about time shows an information object as a radically different fact than it purports to be. Time attributes of objects thus can figure into authenticity determinations. When was the stock option issued? When was the e-mail sent? The possibilities for time to figure into authenticity are endless.

And so can other attributes figure into authenticity issues. If information purports to be associated with "IP address A," (the IP address of a disgruntled employee), saying, "Pay $500,000 to this secret bank account by midnight, or the Chairman will disappear to the Meadowlands forever," but in actuality the document came from "IP address B" (the IP address of the Chairman's hired industrial extortion operative), the object would not be authentic. Indeed, it is probably not possible to make an exhaustive list of all the different attributes of information objects that might be implicated in an authenticity determination.

Accordingly, to learn about the authenticity of digital information we must ask questions about the attributes of the information object in question. First, is it associated with the identity it purports to be associated with? Next, there are questions about the constancy of the information in a record. Constancy or immutability of information, called "integrity," is a key attribute of authenticity of information. Finally, in certain instances, is the *time information* related to the object correct? Was the stock option authorized on that date, or was that record backdated?

Accordingly, learning facts about immutability, identity, and time allows us to test the authenticity of digital records. These can each be explored by means of circumstantial evidence, which will give understanding that is probabilistic, ranging from a downright hunch to an understanding that is fairly certain.

Various circumstantial evidence scenarios are described in the next chapters, as are *eunomic* regimes for each attribute about authenticity, so that advocates can understand how to best prove, and test through cross-examination or contradiction, the various factors going to the weight of the evidence about authenticity. And even if authenticity is not an issue, the attributes about identity, integrity, and time are often relevant in their own right, and very important in the weight of the evidence. But first, Chapter 3 will discuss the rules governing the threshold of admissibility that must be crossed before any item of digital information can be admitted into evidence.

The Existing Scheme Regarding Authenticity

This chapter discusses the concept of authenticity as understood by the Federal Rules of Evidence. It also discusses the requirement that one lay a preliminary foundation about the authenticity of evidence, called "authentication," before such evidence will be admitted by a trial judge. After such admission, the evidence is then weighed by the finder of fact, which will conclude the true facts of the case.

Not every country has rules like this. This is because the United States inherited the jury system, which, for whatever reason, is still alive and thriving here. Even in its original home of England, use of the jury trial is greatly restricted. The jury trial's near-death is the same in most other common law countries.[1] And certainly in most of the rest of the world, judges and magistrates are usually the entities that weigh evidence, not juries.

Accordingly, in the United States our evidence law is concerned at least in part with an area largely irrelevant elsewhere. Noted evidence professor James Bradley Thayer described the peculiarity of our system at the turn of the twentieth century:

> When a man raises his eyes from the common-law system of evidence he is struck with the fact that our system is radically peculiar. Here, a great mass of evidential matter, logically important and probative, is shut out . . . by an imperative rule, while the same matter is not thus excluded anywhere else. English speaking countries have what we call a "Law of Evidence;" but no other country has it; we alone have generated and evolved this large, elaborate and difficult doctrine.[2]

Before discussing the concept of "authentication," we must examine the definition of authenticity and understand how it is only a special type of relevance, because one must understand the ultimate goal before one can understand the test applied to whether one has successfully proved preliminary facts about that goal.

---

1. The English have effectively abolished the civil jury trial. *See* J.R. Spencer, Jackson's Machinery of Justice 72, 73 (8th ed. 1989). Jury trial remains a theoretical entitlement in cases of serious crime throughout the common law world, but plea bargaining and other mechanisms have rendered criminal jury trials ever more exceptional. *See* John H. Langbein, *On the Myth of Written Constitutions: The Disappearance of Criminal Jury Trial,* 15 Harv. J. L. & Pub. Pol'y 119 (1992).

2. James Bradley Thayer, A Preliminary Treatise on Evidence at the Common Law, 1–2 (Boston, Little Brown 1898).

Relevance and Authenticity Under the Federal Rules

The rule dealing with weight of the evidence is called *relevance.* Under the Federal Rules of Evidence, "relevant evidence" means "evidence having any tendency to make the existence of any fact that is of consequence to the determination of the action more probable or less probable than it would be without the evidence."[3]

This refers to the empirical dynamic Locke described. Data taken into the mind creates "facts," really a type of idea about reality. As a result of finding the facts, tribunals actively piece together a mental scheme or impression. The mind constantly tests whether any new idea presented to it agrees with and therefore connects to, or disagrees with and therefore repels, its other ideas. If the proffered data or evidence has no involvement in this dynamic, it has no weight and it is not relevant. "Weight" could just as easily have been called "power," or perhaps even "catalytic function." The law continues to recognize, as it did in its first evidence treatise, that facts are psychological things.

Thus, we have the simplest and most important evidentiary rule: Relevant evidence is admissible. Irrelevant evidence is not admissible.[4] This rule, of course, assumes that a judge can preview the synthetic process and then decide whether a certain fact would be used in the act of synthesis. There is an assumption that the synthetic process is roughly the same in the mind of the judge as in the mind of the jury members. And in order to talk about this assumption, because the judge does not know what is really going on in the jury member's minds, we create a hypothetical, "rational" person on the jury, whose mental functioning of comparing and contrasting evidence is assumed to be similar to the mental functioning of the judge.

Authenticity as a Special Type of Relevance

Given this background on relevance, we can now understand the most fundamental evidentiary concept relating to digital evidence. This is *authenticity.* People involved in disputes will claim that certain written information they possess is probative of facts: For example, they might claim a digital record represents the invoice in question. They will assert facts about a record's content, about the time the record was made, and about either who made the record or who manifested assent to it.

As we have discussed, evidence can have debatable authenticity because a record is claimed to be associated with a *person or entity* other than the truthful entity. Or, it can be debatable because the *content* of a record can have changed over time. Or, the record could have been created or signed at a *time* other than what is stated on or about the record. As we have already discussed to some extent, authenticity means that things are as they are claimed to be.

Authenticity is considered a subset of relevance because, unless an object is authentic, it does not have proper evidentiary weight. The information in, on, or implied by an object that is not authentic does not tend to prove anything in the case, or at least does not tend to prove what its proponents claim it proves. Examining a draft contract nobody saw or signed does not tend to prove facts at issue in the action.

---

3. Fed. R. Ev. 401.
4. Fed. R. Ev. 402.

So what are the rules regarding authenticity? Strangely, the Federal Rules of Evidence do not contain a rule requiring informational records or other objects to be authentic. The requirement appears to be assumed, because of the relevancy paradigm just discussed. The Advisory Committee that drafted the rules considered authenticity to be a special subset of relevance.[5]

There is, however, a wealth of case law holding that documentary evidence must be authentic. *See,* for example, *United States v. Holmquist,* 36 F.3d 154, 166 (1st Cir 1994) ("It cannot be gainsaid that documentary evidence must be authentic") and *United States v. Paulino*, 13 F.3d 20, 22 (1st Cir 1994) (documentary evidence must be authentic; authentication is a condition precedent to admissibility). But the bottom line is that authenticity is required because relevance is required.

Circumstantial Evidence Always Relevant to Authenticity

Usually, whether something is authentic will depend on the weighing of a great many facts. In the consideration of digital evidence, these might be facts about the digital information itself. Or, they could be facts about the outside world. Almost always, both types of facts will be relevant.

THE FOUNDATION CALLED AUTHENTICATION

But the rules do set forth a system by which one can meet a requirement of "authentication." *See* Rule 901(a). Although the term authentication is not explicitly defined, a reading of the rules reveals authentication to be an initial showing about the authenticity of evidence, so that the evidence can be admitted for the jury's determination about authenticity.[6]

Majority Rule of Pure Conditional Relevancy

Again, we cut to the bottom line. Almost any type of circumstantial evidence one can put forward that tends to prove a record is authentic will meet one's burden of authentication, so that a court should then submit the record to a jury for its consideration of the information in the record, and if necessary, for its ultimate determination on the issue of authenticity if that is debated. The rules state the initial burden of proof is "satisfied by evidence *sufficient to support a finding* that the matter in question is what its proponent claims."[7] As we will see, this is a circular definition, because evidence sufficient to support a finding simply assumes there is a quantum of evidence the judge will require to support a finding. It does not define that quantum of evidence; it leaves it to the judge. If the judge, in her discretion, does not believe there is sufficient evidence to have proved

---

5. "Authentication and identification represent a special aspect of relevance." Jerome Michael & Mortimer J. Adler, *Real Proof,* 5 Vand. L. Rev. 344, 362 (1952); John W. Strong, McCormick on Evidence, §§ 179, 185; Edmund M. Morgan, Basic Problems of Evidence 378 (1962); Federal Advisory Committee Note to Subdivision (a) of Rule 901.

6. "Authentication" is a confusing word because the same word is used when discussing information systems, to signify a similar function about confirming the identity of the participants who log on and are accepted into the reading and writing games of information systems. This is discussed in detail in Chapter 6, concerning identity.

7. Fed. R. Ev. 901(a).

the facts of authenticity, one has not met an authentication burden. Few treatises discuss this circularity in the definition, because it formerly did not pose many problems. Our familiar physical records were artifacts; they were testable.

So how do the cases and treatises deal with this circular definition—that one meets one's authentication burden by proving whatever the judge will require in her discretion? By far, the majority view is the "rationality test": So long as it would be *rational* for a jury to conclude the evidence is authentic given the authentication showing, the object should be admitted.[8]

Even here, what exactly does "rational" mean? Is it rational to make an educated guess? And if so, if an educated guess is rational, is it sufficient to support a finding? This will likely be the subject of interesting judicial decisions over the coming years, where thinking judges might rediscover some of the discretion they formerly exercised.

The Federal Rules give nonlimiting illustrations of its concept that parties are entitled to have evidence admitted by proving, through circumstantial evidence, facts sufficient to support a finding that something is what it is claimed to be. The first example, found in Rule 901(b)(1), is of critical significance for digital evidence: that one can meet one's authentication burden by the *testimony* of a person with knowledge that something is what it is claimed to be. This is a minimal to almost nonexistent showing—almost akin to a vouching, or even perhaps an allegation. Our language betrays the real dynamics. Advocates and judges often talk about a "sponsoring" witness who testifies to get an exhibit admitted. All counsel has to do is find someone who, at one time, had some involvement linking such witness to the event in question, and then have that person testify that the record is what the party claims it is in the dispute. There really is no strict requirement that the witness actually know what he or she is talking about.

Commentators gloss over this by pointing out that there is a "light burden of proof," with the "knowledge" requirement of Rule 901(b)(1) liberally construed. A witness may be appropriately knowledgeable through having participated in or *observed the event* reflected by the exhibit.[9] Thus, there is no need to know or remember the information. The rule is satisfied if the witness just observed an event touching on the information. But what event is this? Is it only the event of origination? Does the witness need to have knowledge of events afterwards that might have changed the information? The answer is *no,* because the law evolved during the reign of physical records and there was a somewhat reasonable assumption that changes did not occur, and that if they did, they would probably be apparent. The law incorporates a physical record paradigm into its current foundational tests and precedent.

Along these lines, when the authenticity of records maintained by organizations is at issue, the prima facie showing has been reduced to testimony about how exhibits of the type in question are normally prepared. For example, Weinstein at § 901.03[2] explains

---

8. *See* CHARLES A. WRIGHT & VICTOR J. GOLD, FEDERAL PRACTICE AND PROCEDURE: EVIDENCE § 7104; JACK B. WEINSTEIN & MARGARET A. BERGER, WEINSTEIN'S FEDERAL EVIDENCE § 901.02[3] (hereinafter "WEINSTEIN"); Lorraine v. Markel Insurance Co., 241 F.R.D. 534, 2007 WL 1300739 (D.Md. 2007); United States v. Safavian, 435 F. Supp. 2d at 38; United States v. Meienberg, 263 F.3d 1177, 1180 (10th Cir 2001); *and* Stuckey v. Northern Propane Gas Co., 874 F. 2d 1563 1574 (11th Cir. 1989) (upholding admission of meeting minutes based on "minimal showing" by one witness who testified the minutes "looked like he expected them to look").

9. WEINSTEIN at § 901.03[2].

that Rule 901(b)(1) *does not require personal knowledge about the making of a particular exhibit* if the witness has knowledge of how that type of exhibit is *routinely* made. Authentication is accomplished when the witness identifies exhibits as documents of a type an organization typically develops, and then testifies about the procedures the organization follows in generating and maintaining such records, and about how the document was retrieved.

Clearly, no knowledge, either personal or institutional, about the immutability of the information in the record is required. No testimony is required about any processes that support immutability of information. What we have instead is a quick once-over, with the information then coming into evidence and thereafter affecting the relevancy dynamics discussed previously. If you can introduce evidence of a routine, there is a presumption the routine was followed, even though in fact it might not have been followed in that instance, or even if the "routine" is only a haphazard goal. There is no requirement about the quality of the routine, or how it would ensure immutability. These elements are assumed. The evidence is admitted, and the burden then shifts to the other party to disprove the information going to authenticity. Clearly, this is not a system requiring proof of authenticity, but more of a system forcing participants to disprove authenticity. This might pose problems, however, given that our information infrastructure now makes it impossible to test or disprove the authenticity of information unless certain regimes were followed. As a policy matter, the burden is currently on disprovers, who might have an impossible task. Practitioners should merely understand all this and use it to the benefit of their clients.

ILLUSTRATION OF OPERATION OF RULE 901(B)(1)

Suppose a witness was involved in a closing on a financial transaction that included 25 contracts, and which occurred five years ago. A lawsuit implicates the terms of one of those documents, which is 75 pages long and contains many details. The questioned term is on page 54 of the document near the bottom of the page. There is a dispute over whose version of the writing is the authentic, binding contract. Various competing electronic files have been found on servers, as the parties did not make an official, bound-paper closing book but rather performed an "electronic closing."

The witness, who was involved in the closing those five years ago, honestly believes his employer is correct about its allegations about the proper version of the contract, recently printed off a computer from an electronic file.[10] The witness has absolutely no memory about the term in question found on page 54. Yet, because he was involved in the transaction and can claim to be familiar with an object, he is entitled to testify that the object in question was the object used at closing. The witness was involved in the flurry of e-mails at the time. He saw the first page of the contract and it still looks familiar, like the object at issue. It has the right parties and dates and recitals on it. He guesses it is the right object. A sort of vouching occurs, and it is enough to get the information admitted into evidence as the authentic information object. It thereafter will begin to affect the synthesizing role of the jury, and its determinations about weight.

---

10. See Case Study on the printout of the electronic file problem in Appendix G of this book.

Under Rule 901(b)(1), almost any sort of circumstantial evidence can meet the burden of "sufficient to support a finding." Judges need to ask themselves exactly what the cutoff point is for evidence "sufficient to support a finding." Is it a 5 percent chance, a 1 percent chance of authenticity? To what extent should courts permit juries to guess about authenticity? To what extent is it rational to make an educated guess, based on the vouching of a witness who clearly does not really have personal knowledge that the information at issue has remained constant over time, or is really the right information in any event?

The other illustrative examples of how to "authenticate" evidence show that authentication is an exercise in circumstantial evidence of almost any type that can satisfy the requirement of "rationality." There is no one way to authenticate things. One can have lay people testify about other people's handwriting.[11] One can have experts testify about handwriting through comparison with known specimens.[12] One can bring out, through circumstantial evidence, that certain facts about a piece of evidence lead to the conclusion it is authentic.[13] For example, a letter was authenticated based on the fact it was found in a certain person's suitcase.[14] A court was held to have properly admitted a fax that was circumstantially authenticated, by its responsiveness to a letter that was already in evidence.[15] And in *United States v. Stearns*, 550 F.2d 1167 (9th Cir. 1977), the Court held that even if direct testimony as to foundational matters were absent, the contents of a photograph itself, together with such other circumstantial evidence as bears upon the issue, may justify admission of a photograph (a photo of two stolen boats in the backyard of the defendant).

Continuing with the illustrations found in Rule 901(b), a recording of a voice can be identified by lay opinion based on previous familiarity with the sound of the voice.[16] The speaker on one end of a telephone conversation can be identified through circumstantial evidence about who is assigned to what telephone number, when combined with who identifies himself upon answering.[17] Public records or reports can be authenticated if they are found where they are supposed to be.[18] And a document or data that is 20 years old or older, and found where it would likely be if authentic, is authenticated.[19] Methods provided by other laws, such as Acts of Congress or Supreme Court Rules issued pursuant to statutory authority, can be used to authenticate.[20]

One final illustration is found in Rule 901(b)(9), which allows authentication of the result of a process or system if there is evidence that the process or system produces an accurate result. The Advisory Committee Note gives as an example of this rule "the computer." The Advisory Committee Note on this Rule appears to be a vast oversimplification, and will be discussed in Chapters 7 and 8.

---

11. Fed. R. Ev. 901 (b)(2).
12. Fed. R. Ev. 901 (b)(3).
13. Fed. R. Ev. 901 (b)(4).
14. United States v. Eisenberg, 807 F.2d 1446 (8th Cir. 1986).
15. United States v. Weinstein, 762 F.2d 1522 (11th Cir. 1985), *cert. denied,* 475 U.S. 1110 (1986).
16. Fed. R. Ev. 901 (b)(5).
17. *Id.* at (b)(6).
18. *Id.* at (b)(7).
19. *Id.* at (b)(8).
20. *Id.* at (b)(10).

What all this shows is that whether a piece of evidence is indeed authentic is almost always a question of circumstantial evidence that can implicate facts intrinsic to the record (such as handwriting, signatures, or perhaps metadata), or facts extrinsic to the record (such as where the record is found, what the record replied to, or what a person testifies about a record). What we are talking about is evidence about the attributes of an object, and such evidence can come in many forms, including just where the object was found. And because the jury must also consider the "evidence about the evidence" to make its ultimate conclusion about authenticity, the rules of evidence must be followed in laying an authentication foundation under Article IX.[21]

THE POSSIBILITY OF REQUIRING A MORE ROBUST FOUNDATION TO AUTHENTICATE

Some treatise writers and cases have posited that a more robust showing (more than a showing governed by a rationality test) can, at the discretion of the trial court, be required to assure that reliable evidence is submitted to the jury. *See* Saltzburg et al., *Federal Rules of Evidence Manual* (6th ed. 1994) at 1689. The authors there suggest that certain requirements in the illustrations in the rules, such as Rule 901(b)(2)'s forbidding lay witnesses from studying up on handwriting for purposes of trial, prove that competency and reliability determinations by the court are still allowed. The authors state, "[T]here is no clear showing that Congress adopted a unitary approach to authentication that would deprive the Trial Judge of his or her traditional power to scrutinize possibly unreliable or fabricated evidence." *Id.* at 1689.

Such more traditional competency determinations can be found, for example, in decisions about tape recordings, presumably because of their unusually persuasive effect. *See, e.g., United States v. Branch*, 970 F.2d 1368 (4th Cir 1992), where the Court reiterated a multipronged list of what must be proved to establish the foundation for a tape recording, and *Smith v. City of Chicago*, 242 F.3d 737, 741 (7th Cir. 2001), where the court held the burden to authenticate a tape recording must be proved by "clear and convincing" evidence, even in civil cases. Similar more-robust foundations are required to establish a "chain of custody" showing that an item is indeed the same item and in the same condition as was found with a defendant. *See United States v. Clonts*, 966 F.2d 1366 (10th Cir. 1992), holding that the degree of proof necessary to support a chain of custody will properly depend on the nature of the evidence proffered:

> The degree of proof needed to establish an uninterrupted chain of custody depends upon the nature of the evidence at issue. If the evidence is unique, readily identifiable and resistant to change, the foundation for admission need only be testimony that the evidence is what it purports to be. *United States v. Cardenas*, 864 F.2d 1528, 1531 (10th Cir.), cert. denied, 491 U.S. 909, 105 L. Ed. 2d 705, 109 S. Ct. 3197 (1989). Alternatively, if the evidence is open to alteration or tampering, or is not readily identifiable, the trial court requires a more elaborate chain of custody to establish that the evidence has not been tampered with or altered.[22]

---

21. These are different from admissibility determinations that are not matters of conditional relevancy, which are governed by Rule 104 (a), and where the court is not bound by the rules of evidence in making its admissibility determination.

22. 966 F.2d at 1368.

There is therefore a tension in the authentication requirements under the Federal Rules. The language of Rule 901, and the great weight of comment on the rules, view authentication foundations as issues of conditional relevancy and as governed by Rule 104(b). Under this view, so long as there is evidence whereby a rational jury could find an object authentic, there is a sufficient foundation to admit the evidence. Certain types of records are assumed, on their face, to have a built-in authenticity foundation and therefore are considered "self-authenticating." *See* Rule 902.

However, it is no doubt true that the court, certainly under its residual powers granted by Rule 403, can still exercise discretion to ensure that reliable and nonmisleading evidence is admitted. And clearly, the rule is "sufficient to support a finding." If the court does not feel it would allow a case to go to verdict based on the evidence, it should not admit, even if it were rational to conclude something was authentic.

CASE STUDY

Let us now test these authentication principles on one of the most common problems existing today, the printout of the digital file. We will examine the authentication foundation laid, and then a cross-examination contesting the foundation, and then ask whether the court should admit the evidence as properly authenticated:

Q: Mr. Smith, do you have what has been marked for identification as Exhibit 53 before you there?

A: I do.

Q: What is that?

A: This is a 75-page contract our company entered into five years ago, with the defendant.

Q: I see. Thank you. Now, were you there at the closing as an official representative of the company?

A: I was.

Q: And as part of your duties on behalf of the plaintiff, did you familiarize yourself with Exhibit 53?

A: Yes, I did. I am sure I read it quite closely before we executed the documents.

Q: So, then, you have personal knowledge of its contents?

A: Yes, I do.

Q: And is Exhibit 53 a true and correct copy of the contract that was entered into between the plaintiff and the defendant?

A: Yes, it is.

Move the admission of Exhibit 53, Your Honor.

Opposing Counsel: Objection. Insufficient Foundation, Rule 403. Your Honor, may I have some questions on voir dire?

The Court: Yes. Proceed. But make it quick.

Q: Thank you. Those five years ago, did you commit to memory the terms of the contract?

A: No. Of course not.

Q: So I take it you did not memorize the term that is at issue in this case, the one found on page 54, about the option to renew after four years?

A: No. I did not memorize it.

Q: So you have no personal knowledge of that term, do you?

A: Well, I can read it. It is in the contract.

Q: But you are dependent on what the document says to know anything about that term, is that correct?

A: I suppose so.

Q: So you know personally about as much about that term as I do, because I can read the document, too?

A: Whatever.

Q: Is that right?

A: Yes.

Q: Thank you. Now, is this the document that was signed at the closing?

A: I think so.

Q: I don't see any ink on this copy. Why is that?

A: Well, this particular document was not signed, as it is a stand-alone addendum. The parties just kept electronic files of all the closing documents.

Q: Okay. So how did this show up in court?

A: We printed it off our computer. Just like the defendant printed their copy off their computer.

Q: The one that is different than yours?

A: Yes.

Q: Okay. So when was this printed off your company's computer?

A: I think before a deposition about four months ago.

Q: Well after the lawsuit started, is that correct? About a year after the lawsuit started?

A: Yes.

Q: That was a year after the lawsuit started, correct?

A. Correct.

Q: And where was that electronic file kept in your company?

A: Well, I don't know, other than it is on the network. That is an IT thing.

Q: Could you look at it during the years after the closing, and before it was printed out?

A: Yes. I did, actually, to refer to it a few times. I even downloaded it onto my laptop for study.

Q: And could other people in the company do that? Look at it and download it?

A: Yes. I suppose.

Q: Can you upload things to the network, too?

A: Yes, I often upload things I do at home onto our network.

Q: Well, after things are on the network, can you continue to work on them, so that your work is precise and accurate?

A: Absolutely. That is the way we do things.

Q: Well, what happens when documents are finished?

A: Well, you just stop working on them.

Q: Are there any procedures or technologies that freeze the document from further changes?

A: Well if there are, I don't know about them.

Q: Was that done here?

A: Was *what* done here?

Q: Was some sort of process or procedure put into place to stop edits on this electronic file that is the exhibit in front of you?

A: I don't know.

Q: You know of none?

A: That is right.

Q: Well, when did the disagreement with the defendant over this provision flare up?

A: Probably about nine months before the suit was filed.

Q: And I think that you testified that this was printed out about a year after the complaint was filed?

A: Yes.

Q: And the dispute erupted about nine months before that, meaning that the dispute erupted about one year and nine months before this was printed out, correct?

A: That is right.

Q. During that year and nine months, just how many people had access to this document?

A: Everybody in the division, probably 1,500 people or so.

Q: And could any of those 1,500 people in the division edit it?

A: I doubt it. I certainly did not.

Q: Well, are you aware of any protections that were made against its being edited?

A: Well . . . , no.

Q: So do you know if they could have edited it?

A: No.

Q: Could you have edited it?

A: Well, I don't know what you are getting at there. I resent that.

Q: Well, were you, given the information system in place at your workplace, able to edit this document?

A: I suppose that if I had been inclined to, yes, it was theoretically possible.

Q: Well, how many people accessed this electronic file before it was printed?

A: I have no idea.

Q: Does your company keep data about that?

A: I have no idea.

Q: So you can't testify that this record is in the same condition as it was originally, around the time of the closing, can you?

A: Everything looks in order to me.

Q: But 1,500 people had access to it for several years, and you have no knowledge about whether it was changed, do you?

A: I suppose not.

Q: And you have no memory of the term in question, correct?

A: Yes.

Q: And you have no other records of the term in question, other than this document that was available to be changed by any one of the 1,500 people, right?

A: The only information I have is what you have, the authentic document.

Q: It could have been changed, or it might not have changed—you just would have to guess, right?

A: I know of no evidence of change.

Q: But do you have any evidence it was *not* changed?

A: No. I don't know whether it changed or not.

Q: You would have to guess it was not changed, correct?

A: Again, that is against our company rules and procedures. We just don't change things after closing.

Q: You just don't do that, is that the policy you are referring to?

A: Yes, we just don't do that here.

Q: Do all 1,500 people feel strongly about that?

A: Absolutely.

Q: Has there ever been a violation of that policy?

A: Well, yes, it does come up in our Sarbannes audits yearly. We always then thereafter strive for perfection.

Q: But do you have any information you can rely on that says that this was not edited?

A: Nothing other than our policy, no.

Q: Thank you.

Your Honor, we object that there is insufficient foundation to show the authenticity of this recently printed electronic file.

A Conundrum Regarding Authentication: Trivial Showings

What should the court do here?

The vast majority of courts would overrule any objection and rule the exhibit had been authenticated. It would be submitted to the jury. The reasoning would be that it would be rational for the jury to conclude it was authentic. All this would then go to the weight of the evidence.

But just what has been proved by the authentication evidence? There is a witness who had some general involvement at the time, who knows something was printed off a computer. He really knows nothing else. He had no knowledge of the relevant term of the contract, or whether it has been edited, or really anything about his company's systems other than a general policy that "We don't do that here." The policy, however, is broken regularly, and there is no way to test whether it was broken in this instance or not. There simply is not enough information to test the authenticity of this document, other than to bring out this evidence going to weight. The law seems to allow that it is rational, nevertheless, for a jury to conclude that the document is authentic, meaning that it is the same contract that the other side agreed to long before the dispute arose. *If it came from a party, and the party says it is authentic, it certainly would not be irrational to conclude it was authentic.*

But is this evidence sufficient to support a finding? That will depend on the facts of each case. And it will depend on how the judge views his or her role.

Having a witness with some minimum level of knowledge testify that a document is what it is claimed to be made sense during the time that documents were artifacts—records made of molecules that were static over time. A witness could look at a physical object, ensure himself it was the right object by examining the type of paper it was on, how it felt in his hands, whether there were any obvious signs of change on the document, or whether his handwriting appeared on the document. The upshot was that, if it was the same document he originally handled, and there were no obvious signs of change, the document was likely authentic. The inference is that since the "thing" is present and being held, the record had integrity.

But such assumptions go out the window when we stop dealing with artifacts, and start dealing with pure information objects that can be undetectably edited by any one of 1,500 people, in ignorance of all others, and then printed. The modern electronic file lives not as an artifact one can hold in one's hand, but as pure information that can be reordered at will. Accordingly, without more, having a witness look at the order of the words on the first page of a recently printed electronic file does not logically entitle that witness, or our culture either, to make any assumptions whatsoever about the integrity of the order of the words in the middle of the document on page 54. There is no necessary inference that, since a thing is present, the record has integrity.

The foundational requirement for authentication of digital evidence has thus largely deteriorated into a "trivial showing." There is no necessary showing that because someone with personal knowledge recognizes the subject matter, or the order of some of the words, that all the words are in the authentic order. Clearly, in order to avoid a trivial showing, something along the lines of the chain of custody that is required for certain easily changed artifacts, as in contraband cases, is required.

COLLAPSE OF THE LEGAL DEFINITION OF THE TERM "ORIGINAL"

What of the venerable best evidence rule, found in Article X of the Federal Rules of Evidence? Can't we get around this trivial-showing problem by insisting that an original electronic file be produced?

Unfortunately, the best evidence rule is of no help. That protection, at least as regards digital evidence, has been eviscerated by the rules, the drafters of which not surprisingly could not have foreseen the future evolution of technology when they finalized the rules in the early 1970s. Indeed, in defining "original" in Rule 1001(3), the drafters declared that anything that was printed off a computer was an original so long as the printouts accurately reflect the data currently in the computer. Even if an electronic file had been edited numerous times over several years, as long a printout is accurate, the printout is an original for purposes of Article X.

But an original of what? It is an original of what was printed out, not of the record of digital information. Thus, the definition is almost meaningless. What is printed out is an original of what was printed out. The drafters of Article X gave no thought to the fact that digital files are pure information, and live apart from the world of artifacts, and that such information can be undetectably edited on networks without any ability to test for changes. The reading and writing games occurring in information ecosystems were simply not in mind when this was drafted.

Thus, the concept of originality under the Federal Rules has been reduced to triviality regarding digital information. A large hole in the law has appeared in one of its main assumptions, that with regard to written records there was evidence that could be traced closer to an original or farther away from it—and that there was a requirement to go closer to the original if that was available.

Accordingly, the current system of foundations allows litigants to place into evidence almost anything they want so long as they can get a witness with some nexus to testify that a document is what it is claimed to be. They can employ a sort of legerdemain. If we are to be intellectually honest, there is almost no preliminary burden of proving digital information is authentic.

In the future, in certain defined areas we may want to devise a regulatory scheme, or even a larger system of evidence, that requires legitimate proof of authenticity before digital records are thrown into the ring of evidence. The bottom line is that today, any trivial showing is likely to serve as a foundation for getting digital evidence admitted.

Accordingly, practitioners should know these rules, which are nicely summarized in the summary judgment context in *Lorraine v. Markel American Insurance Company*, 241 F.R.D. 534, 2007 WL 1300739 (D.Md. 2007). They should be prepared to take advantage of them on behalf of their clients, laying the most convincing foundation they can, of course, because often that will be their only attempt to convince the fact finder about the weight of the evidence.

THE WEIGHT OF THE EVIDENCE

Does it do a practitioner any good to understand digital evidence? If a trivial showing is all that is necessary to get something into evidence, then why even bother understanding things?

There are, of course, a multitude of reasons.

First, judges may well begin demanding authentication foundations that do more than constitute trivial showings. They may start ruling that, although it is rational, it is not allowable for juries to in effect guess that a record of information is authentic if an authenticating witness cannot testify with any personal knowledge about integrity of information, dates and times, or the identity of authors, signers, or transmitters. This higher standard has already appeared in at least one case, and may increase in the future, and is exemplified by *In re Vee Vinhnee*, 336 B.R. 437, 2005 WL 3609376 (9th Cir. BAP (Cal.) 2005), discussed in detail in Chapter 8. Unless you know how to oppose the authentication foundation of your opponent, you will miss out on this opportunity to exclude evidence from being admitted.

But remember that the main fight in any battle over truth is not the concept of admissibility, but rather the weight of evidence. If one wants to oppose a record introduced against your cause, you must be able to attack its probative force. Accordingly, there is a wealth of discovery and proof that can occur about the main facets of authenticity: about whether the information in a digital record has stayed the same through time; about the identity of who did what; and about the time at which certain events occurred. And similarly, if one wants to bolster a record, one shores up things through circumstantial evidence and *eunomic* regimes, if possible.

For example, in our case above, the first thing a cross-examiner must realize is that the "document" being handled above is a mere computer printout—the printing of a then-current electronic file. But what do we know about the file before it was printed? Who had access to it? Does its custodian even know where it came from? Is there any trail or history of its evolution? Was it edited? When was it edited? By whom? Does the company that possesses the record have any information about these facts? And if it does not know about these facts, how can it know its records are authentic?

Indeed, a whole world of investigation, and then testing, is available and can be guided by the topics discussed in this book.

CHAPTER 4

Integrity of Information

We now address perhaps the most important of all foundations of digital evidence. In the physical realm, the concept of "original" was important because reading from an original record allowed one to know with some confidence that one was reading information, associated with a known person, that had not changed over time—at least not undetectably so. Original documents were usually authentic documents. Information stayed the same over time and was, indeed, literally etched in stone in some instances. If there was a change, it could usually be discovered upon inspection of the original.

But as we have discussed, when information was liberated from the realm of physical matter, the concept of "original" lost meaning. In the digital realm, examining original artifacts can no longer be used as a test for whether information has changed through time. If the concept of "original" is dead in the digital realm, what concept tests whether information, found in pure information objects, has remained unchanged since it originated?

THE CONCEPT OF INTEGRITY

In the digital realm, the attribute for whether something stays the same through time is called *integrity*. Integrity means an object has remained whole—that it has not changed over time. If an information object has integrity, then it is now as it was when created. Integrity is a principal way we test for authenticity in the digital world.

Because we can no longer depend on original artifacts, we need an ability to test for integrity. How does one know whether digital information has changed through time? It is not, as we have seen, accomplished by examination of the record alone. Digital records, upon examination, allow one to learn about information *in the present*. But very few records contain enough information to allow one to confidently track changes in order to learn the original state of the record. Verification by inspection no longer works in the digital realm.

The Act of Comparison

How then does one perform a test for integrity? Rather than inspecting a record, testing for integrity is done by *comparing* a questioned digital record (called hereinafter an "information object") that purports to be the same as another information object that is trusted. Comparison of objects has replaced examination of one object as the philosophical underpinning for testing authenticity.

Comparison of two sets of digital information can be done either through circumstantial evidence, with the need for logical inferences using what facts one may fortuitously turn up, or it can be done in a more premeditated way that uses tools in an ordered scheme, much like a *demonstration*, or mathematical proof. Such a demonstration of integrity gives us what is often called "strong" knowledge. In this book we will discuss strong evidence of integrity, strong evidence of identity, and strong evidence of time. Or, we will sometimes say that there are "strong associations" of attributes with objects—such as a strong association of time to a digital object. Such *eunomic* schemes, when they concern integrity, take us back to the original idea that writing is a permanent thing though which knowledge about facts can be gained by demonstration.[1] In short, even in the new, malleable digital realm, through *eunomic* planning we can resurrect the permanency of information that lawyers formerly believed they had with the technology of writing.

COMPARISON BY WAY OF CIRCUMSTANTIAL EVIDENCE

As an example of an inferential, circumstantial way to test for integrity, consider a digital record filed in a court. These are often in the file format known as portable document format, or PDF. What some people do not recognize, however, is that PDF files *can* be edited just like other files. Accordingly, what if several years after a court filing, a question arises as to whether a certain PDF file is indeed the authentic record that appeared in a certain court case? Luckily, one would have several records to compare that purported to have been filed at the same time. There would be what was in the court file, but there would also be records in possession of other parties. If all these were identical, then all would appear to have integrity. The chances that identical edits could have been made to all the files, with new files substituted for old ones in their various physically separate repositories without anyone's knowledge, would be small. Circumstantial evidence, gathered through comparing objects and determining if there were differences, combined with the fact objects were in control of different entities, allows an inference of integrity. This is a type of test for integrity.

Accordingly, the comparison of information objects allows us to deduce if information has changed from one object to another object. For example, if it is known that file A existed on January 1, 2005, because its informational content was published in *The New York Times* that day, and file B is revealed to be identical to file A upon comparison, then file B came into existence no later than January 1, 2005 (not accounting for the highly unlikely event that identical arrangements of bits originated independently). We can say that file A and file B have integrity because they corroborate one another. Thus, we have gained knowledge about integrity, and we have also tied it to knowledge about the timing of the existence of information ("This existed no later than X date.").

Back to our example of comparison by circumstantial evidence, if a questioned court filing in the possession of a party, purporting to be authentic, was found to be different from all the other files in the repositories of the many other parties, but all those other files were identical to one another, then a substantial question as to integrity, and there-

---

1. See discussion in Chapter 1 about Gilbert's emphasis of the permanency of writing, and how it therefore allowed lawyers to pull themselves out of mere probability into the more concrete realm of knowledge.

fore authenticity, would have arisen as to the questioned filing. Or, if there were only a single courthouse file, which differed from a questioned purportedly authentic file in the possession of a party, then once again a question would have arisen, although without a reason to trust the reliability of the court file it would not be certain which file, if either, were authentic. The identity of the court system involved—assuming, for example, a U.S. court versus a Nigerian court in various hypotheticals—might be a fact about "place," which might well make a difference in our circumstantial evidence calculations of the probability of what was authentic. What to trust in such a hypothetical?

One can see that the probabilities of what might have changed between two specimens of a file will differ markedly with the facts. Critically, there must be at least two different information objects under the control of two different entities for this method of testing integrity to be available. And without knowing what to trust, you don't get too far. Often, however, there is only one information object, one file, and in that case a comparison test for integrity cannot occur. In that case, one must examine all the circumstantial evidence, digital and real-world, so as to draw inferences, which indeed might not flow at all, given available evidence. But if there are at least two objects that purport to be the same, one can gain valuable information from the act of comparison. Objects known to exist at different times can be revealed to be identical or different. Objects kept in different locations can be revealed to be identical or different, and so on. Using knowledge of "identical or different," we gain not only knowledge about integrity, but about such other attributes as timing of events and so on, depending upon the facts.

One can see this is a hit-or-miss system involving whatever circumstantial evidence is available. And it can be expensive. Indeed, unless other steps are taken in advance, even the simple comparison techniques discussed can be laborious. If you had a 100-page contract, and another purportedly identical 100-page contract with which to compare it, one would have to examine not only all the information on the top-level view of the document to determine any differences, but there could also be questions arising from the comparison of other views, such as metadata.

Audit-Logging-Type Systems for Testing Integrity

Besides testing or checking file integrity bit by bit, there are other ways of handling integrity. Some businesses have begun to organize the various circumstantial-evidence ways of assuring integrity by mandating elaborate procedures for handlers of information. Instead of providing tests to determine whether things are different, these methods try instead to control changes to information, and to keep track of what has been changed.

Some businesses thus try to control when files are edited. They make information objects read-only, and allow alteration only under certain circumstances. And they might keep track in a database of who gained access to any file or record, resulting in a set of information about who was interacting with what questioned information. And there might even be information about how information changed through time—a sort of audit log. But the audit-type information must also be controlled, because if it can be freely edited the system collapses. Such systems are fairly common in financial industries, which protect their communications with customers in read-only mode by mandate of federal regulation or rule. However, whether such a system has been deployed, and how well it has been implemented, depends on the facts. In other words, sometimes it is erroneously assumed that certain records have been kept in a secure fashion. And critically, these systems do not usually provide strict tests of the integrity of a record—up/down, yes/no, and so on. Instead, they often provide only some evidence that allows one to have at least some knowledge about the state of one's records.

EUNOMIC TOOLS FACILITATING TESTS FOR INTEGRITY

Techniques have been developed that make *comparisons* easy and systematic—technological solutions facilitating the comparison of digital information to test for integrity. These developed quite recently as technologists worked on the problem of how to use logic and mathematics to provide such solutions. Taken together, such tools provide a *eunomic* information regime governing integrity.

Chief among such tools are mathematical functions or algorithms called *transformations,* where information, which is mere numbers in the digital world, is transformed into different numbers. Sometimes the transformation is a one-way street and cannot be reversed, and sometimes it is reversible. Often the transformation takes a huge number and reduces it in size.

Using these mathematical functions, ordered regimes for determining integrity can be devised. Such regimes can be folded into interlocking computer applications that work almost without the operator thinking about things. If such schemes are implemented properly, the statistical likelihood of knowledge of a certain attribute—in this case, integrity—rises above mere probability. A demonstration has occurred, and there is a strong showing of integrity, and in many cases a strong showing of identity, of the entity associated with the information in question.

Hashing and Comparison of Hash Results

To understand these new, strong regimes for testing integrity, we first discuss *hashing,* called that because it stems from the use of mathematical equations called *hash functions.* Hashing can be a source of confusion on the part of the legal profession, but it need not be.[2]

A "hash result," a "hash digest," or sometimes just a "hash" is the result of a one-way, mathematical transformation of data according to the use of a hash function.[3] One can

---

2. For an explanation of hashing and how it can be used in discovery, *see* Ralph C. Losey, *Hash: The New Bates Stamp,* 12 JOURNAL OF TECHNOLOGY LAW & POLICY (June 2007).

3. "Hash Function," according to the May 2000 "Glossary" of The Internet Engineering Task Force's (IETF), found at http://www.ietf.org/rfc/rfc2828.txt, has multiple definitions based on different security standards: Hash function is defined as (i) "an algorithm that computes a value based on a data object (such as a message or file; usually variable-length; possibly very large), thereby mapping the data object to a smaller data object (the 'hash result'), which is usually a fixed-size value"; and (ii) "[a] (mathematical) function which maps values from a large (possibly very large) domain into a smaller range. A 'good' hash function is such that the results of applying the function to a (large) set of values in the domain will be evenly distributed (and apparently at random) over the range.

"The kind of hash function needed for security applications is called a 'cryptographic hash function,' an algorithm for which it is computationally infeasible (because no attack is significantly more efficient than brute force) to find either (a) a data object that maps to a pre-specified hash result (the 'one-way' property) or (b) two data objects that map to the same hash result (the 'collision-free' property)."

Finally, a cryptographic hash "is 'good' in the sense stated in the [ii] definition for hash function. Any change to an input data object will, with high probability, result in a different hash result, so that the result of a cryptographic hash makes a good checksum for a data object."

take any given set of digital information, feed it into a hash function, and get a much reduced set of numbers that serves as a functional "fingerprint" of the set of data, which is the "hash result" or "hash digest."[4] The hash result is representative, or shorthand, for the set of data that was hashed.

For example, one could take all the digital information that was on a certain computer hard drive that contained 200 gigabytes of information (or in other words, well in excess of many millions of pages of paper documents) and, by transforming and reducing it with a hash function, get one string of bits that was only one number, 160 bits long. More than 200 billion bytes, taking up many millions of pages, becomes 160 bits (or a number that can be printed on two lines of a page like the one you are reading) that then serves as a fingerprint, representative or shorthand proxy for the larger data set. By design, the output of a hashing transformation (or hash result) will always be the same size no matter how large the original data set transformed by that process. The 160 bits can be reduced even further, by representing some of the binary numbers as hexadecimal numbers. A 160-bit number reduces to a 40-character hexadecimal number. Here is an example: D5CD0351DFAB8F3C1E17EE634DE75BB6A92C13B7.

Some extremely useful attributes of hash functions allow that family of equations to perform services used in *eunomic* regimes. First, the transformation that occurs is irreversible. You may know a hash result, but this does not allow you to know anything about the set of data that was hashed—neither how big it was, nor what type of data it was, whether picture or text, nor anything about it whatsoever. This is useful because it allows one to deal with hash functions without revealing anything about the content of the data set hashed.

Second, it is nearly impossible (the scientists call this "computationally infeasible") to create two sets of data that will reduce to the same hash result, called a "collision" in the world of those that study hash functions.[5] This, in turn, means with near certainty that each hash result is a unique representation of a larger set of data.

Third, given any hash result, it is impossible to create a set of data that will generate that same result.

Hashing digital information, and having the hash results to use, is extremely useful in testing for integrity. Because hashes are extremely small and of consistent size, they can be computationally manipulated more easily than the typically much larger sets of data they represent. As they are unique fingerprints of much larger sets of data, they can be used to efficiently *compare* whether sets of data are identical or different—whether they be files, hard drives, removable drives, pictures, or text irrespective of file format. Hashes are very small, trusted representations of sets of data that can be used as unique proxies for the represented information object. Comparing them achieves the same knowledge of "identical or different" as does comparing the parent objects.

Accordingly, if someone asserts, or wants to test, that a certain purported file or questioned information object is the same as some other file or information object, then

---

4. The two most common hashing algorithms used to determine file integrity are MD5, which creates a 128-bit number typically expressed as a 32-character hexadecimal number; and SHA1, which creates a 160-bit number, usually expressed as a 40-character hexadecimal number.

5. Even in the unlikely event that two files resulted in the same hash value, it would be even more unlikely that the two files could be similar in any other way.

hashes of the two information objects can be used to quickly and easily test whether the objects are identical. *If the objects differ by even one bit of information, then the hashes generated by the objects will be unpredictably different,* and one will be alerted to the difference. One won't know how the objects are different, or why the objects are different, but one does have the critical knowledge that the objects *are* different.

Accordingly, one can compare objects, or one can compare hashes of objects to test for integrity. Hashes are more convenient because they are much smaller and therefore can be manipulated by computers more easily. They can be sent over the Internet more easily, and they can be used in computer applications more easily. For example, because they are smaller it is easier for a trusted third party to store them, and less time-consuming and resource-intensive to encrypt them.

THE "REFERENCE"—A NEW CONCEPT IN THE LAW OF EVIDENCE

A rigid test for integrity in the digital world depends on comparing objects. In order to learn about integrity, we focus on a particular object we want to test. Let us call it the "purported" information object, or the "questioned" information object—the one we want to learn about. Is this object the correct contract, or perhaps the right software to install on a computer after downloading it? We have information and we want to test it to determine if it is authentic.

Critically, we will not have learned about integrity unless we know *against what object* we are supposed to be comparing our questioned object. This is a critical question, and it introduces a new evidentiary concept. The information object against which we compare the questioned object is called the *reference.*

What is a reference? There is something axiomatic about the concept of a reference—something self-defining. There is no route to pure or Platonic knowledge about the identity of a reference. The reference is simply the object we trust as being authentic as compared with any other object. It is the object we choose as the standard of comparison when we do our act of comparing. Because information is no longer tied to artifacts—our beloved originals with a history on the planet and a provenance of possession—we must arrive at our notions of reference differently. We must trace them to the identity of a declarant.

For example, suppose one has downloaded software that is supposed to protect one's computer from different viruses, purportedly published by Microsoft. One obviously would want to use software guaranteed by Microsoft to be the authentic Microsoft version of the software, by which to compare the software one has downloaded from the Internet. One would also want a means by which to compare the software one has downloaded from the Internet to establish that the software downloaded is indeed authentic Microsoft software.

In this instance, what we trust to be Microsoft's software is the reference. One can learn the hash value of that trusted software. One can get this off a trusted website, or in the mail, or perhaps have it sent in secure form over the Internet. Then one can compare the hash value of Microsoft's guaranteed software to the hash value of the questioned software one has downloaded. If the hash values are the same, there is integrity and authenticity, and one can install the software on one's computer with confidence.

Notice how much more convenient it is to compare two very short numbers, such as hash values, than it is to compare all the bits contained in software programs that might contain several hundred megabytes.

The same process works on a digital copy of a government regulation, a contract, an audio or video file, or a photo. It is the same for comparing the entire data set comprising a hard drive to copies of those hard drive data sets (also known as "images"), as one often sees with regard to computer forensics work. The reference is the data set contained on the computer hard drive seized as evidence. The "purported information" is the purportedly forensically sound image of the hard drive seized as evidence, which is on the hard drive the forensicist is analyzing and using to points out facts to the jury.[6] The crucial issue is that one has a questioned information object that purports to be authentic. The way to test its integrity is by comparing it to the reference. Or, one can compare its hash to the hash of the reference to obtain the same knowledge about integrity.

Accordingly, the concept of reference now looms large in the world of evidence. Indeed, it is the closest concept we have to an original in the digital world. The reference is the set of pure information, of which there might be a billion copies, that has been *declared* by an entity as the authentic information. A reference therefore has an identity associated with it; the identity that declares it, and, as we will see, the identity that protects it and defends its immutability. These are most often but not always the same identity. A reference contains the information that is the reference information (the official content), and an implied promise the information will not change through time. A reference by its very nature contains a promised attribute of immutability.

Declaring the Reference: The Implied Promise of Immutability

In the world of physical records of information, there was clearly an act of declaring a reference: the signing of the original. The immutability of the artifact gave protections against change to the information. Such immutability "services" were accepted, and not overly pondered. The act of declaring, by an actor or participant, was clearly what was in mind, and we therefore have the important concept of "signature" in the law. Often there were notaries involved.

But the service of keeping information immutable was left to the writing technology itself. The long-standing physical system of protecting information was a useful technology indeed. It accomplished many functions taken for granted by the law.

The same process of declaring references and keeping information immutable must now happen in the digital realm if we are to retain any philosophical concept of authenticity. Because we no longer necessarily have original writings that are physical manifestations of declarations, we must be even more explicit about our declarations of references. What are the company's authentic financials? The company declares *this information* to be its financial record. The company states it. The company publishes it. The company makes a declaration of a reference of financial information for the future.

---

6. See discussion in Appendix E of integrity testing in the case study "The Role of the Vendor and Specialized Software in the Handling of Digital Evidence."

Thus, in the digital world, one must now be self-conscious about declaring what objects will henceforward be used as references in future tests of integrity.

Critically, in declaring a reference there is an implicit statement by the declarant—a sort of implied promise—that the object of information will be protected by him, or by an independent agent, now and in the future, from changes in the information. The object will be held inviolate and preserved as immutable. If you declare that a certain spreadsheet is the authentic financial record, you are also tacitly asserting you will take action with regard to that information so that it will be protected against unauthorized changes through time. In addition, it will be kept in a fashion making it possible for other information—purporting to be the identical information—to be compared against it so as to allow for a test of integrity of purportedly identical copies.

Thus, a declaration of a reference implicates an actor or an initiator of information—an identity of some sort. It is a promise to hold information immutable, and a promise that it will be testable now and in the future. If the reference shifts and morphs in unknowable, undetectable ways through time, it is no reference at all. One can see how the idea of reference supplants the concept of original in the digital realm. Indeed, an original was just the old-fashioned, physical-evidence way of declaring a reference.

Protecting a Reference as Immutable

Accordingly, a declaration of a reference contains a tacit promise the declarant will preserve referenced information as immutable. In the physical realm, one did this by using stable media such as pen and ink rather than pencil, and perhaps by using a seal, and perhaps by keeping the immutable original record in a safe where it would be protected from tampering. And one tried hard not to lose the record. We still do this today and most likely will never stop, as the physical system of record-keeping is a superb invention. Indeed many people, when they want to keep more formal track of their e-mail, transmute the electronic files into paper printouts and file away the resulting physical artifacts on a file backer, in a cabinet, that might even be locked!

Of course, in the digital realm, the reference, or its hash, must similarly be protected through time if any evidentiary value of a reference is to be maintained.[7] Particularly because we are using the reference to establish that a certain set of data existed in a point in time, we must strongly trust that the reference, or its proxy the reference hash, has not changed since that point in time. Change happens, and change is what we are concerned about in the attribute of integrity. If the information in the reference existed in an insecure location (such as the computer files of a smallish company with an ordinary network, or in the files of a larger company with at least one unscrupulous worker), both the reference information and therefore also its hash could possibly be changed without the knowledge either of those declaring the reference, or those relying on it. The system of digital authenticity would collapse. Given that there is no immutable ink-based original artifact involved, and we deal with undetectably editable information, such susceptibility to change becomes considerably more important in the digital realm than it was in the physical realm.

---

7. Critically, if one keeps just the hash and loses the record itself, there is a loss of the reference. If one only has a hash result, one cannot reverse-engineer the record that gave birth to the hash result.

How can we protect the immutability of digital information?

First, one could use the old-fashioned way to protect references and their hashes: physically secure them, typically by locking them up. One could use a giant vault to protect a record of digital information or its hash result. One could even write a hash down on paper and protect it in a safe, or one could use a super-secure computer system to store reference information. More generally, this objective can be achieved by using a trusted third party, whose role is to protect a digital record or its hash. Indeed, there are now services springing up that provide this function. "We will store your hash values securely." This method works.

Or you could take a somewhat different approach. Instead of locking up information to prevent manipulation, you could spread the information far and wide, which does not prevent change but which might guarantee that change would be easily discovered through the act of comparison with the distributed information. One could, for example, publish either the reference information or the hash of a reference in a newspaper of wide circulation. This would ensure there were numerous physical repositories of the reference or its hash existing on a certain date. The chance that such newspapers could be reprinted, and then substituted, all over the United States, is mathematically almost zero percent. One can trust the digital information object existed on a certain date if one found one or more newspapers with its hash published on that date.

Or, to protect the reference as immutable, one could try to make a digital record uneditable. One could store the record in read-only format on media commonly known as "WORM" or "write once, read many" format. This is a "preventing change" solution, not a "discovering change" solution. Many solutions do exactly that.[8]

Accordingly, there are numerous ways one can protect a reference of digital information so that it can be used in a test of the integrity of purported identical files. There is no single, accepted way to protect information as immutable. It is all a matter of logic and technology.

But there is a specific technology that has become particularly important in the last few years in this regard. Indeed, as illustrated in Stephen Mason's case study "Digital Evidence in Five Nations," this methodology has rapidly been incorporated into the world's legal systems as a way to test integrity of digital information. It is used to confirm *who* declared the reference or *who* protected it as inviolate, and to provide a check of *integrity* on any purported information object that is compared to the reference as identical. Just like locking information up in a safe with trusted guardians protecting it, this solution solves the issue about how to protect the reference or its hash as immutable. It reveals the existence of any unauthorized tampering between the time the reference is protected and the time the purported digital information is tested against the reference.

PROTECTING A REFERENCE BY ENCRYPTION

The last method for protecting a reference set of information is by *encryption*. This is similar to locking up information in a vault, but the method uses logic and math instead

---

8. Although this alternative might make the reference immutable, it would not prevent fraudulent creation of a contradictory reference by those in control of computer environment variables.

of physical matter to create a sort of "virtual vault" that prevents anyone from tampering with the reference inside of it. In this method, a declarant can freeze a reference set of information by making it disappear—by causing it to become unintelligible and uneditable to everyone except those who choose to unfreeze it. The key issue, or main point, is that so long as one retains the encrypted file, the frozen, encrypted version of the information lives on—forever available to those who want to unfreeze it to test it in the future. Each act of unfreezing reveals the information in its authentic state: the state it was in at the time the reference was protected by an entity.[9]

It is perhaps odd that a subject like cryptography should have rapidly evolved to become so important in testing authenticity in our new world of digital information. It is not clear how many years or decades this particular solution to protecting references or their hashes will exist, as increases in computing power affect the demonstrations involved here. However, the system works now and is predicted to work into the foreseeable future. It is being rapidly adopted by national legal systems. Those who want to understand the new foundations of digital information need to understand how this works.

Digital Signatures

Hash functions are not the only type of transformations of information. Encryption, cryptosystems, and cryptograms are transformations as well, although unlike the irreversible hash transformation, encryption techniques are *reversible.* In encryption, an information object, such as, for example, the message "Napoleon is advancing on Borodino," can be scrambled from readable, editable, useable form ("plaintext") into something called "ciphertext," that is unreadable, uneditable, seeming gibberish. But, if one has a "key" to the cryptogram, one can reverse the transformation, and read the message, resurrecting the information object back to its original form. One can "unfreeze" the information.

There are many different types of encryption systems. Traditionally, people sending messages back and forth shared the same key, and the key could both encrypt and decrypt the information with the key. This is called symmetric cryptography.

Then in 1976 something called *public-key cryptography* was introduced by Whitfield Diffie and Martin Hellman of Stanford University.[10] In contrast to symmetric cryptosystems, where users share one key for both encryption and decryption, a public-key cryptosystem uses a pair of related keys: one key for encryption and the other for decryption. The keys are numbers that plug into a mathematical formula, the cryptogram. One key, the *private key,* is kept secret by the system and is only known by one or a very

---

9. The time a reference is declared may be exact, but the time data on the record is not necessarily the correct or accurate time, for reasons explained in Chapter 5. The time of encryption is the time asserted but not necessarily established for the referential declaration, i.e., perhaps not either the actual time of encryption or time of declaration of the reference. Accordingly, references are frozen at a particular exact time, but how accurate any evidence of this time is must be established separately, as explained in the next chapter.

10. Whitfield Diffie & Martin Helman, *New Directions in Cryptography,* IEEE Transactions on Information Theory IT-22, no. 6 (1976): 644–54. *See also* Whitfield Diffie, *The First Ten Years of Public Key Cryptology, in* Contemporary Cryptology: The Science of Information Integrity 136–75 (Gustavus J. Simmons ed., IEEE Press, 1992).

small number of authorized users, while the other key, the *public key*, can be publicly disclosed to anybody—the more, the merrier—perhaps published on, for example, a website, hence the name public-key cryptography. The keys in the key pair are computationally related, in a strong fashion. If a key unlocks a cryptogram, you know you are dealing with the correct, corresponding key on the other end. However, critically, given knowledge of the composition of the public key, it is still impossible to determine the composition of the private key. All you know is that it works, and that the keys are indeed computationally related. This is all a matter of mathematics and logic, the stuff of strong demonstrations in the digital age.

One can encrypt with either the public or private key, and if one encrypts with the public key, one can keep messages secret from people unless they possess the private key. An analogy for public-key encryption is that of a locked mailbox with a mail slot. The mail slot is exposed and accessible to the public; its location is in essence the public key. Anyone knowing the street address can drop a written message through the slot. However, only the person who possesses the private key can open the mailbox and read the message.

But the challenge of protecting a reference or its hash implicates the other mode of public key cryptography, its "authenticity mode," where a *private key* is used to *encrypt* information that is then *decrypted* by the *public key*.

Accordingly, a *digital signature* is the encrypted information object that results when the possessor of a private key encrypts an information object, whether it be a message like "Napoleon is advancing" or an object like a contract, or even elaborate software. Anything in digital form can be digitally signed—encrypted with a private key—and the digital signature is the encrypted information, the cyphertext, of what was signed or encrypted.

So what does this accomplish? Given the math and logic involved, it provides two functions.

The Identity Service Provided by Digital Signatures

First, use of public key cryptography gives strong evidence of who protected the reference. If the public key one uses actually does decrypt the digital signature, and an intelligible record appears, then one knows it was encrypted with the private key related to the public key used. In short, one has strong evidence that the owner of the private key is the entity who signed the information and who encrypted the information. Signing as an act can signify several things (transmitting, agreeing, acknowledging, endorsing), but in any event, one now knows the identity of the person or entity that is the originator of the reference digitally signed. One knows who froze the information, who locked the information up in a virtual vault so as to be forever available to the future.

The Integrity Service Provided by Digital Signatures

Next, one also now has a built-in comparison available so as to test integrity. A classic, simple digital signature presents itself with an unencrypted, plaintext purported information object, and a reference information object that is encrypted in ciphertext (the digital signature). They are almost always attached or logically associated in some fashion. The purported information object—the plain-text object—is accordingly present for testing. One does this by decrypting the digital signature. If the public key, when inserted into the public key cryptogram, works and encrypted information is decrypted so that plaintext appears, one knows who signed the information because there is confirmation the public key and private keys that were used are in fact computationally related. We say that the signature is "verified."

In addition, if the newly decrypted information object is identical to the purported information object one has in plainttext, one knows there is integrity of information during the span of time between the decryption of the information object and the point in time when that object was signed or encrypted. In short, if the purported information object matches the newly decrypted signature, integrity has been proved. And so long as the digital signature lives on and is not edited, it can be decrypted again years hence by other people, who can assure themselves of integrity ad infinitum.

Why is this so? During the time it is encrypted, the information object cannot be read, and any editing will destroy its ability to be decrypted (thereby providing strong evidence of an attempted alteration or modification). Encrypted information is incomprehensible and is also rendered incomprehensible when edited in its encrypted state. One can't tamper with encrypted information, or it will be computationally infeasible to predict what kind of information object will be resurrected when the cyphertext is decrypted after any editing. As long as the encrypted information is there to be decrypted by a public key, the encryption protects the immutability of the reference.

Figure 4.1 is an illustration of such a scheme.

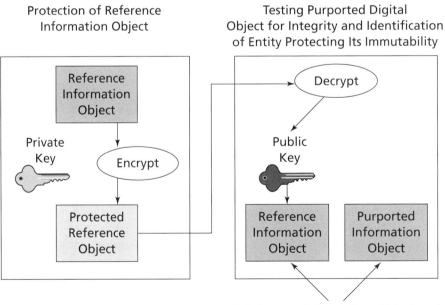

FIGURE 4.1
Simplistic "RSA" Digital Signature Scheme

In reality, encrypting an entire reference information object is not convenient. It takes a lot of time and computing resources. In addition, one is left with an entire object to use to compare against another entire purported object. One might have to determine whether a 10-gigabyte object was identical to another 10-gigabyte object, for example. One would likely make a hash of both objects to facilitate such a comparison, so that one could compare two relatively short numbers to test to see whether they were identical, rather than testing two exceedingly large numbers. For these reasons, protecting the immutability of referenced digital information is not usually accomplished by encrypting the entire object—although that is indeed done and is, theoretically, a pure way to do so.

Another way to accomplish this same type of integrity test lies in the encryption of smaller parts of information rather than on the entire object. And this is where hash values fit into a digital signature scheme. A more advanced form of digital signature incorporates the use of hashes, once again a favorite tool for the act of comparison.

Many different forms of asymmetric or public key cryptography are in use, as well as many different types of encryption algorithms. Indeed, corporate empires have been built by those that market and sell such algorithms. Examples of well-regarded asymmetric key techniques for varied purposes include the Diffie-Hellman key exchange protocol; Digital Signature Standard (DSS), which incorporates the Digital Signature Algorithm (DSA); various "Elliptic Curve" techniques; various password-authenticated key agreement techniques; the Paillier cryptosystem; the RSA encryption algorithm (PKCS); and the Cramer-Shoup encryption.[11] Some asymmetric algorithms are not reversible—algorithms in which one does not extract a plaintext hash value by application of the public key to an encrypted hash value. Instead, the signature verification process only tests to determine if the associated private key produced the encryption. DSA is an example of this type of asymmetric cryptography.

Exploring each of these techniques is beyond the scope of this book, but let us take as an example a typical reversible asymmetric cryptography that can be used in digital signatures: the RSA Digital Signature Scheme using the RSA encryption algorithm. This scheme is often used with hash values in order to test and therefore prove integrity of information.

Let us say that a company named Parmalat wants to declare a reference. It declares it is electronically publishing quarterly financial statements for the quarter ending March 31, 2008. By declaring such a reference, Parmalat is tacitly promising it will preserve that information inviolate and immutable, not in a vault, but in the world of logic and math. Any changes must be known and published, rather than secret and unknown to those using the reference. Parmalat accordingly wants to protect its reference as immutable

---

11. Each of these encryption techniques relies on very difficult mathematical problems. For example, the RSA algorithm depends on the fact that while finding large prime numbers is relatively easy, factoring the product of two such numbers is difficult. If the numbers are sufficiently large, factoring requires enormous processing resources, to the extent that the problem is considered computationally infeasible. Building in such math problems that even computers cannot handle is the key to all these encryption techniques. This is why some thinkers worry about a future where quantum computers simply blow by all the math problems, and make a "quantum leap" to get the answer, thus causing the entire system of cryptography to come crashing down. This possible future has not, however, caused most of the other of the nations we surveyed to abandon cryptography as a way of protecting digital information objects.

for the future. To employ one type of advanced digital signature incorporating the use of hashes, Parmalat would take the referenced information object (the digital file of the quarterly financials ending March 31, 2008) and then would create a hash result using a hash function operating on that information object. Then, instead of signing (encrypting) the reference, here the digital financial statement (as we did in the simple digital signature model), Parmalat would sign (encrypt) the hash of its reference financials. *The encrypted hash result becomes the digital signature.*

The digital signature (encryption of the hash result) is then logically associated or appended to the referenced information object—the financials. The reference information can be stored, together with the logically associated digitally signed hash, for years. There can be 50 million copies of these financials, in the hands of many people worldwide.

What if one wants to do an integrity test later? Suppose two years later one has a digital copy of an information object purporting to be Parmalat's official quarterly financials for the period ending March 31, 2008. As we have discussed, one also has to possess the digitally signed reference object, as one has to possess the reference in order to engage in an act of comparison.

To engage in a test, one uses Parmalat's public key—which one can get from a website and any number of other ways—and decrypts the digital signature to give an expected hash result. This produces an unfrozen, decrypted hash of the reference information.

One then takes the purported financials one is testing, and using the same hash function that was originally used to create a hash of the reference, one creates a hash of the purported financials. One now has a hash of the purported financials, plus a decrypted hash of the reference financials.

One then compares the two hashes, which is equivalent to comparing the two sets of financials, as hashes are proxies of information objects. If the decrypted hash result, which was the digital signature, matches the newly created hash of the purported financials being tested, the two hashes match and the digital files are identical. There is integrity of information. And because Parmalat's public key indeed decrypted the digital signature, we know that Parmalat protected the reference by digitally signing it. Figure 4.2 is diagram of this more sophisticated digital signature model, employing hash digests and utilizing reversible asymmetric cryptography.

Public Key Infrastructures

There is one final point: The cryptographic scheme described here depends on trust, and perhaps on an assumption that there will be a strong and true proof or data about the real-world identity of the owners of public keys. For example, if a one sees information asserting that Microsoft holds a certain public key, so that you can use that public key to decrypt information purportedly digitally signed by Microsoft (like its software), unless it is indeed Microsoft that owns that public key, this system breaks down and indeed becomes insidious. If there is an incorrect assumption about the real-world identity of owners of public keys, users of public keys will be misled.

Accordingly, those interested in providing this solution for providing identity and integrity services have discussed something called a "Public Key Infrastructure," also known as PKI. In order for all this to work, trusted entities called "certification authori-

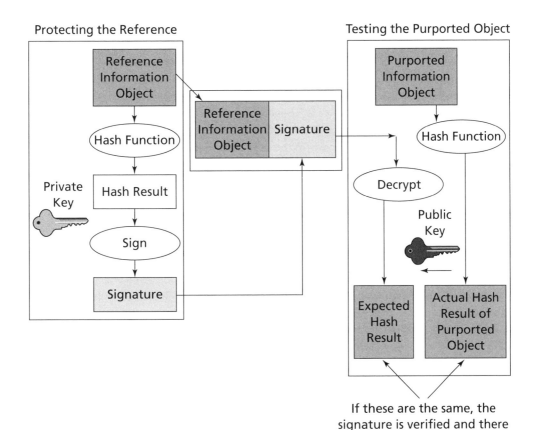

FIGURE 4.2
RSA Digital Signature Scheme Using Hash Function

ties" must issue information about who really holds what public key. These organizations issue certificates proving the identity of who holds what public key.

Whether these certification authorities are doing their job is not usually a technical issue, but rather a business process or business solutions issue. How do they know whom they are dealing with, so that they can then issue credentials to the world about the identity of that person or entity? These are completely separate issues, outside the scope of this book. The ABA's Information Security Committee has published two authoritative works on this topic: the "Digital Signature Guidelines," (http://www.abanet.org/scitech/ec/isc/dsg-tutorial.html) and the "Public Key Infrastructure Assessment Guidelines," or PAG, available at http://www.abanet.org/scitech/ec/isc/pag/pag.html.

Digital signatures are thus a readily available informational solution that can be implemented to test integrity, and to test the identity of a protector of a reference. There are countless ways to do this, but all depend on asymmetric cryptography and the encryption of either a reference, or its hash, with a private key. All depend on a verification that the private key was used to encrypt the reference, and a test or verification that the signature is valid. All depend on the act of comparison, and the more advanced forms of these solutions compare hashes. Exactly how the algorithms work varies in different cases.

But as we have seen, we discuss ever-evolving ecosystems. Processors gain in power. The robustness (or susceptibility) of mathematical formulas used in cryptography and hashing are continually lessened by advances in processing power of computers. Moreover, encryption is an empirical science, and we know an encryption technique is strong only because it has not yet been broken, and because we have reason to believe that it is unlikely to be broken in a specific period using known or anticipated technology.[12] Accordingly, it is not clear how long this specific sort of *eunomic* regime can be employed. Quantum computing, if and when it arrives, may make some of this obsolete, as existing encryption algorithms and hash functions might be broken and new ones emerge.

But even if that happens we still will be left with a new authenticity paradigm for the digital realm: A reference is declared. A reference is protected as immutable for the future. A purported information object is compared against the reference information object. If they are identical, there is integrity of information. Given the logic of this scheme, one can leave the details of any particular *eunomic* solution to technology as it advances.

---

12. Roger Cummings, Senior Principal Software Engineer in the Advanced Technology Standards Group of the Symantec CTO Technology Group, presented at the Storage Security Industry Forum Summit, ABC's of Encryption (Jan. 30, 2008).

CHAPTER 5

Time

The concept of when an event happened is important in the world of digital evidence. Information about time can be one of the foundational elements of authenticity. But time, as a species of evidence, is important to many aspects of proof. When did that event occur? In what order did events occur? Who knew what, when? Did one event happen (grant of a stock option, for example) before or after some other event (a stock price increase, for example)?

Facts about time might be relevant to know, as for example, when a particular person was logged onto a network. Or, one might want to know when a certain transaction happened—for example when the disputed cash was taken out of that ATM in Las Vegas. Was it just before, or just after, the customer made a call claiming to have lost her debit card?

Lawyers need to understand how digital systems record time; what types of time records exist; how a digital system associates time with other computer information; and to what extent one may rely on different types of records as *reliable* and *authentic* records about time, and the timing of events. They need to know how to test such records to either verify them, or disprove them, or perhaps to show that no one can really say anything reliable about the time involved.

As in other types of foundations, there is a *eunomic* way of creating evidence about time that can be strongly trusted when used now or in the future. And, predictably, there is evidence about time that is much less reliable, if not unreliable, because time data (like all computer data) is editable; because it can be manipulated by changes to the apparent time shown in system clocks; and because the way computer programs generate time records may not be understandable. In these circumstances, evidence about time is circumstantial and inferential.

Time has also long played a role in admissibility determinations under the Federal Rules of Evidence. For example, Rule 803(6) provides for the admissibility of hearsay under an exception for "Records of Regularly Conducted Activity." Commonly referred to as the "Business Records Exception," Rule 803(6) has a time element in it and provides in pertinent part that:

> A memorandum, report, record, or data compilation, in any form, of acts, events, conditions, opinions, or diagnoses made *at or near the time* by, or from information transmitted by, a person with knowledge. . . .

It should therefore not be too controversial to note that time is almost always a key evidentiary fact, for many reasons including not only evidentiary and substantive law reasons, but also because the theory of one's case often depends on the timing or sequence of events involved. Isn't one of the first things litigation lawyers do when attacking a case is to build a chronology?

Let us examine how time information is recorded in digital evidence. How does one prove time in the digital world? How does one test statements about time found in digital evidence?

First, of course, data relating to time can be found in digital records because people have entered data, or text, about time into such a record. This is the computer-stored information discussed in Chapter 7. For example, if on a Microsoft Word document one typed the date "September 7, 2007," such a human-generated, computer-stored record clearly relates to time. But just as any other data can be edited, so, too, obviously can such data about time be edited. One could easily edit the word "September" to read "December," and the entry would thereafter read "December 7, 2007." And of course, the date could have been wrong or misleading in the first place.[1]

Unless steps have been taken to ensure the integrity of the Word file through time, such human-generated, time-related data is completely editable, and therefore to that extent, unreliable. It merely represents either what the writer wanted to say when the data was originally written, or what he or someone else decided to write later when the data was edited. It has no necessary temporal association to what happened in the digital world.[2]

Yet there is information about time that *does* correlate to things that actually happen in the digital realm—not solely as a result of input by humans, but as a result of the unfolding of things caused by the system's reading and writing games. This, in essence, is the system making records about its own evolution through time. These data entries are information about time, recorded as the time certain events happened in the digital world.

We discussed the concept of "events" in Chapter 2. An event is the most basic phenomenon in the digital universe. It is a digital "happening," or a digital "occurrence."

DATA ABOUT THE TIME OF EVENTS IS GENERATED AND AUTOMATICALLY RECORDED

As a result of the operation of computer applications, data about the time of an event is often generated and automatically recorded in a record associated with the event

---

1. For example, in a case of computer-generated information gone awry, a program such as Microsoft Word can "autofill" a date within an existing Word document. This happens when Word opens up a document, and Word then displays the date the computer "knows" it is currently, not the actual creation date of the document. Hence, the date on a record can be wrong and misleading because of computer-generated information.

2. An example of this same result in the physical evidence world happened in a case where a plaintiff-inventor seeking to enforce a patent claim had his patent invalidated when, following a forensic analysis involving the testing of the chemical composition of the ink used to write his inventor's logbook, it was determined that fraudulent material was later added to a once-genuine notebook. Aptix Corp. v. Quickturn Design Sys., No. C 98-00762 WHA, 2000 U.S. Dist. LEXIS 3408, at *71 (N.D. Cal. June 14, 2000).

in question. Hence, we have computer-generated records about time. These are often found as *metadata* in a file. Thus, the most common definition of the word "metadata," "data about data," fits well in this context. There is metadata about the time of an event associated with a certain set of data.

For example, one can readily obtain and examine such metadata of any document generated by the Microsoft Word word-processing application (perhaps the most commonly used document generation program on the planet) by selecting the Properties tab under the File menu. As seen in Figure 5.1, one will then find time data entries for different events that occurred in connection with that particular Word file, such as is found on the type of files that most readers probably handle many times each week. One will see a time that the particular application "knows" to be the creation date of a file and has recorded as the creation date of that file. Typically, that certain time known by the application is provided to the application by the system clock of the computing system, or by communication with the operating system, which "tells" the time to the application for its use in data generation. And one will see that the time that a file was modified will be derived from that certain time known to the application as provided to it by either the system clock of the computer or from the operating system's provision of system clock time.

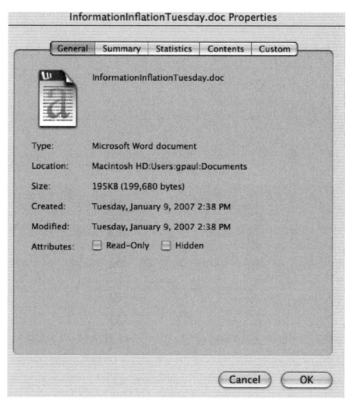

FIGURE 5.1
Computer-Generated Time Information

User	Application	Activity	Date-Time ▽	Duration	Pages Prin...	Location
GPAUL	WINWORD	Checkin	11/20/2007 10:34:51 AM	0:58:18	0	WS-00087420D...
GPAUL	WINWORD	Modify	11/20/2007 10:34:51 AM	0:0:0	0	WS-00087420D...
GPAUL	Winword	Mail	11/20/2007 10:33:13 AM	0:0:0	0	WS-00087420D...
GPAUL	Winword	Mail	11/20/2007 10:32:44 AM	0:0:0	0	WS-00087420D...
GPAUL	OUTLOOK	Checkout	11/20/2007 9:36:33 AM	0:0:0	0	WS-00087420D...
ELABRANT	WINWORD	View	11/20/2007 9:22:39 AM	0:0:0	0	WS-00123F4A4...
ELABRANT	WINWORD	View	11/12/2007 3:29:38 PM	0:0:0	0	WS-00123F4A4...
ELABRANT	WINWORD	View	11/12/2007 3:25:49 PM	0:0:0	0	WS-00123F4A4...
ELABRANT	WINWORD	Checkin	11/27/2006 12:12:01 PM	0:4:19	0	WS-00123F4A4...
ELABRANT	WINWORD	Modify	11/27/2006 12:12:00 PM	0:0:0	0	WS-00123F4A4...
ELABRANT	winword	Print	11/27/2006 12:10:10 PM	0:0:0	3	WS-00123F4A4...
ELABRANT	winword	Print	11/27/2006 12:07:45 PM	0:0:0	3	WS-00123F4A4...
ELABRANT	WINWORD	Checkout	11/27/2006 12:07:42 PM	0:0:0	0	WS-00123F4A4...
ELABRANT	WINWORD	Checkin	11/27/2006 12:06:57 PM	0:10:58	0	WS-00123F4A4...
ELABRANT	WINWORD	Modify	11/27/2006 12:06:56 PM	0:0:0	0	WS-00123F4A4...
ELABRANT	winword	Print	11/27/2006 12:06:52 PM	0:0:0	3	WS-00123F4A4...
ELABRANT	winword	Checkin	11/27/2006 11:55:59 AM	0:0:1	0	WS-00123F4A4...
ELABRANT	winword	Checkout	11/27/2006 11:55:59 AM	0:0:0	0	WS-00123F4A4...
ELABRANT	WINWORD	Create	11/27/2006 11:55:58 AM	0:0:0	0	WS-00123F4A4...
ELABRANT	WINWORD	Checkout	11/27/2006 11:55:58 AM	0:0:0	0	WS-00123F4A4...

FIGURE 5.2
Time Information in a Database-type Program

Or, consider a database program. Many law offices use a program called Interwoven Mailsite. This program keeps track of what happens, and when, to certain identified documents in a firm's document database. In Figure 5.2, taken from a law firm's database records, a document's history was viewed on a screen and then a screenshot was taken of that history. The program labels something called an "activity," which is this program's name for a certain event that occurs on a network. The reader can see what date and time certain events occurred, and where on the network the event occurred. Obviously, the interaction of programs running on this network insert time data about network events as they are associated with a certain document, and record them in a database about the document. Certain users are also identified and associated with those events. Whether these are really the people whose names appear as users will be discussed in Chapter 6.

In Figure 5.2, all these data entries, generated by computer programs and recorded as data about events in the digital world, are time entries. At this writing, there is no standardized way to refer to such computer-generated time data. Many people call these "time stamps," and others call them "time marks" or "time notations." This author prefers to call them time marks, reserving the term "time stamps" for cryptographically protected records about time. But no matter what one calls these time entries, the legal profession needs to understand such digital time information.

WHAT IS THE EVENT DELINEATED BY THE TIME MARK?

Unfortunately, there often is only a cryptic reference to the event delineated by a particular time mark. We all probably intuitively know what "save" means as an event. We probably can determine what it means if the computer has a time mark that a file was "saved" on "Thursday, July 5, 2007 at 5:50 PM." This is the time at which the data stored in volatile (temporary) memory was written to a more permanent storage medium, such as a hard drive or a USB flash drive.

But for the time recorded as delineating other events, things are often not so clear, because there is little if any documentation explaining the often cryptic categories of metadata. For example, in the Word program, what does "Thursday, July 5, 5:50 PM" mean for the time a file was modified? What precisely does "modified" mean? Is it the time of the last edit? Is it the time the edits were saved? Or both? Which is it? If you have been typing away for an hour, haven't you been modifying things? Here, we see the beginning of the problem of understanding what computers mean when we are engaged in reading and writing games with them.

In short, there are events that are considered fairly generic in the world of computers—creating a file, opening a file, closing a file, saving a file, and other things like that. But in total, there are a myriad of different information processing events that can be associated with time. The number of such events is limited only by the discourse that occurs in the digital world, and what the writers of the relevant programs created as possible events.

In addition, the definition of an event can cause confusion about time. Suppose a person started working on an electronic file at his home several months ago. He then e-mailed it to himself at the office, and saved it on a different computer.

He then looks at the properties tab under the file menu heading. It has the "created" date and time not when the file was created, but rather when it was saved to that different computer.[3] Both times are examples of file "creation," but they do not reflect the same event. Accordingly, the time now shown for "creation" is not when the file was created, it is when the file was created on the computer in question. Put another way, the time of creation of a particular file is not necessarily the time of creation of *that* file, as it is understood in another computer. One needs to understand what the computer means when it makes the hearsay statement that a file was "created." It is important to understand what an information system is trying to say when it is talking to you.

WHERE DOES THE TIME DATA ORIGINATE THAT IS FOUND ON A TIME MARK?

So where does the time data originate, which is ultimately placed by the computer's programs in the computer-generated record in question?

It originates in the computer's clock, or its time clock, or if the computer lives on a network, from a time source located within some other computing device in that network.

Most time marks and MAC dates (for Modified/Accessed/Created) are system metadata assigned by the file system (e.g., NTFS, FAT, HFS, etc.). They can be encoded in a number of ways on the media depending upon the number of bytes available to store the information. Earlier operating systems did not allocate as much space to storing data as did later systems, so one often will find false date values when one moves data from an

---

3. This is further complicated where a *different* application is used to subsequently open and edit the document, even where such actions take place on the same computer. For example, the creation date shown for a document generated in Microsoft Word may differ from the creation date shown by the later opening and editing of that same document in, for example, WordPerfect or in OpenOffice.

older operating system to a newer one. Such transfer of files can lead to inaccurate time marks.

Practically all computers, such as a stand-alone computer not on a network, have a system clock linked to the various programs and events that are unfolding in the computer as it reads and writes data and thus causes events to occur. Time and date information are usually pulled from the BIOS, or system, clock on the machine recording the information. E-mail picks up multiple time marks all along the way as it is handed off between servers. Thus, time information inserted in e-mail records needs to be interpreted with care, as different time zones can be implicated. Moreover, because this time information is easily editable, the integrity and trustworthiness of such information is particularly susceptible to reliability challenges.

TIME MARKS CAN BE MANIPULATED BY ALTERATION OF THE TIME CLOCK

But what does this tell us? If one can manipulate the computer's time clock by changing the apparent time on either a stand-alone computer or on a network, one can also manipulate the apparent time as recorded on a time mark. Thus, computer-generated information can be manipulated by human beings even before it ever is born as data in the first place.

For example, this chapter was originally written on Microsoft Word 2004 for Mac, Version 11.3.5. The author called up some of the current metadata for the file. This was done by clicking the Properties tab under the File menu. Figure 5.3 shows the information the computer generated as the metadata for the file.

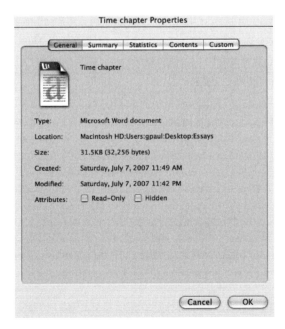

FIGURE 5.3
Current Created and Modified Metadata for an Information Object

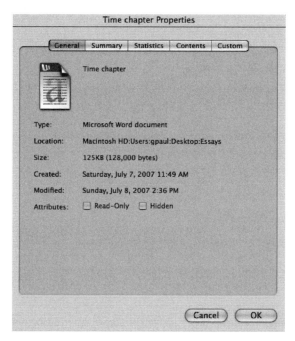

FIGURE 5.4
Change in the "Modified" Time Mark upon Saving a File

Figure 5.4 shows a possible result were one to now save the document to see what has changed, if anything.

It thus appears that by saving the file, one has changed the "modified" time mark on the metadata. Just a few moments earlier, or at about 2:30 PM on Sunday, this modified time mark had read Saturday at 11:42 in the morning. But the author had been working on this for a half-hour on Sunday, apparently without saving it, and then saved it at 2:36 PM on Sunday, July 8. The computer-generated information was updated.

Let us now see if one can alter the time mark. The author changes the clock on his computer by going to the System Preferences tab, and by choosing "Date and Time." He instructs the computer it is July 3.

Let us now call up the metadata without saving the file (Figure 5.5).

The correct time is still in the metadata. The computer has not inserted a new time mark through insertion of computer-generated information. This is because the relevant event, "modified," has not happened since the time clock was altered. The old metadata is still in the file, as the relevant event has not occurred since the time the clock was changed. If some other event happened since the change to the time clock, and assuming the programming instructed a time mark to be recorded somewhere, then a false time mark would have been recorded with respect to that particular event that did happen.

But now, at 2:46 PM on Sunday, July 8, 2007, the author saves the document again. Let us now check the metadata as shown in Figure 5.6.

The "Modified" time mark says it is July 3, 2007. But the document was not created until July 7, 2007! The time shown for the metadata on the Modified time mark has been updated using a clock that has been manipulated to show a false time.

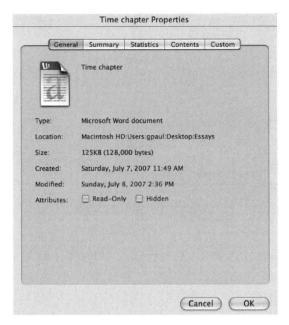

FIGURE 5.5
Metadata After Clock Change, Before Saving Event

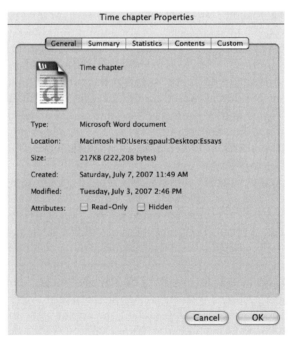

FIGURE 5.6
False Time of Modified Event Achieved by Change in Clock

This example, in fact, shows the importance of time as circumstantial evidence. Here, fortuitously, the file had been created fairly recently, indeed only a day before the tampering with the time clock. Accordingly, the change in the clock leaves a circumstantial evidence artifact—the fact that the Modified time mark is earlier in time than the Created time mark.

But such changes may not be so easy to spot. In other circumstances, they might be impossible or impractically expensive to spot. If the created date were further in the past, things would look "in order" even though the computer-generated metadata was, in fact, false as a result of manipulation of the time clock

The potential for document or metadata time-shifting has recently been recognized by at least one court.[4] The *Telxon* case involved a discovery and spoliation dispute where the court took notice of a party's expert testimony about time, timing of digital data creation or modification, and time-shifting. The court noted that electronic "[w]orkpapers which are at the heart of this case ... were vulnerable to undetectable alteration while the *Telxon* litigation was pending. The *Ennis* case in particular creates strong suspicions that this has been done to at least one document."[5] The *Telxon* court's analysis also referred to expert testimony that "[i]t is possible to alter any document in the database, and if the date on the computer used to alter the document is reset, the incorrect date will be incorporated in the metadata fields as the date of modification."[6] In this instance, the court noted that expert testimony stated that the metadata of certain documents had been altered or deleted, specifically that data had been time- and date-shifted.[7] The matter was ultimately resolved prior to a ruling on the discovery dispute, but the *Telxon* court appeared to criticize the defendant's auditor, PriceWaterhouseCoopers, for violating its duty of preservation, noting that auditing documents were altered "well after the close of the [relevant auditing period] and that [PWC] should have been on notice to preserve these documents. . . ."[8]

The same dynamics are present in networks. Here, rather than a BIOS or system clock setting the time for one computer, there may be a designated network time source, which may be a server clock or other device providing one-time value for all client computers in that network. The network clock sets the time marks for events on the computer-generated records throughout the system.

Once again, so long as that network clock can be manipulated at will, the time records generated are unreliable. As a matter of the statistics of interconnected objects, however, large network-generated time marks are probably somewhat more reliable than stand-alone computers, because it is somewhat more likely that manipulating the time will leave circumstantial evidence inconsistencies that will reveal the manipulation. This is because there are many different sources of records for the same event that can be compared. For example, metadata time values may be contained in a log of a network e-mail server, as well as in the .pst or .msg (e-mail database) files of the computer that generated the e-mail.

---

4. *In re Telxon Corporation Securities Litigation* 2004 WL 3192729 (W.D. Ohio 2004).
5. *Id.* at *35.
6. *Id.*
7. *Id.* at *18
8. *Id.* at *17.

However, even computers that are connected on networks can still have their own individual clocks adjusted. If data is saved locally on the machine's hard drive, and that individual computer's clock is manipulated, then the time recorded may well be false. Accordingly, most time data currently generated in connection with digital informational records is subject to manipulation, and therefore is unreliable to that extent. This means that one cannot necessarily depend on time marks. They might be accurate, but they might not. Exactly how likely accuracy is in any instance is a matter of circumstantial evidence, and accuracy may not be testable without resort to extrinsic evidence, and that evidence may not exist. Time marks are unreliable so long as some person who is part of the "information ecosystem" can manipulate a computer's time clock. In addition, time marks are unreliable because the clock involved could have been wrong, which happens for innocent reasons, such as power outages, time and zone resetting errors, mistakes about AM versus PM, and so on. By taking one's laptop across the country and forgetting to reset its time clock, one will guarantee inaccurate time metadata in files.

AS A FORM OF DATA, TIME MARKS CAN BE EDITED

Accordingly, time marks are inherently unreliable because they are a form of computer-generated information that can be manipulated by humans, or by computer processes acting in accordance with human instruction. But they are unreliable for a more fundamental reason.

They can be undetectably edited.

This can be as easy as using what is called a *hex editor,* a type of text editor that edits the hexadecimal[9] values of a file. Or, there are various types of metadata cleaning tools that allow one to wipe time referencing metadata clean. For example, some law firms use a tool called "Metadata Assistant."[10] If one sends a Word or other Microsoft Office file out of the office, it can first be "scrubbed" of its metadata. A copy of a file for this chapter was sent outside the office to a home e-mail address, but before that it was scrubbed by the Metadata Assistant utility. The "before" and "after" metadata scrubbing "Summary" and "Statistics" sub-tabs in the Properties tab for its MAC information are shown in Figures 5.7 and 5.8 on the following pages.

Indeed, there are now products that facilitate the editing of metadata, including data about time. One program designed to do so is called "Timestomp." Another older application is called "OrdiTouch."

---

9. Refers to the base-16 number system, which consists of 16 unique symbols: the numbers 0 to 9 and the letters A to F. For example, the decimal number 15 is represented as F in the hexadecimal numbering system. The hexadecimal system is useful because it can represent every byte (8 bits) as two consecutive hexadecimal digits. It is easier for humans to read hexadecimal numbers than binary numbers. To convert a value from hexadecimal to binary, one merely translates each hexadecimal digit into its 4-bit binary equivalent. Hexadecimal numbers have either an 0x prefix or an h suffix. For example, the hexadecimal number "0x3F7A" translates to the following binary number: 0011 1111 0111 1010. See *Webopedia* entry for "hexadecimal."

10. Other tools in the market place currently are EZ Clean and 3B Clean. If one "Googles" the words "metadata cleaner," one can find a myriad of products and techniques.

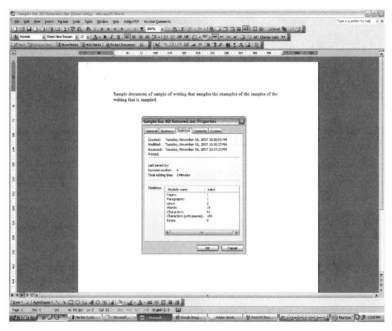

FIGURE 5.7
View of Metadata Before Use of Metadata Assistant

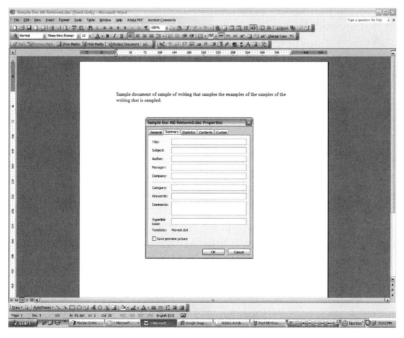

FIGURE 5.8
View of Metadata After Use of Metadata Assistant

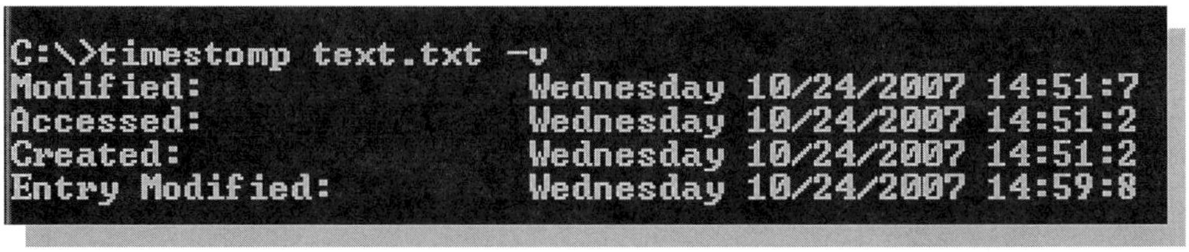

```
C:\>timestomp text.txt -v
Modified:              Wednesday 10/24/2007 14:51:7
Accessed:              Wednesday 10/24/2007 14:51:2
Created:               Wednesday 10/24/2007 14:51:2
Entry Modified:        Wednesday 10/24/2007 14:59:8
```

FIGURE 5.9
Timestomp MACE Value Screenshot

Timestomp is a software utility program designed to permit deletion or modification of time mark–related information on files.[11] The following example of Timestomp program operation is from a website called "Forensics Wiki".

Consider as an example of the operation of this program the "Timestomp MACE Values" screenshot displaying a command prompt window, and showing the MACE values for a document file, under examination, titled "text.txt".[12] The Timestomp program displays information about the time-related metadata in the text.txt file selected for analysis and/or editing. As seen in the screenshot, Figure 5.9, there are four time-mark references of interest, corresponding to data in the file that evidence when it was last modified, accessed, created, or entered into the NTFS Master File Table by the Operating system or manually by the user. Accordingly, anyone using this utility can call up certain time data in the file, in this instance metadata.

Using the Timestomp application, the time/date data can be modified in the form of metadata text editing. Afterwards, one can look at a separate screen to examine one's handiwork. See Figure 5.10, the "Timestomp MACE Change" screenshot.

The data at the bottom of the screenshot shows that there is a modification date that is six years earlier than the creation of the file.

A final screenshot is taken not from the Timestomp application, but rather from the Properties tab of the text.txt file itself. Figure 5.11 shows the same dates as were exhibited by the Timestomp application after editing the file's time metadata. The "Timestomp MACE Change Proof" screenshot is the view given to the handler of the text.txt file by the Operating System's presentation of the Modified time data.

Accordingly, once a digital file is created, the data that is metadata (such as the data about time) can be edited or deleted, just like any data in the file. *The computer-generated information metadata is no more reliable or permanent than any other data.*

This means that time-mark metadata for the myriad of events that occur in the digital world may or may not be authentic. Its authenticity is untestable[13] without extrinsic evidence. It is just data, perhaps a little harder to edit, but editable just the same. Accordingly, there is an authenticity issue with the data in a time mark, just as there is an authenticity issue with any data in a digital record.

---

11. Forensics Wiki ("A Creative Commons licenses Wiki devoted to information about digital forensics"); http://www.forensicswiki.org/index.php?title=Timestomp.

12. MACE Value means "Modified," "Accessed," "Created," and "Entry Modified," all of which are data-generating events to which time values are attached.

13. See Chapter 2 for the concept of *untestability* in the digital world.

```
C:\>timestomp text.txt -m "Monday 1/01/2001 01:01:1 AM"

C:\>dir
 Volume in drive C has no label.
 Volume Serial Number is 3036-18D7

 Directory of C:\

05/26/2007  06:01 PM                      0 AUTOEXEC.BAT
05/26/2007  06:01 PM                      0 CONFIG.SYS
10/24/2007  02:58 PM       <DIR>            Documents and Settings
05/29/2007  01:15 PM       <DIR>            Program Files
01/01/2001  01:01 AM                      0 text.txt
10/24/2007  02:50 PM                  57,344 timestomp.exe
06/18/2007  05:31 PM       <DIR>            WINDOWS
               4 File(s)          57,344 bytes
               3 Dir(s)  11,767,320,576 bytes free

C:\>timestomp text.txt -v
Modified:                    Monday 1/1/2001 1:1:1
Accessed:                    Wednesday 10/24/2007 14:51:2
Created:                     Wednesday 10/24/2007 14:51:2
Entry Modified:              Wednesday 10/24/2007 14:59:8

C:\>
```

FIGURE 5.10
Timestomp MACE Change Screenshot

FIGURE 5.11
Properties Tab View of Time Metadata After Editing with Timestomp

The upshot? Computers do not know the time. A computer system knows only the time expressed to the computer's clock by some external set of processes (ultimately determined by a person) that sets that computer's clock. Computer-generated information in turn expresses only the time "told" to it by the computer system and clock. The record that is made can then be edited in a way that conceals both the act of editing, and thus the edit itself.

Given the intrinsic untestability of most digital data, the current choice for a court's investigation into time issues is to take testimony from people and to assess their credibility—not to test the reliability and trustworthiness of the time value associated with digital data. This has long been an accepted way to establish the admissibility of physical evidence. But the maintenance of the old authentication foundation for the admissibility of computer-generated time evidence has consequences for the future of the world of evidence.

First, there is cost. Testing reliability through circumstantial evidence is expensive. With hourly rates starting at several hundred dollars, it could easily take thousands, if not tens of thousands of dollars to test the time associated with a single record. Many large enterprises generate tens of thousands of records daily in a single network. With such a cost-benefit ratio, most records will go untested.

Second, sticking with a circumstantial evidence method of judging admissibility results in judicial acceptance of an evaluative process that never truly addresses reliability of digital information *qua* digital information; time *qua* time; or that time itself as expressed by zeroes and ones is what it purports to be.

We will be forced to test and adjudicate the reliability and authenticity of the purported computer-generated evidence about time, not based on the digital information itself, but on the credibility of witnesses who need merely testify as to the correctness of both the content and the time associated with digital data content, or that the "computer worked." As can be seen from the *Telxon* and *Vin Vinhnee* cases, the intrinsic probative utility of that testimony is now called into question for computer-generated data.[14]

EUNOMIC SOLUTIONS ABOUT DIGITAL TIME INFORMATION

There are, however, solutions that provide the benefit of a strong "demonstration" of digital information about time. These solutions "anchor" time to digital information, and utilize the concept of "trusted" time as a *eunomic* solution. These solutions fall into two categories: The first of these categories relies on "physical controls." Physical controls, (e.g., segregated data generation sites, physical and software-based access control to these sites), combined with frequent inspections and audits, might help ensure that time data used in a data-generating system is accurate and reliable. These are typically costly and require robust physical security.

The second category utilizes computer hardware and software technology in lieu of brick-and-mortar protections. These solutions involve logic and mathematics. The proper implementation of such solutions can provide accurate time information.

---

14. *In re Telxon Corporation Securities Litigation* 2004 WL 3192729, (N.D. Ohio 2004) at *17–18.

Cryptographically Protected Time Stamps

More cost-effective than physical controls are cryptography-based technologies that can generate computer information that will maintain its integrity (and therefore its authenticity), and testably so, over time. These technologies, commonly referred to as *time stamping,* provide content authentication capability by providing the means to establish that computer-generated information existed as of, and has not been changed since, a defined point in time.

A time stamp is therefore a specialized kind of time mark comprising, contained within, or in some manner associated with metadata or other data. In a time stamp, the time mark is *cryptographically protected*, in the way we have discussed in Chapter 4, so that the integrity of a record is protected. In this instance, there is a declaration of a reference about time, and the reference is protected through cryptography. The record cannot be undetectably edited without a key. This keeps the metadata free from change unless one has the key to the cryptograph.

But the trustworthiness of a time stamp is still limited. A cryptographically protected time stamp is still susceptible to manipulation by the person or entity having control over (1) the computer that generates the data and the time stamp; or (2) the key to the cryptograph. In other words, who is declaring the reference? Is it someone in the information ecosystem?

True, with the protection of cryptography, third parties will not be able to edit time entries, but those in control of the computer-generating information system, or the cryptographic key, will still retain that capability, as they are the ones declaring the reference in the first place. For instance, an insider could backdate a computer clock, and then use that backdated computer clock to cryptographically time-stamp false and misleading information. Even after a digital signing and protection of a reference, one still needs to worry about the reliability of the reference. References are not necessarily accurate; they are just what have been declared by the declarant.

The primary reason for such susceptibility arises from the presence of control over the environmental variables affecting an information system. First, there is no way to ascertain that the time used to create the time stamp is the *correct* time. Second, there is no way to ascertain whether time from that particular time source (correct or incorrect) was even used to generate the time stamp. The opportunity for digital data manipulation will almost always exist where a person or entity has control over system environment variables (including time). A person exerting such control can backdate a computer clock and alter digital data, generate or forge "new" digital data, and even generate seemingly valid digital signatures that may be asserted to be genuine. When we talk about a system being subject to manipulation by those who normally control a system, we say that there is a lack of trust from the perspective of those who are outsiders of that system.

For these reasons, the cryptographic protections afforded by a time stamp are largely ineffective against an insider in control of a computer system. Time-stamped computer-generated information accordingly suffers from susceptibility to manipulation, and therefore lack of reliability, as does a time mark. Because much computer-generated information will be offered into evidence by the entity or person in control of the computer system that generated that data, a time stamp affords limited additional protection against intentional manipulation. If one thinks this is an unlikely scenario, please refer to the case study near at the end of this chapter, entitled "The Option Cases."

TRUSTED TIME STAMPS

Trusted time-stamping technologies provide the most reliable computer-generated time information.[15] Like a simple time stamp, a trusted time stamp cryptographically associates time data with data in a record, through digitally signed time data. Trusted time-stamping technology differs from simple time stamping, however, in that it also provides an auditable, cryptographic association of time from a *trusted time source* with computer-generated information. Trusted time-stamping technologies typically employ protected hardware and robust encryption-related technologies to make computer-generated information trustworthy enough to be relied upon by any third party. Most significantly, time stamping also removes the potential for undetectable manipulation by insiders as well as outsiders to the computer data-generating system. A similar benefit is provided to the data generator deploying the technology; in essence, it permits the data generator to place greater reliance on his digital data in evidentiary assertions.

The goal of trusted time-stamping technologies is to ensure the accuracy, reliability, and trustworthiness of both (1) the *time source* used by a computer system creating digital data; and (2) the *time data associated* with the information being time stamped. A "trusted time stamp" therefore typically consists of a time-stamp process, utilizing a trusted time source plus hashing and encryption technologies to provide provable integrity of digital evidence about time.[16] Thus, not only is there protection of the reference statements about time, through encryption; there is also a reliability of the references themselves, as the declarants of the time information are not insiders, but trusted third parties.

First, in trusted time stamps, time information is derived from a generally accepted source of "correct" time (in the United States, the National Institute of Science and Technology, or NIST). Accordingly, the trusted time source in such technologies is not under the control of anyone in the data-generating process. But just having an accurate and trusted time source available does not accomplish the goal. What is needed is a trusted process for ensuring that time data from that trusted time source is strongly associated with the content sought to be time stamped.

In a trusted time stamp, therefore, the "trusted time" of the trusted time source is *robustly associated*[17] with designated digital data (which could be digital data content,

---

15. *See* Internet Engineering Task Force RFC 3161 (Trusted Timestamps), and ANSI Standard X9F4 9.95 (Trusted Timestamping).

16. Of course, the technology must be *used* in the manner for which it is intended, or in which an *enforced* enterprise policy dictates. For example, if the service is disabled during critical data-generating events, no trusted time stamps will be created, and the capability to provide provably persistent data integrity in this manner and for this data set will be forever lost. Moreover, if a request for a time stamp is deliberately delayed, the probative value of digital evidence as existing at the time relevance is asserted is severely diluted, if not destroyed.

17. "Robust" in this context means strong, and not easily broken. "Association," in turn, means link. Accordingly, a robust association means strongly linked.

metadata, or a combination of both).[18] The robust association of trusted time from a trusted time source occurs typically through two hashing and digital signatures processes. The first digital signature, typically, is the signature applied to the information by the originator of the information. This shows the identity of the originator (declarant), and provides an encrypted hash value for future reference (digital signature of the hash of the reference data). The second digital signature typically is applied by the Time Stamp Authority (the declarant of the time) at or close to the time of the application of the first digital signature. The time value from the trusted time source (which is time information such as date, time, hour, second, and so on, with several possible variations) may be added to the first signed hash, the second signed hash, or both. Again, the second digital signature is typically applied by an entity known as a Time Stamp Authority,[19] as described below. Thus, the second digital signature is from a trusted time declarant, and the time information is a reference protected through encryption.

Providers of a trusted time-stamp services, generally known as a "Time Stamp Authority" (TSA) will adhere to some industry standard and be able to provide adequate testimony in connection with demonstrating such adherence. The TSA will have in place policies and processes to use a trusted time source. It also will have in place additional policies and processes specifically designed to prevent physical or software-based compromise of the trusted time source, and to prevent compromise of (1) the time value derived from that trusted time source; (2) the output of the time source; and (3) the private key of the time-stamp server used to provide time stamps.[20] Industry standards also require that TSAs undergo periodic independent audits to ensure compliance with these policies and processes.

Because the trusted time value must be applied to a fingerprint or hash of the data object in such a way that is itself trusted, the time-stamp server or the entity that otherwise provisions the time-stamp service must: (1) provide auditable and continuing protection to show that the time value used for time stamps can be traced to a national timing authority; *and* (2) be able to show that there are adequate and on ongoing protections to the clock or time source, such that the trusted time-stamp provider is not susceptible to compromise, either from within or without the system. It must also be shown that the private key of the trusted time-stamp server or other provisioning service used to sign the trusted time stamps it generates is physically and logically protected from internal and external compromise.

Trusted time stamping is fairly new to the digital data generation scene, but its importance is underscored by the publication in 2005 of an American National Standards

---

18. For further information on trusted time-stamp technologies and standards, *see* Internet Engineering Task Force RFC 3161 (Trusted Timestamps), and ANSI Standard X9F4 9.95 (Trusted Timestamping).

19. A trusted time stamp may also be generated by adding trusted time values in connection with the application of a first digital signature generated in connection with an identity or attribute-based digital signature schema. As with any other trusted time-stamp schema, the source of the time (i.e., time values) used in a trusted time-stamping schema must be traceable (and generally auditable) back to a trusted time source, such as NIST in the United States.

20. *See* ANSI Standard for Financial Services, X9.95-2005; Carlisle Adams *et al.,* Internet X.509 Public Key Infrastructure Time Stamp Protocol (TSP) RFC 3161 (2001).

Institute policy-based standard for trusted time stamping of computer-generated data used in the financial sector.[21]

A well-planned deployment of trusted time-stamping technologies into a computer data-generation environment could accomplish multiple objectives. First, it would imbue computer-generated information with more inherent reliability, and require a markedly lesser degree of reliance on corroborative circumstantial witness testimony. Second, the deployment of trusted time-stamping technology could provide an efficient method to satisfy the requirements of F.R.E. Rule 901(a) without the requirement of traditional corroborative testimony as to the content of computer-generated information. Such a *eunomic* solution about time information makes it economically possible to test or prove the time, as well as the timing, of events. Otherwise, if one is only proceeding on circumstantial evidence, it may simply be too expensive, or even not possible, to learn the true facts about time.

TYPES OF TRUSTED TIME STAMPS

There are basically two models for trusted time-stamp services: remote (relative to the location of the digital data generation) and local. In a remote scheme, a request for a trusted time stamp will originate at the digital data-generating site. A secure hash of the electronic information will then be generated, again at the digital data-generating site, and then transmitted to the remote trusted time-stamp server, which is run by a third-party time-stamp provider known as a Time Stamp Authority, or TSA. The remote trusted time-stamp server will generate a trusted time-stamp "token" (a signed hash of the information) and transmit the time-stamp token back to the requesting digital data generator. Typically, the remote service model requires that policies be developed and processes put into place that deliver both physical, as well as software-based, protection from compromise to the remote trusted time-stamp provider's infrastructure. A remote (to the requestor) trusted time-stamping service must be able to show, therefore, (1) that it derives the time for its time-stamp server or other provisioning service from a trusted time source; and (2) that its trusted time source for time-stamp service provisioning remains uncompromised.

A remote trusted time-stamp service provides data integrity protection that is somewhat limited by time lag and to the fact it is subject to DoS (denials of service), as well as to the fact that it is not time stamping origination events. Remote services only time stamp the time when the TSA received the hash of certain data, irrespective of its time of origination. This is because the only authenticity service a remote, trusted time stamp can provide is that digital data existed as of the time the provider received the hash of the digital data to time stamp. Remote schemas typically do not time stamp such data-generating events as the creation, modification, transmission by a sender, or receipt by a recipient of a data object. This is because the action generating that data object does not occur at the site of the remote service provider, who is a third party, or stranger, to the data generation, but rather at the site of the data generator, and only significantly after the data-generating event.

---

21. *See* AMERICAN NATIONAL STANDARD FOR FINANCIAL SERVICES, X.9.95 2005 TRUSTED TIME STAMP MANAGEMENT AND SECURITY, American National Standards Institute, 2005.

A locally based trusted time-stamp service provides a closer association of trusted time with data origination—such as the creation, modification, transmission, or receipt of digital evidence.[22] This provides a closer association between the digital data sought to be admitted into evidence, and the relevant time asserted to have attached to that digital data. A locally based trusted time stamp, therefore, provides enhanced potential for authentication, admissibility, surviving a content challenge, and even prevailing over contradictory non-time-stamped data. Accordingly, with a locally based service, an assertion may now be made that specific digital data was created, modified, transmitted, or received, at a provable point in time.

The advantages provided by trusted time stamping of digital information are two-fold. The immediate advantage relates to authentication. Here, a trusted time stamp can help show that digital information has not been changed since the asserted trusted time information was associated with that digital evidence.[23] The second advantage, not yet fully recognized, is that the very process that yields data integrity also provides a significant tool to assert that the digital information *content* thus admitted into evidence must be accurate. While the interpretation of such content remains within the province of a trier of fact, digital information that is time stamped in a trusted fashion may be accorded additional weight when considered against contradictory, non-time-stamped data, or other contradictory nondigital evidence and testimony. Once a player is willing to "freeze" his information in time, it takes on a certain additional weightiness. So long as you want to shuck and jive and stay flexible with your information, as so many companies want to do with their financial information, or their e-mail, you lose credibility.

EXAMPLES AND SUMMARIES OF VARIOUS TIME-STAMP METHODOLOGIES[24]

Digital Signature Method

In this time-stamp method, the TSA uses the private key of an asymmetric key pair to digitally sign the time-stamp info object encapsulated in the time-stamp token. The time-stamp token verification is carried out by performing signature verification using the corresponding public key. The signing key shall be reserved specifically for the purpose of issuing time-stamp tokens. This method may require the use of a Public Key Infrastructure (PKI) in order to authenticate the public key of the TSA and its associated usage.

---

22. A distinction should be made here between the "robust association" referred to in note 17 and "close association" described here. The term "close" refers to "close in time." "Close in time" in turn refers to the generation of a trusted time stamp being as close to the time of the data-generating event as possible. A time stamp generated a week after digital data was created cannot pinpoint the time of data creation, only that such data existed as of one week later. Accordingly, the greater the time interval between data generation and time-stamp generation, the less probative will be any assertion of "time of data generation" (as opposed to time of time-stamp generation). This is true irrespective of the robust association of a time stamp with digital data that can be proven.

23. And is testably so.

24. Excerpted from the ANSI X9.95 Trusted Time Stamp Standard. The American National Standards Institute (ANSI) provides standards that are relevant in many industries, particularly including issues relating to manufacturing and engineering.

MAC Method

In this time-stamp method, the TSA uses a secret key to cryptographically bind the time-stamp info object encapsulated in the time-stamp token with a message authentication code (MAC). The time-stamp token verification is done by authenticating the MAC. The TSA is needed to carry out the verification, and the TSA has to be thoroughly trusted, because there is no external evidence that might detect fraud. The secret key used to compute the MAC is kept secret. The secret key used for each time-stamp token shall be available for later verification. It may be either specific to that time stamp token, or common to a range of time-stamp tokens. Every exchange of information between the different entities (requestor, verifier, and TSA) requires data integrity and data-origin authentication protection. This protection may be provided by various means, for example, over a secured channel, or using public keys that do not need to last longer than the transaction lapse.

Linked Token Method

In this time-stamp method, the TSA uses hash functions to link and cryptographically bind the time-stamp info object encapsulated in the time-stamp token with previously issued time-stamp tokens. The TSA performs such a linking operation either for a single time-stamp info object at a time, or for multiple time-stamp info objects assigned the same time value at once. When multiple time-stamp info objects are linked at once, the TSA first performs an aggregation operation, then performs a linking operation. The TSA maintains the input and output values of the linking operations for subsequent time-stamp token verification and auditing purposes. Each time-stamp token contains a cryptographic binding that time-stamp token verification is done by using this cryptographic binding as input to an operation that computes the result of the linking operation performed by the TSA for the same time value. The TSA is needed to carry out the verification. The TSA performs publishing operations on the output values of the linking operations, resulting in values derived from them being published on widely available online or offline media. Each published value should depend on all time-stamp tokens issued by the TSA since the previous publishing event. The availability of the published values achieves a widely witnessed time-stamping process. Every exchange of information between the different entities (requestor, verifier, and TSA) requires data integrity and data-origin authentication protection. This protection may be provided by any means, for example, over a secured channel, or using public keys that do not need to last longer than the transaction lapse.

Linked and Signed Method

In this time-stamp method, the TSA uses hash functions to link and cryptographically bind the time-stamp info object encapsulated in the time-stamp token with previously issued time-stamp tokens in a way similar to the linked time-stamp method. In addition, the TSA uses the private key of an asymmetric key pair to digitally sign the time-stamp info object encapsulated in the time-stamp token, and includes in the signed attributes the data authenticating the time-stamp info object's participation in the TSA's aggregation and linking operation for the time value contained in it. The TSA maintains the input and output values of the linking operation for subsequent time-stamp token verification and auditing purposes. Each time-stamp token contains data authenticating its participation in the TSA's aggregation and linking operations. The time-stamp token verification is carried out either by performing signature verification using the corresponding public key and/or by carrying out a verification protocol exchange with the issuing TSA. The TSA performs publishing operations on the output values of the linking operations, resulting in values derived from them being published on widely available online or offline media. Each published value should depend on all time stamp tokens issued by the TSA since the previous publishing event. The availability of the published values achieves a widely witnessed time-stamping process.

Transient Key Method

In this time-stamp method, the TSA uses an asymmetric key pair that is generated for a defined interval of time. During the time interval (TN), the TSA uses the private key of the asymmetric key pair to digitally sign the time-stamp info object encapsulated in the time-stamp token. The time-stamp token verification is carried out by performing signature verification using the corresponding public key for the given time interval. The signing key shall be reserved specifically for two purposes. First, the private key will be used to issue time-stamp tokens during the interval of its duty. Second, the private key of the then-current time interval will be used to sign the public key of the asymmetric key pair and the interval information of the subsequent time interval (TN+01). During the interval (TN) a concatenate digest log is created. At the end of the interval, the concatenate digest log is itself digested to create the Meta-Digest TN. The interval information contains the start time for the interval, the stop time for the interval, the public key of the asymmetric key pair, and the digest log of the TST requests received by the preceding time interval. Optionally, the interval information may contain cross-chaining signatures generated by other Transient Key TSAs. At the conclusion of the then-current interval, the private key of the asymmetric key pair is destroyed. The public key is redundantly propagated in an archival process to be made available for verification.

Case Study
The Option Cases

Examples of fraudulent time-based data manipulation are now legion. As of the writing of this chapter, more than 140 public companies are under investigation for backdating stock option grants, most of which are calculated, granted, and recorded by specially designed computer software applications. It is expected that aggregated earnings restatements resulting from backdated option grants will exceed $100 billion.

(continued on next page)

(continued from previous page)

In December 2007, the former CEO of UnitedHealth Group agreed to forfeit more than $600 million in connection with backdated options grants issued to him.[25]

In December 2007, the former Vice President of Human Resources for publicly traded Brocade Communications was convicted by a federal jury on charges of conspiracy and falsifying records in connection with stock options backdating.[26]

In December 2007, a former Human Resources Vice President for publicly traded semiconductor chipmaker Broadcom pleaded guilty to obstruction of justice charges in connection with stock options backdating at that company.

In August, 2007, the former CEO of Brocade Communications, a publicly traded company, was found guilty of criminal charges relating to stock options backdating.[27]

In February 2007, the former General Counsel of publicly traded computer security software firm McAfee, Inc., was indicted for taking part in an options grant backdating scheme.[28] McAfee's former general counsel, who was also the company's compliance officer and a member of its ethics committee, was accused of causing the backdating of stock option grants between 2000 and 2006. McAfee used a computer utility called "Transcentive" to record stock options grants, and this recording included the number of options issued to each employee, the grant date for each grant and, the exercise price for each grant. The Transcentive system was also used to generate reports relating to stock options for financial reporting purposes. The former McAfee general counsel was also accused of causing McAfee's then-controller to change the grant date and exercise price in the Transcentive system so that the exercise price would be lower (ostensibly to guarantee an instant profit to the options grant recipient). Ironically, it was also alleged that the former McAfee general counsel attempted to cover his tracks by having the same then-controller fired for backdating option grants.[29]

(continued on next page)

25. Eric Dash, *Former Chief Will Forfeit $418 Million*, N.Y. TIMES, Dec. 7. 2007: http://www.nytimes.com/2007/12/07/business/07options.html?_r=1&adxnnl=1&oref=slogin&adxnnlx=1197230886-I8TZd9luf//YqsIrd3Q4aQ.

26. *Conviction in Backdating Case*, N.Y. TIMES, Dec. 6, 2007: http://www.nytimes.com/2007/12/06/business/06fund.html?ref=business.

27. Jordan Robertson, *Brocade Exec Guilty in Stock Option Case*, WIRED.COM, Dec. 6, 2007; *see also* Eric Dash & Matt Richtel, *Ex-Brocade Chief Convicted in Backdating Case*, N.Y. TIMES, Aug. 8, 2007: http://www.nytimes.com/2007/08/08/business/08brocade.html?adxnnl=1&adxnnlx=1197232159-zaMvjldS47qZ/7e+w/n5AA.

28. United States v. Kent Roberts, 07-cr-0100 (United States District Court for the District of Northern California, San Francisco Division, Feb. 7, 2007) at. 3–5.

29. *Id.*

(continued from previous page)

In January 2007, Broadcom announced that it would take a $2.2 billion charge (loss) against earnings to account for the backdating of options grants.[30]

In September 2006, the former CEO of Comverse Technologies was indicted (having fled the United States just prior to the issuance of the indictment) for fraudulently backdating stock option grants by altering computer records, resulting in "instant" profits of more than $50 million.[31]

In November 2006, former Computer Associates CEO Sanjay Kumar was sentenced to 12 years in prison in an accounting fraud scandal involving both contract and revenue backdating resulting in a misreporting of more than $2.2 billion in revenues.[32] The company also took an earnings charge of approximately $342 million for "misallocated" stock option grants.[33]

---

30. A $2.2 BILLION CHARGE AT BROADCOM, N.Y. TIMES, Jan. 23, 2007. *See also* Charles Forelle, *Broadcom Sees Bigger Options Hit,* WALL ST. J., Sept. 9, 2006, at A-3.

31. United States v. Jacob Alexander, 06-cr-00628, Docket Item 1-1 (E.D.N.Y 2006); Charles Forelle & James Bandler, *Dating Game—Stock-Options Criminal Charge: Slush Fund and Fake Employees,* WALL ST. J., Aug. 10, 2006, at A-1.

32. In April 2007, Mr. Kumar agreed to repay approximately $800 million restitution: $52 million immediately and the remainder subject to a 20 percent wage garnishment. William L. Bulkeley, *Ex-CA Chief Kumar Agrees to Pay $52 Million in Restitution,* N.Y. TIMES, Apr. 13, 2007.

33. William L. Bulkeley, *Kumar Is Sentenced to 12 Years For Role in CA Accounting Fraud,* WSJ.COM, Nov. 2, 2006, Michael J. de la Merced, *Ex-Leader of Computer Associates Gets 12-Year Sentence and Fine,* N.Y. TIMES, Nov. 3, 2006.

CHAPTER **6**

Identity

The issue of "who" caused an event to occur in the digital realm can be of fundamental importance. Who edited the file? Who changed the financial information? Who downloaded the trade secrets? In this discussion, "who" is an entity that associates with an information object by taking some action concerning it, or that sets in motion an event in the digital realm. Quite typically a "who" authors information, signs information, accesses information, or changes information. Entities act on information. And as we have seen, the notion of *identity* is fundamental to authenticity.

The issue of identity is particularly difficult. For one thing, it is easy to operate anonymously within the digital realm. Furthermore, unlike the issue of time, the issue of identity is multifaceted. There are different types of identity, and no unified type of record or scheme that records identity—if it is recorded at all. Often, in order to conserve resources and boost processing power, businesses consciously choose *not* to record information about the identity of who did certain things in an information system. Furthermore, a "who" can be a machine, a computer program, an interacting complex of programs,[1] an organization or department, an agent, or an individual human being, among other things. There is no limit on the types of digital identities, because identities can be created by the reading and writing games at issue, as any lover of video games can avow. In addition, the complexity of information systems works to meld lesser constituents into larger wholes, which then blurs distinct boundaries of cause and effect.

The issue of identity is therefore complex. Unless there is a *eunomic* regime involved,[2] identity is a circumstantial evidence question of substantial difficulty, and many different types of records and evidence, both digital and real-world, will be implicated. Identity is inextricably intertwined with the issue of the security of information systems.

---

1. The Uniform Electronic Transactions Act (UETA) § 2(6) defines an "electronic *agent*" as a "computer program or an electronic or other automated means used independently to initiate an action or respond to electronic records or performances in whole or in part, without review or action by an individual." The federal Electronic Signature in Global and National Commerce Act, E-SIGN, 15 U.S.C. § 7001 *et seq.,* defines an agent similarly.

2. One such *eunomic* regime that gives strong evidence of identity is the digital signature discussed in Chapter 4. The strong evidence of identity depends on the assumption that only a particular, defined, and known entity has possession of a private key, permitting that entity to asymmetrically encrypt information. If the holders of private keys let others use them, the system breaks down. Or, if there is erroneous or misleading information about the association of real world identities with public keys, the system fails. Threats to unlocking the math in cryptograms could also cause the solution to break down. Thus, as with any system, whether digital signatures work as a solution to the identity issue depend on whether they are implemented properly.

Improved regimes of information and improved security over digital information will improve available evidence of identity in the future. Certain federal regulations, such as Sarbanes-Oxley Act of 2002, and certain initiatives in industry are currently pressuring enterprises to develop systems that create reliable evidence about identity. Unless one is dealing with a well-thought-out regime, obtaining knowledge about "who" did something in the digital realm might well be impossible, as there may either be no records at all, or the records will be unreliable because they are freely editable, or because various real-world identities are doing such things as sharing passwords. Understanding by probability is one's best hope in these circumstances.

ADMISSION TO THE PLAYGROUND: AUTHENTICATION PROTOCOLS

Fundamental to any discussion about proof of digital identity is an understanding that information systems have no intrinsic way of knowing the identity of entities that participate in the systems' reading and writing games. For example, if someone sits down at a computer keyboard, begins typing, and then begins accessing and editing files, a computer has no intrinsic way of knowing who is doing such things. Obviously, without more built-in capability, an information system cannot keep records about who is doing things and certainly will not do so automatically and accurately. The same is true if a computer program begins interacting with another program. "Who" is that program? Does the information system know? And if so, how?

This important reality—information systems' intrinsic lack of knowledge about the identity of who is interacting with them—led to the development of protocols that allowed systems to determine: (1) the purported identity of an interacting entity; (2) whether that entity was indeed who it purported to be; and (3) whether that entity was authorized to interact with the system, to greater or lesser degrees, depending on what was happening. Unless such a system is employed, systems will be insecure, with anyone able to anonymously hop onto a system and edit its records, or indeed, even destroy the system itself. Accordingly, our information ecosystems now generally have evolved something akin to immune systems. They have a way of ferreting out what agents are allowed in, and who should be kept out as unknown or unauthorized.

This protocol is known in IT circles as "authentication," or sometimes as "identification and authentication." It is no coincidence that these are the same words used for highly similar functions in the law of evidence. Under the Federal Rules of Evidence, "authentication" is the foundation laid to show that an item is authentic—that it is what it purports to be—before it is admitted into evidence. Under the Rules, "identification" is the same foundation applied to information about identity. For example when presented with the question, "Did Grandma Cleo sign this letter, or was it really Uncle Bill?," a judge might rule: "Counsel, under Rule 901 (b)(2) you need to identify that signature with testimony by someone familiar with Cleo's handwriting before I admit it."

In the digital information protocol discussed here, authentication (or identification and authentication) refers to the preliminary exchange of information that occurs between an information system and an entity who wants to enter that system to engage in its reading and writing games. The system must be informed as to who the entity purports to be ("identification"), and then confirm that that entity is indeed who it purports to be ("authentication"). After gathering information about the "who," the system then determines what that particular entity is allowed to do, based on its prior programming.

Of course, it is only after this process of identification and authentication that the system can generate records about what an entity did on the system. Before the identification and authentication process, the system has no information about identity except happenstance, extrinsic evidence that can be gathered about who was on a computer system. Information systems can apply an authentication process to people, to other computer systems or programs, and indeed to any type of entity that is defined as a player by the reading and writing games at issue. And as we will see, the reliability of any authentication process varies greatly, depending on the system involved, on the type of authentication process used, and on the business processes in place in the environment surrounding the information system.

Generally, like the digital signature process and its use of a private key, the authentication process largely depends on the knowledge of a secret, or the exclusive possession of a unique item, or on a unique characteristic. The National Institute for Standards and Technology (NIST) has provided a number of definitions associated with this process of identification and authentication ("I&A"). First, it defines identification as "the means by which a user provides a claimed identity to the system," while the subsequent step of authentication is "the means of establishing the validity of this claim."[3]

As observed in the NIST document,

> I&A is a critical building block of computer security since it is the basis for most types of access control and for establishing user accountability. Access control often requires that the system be able to identify and differentiate among users. For example, access control is often based on least privilege, which refers to the granting to users of only those accesses required to perform their duties. User accountability requires the linking of activities on a computer system to specific individuals and, therefore, requires the system to identify users.[4]

Put together, the process of I&A is "a technical measure that prevents unauthorized people (or unauthorized processes) from entering a computer system."[5] According to NIST, I&A is explained as follows:

> Computer systems recognize people based on the authentication data the systems receive. Authentication presents several challenges: collecting authentication data, transmitting the data securely, and knowing whether the person who was originally authenticated is still the person using the computer system. For example, a user may walk away from a terminal while still logged on, and another person may start using it.
>
> There are three means of authenticating a user's identity, which can be used alone or in combination:
>
> - something the individual knows (a secret—e.g., a password, Personal Identification Number (PIN), or cryptographic key);
> - something the individual possesses (a token—e.g., an ATM card or a smart card); and
> - something the individual is (a biometric—e.g., such characteristics as a voice pattern, handwriting dynamics, or a fingerprint).

---

3. NIST Special Publication 800-12: Part IV, "Technical Controls," Chapter 16, "Identification and Authentication."

4. *Id.*

5. *Id.*

While it may appear that any of these means could provide strong authentication, there are problems associated with each. If people wanted to pretend to be someone else on a computer system, they can guess or learn that individual's password; they can also steal or fabricate tokens. Each method also has drawbacks for legitimate users and system administrators: users forget passwords and may lose tokens, and administrative overhead for keeping track of I&A data and tokens can be substantial. Biometric systems have significant technical, user acceptance, and cost problems as well.[6]

Examples of the Authentication Process and How It Generates Evidence of Identity

We can see how the identification and authentication process works on a daily basis, both on a stand-alone computer and on a network, and how the process generates evidence about identity. Because the author has one handy, he will use his MacBook Pro laptop computer for the first demonstration, which operates a variant of Mac OS X operating system, which in turn is built upon a Unix operating system core.

After turning the computer on, there is a blank screen with a dialogue box that says "George Paul's Computer." It is not feasible to operate the computer unless one supplies it with information proving you are George Paul. In this case, it is a password previously programmed by George. More precisely, the password information, if supplied correctly, does not really conclusively prove a person is George Paul—only that the person giving the information knows or has guessed a secret supposedly known only by George. Thus, we immediately see that if more than one person knows a password, the entire system of proving identity starts to break down. In companies where administrative assistants know bosses' passwords, or people share passwords, or there are groups that contain many people all known by the same identity, evidence of identity becomes immediately suspect. Litigators should remember this. The business processes surrounding the ecosystem in question are relevant to knowledge of identity, and any ability to test for evidence of identity.

Back to the example: Upon trying to interact with the information system, the computer states: "You must authenticate to unlock the screen. Mac OS X requires that you type your password." There is a special application running, which Apple calls "loginwindow," which prohibits one from doing anything with the computer—even see its desktop—unless one authenticates oneself to the system. If one types in the password correctly, one will see the desktop, and will start getting whatever other access is allowed by more-detailed programming. As we will see, just because one is granted entry into a system, one does not gain entry to each and every application, and just because one gains access to an application, does not mean that one gains access to each and every record found and potentially accessed by that application. At each successive stage—depending on how the system has been set up—a new identification and authentication process can occur to ensure that the entity knocking at the playroom door is allowed to enter.

Often, after the entity is identified and authenticated, records are then automatically generated, keeping track of what that entity did, accessed, edited, downloaded or otherwise caused to happen in the cordoned-off segment of the play area that the entity was allowed to enter by its successfully asserting its identity.

---

6. Id.

One of the useful things about the Mac OS X operating system is that it allows an administrative user—in this instance, George—to create different user accounts for his laptop. Using a Systems Preferences application, George can create a new user for his laptop, say, by the name of Ingrid. She can be given her own user account and password.

After programming the computer there are two users, George and Ingrid, each with his and her own password. When turning on the computer, one is given a choice to log on either as George or Ingrid. Whom do you purport to be? If you know George's secret information—his password—you can authenticate as George. If you know Ingrid's secret information—her password—you can authenticate as Ingrid.

After successful authentication, the information system will assume the entity it is playing with is either George or Ingrid. It displays Ingrid's desktop to Ingrid, and George's desktop to George. George cannot see Ingrid's private files or information. Ingrid cannot see George's information. Unless she knows George's password, Ingrid cannot log on as George or get access to any of his information.

Thereafter, the system will keep certain logs and records about what Ingrid has done during the time she is controlling the system after authenticating, and what George has done during the time he is controlling the system after authenticating. For example, on the Mac OS X operating system, there is an application called "Activity Monitor." It shows the processes and applications currently running on the computer, and the resources currently being used.

To illustrate how the authentication process helps generate evidence of identity, a screenshot of the Activity Monitor is shown as Figure 6.1. The processes and applications that were initiated during the time the computer was utilized by an identity identified and authenticated as George are listed in the log. The processes and applications initiated during the time the computer was utilized by an identity identified and authenticated by Ingrid are listed as well.

Of interest, there is also a mysterious entity: a user named "root" who is associated with something called the pmTool. It is currently not known what this entity, "root," is. It does show, however, that nonhuman entities do "lurk" and read and write during the time we think we are in control of the system. What was root doing? Might it be relevant to know? It all depends on the facts.

Clearly, if someone other than Ingrid knows Ingrid's password, the entity responsible for those activities is not necessarily Ingrid, but could instead be the other entity that knows Ingrid's password. In fact, because George set up Ingrid's user account, and gave Ingrid her password, he can sign on and authenticate as Ingrid, which is precisely what happened so that these illustrations could be created. Just as with a private key in a digital signature scheme, with its characteristics known only by the unique holder, identities that authenticate need secret passwords, tokens, or other characteristics, and not to have the information become common knowledge. Otherwise, the reliability of the information about identity loses force.

Freely Editable Information about User Identity

But the world of software is not uniform in how it handles identity—one of the complicating factors that makes this a study in circumstantial evidence and usually a matter of probability. Many applications, especially where security of access is not a concern, do not carry an I&A protocol.

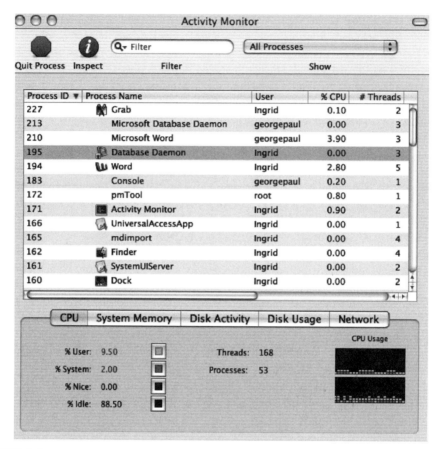

FIGURE 6.1
Log of Activity Showing User Responsible for Activity

For example, using the stand-alone laptop from this demonstration, after either Ingrid or George get access to his or her virtual desktop, one can launch the application Microsoft Word. Microsoft Word will insert information about an identity into the metadata of each document, listing an "author" in the Properties file. For example, George authenticates as himself and enters his system. He then calls up a particular Word file, a version of Grace Power's excellent case study on electronic mortgages and promissory notes (found in Part IV). He goes to the Properties selection of the File menu and the Summary tab, where he sees "gpowers" listed as the author of the file, as illustrated in Figure 6.2.

Critically, however, this metadata about "author" is freely editable without any special utility, merely by using the application. George can edit the author's name, so it now reads "Grace Powers' younger sister," as in Figure 6.3.

After this document is saved, the metadata will thereafter say that the author of the Word record is not Grace Powers, designated by "gpowers," but "Grace Powers' younger sister."

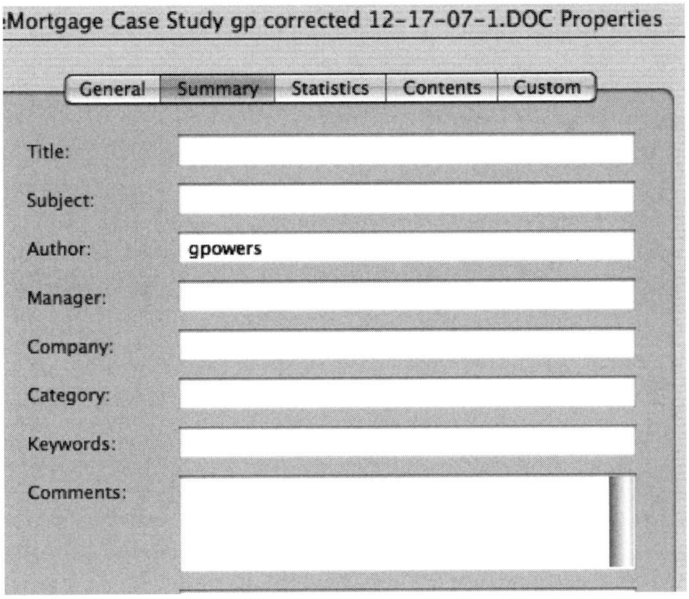

FIGURE 6.2
Metadata Showing "gpowers" as Author of File

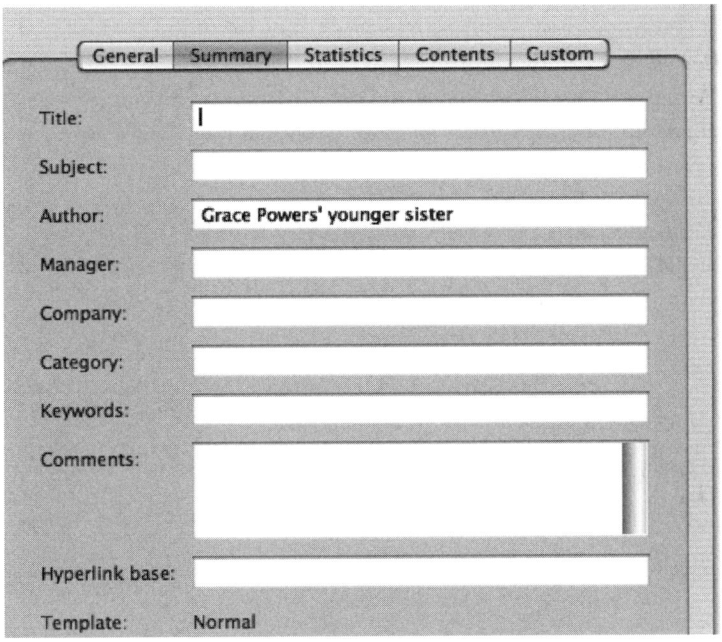

FIGURE 6.3
Edited Metadata about Authorship

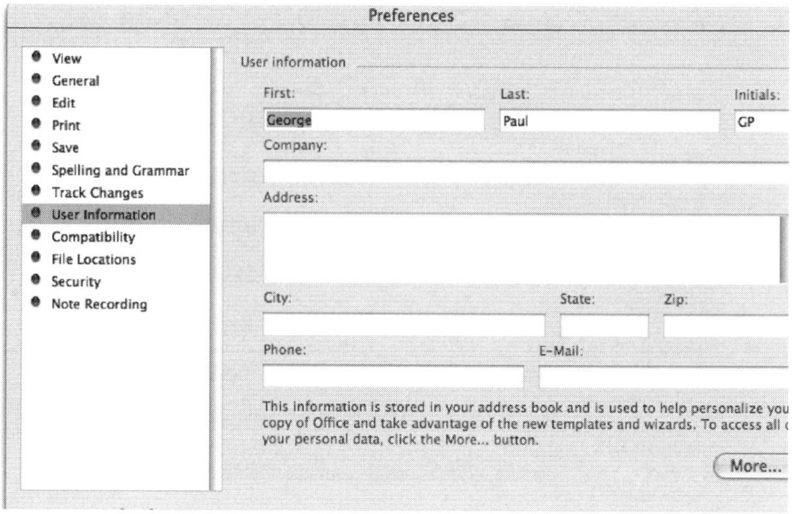

FIGURE 6.4
Preferences about User Information Available in Word

One can even program the Word document to insert false information about authors into all of the files that particular application creates. Word has a "Preferences" selection in the Word menu (Figure 6.4). It, in turn, has a "User" tab, which allows one to program the file to insert metadata about the author of all documents created by that licensed file of Word. Properly configured on George's computer, the Preferences about Users appears as shown in the above figure.

But this, too, is editable. George can change it to anyone he wants, and as a test, edits these preferences about User Information as "Fictional identity 3 Paul" (Figure 6.5).

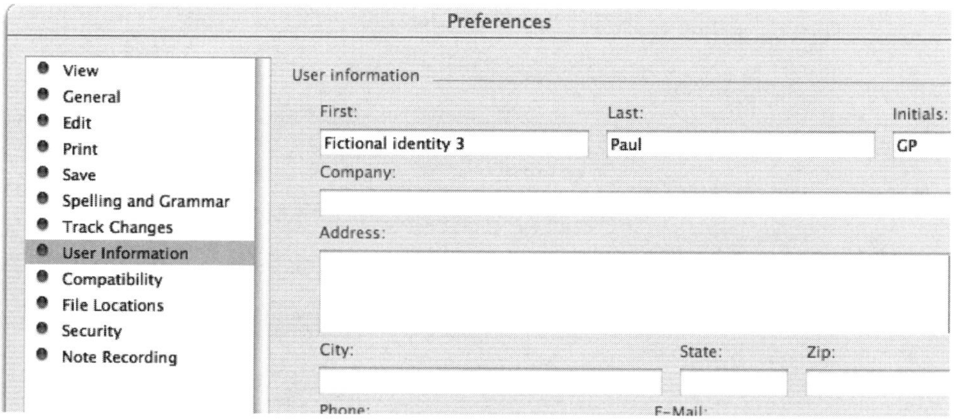

FIGURE 6.5
Edited Preferences about User Information

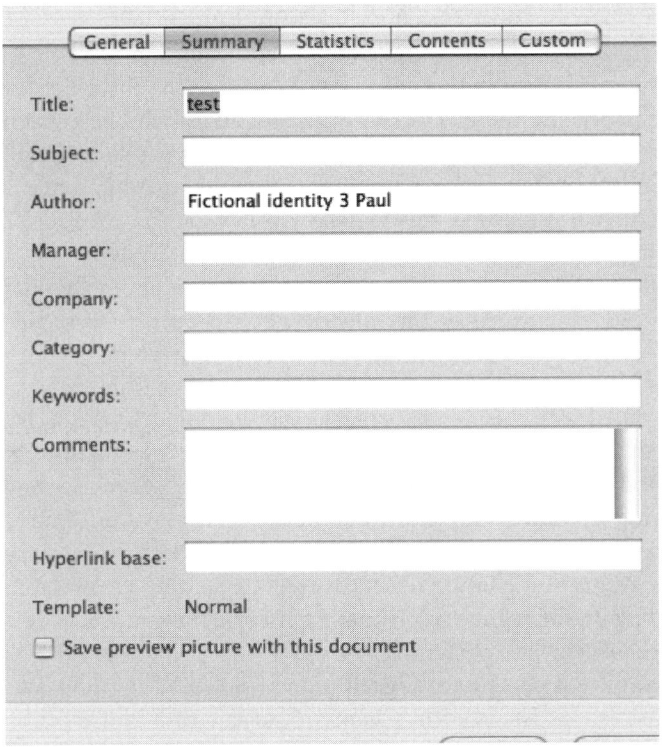

FIGURE 6.6
Unreliable Computer-Generated Information about Authorship

Now that Word is programmed to insert this as the "author," George creates a new Word document named "Test," saves it, and calls up the metadata about the author, found in the Properties window of the file, under the Summary tab. The computer now inserts as metadata that the author of the file is "Fictional identity 3 Paul" (Figure 6.6).

Of course, because the ability to program the computer to insert metadata about authorship is freely editable, George could have instructed the information system to insert automatically, as computer-generated information, that the author of all the Word documents was Grace Powers, Ed Chase, Steve Teppler, Stephen Mason, or anyone. Years later in a lawsuit, if someone checked the metadata of a file created after such programming of preferences, the metadata about the author might be highly misleading.

But on the other hand, it could be accurate, if the business processes at the place where the information system was being used required accurate information about authors and identity to be inserted into a computer's programming. The point here is there is no *eunomic* regime of identity concerning the "author" of these Word files found on the stand-alone computer. This system of creating information about authors in a Word application is quite unlike the system, in the same computer, that keeps track of what Ingrid is doing with the central processing unit and what George is doing with the central processing unit. That log of events, as associated with identity, is tied to an I&A process.

Evidence of Identity in Networks and in Larger Enterprises

The same principles apply in networks. Before George logs on to a computer that is part of a network, he must identify himself and authenticate. At the office, he authenticates with a password. Because there is less information about who he is (as he is not in the actual building), over the Internet he must "log" on to the network using his user ID, his password, and a token that changes numbers randomly every minute or so, which he combines with a secret PIN. If all this matches up to what the network knows about the entity purporting to be George, George is allowed onto the system.

Now that the system has certain *eunomic* information about the identity operating within it, it can create records of that identity. Logs of access to applications, folders, and files can be created. Logs of navigation within the system can be created. Often, but not always, these logs will also contain evidence about what Internet Protocol (IP) address is associated with the identity, such as the IP address of the access point.

Unfortunately, because information systems are unique information ecosystems, there is no one method by which all this information is collected. Some systems create logs of almost everything an entity does. Others do not. This is a matter of business judgment, and a cost-benefit decision that must take into account both security and the need for evidence about events in the future. Each case will depend on its own facts.

But, depending on the regime in place at a network, the concept of I&A will continue to generate useable evidence of identity.

For example, once a person has logged onto a network, an application may require new I&A protocols. As discussed in Chapter 5, at law offices there are often database programs that keep track of Word and other files, and that track the history of documents. These are often integrated with e-mail programs. Accordingly, at some law offices, one must identify and authenticate oneself, as in Figure 6.7, to these applications before gaining access to e-mail records or to the document database.

After one has done this, the database system now has useable evidence of the identity of the entity at the keyboard connected to the network. The database system thereafter will insert this information as data into logs in its database program. For example, in this database program, there is a computer-generated information database called a Document Profile. This database is rather like a network version of metadata, in that it

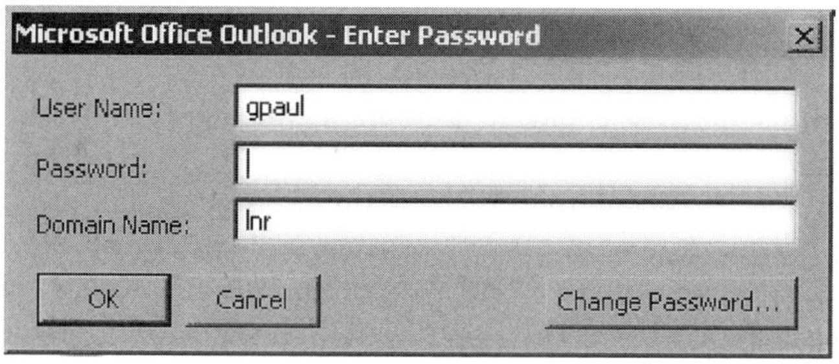

FIGURE 6.7
Authentication Process for an Application Controlling a Database

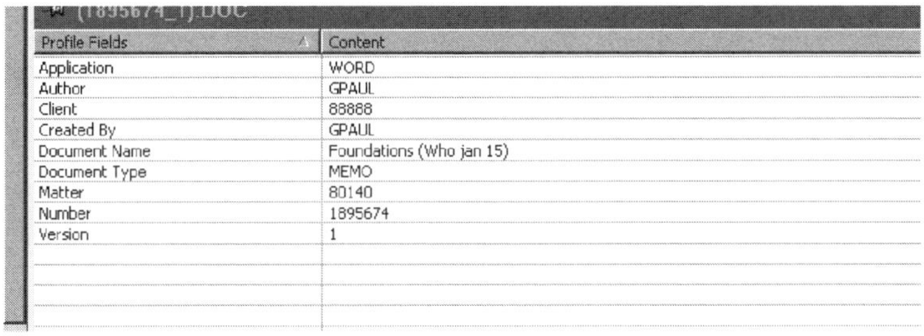

(1895674_1).DOC

Profile Fields	Content
Application	WORD
Author	GPAUL
Client	88888
Created By	GPAUL
Document Name	Foundations (Who jan 15)
Document Type	MEMO
Matter	80140
Number	1895674
Version	1

FIGURE 6.8
Information about Identity Taken from an Authentication Process

shows the identity of the "author." The system uses the information about identity from the entity that authenticated itself to the database program when the actions in question were taken (Figure 6.8).

Other records, such as logs of the history of actions taken with certain documents, can be created and associated with a particular document in a database, such as in Figure 6.9, which inserts information about identity based on the authentication process described. It tracks activity, such as check-out, create a new version, check-in, modify, and view. The program also could track who among those authenticated to the system printed the document, and when, which might be very useful.

Accordingly, for a document that had many users, there might be a significant history of who was doing what to certain information objects. The ability of the system to give information about identity is tied to the authentication protocol.

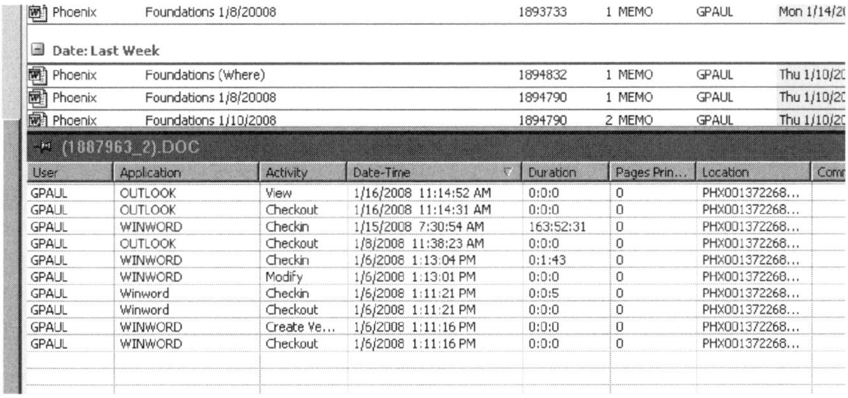

Phoenix	Foundations 1/8/20008	1893733	1 MEMO	GPAUL	Mon 1/14/2(
Date: Last Week					
Phoenix	Foundations (Where)	1894832	1 MEMO	GPAUL	Thu 1/10/2(
Phoenix	Foundations 1/8/20008	1894790	1 MEMO	GPAUL	Thu 1/10/2(
Phoenix	Foundations 1/10/2008	1894790	2 MEMO	GPAUL	Thu 1/10/2(

(1887963_2).DOC

User	Application	Activity	Date-Time	Duration	Pages Prin...	Location	Comr
GPAUL	OUTLOOK	View	1/16/2008 11:14:52 AM	0:0:0	0	PHX001372268...	
GPAUL	OUTLOOK	Checkout	1/16/2008 11:14:31 AM	0:0:0	0	PHX001372268...	
GPAUL	WINWORD	Checkin	1/15/2008 7:30:54 AM	163:52:31	0	PHX001372268...	
GPAUL	OUTLOOK	Checkout	1/8/2008 11:38:23 AM	0:0:0	0	PHX001372268...	
GPAUL	WINWORD	Checkin	1/6/2008 1:13:04 PM	0:1:43	0	PHX001372268...	
GPAUL	WINWORD	Modify	1/6/2008 1:13:01 PM	0:0:0	0	PHX001372268...	
GPAUL	Winword	Checkin	1/6/2008 1:11:21 PM	0:0:5	0	PHX001372268...	
GPAUL	Winword	Checkout	1/6/2008 1:11:21 PM	0:0:0	0	PHX001372268...	
GPAUL	WINWORD	Create Ve...	1/6/2008 1:11:16 PM	0:0:0	0	PHX001372268...	
GPAUL	WINWORD	Checkout	1/6/2008 1:11:16 PM	0:0:0	0	PHX001372268...	

FIGURE 6.9
Logs of Activity Using Authenticated Identities

Quality of Authentication Protocols

Obviously, one area of evidence that will almost always be relevant will be the quality of the authentication protocols, and other information security measures, in place in the information system that gave life to, or that handled, the information object at issue. In the recent past, enterprises in the United States were tolerant of many people sharing passwords and other authentication devices. However, people ultimately discovered that such practices made it impossible to know with any reliability who was doing what on a system, and who was therefore responsible for what the company had done. Accordingly, there is a movement in auditing to make it much more stringently prohibited for people to share authentication protocols, and for such systems to work properly in the nature of business processes.

Indeed, the credit card industry, which handles sensitive digital information that might be misappropriated, leading to theft of funds from banks or theft of digital identity, has staked out a position in this area. A trade association for these entities, the Payment Card Industry (PCI) has formed the PCI Security Standards Council. It, in turn, has published the PCI Data Security Standards (DDS) and "PCI Security Audit Procedures," for use by assessors conducting onsite reviews for merchants and service providers required to validate compliance with Payment Card Industry (PCI) Data Security Standard (DSS) requirements.

One key tenet set forth in the PCI Data Security Standards is Requirement 8: *"Assign a unique ID to each person with computer access,"* which is explained as follows: "Assigning a unique identification (ID) to each person with access ensures that actions taken on critical data and systems are performed by, and can be traced to, known and authorized users."

Explaining the general requirement of the ability to *trace actions to known and authorized users*, subrequirements are explained, such as Requirement 8.1: "Identify all users with a unique user name before allowing them to access system components or cardholder data;" Requirement 8.5: "Ensure proper user authentication and password management for non-consumer users and administrators on all system components;" Requirement 8.5.8: "Do not use group, shared, or generic accounts and passwords;" and Requirement 8.5.8 b: "Examine password policies/procedures to verify that group and shared passwords are explicitly prohibited."

No law requires such a specificity of actions. As we have seen, the United States is technological neutral, leaving us, as a matter of substantive law, with a soup of mere digital circumstances, and often with an inability to prove facts given the untestability of digital information objects.

But as a consequence of the need to determine with whom one wants to do business, and to judge the sort of regimes of information one prefers or demands they should use, certain groups (such as, in this case, the credit card industry), by necessity have now had to start thinking about what is necessary to determine who did what in an information system. The credit card industry is not the only such effort, but it is a prominent part of the economy. Many other sectors now have players joining together to set new rules of the game, so that they can have ordered regimes of information.

Accordingly, evidence of identity depends on the authentication regime employed in conjunction with any information system. It also depends on the quality of the log records, or log files, that applications keep about the identity of the users that log on and that initiate events such as editing, accessing, printing, and so on. Some applications are not written to keep detailed logs. Some applications have the ability to do so, but they are turned off in order to save resources, including processing power and memory. Accordingly, there is no recipe. Each system is set up differently, and the evidence of identity can be different in different circumstances.

LEGAL TESTS FOR ADMISSIBILITY OF EVIDENCE ABOUT IDENTITY

As we have discussed, Article IX of the Federal Rules of Evidence governs not only the authentication foundation, but also "identification." A set of information can be what it purports to be. And so, too, can information about identity be what it purports to be. In the physical realm one may want to "identify" the signer of a letter, or a voice on the other end of a telephone call. Is that really Aunt Michele's signature? Was that Braden's voice on the other end of the phone line?

Evidence Sufficient to Support a Finding

Thus, the rules of evidence already encompass the issue of identifying, for admissibility purposes, the various digital identities that appear in our lawsuits. Who sent that e-mail? Who edited the database? Who launched that missile?

As we have seen, the Federal Rules take a circumstantial evidence approach to such admissibility questions. So long as there is enough circumstantial evidence to "support a finding" of identity—so long, after the foundation has been offered, that it would be rational for the finder of fact to conclude a claimed or purported fact about identity is true—a sufficient foundation of identification has been made, and evidence should be admitted.

Thus, some of the illustrations of circumstantial evidence scenarios, set forth in Rule 901 (b), can apply. There can be testimony by someone with personal knowledge that someone did something in the digital realm: "I was there with him that night. We did it as a lark in the principal's office. It was John who hacked into the computer and changed everyone's test scores!" *See* F.R.E. Rule 901 (b)(1).

Or, there could be distinctive characteristics about certain evidence that pointed, as a matter of circumstantial evidence, to an identity. *See*, for example, the discussion of pattern analysis and lexical fingerprints, later in this chapter, implicating F.R.E. Rule 901 (b)(3) and (4).

Proof of an identity having logged onto a system, as discussed above, by evidence along the lines of "The log of this identity onto our system was done with a token that was issued to John, and that was accompanied by use of John's password," should be considered a sufficient identifying foundation. *See* F.R.E. Rule 901 (b)(9), which governs a process or system used to produce a result, with the showing that that process or system produces an accurate result.

The bottom line is that the foundation for admissibility of evidence about identity is one of circumstantial evidence and only an amount of evidence "sufficient to support a finding" of the claimed fact about identity is necessary for admissibility. Given this foundational burden, almost anything goes in proving identity. It is a question of circumstantial evidence that implicates the inferences that can be drawn from the total-ity of facts about the system and events at issue. Things will be thrown into the weight of the evidence.

Reliability of Evidence

Determining identity must also, to some extent, take into account Article VIII, com-prising the rules about reliability of evidence that will be discussed in the next chapters. In considering circumstantial evidence, resort will be had to computer-generated infor-mation, and to outright hearsay that exists as computer-*stored* information, such as the editable text filled into the Word function "Preferences" identifying an author as "Fic-tional identity 3 Paul." If they understood things, some courts might well reject evidence about identity if it was offered like this, because it would be hearsay. It incorporated human-generated statements, clearly hearsay, about identity. This shows the critical fact: Just because information is computer-generated does not mean that such generation was not using human-entered, hearsay information as data.

Digital evidence is necessarily circumstantial, and some evidence will be weightier than other evidence. Each part of the analysis of the question *who?* in digital evidence therefore can be found along a continuum. How strong is this type of evidence? How reliable is it? Does it require what is called "corroboration," or does it stand on its own? Is the information easy to change or modify? Each of these factors can be evaluated.

TYPES OF IDENTITY

When considering who created or altered a particular piece of evidence, a range of pos-sible entities may be responsible. Some are persons, some are applications or computer systems that directly take their direction from a person, and some are nearly autono-mous systems that record information and create records as part of normal operations.

Establishing individual responsibility may not be feasible or even legally required. Consider, as an example, a SCADA[7] system that monitors and records environmental measurements. Arguably either the programmer who wrote the software or the user account that runs it could be considered the creator of a particular record, but this would not be an important characteristic other than establishing whether or not the application was performing as intended. Indeed, almost all of the information generated by such a system might be computer-generated—the product of reading and writing games of the system as it functions. What can one even make of the concept of "identity" in such a situation?

But generally, there are a number of categories that can be considered when look-ing at who created a particular piece of evidence. Often more than one of these catego-

---

7. SCADA, or "Supervisory Control and Data Acquisition," systems are real-time control systems used for such applications as controlling public utilities or manufacturing processes. SCADA systems are generally highly dis-tributed, highly redundant, and incorporate high levels of security. These systems are semi-autonomous and gather large amounts of data in real time.

ries may apply and will need to be considered and interpreted to establish identity or authorship.

Person: The most obvious creator of a piece of digital evidence is a human being. That person creates a computer file through such actions as sending an e-mail, writing a document, or uploading a digital picture. Depending on the specific nature of the file and operating system, the user's identity (as identified by the operating system) may be recorded in the metadata of the file.

Agent: A person may be designated to act as an agent of another person. For example, an assistant may be granted access to his supervisor's e-mail account with permission to send e-mail on her behalf. In this particular case, while the actor creates the evidence, the direction ostensibly comes from the supervisor. The digital evidence associated with the e-mail or file (as discussed earlier in this chapter) may reflect the agent, the supervisor, or both.

Digital Agent: A Digital Agent is the virtual equivalent of a real world agent. It consists of a software program authorized to act on behalf of a person. For example, a digital agent might monitor stock prices and execute trades based on certain conditions.

Group: A group is simply a collection of persons. Groups may be organizational (such as Legal or Human Resources) or technical (Administrators). Operating systems such as Window, UNIX, and Linux support the concept of both personal and group accounts, with specific permissions tied to each. Creating a new user account in Windows, for example, requires one to be a member of the Administrator group. Therefore, by default, a new user account must have been created by a member of that group, even if the specific account used to create the new user cannot be determined.

Organization: Although the organization, like the group, is a collection of persons, it may also have a legal identity in itself. A corporation has legal standing, and records, while created by persons, may be considered the property of the corporation. Individuals acting as agents of the organization may create evidence in the course of their business that may be deemed to be the property of the corporation. In this respect, the digital evidence is no different than paper documents.

System Software: System software creates records as part of its normal operations. Often these are vital in the context of digital evidence. Examples include telephone call system logs, firewall and intrusion detection logs, and operating-system logs. These may be used to establish the identity of a third party, such as an attacker. While arguably a person is ultimately behind the creation of these entries (either through the programming that instructed the system to log actions or through the action that is logged), the creator of the evidence is more likely a system account or an application.

All these examples show the complexity of the information systems comprising the digital realm. In the digital realm, reading and writing conventions can create novel identities.

TYPES OF RECORDS AND PROCESSES THAT MAY HELP PROVE IDENTITY

A particular piece of evidence may have multiple types of owners and, indeed, multiple owners. How then is ownership or identity regarding a piece of evidence established? There are several types of records generally used.

Operating-System Records

Many, but not all, computer operating systems[8] have the ability to assign "ownership" to a file. These include most versions of Windows and UNIX variants (including Linux). This ownership is based on the user account that created the file originally. Two points are important here: First, the Operating System records ownership based on a user ID. This user ID does not necessarily correspond to the physical user. As discussed, often additional evidence is necessary to confirm that a specific person created that evidence.

Next, a user may create a file that is later modified. For example, a user may write a document using word-processing software. Another user may take that document and use it as a template for a completely different matter. The original user may still be shown as the creator of the file, when the actual creator of the new document is the subsequent user.

As we have seen, file ownership can be changed using the native utilities in the operating system, as well as third-party applications. Simply copying a file from one location to another may change the ownership, depending on the specific operating system and file-copying utility.

Most Windows systems are capable of recording file ownership, but only if certain settings are used (most importantly, the NTFS (standard Windows) file system). UNIX and Linux variants track file ownership by default. In both cases, however, the operating system assigns a user ID to the file. That user ID is a number stored by the operating system and translated to a more user-friendly form (i.e., the user name). In UNIX, the number is called the "uid" and is stored in the password file. When a user requests a file listing, the system will translate the uid of the file into the user name. The listing would typically look something like "sam users file" where "sam" is the user, "users" is the group, and "file" is the filename. If a file from another system is copied to this system, and the second file has the same uid as "sam," the system will interpret "sam" as the owner of the file, even if sam did not create it on the other system.

Application Records

Some applications[9] have the ability to record user data as well. For example, word-processing programs can record the creator of a file in the metadata of the program. Again, this is usually based on the user ID at the time of creation and may be retained if

---

8. Operating System: Software designed to handle basic elements of computer operation, such as sending instructions to hardware devices like disk drives and computer screens, and allocating system resources such as memory to different software applications being run. Given uniformly designed operating systems that run on many different computers, developers of software do not need to concern themselves with these problems, and are provided with a standard platform for new programs. (*American Heritage Science Dictionary,* 2002).

9. Application: A computer program with an interface, enabling people to use the computer as a tool to accomplish a specific task. Word processing, spreadsheet, and communications software are all examples of applications. (*American Heritage Science Dictionary,* 2002).

a file is modified later. Database applications generally have the capability to record user information, assuming the database administrator has enabled that logging. Detailed transaction logging is often not enabled in large databases in order to reduce storage requirements and increase performance. However, where logging has been enabled, the ability to establish provenance is greatly enhanced.

Logical Access Records

One fundamental difference between digital and physical evidence is the ability to create or modify the digital evidence from a distance, over a network. Establishing who had "logical" or virtual access to a particular piece of evidence at a particular time may be used to establish ownership. It may be more useful to refute ownership, by showing that a particular person could not have accessed the evidence at a particular time. As we have discussed, in many environments user access is virtually anonymous at the operating system or application level. For example, web servers often have a default operating system user account. Files created by the web server or by users interacting through it will reference this default account, as opposed to a user account tied to a person. However, the web server or network appliances may log access to the server or application. These records may include connection data and/or user account information. Similarly, if the operating system or application did not log user information (or, as stated previously, if it reflects prior users), but a particular user account was logged in to the local machine, that may also be helpful in establishing logical access.

Logical access records may include connection data (including IP address, browser version, or network name) or user account information. In contrast to system and application records, connection data may exist on multiple machines. If, for example, a user visits a website, the connection data may exist on the user's machine in the form of Internet history and cache files; it may exist on network devices such as proxy servers or firewalls in the form of network connection records, and it may exist on the web server as a record of the user's visit. Correlating the data from multiple sources may serve to strengthen the likelihood that a particular user was the "who" in a particular case.

Physical Access Records

As we have seen in the examples above, computers can do a good job of determining and recording what user account may have created or modified a piece of data. But, absent other information, those records cannot establish physical ownership. A user may claim that someone else used his account to modify data. Establishing physical access to the system at the time of modification can help to confirm or discredit this theory. Physical access can be established through eyewitness testimony, physical access records such as electronic door locks, or access logs. Biometric authentication can be considered as a combination of physical and logical access.

Often more than one of these methods or processes is used to establish identity. For example, operating system or application records may indicate that a certain user ID created a piece of evidence. The user may claim he was not present at the time and that another user compromised the account. Physical access logs or eyewitness testimony can establish that the person was present at the time. While it is still technically possible that another person remotely compromised the system and created the file, absent any supporting evidence, a jury would still be justified in weighing the evidence to discount this possibility.

For example, in *United States v. Simpson*,[10] prosecutors sought to show that the defendant had conversed with an undercover FBI agent in an Internet chat room devoted to child pornography. The government offered a printout of an Internet chat conversation between the agent and an individual identified as "Stavron," and sought to show that Stavron was the defendant. The district court admitted the printout in evidence at trial. On appeal following his conviction, Simpson argued that "because the government could not identify that the statements attributed to [him] were in his handwriting, his writing style, or his voice," the printout had not been authenticated and should have been excluded.[11]

The Tenth Circuit rejected this argument, noting the considerable circumstantial evidence that Stavron was the defendant.[12] For example, "Stavron" had told the undercover agent that his real name was "B. Simpson," gave a home address that matched Simpson's, and appeared to be accessing the Internet from an account registered to Simpson. Further, the police found records in Simpson's home that listed the name, address, and phone number that the undercover agent had sent to Stavron. Accordingly, the government had provided evidence sufficient to support a finding that the defendant was Stavron, and the printout was properly authenticated.[13]

Illustrative Cases Involving Questions of Identity

Certain cases have begun to define the landscape associated with the question of who created a piece of digital evidence. Keep in mind that in many of these cases, digital evidence is being proffered by the state in criminal proceedings where the defendant is challenging its admissibility. Often the defendant does not testify. Accordingly, most of the cases in this area address the bare issue of admissibility, and its "rationality" and "sufficient to support a finding" rules, rather than the more elaborate issue of the weight of the circumstantial evidence going to identity.

Whitaker v. United States[14] involved an appeal of a drug case where certain computer records were allowed into evidence. The defendant attempted to show that printouts of those computer records should not have been admitted by the district court. The defendant attempted to discredit testimony given by an agent regarding electronic records that had been retrieved from a computer. Further, the defendant took issue with the fact that a codefendant had assisted the agent in retrieving the computer records from

---

10. 152 F.3d 1241 (10th Cir. 1998).

11. *Id.* at 1249.

12. *See id.* at 1250.

13. *See also United States v. Tank,* 200 F.3d 627, 630-31 (9th Cir. 2000) (concluding that district court properly admitted chat room log printouts in circumstances similar to those in Simpson); *United States v. Siddiqui,* 235 F.3d 1318, 1322-23 (11th Cir. 2000) (holding that e-mail messages were properly authenticated where messages included defendant's e-mail address, defendant's nickname, and where defendant followed up messages with phone calls). But see *United States v. Jackson,* 208 F.3d 633, 638 (7th Cir. 2000) (concluding that web postings purporting to be statements made by white supremacist groups were properly excluded on authentication grounds absent evidence that the postings were actually posted by the groups); *St. Clair v. Johnny's Oyster & Shrimp, Inc.,* 76 F. Supp. 2d 773, 774-75 (S.D. Tex. 1999) (holding that evidence from a webpage could not be authenticated, because information from the Internet is "inherently untrustworthy")."

14. 127 F.3d 595 (7th Cir. 1997).

Case Study
Example of Circumstantial Evidence: Pattern Analysis

Analysis of the patterns that exist in reality takes many forms, and such patterns can be used as circumstantial evidence of identity. As one example, each person has a "lexical fingerprint," which linguistic analysis can detect. A lexical fingerprint is the language a person uses: certain phrases, vocabulary, and the syntax of communication. A person uses certain phrases, nicknames, initials, acronyms, code words, loose associations, inside jokes, and variants. For example, accounting fraud or accounting flexibility was referred to in one company's data set as "cookie jar" and "cj." "Cookie jar" is a nickname and "cj" are the initials and a variant on the cookie jar name.

This lexical analysis can also be used to detect a redefined use of language. An example is the use of the words "summer projects," which were initially used to refer to projects done in the slow summer period of a business. Over time, the phrase changed to mean any other long-term project that needed to be done, but where there was not enough product development time to do it in the ordinary course of business. So, the term "summer project" came to mean something completely different than its original meaning, but everyone in the company knew what it meant. To an outsider, it would mean something different than to someone inside the company. In other words, language can be private and contextual, and pattern analysis can be used to produce circumstantial evidence of the speakers of such language.

A "hierarchy" of communications refers to its varying levels—with peers using one lexical view, and communication with higher-ups using a different lexical view. More slang, swear words, and foreign language appear in the peer communications than in the higher-ups communications. All of these factors can point to who created the digital evidence, especially if identity and behavior is an issue. A specific example of how a lexical fingerprint can be used is where it is used to identify an author of books or other papers to uncover plagiarism.

In using pattern analysis, the baseline behavior must first be established in order to detect anomalies from that baseline behavior. What is normal behavior for one person or system might be different than another's normal behavior. Expected behavior can be predicted using this methodology. Unexpected behavior can be flagged for further analysis. Ownership or authorship of a writing or behavior can be associated with someone or ascribed to something in an entire data collection using these lexical analysis methods. These methods can be used on an individual, system, group, or company for identification purposes. For example, to establish group behavior, one can compare the expected behavior to the organizational (org) chart to detect unexpected behavior for the company and for individuals. Cliques and other associations can be detected through this type of pattern analysis, and all of these methods can show who created the digital evidence.

the computer. Challenging the requirement that the computer and associated electronic storage and retrieval devices "be in substantially the same condition as when the crime was committed,"[15] the defendant took the position that the codefendant could have altered the evidence "with a few rapid keystrokes."[16] The court, in deciding not to overturn the district court's admission of the evidence, stated that "[t]his is almost wild-eyed speculation and without some evidence to support such a scenario, we will not disturb the trial judge's ruling."[17] Thus, even though some amount of doubt might have been cast as to who created (and who may have altered) certain digital evidence, the court in *Whitaker* looked at the overall facts involved and the lack of evidence supporting the alternative version of reality in deciding to affirm the district court's admission of the evidence. As there was sufficient evidence to support the finding, the evidence was ruled properly admitted.

As a second case involved the Securities and Exchange Commission (SEC) raising the question of whether a particular person to whom an electronic signature[18] was attributed actually created and affixed that electronic signature to a particular document. The SEC found that Bob Guccione, the founder of *Penthouse* magazine, did not "establish and maintain adequate disclosure controls and procedures at Penthouse International, Inc."[19] as required by Section 302 of the Sarbanes-Oxley Act.

Of particular relevance to the notion of who created digital evidence, the SEC alleged that someone other than Mr. Guccione electronically signed a document that was submitted to the SEC but which bore Mr. Guccione's signature. Further, once he had been made aware of the forgery, Mr. Guccione did not notify the SEC. Based on this, the government took the position that Mr. Guccione violated his obligations to shareholders under Sarbanes-Oxley.

In its order (which was based on an Offer of Settlement by Mr. Guccione), the SEC recounted that Penthouse had filed a quarterly 10-Q report for the period ended March 31, 2003, with $1 million improperly characterized as revenue.[20] Included with that 10-Q "was a Sarbanes-Oxley certification bearing the electronic signature of Guccione, as Penthouse's Principal Executive Officer and Principal Financial Officer."[21] Contrary to that statement, however, Mr. Guccione had not reviewed the 10-Q, had not authorized its filing, and "had not authorized use of his electronic signature on the Sarbanes-Oxley certification."[22] Further, the SEC noted that upon finding out about the fraudulently submitted 10-Q (which occurred when Penthouse's auditor resigned), Mr. Guccione and Penthouse did not disclose the forgery in its subsequently submitted Form 8-K. Further,

---

15. *Id.* at 602.

16. *Id.*

17. *Id.*

18. Not to be confused with a digital signature, an electronic signature is a technology-neutral way of using digital technology to sign a message. It can be any sign, symbol, or process one wants it to be, such as clicking on a box that says, "I agree."

19. In the Matter of Robert C. Guccione, Admin. Proc. File No. 3-11800, Accounting and Auditing Enforcement Release No. 2174 (Jan. 24, 2005) (the "Guccione Order").

20. In actuality, the $1 million had been received as an up-front payment for a multiyear agreement related to a website, and so should have been amortized over the term of the agreement.

21. Guccione Order, para. 7.

22. *Id.*

despite evidence of the forgery, Mr. Guccione still vouched for Penthouse's disclosure controls and procedures, "even though he knew that the Company's disclosure controls and procedures were not adequate and had permitted the filing of the Form 10-Q and accompanying Sarbanes-Oxley certification without his review or approval."[23]

In this case, the knowledge that a particular person did *not* create a piece of digital evidence led to the institution by the SEC of a cease-and-desist order on a company that had not instituted adequate controls and procedures over its reporting mechanisms. This was based on electronic evidence, which showed that the electronic signature on the fraudulently filed Form 10-Q was not that of the purported signer.

SOURCES AND CHECKLISTS ABOUT *WHO* DATA

Table 6.1 illustrates numerous sources where information about a digital identity could possibly be found. Anecdotal evidence suggests that there are many more locations where such information could reside than is typically believed. For at least one organization, an initial list of twenty different data sources ballooned into over 200 different data sources after a brainstorming session seeking to establish a data classification policy.

TABLE 6.1
Potential Sources or Repositories of *Who* Data

Types of Data Stores	*Places to Search for Relevant Electronic Data*
Shared Servers or Network	All Network Nodes
Computers	Desktop(s) Laptop(s) Notebooks At Work and at Home
Handheld Devices and PDAs (Personal Digital Assistants)	TREOs BlackBerries Mobile Phones iPods or MP3 Players
Memory Devices	Thumb Drives Memory Stick Memory Cards (from digital cameras, phones, other devices)
Removable Media	DVDs CDs Floppy Drives Tapes

(continued on next page)

---

23. *Id.* at para. 11.

TABLE 6.1 *(continued from prevous page)*
Potential Sources or Repositories of *Who* Data

	Other Removable Media Cards
	Detached Hard Drives
	Zip Drives
	Security Camera Tapes
Archive or Backup Media	Backup Tapes
	Storage Locations:
	• file shares
	• e-mail devices
	• archival tapes
	• hosted e-mails
	• Attachments
	Archives
	Document Management Systems
Databases	Credit Card/Debit Card databases
	VOIP/Phone Logs
	IM Databases
	Business Application Databases (Quicken, Calendar, Address Book, etc.)
	Other Data Entry Systems
Online	Audit Logs
	Access Logs
	Webpages
	Blogs
	Printer Memory Caches
	Copier/Scanner Memory Caches
Deleted/Unused Space	Slack Space
	Deleted/Recovered Files
Other	Desk Drawers
	File Cabinets
	Closets
	Warehouses
	Obsolete Computer Equipment
	Third Parties
	Partners/Licensors
	Escrow Placeholders
	Be creative in your thinking here

Courtesy Cataphora, Inc.

PART III

The Problem of Hearsay and Reliability in Digital Evidence

HAL: I'm sorry you feel the way you do, Dave. If you'd like to check my service record, you'll see it's completely without error.

BOWMAN: I know all about your service record, Hal, but unfortunately it doesn't prove that you're right now.

HAL: Dave, I don't know how else to put this, but it just happens to be an unalterable fact that I am incapable of being wrong.

BOWMAN: Yes, well I understand your view on this now, Hal.

—Stanley Kubrick, 2001: A Space Odyssey (1968)

CHAPTER 7

The Doctrine of Hearsay as Applied to Digital Evidence

The rule against hearsay is a great edifice in the law. If an out-of-court statement was offered to prove the truth of the matter asserted, it was labeled hearsay and excluded from evidence. The rule, generally lax at the beginning of the eighteenth century, became more rigid in the late eighteenth century as lawyers participated in more and more trials, and the importance of testing statements by cross-examination came to be valued. Whereas the concept of authenticity applies to objects, the concept of hearsay applies to statements. The rule formerly only applied to people's statements.

But now, as described in Chapter 2, not only people but also information systems regularly make statements that are then inserted into records. A record in an e-mail program, "You replied on 12/14/2007 8:30 AM," is information inserted by the system, stating that the user sent a reply e-mail at a date and time in reply to someone else's message. Such information can only be understood to be a statement about facts.

Statements by information systems are cropping up frequently, and the future is certain to contain ever more. Why do not the same policies—forbidding introduction of out-of-court statements by people—apply to out-of-court statements by information systems? Why should the statement be admitted if the maker, the system, cannot be cross-examined? In short, what should we do now that information systems regularly make out-of-court statements? How should burdens of proof be allocated? Are there preliminary foundations necessary in order to meet admissibility standards? How much discretion should the judge have? Does everything go to weight? Is there a reason to inquire into the reliability of the system?

The problems are the same the world over, and it does not appear there are well-settled rules in any national jurisdiction. This is not intended to be an exhaustive list of each case that has held every way on the issues, but an introduction into a way of thinking that can be used, depending on what one wants to achieve as an advocate. In addition, Chapter 8 has suggestions about how the law might evolve in this area.

TYPES OF COMPUTER-GENERATED INFORMATION

First, courts and commentators have recognized a distinction between computer-generated and computer-stored evidence. If the system made the statement, it is "computer-generated." If a person input a statement into the system that then preserved a record of it, it is "computer-stored" evidence. Underlying the distinction is the idea that computer-stored evidence is a repetition of data originally entered by a human language writer, while computer-generated evidence is the product of electronic processes, or the statements an information system makes in its reading and writing games.[1]

Such a distinction is surely more sophisticated than the thinking of some courts that uncritically label any evidence derived from a computer as "computer-generated" without examining the nature of the information at issue. When courts apply a blanket label of "computer-generated" to all digital evidence, they necessarily obscure many important points of analysis.[2] This is because computer-stored information is often, if not almost always, hearsay. It is analogous to a person writing down on paper that he was at an intersection and saw that the light was green when the plaintiff's car drove through. The statement contained on the paper, because its maker cannot be cross-examined and is not in court, is hearsay.

The distinction between computer-generated and computer-stored is therefore a step in the right direction. And computer-generated information—the statements of information systems—exists in many different categories. As examples only, and to give a flavor for the wide range of how information systems do different things when they make statements, we will briefly discuss: (1) computer-recorded events; (2) data sets; (3) simulations; and (4) decision trees. There is additional helpful literature on the different types of computer-generated information.[3]

Information systems regularly record events and insert information about the event into a digital record. Take, for example, a transaction carried out at an automatic teller machine (ATM). When a cardholder inserts a card into an ATM, and authenticates himself with a PIN, the information system in the machine allows that person to

---

1. *See, e.g.,* Tatum v. Commonwealth, 17 Va. App. 585 (1993) (holding that caller ID information was not hearsay, because there was no human "out-of-court asserter" and that the caller ID display was based on computer-generated information and not simply the repetition of prior recorded human input or observation).

2. For example, in *State v. Robinson,* 272 Neb. 582, 724 N.W.2d 35 (Neb. 2006), an individual convicted of first-degree murder claimed that cell phone records showing the physical location of certain calls at certain times should be excluded as hearsay. Computer systems automatically recorded each time a phone call was made and what number were connected. At the same time, the information about who owned the cell phones at each end of any recorded call was manually entered and stored in the computer system. *Id.* at 611, 724 N.W.2d at 54. Thus, when the prosecution offered the cell phone records as evidence, those records were the product of both computer-generated information and computer-recorded statements by human beings (each discussed further below). The court did not make any such distinction in its analysis, but instead applied the business records exception to the hearsay rule and held that these records were admissible. *Id.* at 613–17, 724 N.W.2d at 56–60.

3. *See, e.g.,* Rudolph J. Peritz, *Computer Data and Reliability: A Call for Authentication of Business Records Under the Federal Rules of Evidence,* 80 Nw. L. Rev. 956 (1986), which discusses the gaps in the Federal Rules of Evidence for dealing with computer information, and the flaws with how the courts have dealt with them, especially under the hearsay rule. The article also criticizes the general blanket of trust with which the courts at the time of its writing appeared to approach data derived from computers; *see also* Jerome Roberts, *A Practitioner's Primer on Computer-Generated Evidence,* 41 U. Chi. L. Rev. 254 (1973) (discussing in depth the basic concept of computing, and detailing the various points along the path of information through the computer on which evidentiary issues could be encountered); and Leonard J. Nelson, *Garbage In, Garbage Out: The Need for New Approaches to Computer Evidence,* 9 Am. J. Trial Advoc. 411 (1985), which proposed two categories of computer evidence: computer-stored, which, according to the author was treated typically as business records; and simulation, both of which correspond closely to the similarly named categories discussed here. The author also criticizes the blind trust of computer evidence, and points out that a "computer's product is only as good as the input and software." *Id.* at 414. Moreover, the author discusses this type of evidence and its impact on the hearsay and best evidence rule, proposing that the "primary emphasis should be on allowing the opposing party the opportunity to investigate the *reliability* of the [computer] system well in advance of trial." *Id.* at 416 (emphasis added).

carry out a transaction. In addition, the information system will record the "date, time, card number, customer account number, transaction number and type and amount of transaction."[4] The cardholder does not request or necessarily desire this information be recorded, nor does he take any steps to make the recording take place. The information system does it as a result of the reading and writing programmed to occur in the circumstances. In this case, the system is making a record about digital events, sensing and recording what is happening inside itself.

At other times, information systems record real-world events. For example, a computer may have a sensor designed to trigger an alarm if an area reaches a certain temperature. The information system is witnessing some real-world event and making a record of it. Then, when the information is retrieved (to be used as evidence, for example), the digital information is attesting to the event: "It was 145 degrees in the control room at 3:35 AM."

Recording events is, in fact, an extremely common use of information systems. Information about telephone calls is recorded when they occur. And in this regard, information systems are *extremely* similar to witnesses. "Your car was going 127 mph" at impact. "You replied to the email at 8:30 AM." "You visited the website and downloaded sensitive files."

A dataset is the result of an information system performing some kind of analysis or calculation based on input provided either by humans or computer processes. This is an incredibly diverse type of computer-generated information. Examples range from a program performing arithmetic functions such as addition or subtraction on human-entered numbers; to more-complex calculations of statistics; to outputs of video games; to the data being generated by a national defense network; to running totals of credit card transactions. Often, an item of evidence will contain both dataset-type evidence and some other type, such as evidence about events.

Breathalyzer results are examples of such a combination. First, an officer uses a computerized instrument to gather a sample. Pursuant to its programming, a machine instrument records the existence of certain chemical properties. That information is then converted into an electric signal and sent to a computer processor. The system then records a real-world event by means of a sensing instrument.

But then a Breathalyzer program uses the event information sensed, recorded, and provided, and makes calculations to estimate the blood-alcohol content of the individual providing the sample. This is a dataset. Thus, elaborating one step further on the computer-generated/computer-stored dichotomy allows for more-careful analysis, because it reveals additional points of potential error.[5]

Computers are also used to create simulations. These are used to predict outcomes, demonstrate how past events may have occurred, or model the behavior of some element of an object in a certain environment. As described in one article, "[c]omputer

---

4. Stark v. State, 489 N.E.2d 43, 47 (Ind. 1986) (discussing the admission of ATM audit tapes as evidence, and admitting them under an exception to the hearsay rule).

5. See, for example, the information provided at the website of one law firm specializing in DUI defense at http://www.edgelawfirm.com/dui.dwi.facts/3-plus-3. The website gives examples of how law enforcement officers can trick the Breathalyzer into gathering an unrepresentative sample, and how the machine can be programmed to display information in a way that masks certain indicators of its reliability.

simulations have been used for such diverse tasks as estimating the effects of emissions from multiple sources on air quality in the surrounding areas, estimating reaction times in an auto accident case, evaluating the feasibility of an auto failsafe skid device, and constructing hypothetical markets in antitrust cases."[6]

A *decision tree* functions like an information flowchart, leading an inquirer through a path to a destination that depends on answers to questions along the way. The *WebMD Symptom Checker*[7] is a good example. The Symptom Checker asks a user various questions about medical symptoms, and based on the answers, asks follow-up questions until it can provide a more ultimate answer about a "diagnosis." Lawyers also use decision trees to predict the outcomes of lawsuits, and one could program a computer to perform such a decision tree analysis.

But this brings up the point that human judgments are incorporated into programming the games that will ultimately result in a computer-generated statement—in this case, in instructing the program where to go based on earlier states. Is there really a 50/50 chance you will win the motion for summary judgment, or more like a 70/30 chance? Does a computer decide this based on a program, or is this percentage programmed in, using human judgments? Accordingly, decisions of human programmers might severely affect what an information system generates as information, many steps later, when it inserts computer-generated information into a record.

Back to the *WebMD Symptom Checker*, it might state after numerous questions and answers that, "You have gout." But is that accurate just because a computer said it? How much depends on what a computer is doing and how much depends on subjective judgments of programmers? And how much depends on the skill of the operator? The same points can be made regarding the results of many computer operations.

Accordingly, given the potentially infinite variety of reading and writing games that can occur in an information system, it is no surprise that there are different broad categories of computer-generated information. We have discussed four here, and the list is far from exhaustive. But the different types of statements, "You have gout" versus "You replied on 12/14/2007 at 8:30 AM," show that different types of analyses about the reliability of the information might well be in order in different circumstances.

IS SUCH COMPUTER-GENERATED INFORMATION CONSIDERED HEARSAY BY THE COURTS?

Is "You replied on 12/14/2007 at 8:30 AM" considered hearsay by courts? Courts and commentators often take the position that such information is not hearsay. The leading case for this proposition is *State v. Armstead*.[8] There, the Louisiana Supreme Court distinguished between "computer-generated data" and "computer-stored human statements."[9] The court held that a computer printout of certain telephone traces was

---

6. Nelson, *supra* note 3 at 417.

7. http://symptoms.webmd.com/symptomchecker.

8. 432 So. 2d 837 (La. 1983).

9. *See id.* at 840 n.3. "Computer-stored data" or "computer-stored information," as the terms suggest, is information input into the computer by a person. The computer functions similar to a storage device.

"computer-generated data," and thus not hearsay because the computer had recorded the source of the incoming calls independent of a human being's activities.[10] The court determined the printout was therefore not a "statement" within the meaning of the hearsay rule, because the assertions were not made by a person. The *Armstead* court's reasoning is endorsed by many of the courts that perform a full hearsay analysis of whether computer-generated information falls within the hearsay rule.[11]

However, in some cases, courts simply assume that computer-generated information is hearsay, without performing an analysis, seemingly avoiding the preliminary issue. These courts analyze objections to admissibility by searching for a hearsay exception, which they nearly always find.[12] And courts that hold that computer-generated information is hearsay often complicate matters by using the term "computer-generated information" loosely, lumping all evidence that comes from a computer together, and failing to focus on whether what is really at issue is computer-*stored* information—often usually hearsay under anyone's definition. For example, in *United States v. Briscoe*,[13] the court considered computerized "telephone records [that] listed the telephone numbers, the names of the subscribers placing calls to, as well as the subscribers receiving calls from, the three telephone numbers that were the subjects of [a] DEA wiretap investigation, the date, time and length of the call" to be hearsay, but did not parse out which information,

---

10. *See id.* at 840.

11. *See* United States v. Hamilton, 413 F.3d 1138, 1142–43 (10th Cir. 2005) (computer-generated "header" created when images were uploaded to the Internet not hearsay because no human involved); United States v. Khorozian, 333 F.3d 498, 506 (3d Cir. 2003) (fax machine "header" was not hearsay because a statement is something uttered by "a person," so nothing "said" by a machine . . . is hearsay); Hawkins v. Cavalli, No. C 03-3668 PJH, 2006 U.S. Dist. LEXIS 73143, 2006 WL 2724145, at *11–*13 (N.D. Cal. Sept. 22, 2006) (records of computer file access dates ruled not hearsay because a human was not responsible for setting and coordinating the computer's recording of access dates. Rather, the access dates were completely computer-generated with no human input); United States v. Duncan, 30 M.J. 1284, 1287–90 (N.M. Ct. Crim. App. 1990) (ATM records likely not hearsay under *Armstead* precedent); People v. Hawkins, 121 Cal. Rptr. 2d 627, 640–43 98 Cal. App. 4th 1428; 2002 Cal. App. LEXIS 4203; 2002 Cal. Daily Op. Service 4940; 2002 Daily Journal DAR 6235 (Ct. App. 2002) (records of computer file access dates not hearsay because no human declarant); People v. Holowko, 486 N.E.2d 877 (Ill. 1985) (telephone records not hearsay following *Armstead* case); State v. Colwell, No. 05-0280, 2006 WL 468732, at *2–*3 (Iowa Ct. App. Mar. 1, 2006) (unpublished table decision) (telephone trace records); State v. Armstead, 432 So.2d 837, 840 (La. 1983); State v. Dunn, 7 S.W.3d 427, 431–32 (Mo. Ct. App. 1999) (citing State v. Hall, 976 S.W.2d 121, 147 (Tenn. 1998)) (telephone trace records not hearsay); State v. Modest, 944 P.2d 417 (Wash Ct. App. 1997) (telephone trace report); Ly v. State, 908 S.W.2d 598 (Tex. App. 1995) (printout from electronic device that monitored appellant's location held not hearsay); Burlson v. State, 802 S.W.2d 429, 437–38 (Tex. App. 1991) (computer display showing files were missing); Gray v. Fairview Gen. Hosp., No. 82318, 2004 WL 527936, at *2–*3 (Ohio Ct. App. Mar. 18, 2004) (unreported disposition) (computer-aided device analysis of mammogram not hearsay); Luginbyhl v. Commonwealth, 618 S.E.2d 347 (Va. Ct. App. 2005) (Breathalyzer).

12. *See* United States v. Salgado, 250 F.3d 438, 451–53 (6th Cir. 2001) (holding that phone records qualified under business records exception); United States v. Walt, Nos. 95-50328, 95-50329, 1997 WL 362205, at *3–*4 (9th Cir. July 1, 1997) (unpublished table decision) (same); United States v. Blackburn, 992 F.2d 666, 670–73 (7th Cir. 1993) (holding that computer analysis of eyeglass lens prescription qualified under residual exception); State v. Estill, 764 P.2d 455 (Kan Ct. App. 1988) (holding that phone trace records qualified under business records exception); Commonwealth v. McEnany, 732 A.2d 1263, 1272–73 (Pa. 1999) (holding that telephone call records qualified under business records exception); Jack Parker Indus. v. FDIC, 769 S.W.2d 700, 703 (Tex. App. 1989) (holding that computer-generated "interest accrual statement" qualified under business records exception); State v. Ben-Neth, 663 P.2d 156, 158–60 (Wash. Ct. App. 1983) ("Computer-generated evidence is hearsay. . . .").

13. 896 F.2d 1476, 1493–95 (7th Cir. 1990).

if any, was generated by a computer. The court simply assumed that the collective evidence was hearsay and analyzed the problem under the business records exception.[14]

This casual characterization of evidence coming from information systems renders the jurisprudence in the area somewhat murky. But, in many of the cases where courts actually analyze the hearsay issue, computer-generated evidence is rendered nonhearsay following the *Armistead* rationale, reasoning that if you are not a human being, you cannot make a statement, and therefore hearsay cannot be involved, as there is no statement involved.

THE "BUSINESS RECORDS" EXCEPTION AS APPLIED TO INFORMATION SYSTEMS

Many of the decisions that admit computer-generated information do so on the rationale that such statements qualify under the "business records exception" to the hearsay rule, now codified under Rule 803(6).

The business records exception originated early in the nineteenth century. What animated the rule was reliability and indeed, written into the exception is a specific caution about "trustworthiness." Through the years, the exception has become diluted in its application.

Now, *regularity* of preparation has become the key to admitting business records, including records containing computer-generated information. And if regularity is the test, almost any computer-generated information qualifies, without any showing of reliability. Accordingly, both the hearsay rule—and the main exception used to test admissibility of statements of information systems under it—become trivial, without any meaningful competency determination by a court. The ability to exclude out-of-court statements, the hearsay rule, appears to have largely evaporated with regard to computer-generated information. Rather, in almost every case, all computer evidence is admitted and things go to weight of the evidence. That may be our final, preferred policy, after rule makers and thinkers address this issue during the coming years, but in the meantime practitioners should acknowledge the reality of where the law has drifted.

History of the Exception

The business records exception is one of the oldest exceptions to the hearsay rule. It originated as an outgrowth of the English common law "shop book" rule. In England, a rule emerged whereby courts received into evidence the shop books of businesspeople as evidence of goods sold or services rendered.[15] The purpose was to circumvent the prohibition against a party appearing as its own witness. By 1832, the shop-book rule was firmly grounded in English common law, and its scope included all entries made in the ordinary course of business.[16]

---

14. *See also Salgado,* 250 F.3d at 451–53 (subscriber information and location of installed telephone included in printouts) and *Ben-Neth,* 663 P.2d at 158–60.

15. The shop-book rule generally permitted the introduction of shop books only to prove amounts due; further, the books had to be properly authenticated, and the makers of the records had to be examined. *See* 5 J. WIGMORE, EVIDENCE § 1520, at 365 (3d ed.)

16. MCCORMICK ON EVIDENCE § 285 (5th ed. 1999).

For many years, U.S. courts recognized the shop-book rule, which then gradually merged into a "business records exception." The common law version of the business records exception had four elements: (1) the record was an original entry made in the routine course of business; (2) the entries were made upon the personal knowledge of the recorder or someone reporting to him; (3) the entries were made at or near the time of the transaction; and (4) the recorder and his informant were unavailable.[17] Under the common law rule, however, the writer of the record did have to appear at trial "if available."[18]

Although the common law exception was not unduly burdensome when applied in the context of simple, journal-and-ledger business organizations, "some of the common law requirements were incompatible with modern conditions."[19] In particular, the requirement to produce *all available* participants in the process of recording information "was a needless and disruptive burden in view of the unlikelihood that any of those involved would remember a particular transaction or its details."[20] Judge Learned Hand noted the unreasonableness of the common law rule: "Unless [records] can be used in court without the task of calling those who at all stages had a part in the transaction recorded, nobody need ever pay a debt, if only his creditor does a large enough business."[21]

When courts seemed unable to resolve the difficulties with the common law rule, relief was sought through legislation. Codifications of the common law exception came first as the Commonwealth Fund Act and the Uniform Business Records as Evidence Act,[22] then as the Business Records Act,[23] and finally in Rule 803(6) of the Federal Rules of Evidence, adopted in 1975. The statutory versions of the exception highlighted one primary feature: They made the exception available "without regard to unavailability of [the] declarant."[24] When summarizing the pragmatic underpinnings of this statutory change, one commentator stated:

> [T]he size and complexity of economic and political institutions has attenuated the requirement that each and every employee representing a link in the chain from transaction to offered evidence appear and testify unless unavailable. Even if all the employees are available, it makes sense to avoid parading them to the witness stand in order to minimize the expense and disruption to the institution as well as the lengthy process of so qualifying every business record.[25]

The business records exception was justified on grounds of trustworthiness, practicality, and necessity. One commentator explained its rationale:

> The theory underlying the business records exception is similar to the theory underlying other exceptions—unusual reliability, which is inferred from the belief that regularly

---

17. McCormick on Evidence §§ 244 (3d ed. 1984).

18. McCormick on Evidence § 286 (5th ed. 1999) ("The impetus for receiving these hearsay statements at common law arose when the person or persons who made the entry, and upon whose knowledge it was based, were unavailable because of death, disappearance, or other reason.").

19. *Id.* § 260.

20. *Id.*

21. Mass. Bonding & Ins. Co. v. Norwich Pharmaceutical Co., 18 F.2d 934, 937 (2d Cir. 1927).

22. McCormick on Evidence § 286 (5th ed. 1999).

23. 28 U.S.C. § 1732(a) (1970).

24. McCormick on Evidence § 286 (5th ed. 1999).

25. Rudolph J. Peritz, *Computer Data and Reliability: A Call for Authentication of Business Records Under the Federal Rules of Evidence,* 80 Nw. U. L. Rev. 956, 964 (1986).

kept records have a high degree of accuracy. Their very regularity and continuity are presumed to train the recordkeeper in habits of precision.

Moreover, financial records periodically are balanced and audited. Finally, the entire business of the nation and many other activities function in reliance upon records of this kind. In short, not only do courts see the practice and environment as encouraging the making of accurate records, but they also rely upon business reliance. The courts' reliance on business reliance has supported liberalized admissibility and has decreased formal demands for assurances of trustworthiness.[26]

Taking into consideration these underlying theories of reliability, Congress enacted Rule 803(6) in July 1975. As applied by courts today, a business record must satisfy four requirements to be admissible under Rule 803(6):

1. It must have been made in the course of a regularly conducted business activity;
2. it must have been kept in the regular course of that business;
3. the regular practice of that business must have been to have made the record; and
4. the record must have been made by a person with knowledge of the transaction, or from information transmitted by a person with knowledge.[27]

And importantly, business records meeting these criteria are admissible "*unless the source of information or the method or circumstances of preparation indicate lack of trustworthiness.*"[28] The information must be presented through "the testimony of the custodian or other qualified witness."[29]

But over the past decades, "courts have relaxed the substitute conditions of circumstantial trustworthiness for business records in deference to the exigencies of modern business practices and the desire for an efficient trial process."[30] The relaxation of standards is attributed to the vast quantities of evidence produced by businesses in the course of complex litigation and courts' reluctance to exclude relevant information.[31]

Some judges express concern that courts so readily "insert a presumption of trustworthiness into the business records rule."[32] They reiterate the concerns Justice Douglas espoused in *Palmer v. Hoffman*,[33] the famous case that addressed the issue of whether a

---

26. *Id.* at 963; *See also* Paula Noyes Singer, *Proposed Changes to the Federal Rules of Evidence as Applied to Computer-Generated Evidence,* 7 RUT. J. COMPUTERS, TECH. & L. 157, 177 (1979–80) ("The element of unusual reliability of business records has been said variously to be supplied by systematic checking, by regularity and continuity which produce habits of precision, by actual experience of business in relying upon them, or by a duty to make an accurate record as part of a continuing job or occupation.").

27. United States v. Salgado, 250 F.3d 438, 451 (6th Cir. 2001) (citing United States v. Weinstock, 153 F.3d 272, 276 (6th Cir.1998)).

28. Fed. R. Evid. 803(6).

29. *Id.*

30. Peritz, *supra* note 25, at 963–64.

31. Jack Call, *Legal Notes, available at* https://www.ncsconline.org/WC/Publications/KIS_PreCriJSJV22No1 .pdf ("The reluctance to exclude even unreliable evidence stems from the fact that it deprives the fact finder of relevant information in a case. Consequently, the general preference adhered to in the law is to permit a jury to hear evidence of questionable reliability and leave to the jurors' good judgment the question of whether the evidence should be believed.").

32. Lacy v. CSX Transp., Inc., 205 W. Va. 630, 654 (1999).

33. 318 U.S. 109; 63 S. Ct. 477; 87 L. Ed. 645; 1943 U.S. LEXIS 988 (1943).

statement given by a train engineer following a railroad accident could be introduced as a business record. Douglas predicted that "[r]egularity of preparation would become the test rather than the character of the records and their earmarks of reliability."[34] He went on to conclude that if regularity of preparation became the test under the business records exception:

> [t]he result would be that the [exception] would cover *any system of recording events or occurrences* provided it was "regular" and though it had little or nothing to do with the management or operation of the business as such. . . . The probability of trustworthiness of records because they were routine reflections of the day to day operations of a business would be forgotten as the basis of the rule.[35]

One dissent in a case recently lamented that "the day rued by Justice Douglas—when regularity of document preparation would supersede concerns for trustworthiness—has already arrived."[36]

THE ERODING FOUNDATIONAL REQUIREMENTS OF RULE 803(6)

Under the Federal Rules of Evidence, documents must clear at least two hurdles to be admitted into evidence. First, the document must be authenticated, as discussed in Part II. Next, documents containing out-of-court statements require a showing that the statement either is defined as not hearsay, or meets one of the hearsay exceptions if it *is* hearsay.

There is no stand-alone requirement that any statement or assertion admitted into court be the result of a reliable process. Courts, like the one in *Armstead* that exclude computer-generated statements from the ambit of the hearsay rule have likened such statements to a scientific test (e.g., "We therefore view the computer-generated data in this case as demonstrative evidence of a scientific test or experiment.") and therefore do a sort of abbreviated reliability analysis, but those early cases conceived of what they were viewing as a "machine." Indeed, in the early cases that analyzed computer information, such as during the *Armstead* period of the early 1980s, a high percentage of cases involved mainframe and dedicated, batch-processing computer operations—and, of course, no cases at all involving the networked information systems we have today. Concluding that the statement "You replied on 12/14/2007 8:30 AM" is "demonstrative evidence of a scientific test or experiment" now seems awkward and unworkable, and most cases did not take up the analogy.

Instead of relying on the *Armstead* rationale that computer-generated information is demonstrative evidence of a scientific test, more than any other argument, practitioners now commonly use the business records exception of Rule 803(6) to admit computer-generated hearsay into evidence.

As will be discussed in Chapter 8, when this approach of using Rule 803 (6) first appeared, a few courts made a stab at requiring computer-generated statements to meet

---

34. 318 U.S. at 114.

35. *Id.* at 113–14 (emphasis supplied); *see also* Bowman v. Kaufman, 387 F.2d 582, 587 (2d Cir. 1967) (observing that liberal construction of federal business records act "does not mean that any particular business record may be admitted without carefully scrutiny of its reliability for the purpose for which it is offered as evidence").

36. *Lacy,* 205 W. Va. at 655.

additional, beefed-up foundational requirements of reliability. For example, in *United States v. Scholle*,[37] the Eighth Circuit emphasized that not only must the requirements of the Hearsay Rule be satisfied, "but in addition the original source of the computer program must be delineated, and the procedures for input control including tests used to assure accuracy and reliability must be present." And the Sixth Circuit, in *United States v. Russo*,[38] required expert testimony regarding: (1) the mechanics of data input control designed to ensure accuracy; (2) the nature of the information constituting the input; and (3) the business's reliance on the printout in the ordinary course of activities.[39]

But over the past twenty-five years, courts have overwhelmingly declined to follow these policy feelers, instead showing little hesitancy in accepting computerized records into evidence irrespective of reliability. Courts have taken the liberal standards for admitting normal, manually prepared business records and applied them to computer-generated data. One commentator noted, "Despite the fact that computerized records are often easier to tamper with than traditional records, the standards for admitting computer-generated records are ordinarily no more stringent than those for admitting other business records."[40]

Today, the majority of courts do not require any extra foundational testimony for computer-generated records, and indeed, computerized records are often for some reason considered more reliable than the "original entry books" the exception was founded upon.[41] Several courts have held that computer-generated data has "a prima facie aura of reliability"[42] because the data is "not even touched by the hand of man."[43]

Bypassing the Authentication and Trustworthiness Requirements

Today, most courts bypass authentication and reliability hurdles altogether, requiring the proponent of computer-generated evidence only to meet the requirements of the business records exception.[44] One commentator offered the following explanation for the fact that many courts are now bypassing an Article IX authentication requirement for computer records:

---

37. 553 F.2d 1109 (8th Cir. 1977).

38. 380 F.2d 1228 (6th Cir. 1973).

39. Rudolph J. Peritz, *Computer Data and Reliability: A Call for Authentication of Business Records Under the Federal Rules of Evidence,* 80 Nw. U. L. Rev. 956, 964 (1986), n.31, at 967 (citing *Russo,* 380 F.2d at 1240–41).

40. Stephen A. Saltzburg, *et al.,* Federal Rules of Evidence Manual § 803.02[7][f] (9th ed. 2006).

41. *See* McCormick § 294.

42. Canadyne-Georgia Corp. v. Bank of Am., N.A., 174 F. Supp. 2d 1337, 1343 (M.D. Ga. 2001) (quoting Olympic Ins. Co. v. H.D. Harrison, Inc., 418 F.2d 669, 670 (5th Cir. 1969).

43. United States v. Vela, 673 F.2d 86, 90 (5th Cir. 1982).

44. Orin S. Kerr, U.S. Dept. of Justice, U.S.A. Bull. Vol. 49, No. 2, *Computer Records and the Federal Rules of Evidence* (2001), *available at* http://www.usdoj.gov/criminal/cybercrime/usamarch2001_4.htm ("Prosecutors may note the conceptual overlap between establishing the authenticity of a computer-generated record and establishing the trustworthiness of a computer record for the business record exception to the hearsay rule. In fact, federal courts that evaluate the authenticity of computer-generated records often assume that the records contain hearsay, and then apply the business records exception."). *See, e.g.,* United States v. Linn, 880 F.2d 209, 216 (9th Cir. 1989) (applying business records exception to telephone records generated "automatically" by a computer); United States v. Vela, 673 F.2d 86, 89–90 (5th Cir. 1982) (same). . . . As a practical matter, however, prosecutors who lay a foundation to establish a computer-generated record as a business record will also lay the foundation to establish the record's authenticity.

[T]he business records exception to the hearsay rule effectively incorporates an authentication requirement. In particular, if all other requirements for the exception are met, business records are admissible, "unless the source of information or the method or circumstances of preparation indicate lack of trustworthiness." This criterion is analogous to the Rule 901(a) requirement that there must be "evidence sufficient to support a finding that the matter in question is what its proponent claims." Thus, evidence that is excluded on authenticity grounds should also be excluded as hearsay.

With this in mind, some courts bypass an explicit authenticity analysis and instead look to the requirements of the hearsay exception to determine whether the proponent has established a proper foundation. Courts do so not because of the more stringent requirements of the exception, but rather because they recognize computers as inherently reliable.[45]

In addition to bypassing authentication, courts also now overlook the caveat in Rule 803(6) that allows admission "unless the source of the information or the method or circumstances of preparation indicate lack of trustworthiness."[46] Courts overwhelmingly find that problems concerning the accuracy of computer-generated evidence go to the weight of the evidence, not admissibility.[47] For example, in *United States v. Catabran*,[48] the Ninth Circuit held that a computer printout of a business ledger was admissible, despite the appellant's objections that errors in the operation of the computer program made the evidence unreliable.[49] The court dismissed the argument, reasoning that the possibility of such errors went to the weight, not the admissibility, of the evidence.[50]

When courts exclude both the trustworthiness caveat from their 803(6) foundational inquiry, and an explicit preliminary authenticity analysis as a prerequisite for admission, there is a high probability (if not certainty) that any out-of-court statement made by an information system will be admitted. This is significant, because jurors give

---

Evidence that a computer program is sufficiently trustworthy so that its results qualify as business records according to Fed. R. Evid. 803(6) also establishes the authenticity of the record. *Compare* United States v. Saputski, 496 F.2d 140, 142 (9th Cir. 1974)."); Peritz, *supra* note 39, at 984 ("[C]omprehensive authentication of computer system's printouts of business records would be redundant because it would force the proponent to prove trustworthiness twice.").

45. Leah Voigt Romano, Note, *Electronic Evidence and the Federal Rules,* 38 Loy. L.A. L. Rev. 1745, 1770 (2005).

46. Fed. R. Evid. 803(6); *see* Peritz, *supra* note 25, at 969.

47. *See* James E. Carbine & Lynn McLain, *Proposed Model Rules Governing the Admissibility of Computer-Generated Evidence,* 15 Santa Clara Computer & High Tech. L.J. 1, 15 (1999); Romano, *supra* note 45, at 1751; Peritz, *supra* note 25, at 972; United States v. Catabran, 836 F.2d 453 (9th Cir. 1988) (holding that errors in the inventory records attributable to incorrect data entry or the operation of the computer program went to weight, not admissibility); United Sates v. Vela, 673 F.2d 86, 90 (5th Cir. 1982); United States v. Verlin, 466 F. Supp. 155 (N.D. Tex. 1979) (dismissing the defendant's argument that the computer was functioning inaccurately and stating that reliability questions go to the weight of the computerized statements as evidence, not to their admissibility).

48. 836 F.2d 453, 458 (9th Cir. 1988).

49. United States v. Catabran, 836 F.2d 453, 458 (9th Cir. 1988) ("[Appellant] argues that the computer program created inaccurate inventory figures because of the markup it applied. Miss Keys testified that the computer calculated a certain markup automatically, but that she could, and did, override that function for inventory sold at less than the suggested price. Although there was some contradiction concerning this issue, we conclude that the district court did not abuse its discretion . . . .").

50. *Id.*

computer-generated evidence a high level of credibility,[51] much as scientific evidence is interpreted by jurors to have an "aura of credibility."[52] This is problematic, as under the existing scheme, opponents challenging the accuracy and reliability of computer-generated statements cannot keep the statements out of evidence, even if there is substantial proof indicating a "lack of trustworthiness."

United States v. Casey[53] illustrates the difficulties a party faces in challenging the admissibility of computer-generated evidence. In *Casey*, the appellant argued that the trial court judge abused his discretion when admitting into evidence computer records of phone bills, because the "testimony of a computer expert and the evidence offered at trial clearly established that the records were untrustworthy."[54] The appellant's expert testified that the system was "not reliable," and pointed out many of the system's vulnerabilities.[55] Other witnesses testified that the phone bills "were often wrong and the system occasionally 'crashed.'"[56] The custodian of the records acknowledged there were "some problems" with the system, adding however that the system was "generally reliable" and that the management company "relied upon it for reservation and billing."[57] The appellate court upheld the admission of the evidence, stating: "[W]e see the evidence as only creating some questions as to the reliability of the system, which goes to weight rather than admissibility."[58]

The *Casey* ruling highlights the current framework. First, it shows that despite testimony from experts and other witnesses that a computer system does not function properly in all instances, statements by a record's custodian that a system is "generally reliable" because it is "used in the regular course of business activity," are sufficient to get a record admitted. Second, the *Casey* ruling shows how courts ignore the trustworthiness caveat of Rule 803(6). The *Casey* court admitted in its opinion that the evidence created "some questions as to the reliability of the system," implying the source of the information indicated a "lack of trustworthiness." But instead of making this an issue of a pre-

---

51. United States v. Trenkler, 61 F.3d 45, 57 (1st Cir. 1995) (Torruella, J., dissenting) ("Not only is [computerized evidence] rank hearsay evidence, it is hearsay evidence wrapped in a shroud of "scientific" authenticity. This is not a paid government expert testifying that, *in his opinion,* the two devices were built by the same person; this is a *computer* declaring that the two devices were built by the same person. Computers deal in facts, not opinions. Computers are not paid by one side to testify. Computers do not have prejudices. And computers are not subject to cross-examination. Moreover, the chart of the EXIS queries performed by Scheid, and the printouts of the results of those queries, were introduced into evidence and presented as exhibits to the jury. Consequently, the jury had this misleading, physical evidence with them in the jury room during deliberations. Does it not stand to reason that the lay juror will accord greater weight to a computer's written findings than to the testimony of a government expert witness? The common sense answer is, of course.").

52. *Id.* at 67, n.41 ("Scientific evidence impresses lay jurors. They tend to assume it is more accurate and objective than lay testimony. A juror who thinks of scientific evidence visualizes instruments capable of amazingly precise measurement, of findings arrived at by dispassionate scientific tests. In short, in the mind of the typical lay juror, a scientific witness has a special aura of credibility.") (citing EDWARD IMWINKELRIED, EVIDENCE LAW AND TACTICS FOR THE PROPONENTS OF SCIENTIFIC EVIDENCE, *in* SCIENTIFIC AND EXPERT EVIDENCE 33, 37 (E. Imwinkelried ed. 1981); *see also* State v. Damon, 119 P.3d 1194 (Mont. 2005) (finding that jurors are inclined to give more weight to evidence that is presented under the imprimatur of science than to nonscientific evidence).

53. 45 M.J. 623, 625 (N.M. Ct. Crim. App. 1996).

54. United States v. Casey, 45 M.J. 623, 625 (N.M. Ct. Crim. App. 1996).

55. *Id.* at 626.

56. *Id.*

57. *Id.*

58. *Id.* at 627.

liminary determination for admissibility under Rule 104(a), the court diverted the issue to the jury as a matter of weight. It appears the rules were not followed.

Casey is indicative of how courts almost always concern themselves with only two of the foundational requirements of the hearsay exception—whether the records are kept in the course of a regularly conducted business activity, and whether the custodian of the records demonstrates sufficient familiarity with the record-keeping system.[59] By bypassing the authentication requirement, and by ignoring the trustworthiness caveat of the foundational requirement, courts have essentially removed two foundational prerequisites required by the rules.

The two remaining foundations are not checks on accuracy. To prove the first foundation, the proponent must establish that the record was "kept in the course of a regularly conducted business activity."[60] As discussed above, courts have significantly expanded what constitutes a "regular business activity" to include almost any sort of regularly prepared record or recorded event, even if it does not directly relate to the daily operations of the business.[61] Thus, courts rarely exclude computer-generated evidence because it fails the "regularly conducted activity" foundation.[62]

The second foundation—whether a custodian of the record demonstrates sufficient familiarity with the record-keeping system—also usually poses few problems for proponents of computer-generated evidence. The rule "does not require that the custodian personally gather, input, and compile the information memorialized in a business record."[63] In fact, the custodian of the records does not have to be in control of or have

---

59. Romano, *supra* note 45, at 1770.

60. United States v. Dreer, 740 F.2d 18, 20 (11th Cir. 1984).

61. United States v. Linn, 880 F.2d 209, 216 (9th Cir.1989) (holding that a computer printout showing a call placed from a hotel room was admissible as a business record where the record was generated automatically and was retained in the ordinary course of business); State v. Robinson, 724 N.W.2d 35 (Neb. 2006) (finding that computer-generated records from telephone companies were admissible under the business records exception to the hearsay rule even though the records were created for trial and were not of the type normally sent to customers; the records and the information contained therein were made in the regular course of business, and preparing the printouts for litigation purposes did not deprive the printouts of their character as business records); United States v. Briscoe, 896 F.2d 1476, 1494–95 (7th Cir. 1990) (holding that telephone subscriber data entered into the computer contemporaneous with the placing of each telephone call and maintained in the regular course of business for billing purposes was admissible); United States v. Miller, 771 F.2d 1219, 1237 (9th Cir.1985) (upholding the admission of computer-generated toll and billing records made contemporaneously by the computer itself); State Treasurer, Dept. of Educ. v. Johnson, No. 210280, 1999 WL 33433525 (Mich. App. Oct. 29, 1999) ("To the extent that defendant contends that certain exhibits did not constitute business records because they were generated three days before trial, we note that the trend among courts has been to treat computer records like other business records and not to require the proponent of the evidence initially to show trustworthiness beyond meeting the general requirements of the rule. The fact that the organization relies upon the record in the regular course of its business may itself provide sufficient indication of reliability, absent realistic challenge, to warrant admission. [2 MCCORMICK ON EVIDENCE (4th ed.), § 294, pp 283–85 (1992).] Defendant has made no showing that the information contained in the computer-generate exhibits is unreliable.").

62. *See, e.g.,* Commonwealth. v. McEnany, 732 A.2d 1263, 1273 (Pa. Super. 1999) (finding that Cellular One's computer that systematically and contemporaneously creates a record of every telephone call made on its system, regardless of whether the phone call is ultimately answered, were made in the regular course of Cellular One's business at or near the time the telephone calls were made, and thus were admissible); *but see* Ozark Appraisal Servs., Inc. v. Neale, 67 S.W.3d 759, 761–65 (Mo. Ct. App. 2002) (finding that the hearsay objection should have been upheld because the defendant conceded that the computerized summary of billing records was produced specifically for litigation, not in the regular course of litigation).

63. United States v. Weinstock, 153 F.3d 272, 276 (6th Cir. 1998).

individual knowledge of the particular corporate records, but need only be familiar with the company's record-keeping practices.[64] Likewise, "[t]o be an 'other qualified witness' under the rule, it is not necessary that the person laying the foundation for the introduction of the business record have personal knowledge of its preparation."[65] The foundational witness is not required to have any specific knowledge of the accuracy or integrity of the computer system; rather, the witness must merely establish that the business relied on the computer-generated records in question.[66]

For example, in *United States v. Salgado*,[67] the Sixth Circuit found no error in the admission of a printout of computer-generated telephone toll records. The court stated that the foundation was sufficiently provided by a witness who testified that the telephone company relied on the computer-generated records to ensure the accuracy of its billing.[68] The court further reasoned that there was no need to present evidence of any programming features in place to guarantee the accuracy of the records, nor did the witness have to be a computer programmer.[69] The witness only had to demonstrate familiarity with the record-keeping system.[70]

---

64. *Id.* (citing *In re Custodian of Records of Variety Distrib., Inc.*, 927 F.2d 244, 248 (6th Cir. 1991)).

65. Dyno Construction Co. v. McWane, Inc., 198 F.3d 567, 575–76 (6th Cir. 1999).

66. *See* United States v. Vela, 673 F.2d 86 (5th Cir. 1982) (where telephone company records were properly admitted in a drug case, even without testimony that the computers were in proper working order); United States v. Miller, 771 F.2d 1219 (9th Cir. 1985) (holding that a custodian could lay the foundation for computerized records even though he had no knowledge of the maintenance and technical operation of the computer); United States v. Linn, 880 F.2d 209 (9th Cir. 1989) (finding that a hotel's director of communications could lay foundation for a computer record of telephone calls, even though he was not a computer programmer); Brandon v. State, 396 N.E.2d 365, 371 (Ind. 1979) (finding sufficient foundational testimony when a witness testified that the computer equipment used was "standard" and that it "had been used by the company for several years"); State v. Schuette, 44 P.3d 459, 463 (Kan. 2002) ("The foundation requirement of reliability is satisfied through witness testimony that the caller ID device is or has in the past been operating properly."); Stanley A. Kurzban, *Authentication of Computer-Generated Evidence in the United States Federal Courts*, 35 IDEA 437, 441 (1995) ("Someone who is a "qualified witness" may be anyone from someone present when a computer automatically records an event to a senior programmer/analyst who uses a business's application program.").

67. 250 F.3d 438 (6th Cir. 2001)

68. *See Salgado, supra* note 27 ("The government is not required to present expert testimony as to the mechanical accuracy of the computer where it presented evidence that the computer was sufficiently accurate that the company relied upon it in conducting its business.") (citing United States v. De Georgia, 420 F.2d 889, 893 n.11 (9th Cir. 1969); United States v. Weinstock, 153 F.3d 272, 276 (6th Cir. 1998) (witness not required to know personally how company performed safety checks); United States v. Moore, 923 F.2d 910, 915 (1st Cir.1991) (not required that computers be tested for programming errors before computer records can be admitted under Rule 803(6)); United States v. Briscoe, 896 F.2d 1476, 1494–95 (7th Cir. 1990) (showing that computer was regularly tested for internal programming errors not a prerequisite to the admission of computer records).

69. *Id.* ("The record indicates that [the witness] testified that South Central Bell relied on these computer-generated records to ensure the accuracy of its billing. He was not required to testify concerning any programming features which were in place to guarantee accuracy.").

70. *Id.* ("[The witness] testified that he was not the individual who programmed the computer. However, it is not necessary that the computer programmer testify in order to authenticate computer-generated records."); *see also* United States v. Hayes, 861 F.2d 1225, 1228 (10th Cir. 1988) (proper foundation laid for IRS computer records under Fed. R. Evid. 803(6), where IRS employees testified that "tax records were kept in the ordinary course of business and that it was the regular practice of the IRS to keep such records").

CONCLUSION

Casey and *Salgado* are examples of how many courts currently apply the business records exception to computer-generated information. The inconsistency with which courts have handled computer-generated evidence—some courts consider it hearsay, others do not; some courts require extra foundational testimony, others do not—shows the problems created when courts apply old legal concepts to new situations. One commentator explained that "[t]he danger attendant to applying familiar legal concepts like the shop-book rule to new situations is that traditional concepts might predispose judges to treat new situations as if they were not new at all. Important differences would elude consideration."[71]

Clearly, when applying the rationale of the business records exception to computer-generated evidence, "important differences" have "eluded consideration." For example, computer-generated evidence does not become more accurate from "regularity of preparation." Unlike humans, where repeated action trains an individual "in habits of precision," computers do not become more accurate each time they produce a result. Although computers are more consistent than their human counterparts, if programmed or implemented incorrectly, they will be consistently wrong. Computers also usually lack the reflective capacity to recognize errors in their computations and immediately correct their mistakes.

Just because businesses rely on faulty computer programs does not necessarily mean that courts should follow suit. Without requiring some preliminary showing of reliability, a court will simply have no idea what caliber of information system produced the result or what measures, if any, the business took to protect the integrity of the system. When considering the duty judges have to ensure the accuracy of evidence considered by the jury, blindly admitting computer-generated evidence without any foundations is a system that, in essence, does away with the hearsay rule and that allows everything to go to the weight.

---

71. Peritz, *supra* note 25, at 964.

CHAPTER 8

The New Foundation of System Reliability

What should the rules be for the admissibility of statements made by information systems? These statements originate through reading and writing games, and accordingly, the reliability of such statements is implicated. Moreover, the statements live on as "data" in those systems for an indefinite period before they are examined by courts. Accordingly, they are subject to change over time.

Is such information hearsay? And if not, what is it? And if so, is there an appropriate exception to the hearsay rule that is applicable? And if no exception currently exists that makes sense, what legal doctrine should control admissibility?

As we have seen, the existing jurisprudence is confusing. Many cases hold that the statements in computer-generated information are not hearsay. Other cases analyze the admissibility of such statements under an exception to the hearsay rule. Still other cases properly recognize there is an authenticity component that must be addressed before evidence should be admitted, but most do not.

What is needed is a doctrine that satisfies both our evidentiary policies (including the right to test statements in court), and that recognizes what occurs when statements are generated by an information system. Critically, the doctrine must recognize what is making the statement is a *system*. Given that information systems are usually unique, there is no easy or simple recipe to guide any preliminary analysis by trial courts. The challenge is exacerbated by the fact that such systems are *complex*, meaning that no one person, or even one small group of people, can understand or explain them fully.

This book suggests that a new doctrine of *system reliability* should supplement the concept of business records when one analyzes statements made by information systems. *System reliability* is a two-pronged concept. At issue are both the concept of *reliability* (the accuracy and trustworthiness of the end product of the reading and writing games producing the statement) and the concept of *authenticity* (primarily *integrity*, given that information in systems is subject to change).

THE NEED FOR MEANINGFUL COMPETENCY DETERMINATIONS BY COURTS

But first, let us examine the issue of the power of trial courts to require foundations. When the law of evidence began to solidify in the early eighteenth century, the trial judge had substantial discretion to admit or exclude, and even to comment on, the evidence before the trier of fact. Trial courts ruled on the competency of evidence—its overall reliability and appropriateness to be considered by the jury. Over time, particularly as evidence rules became codified and as lawyers became much more involved in trials, such discretion was whittled away. Courts began to apply formalistic rules, many based on the assumption that so long as it was *rational* for a jury to consider something, it should be admitted. Accordingly, the first issue we discuss is the issue of the meaningfulness of the *foundation* necessary to get computer-generated information into evidence.

The case most modern in its approach is *In re Vee Vinhnee*.[1] It shows that the venerable role of the trial court in making competency determinations is not dead. In *Vinhnee*, the court ruled that a major financial institution provided only a trivial foundation for the authentication of its financial records. It held the institution had not met its authentication burden, and excluded the records from evidence.

Vinhnee is a consumer bankruptcy case. Vinhnee's creditor American Express filed a complaint alleging that certain of his credit card debt was nondischargeable under 11 U.S.C. § 523(a)(2)(A), which governs nondischargeability because of fraud. The court scheduled a trial whereby American Express would prove its nondischargeability case.

But Vinhnee did not appear. In its role of deciding whether his credit card debts were fraudulent, and in a case for which it was also acting as the trier of fact, the court had to assure itself of the reliability and continuing integrity of the information American Express was moving into evidence about the nature and amount of Vinhnee's debt.

When the court recognized that everything was going to be decided based on statements made by American Express's information systems, the court demanded a meaningful foundation from American Express about how its systems had produced their statements.

The trial court wanted an authentication foundation regarding the computer and software utilized in order to "assure the continuing accuracy of the records." The witnesses at the trial knew nothing about this subject, and the court agreed to reconvene the trial so that American Express could lay the foundation about the integrity of its records. The court also apparently pointed out Professor Imwinkelried's treatise, *Evidentiary Foundations*, to counsel for American Express.

At the reconvention of the trial, the witness designated to lay the foundation was only able to give conclusions—the sort of trivial showing discussed in Chapter 3.

The witness testified that:

1. American Express used a state-of-the-art mainframe computer;
2. The system had been used for quite some time to produce such billing statements;
3. The system was highly accurate; and
4. The data in the system was fed into it from electronic feeds from service merchants, and that the computer kept these accounts accurate and *did not change the numbers.*

But even with this foundation, as guided by Imwinkelried's treatise, the court excluded the evidence. It ruled that the witness was not qualified to lay the foundation. More

---

1. 336 B.R. 437, (9th Cir. BAP Cal. 2005).

importantly, it ruled there had not been sufficient evidence to warrant a conclusion that the "*American Express computers are sufficiently accurate in the retention and retrieval of the information contained in the documents.*"

The appellate court ruled the trial court was justified in excluding the evidence based on lack of a proper authentication. It focused on the issue of integrity: "There is no information regarding American Express's computer policy and system control procedures, including control of access to the pertinent databases, control of access to the pertinent programs, recording and logging of changes to the data, backup practices, and audit procedures utilized to assure the continuing integrity of the records. All of these matters are pertinent to the accuracy of the computer in the retention and retrieval of the information at issue."[2]

Thus, *Vinhnee* is not about reliability of reading and writing games in the first instance; it is concerned with integrity of information. It is noteworthy because, to date, it is the most important case that has demanded a nontrivial foundation for authentication of computer-generated statements.

To meet the authentication foundation, it appears what the court was looking for was something like this hypothetical examination of a qualified American Express representative:

Hypothetical Examination

Q: After the amount of the credit card charges are entered into the account number database for a cardholder such as Mr. Vinhnee, what happens?

A: They remain in that format and cannot be changed.

Q: Can the amounts owed, or dates of charges, or other data, be edited under any circumstances?

A: Well, technically yes, if we need to make a correcting entry. But there are protections in the system that result in only authorized persons editing data, and in that instance a detailed log is kept.

Q: Why can't anybody in the company just edit the data?

A: The database is read-only. It is not possible to change the numbers unless a special administrative procedure is invoked. That requires two separate departments to be involved, and managers must agree to change any account balance.

Q: So what you are saying is that it is not possible to change any data unless two mangers agree and sign off?

A: Yes, and they have certain passwords and security tokens that only they possess that must be used for the system to initiate changes. And there is something else.

Q: What is that?

A: The system is backed up nightly, the records are "hashed," and a digital signature is applied by the comptroller so that we have a dependable audit trail of what all accounts were on at least a 24-hour rolling basis.

Q: Is it possible to change the figures without invoking the procedure you have described?

A: No. It is not.

---

2. 336 B.R. at 446, 447.

Q: What happens if there is a change to the data in an account?

A: That change is then logged by our audit department, which creates a complete audit log of any and all changes to any account.

Q: So if I wanted to test whether Mr. Vinhnee's account information had ever changed since the data was first input into it, I could look at the audit department records?

A: Yes, they would definitely have the information.

Q: And have you checked the audit department's records on Mr. Vinhnee?

A: Yes, there has been no editing or change of any of his account information since it originally was input into his account number file.

Q: Thank you. So how do I know that this printout is an accurate printout of his account information?

A: We have a system that prints a view of information from the existing account balance of Mr. Vinhnee. It only prints the current account balance, as verified by our auditing department.

Q: Thank you.

Because *system reliability* includes an authenticity component, and because there is a need to authenticate evidence in any event, practitioners should be prepared to lay meaningful foundations about *integrity of information* when they seek to introduce evidence about computer-generated information.

THE REMAINING ELEMENTS OF A FOUNDATION BASED ON SYSTEMS RELIABILITY

Accordingly, in any systems reliability approach, integrity of information is part of the equation. We have seen that the existing rules already encompass the concept, as the business records exception is commonly understood to include an authenticity component. Indeed, in its discussion of admissibility, the *Vinhnee* court used the business records exception as the overarching substantive test governing reliability. Was this appropriate?

Not completely. It is time for the law to recognize that the business records exception—now called the "records of regularly conducted business activity" exception to the hearsay rule—arose in the first third of the nineteenth century, at a time when business records were created by human beings, inserting information about financial transactions into books and records that were generally auditable. If changes were made in the financial books (which were kept with pen and paper in hardbound volumes), there was formalized evidence of the change that could be discovered: the correcting entry.

But now, computer-generated information can be anything from the measurement and recording of an event, to a complex simulation, to the final outcome of elaborate processes linking together many subprocesses; to statements such as "You have gout." The venerable shop-book rule evolved to encompass records of *human-entered* data. It did not encompass a complex system emerging from layers of nested reading and writing games, where systems enter information into other systems—behavior that ultimately results in a system making a statement.

Efforts to Expand Foundations Beyond the Business Records Exception

When lawyers first grappled with this issue, and with introducing computerized evidence at trial, courts toyed with the idea of requiring supplementary foundational testimony to qualify computerized records under the business records exception.

An example is *United States v. Scholle*.[3] Scholle was a lawyer who was convicted of a drug charge. At trial, Scholle objected to the introduction into evidence of computer printouts, and the accompanying testimony of Donald Johnson, who was Section Chief of the Investigative Service Section of the Drug Enforcement Administration (DEA). The printouts were the product of a "computer retrieval system" called System to Retrieve Information from Drug Evidence (STRIDE), which was developed by Mr. Johnson, who testified as to its operation. The system computerized the physical characteristics of drugs seized and tested in eight regional laboratories across the country. Its input includes types of drugs, their potency, components, dilutants, location collected, date analyzed, packaging information, and price. The information so compiled was retrieved by Mr. Johnson daily to determine what elements current drug traffic might have in common in an attempt to detect new trends, new drugs, or any other information to which state and local drug enforcement agencies should be alerted, such as a tie-in pointing to a possible conspiracy involving a particular drug.

Through Mr. Johnson, the government introduced a STRIDE printout reflecting information concerning cocaine received from the Minneapolis DEA District Office. In introducing the computer printout, the government sought to establish the inference that the cocaine sold at the distribution end of the conspiracy in the *Scholle* case was the same cocaine that had been acquired at the importation end of the conspiracy. The government contended the computer evidence was properly admitted as compilations of business records. It invoked the business record exception.

The defense argued the computer printout was admitted erroneously in that it was without foundation.

In reviewing the foundation established for the reliability of the computer printout evidence, the appellate court noted that it had recognized the propriety of treating routinely made and recorded laboratory analyses of drugs as business records admissible under the Federal Business Records Act, 28 U.S.C. § 1732.4; *United States v. Parker*, 491 F.2d 517, 520 (8th Cir. 1973); *see* Federal Rule of Evidence 803. It noted there were two basic requirements for a business record to be admissible. The record must have been made in the regular course of business; and the regular course of business must have been to make such records contemporaneously or within a reasonable time thereafter.[4]

The court then made its brief stab at suggesting a new foundation:

> Even where the procedure and motive for keeping business records provide a check on their trustworthiness (*United States v. Fendley, supra*), the complex nature of computer storage calls for a more comprehensive foundation. Assuming properly functioning equipment is used, there must be not only a showing that the requirements of the Business Records Act have been satisfied, but in addition the original source of the computer program must be delineated, and the procedures for input control including tests used to assure accuracy and reliability must be presented. *United States v. Russo, supra*.

---

3. 553 F.2d 1109 (8th Cir. 1977).
4. United States v. Anderson, 447 F.2d 833, 838 (8th Cir. 1971).

In this case Mr. Johnson, being the founder of STRIDE and qualified by training, experience and position to testify about the system, adequately established that the disputed printouts reflected drug analyses computerized routinely during the regular course of business at the Drug Enforcement Administration, and also described in detail the source of the information upon which the printout was based. The government presented very little evidence concerning the mechanics of how input from eight widely dispersed laboratories is controlled or tested for its accuracy and reliability.

We do not quarrel with the theory underlying the use of STRIDE data in drug investigations or prosecutions. We require only that there be sufficient proof of its trustworthiness as well as an adequate opportunity for rebuttal. In evaluating the admission of the disputed printout, we must consider the reliability of what goes into the computer as well as the reliability of what comes out.

The trial court and counsel engaged in a protracted and in some respects inconclusive dialogue concerning the foundation laid for reception of the computer evidence. We have scrutinized the transcript of this dialogue and of the Johnson testimony with care and are convinced that although the foundation for reception of the evidence could well have been more firm we cannot say that the trial court erred in admitting it. Any evidentiary shortcoming thereafter became a matter of weight to be given to the evidence rather than one of admissibility.

Here, the suggested standard was *"the original source of the computer program must be delineated, and the procedures for input control including tests used to assure accuracy and reliability must be presented."*

Is it clear what this means?

One can see the emergence of two trends that continue to this day: First, even where the court believes something must be shown in addition to just meeting the business records exception, the enunciation of the suggested standard is general and also vague, in that it does not really announce what courts should do.

Next, even though this was a criminal matter, the court was satisfied with a trivial showing in the case. Although it is hard to know without a more comprehensive record, it appears the court accepted a sketchy foundation—just as the American Express lawyers apparently expected the court to do in *Vinhnee.* Typically, the court ruled that more foundation could have been given, but that everything apparently was a matter of weight.

But there is another line of cases, typified by *United States. v. Vela.*[5] The issue there was the accuracy of billing records, just as it was in *Vinhnee,* although the ultimate issue was not whether or not debt would be discharged, as in *Vinhnee,* but whether the criminal defendant, Vela, should be incarcerated.

At trial, an employee of Southwestern Bell described as custodian of the records, sponsored copies of telephone bills being used as evidence against Mr. Vela. He testified that the copies were made from microfiche records prepared by the comptroller's department of the company, that the records were prepared in the usual course of the company's regularly conducted business activity, and that it was part of that activity to prepare such records. When questioned by Vela's counsel, the employee explained the process by which automatic call-identification equipment registers the dialing of long-

5. 673 F.2d 86 (5th Cir. 1982).

distance telephone calls on electronic tapes. The tapes were then transmitted to the comptroller's office, where the information is transferred onto billing tapes. Computers were used at two stages: first, in the recording of the initial dialing; and second, in the computation and preparation of bills in the comptroller's office. The testifying employee vouched only for the general reliability of the process. He was unable to identify the brand, type, and model of each computer, or to vouch for the working condition of the specific equipment during the billing periods covered.

The district court admitted the bills under Rule 803(6), declaring that they "*would be even more reliable than . . . average business record(s) because they are not even touched by the hand of man.*"

Vela's counsel attacked admissibility of the phone bills under Rule 803(6), claiming the prosecution did not lay a satisfactory foundation. Vela did not dispute that, insofar as the custodian of the records testified the records were kept in the regular course of business, the dictates of Rule 803(6) were satisfied. Instead, Vela made an argument that there should be a reliability requirement. Vela argued that by failing to establish that the computers involved in the billing process were in proper working order, a satisfactory foundation had not been made, and that he had been denied confrontation rights.

The appellate court then addressed the critical point: Vela's suggestion there was a unique foundational requirement for the admission of computerized business records under Rule 803(6), together with his citations of *United States v. Scholle*, 553 F.2d 1109, 1125 (8th Cir.) and *McCormick's Handbook of the Law of Evidence*, 733–34 (2d ed. 1972).

The court refused to treat computer records any differently than any other type of business record, noting that "this court has previously held that 'computer data compilations . . . should be treated as any other record of regularly conducted activity.'"[6] Like the computer records in the *Rosenberg* case, the telephone company's long-distance billing records are "sufficiently trustworthy in the eyes of this disinterested company to be relied on by the company in conducting its day to day business affairs."[7] . . . "This court has previously stated that computer evidence is not intrinsically unreliable.[8] Vela's arguments for a level of authentication greater than that regularly practiced by the company in its own business activities go beyond the rule and its reasonable purpose to admit truthful evidence. The court did not abuse its discretion in admitting the bills nor deny Vela his confrontation rights. At best, the arguments made go to the weight that should be accorded the evidence, not its admissibility."[9]

The policy rationale is that if an information system was good enough for a company to use, all its statements were good enough for the jury to consider as evidence. The court held that when information systems generated statements, they should be treated no differently than the venerable shop books of the mid-nineteenth century.

Since these two leading cases were decided, the case law authority has been scattered. A few courts hold that some sort of reliability foundation must be laid. These either use

---

6. *Rosenberg v. Collins*, 624 F.2d at 665.
7. *Id.*
8. *United States v. Fendley*, 522 F.2d 181, 187 (5th Cir. 1975); *Olympic Insurance Co. v. H. D. Harrison, Inc.*, 418 F.2d 669, 670 (5th Cir. 1969).
9. *See United States v. Scholle*, 553 F.2d at 1125.

stand-alone reasoning relating to the world of computers, or get there from Rule 803 (6)'s requirement that there can be no indicia of untrustworthiness if evidence is to be admitted under the business records exception. Some courts hold that the trustworthiness issue is for the opponent of the evidence to address, going to the matter of weight. Most courts simply brush over things cursorily and hold that if a foundation for the business records exception to the hearsay rule is shown, the evidence can be admitted. At least one court, *Vinhnee*, has addressed the authenticity issue, but it is in the extreme minority.

The Singer Proposal

About the same time that courts began grappling with these issues, commentators began writing that the business records exception to the hearsay rule was inadequate to handle computer-generated information. For example, in her article published in 1979, *Proposed Changes to the Federal Rules of Evidence as Applied to Computer-Generated Evidence,* 7 RUT. J. COMPUTERS, TECH. & L. 157, 177 (1979–80), Paula Noyes Singer predicted some of the problems courts would encounter as a result of the prevalent role computers would soon play in business operations. Singer set forth a proposed foundations scheme, and importantly, used the concept of *reliability*, asserting: "[I]t is necessary to demonstrate the reliability of the process which created the evidence. The reliability of computer-generated evidence depends upon: (1) the equipment; (2) the programs; (3) the data entry process; (4) the presence or absence of application controls over the EDP system; and (5) the presence or absence of system security."[10]

Singer forecasted that judges would not apply the rules correctly, because they lacked a "fundamental understanding of electronic data processing."[11] To aid judges in making reliability determinations, Singer proposed adding a new section to the Rule 901 authentication requirement that would specifically pertain to computer-generated evidence. Singer outlined the following suggested new rule, Federal Rule of Evidence 901(c):

> (c) *Computer Program or System.* Evidence describing a computer program or system of computer programs used to produce a result and showing, by a description of the computer hardware, programming method, stored data base, operation of the system, system security, and specific application controls, that the program or system produces an accurate result, satisfies the authentication requirement for a computer programmer or system. Voluminous testimony should not be required to lay a foundation for the computer system or process. For instance, the explanation of the computer hardware need not be more than an overview by the manufacturer of the central processing unit and of the types of input/output devices used by the system.[12]

Singer's proposal, interestingly, was inserted into Article IX of the Rules, rather than Article VIII, which governs hearsay and which therefore could be considered more appropriate for her reliability concerns. But Singer's approach was advanced, in that it tacitly acknowledged that the maker of the statement in question was a *system*. Such

---

10. Paula Noyes Singer, *Proposed Changes to the Federal Rules of Evidence as Applied to Computer-Generated Evidence,* 7 RUT. J. COMPUTERS, TECH. & L. 157, 177 (1979–80) at 163.
    11. *Id.* at 158.
    12. *Id.* at 174.

things as "system security" were mentioned, and a mention is made of a *system* producing an accurate result. Singer's proposal is certainly a good place to start as policy makers, rule drafters, and judges all contemplate what to do about this issue over the coming years.

Second Edition of the Manual for Complex Litigation

As another example, in the early 1980s the authors of the *Manual for Complex Litigation* made six recommendations on how courts should handle computerized data, which were thereafter set forth in the *Manual for Complex Litigation (Second)*.[13] The *Manual* hoped to persuade judges to make it clear that the burden of going forward with evidence of a system's "trustworthiness" was on the proponent of the evidence.[14] In particular, the *Manual* proposed a four-step foundational process:

> The proponent should offer proof that (1) the document is a business record; (2) the document has probative value; (3) the computer equipment used is reliable; and (4) reliable data processing techniques were applied.[15]

The *Manual* proposed including a requirement that the proponent use expert testimony to establish the reliability and accuracy of computer processing systems.[16] It is not clear what happened to these proposals. They are not found in the current *Manual for Complex Litigation*. Courts were probably unwilling to request litigants to go the expense of doing all that.

State Court Initiatives

In addition, various other bodies have taken up the question. As one example only, in the 1990s, under a grant from the State Justice Institute, the Standing Committee on Rules of Practice and Procedure of the Court of Appeals of Maryland studied whether new rules should be created to address computer-generated evidence. The standing committee concluded that the existing rules of evidence adequately dealt with the admissibility of computer-generated evidence, but that new rules of procedure would be helpful. In doing so, the committee generated reports on various ways to handle the reliability determination.

These discussions were the subject of a law review article by James E. Carbine and Lynn McLain, *Proposed Model Rules Governing the Admissibility of Computer-Generated Evidence*. Among the alternatives (which were not adopted), the most advanced form of reliability foundation took the *Manual's* 1980s burden-shifting approach one step further by adding an additional section to rule 803(6).[17] It designated the existing text of Federal Rule of Evidence 803(6) as part (a), and added a new part (b) as follows:

---

13. *See* Rudolph J. Peritz, *Computer Data and Reliability: A Call for Authentication of Business Records Under the Federal Rules of Evidence,* 80 NW. U. L. REV. 956, 964 (1986), at 973.

14. *Id.* at 975 ("The Manual's purpose is to guide judges in requiring proponents to offer evidence of computer system reliability.").

15. *Id.* at 974.

16. *Id.* at 975.

17. James E. Carbine & Lynn McLain, *Proposed Model Rules Governing the Admissibility of Computer Generated Evidence,* 15 SANTA CLARA COMPUTER & HIGH TECH. L.J. 1, 15, 16.

> (b) If a record offered under subsection (a) of this Rule is computer generated, the court also must be satisfied under Rule 104(a) as to: (i) the reliability of the systems and application processing program(s) used, including the security of the system; (iii) the reliability of the input process, including the relevance and reliability of the underlying data, the integrity and completeness of the input data, and the accuracy of the input method; (iv) the reliability of the output, including the propriety of the request, the absence of transmission errors, and the security of the output.[18]

Adding Rule 803(6)(b) would ensure that a judge would make a preliminary determination of *reliability* under Rule 104(a), so that jurors would only see computer-generated evidence if the judge was satisfied by a preponderance of the evidence that the information was reliable.[19] The authors of the article noted that adding the requirements, but placing them in Uniform Rule of Evidence 901(b)(9), on the other hand, would make them Rule 104(b) questions for the jury. Rule 104(b) is, accordingly, a more liberal standard of admission, under which evidence is admissible if the judge finds a reasonable jury could find the authenticating factors met. This is the "rationality test" we discussed in Chapter 3, regarding authentication.

At least one court has recently used a reliability approach. In *State v. Polanco*,[20] a criminal defendant objected to the admission of a computer-generated map that revealed the distance between two locations. Did he sell drugs less than 1,500 feet from a school? The court did not fully explain how the computerized map was created, but it was essentially generated by a computer compiling various types of data.[21] The exhibit in question contained a circle drawn around a certain area to indicate relative distance, which the computer also calculated.[22]

The court evaluated the evidence under the business records exception to the hearsay rule.[23] Because it was computer-generated, however, the court also required an additional burden on the sponsoring party, in essence doing what Mr. Vela's counsel had proposed, but which the U.S. Fifth Circuit Court of Appeals had refused to require:

> Computer generated exhibits present "structural questions of reliability that transcend the reliability of the underlying information that is entered into the computer." To accommodate that heightened concern, a court is not permitted to admit a computer generated exhibit into evidence unless the proffering party also (1) presents a witness whose knowledge of computers is sufficient to enable direct and cross-examination concerning the process used to generate the exhibit and (2) lays a foundation, through that witness, sufficient to support a finding that the process and equipment involved in generating the exhibit were adequate for that purpose.[24]

Thus, the court in *Polanco* added another hurdle to admission because evidence was computer-generated. After discussing the evidence briefly, the court upheld the admission of the map evidence.

---

18. *Id.*
19. *Id.*
20. 797 A.2d 523, 533–39 (Conn. App. 2002).
21. *Id.* at 533–34.
22. *Id.*
23. *Id.* at 534–35.
24. *Id.* at 538 (citations omitted).

TOWARDS A NEW SYSTEMS RELIABILITY STANDARD

This book will not attempt the ambitious goal of laying out a comprehensive scheme for describing under what circumstances any and all computer-generated information should be admitted into evidence. It does, however, touch on highlights and make comments for those in the future who will grapple with this challenging issue.

First, this will be a serious concern of the future. Indeed, many of the opinions authored in this area were written before the networking revolution of the early 1990s—before the advent of the World Wide Web and the omnipresence of e-mail. Information systems increasingly permeate our lives. We use them more and more at work, and at home, for a wide variety of things. They now recognize our voices and take commands, even in cars, whereas just a few years ago, such capabilities were considered a futuristic joke about a state of affairs that would not be possible for centuries.[25] Clearly, the number and complexity and subjectivity of statements that information systems will generate and insert into records will undoubtedly grow for the foreseeable future. Information systems have become part of our society. And given that growth and change in complex systems technology is exponential, it is simply impossible to predict the extent to which information systems will be making statements ten, twenty, or thirty years hence. It will probably be shocking from the perspective of the current day.

Statements of Information Systems Are Hearsay

Next, we must acknowledge that computer-generated information really is hearsay. These are statements, and they often take the form of declarative sentences and not mere numbers or results of calculations.

Consider that the hearsay rule was intended to mitigate problems that would otherwise arise when an out-of-court statement was considered as evidence. Among the dangers implicated were perception, memory, narration, and sincerity of the maker of the statement.[26] If the statement-maker was not present for cross-examination, such attributes could not be tested for benefit of the finder of fact. In cases like *Armstead*, courts simply assumed that computer-generated information presented none of the dangers, and that the policy reasons underlying the hearsay rule therefore did not figure into the analysis.[27] Implicit in this approach is the idea that computers are inherently reliable, and that cross-examination is not necessary to determine the truthfulness of the information

---

25. A quite funny scene in a 1986 Star Trek movie, *Star Trek IV: The Voyage Home,* occurs when, after he has been transported back in time to the 1980s on Earth, Scotty finds a computer and starts talking to it, expecting a response from it.

26. *See* 2 MCCORMICK ON EVIDENCE § 245 (Kenneth S. Broun ed., 6th ed. 2006).

27. *See* State v. Armstead, 432 So.2d 837, 840–41 (La. 1983) ("With a machine . . . there is no possibility of a conscious misrepresentation, and the possibility of inaccurate or misleading data only materializes if the machine is not functioning properly."); *see also Justice Department's Word on Electronically-Created Evidence,* CRIM. PRAC. GUIDE, Mar. 2001, at 39, 42–43 ("Th[e] rationale [behind the hearsay rule] does not apply when an animal or a machine makes an assertion."); PAUL R. RICE, ELECTRONIC EVIDENCE 275–77 (2005) ("The problems of hearsay . . . arise only when there is direct human influence over the recorded statement's existence."); Adam Wolfson, Note, *"Electronic Fingerprints": Doing Away With the Conception of Computer-Generated Records as Hearsay,* 104 MICH L. REV. 151, 161 (2005) ("[N]one of the rationales for the hearsay rule relate to authenticated computer-generated records. . . .").

they produce.[28] With this in mind, let us consider just one of these factors—the issue of narrative.

A human witness's in-court statement can be tested through cross-examination to ensure that the language articulated by the witness accurately represents what is being described, or at least that the witness and the court are on the same page in their language games. Language is an elastic invention, and its use is often if not almost always ambiguous, thus necessitating testing and probing about what is really meant, and the boundaries and concreteness of the assertion.

Computer-generated information is similarly composed of language. The statements made by information systems might be dubious, since a human programmer told the computer what to say under certain circumstances. The true maker of the statement the system outputs is thus twice-removed from the judicial proceeding, each level of removal increasing the risk of miscommunication.

There is thus no compelling reason to conclude that information generated by computers is substantially less subject to problems of narrative than when humans exclusively are involved. If a computer printout consists only of a number, what does the number mean and under what circumstances? What does a date for file creation mean, and on which computer? Computer-generated information might consist only of disembodied numbers, phrases, and symbols, and it should not be assumed that such information will be easily put into context and rendered clear in meaning simply because it comes from a computer. In fact, the opposite is true. Even something as simple as a date might need clarification to resolve ambiguity.[29]

Further, regarding the narrative issue, computers appear to communicate in terms of art, understood primarily by their programmers but not necessarily by the society that reads the statements. For example, the author received an e-mail sent to him the evening of Thursday, December 13, 2007, from a member of his firm in the Research Services department. Friday morning, the 14th, he started on a reply to the e-mail. Thinking for a few moments, he decided *not* to reply to the e-mail. He closed the reply and did not save or send anything.

However, note in Figure 8.1 what the information system said happened. The information system creates information stating the author *did* reply to the e-mail, at a certain date and time.

But he did *not* reply—he only thought about replying. He started to, but then decided not to. He never transmitted a reply to Ms. Bundy.

What is happening here? Did the program malfunction? Was it a one-shot failure?

Obviously, there is something strange going on with the concept of narrative—what the system is saying based on what information it can "perceive" or read. Apparently, the

---

28. *See* Hawkins v. Cavalli, No. C 03-3668 PJH, 2006 WL 2724145, at 13 (N.D. Cal. Sept. 22, 2006) (stating that the court presumed nonhearsay printouts of computer access dates to have such a high degree of reliability that they would have otherwise fallen under the residual exception); People v. Mormon, 422 N.E.2d 1065, 1073 (Ill. App. Ct. 1981) ("In the light of the general use of electronic computing and recording equipment in the business world and the reliance of the business world on them, the scientific reliability of such machines can scarcely be questioned.") (quoting People v. Gauer, 288 N.E.2d 24 (Ill. App. Ct. 1972)).

29. *See*, for example, GEORGE L. PAUL & BRUCE H. NEARON, THE DISCOVERY REVOLUTION 102 ex. 5-2 (2006), for a computer printout that shows a document's date of creation as "(D:20040724013707)."

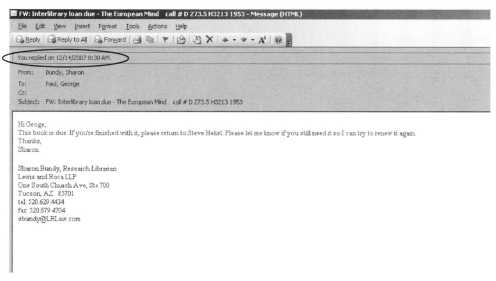

FIGURE 8.1
False Hearsay Generated by Information System

application is programmed to record information stating that a recipient replied to an e-mail if the reply dialogue box is open for a certain amount of time, during which time something happens in the system generating a statement that there has been a reply. Why the system does not wait for an actual transmission of a reply e-mail, before stating that a reply was sent, is unknown. Thus, having "replied" to an e-mail does not mean, in the syntax and semantics of this particular statement, that one actually did reply to an e-mail. Rather, "replied" means that one opened up the reply dialogue box for a certain period of time. "Replied" in this instance means *began* the process of replying, but not replying. This is misleading and could easily lead to false inferences about facts—such as, in other circumstances, that there was spoliation of evidence. No e-mail will be found in the "Sent" folder, another repository of computer-generated information, and the two statements made by the same application will contradict one other. There is no dictionary provided to define what the system means when it states there was a "reply" to an e-mail.

This simple example highlights that we are not just discussing collections of human entries of information, the paradigm of the shop-book rule. We discuss agents and programs and groups of programs writing to one other, and reading each other's information, and then various statements being entered into records without any thought of them being used as evidence. As many decisions and commentators observe, this great discourse in our information systems is subject to error. And when things go wrong, they tend to go consistently wrong.

For example, a system can have been designed wrong, or have been designed wrong in an upgrade. It might take several years to discover errors producing erroneous narratives about events in the system. A famous example is the THERAC-25 radiation treatment device, used in radiation therapy for cancer patients, originally marketed by Atomic Energy of Canada, Ltd. (AECL). The TERAC-25 had two modes of operation:

1. X—X-rays, 25 MeV (25 Krads)
2. E—electron beam, 200 rads

Unfortunately, because of improper software design, several cancer patients undergoing treatment in E mode were subjected to accidental X-ray exposure (at 125 times the recommended radiation dose for their illnesses), and some died resulting from a design flaw in the THERAC-25.

The accidental exposure came from the following sequence of events:

1. Technician enters "X" on the keyboard.
2. Screen indicates "X-ray Mode."
3. Technician immediately recognizes a mistake and edits it, using the "UP" key to cursor back over the "X."
4. Technician enters "E."
5. Screen indicates "Electron Beam Mode."
6. Technician sees this is the right setting and hits the "RETURN" key.
7. Screen indicates "Beam Ready."
8. Technician enters "B" to fire the beam.

The problem was this: Even though the technician had done everything correctly, the mere fact he had erroneously entered "X," but then immediately caught his mistake and finished programming the machine in less than eight seconds, after instructing it to administer electrons, the machine nevertheless went on to administer a serious and sometimes fatal dose of X-rays, rather than electrons. In one celebrated case, the radiological physicist and oncologist on duty could see nothing wrong with the device—and ran it through a series of prescribed tests that showed nothing abnormal. And the patient injured by the X-ray had no visible sign of burns. But that patient, Voyne Ray Cox, died four months later.[30]

Or, similar to incorrect design, a system can have been implemented incorrectly. Judicial decisions often naively state that such-and-such hardware is reliable, or such-and-such software is reliable. However, especially as one goes up the level of complexity of systems, hardware and various types of software are implemented in a process that is subjective and for which there is no one right way to do things. Indeed, code almost always is custom-written in such implementations. This is why companies hire expensive consultants to implement systems. If hardware and software were just commodities, one could buy them as products off the shelf. But this is not how it works.

In a noted example of an implementation mistake, a $125 million satellite, the Mars Climate Orbiter funded by the U.S. government, crashed into the planet Mars and was destroyed because of something so simple as a failed translation of English system measurement units into metric units. Apparently, one group of programmers was using the English system and another was using metric, and they failed to recognize they were not

---

30. See sci.engr.* FAQ on Failures: THERAC-25, from the Barrret Engineering Consulting website, http://www.tcnj.edu/~rgraham/failures/THERAC25.html.

using the same units and so needed to convert. And this was in an engineering project that was hundreds of millions of dollars in scope.

Systems can be deployed improperly, configured improperly, or be the subject of operator error. This, of course, happens all the time, and it is therefore disingenuous to conclude, as have some courts, that computers' statements need not be scrutinized because they are "not even touched by the hand of man." And it is simply not possible to predict what types of erroneous statements will occur under what circumstances. Because there are literally millions of such systems—each a unique information ecosystem in its own way communicating with its resident human operators, implementers, deployers—and designers, the variation in the possibilities for erroneous information is large. How many time marks on e-mails or other records around the United States are seriously wrong and misleading, for whatever reason? Tens of millions? Mistakes occur because such systems depend on a great many variables that affect statements in hard-to-predict ways. Clocks can innocently have the wrong time.

Statements of information systems are therefore hearsay. The policy reasons animating the hearsay rule mean it is an abandonment of our values to admit such statements into evidence without at least thinking about whether it is fair to admit them, and to test their reliability in the adversary process, at least going to the weight of the evidence.

There Must Be a New Exception to the Hearsay Rule

But, notwithstanding their existence as hearsay, such statements will and must be admitted into evidence. There are too many such statements, and they are too important as evidence about our daily lives. Accordingly, there must be a properly considered exception to the hearsay rule. The business records exception is a creature of the mid-nineteenth century. But this problem is one of the late twentieth century and early twenty-first. It implicates not a compendium of human-entered statements, like the shop books of old, but the statements of information systems' reading and writing games. We need a new exception, or at least a consistent refinement to the closest one we have, Rule 803(6). As discussed, this exception should probably be called *systems reliability*.

Accordingly, proponents of computer-generated information will need to lay a foundation to qualify statements as reliable under a systems reliability exception. Just like other determinations under Article VIII, this adjudication should be governed by Rule 104(a), not Rule 104 (b). The court will act as a trier of fact to determine the competency of the evidence. It will not just determine whether it would be rational for the jury to find something, such as in the conditional relevancy determinations currently made under Article IX.

Marginal Utility as Informing the Court's Rule 104 (a) Determination

All evidence needs to be authenticated under Article IX. But how stringent should the reliability determination be for the statements of information systems to be considered prima facie reliable in an Article VIII foundational determination? Does each case compel a proponent to prove the reliability of every system, de novo?

No. As many cases recognize, once there is a familiarity with a particular system or process, over time, less and less of a foundational showing is required before evidence is admitted. Do we need litigants proving how a Word application inserts information as metadata, as a foundation to each and every admission of such metadata? No. But of course, the opponent of the evidence is free to litigate the reliability of the process in question in every case, and to argue the weight of the evidence.

Accordingly, courts should have broad and powerful discretion about how much to require in each case as a matter of a foundational showing. If a piece of computer-generated information is duplicative, and merely adds to what is already a substantial weight of evidence, and comes from a commonly trusted system, perhaps less of a showing is necessary than when it is practically the only evidence in the case, as occurred with *Vinhnee.*

Further, if the computer-generated information comes from a custom designed, custom-implemented, sparsely distributed or marketed application, or a new application, then a different approach is appropriate than if, for example, a common e-mail system, operating in a common configuration, is examined. Courts, in their opinions, generally skip over this important aspect. In some instances, a computer program may only have been written for one or two users. In other instances, many tens of millions of users might use a program daily, and are presumably reporting to publishers about any problems. The foundational determination should take this into account.

Thus, the foundational showing depends on the facts of the case, and this is somewhat similar to the marginal utility approach courts are now directed to take in discovery of electronically stored information under the new Rule 26 (b)(2)(B). If it is very expensive to obtain information from a system, that is not reasonably accessible because of system complexity, and it holds little prospect of being useful or powerfully relevant in the case, then courts may order that costs of obtaining such information be shifted to the requester.

Similarly, if someone objecting to computer-generated information is in essence complaining about something that is undisputed, or from a system known to be reliable, the court might employ a lesser burden in the Rule 104 foundational showing than if someone demands a showing of system reliability for a new or idiosyncratic system, a system with little marketplace acceptance, or in a case where the computer-generated statements loom large as uniquely powerful pieces of evidence. Here, the trial court returns to its former position as a powerful organ, making competency determinations.

Probably the best example of this marginal utility principle in action is the famous case of *State v. Swinton.*[31] There, the stakes were high. The defendant, Alfred Swinton, was on trial for murder and sexual assault—having been accused of being a serial rapist and murderer. Among the evidence in the case were bite marks on each of the victim's breasts. The issue was the foundation laid to allow the admission of digital imaging technology, whereby the prosecution proved that the bite marks on the victim matched up to Swinton's bite patterns.

The bite mark evidence was particularly important in the case. And the technology involved was not off-the-shelf, and needed to be understood by the court. The court required an extensive foundation, and in the appellate opinion, the court spent many pages exploring the authority for admitting computer-generated imaging evidence.

---

31. 847 A.2d 921 (Conn. 2004).

The case is an interesting read, and is clearly one, if not the leading, case where a court explored the reliability of computer-generated information.

Pretrial Discovery Is Necessary for Fairness

From the author's perspective as an experienced trial lawyer, the bottom line is that almost all evidence passes preliminary foundational muster and is admitted. Courts simply do not like making ultimate weight determinations in jury trials. They want the jury to do that. It would be unusual evidence indeed that could not be admitted if the proponent knew what she was doing.

Accordingly, the litigants, who might want to battle about the merits of the reliability of evidence after it is admitted, need to have discovery about the facts going to system reliability. This concern is highlighted in the interesting opinion written in *Commonwealth v. Klinghoffer*[32] In *Klinghoffer*, the Supreme Court of Pennsylvania granted an appeal, but then dismissed it as improvidently granted. Justice Larsen dissented, objecting that there were very good reasons to decide the appeal—whose issue was the "scope of the evidentiary foundation which should be required prior to the admission of a computer-generated expert opinion on a critical issue."

Andrew Klinghoffer was convicted of two counts of vehicular homicide, occurring after he crossed over two lanes on the Benjamin Franklin Bridge in Philadelphia. The key issue in the case was the speed Klinghoffer was going at the time of the accident. He stated to police after the crash that he had been going 55 to 60 miles per hour. The state, however, introduced a statement of a computer system called "Applecrash," which stated that Klinghoffer was going 75 mph. What was the foundation for the statement of Applecrash? Justice Larsen put the issue this way:

> When an expert opinion on a crucial issue in a trial is generated by a computer program, how much information about that program and the data that went into it should the trial court require of its proponent in order to prima facie establish the reliability of that computer opinion, i.e., what is an adequate evidentiary foundation to permit the introduction of such an expert computer opinion? *Also, how much pretrial discovery of such information and data is the opponent entitled to, and when is he entitled to it, in order to ensure a fair and adequate predicate for effective cross-examination of the expert witness and a fair and adequate basis on which to challenge the accuracy of the computer generated opinion?*[33]

Critically, in *Klinghoffer*, the expert running the Applecrash program that calculated the speed at 75 mph had failed to preserve a record of what he input into the program, and thus had to prepare for the trial, from *memory*, a one-page sheet that contained *some* of the input. Again, Justice Larsen's concern appears justified:

> Suffice it to say that it is not clear precisely what data Dr. Thomas fed into and utilized in running the Applecrash program to generate the computer's opinion on the speed of appellant's vehicle, and the parties are in dispute as to when appellant discovered that the Applecrash program had been used, when he received that programming

---

32. 564 A.2d 1240, 522 Pa 562, 564 A. 2d 1240 (Pa. 1989).
33. 522 Pa. 562 at 553 (emphasis supplied).

information, and as to the completeness of the information which Dr. Thomas recalled utilizing. The point is, should a reviewing court have to guess, or should we not establish specific guidelines for the admissibility of computer generated expert opinions and pretrial discovery of the programming information and data that went into the computer, and require that a proper foundation meeting those guidelines be demonstrated on the record.

As the trial judge candidly stated as he struggled with the issue of the admissibility of and foundation for the computer generated expert opinion: "It's a very esoteric field. . . . The computer world is still a great mystery to me as it is to ninety-nine point nine nine percent of the population." Notes of Testimony, Trial at 5.39. The judge's point is well taken, although his percentage estimate of the computer ignorant might be subject to debate.

Despite the court's frank acknowledgment of the esoteric nature and "mystery" of computer programs such as Applecrash, it decided that cross-examination would be sufficient to point out and uncover the potential gaps and flaws in an expert opinion generated by such a program. *However, without adequate information as to the precise data that went into that program and sufficient time to analyze the data and the program, the effectiveness of cross-examination is, it seems to me, seriously undermined.*

Because the record in this case contains no information about the programming relied upon by plaintiff's experts, neither we nor defense counsel have any way of knowing whether it was complete or accurate.

* * *

As the saying goes, "garbage in—garbage out." If computer generated evidence and expert opinions are to be used to deprive a person of his liberty as here (and such use of computer evidence can be expected to be made with increasing frequency), surely the judicial system must demand a high degree of reliability *and disclosure of adequate information as to programming and input to allow meaningful cross-examination,* and to permit the jury to determine whether any garbage went into and contaminated the computer program. Moreover, we must require disclosure of the necessary information to the opponent prior to trial to allow sufficient time to locate a qualified expert in the field who speaks the unique foreign language of the particular computer program who can assist the opponent and his advocate in meaningfully interpreting the data and program and in challenging the accuracy of the results. While there are some exceptions, as a rule I would not expect our judges, juries or lawyers to be well-versed in the foreign computer language used, nor to have the requisite expertise and knowledge to understand how a computer generated a particular opinion. On the other hand, it is easy for a layman to grasp the computer's final result, for example "defendant was traveling at 75 mph," and to be seduced by the magic and technology which enables a computer to analyze staggering amounts of information and variables and transform that data into a conclusion.

Such a conclusion—a computer generated expert opinion—might be accurate and useful in litigation, but only if the information fed into the program, the program itself, and the operation of the program have been accurate and complete. Neither computer nor its programmer is infallible, and unless there is, on the record, sufficient information and data about the program and the programming to establish a proper foundation and to permit meaningful cross-examination, a jury's verdict that may have been influenced by a computer generated opinion on a critical issue will be suspect. It has been said that only a small (two digit) number of men and women truly understand the formulae, processes, equations and reasoning that led to Einstein's theory of relativity and his landmark conclusion E = MC². Obviously more people understand the workings and language of computers, but not so many that I would allow the use of computer generated opinions and evidence at trial without adequate assurances of reliability and meaningful opportunity to permit the parties and advocates to effectively challenge the accuracy of such computer conclusions before the finder of fact.

For the foregoing reasons, I dissent from the majority's disposition of this case.[34]

Accordingly, yet another rule in any new scheme should be that courts, in making their admissibility determinations, should keep in mind whether the proponent of the computer-generated statements has been forthcoming in discovery about all aspects of the system at issue. If not, it would seem fair that a court could refuse to admit the evidence, as the foundational hearing on reliability could not proceed in fairness. Nor, obviously, could the case proceed fairly before a jury. This is not a theoretical concern. There have been situations, over voting machines, for example, where one party insists the machine is reliable, while simultaneously refusing to allow inspection of its reading and writing games. Certainly, one would hate to find oneself in jail because of the statements of a system, when one was deprived of the ability to test how those statements came about. Accordingly, full discovery long before trial appears required if any statement of an information system will be admitted into evidence.

Towards a Systems Reliability Test

Accountants have their own test for and definition of reliability, found in certain Financial Accounting Standards Board (FASB) standards. Lawyers need one as well. And when we talk about the reliability of a computer system, remember that we are talking about something akin to an ecosystem, even perhaps a new form of life. It is a behavior with emergent properties, often so complex in its operation as to defy the ability of any one person, or small group of people, to explain it.

How can the legal system fashion a test for reliability, then? Others will need to articulate the precise standards. However, courts may need to assume the role of information ecologists from this point forward. How does the information travel through the system? Starting with the assertion, "You replied on 12/14/2007 at 8:30 AM," and working backwards, how do we get to that erroneous statement, based on what other information being input into the system, and based upon what programs?

What was the environment of the system? Where was it? What is the history of the system? Is it off-the-shelf or custom-designed or implemented? Is there any evidence of malfunction on other occasions? How much of a role does human input cause in the statement that is output? Is there the possibility of configuration error? Critically, is there a theory of mistake, or error, and a demonstrated problem (akin to an assertion there was an 9-foot-tall man?) Or, is there just a complaint: "How do I know this works?"

All these factors, and possibly more, can affect the reliability of an information system. There needs to be discretion in the trial court, a competency determination made under Rule 104(a), a marginal utility analysis, and full disclosure long before any trial so that the advocates can develop the issues of system reliability.

---

34. 522 Pa 562 at 565, 566 & 570 (emphasis supplied).

Authenticity Concerns

Finally, just as the court was concerned in *Vinhnee*, so too should all courts be concerned about how an information system protects the integrity of its records. Who has access to what records? Is there an audit trail of who had access to the records in question? Can they be edited? Is there some sort of integrity mechanism, such as a digital signature? What, exactly, is the procedure for ensuring integrity and authenticity? These are part of the prerequisite for admissibility under Article IX of the Federal Rules, but also should be considered part of the overall reliability of the system under Article VIII—as demonstrated by the analysis in *Vinhnee*.

CONCLUSION

How to understand the workings of a complex system, such as the human brain, the climate, the economy, or an information system is one of the most difficult challenges facing modernity. It will take the law some time to develop a cogent articulation of how it should gauge the reliability of information systems. But it really has no choice but to do so.

PART IV

Case Studies

Eunomic Solutions in a Commonly Used Application

*Ed Chase**

Can the principles in this book be economically implemented on a day-to-day basis? For example, is it possible to easily create an electronic document that can be strongly tested for authenticity at a later time? Is it possible to create a document that has a strong association with identity? Is it possible to build in a strong test for integrity of information?

In other words, is eunomia *achievable in the near term for the common handler of digital information?*

Importantly, there are already products on the market that achieve such goals with everyday business applications that create documents. This exhaustive case study, authored by Ed Chase, will examine a readily available electronic document format that can help users: (1) prove the integrity of digital information and preserve the content of a digital document over time; (2) establish the identity of "signers"; (3) maintain the times and dates of "signature events"; and (4) support mechanisms to provide for new concepts like "electronic originality." These may all be accomplished in "strong" fashion, in a eunomic *regime using mathematics and logic. All these features are currently achieved through software applications that take advantage of the digital signature features of the Portable Document Format (PDF).*

THE PORTABLE DOCUMENT FORMAT

"PDF" is an electronic file format for documents that was originally developed in the early 1990s by Adobe Systems, Inc. The *PDF Reference* (first published in 1993) (see Bibliography) contains detailed information about the PDF file format, providing software developers with the information required to build software applications that read, write, or manipulate PDF files. With the publication of the *PDF Reference,* Adobe allowed third parties to use the specification to build various applications that supported PDF.

---

*Ed Chase is a Solutions Architect at Adobe Systems, Inc. Ed has been closely involved with the development of electronic document formats, data and metadata standards, and electronic signature solution across the financial services, government, and life sciences industries. He has contributed to the development of industry guidance and standards around PDF, XML, and information security through organizations such as OASIS (the Organization for the Advancement of Structured Information Standards), MISMO (the Mortgage Industry Standards Maintenance Organization), the SAFE (Signatures and Authentication for Everyone) Bio-pharma Association, and AIIM (The Enterprise Content Management Association).

In 2001, the first ISO (International Organization for Standardization) standards based on PDF were published. The PDF/X (see Bibliography) ISO standard is an *open standard* for the printing industry. The term "open standard" has a variety of interpretations, but generally indicates some level of public availability to the specification, and a visible, consensus-based development process. PDF/X was followed by other specialized PDF ISO standards, including PDF/A for archiving and PDF/E for engineering documentation (see Bibliography). These PDF ISO standards target different industries, but they are all subsets of the full PDF specification and are based on versions of Adobe's published and publicly available PDF Reference. As of September 2007, Adobe began work with an ISO Technical Committee to submit the full PDF specification to ISO for approval as a formal, open standard, named ISO 32000. The plan is for ISO 32000 to be maintained and further developed by this technical committee with the objective of protecting the integrity and longevity of PDF. The significance of these standards processes is that they allow anyone to not only use, but also to develop the PDF specification itself, in the manner of other standards such as HTML (HyperText Markup Language) and XML (eXtensible Markup Language) (see Bibliography).

Differentiation must be made between the PDF *file format* and those *software applications* that are used to create and manipulate documents utilizing such file formats. While the PDF file format is published and publicly available, many of the software applications that utilize it may be commercial and proprietary. While Adobe itself develops and sells the commercial PDF application Adobe Acrobat, and freely distributes the Adobe Reader PDF viewer, there are numerous other PDF applications of many types, both commercial and open-source. Companies such as Apple and Microsoft include various levels of PDF functionality in their operating systems or office software suites. Numerous other developers sell commercial PDF software, and many free open-source variants of PDF software also exist. Such developers and projects include Adlib, Ghostscript, iText, Image Solutions, and Xpdf.

EUNOMIC FEATURES OF PDF

This case study discusses the *digital signature* functionality of PDF, and how this technology supports many of the general concepts associated with both traditional signatures and electronic signatures. It should be noted that PDF signature technologies may be implemented in different ways. While the PDF technical specifications do encourage implementers to create PDF signatures that are interoperable at a basic level, not all PDF signature implementations incorporate all of the features that will be discussed, nor do all implementations incorporate them in the same way or at the same level of "trustworthiness." When evaluating the trustworthiness of any particular PDF signature, it is critical to consider all aspects of the signature technologies and the signature process itself. Individual weaknesses in parts of the process or technology may lower the overall trustworthiness of the entire system.

PDF was originally developed by Adobe Systems as a form of "electronic paper." In the years since its initial release, PDF has been updated to included new capabilities, including those necessary to support electronic security and authenticity requirements. Beginning as a representation of the printed page, PDF now includes most of the features found in interactive formats like HTML (see Bibliography), such as links, book-marks, flowable and dynamic content, events, embedded XML (see Bibliography), data, and multimedia. It also includes features like annotations and commenting, as well as security capabilities to restrict access or user permissions.

INCORPORATION OF DIGITAL SIGNATURES TO ACHIEVE STRONG INTEGRITY AND IDENTITY FUNCTIONS

Importantly, in 1999, PDF version 1.4 introduced support for a form of "electronic sig-nature." An "electronic signature" is a technology-neutral term that means any type of "sound, symbol, or process" that is utilized to sign a message or document. An elec-tronic signature can be something as simple as a check-box acknowledgment, or an "I agree" button on an eCommerce website. The term "electronic signature" implies no specific technology, security, or trust requirement. The term has been incorporated into substantive law, in the UETA act, ESIGN, and the UNCITRAL Model Law on Electronic Signatures (see Bibliography).

By contrast, however, the term "digital signature" is a specific form of technology. As discussed in Chapter 4, the essence of a digital signature is a technology-specific mecha-nism based on cryptographic principles. Accordingly, digital signatures can provide a strong test and therefore assurance of integrity, as well as a test and assurance of iden-tity, provided that only a unique person has control of a private key. If there is also some control over a source of time, then a digital signature process can also create a strong association with trusted time (see Chapter 5).

While an "electronic signature" can be almost any sort of electronic acknowledgment process, a digital signature is based on a specific type of technology. *Digital signatures* are based on a *public key cryptography*. Public key cryptography itself is a technical sub-ject that will not be covered in detail here, but understanding digital signatures—even conceptually—does require a very basic understanding of what public key cryptography provides. Public key cryptography is based on pairs of unique electronic "keys."

One key is known only to and secured by its owner (the private key), and the other key is freely distributed (the public key). These keys function in a one-way manner—a message locked with the private key can only be unlocked with the public key. Con-versely, a message locked with the public key can only be unlocked with the private key.

The most basic use of public key cryptography is to encrypt data communicated between two (or more) parties. In a typical public key cryptography encryption pro-cess, data will be encrypted with the intended recipient's public key, ensuring that only a recipient possessing the corresponding private key will be able to decrypt and access the document. But for digital signature applications, the encryption occurs with the private key. Because the private key presumably is unique and known only to the signer, the fact a record could be decrypted using the corresponding public key provides strong evidence of identity.

HASH FUNCTIONS

As discussed in Chapter 4, a *hash function* is a mathematical algorithm that generates a unique "digital fingerprint" of a given electronic document (or any electronic data set).

A *hash value* is the value that results from applying a hash function to an electronic document. A hash value is not an encryption or encipherment of a document; rather, it is a small, fixed-length, seemingly random string of data. Hash values are not random, however. They can be reproduced identically each time the same hash function is applied (in the same way) to the same electronic document. As discussed in Chapter 4, two very important features of hash functions are: first, that actual data can not be recovered from the hash value of a document; and second, that two different documents do not produce the same hash value. Even if they are only different by the smallest of digital elements, documents or data sets can have materially different hash values.

At the most basic level, a digital signature is created by first encrypting the hash value of a document with the private key of the signer. This digital signature may then be appended to the document itself (see Figure A.1). The resulting digitally signed document can then be verified by another party by decrypting the encrypted hash value with the signer's public key, and then separately recalculating the document's hash value. If the recalculated hash value matches the decrypted hash value from the digital signature, then the digital signature is valid (see Figure A.2). Of course, if the hash values of the documents are the same, there is strong evidence that digital information has not changed, and integrity of information has been proved. There are other significant aspects to overall digital signature validity, but the encryption and decryption of the hash value is the core functionality that most other elements of the technology are built upon.

PDF DIGITAL SIGNATURES

In addition to being used for paper-and-ink replacements, digital signatures are used for many other purposes, including securing machine-to-machine communication, and

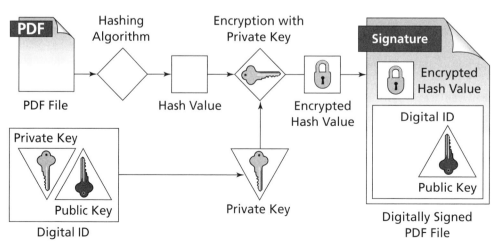

FIGURE A.1
The Basic Digital Signature Creation Process

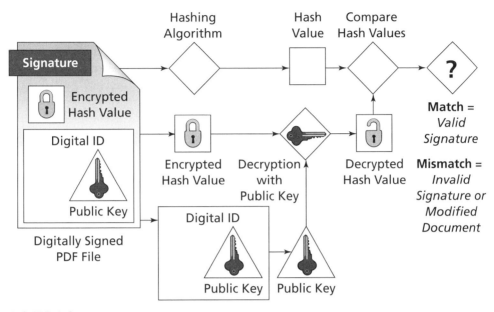

FIGURE A.2
The Basic Digital Signature Verification Process

validation of application software components to protect from corruption or malicious software.

The rest of this case study will explore how PDF digital signatures implement real world digital foundational requirements—establishing the identity of signers, preserving integrity of documents, maintaining the times and dates of signature events, and supporting mechanisms to provide for new concepts such as electronic originality.

IDENTITY

Issues relating to the foundation of *identity* are covered in Chapter 6. It is often important to know the identity of the actor that originated an event that unfolded in the digital realm. Who, for example, really signed the document? Who made the edit? Who filled out the form? Who caused the realm of bits to change the information it recorded?

At issue here is the question of how we know "who" did something, and what, in fact, does it mean to know "who"? The issue of *identity* is somewhat epistemological—it can be defined as the collection of those facts about an individual or organization that differentiate that individual from others. A person's name, social security number, driver's license number, age, gender, and physical description are all facts that contribute to an individual's identity. Different sets of facts may be more or less relevant or appropriate in different identity contexts. For example, the identity facts in a passport (name, address, date of birth, physical description, passport number) are generally a much stronger basis for personal identification than the facts presented by a library card (name, address, card number), but nevertheless, in the context of a library, it is probably not possible to check out books with a passport. Conceptual identities are traditionally represented by physical objects—documents or identification cards.

The relative level of trust with which any given physical identity card will be treated depends on several factors:

- Issuer: Who provided the identity card? Is it someone I trust? Is it a government or a private corporation?
- Identity Proofing: What steps were taken by the issuer to establish that this identity does in fact describe this person? Did they appear in person? What is the history and source of the information (antecedent data) presented in this identity?
- Tamper-proofing or tamper evidence: Is this identity what it purports to be? Has it been altered or fraudulently manufactured?

LEVELS OF ASSURANCE IN DIGITAL IDENTITY

The accepted level of trust for any given identity is known as its "level of assurance." A passport is a physical identity card with a very high level of assurance. A library card usually has a relatively low level of assurance. These concepts extend into forms of electronic identity as well.

An electronic identity is simply an extension of identity concepts into a machine-readable form. In a PDF digital signature, the identity of the signer can be established through a *digital identity* (*digital ID*). There are various types of digital IDs that can provide different levels of assurance. They share the same basic requirements of issuance, proofing, and physical and electronic tamper evidence, as well as identity-management infrastructures and authentication mechanisms. Collectively, these elements contribute to the assurance level of any digital ID. As with physical identity cards, there are many technical and nontechnical facets to digital ID issuance and management. Note that a weakness or shortcoming in any of these elements of identity can constitute an overall lowering of assurance for not just the associated digital identities, but also for any digital signatures that may have been created by them.

Just as a digital signature is a specific type of electronic signature, a digital identity can be thought of as a specific type of electronic identity. An electronic identity is simply a collection of identity facts stored electronically. An electronic identity can simply be the information in a service such as an online account with a web retailer or investment portal. Logging in to the website establishes your identity to that particular service.

A digital identity, however, can be electronic identity information in the form of a *digital certificate* that is bound to a public/private key pair. A collection of digital identities and the systems that manage and support them is known as a *public key infrastructure* (PKI). Digital IDs can be used to create digital signatures in PDF documents. PDF digital signatures can directly incorporate information from a digital identity, and as with most types of digital signature, include a hash value that was encrypted with a digital ID's private key. Digital IDs may be associated with an individual or with an organization. The use of digital IDs is not limited to digital signatures; they can also be used for applications such as access control, or for electronic identity authentication for confidentiality purposes.

ISSUANCE OF DIGITAL IDS

The issuance process for digital IDs is critical to the overall assurance of a PKI and any associated digital signatures. The foundation of the issuance process is the establishment and verification of the identity of an individual or organization that will be issued a digital ID. Elements to consider include whether or not an individual was seen in-person by the issuer ("in-person proofing"); the nature and verification methods of other forms of identity (antecedent data); and how the public and private keys for the digital ID are electronically generated, transferred, or installed. It is also important to consider how the digital ID is stored and accessed once issued. Storage and access of higher-assurance digital IDs should provide for both physical and electronic tamper evidence. Passwords to restrict access and physical hardware tokens or smart cards, or server-managed storage all provide increased tamper evidence as well as access control. Diligence by the individual in maintaining secure control of the private key can also affect the level of assurance one has in the digital ID and the digital signatures created with it. Standards do exist for issuance policy and assurance level, though in the United States most are not currently targeted at issuance to the general public. Examples and additional information about issuance and assurance can be found in the National Institute of Standards and Technology's (NIST's) Special Publication 800-63 *Electronic Authentication Guidelines*, and the European Union's Directive 1999/93/EC on a community framework for electronic signatures (see Bibliography).

AUTHENTICATION

As discussed in Chapter 6, storing identity information electronically requires the introduction of the concept of *authentication*, or *authenticating,* to unlock the use of an electronic identity. Authentication is a confusing word for lawyers who are not information security specialists, because it is so close to the older and more general word "authenticity," and to the same word "authentication," which is the preliminary foundation laid to admit a document or thing into evidence. What authentication, or authenticating, means in the parlance of information security circles is determining that a user, the "who," is the authentic person or agent whom they purport to be.

Authenticating means "challenging" or "testing" a "who" in some manner before allowing the electronic identity to be used. Consumer-level authentication is often simply a user name and/or passphrase on a website. More high-assurance authentication can incorporate elements like hardware devices (tokens, smart cards), biometrics (fingerprint readers), and/or "out of band" questions (offline information known only to an account holder). The more disparate elements that are introduced, the higher the "factor" of the authentication. *Multifactor* authentication means employing not just multiple steps, but multiple methods of authentication. A simple user name and passphrase is *single-factor*, while a smart card (credit-card-sized device with an embedded microchip) or biometric (matching a person's physical characteristics such as fingerprints or retinal patterns to a known sample) and passphrase is considered *two-factor*. A smart card, biometric, and passphrase together would be considered a very strong *three-factor* authentication method. Assessing some authentication factors can be difficult. Requiring two different passwords does not constitute two-factor authentication in most cases, but requiring a password and the person to identify random charges from a bank statement may be considered two-factor in some circumstances. Standards for authentication vary by identity type, but authentication is generally a factor in assurance. For digital IDs and digital signatures in PDF, stronger authentication methods can provide a higher assurance of identity, which contributes to higher assurance digital signatures.

PKI Hierarchies

One powerful feature of a PKI is the ability to share, link, or "federate trust" between parties. This means that unlike a single-purpose electronic identity that may be limited to a particular web application or service, the digital IDs in a PKI have a higher degree of portability; trust is not necessarily limited to a single application or organization. PDF signatures can include this information to better establish the trustworthiness of a signature. A trust model in a PKI starts with a "trust root" or "trust anchor" digital ID or *root certificate*. A root certificate is a digital ID that is trusted by all other digital IDs in a PKI. A root certificate's private key must be stored very securely, and its usage is closely regulated by strict policies and procedures. The typical role of the root certificate is to digitally sign other digital IDs. Typically, in a commercial or enterprise PKI, a root certificate does not sign the digital IDs of individual users; rather, it signs *intermediate certificates*. Intermediate certificates are usually used to sign the digital IDs of individual users ("end entities" in a PKI). Intermediate certificates' categories and tiers may reflect different divisions within an organization, or different levels of assurance. Intermediate certificates are used to sign not only individual digital IDs, but also the digital IDs used by networked services, and digital IDs of systems that support the PKI itself. A PDF signature can contain the digital identity of the signer as well as any intermediate certificates and the root certificate itself. Including certificates inside the signed document makes the signature more portable and archivable; it ensures that certificates will be available for the signature verification process even if the application verifying the document does not have access to the PKI resources associated with the certificates and digital IDs.

REVOCATION AND EXPIRATION

As with many physical identity cards, digital IDs generally have expiration dates. Digital IDs may also be revoked by their issuer for various reasons, including fraud, theft, cancellation, or end of employment/association with issuing organization. *Revocation-checking* is an optional (but recommended) functionality of a PKI to provide up-to-date information about the status of a digital ID. Revocation-checking may be performed at any time (with network access to the PKI) by a software application that supports it, and is commonly performed as part of the process when a digital signature is created and/or verified. The most common forms of revocation checking today are CRL (Certificate Revocation List) and OCSP (Online Certificate Status Protocol) servers. These are typically supplied by network resources that can be located by a software application using information found in the digital ID, though some types of information may be cached locally on a user's computer. To access a CRL, an application downloads it from a specified location. A CRL should enumerate all digital IDs that have been revoked by the issuer. OCSP information is obtained from an OCSP service by requesting information about the status of a specified digital ID. CRLs and OCSP messages themselves are usually digitally signed to better attest to their authenticity, and may include other features for additional assurance. Applications that create PDF signatures should support revocation-checking at signing and verification. Some applications may also support the embedding of revocation information into a PDF at the time of signing. The embedding of revocation information is supported in PDF digital signatures, and it can provide additional portability and long-term viability for a digital signature by reducing the dependency on remote PKI resources over time. Embedding revocation information can also provide additional assurance around the time of signing (see the discussion of time later in this chapter for more information).

SELF-SIGNED CERTIFICATES AND OTHER SCENARIOS

Although trust can be established for PDF digital signatures through path-building and validation in PKI, there are other models for sharing trust around PDF signatures. While the specific type of technology may differ from PKI models, the underlying requirements of identity management and trust are the same—issuance, authentication, and tamper evidence. The application of these elements in any trust model should be evaluated for consistent and appropriate levels of assurance. For example, some PDF software applications provide users with the capability of creating "self-signed" digital IDs that can be used to create PDF digital signatures. Self-signed digital IDs share many features with digital IDs in a PKI, but they do not chain to a trusted root certificate. This means that while a PDF digital signature created with a self-signed digital ID may provide document integrity (see "Integrity of Information," below), it does not by itself provide identity in the manner of a digital ID associated with a PKI. However, self-signed digital ID signatures may be combined with other mechanisms of identity to provide levels of assurance similar to those of PKI-based digital IDs. An example of this would be a web portal that authenticates users and allows them to submit PDF documents that were signed with self-signed digital IDs. In this case, the proof of integrity would be provided by the PDF digital signature, but the proof of identity would be provided by the records of the user logging in before uploading the PDF. This type of system is not necessarily as flexible or portable as one based fully on PKI, but when implemented with the appropriate controls, it can provide a similar level of assurance for certain applications.

Accordingly, the PDF file format allows the creation of a foundation for identity. An electronic signature, often a digital signature, can be used so that there can be strong or trusted verification that a certain person or entity was in fact the person or entity that caused an event to occur—usually by "signing" a transaction, such a sending an e-mail or signing a contract or letter, for example.

INTEGRITY OF INFORMATION

In technology terms, a document's *integrity* can have different definitions, depending on the context. Integrity features can be either a capability to *resist* modification, or be a means of providing *evidence* of modification. PDF digital signatures, by themselves, are not a means of *preventing* document modification. Other technologies, such as digital rights management and encryption, are focused on blocking or directly resisting the modification of documents. While some technologies combine these elements with electronic signature features, PDF signatures are mainly intended to provide an integrity foundation by providing *evidence* of modification of documents—not to block or prevent modification directly. This form of integrity, or *modification-detection* capability, is sometimes referred to as a *tamper-evident* functionality. With this function, an electronic document or file becomes "testable" as to the integrity of the file or data involved.

INTEGRITY BUILDS ON IDENTITY

Integrity alone does not create a digital signature. To be considered a digital signature, integrity must build upon identity. If a document's integrity is not bound to an identity (in a trustworthy manner), then such integrity could conceivably have been provided by *any* identity. For example, consider a paper check, or bank draft. Paper checks have physical tamper-evident features designed to provide evidence of any modification of their written content. However, if a fraudulent user had access to *blank* checks, then the tamper-evident features would be of little or no value to integrity, because a fraudulent user could *create* checks that showed no evidence of tampering and circumvention of tamper-evidence features. Unless the recipient or bank verified the *identity* on the check—in the form of matching physical signatures—the *integrity* features alone would provide no protection. This holds true to an even greater extent for electronic documents, which can be much simpler to create or duplicate, or undetectably modify.

Accordingly, digital signatures in PDF *bind* identity to integrity by using the private key that is likewise bound to a signer's digital identity to encrypt the hash value of a document. Similar to authentication, the integrity features are only as strong as the digital identity used to create them: the lower the assurance level of a digital identity, the lower the assurance level of those digital signatures that are created with it. Similarly, if the holder of the private key, which is usually stored in a hardware or software token, loses control of that key, then the use of a private key to give identity evidence fails as a complete regime.

BASIC INTEGRITY

Integrity in a basic digital signature works in a simple manner. A simple digital signature (see Figure A.3) offers integrity of the signed content through its ability to indicate whether or not the content has been modified since the signature was created. This modification detection may be very precise to the level of a single character, blank space, color, or even pixel (a pixel, or *picture element,* is the single smallest displayed point in an electronic image).

However, at this basic functionality level, a signature, and therefore the integrity of the file, is simply either valid or not valid. This means that the capability of a simple signature is limited to application in simple processes.

Most real-world processes, however, are considerably more complex than this simple example. Documents are often modified in acceptable ways during their life cycle. Documents are edited, forms are completed, metadata is changed, and multiple parties may execute multiple signatures. To be effective in real-world processes, these and other changes all need to be accommodated in an auditable manner without causing a digital signature to invalidate absolutely.

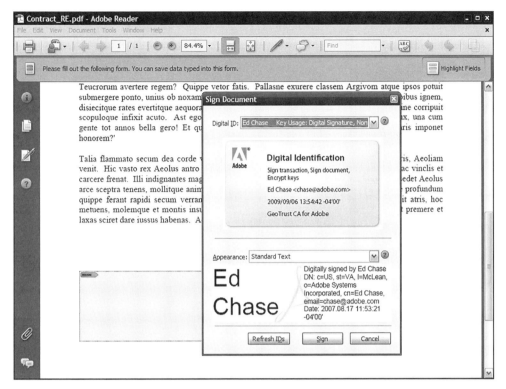

FIGURE A.3
Digitally Signing a PDF Document with Adobe Reader

Adobe product screen shot reprinted with permission from Adobe Systems Incorporated.

PDF digital signatures can extend the simple digital signature concept with function-ality that supports these and other real-world document requirements. PDF documents can be digitally signed, edited, and digitally signed again—multiple times—while pre-serving both the original signed versions as well as all changes and new digital signatures that are applied.

Paper documents can be easily signed and edited between signatures. PDF takes this a step further, not only supporting this sort of intuitive workflow, but also adding audit-ability and accountability to the process. PDF documents can retain not just the final version, but also versions, changes, and metadata between. This means that modifying a digitally signed PDF document does not necessarily "invalidate" a document's digi-tal signature. Modifying a digitally signed PDF usually results in the creation of a new internal "version"" of the document, while retaining all previously signed versions. See Figure A.4.

INCREMENTAL UPDATES

Most electronic document formats are designed for in-line authoring and editing. Word processor or office-type documents are often referred to as "native-file formats" in that

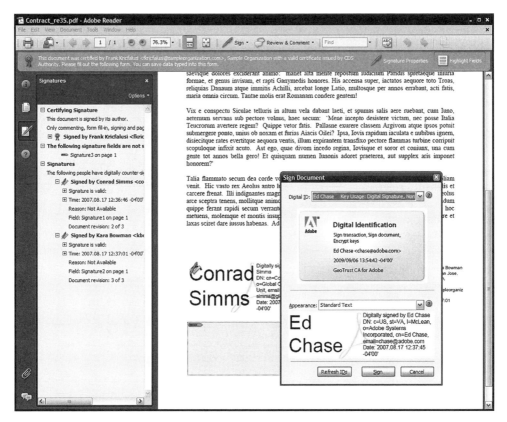

FIGURE A.4
Multiple Digital Signatures in a PDF Document with Adobe Reader.

Adobe product screen shot reprinted with permission from Adobe Systems Incorporated.

they are a file format designed specifically to accommodate direct editing in a particular software application. When a word processor changes a block of text in its native-file format, those changes are made directly to the section of text being modified in the native file. As discussed throughout this book, this means that the changes replace the original text, in many cases removing it altogether. The file size of a native-format document increases or decreases as text and other elements are added or removed, a simple reflection of the current state of the document. While this is a suitable mechanism for the first stages of individual authoring, it is not well-suited for controlled, shared, auditable, or signed documents. Because they have difficulty managing modifications or versions, most native-file formats only support the most basic tamper-evident or digital signature features. PDF however, uses a different approach.

PDF is not a native-file format. The most common PDF files are created by capturing a document from its native application during a virtual printing process. A PDF generating application effectively "prints" the native document through the authoring application into a PDF file, compressing, condensing, and organizing the output. This results in a compact and portable document that no longer depends on its original authoring application for viewing. A PDF created in this manner is not simply a bitmap image.[1] However, it is no longer directly editable in the same manner as a native-file format.

PDF accommodates modifications differently than most native-file formats. When modifications are made to a PDF document, the changes do not directly alter the corresponding sections of original file. Instead, the changes are added at the end of the PDF file, while instructions within the PDF are changed to reflect this (see Figure A.5). The new instructions will direct a PDF viewing application to use the updated sections instead of the originals. This means that PDFs (when digitally signed) can only increase in file size (unless digital signatures and modifications are stripped out through a process sometimes referred to as "flattening"). When a PDF viewer renders a modified PDF document, it substitutes the latest modified sections for the original sections. To the user, the document simply appears to have been directly modified, yet all previous content is still retained.

This document-versioning capability is effectively combined with digital signatures in PDF. Each time a PDF document is digitally signed, a new signed version is created that incorporates any changes since any previous signed version. This means that a PDF document can not only be digitally signed multiple times, but it can also indicate what, if any, modifications have occurred between digital signatures (see Figure A.6). Accordingly, an audit trail of the versions that each user signed is created that can be tested for integrity, and therefore, for authenticity (see Figure A.7).

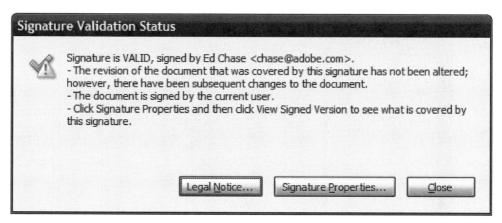

FIGURE A.5
Signature Validation Status of a PDF Document with Adobe Reader

Adobe product screen shot reprinted with permission from Adobe Systems Incorporated.

---

1. A "bitmap" or "raster" image is a data file representing a generally rectangular grid of pixels, or points, each with assigned color values. Digital photographs and scanned images are generally bitmap images.

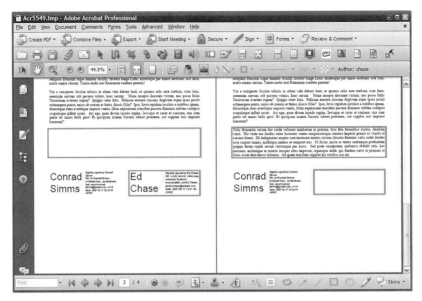

FIGURE A.6
Examining Changes Between Signatures with Adobe Acrobat

Adobe product screen shot reprinted with permission from Adobe Systems Incorporated.

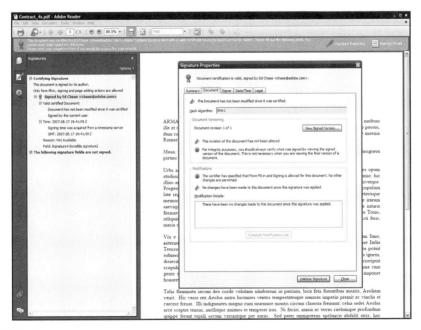

FIGURE A.7
A Certified Document with Permissions in Adobe Reader

Adobe product screen shot reprinted with permission from Adobe Systems Incorporated.

TIME EVIDENCE IN PDF

As discussed in Chapter 5, the time a digital event happened is often an important fact. Accordingly, many transactions require or benefit from the definitive establishment of the time and date at which they occurred. Many basic electronic signatures do not provide this information, or may only provide it in an ad-hoc or secondary manner. For example, it may be possible to estimate when an individual sent an e-mail or submitted a web form based on server or system logs, but these mechanisms tend to be reactive or forensic in nature, and were not designed specifically as features to give useable and strong evidence of the time of events.

There are a number of methods for establishing the time and date at which a digital signature occurred. As with testing authenticity, a trusted identity plays an important role in the proof of time. Time verification must be associated with a trusted identity or service to avoid being arbitrary or ambiguous. Evidence of time verification should also ideally be logically associated with and/or embedded within a signed document to avoid long-term dependencies on external systems. In its association with a document, evidence of time should also provide integrity features, and/or be subject to the integrity features of a signed document. PDF can directly support several methods for establishing the time of a PDF digital signature, including the capture of time values from revocation information, and the use of industry standards for *trusted time stamps* (see discussion later in this chapter).

THE TIME OF SIGNING

When a PDF digital signature is applied without any special consideration for time, the time of signing that is recorded by the signature is generally obtained directly from the signing computer's operating system itself. Time and date values obtained in this manner may or may not be accurate. As discussed in Chapter 5, many users have direct control over their computer's time settings and are able to manually adjust the time. It is possible for a user with this access to purposefully back-date her computer, or to forget to reset the time after a system malfunction. If she then digitally signs a PDF document without any definitive time source, the time and date of the digital signature will reflect the incorrect time obtained from the computer. Only in situations where a user does not have the ability (via system administrator permissions) to alter the time settings for his or her computer can the system time alone be considered definitive. However, in such a scenario, the determination of the time of signing becomes a separate element or proof outside the document, and will necessitate examination of policies and procedures and whether they were followed in the questioned instance.

TIME FROM REVOCATION INFORMATION

One opportunity for testing or verifying the time of signing is to consult *revocation information* that may be embedded within a digitally signed PDF document. The existence of any revocation information relies on the digital identity used for signing being part of a PKI that supports revocation-checking. Embedding of revocation information at the time of signing is an optional feature for PDF digital signatures. Embedded revocation information's main feature is to provide a long-term and self-contained record of the sign-time validity status of the signer's digital ID. For this information to be able to verify the status of a digital ID at the time of signing, it must include the time and date ranges of its own validity. This information can then be used to determine or verify the time and date of signing. The range and precision of this information varies. Revocation methods such as OCSP (Online Certificate Status Protocol: see Figure A.8) can help identify time and date of signing to within seconds or minutes, while other

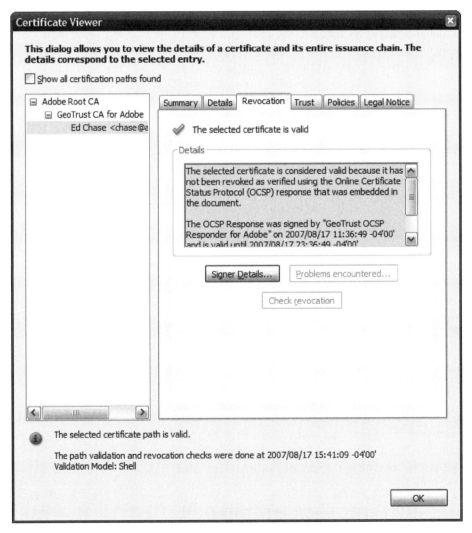

FIGURE A.8
Viewing a Certificate Path and Embedded Revocation Information
with Adobe Reader

Adobe product screen shot reprinted with permission from Adobe Systems Incorporated.

methods such as a CRL (Certificate Revocation List) may be limited to a range of hours or days. Revocation information is usually itself obtained in a digitally signed format from a trusted PKI resource identified within the signer's digital ID. The benefit of this approach to time authentication is that it takes advantage of common trusted PKI infrastructure features and components. The potential drawbacks are that this information is not necessarily intended as a definitive source of time, and depending on the revocation method, it may not provide a suitable degree of precision for all transactions. Revocation information can also be used in conjunction with other methods, such as trusted time stamps, to provide even stronger levels of assurance around time.

TRUSTED TIME STAMPS

As discussed extensively in Chapter 5, a *trusted time stamp* is a formal method of determining the time of a digital event. Trusted time stamps in PDF are generally based on the Internet Engineering Task Force (IETF) standard RFC 3161 (see Bibliography), as discussed here, but may employ other methods. A trusted time stamp incorporates a trusted source of time, includes its own internal digital signatures to authenticate the time value, and is bound to the digitally signed document (see Figure A.9). In a PDF document, trusted time stamps are used in directly in conjunction with a PDF digital signature, and are applied during their creation process. A time-stamped PDF digital signature can provide high-assurance verification of the time that a digital signature was created. Trusted time stamps do require specialized PKI components or services in the form of a *time stamp authority* (TSA). A TSA may be an actual service within an organization's PKI, or it may be a third-party service operated by an outside organization. The time values used for trusted time stamps are usually provided by a link to a secure and highly accurate time source, such as a government agency's atomic clock.

When creating a trusted time stamp, an application first sends a request, along with a hash value to a specified TSA. In PDF signatures, this is not the hash value of the document itself; rather, it is the hash value of the *digital signature* that will be associated with the time stamp. Because the digital signature already contains a signed hash value for the document content, this means that the hash value that is sent to the TSA is able to authenticate time for *both* the document content as well as the digital signature itself.

The use of third-party TSA services can introduce additional safeguards against errors or deliberate tampering, because they can be neutral parties outside the control of an organization or its other PKI providers. Because only hash values are transmitted as part of the trusted-time-stamp process, third-party TSAs can generally provide this additional assurance without exposing any potentially confidential data to them in the process. As with other PKI services, trust for a TSA is provided by the digital IDs that it uses to digitally sign its time stamps. To fully verify a time-stamped PDF, the verifying application must be able to validate the TSA's identity through the same PKI methods used to validate the digital IDs of the signer or the revocation information. The digital ID of a TSA must be traceable to a source trusted by the organization. The TSA's digital ID does not necessarily need to be traceable to the same source of trust as the digital ID of the signer, though its security and assurance levels should be at a commensurate level with other PKI elements in the organization.

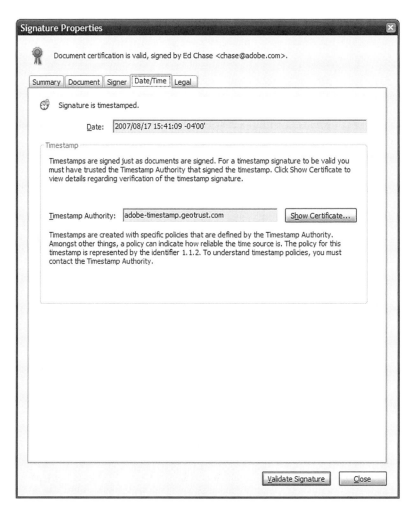

FIGURE A.9
Viewing Time Stamp Information in Adobe Reader

Adobe product screen shot reprinted with permission from Adobe Systems Incorporated.

USABILITY, CONTEXT, AND PRESERVATION

Interpreting the contents and "validity" of any digital signature may present a number of challenges for casual users. It can be difficult for software developers to take a simple or generic approach, because PDF documents are used in many different workflows and in different industry-, legal-, or regulatory-specific rules around what constitutes a "valid" digital signature. PDF offers a variety of ways to visually display signature elements, status, and details. The on-document representation of a PDF digital signature is known as a *signature appearance*. A signature appearance may reflect information from the digital ID of the signer, and may include the time and date of signing (see earlier discussion of "Time Evidence in PDF" for more information), as well as images, seals, logos, or images of handwritten signatures. A signature appearance may also include a "reason for signing."

The reason-for-signing concept is the source of many differences in opinion and implementation across industries and locales. Some regulations, such as the FDA's 21 CFR Part 11 (see Bibliography), specifically require that electronic signatures include such information, while many banking applications specifically prohibit its use on some documents out of concern it may alter the context of the signature or change the meaning of the document. PDF supports the use of a reason for signing as required, but its presence can be enabled or disabled as required by many PDF signing applications. If a reason for signing is captured as part of the signing process, it will generally become part of the signature and thus part of the digitally signed PDF document.

In many PDF software applications that support signing, signature appearances are not generally exclusive to any particular digital ID (see Figures A.10 and A.11). It is usually possible to use a single digital ID with multiple signature appearances or a single signature appearance with multiple digital IDs. A PDF signature appearance will generally display only a limited amount of the available information for a digital signature. PDF viewing applications that support signature verification may be capable of accessing more-detailed signature information, including digital identity, revocation and trust chain details, versioning information, time information, and other specific details. The access to digital signature information in a PDF is implementation-specific, and may not be supported by all PDF viewers.

VISUAL APPEARANCES

PDF digital signatures may or may not be visible on a page in a document. "Invisible" signatures contain most of the same information as their visible counterparts, with the exception of appearance information or images. Both visible and invisible signatures

FIGURE A.10
Four Examples of Signature Appearances in Adobe Reader

FIGURE A.11
Signature Status in Adobe Reader
(Left to right) Valid; Unknown identity; Invalid; Valid with modifications.

Adobe product screen shot reprinted with permission from Adobe Systems Incorporated.

have the capability to support the identity and integrity features discussed in the previous sections, and both certification and approval signatures may be visible or invisible. While visible signatures are often interactive in a PDF viewer, allowing a user to select them directly to view signature information, invisible signatures generally require a PDF viewer with the ability to display signature information in a separate window or interface. Any visual representation of a PDF digital signature should always be examined beyond a cursory glance at the appearance. A verifier should examine visual signature appearances by interacting with them and establishing that the signature appearance does correspond to an actual digital signature and is not merely an image of a signature appearance. Desktop PDF software applications that support digital signatures may also offer alternative methods for examining digital signatures, such as dedicated windows that may enumerate status and details for all signatures for a given document (see Figure A.11). Such interfaces are helpful in verifying the correspondence of signature images and digital signatures in a document, and should always be used if available.

HANDWRITTEN SIGNATURES

While the concepts of digital signatures are finding more mainstream usage, it is not uncommon for many users to attribute a significant level of trust to an image of an individual's handwritten signature, stamp, or seal on an electronic document. Without additional technology features or process controls, there is very little technical reason for an individual to trust such an imaged signature, often even less so than a physical signature on paper. Image-only signatures are easily reproducible and transferable with even the simplest software applications. In a PDF, handwritten signature images may appear as part of a signature appearance, though this should always be verified by examining the signature appearance and verification state, rather than relying on the signature appearance alone (see Figure A.12). These signature images may be captured from a touchscreen tablet PC, signing pad, scanned image, or other means, and are usually bound to a document through the digital signature. In most cases, handwritten signature images in digital signature fields are simply a visual addition to a digital signature, and offer no additional assurance beyond the digital signature itself. However, some PDF applications employ specialized biometric-capable signature pads and software that capture and incorporate additional identifying information from the physical signature. These features are not native to PDF signatures, but are implemented as extensions (extensions

Handwritten or "digitized" signature.　　Digitized signature with status icon.

FIGURE A.12A AND B
Digital Signature with Status Icon and Appearance in Adobe Reader

are permitted in PDF), and access to their additional functionality may require application plug-ins or specialized software.

CONTEXT

An electronic or digital signature may authenticate either part or all of a given document. This varies, depending on the application type, as well as technology or other factors. In the case of a simple web form, an electronic signature may only authenticate the *data* in the form fields, not the form fields themselves. Likewise, electronically signed data rendered in a web browser may be formatted by way of an external "stylesheet" (a stylesheet is a template to provide formatting for unformatted data) or other formatting mechanism that flows the data into a template to produce the final document. In these and similar scenarios, an electronic signature does not necessarily authenticate the entire document, only the unformatted data. While this may be appropriate in some situations, it may result in signatures that lack context, have external dependencies, or are not suitable for preservation. In such situations where signed data has dependencies on external systems or on templates or other documents, those external resources themselves may or may not be authenticated at all, or not at an appropriate level of assurance to match the signed data itself. This can result in documents and electronic signatures that are less portable between individuals or systems, and it has the potential to create ambiguous situations where only *part* of a transaction may be authenticated.

For example, a scenario such as this could result in the authenticated sections of a purchase order containing the items to be purchased, but not the terms of the sale, resulting in potential ambiguity over exactly what was electronically signed. A PDF digital signature usually authenticates the entire document. This means that both the data and the presentation of that data are "signed" as part of the signature process (see Figure A.13). A PDF digital signature can authenticate a document's text, formatting, embedded fonts, layout, images, pagination, metadata, form data, annotations, scripts, attachments, and comments. This reduces the reliance on unsigned external dependencies when viewing, signing, or verifying signatures. It makes the document more self-contained, and provides a more portable and transferable record than data-only signatures. There are certain situations where PDF forms may use data-only signatures, or XML digital

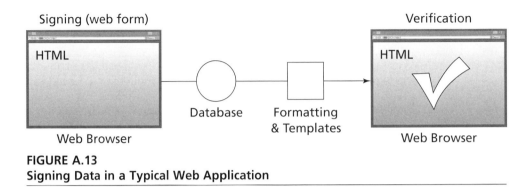

FIGURE A.13
Signing Data in a Typical Web Application

signatures, instead of PDF digital signatures. These implementations are subject to the same implications of context as the web-based form example just discussed.

To verify the signature in a typical web application, the "document" must be reconstructed as it appeared to the signer, including the application of external formatting, to fully evaluate the signature and its content. In a PDF, however, the entire document is typically signed, providing integrity for both data and presentation context.

PRESERVATION

The preservation capability of a document is related to context, but has broader implications. Preservation is more indicative of the overall long-term ability of the entire document to be viewed accurately and consistently. There are many different types of electronic "documents". An electronic document can be a "native file format," an XML data file or HTML webpage, a scanned image of a paper document, or a PDF file. Most electronic document types are not ideal for long-term preservation roles. Native-file formats usually depend heavily on their application software and resources of their host operating system. Over time, applications and operating systems become obsolete and are replaced. Newer versions do not always provide the same resources to accurately or

FIGURE A.14
Signing a PDF

consistently support older formats. HTML and XML have variable views. This flexibility makes them ideal for some situations, but also means that they may not always view or print consistently with different systems or software applications. Scanned or bitmap images are a basic means of preserving visual content exactly, and can produce very precise results, but they lack the ability to support selectable, searchable text or structured data, making them difficult to use for searches or retrieval of accurate information.

PDF documents can provide the benefits of each of these formats, without many of the drawbacks. PDF can provide the accurate and precise layout and formatting of image files, but can also include multipage, selectable, searchable text. PDF files can also include the specific resources used to create the document. Embedded elements such as fonts, color settings, metadata, and structure information can provide the information needed to render a PDF with a high degree of consistency and accuracy using many different types of computer hardware and software. The PDF/A standard (see Bibliography) was developed with the cooperation of Adobe, the National Archives and Records Administration, the U.S. courts, and the Internal Revenue Service to better identify the features of PDF best suited to long-term preservation and archiving. Preservation time frames for document formats are especially critical, considering that many basic native-file format documents lack reliable application support after durations of less than ten years. Many documents (such as mortgage documents) now have preservation requirements exceeding forty years, making a long-term capable format like PDF a much more suitable option. The ISO PDF/A standard provides guidance on PDF preservation, and may be used as a guidance when using PDF in an archival role. PDF/A itself is not the ideal format for all PDF files, however. In many cases, PDF/A does not support the requirements of electronic documents during the active phases of their life cycle, and is primarily targeted at static content entering its archival phase. Archival PDF documents are often converted to strict PDF/A conformance at the end of their active life cycle. Even when strict PDF/A compliance is not desirable, the PDF/A standard can also be consulted more generally for guidance on the effects of various PDF features on the self-contained nature and representational fidelity of PDF files over their entire life cycle (see Bibliography).

CONCLUSION

Appendix A has described the basic elements of PDF's digital signature functionality, which provides the function of a strong test for integrity, a strong test for identity, the possibility of trusted time information, and ways in which user of an information system can customize such functionalities, including who is authorized or has permission to do what, and what appears to what users. These capabilities can be applied to many types of digitally signed documents in wide range of different use cases. PDF can support many different levels of assurance for digital signatures, and PDF can be part of systems that meet many electronic signature laws and regulations. When implemented appropriately, the concepts of identity, integrity, preservation, time, and originality all can be met through the use of PDF and PDF-based systems.

It is critical to reiterate that PDF by itself, or any document format or technology alone, is rarely sufficient to meet the requirements for electronic signatures that are as readily accepted as their paper counterparts. Legally binding electronic signatures must include process-appropriate policy and procedure around each of these core concepts. Taking this into consideration, though, the core strength of PDF is that when implemented in such a manner, it can provide the ability to incorporate significant evidence around these concepts directly into the electronic document itself. While many electronic signature systems rely on numerous different systems to provide signature evidence for a single transaction, PDF can create a stand-alone, self-contained electronic signature record.

BIBLIOGRAPHY

Adobe Systems, "PDF Reference, Sixth Edition, version 1.7," Adobe Systems, http:// www.adobe.com/devnet/pdf/pdf_reference.html

International Organization for Standardization (ISO). The following standards are available through http://www.iso.org/:
- ISO 15930-1:2001, *Graphic technology—Prepress digital data exchange—Use of PDF—Part 1: Complete exchange using CMYK data (PDF/X-1 and PDF/X-1a)*
- ISO 19005-1. *Document management—Electronic document file format for long-term preservation—Part 1: Use of PDF (PDF/A)*
- ISO/DIS 24517, *Document management—Engineering document format using PDF—Part 1: Use of PDF 1.6 (PDF/E)*

World Wide Web Consortium (W3C). The following publications are available through the W3C Web site at http://www.w3.org/:
- Extensible Markup Language (XML) 1.1 http://www.w3.org/TR/xml11/
- HTML 4.01 Specification http://www.w3.org/TR/html401/

United Nations Commission on International Trade Law, "UNCITRAL Model Law on Electronic Signatures", UNCITRAL, http://www.uncitral.org/uncitral/en/uncitral_ texts/electronic_commerce.html

Electronic Signatures In Global and National Commerce Act (ESIGN), http://frwebgate .access.gpo.gov/cgi-bin/getdoc.cgi?dbname=106_cong_public_laws&docid=f:publ229 .106

Uniform Electronic Transactions Act (UETA), National Conference of State Legislatures, http://www.ncsl.org/programs/lis/CIP/ueta-statutes.htm

NIST's Special Publication 800-63 Electronic Authentication Guideline, National Institute of Science and Technology, http://csrc.nist.gov/publications/nistpubs/800-63/ SP800-63V1_0_2.pdf

EU Directive 1999/93/EC on a Community framework for electronic signatures, http:// www.signatur.rtr.at/en/repository/legal-directive-20000119.html

Internet Engineering Task Force (IETF) Requests for Comments (RFC) 3161, Internet X.509 Public Key Infrastructure Time-Stamp Protocol (TSP), http://www.rfc-editor .org

Title 21 Code of Federal Regulations (21 CFR Part 11), http://www.fda.gov/ora/compliance_ ref/part11/

eMortgages: A Specialized *Eunomia* Designed by a Group of Players

*Grace Powers**

Appendix A examined how a commonly used electronic document format, the Portable Document Format (PDF), can provide provable integrity and identity attributes for digital information, so that users of everyday digital records can strongly prove or test the authenticity of those records at future times. Thus, there are eunomic *regimes for stand-alone digital records like letters, memos, invoices, and so on. Any record that can be created in PDF format can have strongly provable integrity, as well as provable identity associations, depending on the implementation of signature functions.*

This case study illustrates that through careful planning, a group of players—if working together according to rules—can create highly specialized eunomic *regimes. Grace Powers explains how players in the mortgage industry joined together in a carefully-thought-out* eunomic *regime to recreate the concept of an original, unique negotiable instrument. Because there can be unlimited numbers of identical digital records, how could one have a digital promissory note? Why would there not be a risk that the note could be exactly copied, and the maker thereby owe not one mortgage, but many? What would this risk do to the transferability of the note, and indeed, to the foundation of the entire mortgage industry?*

Because logic and math can be combined in an ordered regime, whereby participants agree to abide by rules, there is a eunomic *digital solution even for these challenges. Lockean demonstrations are possible. Accordingly, this case study examines how the mortgage industry is attempting to achieve its goals in the digital world, including creating an analog of "originality" for digital promissory notes, among other things. One will see that the substantive law guides many of the outcomes.*

The key elements of a paper promissory note are that it records certain information (such as amount owed and other terms and conditions); that there is a record of "signing" or agreement to terms; and that there is only one such agreement that can be possessed

*Grace Powers is First Vice President and Senior Legal Counsel at Countrywide Financial Corporation in Calabasas, California, and is co-chair of the Mortgage Industry Standards Maintenance Organization's eMortgage Legal Issues Workgroup. The author would like to thank Bill Hultman, Dan McLaughlin, Igor Derensteyn, Jessica Bass, Ed Chase, Harry Gardner, and Matthew Powers for their invaluable comments on this chapter. The views expressed in this chapter are the author's own and do not necessarily represent the views of Countrywide Financial Corporation.

or owned. As one sees in Powers's scholarly explanation, a digital original is created by means of a registry, which tracks the "location" of the authoritative copy of the electronic note; the identity of the owner; and the electronic fingerprint (hash value) of the note. This creates a proxy for an original artifact by prohibiting anyone but the owner of the note from transferring the note, through several eunomic safeguards. For example, before any transfer, the owner must send a message to the registry, which message presents the fingerprint of the electronic note and the mortgage identification number. In addition, the message has to be digitally signed using a digital certificate issued by an accredited issuing authority.

eMORTGAGES: A DIGITAL ANALOG TO AN ORIGINAL PAPER PROMISSORY NOTE

The Paper Chase in the Mortgage Industry

The business of making loans, at its core, is an inherently inefficient process. Contributing to this inefficiency is the required participation of many unrelated players, including mortgage lenders, consumers, brokers, appraisers, closing agents, title insurers, investors, loan servicers, and document custodians. The volume and type of information that must be exchanged between such parties to evaluate a loan application, approve, close, and sell the loan slows down the process to the extent that it typically takes thirty to sixty days to complete a purchase-money loan transaction. In this age, that is a long time.

Additionally, the custom of having paper loan documents manually signed with a pen by borrowers adds to the potential for delay, because if there are errors or missed signatures on the loan documents, new documents have to be created, sent to the closing table, and signed again. Once signed, the paper loan documents must be sent back to the lender, manually reviewed for errors, imaged, transferred to third-party servicers and investors, and stored in vaults or document warehouses where they sit (sometimes never to be seen again). Although the mortgage industry has made progress automating certain processes, the industry continues to deal with an ever-growing mountain of paper and its associated costs.[1]

The mortgage industry, accordingly, has become interested in using electronic commerce to make these mortgage processes more efficient. Most of the innovation has been focused on automating the transfer, processing, indexing, storage, and validation of loan data (i.e., automated document preparation, automated underwriting, and automated compliance tools). One of the best examples of the use of electronic commerce is how the mortgage industry virtually eliminated the need to prepare assignments of mortgages whenever the mortgages were transferred to subsequent lenders and investors. In 1995, the Mortgage Bankers Association (MBA),[2] the national trade association for the real estate finance industry, created the Mortgage Electronic Registration Systems, Inc.[3]

---

1. *See* MISMO eMortgage Workgroup, *Cost Benefits of an eClosing Process,* version 1.0 (Apr. 27, 2006) *available at* http://www.mismo.org/SpecificationsAndGuidance/eMortgageSpecificatons.htm, at 6.

2. At that time, the MBA was known as the Mortgage Bankers Association of America. The MBA is headquartered in Washington, D.C. More information about the MBA can be found at http://www.mortgagebankers.org/.

3. MERSCORP, Inc., is the operating company that owns MERS System and MERS eRegistry and the parent company of Mortgage Electronic Registration Systems, Inc.

(MERS˚). In creating the MERS system, the MBA took as a model the Depository Trust Corporation (DTC), a participant-owned corporation that revolutionized the national securities market by allowing DTC participants to record securities transactions electronically, thereby eliminating the need to transfer paper stock certificates back and forth.[4]

The MERS system is a members-only service[5]—lenders, servicers, and others who wish to use the system must become MERS members and agree to abide by membership terms and conditions. This membership requirement creates a certain level of trust among MERS members that the transactions on the system can be relied upon. The system enables borrowers to name MERS as the mortgagee of record or nominee for a given lender on deeds of trust or mortgages that are recorded in county land records. The loans are then registered on the system and are assigned a unique mortgage identification number (MIN) for tracking purposes within the system. With the MIN, system users can electronically track changes in servicing and ownership rights over the life of the loan.[6] Therefore, if the originating lender were to sell the registered loan, there would be no need to file an assignment in the county land records to change the lienholder on the deed of trust or mortgage, because this information will automatically be tracked in the MERS system. Additionally, for lenders and investors who deal with mortgage loans on a national basis, the system acts as the centralized resource for tracking lienholder information rather than having to deal with over 3,000 counties nationwide to obtain the same information.

Was a Paperless Future Possible?

While the MERS system reduced the use of assignments, lenders were still left with paper promissory notes, deed of trusts, mortgages, and the mountain of consumer disclosures that are prevalent in the highly regulated business of mortgage lending. For the mortgage industry, the idea of a paperless future includes electronic mortgage documents (eMortgages), where the critical loan documentation—at a minimum the promissory note—is created, executed, transferred, and stored electronically.[7] The biggest stumbling block to eMortgages was the question of how to create an electronic promissory note (eNote) that can be freely transferred to subsequent owners (i.e., investors), while providing those owners the same assurances of authenticity and good title that are available under the laws governing paper promissory notes. In addition, the quandary of how to

---

4. Carson Mullen, *MERS: Tracking Loans Electronically,* Mortgage Banking (May 2000), available at http://www .mersinc.org/MersProducts/publications.aspx?mpid=1, at 64.

5. Although the MERS System is a members-only service for registrations and transactions, there is free public access via the Internet, and a toll-free telephone number for homeowners to access information about their mortgage loan on the MERS System. This free access also allows the title industry to determine the current mortgage servicer for a mortgage when MERS is the mortgagee.

6. *See* MISMO eMortgage Workgroup, *eMortgage Guide,* v. 2.0 (April 2006) ("eMortgage Guide") *available at* http://www.mismo.org/SpecificationsAndGuidance/eMortgageSpecificatons.htm, at 6. For more information on the MERS System, see the MERS website at www.mersinc.org. According to the MERS website, use of the MERS System will save $25 or more per loan.

7. MBA Residential Technology Committee, eMortgage Adoption Task Force, *eMortgage Glossary of Key Terms* v. 1.0 (Mar. 9, 2007) *available at* http://www.mortgagebankers.org/emortgage.

create an analog of the fact that there should be only one note, not many thousands or millions, must be resolved.

A paperless mortgage environment would eliminate the manual processes associated with paper and reduce the costs of printing, data re-entry, imaging, shipping, storing, managing, and disposing of paper records. An eMortgage process would also create the potential for more-efficient risk management through automated compliance and loan guideline checks, automated data transfer, and more-central controls over data security and record retention.[8] With robust back-up, off-site storage, indexing, and recovery programs, an eMortgage process can virtually eliminate lost loan documents and provide faster recovery from system failures caused by natural disasters or other unforeseen circumstances. Mortgage lenders who successfully implement eMortgages can market to consumers their opportunity to obtain faster loan decisions, shorter waits between loan approval and closing, the ability for advance review of loan terms and conditions, and less time spent at the closing table.

This case study discusses how the mortgage industry created an electronic analog to the paper promissory note by leveraging the concept of the MERS system in the creation of the MERS eRegistry. It will also discuss: (1) the importance of the promissory note to the mortgage industry; (2) historical fears regarding eNotes; (3) background on how the Electronic Signatures in Global and National Commerce Act and the Uniform Electronic Transactions Act paved the way for eNotes; (4) the functionality of the MERS eRegistry; (5) how the authenticity of an eNote can be validated; and (6) the challenges presented by technology obsolescence for records, including eNotes, that need to be retained for up to several decades.

Paving the Way for eMortgages—E-SIGN and UETA

The federal Electronic Signatures in Global and National Commerce Act (E-SIGN) and the state-enacted Uniform Electronic Transactions Act (UETA) were drafted to ensure that electronic transactions could enjoy the same validity and legal effect as transactions memorialized in paper.[9] The drafters of E-SIGN and UETA intended that the laws should facilitate the development of technology and not dictate any specific technology requirements for the creation of electronic contracts or other records.[10]

---

8. *See* eMortgage Guide, *supra* note 6, at 5. MISMO was established in 1999 by the Mortgage Bankers Association to develop, promote, and maintain voluntary electronic commerce standards for the mortgage industry.

9. *See* E-SIGN at 15 U.S.C.A. § 7001(a), and Section 7 of UETA. UETA was promulgated in 1999 by the National Conference of Commissioners on Uniform Laws (NCCUSL); see www.nccusl.org for a copy of UETA and other model acts. As of September 2007, forty-six states and the District of Columbia have adopted UETA in some form. Despite the introduction of UETA as a model act for adoption by the states, Congress became concerned regarding the slow pace of states enacting UETA and, for some states, making substantial changes to the uniform version of UETA. As a result, E-SIGN was enacted on June 30, 2000, to establish a uniform national standard for the treatment of electronic records and signatures. E-SIGN shares many of the same provisions in UETA, but adds special consent requirements for consumer disclosures. Discussion of the interaction between the federal E-SIGN and the state-enacted UETA and the preemption issues are beyond the scope of this chapter. For an a discussion of the relationship between E-SIGN and UETA, see Jeremiah S. Buckley, John P. Kromer, Margo H. K. Tank & R. David Whitaker, *The Law of Electronic Signatures and Records* (Glasser LegalWorks 2004) at 2.3-1 to 2.3-23.

10. *See* Prefatory Note to official version of the UETA as approved by the Conference of Commissioners on Uniform State Law (July 1999) *available at* www.nccusl.org; 15 U.S.C. § 7004.

UETA and certain provisions in E-SIGN set forth the basic rules of validity of electronic signatures and records, as follows:

- A record or signature may not be denied legal effect or enforceability solely because it is in electronic form;
- A contract may not be denied legal effect or enforceability solely because an electronic record was used in its formation;
- Any law that requires "a writing" will be satisfied by an electronic record; and
- Any signature requirement in the law will be met if there is an electronic signature.[11]

Both UETA and E-SIGN define a "record" as information that is inscribed on a tangible medium or that is stored in an electronic or other medium and is retrievable in perceivable form.[12] An "electronic record" is similarly defined under E-SIGN and UETA as a record created, generated, sent, communicated, received, or stored by electronic means.[13] As a result, any type of document, contract, or other record of information could meet the definition of an electronic record if it were created, used, or stored in a medium other than paper.

The Note: The Most Important Asset in the Mortgage Industry

The promissory note, which represents a mortgage loan, is the key document traded by lenders and investors on the secondary market. The secondary market refers to the market in which lenders and investors (such as Fannie Mae and Freddie Mac)[14] buy and sell existing mortgages and mortgage-backed securities.[15] This provides lenders with the liquidity to make additional mortgage loans.

In the paper world, a promissory note can be transferred from one party to another if it meets the negotiable instrument requirements of Uniform Commercial Code (UCC) Article 3. UCC § 3-104 provides that a negotiable promissory note must be:

- in writing;
- signed;
- an unconditional promise to pay a specified sum of money;
- payable on demand or at a definite time; and
- payable to the order of a named payee or to the person in possession of an instrument.

A promissory note that meets the above requirements can then be "negotiated" or transferred by physical delivery of the note from the original payee to a third party, with

---

11. UETA § 7. *See also* similar provision in E-SIGN at 15 U.S.C.A. § 7001(a).

12. UETA § 2(13); E-SIGN at 15 U.S.C.A. § 7006(9).

13. UETA § 2(7); E-SIGN at 15 U.S.C.A. § 7006(4).

14. Fannie Mae (the Federal National Mortgage Association) and Freddie Mac (the Federal Home Loan Mortgage Association) are government-sponsored enterprises (GSEs) that are authorized to make loans and loan guarantees. These GSEs buy and pool mortgages, then sell them as mortgage-backed securities to other investors. For more information, see Fannie Mae and Freddie Mac's websites at www.fanniemae.com and www.freddiemac.com, respectively.

15. A mortgage-backed security is a debt instrument or security that provides investors with an undivided interest in a pool of mortgage loans of similar maturities and interest rates.

an indorsement[16] and instruction to the borrower to make all future payments to the new note holder. If the third party takes delivery of the note (1) for value; (2) in good faith; and (3) without notice of defenses to payment or claims of third parties to an interest in the note, the third party qualifies as a "holder in due course" of the note.[17] As a holder in due course, the third-party transferee would be entitled to collect the debt evidenced by the promissory note from the borrower, despite many defenses a borrower may have.[18]

One of the issues for the mortgage industry, therefore, is to ensure that electronic promissory notes are as freely negotiable as their paper counterparts.

eNotes as Transferable Records under E-SIGN and UETA—UCC Article 3 Equivalence

While physical possession of a paper note plays an important role in negotiability, it is problematic to obtain physical possession of an *original* electronic note because of the potential for the creation of multiple, perfectly identical copies. The drafters of UETA and E-SIGN recognized this challenge and created substitutes for a paper negotiable instrument and possession with the concepts of "transferable record" and "control."[19] These concepts would create a parallel mechanism that would allow one party to transfer an eNote to a third party, and enable the third party transferee to have the same rights and defenses as a holder, holder in due course, or purchaser of a paper note under the UCC.[20]

---

16. In the mortgage industry, notes are typically "indorsed in blank," which allows the instrument to be payable to bearer, and may be negotiated by transfer of possession alone until specially indorsed to a specific person. *See* UCC § 3-205. Although E-SIGN uses the term "endorsement," both UETA and the UCC use the term "indorsement"—both terms have the same meaning.

17. UCC § 3-302.

18. Generally, the only defenses that can be raised against a holder in due course are uncommon ones, such as: (1) discharge in bankruptcy; (2) infancy; (3) duress; (4) lack of legal capacity; (5) illegality of the transaction; and (6) fraud in the inducement. *See* UCC § 3-305(a)(1).

19. Comment 1 to UETA Section 16 reveals the drafters' recognition of the importance of negotiability for electronic notes, as follows:

> Current business models exist which rely for their efficacy on the benefits of negotiability. A principal example, and one which informed much of the development of Section 16, involves the mortgage backed securities industry. Aggregators of commercial paper acquire mortgage secured promissory notes following a chain of transfers beginning with the origination of the mortgage loan by a mortgage broker. In the course of the transfers of this paper, buyers of the notes and lenders/secured parties for these buyers will intervene. For the ultimate purchaser of the paper, the ability to rely on holder in due course and good faith purchaser status creates the legal security necessary to issue its own investment securities which are backed by the obligations evidenced by the notes purchased. Only through their HIDC status can these purchasers be assured that third party claims will be barred. Only through their HIDC status can the end purchaser avoid the incredible burden of requiring and assuring that each person in the chain of transfer has waived any and all defenses to performance which may be created during the chain of transfer.

20. See Comment 1 to Section 16 of UETA, which states:

> The importance of facilitating the development of systems which will permit electronic equivalents is a function of cost, efficiency and safety for the records. The storage cost and space needed for the billions of paper notes and documents is phenomenal. Further, natural disasters can wreak havoc on the ability to meet legal requirements for retaining, retrieving and delivering paper instruments. The development of electronic systems meeting the rigorous standards of this section will permit retention of copies which reflect the same integrity as the original. As a result storage, transmission and

UETA and E-SIGN define a "transferable record" as an electronic record: (1) that would be a note under UCC Article 3 if the electronic record were in writing; and (2) in which the issuer (i.e., borrower) of the electronic record has expressly agreed that it will be treated as a transferable record.[21] E-SIGN additionally requires that the electronic record must relate to a loan secured by real property.[22] The key to transferability of an electronic record under UETA and E-SIGN is "control," which is basically the equivalent of possession in the paper world.

Critically, a person has control of a transferable record (eNote) if the system employed for evidencing the transfer of interests in the eNote reliably establishes that person as the person to whom the eNote was issued or transferred.[23] Using such a system, a party can transfer control of an eNote to a third party, thereby giving the third party the exclusive right to enforce or transfer ownership of the underlying debt obligation. Additionally, if the third-party transferee takes control for value, in good faith, and without notice of any defenses, the third-party transferee will enjoy the same rights and defenses as a holder in due course of an equivalent paper negotiable instrument under the UCC.[24]

Although the concept of "control" is a stand-alone provision, E-SIGN and UETA provide a safe harbor for determining that a system for transferring interests in the eNote is adequate. Under the safe harbor, a person is deemed to have control if the eNote is created, stored, and assigned in such a manner that:

1. A single authoritative copy exists that is unique, identifiable, and unalterable without detection.
2. The authoritative copy identifies the person asserting control as either to whom the transferable record was issued or the issuer.
3. The authoritative copy is communicated to and maintained by the person asserting control or its designated custodian.
4. Copies or revisions that add or change an identified assignee of the authoritative copy can be made only with the consent of the person asserting control.
5. Each copy of the authoritative copy and any copy of a copy is readily identifiable as a copy that is not the authoritative copy.
6. Any revision of the authoritative copy is readily identifiable as authorized or unauthorized.[25]

The system for evidencing the transfer of interests can use either a third-party registry or technological safeguards, as long as such system is shown to reliably establish the identity of the person entitled to payment under the eNote.[26] The drafters of UETA and E-SIGN, however, felt that the use of a third-party registry, similar to registries currently

---

other costs will be reduced, while security and the ability to satisfy legal requirements governing such paper records will be enhanced.

21. UETA § 16(a); 15 U.S.C.A § 7021(a)(1)(A) & (B).
22. 15 U.S.C.A § 7021(a)(1)(C).
23. UETA § 16(b); 15 U.S.C.A. § 7021(b).
24. UETA § 16(d); 15 U.S.C.A. § 7021(d).
25. UETA § 16(c); 15 U.S.C.A. § 7021(c).
26. UETA § 16, cmt. 3.

in place for securities entitlements under Article 8 of the UCC, and in the transfer of cotton warehouse receipts under the program sponsored by the U.S. Department of Agriculture, would be the most effective way to satisfy the safe harbor requirements for control.[27] In addition, a third-party registry could ensure that the transferable record remains unique, identifiable, and unalterable, while also providing the means to assure that the transferee is clearly noted and identified.[28] Additionally, it was vitally important that the registry be able to securely and demonstrably transfer the record to others in a manner which assures that only one "holder" exists.[29]

The MERS eRegistry Achieves a "Control" Function

Although a third-party registry seemed to be a viable solution to meet the safe harbor requirements for control under E-SIGN and UETA, the mortgage industry still needed to determine how to create such a registry. If a registry were simply designed to store information about the ownership of an eNote and its location, this would not comply with all of the safe harbor elements for control.[30] The registry, by itself, would be unable to prove that a particular eNote is the single authoritative copy that is unique, identifiable, and unalterable, because the registry information (i.e., ownership and location information) would not be enough to ensure document integrity (i.e., the eNote contains the same information as it did at the time it was originally executed by the borrower).

In 2002, an early example of a preliminary eNote registry was not regarded as feasible or cost-effective for the mortgage industry. Fannie Mae was the first investor to announce its willingness to purchase eNotes, but required lenders to deliver the eNote directly to Fannie Mae, and to use Fannie Mae's proprietary interim registry to register and track the person in control of such eNotes.[31] Unfortunately, there were several issues with this solution: (1) a proprietary interim registry owned and controlled by one investor appeared to restrict the sale of eNotes to one investor;[32] and (2) document custodians were concerned that delivery of the eNote to Fannie Mae would obviate the need for their services, which include taking custody and maintaining the mortgage loan files and certifying such mortgage loans for sale to investors. To foster eMortgage adoption, the mortgage industry quickly realized that a national centralized eNote registry, not a proprietary system solely owned by one investor, would be a more appropriate solution.

---

27. *Id.*

28. *Id.*

29. *Id.*

30. *See* Fannie Mae and Freddie Mac, *Delivering Mortgages in the Electronic Age: The Case for a Central Electronic Mortgage Note Registration System as a Vehicle for Complying with the UETA and E-SIGN Safe Harbor* (Mar. 8, 2002), *available at* http://www.efscouncil.org/frames/Forum%20Members/Fannie_RegistryWhitePaper.doc, at 6.

31. *See* Fannie Mae, Ann. 02-08: Selling Electronic Mortgages to Fannie Mae (06/28/02) ("Selling eMortgages to Fannie Mae"), *available at* https://www.efanniemae.com/sf/guides/ssg/annltrs/pdf/2002/02-08.pdf. at 4.

32. In 2001, Freddie Mac published preliminary specifications for eMortgages but was not ready to accept eNotes for purchase. *See* Freddie Mac, Preliminary Specifications for Electronic Loan Documentation (June 2001), *available at* http://www.freddiemac.com/singlefamily/elm/pdf/specifications.pdf.

The MBA, through meetings with industry participants such as Fannie Mae, Freddie Mac and others, set out to create requirements for a national eNote registry. In creating such requirements, the group made the following assumptions:

1. Proprietary electronic custodial repositories (i.e., electronic vaults) would exist to store eNotes.[33]
2. When an eNote was sold, the electronic file could be transferred from the seller's e-vault to the buyer's (or it may remain in place, if the buyer and seller have a business relationship that allows for that) (see Figure B.1 for an illustration of electronic vault transfers).[34]
3. Any electronic copy of an eNote is identical to any other—because they are simply bit-for-bit copies of computer files, no one copy of an eNote can contain data that would identify it as the authoritative copy (the electronic equivalent of the paper copy with wet-ink signatures).[35]
4. Some external mechanism is required to resolve the question of which of the (potentially many) copies of an eNote is the authoritative copy, and thus identify ownership of the eNote.

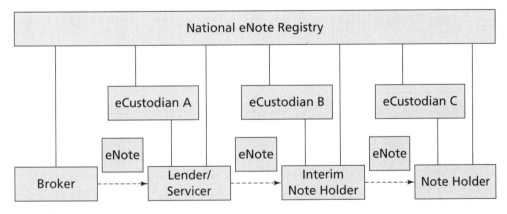

FIGURE B.1
Sample eNote Process Flow
The diagram maps transfers of the eNote from loan broker to ultimate investor and to their respective electronic vault custodians (eCustodians).

Source: MBA eNote Registry Requirements Document. Used with permission.

---

33. MBA, National eNote Registry Requirements Document, version 1.0 (Mar. 7, 2003), *available at* http://www.mersinc.org/MersProducts/publications.aspx?mpid=5, at 2. Today, paper promissory notes are stored in physical vaults run by document custodians, which are typically required by investors to be financial institutions or a subsidiaries thereof, subject to regulation by a federal agency, such as the Federal Deposit Insurance Corporation (FDIC), the Board of Governors of the Federal Reserve System, the Office of the Comptroller of the Currency (OCC), the Office of Thrift Supervision (OTS), or the National Credit Union Administration (NCUA).
34. *Id.*
35. *Id.*

5. The assurance of this external mechanism will be required by secondary market investors for them to accept delivery of an eNote.
6. Based on this need, the National Registry will allow eNotes to be registered and uniquely identified for tracking and verification. It will store information on the controller and location of the Authoritative Copy of the eNote.
7. The National Registry will not store the actual eNote, but only identifying information about it.[36]

On March 7, 2003, the MBA published the National eNote Registry Requirements Document, which defined the concepts, key assumptions and terms, and high-level business requirements for the registry.[37] Based on these requirements and the existing infrastructure used for the MERS system, MERSCORP, Inc., with industry support, created the MERS eRegistry. The MERS eRegistry was designed to comply with the safe harbor requirements of E-SIGN and UETA's transferable-records provisions, including those requirements dealing with ensuring the document integrity of an eNote. It is important to note, however, that the MERS eRegistry does not store the actual eNote—investors would likely delegate the storage and maintenance of eNotes to document custodians with electronic vaults. On July 23, 2004, the first eNote was registered on the MERS eRegistry.[38]

ANATOMY OF AN eNOTE

The MERS eRegistry was designed to function as a definitive source to find information on the person in control (controller) and the location of an eNote. However, the mortgage industry still needed to create standards and guidance for eNote processes to ensure eNotes could operate with the eRegistry to meet the safe harbor requirements and answer questions about ensuring eNote authenticity. For example, if eNotes can be freely duplicated, how do you prevent an unscrupulous lender from selling an eNote to multiple investors? How do you know that an eNote has not been modified since it was executed by the borrower? How can you affix a borrower's electronic signature in such a way that (1) it legally binds a borrower in the same way a wet-ink signature would; and (2) the signature can be attributed directly to the borrower? These questions highlight the challenges of creating a proxy for an original paper document in the digital realm.

This section discusses some of the standards and guidance for eNote processes created by MERS, the MBA, the Mortgage Industry Standards Maintenance Organization (MISMO), Fannie Mae, and Freddie Mac to address these questions. Specifically, it covers some of the considerations for the creation of eNotes, such as document file formats and data, transferable record agreement language, MERS eRegistry required language, electronic signature processes, tamper-evident digital signatures, and systems integration with the MERS eRegistry.

---

36. *Id.*
37. *Id.*
38. MERS Press Release, First Electronic Note Registered on the MERS eRegistry, *available at* http://www.mersinc.org/newsroom/press_details.aspx?id=161. As of September 2007, the MERS eRegistry had over 3,400 eNotes successfully registered.

Document Format and Data Extraction

In general, eNotes need to be created using a document file format, which is a technical specification that a computer program uses to render, manipulate, and store information contained in a particular file. E-SIGN and UETA do not require specific document file formats or technologies for the creation of electronic records.[39] As a result, the decision of which document file format a lender should use to create eNotes will depend on what file formats the investors will accept, the lender's technology infrastructure, and other business considerations.

Currently, the MERS eRegistry has the ability to register eNotes in the MISMO SMART document format[40] and the Portable Document Format (PDF).[41] Both of these formats, when implemented properly, allow for document data (i.e., XML[42] data) to be extracted for automated processing by lenders and investors. Readers or viewers, both proprietary and open source, are available for these document formats, which enable viewing and signing of the electronic documents.

Transferable Records Agreement

As discussed previously, one of the required elements for an eNote to be considered a transferable record is the borrower's agreement that the eNote be treated as such. This language could be drafted any number of ways, and could be included within the eNote itself or on a separate agreement. A good example of this language can be found in the Fannie Mae and Freddie Mac required eNote clause for their uniform instruments:

> I expressly state that I have signed this electronically created Note (the "Electronic Note") using an electronic signature. By doing this, I am indicating that I agree to the terms of this Electronic Note. I also agree that this Electronic Note may be Authenticated, Stored and Transmitted by Electronic Means (as defined in Section 11(F)), and will be valid for all legal purposes, as set forth in the Uniform Electronic Transactions Act, as enacted in the jurisdiction where the Property is located ("UETA"), the Electronic Signatures in Global and National Commerce Act ("E-SIGN"), or both, as applicable. In addition, I agree that this Electronic Note will be an effective, enforceable and

---

39. This technology-neutral stance is deliberate, as evidenced by the prefatory note to UETA, which states that UETA was meant to provide "a solid legal framework that allows for the continued development of innovative technology to facilitate electronic transactions." *See* Prefatory Note to the Uniform Electronic Transactions Act (1999), *supra* note 10.

40. The MISMO SMART document format stands for Secure, Manageable, Archivable, Retrievable, and Transferable. SMART documents are electronic documents that bind data and presentation together in a single file. For more information on SMART documents, *see generally* http://www.mismo.org/specificationsandguidance/emortgagespecificatons.htm.

41. *See* MERS eRegistry, *Procedures Manual,* version 3.5 (June 4, 2007) ("eRegistry Procedures Manual") and MERS eRegistry, *PDF Guidelines* (Apr. 15, 2007), *both available at* http://www.mersinc.org/MersProducts/manuals.aspx?mpid=5. Investors may require sellers to present a copy of an eNote to the MERS eRegistry for calculation of the hash value—at this writing, this is only possible with the SMART document format. PDF eNotes would need to be registered using a "data point registration," in which the lender presents the hash value of the eNote rather than a full copy of the eNote.

42. XML is the abbreviation for Extensible Markup Language, a specification developed by the World Wide Web Consortium (W3C). Originally designed to meet the challenges of large-scale electronic publishing, XML is also playing an increasingly important role in the exchange of a wide variety of data on the web and elsewhere. For more on XML, see http://www.w3.org/XML/.

valid Transferable Record (as defined in Section 11(F)) and may be created, authenticated, stored, transmitted and transferred in a manner consistent and permitted by the Transferable Records sections of UETA or E-SIGN.[43]

MERS eRegistry Required Language

Similar to what is used in the existing MERS system, a unique numerical identifier, known as the MIN, is required to be included in an eNote to identify the eNote within the eRegistry. A MIN is an 18-digit number that is permanently assigned to an eNote, and consists of a MERS member organization ID number (Org ID), a lender sequence number (i.e., loan number), and a check-digit calculated with a specific mathematical algorithm.[44] The MIN number on the eNote is required to be the same MIN number for the corresponding mortgage or deed of trust registered on the system, so that they can be cross-referenced. Additionally, the eNote must contain language referring to the eRegistry as the definitive source to determine the identity of the person in control of the eNote.[45] For example, the Fannie Mae and Freddie Mac eNote clause sets forth their required eRegistry language:

> Except as indicated in Section 11(D) below, the Note Holder and any person to whom this Electronic Note is later transferred will be recorded in a registry maintained by MERSCORP, Inc., a Delaware corporation, or in another registry to which the records are later transferred (the "Note Holder Registry"). The authoritative copy of this Electronic Note will be the copy identified by the Note Holder after loan closing or, if this Electronic Note has been transferred, by the Loan Servicer (as defined in the Security Instrument), in the Note Holder Registry as the authoritative copy. The current identity of the Note Holder and the location of the authoritative copy will be available from the Loan Servicer. Any copy of this Electronic Note other than the authoritative copy identified in the Note Holder Registry is a nonauthoritative copy.[46]

Electronic Signature Process

The signing of an eNote requires certain processes to be in place to ensure enforceability and document integrity. The borrower will typically sign an eNote on an electronic closing system that has electronic signature capture functionality. An "electronic signature" is defined by E-SIGN and UETA as any sound, symbol, or process attached to or logically associated with a record, and executed or adopted with the intent to sign the record.[47] The most common electronic signatures in use by the mortgage industry today are (1) click-through signatures; (2) handwritten electronic signatures (i.e., stylus on a sig-

---

43. Fannie Mae, Guide to Delivering eMortgage Loans to Fannie Mae, version 2.5 (March 2007) ("Fannie Mae eMortgage Guide") *available at* https://www.efanniemae.com/sf/guides/ssg/relatedsellinginfo/emtg/pdf/emortgage deliveryguide.pdf; Appendix A and Freddie Mac, eMortgage Handbook: Requirements for Participating in Freddie Mac's eMortgage Initiative, version 1.0 (December 2005) ("Freddie Mac eMortgage Handbook"), *available at* http://www.freddiemac.com/singlefamily/elm/pdf/eMortgage_Handbook.pdf, Appendix A.

44. The algorithm used for the check-digit is a MOD 10 Weight 2 Algorithm. *See* eRegistry Procedures Manual, *supra* note 41, at 15.

45. For more details about the eNote registration process, *see generally* eRegistry Procedures Manual, *supra* note 41.

46. Fannie Mae eMortgage Guide and Freddie Mac eMortgage Handbook, *supra* note 43, Appendix A.

47. UETA § 2(8); 15 U.S.C.A. § 7006(5).

nature module or tablet PC); and (3) digital signatures.[48] Regardless of what signature method is chosen, the electronic closing system should be designed to prove compliance with E-SIGN and UETA's electronic signature definition. In addition, some electronic signature implementations provide evidence of signature attribution and authentication.

Attachment or Logical Association

In a paper-based transaction, the association of a signature to a document is generally shown by such signature being physically affixed to a particular document. Although E-SIGN and UETA do not necessarily require a viewable signature on an electronic document, a signature symbol viewed on an eNote is the preferred way to show attachment or logical association. A viewable signature symbol also has the advantage of custom—consumers are used to click-signing or handwriting their electronic signature on a signature pad and obtaining visual confirmation that a document was signed.

Evidence of Intent

The validity of an electronic signature requires the intent by the signer to sign and be bound to a particular record. Evidence of intent can be found within the electronic document itself and/or the surrounding circumstances in which the document was signed. For example, in a paper-based transaction, intent can be inferred by a borrower affixing his or her signature on a signature line that appears immediately after language such as, "By signing below, I agree to the terms and conditions." In an eNote process, for example, intent can be inferred if the electronic closing process requires a borrower to scroll down to the end of an electronic document before activating a click-sign button that appears after language such as "By clicking the 'I agree' button below, I agree to the terms and conditions. I understand that my electronic signature is legally binding."

Signature Attribution

Although E-SIGN and UETA provide that electronic signatures are legally equivalent to wet-ink signatures, attribution remains an issue. Signature attribution for ink signatures can be done through the use of the signer's name (if readable), through handwriting comparison, or, in certain circumstances, through a notary witnessing a person signing a document and acknowledging such act. With the exception of when a notary is present during the signature process, attribution of other electronic signatures may be more complex. UETA provides guidance in this area by stating that an electronic record or electronic signature is attributable to a person if it was the act of the person. An act of a person includes an act done by the agent of a person, as well as an act done by an electronic agent (i.e., computer, signing pad) of a person.

The UETA commentary provides some examples of electronic acts in which the record and signature would be attributable to a person, as follows:

- The person types his or her name as part of an e-mail purchase order;
- The person's employee, pursuant to authority, types the person's name as part of the e-mail purchase order;

---

48. For more information on legal issues related to electronic records and signatures, see Standards and Procedures for electronic Records and Signatures, version 1.0 (September 2003) available (for purchase) at www.spers.org.

- The person's computer, programmed to order goods upon receipt of inventory information within particular parameters, issues a purchase order that includes the person's name, or other identifying information as part of the order.

The act of the person may be shown in any manner, including showing the efficacy of any security procedure applied (i.e., access controls, user ID and password, etc.) to determine the person to which the electronic record or electronic signature was attributable. For example, if the electronic closing system requires a borrower to log in with a user ID and password[49] before being able to electronically sign the eNote, this can be evidence of signature attribution. Additionally, some document formats provide for electronic signatures that contain information about a particular signature. For example, PDF supports electronic signatures that may contain additional information about a particular signature. This capability can be used to capture additional attribution information such as signer e-mail address, signer passwords, and other information (although some of this information may be encrypted if it is sensitive or confidential).[50]

UETA provides that the effect of an attributed electronic record or signature can be determined from the context and surrounding circumstances at the time of its creation, execution, or adoption, including the parties' agreement, if any, and as otherwise provided by law. This means that even if proper attribution occurs, the legal enforceability of such record and signature may still be dependent on other factors (i.e., intent, legal age, capacity, proper authority, etc.).

Signer Authentication (Verification of Signer's Identity)

To ensure enforceability of a mortgage transaction, as well as to minimize the risk of fraud, a lender needs to ensure that its customers are who they purport to be. The signing process can, but does not necessarily, include an identity authentication component. In a paper loan closing, authentication can be performed by a notary verifying a borrower's identity by reviewing the borrower's driver's license or passport. This in-person verification could also work with an electronic loan closing, although many states do not require the promissory note to be notarized. While not common for loan transactions, borrowers can sign electronic mortgage documents using digital signatures. The use of digital signatures can be used to validate a borrower's identity, as well as ensuring the integrity of the signed document. As described elsewhere in this book, digital signature technology is based on public/private key cryptography, and is used in secure messaging, public key infrastructure (PKI), virtual private networks (VPN), web standards for secure transactions, and electronic signatures.[51] Digital signatures use public key cryptography (PKC), which employs an algorithm using two different but mathematically related keys: a private key for creating a digital signature or transforming data

---

49. This is a simple example. In high-value transactions, two-factor (two-credential) authentication or layered security is recommended. Credentials are (1) something the user knows; (2) something the user has; and (3) something the user is. *See* Federal Financial Institutions Examination Council (FFIEC), Authentication in an Internet Banking Environment (Oct. 13, 2005), *available at* http://www.ffiec.gov/ffiecinfobase/resources/info_sec/2006/frb-sr-05-19.pdf .

50. MISMO, E-SIGNed PDF Guidelines, version 1.0 (Feb. 5, 2007), *available at* http://www.mismo.org/specificationsandguidance/emortgagespecificatons.htm, at 18.

51. *See* eMortgage Guide, *supra* note 6, at 36.

into a seemingly unintelligible form, and a public key for verifying a digital signature or returning the data to its original form. If a public and private key pair is associated with an identified signer (i.e., borrower), the digital signature created with the keys can attribute the signed data to the signer.[52]

Electronic Closing System Audit Trails

In addition to signature processes, the electronic closing system can also be designed to provide signer information through system audit trails. In a paper loan-closing scenario, parties rely heavily on documentary evidence (i.e., the closing file, mortgage loan file checklists, closing instructions, written participant dates and signatures, etc.) and on participant recollection to recreate what occurred during a particular paper closing transaction. Participant recollection may not always be reliable, especially when there is a large time gap between the loan closing and when participant recollection is required. In an electronic loan closing scenario, a closing system audit trail could be designed to provide a more reliable, less subjective record of events than participant recollection alone.

Audit trail information could include:

- Time, date, and record of uploading of the eNote to the electronic loan closing system;
- Information regarding who logged in to the electronic closing system, including date and time of log-in;
- Duration of loan closing session;
- Sign-out information, including date and time;
- Which documents in the electronic loan-closing system were accessed, including date and time of access;
- How a particular document was handled within the loan-closing system, including date and time of action:
  - Viewing;
  - Editing;
  - Initialing and signing;
  - Notarization;
  - Tamper-evident sealing;
  - Transferring document out of the closing system; and
  - Time and date information for the above events.
- Who accessed and performed the above document-handling events.[53]

From an evidentiary standpoint, a system audit trail can provide valuable information as to what occurred during an electronic loan closing. However, before audit trail information can be relied upon, the lender must ensure that the information captured is the information that would be useful if needed, and that the information is accessible for

---

52. An in-depth discussion on digital signatures and PKI is beyond the scope of this appendix. For more information, see American Bar Association, *Digital Signature Guidelines Tutorial,* available at http://www.abanet.org/scitech/ec/isc/dsg-tutorial.html.
53. MISMO, eMortgage Closing Guide, version 1.0 (Apr. 27, 2006) ("eMortgage Closing Guide") *available at* http://www.mismo.org/SpecificationsAndGuidance/eMortgageSpecificatons.htm, at 44.

as long as a cause of action or claim may be brought concerning the particular loan. The system audit trail is only useful if the information can be accessed and retained by the party who actually needs to rely on it.

Tamper-Evident Digital Signature Requirement

After all signatures on an eNote are captured, registration of the eNote on the MERS eRegistry requires that a tamper-evident digital signature (including date and time stamp) be applied to ensure the integrity of the eNote contents. A tamper-evident digital signature (also known as a "tamperseal") is the process of digitally signing a document with a valid digital certificate such that if a document is modified, the modification can be easily detected. In cases where the digital certificate references an individual or business entity, these digital signatures can provide proof of the identity of the signing party.[54] An important part of the tamperseal is the tamperseal date and time, which can be used to detect potential fraud if there are unreasonable time discrepancies between steps in the process.

Although it is possible to use certificates of any assurance level (including self-signed certificates) to apply a tamperseal on an eNote, lenders and investors may require tamperseals to be applied using a digital certificate issued by an accredited certification authority. For example, the MBA's nonprofit subsidiary, the Secure Identity Services Accreditation Corporation (SISAC), accredits digital identity credential issuers for the mortgage industry. SISAC describes its accreditation framework as:

> based on minimum standards for four major components of an identity management solution, and specifically, a Public Key Infrastructure (Identification & Authentication (I&A), Issuance, Validation and Publication.) Once a commercial identity credential provider has demonstrated that its PKI meets the minimum standards for these components, it will receive an official SISAC accreditation certificate. SISAC certifications will be administered through a contract arrangement with approved firms of nationwide auditing capacity. SISAC certifications are equally applicable to both the commercial and residential industries, as the certification focuses on enterprise-wide PKI programs and not transaction-based programs. Further, and to promote interoperability outside the mortgage industry, SISAC's PKI standards are modeled after the U.S. Federal PKI standards. In some cases however, SISAC defined additional requirements that are not addressed in the Federal requirements. For example, SISAC has defined financial liability requirements for an Accredited Issuing Authority (AIA), while the Federal standard defines none.[55]

As discussed in the following pages, SISAC-accredited digital certificates are a prerequisite for MERS eRegistry usage.

MERS eREGISTRY

eRegistry Integration

Lenders, investors and others who wish to use the MERS eRegistry must submit a MERS membership application and execute an eRegistry addendum. MERS will assign a

---

54. *Id.* at § 3.5.
55. *See* SISAC, Executive Summary, *available at* http://www.sisac.org/executive_summary.html.

MERS Org ID to each member company. Member companies must also integrate their respective systems with the MERS eRegistry because transaction requests are submitted through a secure system-to-system interface (i.e., VPN or frame relay). Members must also obtain an organization or individual (medium- or high-assurance level) digital certificate from a SISAC-accredited issuing authority for signing transaction request messages to the MERS eRegistry. The MERS eRegistry assigns appropriate transactions access to each member based on their lines of business and their rights in a particular eNote. For example, if a member is a document custodian only and does not originate loans, the member would not be able to initiate a transfer of control request; such requests can only be initiated by the person in control or its delegatee if specifically authorized (see Table B.1.)[56]

To initiate any transactions, such as an eNote registration, members are required to submit XML-format request messages to the MERS eRegistry. Each message must be digitally signed with an individual or organizational SISAC-accredited digital certificate. To ensure the request is genuine and that all the information is present for a complete registration record, the eRegistry validates:

1. That the digital certificate included in the registration request is valid and not revoked, and that it matches the certificate information stored in the MERS eRegistry database for the member;

TABLE B.1
Roles of Rights-Holders on the eRegistry System for Transfers of Control and Location

Transfer of Control and Location	Current Controller	Current Location	Current Delegatee	New Controller	New Location
Initiate Transfer Request	Yes	No	No	No	No
Receive Pending Transfer Notice	No	Yes	Yes*	Yes	Yes
Initiate Transfer Confirmation Request	Yes	No	No	Yes	Yes
Receive Transfer Completion Notice	Yes	Yes	Yes*	Yes	Yes

Yes* - Only if Delegatee Present on MIN

Source: MERSCORP, Inc. Used with permission.

---

56. For comprehensive technical information on the roles of rights holders for transactions on the MERS eRegistry system, see the MERS eRegistry Integration Handbook Series at www.mersinc.org.

2. That the requesting party is registered as an active member and is the originating lender of the eNote loan; and

3. That the registration information is complete, including the MIN, signature value (or hash value) of the tamperseal, tamperseal date and time, the eNote in SMART format (if required by the investor)[57] and certain loan data (i.e., borrower name, property address, etc.) (see Figure B.2).

If the registration request is accepted, the MERS eRegistry (1) sends a message to the person in control indicating a successful registration; and (2) stores, in the MERS eRegistry database, the signature value of the tamperseal of the eNote and certain loan data, such as borrower information, property information, and lien type. Additionally, a registration record is created for the eNote that contains information on the controller, the location of the authoritative copy, a transaction history, and other information.

For other transactions, the MERS eRegistry performs similar validation for each transaction request submitted as described above. Additionally, the MERS eRegistry requires the affected members on a particular transaction (i.e., transferees, document custodians, and servicers) to actively accept confirmation of a transfer transaction (i.e., transfer of control) through an XML response back to the eRegistry that is digitally signed using a party's SISAC-accredited digital certificate before the transfer can be effective. Examples of transactions that can be initiated on the eRegistry are:

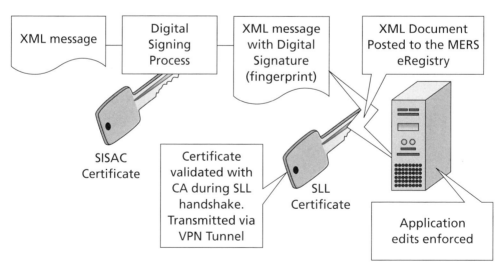

FIGURE B.2
How XML Messages from Members are Validated by the eRegistry

Source: MERSCORP, Inc. Used with permission

---

57. If the eNote is presented during registration, the MERS eRegistry will calculate and store the signature value of the tamperseal and compare it with the tamperseal value on the registration request message. *See* eRegistry Procedures Manual, *supra* note 41, at 19.

- Transfers of Control: To sell an eNote to an investor;
- Transfers of Location: To designate a document custodian/electronic vault;
- Transfers of Delegatee: To designate a loan servicer;
- Change Data—Updates: To correct loan data, update delegatee/location information;
- Change Data—Modifications: To record an eNote modification (i.e., change in terms or loan workout);
- Change Data—Assumptions: To change any borrower on the eNote; and
- Change Data—Status: To report payoffs, charge-offs, transfer of eNote information to a proprietary registry, conversion of eNote to paper, and registration reversal.

Illustration of MERS eRegistry Functionality

To assist in the illustration of the MERS eRegistry, it is important to understand the new terms and definitions that are being used by the mortgage industry for eNotes. Table B.2 translates this new vocabulary from the paper to the electronic world.

Figure B.3 illustrates the eNote registration process, and Figure B.4 illustrates the transfer of control and location process after an eNote is sold to another investor.[58]

> *Step B.3-1*: Originating Lender creates an eNote with all required language, including the reference to the MERS eRegistry and the MIN, and delivers the eNote to the eClosing System.

> *Step B.3-2*: Closing Agent conducts the loan closing, and Borrower electronically signs the eNote using the eClosing system's signature functionality.

TABLE B.2
Translation from Paper to Electronic Documents

Paper World	*Electronic World*
Original Note with Wet-ink Signature	Authoritative Copy of eNote (AC)
Possession	Control
Investor / Holder	Controller
Custodian	Location (Electronic Vault)
Indorsement	Transfer of Control on eRegistry
Chain of Indorsements	Transferable Record Audit Trail
Servicer	Delegatee (of Controller)

---

58. This illustration has been simplified for the purposes of showing the basic MERS functionality. For a more in-depth description of a typical eNote process flow, including loan servicing functions, see eMortgage Guide, *supra* note 6, at § 6.5.

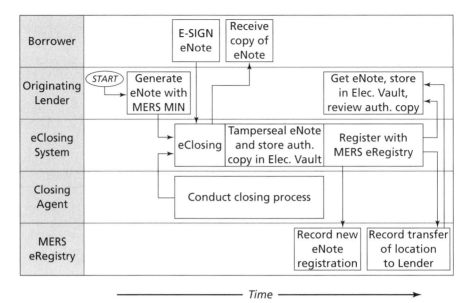

FIGURE B.3
Sample Process Flow from eNote Creation to Registration on the MERS eRegistry

Step B.3-3: After all signatures are captured, the eClosing System applies a final tamperseal to the eNote, and the eNote is stored in the eClosing System's vault. The Borrower receives a copy of the signed eNote.

Step B.3-4: Originating Lender receives delivery of the eNote from the eClosing system and stores it in its own electronic vault. After reviewing the eNote for accuracy and compliance, the Originating Lender sends a registration request to the MERS eRegistry.[59]

Step B.3-5: Once the MERS eRegistry has performed all validations, the eNote registration record will reflect the following information:

Controller   =   Originating Lender
Location   =   Originating Lender

Delegatee   =   Originating Lender

Additionally, the MERS eRegistry will store the hash value of the tamperseal to validate future transactions with the associated eNote, as well as certain borrower information, lien priority type and property information.[60]

---

59. MERS requires that eNotes be registered within one business day of eNote execution and tampersealing. Investors may not accept eNotes for purchase if there is a large unexplained time gap between tampersealing and eNote registration.

60. *eRegistry Procedures Manual*, *supra* note 41, at 22.

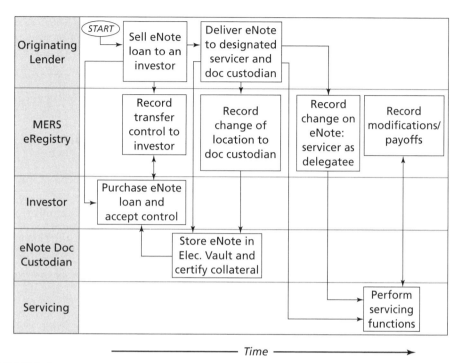

FIGURE B.4
Sample eNote Process Flow from Sale of eNote to Loan Servicing

Step B.4-1: The Originating Lender sells the eNote loan to the Investor. To complete the sale, the Originating Lender delivers a copy of the eNote to investor's designated document custodian, eNote Doc Custodian, and the designated loan servicer, Servicing.

Step B.4-2: The Originating Lender will submit requests to the MERS eRegistry to transfer control to Investor, transfer location to eNote Doc Custodian, and transfer delegatee to Servicing.

Step B.4-3: The MERS eRegistry will notify Investor that a transfer of control is pending and what the expiration date shall be for the transfer of control request. Prior to the expiration date, the Investor must send a digitally signed XML message to the MERS eRegistry confirming acceptance of control. Depending on investor requirements, the acceptance confirmation may present the hash value of the tamperseal as an additional validation that the investor has an accurate copy of the subject eNote.[61] The same type of notifications and requests for confirmation will be sent to the eNote Doc Custodian and Servicing.

---

61. Investors may want to include the tamperseal hash value in their acceptance confirmation to validate that the eNote, in which they are accepting control, is the actual eNote registered on the MERS eRegistry.

Step B.4-4: Once the MERS eRegistry obtains confirmations from investor, eNote Doc Custodian, and Servicing, the eNote transaction information will be updated to show:

Controller   =   Investor
Location   =   eNote Doc Custodian
Delegatee   =   Servicing

The MERS eRegistry will also capture transaction history information (see Figure B.5).

Step B.4-5: Servicing, as the delegatee, will have rights to update the eNote information on the MERS eRegistry with any loan servicing functions, such as loan modifications and payoffs, by submitting requests to change the eNote informa-

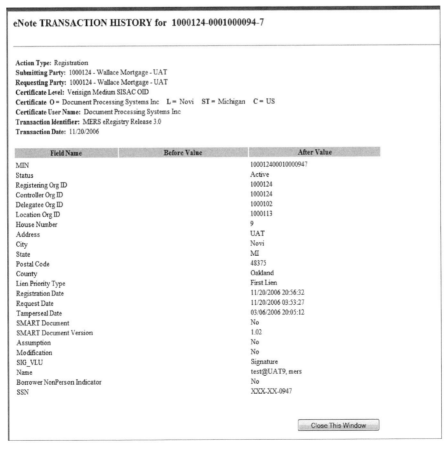

FIGURE B.5
Sample MERS eRegistry Database Registration Transaction Information

MERS eRegistry screen shot reprinted with permission from MERSCORP, Inc.

tion data ("change data" requests). The same validation that takes place with registration and transfer requests will also be required for change data requests.

Figure B.6 is a screenshot of the MERS eRegistry database with eNote information,
including the property address, borrower name, and last four digits of the social security
number, controller, delegatee, location, pending transfers, and other eNote information.

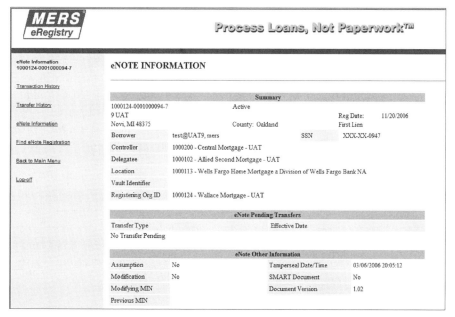

FIGURE B.6
Sample eNote Information on the MERS eRegistry

MERS eRegistry screen shot reprinted with permission from MERSCORP, Inc.

How the MERS eRegistry Meets the Control Requirements of E-SIGN and UETA

This section discuss how the MERS eRegistry, in combination with the eNote processes
and guidance developed by the mortgage industry, meets the six safe harbor requirements for establishing control under E-SIGN and UETA.[62] Each element of the safe harbor will be discussed separately below with an explanation of how the MERS eRegistry
meets the requirement.

1. A single authoritative copy exists that is unique, identifiable, and unalterable without detection.

To qualify as an authoritative copy, an eNote must be unique, identifiable, and unalterable (with limited exceptions). As referenced within the eNote, the MERS eRegistry is

---

62. *See* the MERS website at www.mersinc.org for a formal legal opinion on how the MERS eRegistry satisfies
E-SIGN and UETA's transferable record requirements, and for more information on eNote registration requirements.

the single definitive source to determine the location of the authoritative copy of the eNote. By default, other copies of the eNote that are not stored in the location named by the MERS eRegistry are not the authoritative copies and therefore, the authoritative copy is unique and can be readily identified. Additionally, an eNote is identifiable because the MERS eRegistry stores the tamperseal and MIN of an eNote, along with borrower and property information. No other eNote with the same MIN can be registered. This safe harbor element also requires the eNote to be unalterable, except with the permission of the person asserting control. The MERS eRegistry meets this requirement by mandating that the hash value of the tamperseal be presented by the controller (or its delegatee if authorized) when initiating a (1) transfer of control; or (2) change update— modification. This prevents unauthorized parties from making changes to the controller or modifying the eNote, thereby meeting the unalterable requirement. Although an unauthorized party in possession of an identical copy of an eNote could alter that copy of the eNote, such alterations would not be recognized, because third parties could easily determine from the MERS eRegistry that the unauthorized party is not the controller, and the eNote in the unauthorized party's possession is not the authoritative copy.

2. The authoritative copy identifies the person asserting control as either to whom the transferable record was issued or the issuer.

The eNote provides notice that the MERS eRegistry is the definitive source to determine the identity of the controller. The eRegistry only allows one controller to be named at any one time for a particular eNote and tracks all transfers of control. Additionally, the MERS eRegistry validates the identity of the controller upon initial eNote registration and requires validation and confirmation for any transfer request.

3. The authoritative copy is communicated to and maintained by the person asserting control or its designated custodian.

The controller of the authoritative copy or its designated custodian would be equivalent to the person in possession of a physical promissory note in the paper world. In the MERS eRegistry, the controller always has the ability to designate the location of the authoritative copy. If the controller wishes to transfer location, the new document custodian (or location) would be required to send a confirmation of acceptance that includes the signature value of the tamperseal, which provides evidence that the document custodian has custody of the authoritative copy.

4. Copies or revisions that add or change an identified assignee of the authoritative copy can be made only with the consent of the person asserting control.

Only the controller (or a delegatee if specifically authorized) can transfer control of an eNote. The MERS eRegistry also validates the controller's transfer-request transactions and requires transferees to confirm acceptance.

5. Each copy of the authoritative copy and any copy of a copy is readily identifiable as a copy that is not the authoritative copy

Based on the language in the eNote, all copies that are in locations other than the location designated on the MERS eRegistry for the eNote are, by default, not the authoritative copies.

6. Any revision of the authoritative copy is readily identifiable as authorized or unauthorized.

Revisions to an authoritative copy, such as modifications to an eNote, must be identifiable as authorized or unauthorized revisions. Whenever an eNote modification is created and agreed upon by the controller and the obligor (i.e., borrower), the controller is required to register the eNote modification on the MERS eRegistry with the same MIN as the original eNote. Both the hash values of the original eNote and eNote modification are stored by the MERS eRegistry upon successful registration. The MERS eRegistry eNote information will reflect that the eNote has a modification associated with it, and the transaction history will reflect when and by whom the modification was registered.

THE eNOTE FINGERPRINT— VALIDATING THE AUTHORITATIVE COPY

One of the key ways to ensure that modifications to an eNote are detected is the application of a tamper-evident digital signature after all borrower signatures have been collected. This section will illustrate how a party can validate the integrity of an eNote (see Figure B.7).

Step B.7-1: Create a hash value of the contents of the document using an algorithm function. (Hash algorithms seek to provide unique compact representations of a much larger input data).[63]

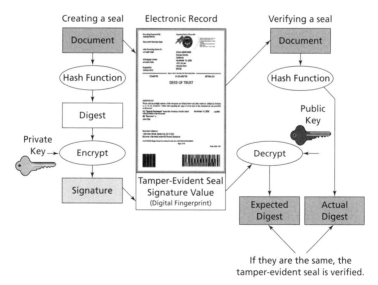

FIGURE B.7
Process to Create and Validate a Tamper-Evident Digital Signature

Source: Countrywide Home Loans, Inc. Used with permission.

---

63. One should carefully consider which algorithm function to use to create hash values of electronic documents. It is possible for weak algorithms to exist and raise the risk of spoofing (i.e., creating a modified electronic document with the same hash value as the original one).

Step B.7-2: Encrypt the resulting hash value with the signer's private key that is part of the SISAC-accredited digital certificate.

Step B.7-3: Embed the hash value, along with the public key from the SISAC-accredited digital certificate, within the tamper-evident digital signature applied to the document.

Step B.7-4: In order for a third party to validate that the document has not been altered since the tamper-evident seal was applied, the third party would create a hash value based upon the contents of the document using the same mathematical function used in Step B.7-1.

Step B.7-5: The third party would decrypt the encrypted value using the public key embedded within the tamper-evident digital signature.

Step B.7-6: Then the third party would compare the calculated hash value with the encrypted hash value. If these values are the same, then this would constitute evidence that the document has not been modified.[64]

Because hash values are calculated based on the contents of the document, if even one character or pixel on document has been modified, the calculated hash values would be completely different (see Figure B.8a and b).

FIGURE B.8a
Example of Hash Value Calculations[65] on an eNote in which One Number in the Interest Rate is Subsequently Modified

64. For more on the digital signature process, see UNCITRAL Model Law on Electronic Signatures with Guide to Enactment 2001, Part Two, ¶ 62 (July 5, 2001).

65. For the purposes of this example, the author is using an SHA-1 algorithm to calculate the hash value, which results in a hash value that is 160 bits long (which can be represented in a string of 40 hexadecimal characters). SHA

FIGURE B.8b

Multiple tamperseals can also act as checkpoints in an electronic document to track modifications. For example, a lender can create a mortgage document in PDF format and apply a tamperseal prior to sending the document to the closing table. At loan closing, the mortgage document is signed by the borrowers and notarized before it is tampersealed again by the electronic loan-closing system (see Figure B.9). The first tamperseal takes a snapshot of the document at the time the lender sealed the document; the second tamperseal takes a snapshot of the document at the time the loan-closing system sealed the document. In some PDF implementations, the effect of the two tamperseals results not only in being able to detect that the document has been modified, but also what the modifications were.

Do I Have an Original eNote?

The MERS eRegistry allows a MERS member to validate whether an eNote a member possesses is the same one that was registered on the eRegistry. To validate the eNote, the member must submit the eNote's MIN, tamper-evident digital signature hash value, and the document type (i.e., note, modification).[66] The MERS eRegistry compares the hash value submitted by the member to the hash value stored for the eNote associated with

---

stands for Secure Hash Algorithm. This algorithm is designed by the National Security Agency (NSA) and published by the National Institute of Standards and Technology (NIST). Mortgage lenders and investors may choose to use other algorithms (i.e., SHA-512) that result in hash values that are longer than SHA-1. For more information on the different SHA algorithms and usage recommendations, see the NIST website at www.nist.gov.

66. MERS eRegistry Integration Series: Business Process Analysis, Release 3.5 (June 4, 2007) *available at* http://www.mersinc.org/MersProducts/manuals.aspx?mpid=5, at 18.

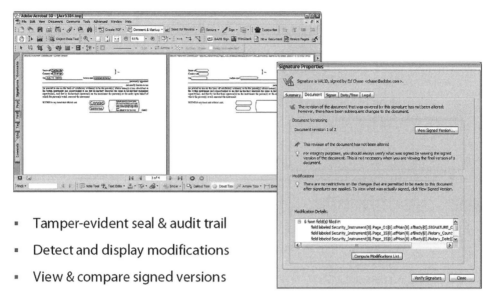

- Tamper-evident seal & audit trail

- Detect and display modifications

- View & compare signed versions

FIGURE B.9
Sample of a PDF Document with Two Tamperseals
Two tamperseals allow for the original and modified versions to be compared and any modifications flagged. In this example, the original tampersealed document was subsequently modified to add the notary information and signature.

Adobe product screen shot reprinted with permission from Adobe Systems Incorporated.

the same MIN, and sends an XML message back to the member indicating success or failure of the validation (see Figure B.10).

Once again, submission of the eNote hash value (or fingerprint) validates that the member requesting the transaction or inquiry has the correct eNote with the correct data. This also ensures the integrity of the data on the MERS eRegistry by limiting transactions and inquiries to those members who can present the matching eNote fingerprint.

THE LAST FRONTIER: TACKLING THE PROBLEM OF TECHNOLOGY OBSOLESCENCE

UETA provides that if a law requires that a record be retained, the requirement is satisfied by retaining an electronic record of the information in the record that: (1) accurately reflects the information set forth in the contract or other record after it was first generated in its final form as an electronic record or otherwise; and (2) remains accessible for later reference.[67] E-SIGN's record retention requirements mirror the UETA provisions except for the added requirement that the record must "remain accessible to all persons

---

67. This UETA provision is consistent with Rule 1001(3) of the Federal Rules of Evidence and the Uniform Rules of Evidence.

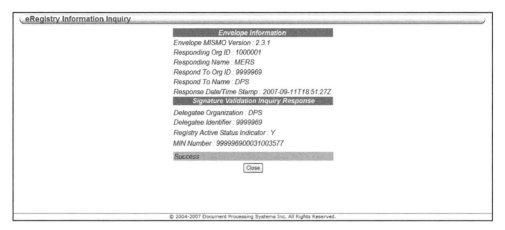

FIGURE B.10
Sample Response to a MERS Member Requesting a Signature Validation
The "Success" notation indicates that the eNote hash value held by the member matches
the eNote hash value on the registry.

Source: Document Processing Systems, Inc. Used with permission.

who are entitled to access by statute, regulation, or rule of law, in a form that is capable
of being accurately reproduced for later reference, whether by transmission, printing, or
otherwise."[68] If an electronic record is retained in compliance with these requirements,
E-SIGN and UETA provide that such record will meet any legal requirement for a record
"to be presented or retained in its original form."[69] As long as there is reliable assurance
that the electronic record accurately reproduces the information, such information will
be effective for all audit, evidentiary, archival, or similar purposes.[70] E-SIGN and UETA
switch the focus of record retention from the concept of "originality" to the concept of
"integrity."[71]

---

68. 15 U.S.C.A. § 7001(d)(1)(B).
69. UETA § 12(d); 15 U.S.C.A. § 7001(d)(3).
70. UETA § 12(d), cmt. 1.
71. Comment 1 to UETA § 12(d) provides a good discussion on why the concept of originality is so problematic, as follows:

> In an electronic medium, the concept of an original document is problematic. For example, as one
> drafts a document on a computer, the "original" is either on a disc or the hard drive to which the
> document has been initially saved. If one periodically saves the draft, the fact is that at times a docu-
> ment may be first saved to disc then to hard drive, and at others vice-versa. In such a case, the "origi-
> nal" may change from the information on the disc to the information on the hard drive. Indeed, it
> may be argued that the "original" exists solely in RAM and, in a sense, the original is destroyed when
> a "copy" is saved to a disc or to the hard drive. In any event, in the context of record retention, the
> concern focuses on the integrity of the information, and not with its "originality."

The consequences of being unable to reproduce an electronic record are severe. E-SIGN provides that if one is unable to reproduce such record:

> the legal effect, validity or enforceability of an electronic record of such contract or other record may be denied if such electronic record is not in a form that is capable of being retained and accurately reproduced for later reference by all parties or persons who are entitled to retain the contract or record.[72]

Record retention could potentially pose a problem for eNotes because financial institutions are generally required to retain such documents for the life of the loan plus seven years, which for some products could be up to fifty-seven years. There is no guarantee that the hardware, software, and operating system used to create and store the eNote will still function in such a way that the eNote remains accessible and accurately reproducible. Digital certificates, hash values, audit trails, and document formats all have the potential for failure over time. Fortunately, the provisions in E-SIGN and UETA make it clear that the content of the record, rather than the medium, is important for record retention and other requirements. The commentary to the official version of UETA recognizes that technology tends to become obsolete and, as a result, within a five- to ten-year period, a corporation may need to evolve through one or more generations of technology.[73] Additionally, a corporation may need to convert information stored in one medium to another to satisfy E-SIGN and UETA's requirements for continued accessibility to the information contained in an electronic record.

For eNotes, this means that the document custodians who operate electronic vaults will need to maintain hardware and software necessary to access and accurately reproduce the eNotes in their custody, as well as implement data backups, offline storage, and document recovery.[74] Additionally, document custodians will need to perform periodic checks of the electronic vault systems to ensure that the eNotes continue to comply with E-SIGN and UETA's record retention requirements. If a document custodian foresees or discovers a system integrity problem, the custodian may need to convert these eNotes to another technology format, or even to paper.[75]

Regardless of the technological and process safeguards the mortgage industry has implemented for eNotes, lenders and other interested parties can always rely upon traditional methods of introducing eNote evidence for litigation purposes. For example, the document custodian could submit an affidavit asserting that an eNote that has been converted from one format to another accurately reflects the information that was contained in the original eNote, and describing the reliability of the document conversion process. If the eNote were completely lost, a document custodian could submit a lost note affidavit pursuant to UCC § 3-309, which governs the enforcement of lost, destroyed, or

---

72. 15 U.S.C.A. § 7001(e).

73. UETA § 12; cmt. 3.

74. *See* OCC Advisory Letter, Electronic Record Keeping, (AL 2004-9), *available at* http://www.occ.treas.gov/ftp/advisory/2004-9.doc.

75. Fannie Mae and Freddie Mac require the eNote to contain the borrower's specific agreement authorizing conversion to paper. *See* Fannie Mae eMortgage Guide and Freddie Mac eMortgage Handbook, *supra* note 43, Appendix A.

stolen negotiable instruments. Finally, there is always evidence outside of the eNote that can be called upon, such as witnesses, payment history, notary journals, and the like.

CONCLUSION

The volume of eNotes originated by the mortgage industry is small, but growing, as lenders, title insurers, closing agents, and investors integrate with the MERS eRegistry and implement their eNote processes. Several years from now, the origination and sale of eNotes will no longer be a novel idea, but business as usual. The acceptance of the MERS eRegistry as the solution for a transferable and original eNote is a testament to the collaboration among the mortgage industry players in pursuit of the common goal of a paperless environment.

Evidentiary Requirements for Electronic Notarization and the Legalization of Certified Electronic Documents

*Timothy S. Reiniger**

Notaries have long been critical components in authenticating documents. If a document has been notarized, it is "self-authenticated" under Federal Rules of Evidence Rule 902. No witness or other extrinsic evidence is necessary to provide the authentication foundation. The document comes directly into evidence, where the opposing party can challenge its authenticity with controverting evidence.

In the traditional physical realm, notaries confirmed the identities of signers, their intent to be bound by the document to be signed, and the completeness of the document to be signed. After witnessing the act of signing, or the affirmation of a signature, they provided the notarial act of attesting to the signature by applying their seal and other official information to the physical document. The act of the notary proved identity, intent, and the genuineness of the entire record at the time of signing. The notary made an official record of the date. As for continuing integrity of the information in the document, the notarial system then depended, like the rest of society, on the physical nature of the artifact to preserve the integrity of the document that had been notarized. One of the keys to the system was a physical seal, also an artifact of sorts that could be traced to the notary.

But how can such a process work in a digital world? If you are signing something electronically, as a notary might do in an electronic transaction dealing with digital information, how do we know it was really the notary who signed something? How does the notary prove his or her own identity? And when one cannot apply a physical seal, what does one do? How can there be an assurance of integrity, as the electronic document being signed and notarized might thereafter be edited?

As Tim Reiniger points out here, because the notarial act itself is self-proving, electronic documents authenticated by the notarial act require that the electronic notarial seal information, and electronic notarial certificate be attached to or logically associated with the underlying document in such a manner that the identity of the notary can be independently verified—and any alterations to the signatures or document contents rendered evident.

---

*Executive Director of the National Notary Association and member of the California and New Hampshire Bars. The author hereby acknowledges and thanks William A. Anderson of the National Notary Association for his invaluable assistance with the preparation of this appendix.

Accordingly, the notarial profession has now embarked on devising a eunomic regime that allows people dealing with digital evidence to conduct strong tests of identity (including the identity of the notary); integrity of information (of both the document itself, and the information on the document from the notary); and information about the time of notarization. Thus identity, integrity, and time, as the three main components of authenticity, can be handled in a fashion that will allow strong tests, or strong proof, in the future should questions arise.

BACKGROUND ON NOTARIES AND THEIR LEGAL AUTHORITY

In General

Evidentiary Function of the Notary

For both paper and electronic documents, the essential function of the notary[1] is to attest the genuineness of writings and acts of execution and, thereby, to authenticate documents for purposes of admissibility and proof in court proceedings, as well as for public recording purposes.[2] The notary's official witnessing act attributes a signature and document to a particular individual by formally attesting the signer's identity and intent, denoting the complete and original document, and protecting against forgery.[3] Because the notarial act under seal is self-proving, documents authenticated in this manner are rendered self-authenticating and admissible in court on their face.[4] Proof of execution before a notary is required by federal and state laws for many important legal documents, including property deeds, advance health care directives, and powers of attorney.

Authentication by Seal

Under the Federal Rules of Evidence and the evidence rules of nearly every state, notarized documents *under seal* are admitted without further proof.[5] Specifically, Rule 902(1)

---

1. Throughout this appendix, the term "notary" shall be used to mean "notary public."

2. *See generally* MICHAEL L. CLOSEN, ET AL., NOTARY LAW & PRACTICE: CASES AND MATERIALS (Nat'l Notary Ass'n 1997) and CHARLES N. FAERBER, 2007–2008 U.S. NOTARY REFERENCE MANUAL (Nat'l Notary Ass'n 2007).

3. Specific information concerning the various state requirements for the notary to attest the signer's identity and intent, as well as the integrity of the executed document, is available at http://www.nationalnotary.org/commission.

4. *See generally* EDWARD W. CLEARY, McCORMACK ON EVIDENCE § 228 (3rd ed. 1984).

5. The following state rules of evidence incorporate in whole or in part: FED R. EVID. 902 (1), (2), & (8). Rendering as self-authenticating a document under a notary public's seal of office as well as a document accompanied by a certificate of acknowledgment: ALA. R. EVID. 902 (Loislaw 2007); ALASKA R. EVID. 902 (Loislaw 2007); ARIZ. R. EVID. 902 (Loislaw 2007); ARK. R. EVID. 902 (Loislaw 2007); COLO. R. EVID. 902 (Loislaw 2007); DEL. UNIF. R. EVID. 902 (Loislaw 2007); FLA. ANN. STAT. § 90.902(1)(a) (LexisNexis 2007)(acknowledgment act provision not included); HAW. R. EVID. 902 (Loislaw 2007); IDAHO R. EVID. 902 (Loislaw 2007); IND. R. EVID. 902 (Loislaw 2007); IOWA R. EVID. 902 (Loislaw 2007); KY. R. EVID. 5-902 (Loislaw 2007); LA. CODE EVID. ANN. ART. 902 (Loislaw 2007); ME. R. EVID. 902 (Loislaw 2007); MD. R. 5-902 (Loislaw 2007); MICH. R. EVID. 902 (Loislaw 2007); MINN. R. EVID. 902 (Loislaw 2007); MISS. R. EVID. 902 (Loislaw 2007); MONT. R. EVID 902 (Loislaw 2007); NEB. REV. STAT. § 27-902 (LexisNexis 2007); N.H. R. EVID. 902 (Loislaw 2007); N.J. R. EVID. 902 (Loislaw 2007); N.M. R. EVID. 902 (Loislaw 2007); N.C. GEN. STAT. §8C-9-902 (Loislaw 2007); N.D. R. EVID. 902 (Loislaw 2007); OHIO R. EVID. 902 (Loislaw 2007); OKLA. STAT. TIT. 12 § 2902 (Loislaw 2007); OR. R. EVID. 902 (Loislaw 2007); PA. R. EVID. 902 (Loislaw 2007); R.I. R. EVID. 902 (Loislaw 2007); S.C. R. EVID. 902 (Loislaw 2007); S.D. R. EVID. 19-17-2 AND 19-17-9 (Loislaw 2007); TENN. R. EVID. 902 (Loislaw 2007); TEX. R. EVID. 902 (Loislaw 2007); UTAH R. EVID. 902 (Loislaw 1996); VT. R. EVID. 902 (Loislaw 1983); WASH. R. EVID. 902 (Loislaw 1996); W.VA. R. EVID. 902 (Loislaw 2007); WIS. STAT. § 909.02 (Loislaw 2007); WYO. R. EVID. 902 (Loislaw 2007). *See also* CAL. EVID. CODE §§ 1451 & 1452(f) (LexisNexis 2007).

requires that documents under seal of a public officer be treated as self-authenticating. The evidentiary effect of self-authentication is to create a rebuttable presumption of document authenticity and to permit admissibility.[6] The notarial certificate, to which the seal is affixed, provides prima facie or presumptive evidence of the due execution of the document and attribution of the principal.[7] In addition to removing the need for a testifying witness, self-authentication also shifts to the opposing party the burden of going forward with evidence on the issue.[8]

Authentication of a document under seal involves the inference of three items: (1) the notary is who he or she claims to be; (2) the seal is genuine; and (3) the seal was affixed by the named notary.[9] Concerning the first inference, because the notary is a "public officer," the notarial seal authenticates a document without the need for extrinsic evidence to prove the genuineness of the notary's identity and officer status.[10] The notarial seal thus provides prima facie proof of the individual's capacity as a notary.[11] With respect to the second and third inferences, the seal and official capacity to use the seal are presumed genuine because any forgery of the seal is fairly easy to detect.[12]

---

6. CLEARY, *supra* note 4, at 700; *see also* PAUL R. RICE, ELECTRONIC EVIDENCE LAW & PRACTICE at 248, 249 (American Bar Association 2005).

7. *See, e.g.,* CAL. EVID. CODE § 1451 (a certificate of acknowledgment or proof of a writing other than a will is prima facie evidence of the facts recited in the certificate and the signatures contained in the underlying document); COLO. REV. STAT. § 38-35-101(2) (LexisNexis 2006) (prima facie evidence of proper execution of deed); IND. CODE ANN. §§ 32-21-9-2 & 33-42-2-6 (certificate under seal is prima facie evidence of due execution); LA. CIV. CODE PROC. ART. 1836 (LexisNexis 2006) (prima facie proof of due execution); MICH. COMP. LAWS § 55.307(1) (Lexis-Nexis 2007); MO. ANN. STAT. § 490.410 (LexisNexis 2007 (prima facie evidence of due execution of deed); N.J. STAT. ANN. § 2A:82-17 (prima facie evidence of due execution); N.Y. CONS. LAWS § 137 Exec. (presumptive evidence of facts in certificate); 21 P. S. § 46 (LexisNexis 2006) (certificate under seal is presumptive evidence of facts in certificate); UTAH CODE ANN. § 78-25-7 (LexisNexis 2006) (prima facie evidence of due execution); WASH. REV. CODE ANN. § 64.08.050 (certificate under seal is prima facie evidence of due execution); WIS. STAT. ANN. § 134.01(4)(c) (LexisNexis 200) (presumptive evidence facts in certificate); & WYO. STAT. ANN. § 32-1-104(a) (2006) (presumptive evidence of facts in certificate). *See also* UTAH CODE ANN. § 69-1-4 (LexisNexis 2006) & WASH. REV. CODE ANN. § 5.52.050 (electronically transmitted instrument under seal is prima facie proof of due execution of the original). *See also* Briggs v. Glass, 420 So.2d 46, 47 (Ala. 1982); Fares v. Morrison, 54 Cal. App.2d 773, 775 (1942); Westmoreland v. Tallent, 274 Ga. 172, 174 (2001); Curtis v. Curtis, 75 N.E.2d 881 (Ill. 1949); Valeriano-Cruz v. Neth, 14 Neb. App. 855, 861 (2006); Smith v. Smith, 44 A.D.3d 1081 (NY 3d Dept 2007); Limor v. Fleet Mortgage Group (*In re Marsh*), 12 S.W.3d 449, 453 (Tenn. 2000); and Mortgage Associates, Inc. v. Hendricks, 51 Wis.2d 579 (1971).

8. *See supra* note 6; FED. R. EVID. 301. However, in some states, the presumption of due execution can be defeated only by clear and convincing evidence to the contrary. *See, e.g., In re Adoption of X.J.A.,* 284 Kan. 853 (2007); Thompson v. Shell Western E&P Inc., 607 So.2d 37, 40 (Miss. 1992); Dencer v. Erb, 142 N.J. Eq. 422, 426 (Ch. 1948); Chianese v. Meier, 285 A.D.2d 314, 320, 729 N.Y.S.2d 460, 466 (1st Dept 2001); Wayt v. Urbigkit, 157 P.3d 1057, 1061 (Wy. 2007).

9. 7 JOHN WIGMORE, EVIDENCE § 2161 (1978).

10. Pierce v. Indseth, 106 U.S. 546, 549; 1 S. Ct. 418 (1883) ("the Court will take judicial notice of the seals of notaries public for they are officers recognized by the commercial law of the world").

11. *See* Limor v. Fleet Mortgage Group *(In re Marsh),* 12 S.W.3d at 453 (affixation of the seal is prima facie proof of official character or that the notary is a notary). Idaho courts take judicial notice of the seals of notaries public (IDAHO CODE § 9-101[7]). *See infra* note 328 for a listing of states that presume a notary's official character without further proof as long as the office title is indicated in some way.

12. WIGMORE, *supra* note 9. California presumes a seal to be genuine and its use authorized if it purports to be the seal of a notary public within any state of the United States (CAL. EVID. CODE § 1452[f]) (LexisNexis 2007).

When a notary has attempted to authenticate a document merely with a signature, Rule 902(2) requires that the notary's signature and official capacity, in turn, be certified by a higher jurisdictional public officer who possesses a seal of office. This higher-level seal must then be affixed to effect self-authentication of the document. The drafters of the Federal Rules of Evidence recognized that the risk of forgery is reduced by the requirement of authentication by a public officer who possesses and affixes a seal.[13]

Similarly, acknowledgment act certificates are self-authenticating pursuant to FED. R. EVID. 902(8) and the rules of evidence of nearly every state. In states that grant non-notaries the power to take acknowledgments, this rule treats documents as self-authenticating even where a seal is not required.[14]

E-Document Authenticity Standard

Authenticity of executed electronic documents requires proof of origin (identity of the signer); signer intent to execute or adopt the writing; and content integrity (whether the document has been altered).[15] A critical part of the authentication inquiry is whether safeguards have been implemented to assure the continuing accuracy and integrity of the originally created record.[16]

Concerning electronically notarized documents, an international and national e-document authenticity standard has emerged that reflects the evidentiary need for electronic documents to have the capability of authenticity testing.[17] This standard requires that any relying party be able to verify the origin and integrity of the notarized electronic document.[18] Establishing the authenticity of a notarized document thus requires the capability, in perpetuity, of independently authenticating the notary, and verifying whether the content of the electronic document is complete and unaltered.

---

13. *See* Advisory Committee Notes to Fed. R. Evid. 902(2) (1972 Proposed Rules). *See also* Karla J. Elliott, *The Notarial Seal – The Last Vestiges of Notaries Past,* 31 J. MARSHALL L. REV. 903, at 908 (1998) ("The embosser seal provides maximum safeguards against forgery and fraud by providing and obvious, tactile means by which to verify an original document.").

14. *See, e.g.,* N.H. REV. STAT. ANN. § 455-A (in New Hampshire, a Justice of the Peace and Quorum for the State is not required to affix an official seal).

15. JANE K. WINN & BENJAMIN WRIGHT, THE LAW OF ELECTRONIC COMMERCE, § 20.05 (4th ed. Aspen Publishers, Inc. 2007).; RICE, *supra* note 6, at 222; Thomas J. Smedinghoff & Ruth Hill Bro, *Moving with Change: Electronic Signature Legislation as a Vehicle for Advancing E-Commerce,* 17 J. MARSHALL J. COMPUTER & INFORMATION LAW 723, at 731 (1999); *See also* Stephen Mason, *Electronic Signatures in Practice,* 6 J. HIGH TECH L. 149, at 158 (2006) for discussion of authentication of electronic documents generally in common law countries.

16. See *In re Vinhnee,* American Express Travel Related Service Co. v. Vinhnee, 336 B.R. 437 (9th Cir. B.A.P. 2005) (proponent failed to authenticate computer generated business records because of an inability to assure content integrity from the time they were originally created). *See generally* George L. Paul, *The "Authenticity Crisis" in Real Evidence,* 15 PRAC. LITIGATOR No. 6, at 45–49 (2004).

17. *See infra* in "Authenticating Electronic Public Documents for Interstate and International Use" the discussion of the nonrepudiation standards for electronic notarization, electronic Certificates of Authenticity, and e-Apostilles promulgated by the National Association of Secretaries of State and the Hague Conference on Private International Law.

18. National e-Notarization Standards, Standards 14 and 15 (Nat'l Ass'n of Secretaries of State 2006), *available at* http://www.nationalnotary.org/commission; First International Forum on e-Notarization and e-Apostilles, Conclusions 15 and 18 (Nat'l Notary Ass'n 2005), *available at* http://www.e-app.info.

Attributing (Authenticating) Electronic Notarial Acts

Under the Uniform Electronic Transactions Act (UETA), authentication of the origin and contents of a document to a particular individual is termed "attribution".[19] While not requiring the use of any one method to prove that an electronic signature is attributable to a person or document, the UETA importantly does provide that attribution may be proven by means of a security procedure.[20]

Electronic notarization is a security procedure for authenticating or attributing the principal signer.[21] As defined by Section 2(14) of UETA, a security procedure is:

> A procedure employed for the purpose of verifying that an electronic signature, record, or performance is that of a specific person or for detecting changes or errors in the information in an electronic record. The term includes a procedure that requires the use of algorithms or other codes, identifying words or numbers, encryption, or callback or other acknowledgment procedures.

Just as in the paper world, the act of electronic notarization authenticates an executed document by proving attribution of the electronic signature and document to the signatory.[22] When the electronic notarization process is performed in the manner of a security procedure, by incorporating encryption or similar technology, subsequent changes to the electronic signatures and document can be detected.[23]

The two-pronged function of electronic notarization as a security procedure—to verify the signer and the integrity of the signatures and document—in evidentiary terms renders both the underlying electronic document self-authenticating, and the notarial act, itself, self-proving. Performing the electronic notarization in the manner of a security procedure also serves to provide presumptive evidence of attribution of the electronic document as the act of the signer, and attribution of the electronic notarial certificate as the act of the specific notary.[24]

---

19. Unif. Elec. Transactions Act § 9(a) & com. (Nat'l Conf. of Comm'rs on Unif. State Laws 1999). The UETA has been adopted in every state and the District of Columbia except Georgia, Illinois, New York, and Washington.

20. *Id.*

21. UETA, *supra* note 19, at § *2(14)*; Ariz. Rev. Stat. § 41-351(9) (LexisNexis 2007); Daniel J. Greenwood, Electronic Notarization: Why It's Needed, How It Works, and How It Can Be Implemented to Enable Greater Transactional Security 10 (Nat'l Notary Ass'n 2006), *available at* http://www.nationalnotary.org/commission. The four states that have not enacted the UETA also recognize attribution by security procedure: Ga. Code Ann. § 10-12-4(j) (notary is required to use a secure or advanced electronic signature); 5 Ill. Comp. Stat. Ann. § 175/10-110(b) (authentication by security procedure expressly incorporated); 9 NYCRR 540.5(d) (procedures by government entities and public officers required for ensuring authenticity and integrity of records); Wash. Rev. Code Ann. § 19.34.340 (authentication by digital signature).

22. Greenwood, *supra* note 21, at 10.

23. *See* ABA Subcommittee on eTrust: eNW Whitepaper on eNotarization at 3.3 (American Bar Association, 2006), *available at* http://www.nationalnotary.org/commission ("[T]he document being proffered must contain or be accompanied by evidence that it has not changed since it was first generated in its final form (see Section 12, UETA), or if it has changed, what those changes were and their significance, if any.").

24. *See, e.g.,* Ariz. Rev. Stat. § 44-7033 (LexisNexis 2007); 5 Ill. Comp. Stat. Ann. § 175/10-120(b) (LexisNexis 2007).

Nature of Public Office

A notary is a public officer.[25] The primary duties of the office are to take acknowledgments of instruments, administer oaths and affirmations, execute jurats, certify copies of documents, witness and attest signatures, and perform other acts as specified by law.[26]

The U.S. Supreme Court has recognized notaries as public officers whose official acts, without further proof, are given legal recognition beyond the borders of the originating jurisdiction.[27] Consistent with this approach, the Minnesota Supreme Court has observed, "A public notary is considered not merely an officer of the country where he is admitted or appointed, but as a kind of international officer, whose official acts, performed in the state for which he is appointed, are recognized as authoritative the world over."[28]

Commission

Authority to perform notarial acts is granted to persons who have qualified and applied for a notary public commission with a state's notary appointing official.[29] To qualify for a commission, typically a person must be 18 years of age or older, maintain residency or

---

25. *See* ALA. CODE § 40-1-123 (LexisNexis 2007); ARIZ. REV. STAT. § 41-312(C), § 41-353(D) (LexisNexis 2007); ARK. CODE ANN. § 23-38-207 (LexisNexis 2006); CAL. GOV'T CODE § 6106 (LexisNexis 2007); COLO. REV. STAT. § 11-41-128 (LexisNexis 2006); D.C. CODE ANN. § 22-1404 (LexisNexis 2007); FLA. STAT. § 443.141(3)(a)(1) (LexisNexis 2007); GA. CODE ANN. § 7-1-788 (LexisNexis 2007); HAW. REV. STAT. ANN. § 12-7 (LexisNexis 2006); KY. REV. STAT. ANN. §§ 14.090(2) (LexisNexis 2007); LA. REV. STAT. ANN. § 42:282 (LexisNexis 2006); MD. CODE ANN. CTS. & JUD. PROC. § 2-212(c)(2) (LexisNexis 2006); MASS. GEN. LAWS ch. 267, § 1 (LexisNexis 2007); ME. REV. STAT. ANN. tit. 5 § 87 (LexisNexis 2006); MICH. COMP. LAWS § 750-248(1) (LexisNexis 2007); MINN. STAT. ANN. § 609.65 (LexisNexis 2006); N.Y. CONS. LAWS § 8021 11(b)(1) N.Y.C.P.L.R. (LexisNexis 2007); N.C. GEN. STAT. § 10B-3(13) (LexisNexis 2006); N.D. CENT. CODE § 12.1-01-04(22) (LexisNexis 2007); OR. REV. STAT. § 194.152 (LexisNexis 2006) (some notaries are considered public officials and some are not); R.I. GEN. LAWS § 11-17-1 (LexisNexis 2006); S.D. CODIFIED LAWS § 15-6-45(a) (LexisNexis 2005); TENN. CODE ANN. § 8-21-1201 (LexisNexis 2007); TEX. GOV'T CODE ANN. § 406.005(b) (LexisNexis 2006); VA. CODE ANN. § 17.1-270 (LexisNexis 2007); VT. STAT. ANN. tit. 13 § 1801 (2007); W.VA. CODE ANN. § 21-5-3. The following states reference notaries as notarial officers: DEL. CODE ANN. tit. 29 § 4321 (LexisNexis 2007); IOWA CODE ANN. § 9E.2(3) (LexisNexis 2006); MONT. CODE ANN. § 1-5-602(3) (LexisNexis 2005); NEB. REV. STAT. § 64-202(3) (LexisNexis 2007); NEV. REV. STAT. ANN. § 240.005. *See also,* State *ex rel.* Pickett v. Truman, 64 S.W.2d 105 (Mo. Banc. 1933); Smith v. Johnson, 231 N.E.2d 81 (Ohio App. 1967); Opinion of the Justices, 73 N.H. 621, 622 (1906); People v. Rathbone, 145 N.Y. 434, 437 (1895). For a survey of relevant cases pronouncing that notaries are public officials, see Michael L. Closen, *The Public Official Role of the Notary,* 30 J. MARSHALL L. REV. 651, at 652 n.4 (1998).

26. These "other acts" are wide and varied. For example, notaries can solemnize weddings (Florida, Louisiana, Maine and South Carolina); open and inventory the contents of safe deposit boxes (New York and many other states); perform protests of negotiable instruments (many states); qualify parties to bills in chancery (Tennessee); and subpoena witnesses to appear in court to testify (Connecticut, Ohio).

27. Smith v. Gale, 144 U.S. 509 (1892); Pierce v Indseth, 106 U.S. at 549; Britton v. Niccolls, 104 U.S. 757 (1881).

28. Wood v. St. Paul City Ry. Co., 44 N.W. 308, 308 (Minn. 1890).

29. The secretary of state appoints notaries in American Samoa (Secretary of State within the Office of Governor), Arizona, Arkansas, California, Colorado, Connecticut, Idaho, Illinois, Iowa, Kansas, Kentucky, Maine, Michigan, Missouri, Montana, Nebraska, Nevada, New Jersey, New York, North Carolina, North Dakota, Ohio, Oklahoma, Oregon, Pennsylvania, South Dakota, Texas, and Wyoming. Other appointing officials include the governor (Delaware, Florida, Indiana, Louisiana, Maryland, Massachusetts, Minnesota, Mississippi, New Hampshire, New Mexico, Rhode Island, South Carolina, Tennessee, West Virginia, Virginia and Wisconsin); lieutenant governor (Alaska, Utah and U.S. Virgin Islands); attorney general (Guam, Hawaii and Northern Marianas); county probate judge (Alabama); mayor (District of Columbia); superior court clerk (Georgia); supreme court (Puerto Rico); county superior judge (Vermont); and Director of the Department of Licensing (Washington).

employment in the state or jurisdiction where application is made, possess good moral integrity, and take an oath of office. Certain states require notaries to take an educational course[30] on the duties and ethical conduct of the notary public office, or pass an examination[31] on state laws and rules governing the performance of notarial acts. In thirty-five states, notaries must post a bond conditioned for the faithful performance of official duties.[32]

Qualification and commissioning procedures for lawyers are also varied. Certain states grant automatic notarial powers to lawyers, including Maine, Connecticut (for taking acknowledgments only); New Hampshire (for administering oaths related to taking testimony); and New Jersey (for taking acknowledgments and proofs). Ohio[33] and Wisconsin[34] automatically qualify lawyers, but they must formally apply for a commission.[35]

Presumption of Validity

As a public officer, the notary's official acts and all certified facts enjoy an evidentiary presumption of having been validly performed.[36] Accordingly, absent rebuttal evidence,

---

30. CAL. GOV'T CODE § 8201(a)(3) (LexisNexis 2007); FLA. ANN. STAT. § 668.50(11)(b) (LexisNexis 2007); MO. ANN. STAT. § 486.225(6) (LexisNexis 2007); N.C. GEN. STAT. § 10B-8(a) (LexisNexis 2006); OR. REV. STAT. § 194.022(h) (LexisNexis 2006); 57 PA. CONS. STAT. ANN. § 151(c) (LexisNexis 2006). Puerto Rico notaries public must fulfill the educational requirements for lawyers.

31. CAL. GOV'T CODE § 8201(a)(4) (LexisNexis 2007); CONN. GEN. STAT. ANN. § 3-94b(b)(3) (LexisNexis 2006); 17 D.C. MUN. REGS. § 2402.3 (Loislaw 2007); LA. REV. STAT. ANN. § 35:191(C)(2)(a) (LexisNexis 2006); NEB. REV. STAT. ANN.§ 64-101.01 (LexisNexis 2007); N.C. GEN. STAT. § 10B-8(b) (LexisNexis 2006); N.Y. EXEC. LAW. § 130 (LexisNexis 2007); OHIO REV. CODE ANN. § 147.02(B) (LexisNexis 2007); OR. REV. STAT. 194.022(g) (LexisNexis 2006); UTAH CODE ANN. § 46-1-3(5) (LexisNexis 2006). Puerto Rico notaries public must fulfill the examination requirement for lawyers. Applicants for a Hawaii and Maine notary commission also must pass an examination.

32. States and jurisdictions with bond requirements (in parentheses) are: ALA. CODE § 36-20-3 ($10,000); ALASKA STAT. § 44.50.034 ($1,000); ARIZ. REV. STAT. § 41-312(B) ($5,000); ARK. CODE ANN. § 21-14-101(d)(1) (LexisNexis 2006) ($7,500); CAL. GOV'T CODE § 8202 ($15,000); D.C. CODE ANN. § 1-1203 ($2,000); FLA. ANN. STAT. § 117.01(7)(a) ($7,500); HAW. REV. STAT. ANN. § 456-5 (LexisNexis 2006) ($1,000); IDAHO CODE ANN. § 51-105(2) ($10,000); 5 ILL. COMP. STAT. ANN. § 312/2-105 ($5,000); IND. CODE ANN. § 33-42-2-1(e) ($5,000); KAN. STAT. ANN. § 53-102 (LexisNexis 2006) ($7,500); KY. REV. STAT. ANN. §§ 423.010–.990 (amount varies by county); LA. REV. STAT. ANN. § 35:71(A)(1) (LexisNexis 2006) ($10,000—lawyers are exempt); MICH. COMP. LAWS § 55.273(2) ($10,000—lawyers are exempt); MISS. CODE ANN. § 25-33-1 (2007) ($5,000); MO. ANN. STAT. § 486-235(1) ($10,000); MONT. CODE ANN. § 1-5-405(1) (LexisNexis 2005) ($10,000); NEB. REV. STAT. § 64-102 ($15,000); NEV. REV. STAT. ANN. § 240.030(1)(c) ($10,000); N.M. STAT. ANN. § 14-12A-4 (B) ($10,000); N.D. CENT. CODE § 44-06-03 ($7,500); OKLA. STAT. ANN. tit. 49, § 2(A) (LexisNexis 2006) ($1,000); 57 PA. CONS. STAT. ANN. § 154 (LexisNexis 2006) ($10,000); S.D. CODIFIED LAWS § 18-1-2 (LexisNexis 2005) ($5,000); TENN. CODE ANN. § 8-16-104(a) ($10,000); TEX. GOV'T CODE ANN. § 406.010(a) (LexisNexis 2006) ($10,000); UTAH CODE ANN. § 46-1-4(1) (LexisNexis 2006) ($5,000); WASH. REV. CODE ANN. § 42.44.020(5) ($10,000); WIS. STAT. ANN. § 137.01(1)(d) (LexisNexis 2006) ($500—lawyers exempt); WYO. STAT. ANN. § 32-1-104(a) (LexisNexis 2006) ($500); 4 LPRA § 2001 (LexisNexis 2006) ($15,000); 3 V.I. CODE R. 773(b) ($5,000 or $10,000 in property).

33. *See* OHIO REV. CODE ANN. § 147.01(B).

34. *See* WIS. STAT. ANN. § 137.01(2)(a) (LexisNexis 2006).

35. In 2005, Missouri enacted a statute defining a notary public as "any person appointed and commissioned to perform notarial acts, including an attorney licensed to practice in this state" (MO. ANN. STAT. § 486.200[5] (LexisNexis 2007)). The secretary of state currently does not interpret this statute as granting lawyers automatic notarial powers.

36. *See, e.g.,* Eveleigh v. Conness, 933 P.2d 675, 682 (Kan. 1997) ("presumption that a public office has performed the duties of his or her office faithfully"); Gombach v. Department of State, 692 A.2d 1127, 1132 (Pa. Commonw. Ct. 1997) ("[A] notary commission notifies the public that the Commonwealth believes the notary can be trusted properly."); *In re Medlin,* 201 B.R. 188, 192 (E.D. Tenn. 1996) ("presumption that sworn public officers have properly executed their duties absent evidence to the contrary").

the notarial act is self-proving, and the certified facts are received into evidence without further proof of the notary's official authority or seal.[37] In some states, successful rebuttal requires clear and convincing evidence.[38]

Notarial Seal of Office

The notarial seal is a particular sign or written mark made to attest the formal execution of a document.[39] Information contained in the seal identifies the individual as a duly commissioned notary imbued with authority to perform official acts.[40] The notarial seal authenticates or attributes the official act as the act of a notary.[41] The evidentiary func-

---

37. By statutory means, the following states presume the official character of the notary and the lawful performance of the duties: ALASKA STAT. § 09.63.060 (LexisNexis 2007); ARIZ. REV. STAT. § 33-502(A) (LexisNexis 2007); CAL. EVID. CODE §§ 1453(c) & 1452(f) (notary's signature and seal presumed genuine); COLO. REV. STAT. § 12-55-204(1) (LexisNexis 2006); 29 DEL. CODE § 4323(c) (2007); D.C. CODE ANN. § 42-143(c) (LexisNexis 2007); GA. CODE ANN. § 9-10-113 (2006); 765 ILL. COMP. STAT. ANN. § 30/3(a) (LexisNexis 2007); IND. CODE ANN. § 34-37-1-5 (LexisNexis 2007); KAN. STAT. ANN. § 53-504 (LexisNexis 2006); ME. REV. STAT. ANN. tit. 4 § 1012(1) (LexisNexis 2006); MICH. COMP. LAWS § 565.263(1) (LexisNexis 2007); MINN. STAT. ANN. § 358.43(c) (LexisNexis 2006); MONT. CODE ANN. § 1-5-604(4) (LexisNexis 2005); NEV. REV. STAT. ANN. § 240.1635(3) (LexisNexis 2007); N.H. REV. STAT. ANN. § 456-B:3 III (LexisNexis 2007); N.M. STAT. ANN. § 14-14-3(C) (LexisNexis 2007); N.C. GEN. STAT. § 10B-99(a) (LexisNexis 2006) (notarial acts are given a presumption of regularity); N.D. CENT. CODE § 47-19-14.2(1) (LexisNexis 2007); OKLA. STAT. ANN. tit. § 49-114(C) (LexisNexis 2006); OR. REV. STAT. § 194.525(3) (LexisNexis 2006); S.C. CODE ANN. § 25-1-630(E) (LexisNexis 2006); VA. CODE ANN. § 55-118.2(a) (LexisNexis 2007); WASH. REV. CODE ANN. § 42.44.080(9) (LexisNexis 2007); W. VA. CODE ANN. § 39-1A-2(a) (LexisNexis 2007); WIS. STAT. ANN. § 706.07(3)(c) (LexisNexis 200).

38. See, e.g., Colburn v. Mid-State Homes, Inc., 266 So.2d 865 (Ala. 1972) (the acknowledgment is conclusive of the facts therein absent proof of fraud or duress); Witt v. Panek, 97 N.E.2d 283, 285 (Ill. 1951) ("the certificate of acknowledgment can be overcome only by proof which is clear, convincing and satisfactory, and by disinterested witnesses"); Waitt Bros. Land, Inc. v. Montange, 257 N.W.2d 516 (Iowa 1977); Jensen v. Skibiski, 28 So.2d 328 (Fl. 1947) (being a quasi-judicial act, the acknowledgment is conclusive of the facts therein absent proof of fraud or duress); Murdock v. Nelms, 212 Va. 639, 641 (1972) (the acknowledgment is a judicial act that imparts absolute verity and cannot be impeached except for fraud); Evans v. Bottomlee, 148 S.E.2d 712 (WV 1966) (being a quasi-judicial act, the acknowledgment is conclusive and cannot be impeached except for clear and satisfactory proof of fraud or collusion).

39. See CAL. CODE OF CIVIL PROCEDURE § 1930 (LexisNexis 2007); MONT. CODE ANN. § 1-4-201 (LexisNexis 2005); OR. REV. STAT. § 42.110 (LexisNexis 2006); Van Den Borre v. State, 596 So. 2d 687, 691 (Fla. App. 4. Dist. 1992); King v. Guynes, 42 So. 959,960 (La. 1907) ("The purpose of a 'seal' is to attest in a formal manner to the execution of an instrument."). See also BLACK'S LAW DICTIONARY, at 1210 (West 1979).

40. "The seal ensures that the Notary's credentials are present and legible." Douglas M. Fischer, The Seal: Symbol of Security, NAT'L NOTARY MAG., Nov. 1995, at 12.

41. ALA. CODE § 36-20-4 (LexisNexis 2007); ALASKA STAT. § 44.50.062(5) (LexisNexis 2007); ARIZ. REV. STAT. § 41-313(C)(3) (LexisNexis 2007); CAL. GOV'T CODE § 8207 (LexisNexis 2007); D.C. CODE ANN. § 1-1204 (LexisNexis 2007); FLA. STAT. § 95.03 (LexisNexis 2007); GA. CODE ANN. § 45-17-6 (2006); HAW. REV. STAT. ANN. § 456-3 (LexisNexis 2006); 5 ILL. COMP. STAT. ANN. § 312/3-101 (LexisNexis 2007); IND. CODE ANN. § 33-42-2-4(b) ("All notarial acts not attested by a seal as described in subsection (a) are void") (LexisNexis 2007); KAN. STAT. ANN. § 53-105 (LexisNexis 2006); MD. CODE ANN. STATE GOV'T. § 18-108(a) (LexisNexis 2006); MASS. GEN. LAWS ch. 59, § 31 (LexisNexis 2007); MINN. STAT. ANN. § 359.03 subd. 1 (LexisNexis 2006); MISS. CODE ANN. § 25-33-3 ("and his official acts shall be attested by his seal of office") (LexisNexis 2007); NEB. REV. STAT. § 64-210 (LexisNexis 2007); NEV. REV. STAT. ANN. § 240.040 (LexisNexis 2007); N.M. STAT. ANN. § 14-12A-18(B) (LexisNexis 2007); N.D. CENT. CODE § 6-02-05 (LexisNexis 2007); OKLA. STAT. ANN. tit. 49, § 5 (LexisNexis 2006); OR. REV. STAT. § 194.152 (LexisNexis 2006) (a document without an imprint of the official seal of the notary shall be of no effect); 57 PA. CONS. STAT. ANN. § 158 (LexisNexis 2006); TENN. CODE ANN. § 66-22-110 (2007) (acknowledgment without a seal is void); TEX. GOV'T CODE ANN. § 406.013(a) (LexisNexis 2006); UTAH CODE ANN. § 69-1-4 (LexisNexis 2006); WASH. REV. CODE ANN. § 65.52.050 WIS. STAT. ANN. § 137.01(4)(b) (LexisNexis 2006) WYO. STAT. ANN. § 32-1-106(a) (2006).

tion of the seal is to render the notarial act self-proving and the underlying document self-authenticating or admissible without further proof.[42]

Forty-nine states and the District of Columbia prescribe the form and content of the notarial seal.[43] With paper notarizations, the notarial seal appears in one of three forms: (1) impressed or embossed sign; (2) imprinted or stamped sign; and (3) handwritten (scrolled) or typed mark.[44] Information in the seal typically includes a combination of the notary's name, title, county, commission number, and commission expiration date.[45]

Forty-three states mandate one specific form for the notary's seal, most commonly an imprint.[46] Seven states permit the notary to use any of the three general forms for affixing information concerning commission and official capacity.[47] A certificate of notarization, containing some form of seal informational elements of a duly commissioned notary, constitutes a lawful notarization in those jurisdictions that do not mandate an impress or imprint of the notarial seal.[48]

---

42. *See supra* note 5. *See also* WIGMORE, *supra* note 9, §§ 2161, 2165.

43. The following states mandate a specific form for the notarial seal: ALA. CODE § 36-20-4 (LexisNexis 2007); ALASKA STAT. § 44.50.064 (LexisNexis 2007); ARIZ. REV. STAT. § 41-312(B)(2) (LexisNexis 2007); ARK. CODE ANN. § 21-14-106(a)(4), § 21-14-107(b)(1) (LexisNexis 2006); CAL. GOV'T CODE § 8207, CIV. CODE § 1193 (LexisNexis 2007); COLO. REV. STAT. § 12-55-112(2) (LexisNexis 2006); CONN. GEN. STAT. ANN. § 3-94j(a) (LexisNexis 2006); 29 DEL. CODE § 4309(b) (2007); D.C. CODE ANN. § 1-1204, § 42-147 (LexisNexis 2007); FLA. ANN. STAT. § 117.01(5)(b), § 117.05(3)(a) (LexisNexis 2007); GA. CODE ANN. § 45-17-69(a)(1) (2006); HAW. REV. STAT. ANN. § 456-3 (LexisNexis 2006); IDAHO CODE ANN. § 51-106(1) (2007); 5 ILL. COMP. STAT. ANN. § 312/3-101 (Lexis-Nexis 2007); IND. CODE ANN. § 33-42-2-4(a) (LexisNexis 2007); IOWA CODE ANN. § 9E.14(1) (LexisNexis 2006); KAN. STAT. ANN. § 53-105 (LexisNexis 2006); ME. REV. STAT. ANN. tit. 5 § 951 (LexisNexis 2006); MD. CODE ANN. STATE GOV'T. § 18-108(a), § 19-107(a) (LexisNexis 2006); MASS. EXEC. ORDER NO. 455 § 5(c) (Apr. 2004); MINN. STAT. ANN. § 359.03 subd. 1 (LexisNexis 2006); MISS. CODE ANN. § 25-33-3 (LexisNexis 2007); MO. ANN. STAT. §§ 486-380, 492-370 (LexisNexis 2007); MONT. CODE ANN. § 1-5-416(1)(d) (LexisNexis 2005); NEB. REV. STAT. § 64-210(1) (LexisNexis 2007); NEV. REV. STAT. ANN. § 240.040 (LexisNexis 2007); N.H. REV. STAT. ANN. § 455:3 (LexisNexis 2007); N.M. STAT. ANN. § 14-12A-18(A) (LexisNexis 2007); N.C. GEN. STAT. § 10B-36(a) (LexisNexis 2006); N.D. CENT. CODE § 44-06-04, § 47-19-32 (LexisNexis 2007); OKLA. STAT. ANN. tit. 49, § 5 (LexisNexis 2006); OH. REV. CODE § 147.04 (LexisNexis 2007); OR. REV. STAT. § 194.031(1) (LexisNexis 2006); 57 PA. CONS. STAT. ANN. § 158(a) (LexisNexis 2006); S.C. CODE ANN. § 26-1-60 (LexisNexis 2006); S.D. CODIFIED LAWS § 18-1-3 (LexisNexis 2005); TENN. CODE ANN. § 8-16-114(a) & (b) (LexisNexis 2007); TEX. GOV'T CODE ANN. § 406.013(a) (LexisNexis 2006); UTAH CODE ANN. § 46-1-16(2)(a) (LexisNexis 2006); VA. CODE ANN. § 47.1-16C (LexisNexis 2007); WASH. REV. CODE ANN. § 42.44.090(1) (LexisNexis 2007); W. VA. CODE ANN. § 29C-4-102(a) (LexisNexis 2007); WIS. STAT. ANN. § 137.01(3)(a) (LexisNexis 2006); WYO. STAT. ANN. § 32-1-106(a) (LexisNexis 2006). The following states prescribe seal informational content but permit multiple forms: KY. REV. STAT. ANN. § 423.010 (LexisNexis 2007); LA. REV. STAT. ANN. § 35:12 (LexisNexis 2006); MICH. COMP. LAWS § 55.287(2) (LexisNexis 2007); N.J. STAT. ANN. § 52:7-19 (LexisNexis 2007); N.Y. CONS. LAWS § 137 Exec. (LexisNexis 2007); R.I. GEN. LAWS § 34-11-1.1 (LexisNexis 2006).

44. *Id. See also* ARTHUR LINTON CORBIN, CONTRACTS 3241 (one-volume ed. 1952); RESTATEMENT (SECOND) OF CONTRACTS § 96 cmt. a (1981).

45. *See supra* note 43.

46. *Id.*

47. These states include Kentucky, Louisiana, Michigan, New Jersey, New York, Rhode Island, and Vermont. While Vermont preserves the authenticating evidentiary function of the notarial seal, Vermont does not require the seal for enforceability and is the only state that leaves the content and form entirely to the discretion of the notary. FAERBER, *supra* note 2, at 183, 191, 231, 301, 319, 415 & 471.

48. *See, e.g.,* WIGMORE, *supra* note 9, at § 2165.

LEGAL REQUIREMENTS FOR EVIDENCING THE NOTARIZATION OF ELECTRONIC DOCUMENTS

In General

Authorization

The federal Electronic Signatures in Global and National Commerce Act ("E-SIGN")[49] and the widely enacted UETA authorize the use of electronic signatures and seals by notaries public.[50] E-SIGN is modeled after the UETA and contains the same notary-related provisions and definitions.[51] Commensurate with their policy of technological netutrality, while authorizing e-notarization, neither E-SIGN nor the UETA specifies the manner for performing the electronic notarial act. Because notaries are principally governed by state law, this discussion will focus on the UETA and the pertinent language variations in the state enactments.

Section 11 of the UETA gives notaries the authority to act electronically using any type of electronic signature.[52] An electronic signature satisfies any requirement for a handwritten signature[53] and expresses the principal's intent to be bound by the document.[54] Section 11 also requires that any other information required by a state law to be included for the notarial act—such as the notary's name, title, commission number, commission expiration date, and seal image—must be attached to or logically associated with the notary's electronic signature or the electronic document.

Of the forty-six enactments of the UETA to date, six states have amended or qualified Section 11 in various ways. California and Indiana replaced the phrase "electronic signature of the person authorized to perform these acts," with "the electronic signature of the notary public,"[55] clarifying that only a *notary public*, and not just any non-notary who has been statutorily granted notarial powers, may perform electronic notarizations. Hawaii's version provides that those documents made under seal are satisfied if the electronic signature or seal of the officer are attached to or logically associated with the signature or record.[56]

Florida made two substantive changes. First, neither a rubber stamp nor impression-type seal need be used for an electronic notarization.[57] Second, all first-time applicants for a notary public commission must take a course of instruction on notarization and *electronic notarization* before commencing official duties.[58]

---

49. 15 U.S.C.A. §§ 7001 *et seq.*

50. *See* UETA, supra note 19, at § 11. ("If a law requires a signature or record to be notarized, acknowledged, verified, or made under oath, the requirement is satisfied if the electronic signature of the person authorized to perform those acts, together with all other information required to be included by other applicable law, is attached to or logically associated with the signature or record.").

51. Electronic Signatures in Global and National Commerce Act ("E-SIGN") 15 USC § 7001(g).

52. An electronic signature is any "an electronic sound, symbol, or process attached to or logically associated with a record and executed or adopted by a person with the intent to sign the record." UETA § 2(8) (1999).

53. *Id.* § 7(d).

54. *Id.* § 2(8).

55. CAL. CIV. CODE § 1633.11(a) (LexisNexis 2007); IND. CODE ANN. § 26-2-8-110 (LexisNexis 2007).

56. HAW. REV. STAT. ANN. § 489E-11 (LexisNexis 2006).

57. FLA. ANN. STAT. § 668.50(11)(a). *See* FLA. ANN. STAT. § 117.021(2) for security requirements.

58. *Id.* § 668.50(11)(b).

Kansas specifically authorized the Secretary of State to promulgate rules and regulations establishing procedures for an electronic notarization.[59] These rules were published effective December 30, 2005.[60]

In enacting the UETA, Pennsylvania postponed the effective date of its section on notarization until thirty days after a notice was published in the *Pennsylvania Bulletin* by the Secretary of the Commonwealth indicating that the section no longer conflicted with the requirements and procedures for electronic notarization, acknowledgment, and verification.[61] The required notice was subsequently published in the *Pennsylvania Bulletin* on December 30, 2005.[62]

Notary Registration Requirement

Coincident to the enactment of the UETA and E-SIGN, states have considered whether a notary public commission authorizes a notary to perform electronic acts, or whether an additional authorization is necessary. Arizona and Virginia have taken one approach by requiring "electronic notaries"[63] to obtain a separate commission to perform electronic acts, including submission of a separate application and application fee, and oath of office.[64]

The states of Colorado, Kansas, Minnesota, North Carolina, and Pennsylvania have taken a second approach. These states stop short of mandating a separate commission, opting instead to have notaries register for authorization to perform electronic acts. This registration informs the commissioning official that the notary public possesses the technology, tools, and capability to perform electronic acts, and can require the notary to enumerate the technology or technologies the notary will use to create an official electronic signature and/or electronic notary seal.[65]

National Association of Secretaries of State Standards

In 2005, the National Association of Secretaries of State (NASS) established the National e-Notarization Commission to study and propose national standards for electronic notarization. Chaired by North Carolina Secretary of State Elaine Marshall and comprised of secretaries of state, state notary regulating officials, state attorneys general, and federal government representatives, the commission developed standards that were adopted by NASS in July 2006. The resulting standards reflect the need for the electronic notarial act to be self-proving and to provide the capability of document authenticity testing and nonrepudiation.[66]

---

59. KAN. STAT. ANN. § 16-1611(b) (LexisNexis 2006).

60. KAN. ADMIN. REG. §§ 7-43-1 *et seq.* (Loislaw 2007).

61. 73 PA. CONS. STAT. ANN. § 2260.5101(1) (LexisNexis 2006).

62. 35 PA. B. 7068 (Dec. 31, 2005), http://www.pabulletin.com/secure/data/vol35/35-53/2416.html.

63. *See* ARIZ. REV. STAT. § 41-351(7) (The term "electronic notary" is defined as "any person commissioned to perform notarial acts under this article.").

64. *See id.* § 41-353. VA. CODE ANN. § 47.1-7 (LexisNexis 2007).

65. 8 COLO. CODE REG. § 1505-11, Rule 2 (Loislaw 2007); KAN. ADMIN. REG. § 7-43-2(d) (Loislaw 2007); N.C. GEN. STAT. § 10B-106 (LexisNexis 2006); MINN. STAT. ANN. § 359.01(subd. 5) (LexisNexis 2006); 35 PA. B. 7068 (Dec. 31, 2005), http://www.pabulletin.com/secure/data/vol35/35-53/2416.html.

66. NATIONAL E-NOTARIZATION STANDARDS, Standard 13 (Nat'l Ass'n of Secretaries of State 2006). The ABA defines the term "non-repudiation" as "[s]trong and substantial evidence of the identity of the signer of a message and of message integrity, sufficient to prevent a party from successfully denying the origin, submission or delivery of the message and the integrity of its contents." DIGITAL SIGNATURE GUIDELINES § 1.20 (American Bar Association 1996).

The NASS National e-Notarization Standards require an electronic notarization to give relying parties the ability to independently verify the notary and detect alterations to the signatures and document.[67] The principal must be physically present before the notary at the time of the electronic notarization,[68] and the notary must identify the principal using the same methods of identification as for paper-based acts.[69] NASS rejected the idea that in an electronic environment, "physical appearance"[70] can be established through video-conference links, audio-visual hookups, or similar technology.[71] An electronic notarization also must be performed securely and reliably. Any electronic signature, seal, and certificate of a notary must identify the notary public who is authorized to perform the electronic act and provide a means for subsequently testing the integrity of the contents and signatures.

Notary's Electronic Signature

The NASS standards adopt the UETA's definition of electronic signature[72] and add a definition for the notary's electronic signature.[73] No particular technology for the notary's electronic signature is specified, but an electronic notary signature must be attached to or logically associated with the electronic document so that removal or alteration of the electronic signature is detectable, and renders evidence of the change so as to invalidate the electronic notarial act.[74] A notary may use any type of electronic signature as long as it meets the following criteria:

> The notary public's electronic signature is deemed to be reliable if the following requirements are met: a) it is unique to the notary public, b) it is capable of independent verification, c) it is retained under the notary public's sole control, d) it is attached to or logically associated with the electronic document, and e) it is linked to the data in such a manner that any subsequent alterations to the underlying document or electronic notarial certificate are detectable and may invalidate the electronic notarial act.[75]

Electronic Notarial Seal

The NASS standards provide for the use of an electronic notarial seal, defined as "information within a notarized electronic document that includes the notary public's name, jurisdiction of appointment, commission number, and commission expiration date, and generally corresponds to data in notary public seals used on paper documents."[76]

---

67. NATIONAL E-NOTARIZATION STANDARDS, Standards 5–11.

68. *Id.* Standard 1.

69. *Id.* Standard 2.

70. "'Physical appearance' and 'appears before the notary' mean that the principal and the notary public are physically close enough to see, hear, communicate with, and give documents to each other without reliance on electronic devices such as telephones, computers, video cameras or facsimile machines." *Id.* Definition 10.

71. Of note is the fact that in 2006, the Utah legislature enacted Senate Bill 20, which repealed a law allowing an acknowledgment to be made "either in the presence of the notary or by an electronic communication that is as reliable as an admission made in the presence of a notary."

72. *Id.* Definition 6.

73. *Id.* Definition 9.

74. *Id.* Standard 5.

75. *Id.* Standard 7.

76. *Id.* Definition 5. The definition is based virtually verbatim upon the Model Notary Act (2002) definition in § 14-6 (Nat'l. Notary Ass'n. 2002).

The electronic notary seal must be affixed to or logically associated with the electronic document in such a manner that removal or alteration of the electronic seal is detectable, provides evidence of the change, and as a result invalidates the electronic notarial act.[77] The notary's electronic seal must meet the same five-point reliability test as for an electronic signature.[78] The electronic seal also may function as the electronic signature.[79]

Electronic Notarial Certificate

As with paper-based acts, the NASS standards require a notary to complete a certificate to evidence an electronic notarial act.[80] This electronic certificate contains important evidentiary facts certified or attested to by the notary in an electronic notarization, such as the date and place of the act, the name of the signer or signers personally appearing before the notary, and the type of notarization performed. In order to preserve a trustworthy record of what was signed by the principal and notary, the electronic notarial certificate must be affixed in such a manner as to render both the certificate and the underlying document tamper-evident.[81]

State Law Requirements for Manner of Performing e-Notarization
In General

Electronic notarization is a security procedure that attributes the signature to the principal signer and renders the electronic notarial act self-proving.[82] By attaching the seal information in a manner that enables independent verification of the notary and tamper evidence of the electronic document, the notary's evidentiary function of rendering documents self-authenticating is preserved.[83] While physically affixing the imprint or impress of the paper seal image does not apply to an electronic document, the information concerning the notarial seal nevertheless must be attached.[84] E-SIGN and the UETA defer to other state laws and regulations for direction on how the notary's seal information is to be attached to a document or for detailing a specific security procedure to be used by the notary in attributing the signature to the principal.[85]

---

77. NATIONAL E-NOTARIZATION STANDARDS, Standard 8.

78. *Id.* Standard 9.

79. *Id.* Standard 4 cmt.

80. *Id.* Definition 7 ("'Electronic notarial certificate' means the portion of a notarized electronic document that is completed by the notary public, bears the notary public's electronic signature and/or official electronic seal, official title, commission number, commission expiration date, any required information concerning the date and place of the electronic notarization, and states the facts attested to or certified by the notary public in a particular electronic notarization.").

81. *Id.* Standard 6 ("When performing an electronic notarization, a notary public shall complete an electronic notarial certificate, which shall be attached to or logically associated with the electronic document such that removal or alteration of the electronic notarial certificate is detectable and will render evidence of alteration of the document containing the notary certificate which may invalidate the electronic notarial act.").

82. *See supra* note 21 and accompanying text. Although E-SIGN is silent on the matter, procedures and methods for authenticating or attributing signers are set forth by state law.

83. NATIONAL E-NOTARIZATION STANDARDS, "Form and Manner of Performing the Electronic Notarial Act," cmt. ("Although UETA, URPERA, and the federal E-SIGN law can be read to have eliminated the need for a physical seal image as a requirement for determining whether an electronic document is an 'original' versus a copy, the seal requirement remains essential to authenticating documents under federal and state rules of evidence.").

84. *See* ABA SUBCOMMITTEE ON ETRUST: ENOTARIZATION, *supra* note 23, at 1.0.

85. *Id.* "Registration Requirement," cmt. ("The important matter is that all of the notary public's identifying and commissioning information be made a part of, or a secure attachment to, the underlying notarized electronic document.").

In performing the electronic notarization as a security procedure, states either require or permit the notary to use any combination of the following forms or methods for attaching the seal information: (1) the seal information combined with a secure electronic signature;[86] (2) a secure electronic notarial seal combined with a secure electronic signature;[87] (3) an electronic image of the paper seal imprint or impress;[88] (4) an electronic image of the paper seal imprint as well as an electronic image of the holographic signature;[89] and (5) the seal information combined with a document authentication number.[90]

E-Notarization Performed as a Form-Specified Security Procedure

Fourteen states now prescribe either a specific method or specific security criteria for performing the electronic notarial act in the manner of a security procedure: Arizona, Arkansas, California, Colorado, Florida, Georgia, Illinois, Kansas, Minnesota, North Carolina, Nevada, Pennsylvania, Virginia, and Washington. Various forms or methods are required.

Several states require the use of an electronic notary signature or seal that identifies the notary public and is unique to that notary.[91] In the states of California (electronic advance health directives), Kansas, Minnesota, Nevada, Pennsylvania, and Washington, use of a digital signature is the specified method.[92] In the states of Arizona, Arkansas, Florida, Georgia, Illinois, North Carolina, and Virginia, a secure electronic signature is required that is unique to the notary, capable of independent verification, under the notary's sole control, and linked to the electronic document so as to show evidence of alterations or forgery.[93]

---

86. ARIZ. REV. STAT. §§ 44-7011 & 44-7034 (LexisNexis 2007); ARK. CODE ANN. §§ 19-11-203(29) & 25-31-104(b)(3) (LexisNexis 2006); CAL. PROBATE CODE § 4673(b) (LexisNexis 2007); (electronic advance health directives); FLA. ANN. STAT. § 117.021(2) (LexisNexis 2007); GA. CODE ANN. §§ 10-12-3(6) & 10-12-4(j) (2006); 5 ILL. COMP. STAT. ANN. § 175/10-110 and 14 ILL. ADMIN. CODE 100.30 (LexisNexis 2007); KAN. ADMIN. REG. § 7-43-3(a) (Loislaw 2007); NEV. REV. STAT. ANN. § 720.150(5) and NEV. ADMIN. CODE § 720.770 (LexisNexis 2007); 35 PA. B. 7068 (Dec. 1, 2005), http://www.pabulletin.com/secure/data/vol35/35-53/2416.html; WASH. REV. CODE ANN. § 19.34.020(11) and § 19.34.340 (LexisNexis 2007).

87. MINN. STAT. ANN. § 358.47(a) (LexisNexis 2006); N.C. ADMIN. CODE tit. 18 ch. 7 §§ 07C.0401(a-d) & 07C.0402(a-d) (Loislaw 2007); VA. CODE ANN. § 47.1-16(B), (D) (LexisNexis 2007).

88. California (except for electronic advance health directives).

89. N.C. ADMIN. CODE tit. 18 ch. 7 §§ 07C.0401(e) & 07C.0402(e) (Loislaw 2007), *available at* http://www.nationalnotary.org/commission.

90. COLO. REV. STAT. § 12-55-106.5 (LexisNexis 2006).

91. ARIZ. REV. STAT. §§ 41-351(8), (9) & 44-7034 (LexisNexis 2007); ARK. CODE ANN. §§ 25-31-103(1) & 25-31-104(b)(3) (LexisNexis 2006); 8 COLO. CODE REG. § 1505-11 Rule 1(1) (Loislaw 2007); FLA. ANN. STAT. § 117.021(2) (LexisNexis 2007); GA. CODE ANN. §§ 10-12-3(6) & 10-12-4(3)(j) (2006); KAN. STAT. ANN. § 16-1602(d) and KAN. ADMIN. REG. § 7-43-3(a) (LexisNexis 2006); MINN. STAT. ANN. § 325K.23 (LexisNexis 2006); NEV. REV. STAT. ANN. § 720.150(5) and NEV. ADMIN. CODE § 720.770 (LexisNexis 2007); N.C. GEN. STAT. § 10B-117 and N.C. ADMIN. CODE tit. 18 ch. 7 §§ 07C .0401 & 07C .042 (LexisNexis 2006); WASH. REV. CODE ANN. §§ 19.34.020(11) & 19.34.340 (LexisNexis 2007).

92. CAL. PROBATE CODE § 4673(b) (LexisNexis 2007); KAN. ADMIN. REG. § 7-43-3(a) (Loislaw 2007); MINN. STAT. ANN. § 325K.23 (LexisNexis 2006); NEV. REV. STAT. ANN. § 720.150(5) and NEV. ADMIN. CODE § 720.770 (LexisNexis 2007); 35 PA. B. 7068 (Dec. 1, 2005), http://www.pabulletin.com/secure/data/vol35/35-53/2416.html; WASH. REV. CODE ANN. §§ 19.34.020(11) & 19.34.340 (LexisNexis 2007).

93. ARIZ. REV. STAT. §§ 44-7031 & 44-7034 (LexisNexis 2007); ARK. CODE ANN. §§ 19-11-203(29) & 25-31-104(b)(3) (LexisNexis 2006); FLA. ANN. STAT. § 117.021(2) (LexisNexis 2007); GA. CODE ANN. §§ 10-12-3(6) & 10-12-4(j) (2006); 5 ILL. COMP. STAT. ANN. § 175/10-110 and 14 ILL. ADMIN. CODE 100.30 (LexisNexis 2007); N.C. ADMIN. CODE tit. 18 ch. 7 §§ 07C.0401(a-d) & 07C.0402(a-d) (Loislaw 2007); VA. CODE ANN. § 47.1-16(B), (D) (LexisNexis 2007).

Minnesota, Pennsylvania, and Virginia specify that the notary's electronic signature and accompanying seal information be attached in a manner so as to attribute the signature as the act of the notary identified on the official commission.[94]

States further set requirements for securing the notary's electronic signature from loss, theft, or use by any other person.[95] These rules correspond to similar rules for paper-based signatures and seals.[96] As long as the electronic signature or seal is used only by the notary and is kept secure from unauthorized or wrongful use by others, the public can have confidence that any electronic document bearing the notary's signature or seal is authentic.

California and North Carolina require notaries to affix an actual image of the notary's physical seal[97] to all[98] electronic notarizations. However, under California's electronic recording statute, three specific types of documents are exempted from this electronic image requirement: an assignment of a deed of trust, substitution of trustee, and deed of reconveyance.[99]

The state of Colorado adopts a unique approach. Each notary who has registered intent to notarize electronically with the Secretary of State is assigned an individually unique accounting system validation number and a set of Document Authentication Numbers (DAN). Each DAN includes the accounting system validation number issued to the notary, and a randomly generated number that when used together may constitute the notary's electronic signature and identify both the individual notary and the document to which the DAN has been affixed.[100] The notary then uses a different DAN for each electronically notarized document.[101] The notary may use a DAN as an electronic signature if the notary's name, the words "NOTARY PUBLIC" and "STATE OF COLORADO," and the words "my commission expires," followed by the expiration of the notary's commission are included with each DAN affixed to an electronic

---

94. MINN. STAT. ANN. § 359.47(a) (LexisNexis 2006); 57 PA. CONS. STAT. ANN. § 155(c) (LexisNexis 2006); VA. CODE ANN. § 47.1-16(B) (LexisNexis 2007)).

95. VA. CODE ANN. § 47.1-14(G) (LexisNexis 2007); N.C. GEN. STAT. §§10B-125(a), 10B-126(a) & (b) (LexisNexis 2006).

96. ALASKA STAT. § 44.50064 (LexisNexis 2007); ARIZ. REV. STAT. §§ 41-312(C), 41-323(B) & (C) (LexisNexis 2007); ARK. CODE ANN. §§ 21-14-107(d) & (e) (LexisNexis 2006); CAL. GOV'T CODE § 8207 (LexisNexis 2007); COLO. REV. STAT. § 12-55-118 (LexisNexis 2006); FLA. ANN. STAT. § 117.05(3)(c) & (e) (LexisNexis 2007); IDAHO CODE ANN. § 51-119(4) (2007); 5 ILL. COMP. STAT. ANN. § 312/7-107 (LexisNexis 2007); MASS. EXEC. ORDER No. 455 § 5(c) (Apr. 2004), *available at* http://www.sec.state.ma.us/pre/prepdf/execorder445.doc; MO. ANN. STAT. §§ 486-285(3) & 486-380 (LexisNexis 2007); NEV. REV. STAT. ANN. § 240.143 (LexisNexis 2007); N.M. STAT. ANN. §§ 14-12A-18(A) & (E) (LexisNexis 2007); N.C. GEN. STAT. §§ 10B-36(a) & 10B-60(f) (LexisNexis 2006); N.D. CENT. CODE § 44-06-04 (LexisNexis 2007); OKLA. ADMIN. CODE 655:25-5-2 (Loislaw 2007); OR. REV. STAT. § 194.990(1)(c) (LexisNexis 2006); 57 PA. CONS. STAT. ANN. §§ 158(d) & (e) (LexisNexis 2006); UTAH CODE ANN. § 46-1-16(2) (LexisNexis 2006); WASH. REV. CODE ANN. § 42.44.090(4) (LexisNexis 2007); W. VA. CODE ANN. § 29C-6-204 (LexisNexis 2007).

97. CAL. GOV'T CODE § 8207 (LexisNexis 2007); N.C. ADMIN. CODE tit. 18 ch. 7 § 07C.0402 (Loislaw 2007).

98. California's Electronic Recording Delivery Act of 2004 (GOV'T CODE §§ 27390 *et seq.*) does not allow real property documents affecting consumers, including deeds of trust and conveyance deeds, to be electronically notarized and submitted for digital electronic recording in the state.

99. CAL. GOV'T CODE § 27391(e) (LexisNexis 2007).

100. COLO. REV. STAT. § 12-55-112(4.5)(b) (LexisNexis 2006); 8 COLO. CODE REG. § 1505-11 Rule 1 (Loislaw 2007).

101. 8 COLO. CODE REG. §1505-11 Rule 2(4)(b) (Loislaw 2007).

document.[102] If the notary elects to use a different type of electronic signature, such as a digital signature, a DAN still must be used in the electronic notarization.

E-Notarization Performed as a Form-Unspecified Security Procedure

Thirty-six states and the District of Columbia at this writing have not prescribed a specific method for securely attaching the required seal information to an electronic document.[103] Nor have these states yet mandated a type of security procedure to be used in performing an e-notarization or to ensure non-repudiation. As a result, the notary is not limited to using one type of security procedure or method.

E-Notarization Performed as a Security Procedure—Time-Stamping

Time-stamping helps to ensure signer and document non-repudiation by providing strong and verifiable cryptographic evidence that a specific electronic record existed at a specific moment in time. Time-stamping an electronic record thus gives relying parties verifiable proof of when a certain act has taken place. Currently, only Arizona requires the electronic notarial act to include time-stamping.[104]

Electronic Notary Journal

An important aspect for establishing the veracity of a notarization and ensuring non-repudiation is the creation of a record of the notarial act in a bound or electronic journal. Nearly half the states require notaries to log the pertinent facts of each notarization performed in an official journal or record book.[105] E-SIGN and the UETA authorize the use of electronic journals. Virginia requires the use of an electronic notary journal for all electronic notarial acts.[106]

The journal entry preserves an entirely separate and independent record of the transaction, which can be of great value in the event that the document is later lost, damaged,

---

102. 8 Colo. Code Reg. § 1505-11 Rule 2(4)(c) (Loislaw 2007).

103. Of these, rules are forthcoming from Alaska and Oregon.

104. Ariz. Rev. Stat. §§ 41-355 & 41-356 (LexisNexis 2007).

105. Ala. Code § 36-20-6 (LexisNexis 2007); Ariz. Rev. Stat. § 41-319(A) (LexisNexis 2007); Cal. Gov't Code § 8206(a) (LexisNexis 2007); Colo. Rev. Stat. § 12-55-111(1) & (4) (LexisNexis 2006) (where notaries must keep a journal for all electronic acts); D.C. Code Ann. § 1-1211 (LexisNexis 2007); Fla. Ann. Stat. § 117.01(4) (LexisNexis 2007); Haw. Rev. Stat. Ann. § 456-15 (LexisNexis 2006); Ky. Rev. Stat. Ann. § 423.030 (for notarial protests only); Me. Rev. Stat. Ann. tit. 19-A § 654 (for marriages only); Md. Code Ann. St. Gov. Art. 18 § 107 (LexisNexis 2007); Mass. Exec. Order No. 455, § 11(a) (April 2004), Miss. Code Ann. § 25-33-5 (LexisNexis 2007); Mo. Ann. Stat. § 486-260 (LexisNexis 2007); Neb. Rev. Stat. § 64-101(6) (notaries must "faithfully discharge the duties pertaining to said office and keep records according to law"); Nev. Rev. Stat. Ann. § 240.120(1) (LexisNexis 2007); N.D. Cent. Code § 44-06-08 (for notarial protests only); Ohio Rev. Code Ann.§ 147.04 (for notarial protests only); Okla. Stat. Ann. tit. 49, § 7 (LexisNexis 2006) (for notarial protests only); Or. Rev. Stat. § 194.152 (LexisNexis 2006); 57 Pa. Cons. Stat. Ann. § 161(a) (LexisNexis 2006); Tenn. Code Ann. § 18-16-118 (LexisNexis 2007) (notaries must keep a journal in order to charge a fee); Tex. Gov't Code Ann. § 406.014 (LexisNexis 2006); Utah Code Ann. § 46-1-13 (LexisNexis 2006) ("A notary may keep, maintain, and protect as a public record, and provide for lawful inspection a chronological, permanently bound official journal of notarial acts, containing numbered pages."); 4 LPRA § 2071 (LexisNexis 2006) (protocol of original deeds and acts executed by a notary), and § 2092 (registry of affidavits).

106. Va. Code Ann. § 47.1-14(C) (LexisNexis 2007).

or contested. A document signer's signature[107] and even a thumbprint[108] captured in the journal are compelling, if not irrefutable, evidence that the identified signer was physically present before the notary on the date of the notarization.

AUTHENTICATING ELECTRONIC PUBLIC DOCUMENTS FOR INTERSTATE AND INTERNATIONAL USE

General Principle

When a document executed in one place is to be submitted in a court or office of another state or foreign jurisdiction, certification of the notary's identity and official status may be required as a prerequisite for that document to be recognized or received into evidence in that other court or office.[109] The current methods and treaties of authentication for traditional paper documents apply to electronic documents.

Because notarial acts do not expressly fall within the terms of the Full Faith and Credit Clause of Article IV of the U.S. Constitution,[110] many states have enacted statutes that presume the validity of official acts performed by notaries in other states and foreign nations.[111]

Certificates of Authenticity (Appointment)

State, county, and judicial officials have the legal obligation, when requested, to verify the authority of a notarial officer performing electronic notarizations.

Standards for electronic certificates of authenticity and apostilles have been established by NASS. As prerequisites to issuing certifications and apostilles, electronic notarial acts must meet certain basic requirements to ensure non-repudiation:

> a) the fact of the notarial act, including the notary's identity, signature, and commission status, must be verifiable by the commissioning official and b) the notarized electronic document will be rendered ineligible for authentication by the commissioning official if it is improperly modified after the time of notarization, including any unauthorized alterations to the document content, the electronic notarial certificate, the notary public's electronic signature, and/or the notary public's official electronic seal.[112]

---

107. Cal. Gov't Code § 8206(a)(2)(A) (LexisNexis 2007); Haw. Rev. Stat. Ann. § 456-15(3) (LexisNexis 2006); Handbook for MD Notaries Public (MD Sec'y of State 2006) at 7; Mass. Exec. Order No. 455, § 11(c)(4) (April 2004); Mo. Ann. Stat. § 486-260(4) (LexisNexis 2007); Nev. Rev. Stat. Ann. § 240.120(1)(d) (LexisNexis 2007); Or. Admin. Rules § 160-100-120(6).

108. Cal. Gov't Code § 8206(a)(2)(G) (required for all deeds, quitclaim deeds, and deeds of trust affecting real property).

109. A discussion of the background of interstate and international recognition of notarial acts is outside the scope of this appendix. *See generally* Closen, *supra* note 25, at 217–36, 455–81; Keith D. Sherry, cmt., *Old Treaties Never Die, They Just Lose Their Teeth: Authentication Needs of a Global Community Demand Retirement of the Hague Public Documents Convention,* 31 J. Marshall L. Rev. 1045–83 (1998).

110. No case interpreting the Full Faith and Credit Clause of Article IV has ruled specific "notarial acts" to be "public acts" within the meaning and application of the text.

111. Examples of such laws are (1) The Uniform Law on Notarial Acts, adopted in Delaware, the District of Columbia, Kansas, Minnesota, Montana, Nevada, New Hampshire, New Mexico, Oklahoma, Oregon, and Wisconsin; and (2) the Uniform Recognition of Acknowledgments Act, adopted in Alaska, Arizona, Colorado, Connecticut, Illinois, Kentucky, Maine, Michigan, Nebraska, North Dakota, Ohio, South Carolina, Virginia, West Virginia, and the U.S. Virgin Islands.

112. National E-notarization Standards, Standard 13.

Thus, the NASS requirements for electronic certifications and apostilles follow the same e-document authenticity standard as that of the Hague Conference on Private International Law ("the Hague") regarding e-apostilles: The fact of the issuance of the certification or apostille must be independently verifiable, and the certification or apostille must be invalidated if the underlying document is improperly modified.[113]

Provisions for the electronic certificate of authenticity are contained in the Model Notary Act of 2002:

> On a notarized electronic document transmitted to another state or nation, electronic evidence of the authenticity of the official signature and seal of an electronic notary of this [State], if required, shall be attached to, or logically associated with, the document and shall be in the form of an electronic certificate of authority signed by the [commissioning official] in conformance with any current and pertinent international treaties, agreements, and conventions subscribed by the government of the United States.[114]

The Model Notary Act also includes the content for an authentication certificate for electronic documents.[115]

North Carolina and Virginia have enacted the first laws specifying how their respective secretaries of state must issue electronic certifications and apostilles.[116] North Carolina's law follows the Model Notary Act, while Virginia's law tracks more closely to the National e-Notarization Standards.

E-Apostilles and the Hague Conference on Private International Law

To effectuate legal recognition of notarized documents that cross national borders, the Hague oversees the Convention Abolishing the Requirement of Legalization for Foreign Public Documents (the "Convention"), a treaty currently subscribed to by 93 nations and over 1000 Competent Authorities.[117] The Convention eliminates the often time-consuming and costly requirement of diplomatic and consular authentication and replaces its burdensome method of requiring a chain of authenticating certificates beginning with the signature and seal of the issuer and several intermediary authorities.

The Hague has determined that the spirit and letter of the Convention do not pose an obstacle to usage of technology, and that the interpretation of the Convention in the light of functional equivalence thus permits competent authorities to issue electronic apostilles.[118] For e-apostilles and electronically notarized documents, the Hague has established an e-document authenticity standard based on a nonrepudiation standard. Accordingly, an electronic public document with an electronic notarization or an electronic apostille must be independently verifiable, and must be invalidated if it

---

113. *Id.* Standards 14 & 15.

114. Model Notary Act, *supra* note 76, at § 20-1.

115. *Id.* § 20-2.

116. N.C. GEN. STAT. § 10B-38 *et seq.* (LexisNexis 2006); VA. CODE ANN. § 47.1-11.1(A) (LexisNexis 2007).

117. For the current official list of member and non-member states party to the convention, refer to the list at http://www.hcch.net/.

118. First International Forum on e-Notarization and e-Apostilles, *supra* note 18, Conclusion 1.

is improperly modified.[119] These requirements do not require the use of a particular technology.[120]

The Hague encourages all competent authorities to issue e-apostilles.[121] Under the auspices of the Electronic Apostille Pilot Program (e-APP) between the Hague and the National Notary Association (USA), on February 15, 2007, Kansas became the first competent authority to send an e-apostille attached to an electronically notarized document. Subsequently, Rhode Island and Belgium each adopted a completely electronic register under the e-APP. Colombia has become the first jurisdiction to implement both an electronic register and a system to issue *all* of its e-apostilles electronically.[122]

---

119. *Id.* Conclusions 15 & 18.

120. *Id.* Conclusions 16 & 19.

121. *Id.* Conclusion 13.

122. Information concerning the e-APP and the implementation of electronic registers and electronic apostilles generally is available at http://www.e-app.info.

Digital Evidence in Five Nations

Stephen Mason*

The discussion in this chapter provides a broad outline of how digital evidence is treated by the laws of Argentina, France, Germany, Japan, and the Russian Federation (covering its Arbitration Proceedings Code). The chapter comprises a summary of the content of the relevant chapters for these jurisdictions taken from the text International Electronic Evidence.[1] *For the benefit of the reader, and to understand the extent of text that was potentially covered in the book, the guidance provided to each author of the discussion of each country is set out at the end of the case study.*

In marked contrast to the United States, and in following their own jurisprudence, some nations recognize a legal difference between (1) digital evidence that takes advantage of the hashing and cryptography employed by digital signatures, and (2) "ordinary" digital evidence, such as an e-mail that is sent without a digital signature. In the main, this is achieved by providing for presumptions about legal effect; providing that a digital signature satisfies the legal requirement of a "signature" in certain circumstances, and sometimes holding that other types of electronic signatures do not satisfy the legal requirements of a signature; and in presumptions about the admission of evidence that may or may not include a digital signature.

*Stephen is barrister (www.stephenmason.eu) and a member of the IT Panel of the General Council of the Bar of England and Wales. He is the author and general editor of *Electronic Evidence: Disclosure, Discovery & Admissibility* (LexisNexis Butterworths, 2007) and *International Electronic Evidence* (British Institute of International and Comparative Law, 2008). He is the author of *Electronic Signatures in Law* (Tottel, 2nd edn, 2007) and *E-Mail, Networks and the Internet: A Concise Guide to Compliance with the Law* (xpl publishing, 6th edn, 2006). He is the founder and general editor of the *Digital Evidence and Electronic Signature Law Review*.

1. Stephen Mason, general editor, *International Electronic Evidence* (British Institute of International and Comparative Law, 2008), covering the following jurisdictions: Argentina, Austria, Belgium, Bulgaria, Croatia, Cyprus, Czech Republic, Denmark, Egypt, Estonia, Finland, France, Germany, Greece, Hungary, Iceland, Italy, Japan, Latvia, Lithuania, Luxembourg, Malta, Mexico, Netherlands, Norway, Poland, Romania, Russia, Slovakia, Slovenia, Spain, Sweden, Switzerland, Thailand, and Turkey.

ARGENTINA[2]

Argentina is a federal state comprising 23 separate provinces, each with its own Civil Procedure Code. There are two approaches to digital evidence. Digital evidence can be an object in relation to an action, such as effecting a payment over the Internet. Second, digital evidence may be considered as the representation of facts or acts that are legally relevant. An example is the evidence of payment in relation to a contract formed over the Internet. In this instance, the evidence is not a fact by itself, but provides evidence of the action of making the payment.

The Firma Digital Ley 25.506 (Digital Signatures Law 25.506) was passed in 2001. Article 3 provides that a digital signature meets the requirements of a manuscript signature, and through the application of articles 2, 7 and 8, two presumptions follow: where a digital signature is affixed to a digital document, the signature was that of the person whose private key was used, and the content of the record has not changed through time. Thus, the presumptions of identity and integrity are addressed in substantive law.

Admissibility

There are no specific rules in relation to digital evidence in the Código Procesal Penal (Federal Code of Criminal Procedure). Article 206 of the Code provides for the principle of the freedom of evidence in criminal investigations, and provides that the only limit on the nature of the evidence adduced in criminal proceedings are those relating to the marital status of the accused or the witnesses, if this is relevant:

> *Limitaciones sobre la prueba*
> Art. 206. No regirán en la instrucción las limitaciones establecidas por las leyes civiles respecto de la prueba, con excepción de las relativas al estado civil de las personas.

> *Limitations of the evidence*
> Art. 206. There are no limitations established by the civil law regarding the evidence governing an investigation, except for those relating to the civil status of individuals.

This means that because digital evidence is not prohibited, it is therefore received into evidence.

Both civil and criminal trials are governed by the procedural codes of the individual province. However, the admissibility of evidence in civil proceedings is set out in article 378 of the Código Procesal Civil y Comercial de La Nación Ley 17.454 (National Civil and Commercial Procedure Code), which provides for the principle of the freedom of proof, although evidence cannot be adduced that might damage morals, the freedom of the litigants or third parties, or where it is expressly forbidden. Where a form of evidence is not listed in the Code, it can be admitted, as is evidence in digital format, by analogy with other forms of evidence. The judge also has a discretion to admit other forms of evidence if it is considered necessary.

---

2. For more detail, see Dr Mercedes Rivolta and Dr Pablo Fraga 'Argentina' in Stephen Mason, general editor, *International Electronic Evidence* (British Institute of International and Comparative Law, 2008).

The validity of digital documents and electronic signatures are recognized by the Firma Digital Ley 25.506 (Digital Signatures Law 25.506). Article 6 provides a definition of a digital document:[3]

> ***Documento digital***. Se entiende por documento digital a la representación digital de actos o hechos, con independencia del soporte utilizado para su fijación, almacenamiento o archivo. Un documento digital también satisface el requerimiento de escritura.

> A digital document is a digital representation of acts or facts, regardless of the storage device where it is stored. A digital document also satisfies the writing requirement.

The concept of "original" is also considered in the context of the probative value of a digital document that has been signed, together with any reproduction, as set out in Article 11:

> **Original.** Los documentos electrónicos firmados digitalmente y los reproducidos en formato digital firmados digitalmente a partir de originales de primera generación en cualquier otro soporte, también serán considerados originales y poseen, como consecuencia de ello, valor probatorio como tales, según los procedimientos que determine la reglamentación.

> **Original.** The digitally signed electronic documents and those digitally signed reproduced in digital format from first generation originals in any other storage device, shall also be considered originals and will be, as a consequence, valid as evidence according to the procedures specified by the regulation.[4]

Under the principle of the freedom of proof, the parties and the judge may introduce any item of evidence into legal proceedings, including evidence in digital form. Documents in digital format may be considered a private or public instrument, but the nature of the document does not preclude it from being adduced into evidence. Article 1190 of the Código Civil de la República Argentina (Civil Code) enables contracts to be proved by methods adopted by local procedural codes, and provides for a variety of forms of evidence that can be admitted: public instruments, individual instruments that may be signed or unsigned, judicial or non-judicial confession of the parties, judicial oath, legal or judicial presumptions, and by witnesses.

Legal Preference for Digital Signatures by Means of Presumptions

Contrary to the approach taken in the United States, Argentina has adopted the functional equivalent concept in its approach to electronic signatures,[5] which means that the

---

3. The English translation is from the Firma Digital web site at http://www.pki.gov.ar.
4. Although this is the official translation of article 11, perhaps an alternative translation might be as follows: 'Original. An electronic document will be considered an original and will, as a consequence, be valid as evidence in accordance with the procedures specified by the regulation, provided that the document is signed with a digital signature and reproduced in digital format from the first version of the document, whatever the storage device upon which it is stored.'
5. There are three broad terms used to describe the various approaches to the introduction of legislation relating to electronic signatures: the functional equivalent concept, the minimalist approach and the two-tier approach. For a discussion of the response across 98 jurisdictions, see Stephen Mason, *Electronic Signatures in Law* (Tottel, 2nd edn, 2007) Chapter 9.

law tends to be prescriptive in nature, with the intention of establishing a particular type of technology as a means to replace a manuscript signature in the digital environment. This means the digital signature is considered to have a greater legal effect than that of an electronic signature in any other format. A digital signature is defined in Article 2, and it is to be noted that a digital signature requires the inclusion of an intermediary, in this instance, the Application Authority:

> **ARTICULO 2º—Firma Digital.** Se entiende por firma digital al resultado de aplicar a un documento digital un procedimiento matemático que requiere información de exclusivo conocimiento del firmante, encontrándose ésta bajo su absoluto control. La firma digital debe ser susceptible de verificación por terceras partes, tal que dicha verificación simultáneamente permita identificar al firmante y detectar cualquier alteración del documento digital posterior a su firma.

> **ARTICLE 2—Digital Signature.** A digital signature is the result of applying a mathematical procedure to a digital document, that requires information controlled exclusively by the signing party and which is under his absolute control. The digital signature must be verifiable by third parties, such that this verification will simultaneously permit the identification of the signing party and any alteration of the digital document after it has been signed.

The Ley De Firma Digital Nº 25.506 passed by Argentina in 2001, which is similar to those passed by certain other South American countries, provides for the functional equivalent of a manuscript signature in Article 3, in that a digital signature is considered to be the equivalent of a manuscript signature:

> **ARTICULO 3º—Del requerimiento de firma.** Cuando la ley requiera una firma manuscrita, esa exigencia también queda satisfecha por una firma digital. Este principio es aplicable a los casos en que la ley establece la obligación de firmar o prescribe consecuencias para su ausencia.

> **ARTICLE 3.—On the requirement of signature.** When the law requires a handwritten signature, this requirement is also met by a digital signature. This principle is applicable to those cases in which the law establishes the obligation of signing or prescribes consequences for the absence of a signature.

Where a digital signature is used, the legislation requires it to be verified by a third party by way of the Application Authority, and the verification provides two presumptions by means of Articles 7 and 8.

Article 7 provides that a digital signature is presumed to belong to the holder of the certificate that enables the private key to be verified, and Article 8 provides that once the verification procedure is complete, there is a presumption that a digital signature affixed to a digital document is true, and the document has not been modified from the moment it was signed. In addition, there is a requirement that the digital signature be controlled by the signing party and be under their absolute control, as provided for in Article 2. The presumptions are rebuttable, although the burden of proof has been reversed under the provisions of Article 10. It is for the signing party, where they claim that they did not affix the private key to the document, to prove they did not do so.

By comparison, other forms of electronic signature (name typed at the bottom of an e-mail, e-mail address, biometric measurement of a manuscript signature, scanned manuscript signature, PIN) are not recognized as the functional equivalent of a manuscript signature unless the parties recognize it, on the basis of the principle of autonomy, as provided in article 1197 of the Civil Code.

Two cases have occurred that illustrate the way the law has been interpreted and applied. In the case of *Huberman Fernando Pablo c/Industrias Audiovisuales Argentinas SA s/despido*,[6] it was decided that an e-mail sent by an employee was not an acceptable method of a resignation without the inclusion of a digital signature, and in *Cooperativa de Vivienda Crédito y Consumo Fiduciaria LTDA c/Becerra Leguizamón Hugo Ramón s/incidente de apelación*,[7] it was decided that an e-mail without a digital signature affixed is not recognized as a document signed by the parties under the terms of Law 25.506. The decisions in both cases reflect the fact that only digital signatures are recognized as an equivalent to a manuscript signature in the absence of an agreement between the parties that another form of electronic signature is acceptable. If a party relies on such a signature, it is for them to prove its validity, as provided for in article 5.

Liability of the Sender and Recipient

The holder of a digital certificate in Argentina has a number of duties imposed upon them in article 25, in that they must maintain exclusive control of the digital signature creation data, not to share it, and to prevent it from being publicly known; to use a technically reliable digital signature creation device; to request the certification authority to revoke their certificate if there are any circumstance that might have compromised the privacy of the signature creation data, and to inform the certification authority without delay of any change in any of the data which has been subject to verification contained in the digital certificate. Conversely, the Argentine government, in article 23 of Ley de Firma Digital Nº 25.506, have imposed a mild form of limitation on the recipient of a digital signature, in the form of a rule against relying on the validity of the certificate in the following circumstances:

> ARTICULO 23.—Desconocimiento de la validez de un certificado digital. Un certificado digital no es válido si es utilizado:
> a) Para alguna finalidad diferente a los fines para los cuales fue extendido;
> b) Para operaciones que superen el valor máximo autorizado cuando corresponda;
> c) Una vez revocado.

> ARTICLE 23.—Lack of recognition of the validity of a digital certificate. A digital certificate is not valid if it is used:
> a) For a purpose different from that for which it was issued;
> b) For transactions that exceed the maximum value authorized when applicable;
> c) Once it has been revoked.

Experts

Experts participate in both civil and criminal proceedings in Argentina, and must be briefed by the parties or appointed by the judge. Article 464 of the National Civil and

---

6. (29884/02 S. 56885 - CNTRAB - SALA VI - Buenos Aires, 23 de febrero de 2004 (Published in http://www.elDial.com.ar Cite: elDial AA1E25).

7. CNCOM - SALA A 16645/2006 - Buenos Aires, junio 27 de 2006 (Published in http://www.elDial.com.ar Cite elDial - AA379B).

Commercial Procedure Code provides that the expert is required to have a relevant degree in the area that is the subject of analysis, although where there is no specific qualification available, the court will admit the evidence or opinion of a person that has provided satisfactory evidence of their expertise. There are no criteria, policies or guidelines in respect of how digital evidence is obtained, produced, preserved, and presented. As there are no specific rules or obligations relating to digital evidence specialists, the general rules apply, and a judge can obtain an opinion from a variety of sources in accordance with the provisions of article 476 of the National Criminal Procedure Code.

FRANCE[8]

There is no unique definition of what constitutes evidence in France, although two different notions are evident: the demonstration of a judicial fact, such as proof that damage occurred, or the demonstration of a judicial act, such as evidence of a contract. Electronic evidence in civil proceedings is governed by Loi no 2000-230 du 13 mars 2000 portant adaptation du droit de la preuve aux technologies de l'information et relative à la signature électronique (Act n°. 2000-230 on Adaptation of the Law of Evidence on Information Technology and Relevant to e-signatures),[9] and although there is no general definition of what constitutes electronic evidence, the term *numérique* (numeric), which is often used to describe electronic evidence (*preuve numérique*), provides a form of definition:[10]

> *Numérique (adj.):*
> Se dit, par opposition à analogique, de la représentation de données ou de grandeurs physiques au moyen de caractères - des chiffres généralement - et aussi des systèmes, dispositifs ou procédés employant ce mode de représentation discrète (en anglais: digital, numerical, numeric).

> *Digital (adjective):*
> In opposition to analogue, this term means the representation of data or physical quantities by means of characters—generally numbers—as well as systems, devices or methods employing this mean of discrete representation.

The same regulation defines data as follows:

> *Donnée (n. f.):*
> Représentation d'une information sous une forme conventionnelle destinée à faciliter son traitement (en anglais: data).

> *Data (feminine noun):*
> Representation of information in a conventional form intended to facilitate its treatment.

---

8. For more detail, see David Benichou, judge and Ariane Zimra 'France' in Stephen Mason, general editor, *International Electronic Evidence* (British Institute of International and Comparative Law, 2008).

9. Entered into force on the 13 March 2000, amending the Civil Code, except where the provisions require specific regulations to enter into force (décrets or arrêtés d'application).

10. Arrêté du 22 décembre 1981 relatif à l'enrichissement du vocabulaire de l'informatique (Journal officiel du 17 janvier 1982).

The passing of Loi no 2000-230 du 13 mars 2000 portant adaptation du droit de la preuve aux technologies de l'information et relative à la signature électronique (Act No. 2000-230 of 13 March 2000 on the adaptation of the law of evidence to information technology and related to electronic signatures) and Loi no 2004-669 du 9 juillet 2004 relative aux communications électroniques et aux services de communication audiovisuelle (Act No. 2004-669 of 9 July 2004 on electronic communications and audiovisual communication services), have served to encourage the introduction of the term "electronic" into legislation, one example being the Code des postes et des communications électroniques, Loi n° 2004-669 du 9 juillet 2004 relative aux communications électroniques et aux services de communication audiovisuelle (Act No. 2004-669 of 9 July 2004 on electronic communications and audiovisual communication services), which replaced the Code des postes et telecommunications, in which the term *télécommunications* was replaced with *communications électroniques*.

As pointed out by David Benichou and Ariane Zimra in their chapter, "The lack of a specific definition of electronic evidence in the French legal system leads to several important points including the fact that electronic evidence is above all evidence, distinguished by being carried by a specific medium. Electronic evidence is only an electronic form of classical evidence." The main difference in French law is between the rules of evidence in respect of civil and criminal proceedings. Since the passing of Loi no 2000-230 du 13 mars 2000, writing in digital format has the same value as that of writing on paper in civil proceedings, although digital and analogue evidence has always been admitted into criminal proceedings.

Proof in Civil Proceedings

In civil proceedings, some forms of evidence can be more valuable than other forms, and specific forms of proof are required for some forms of legal action. Five forms of evidence are prescribed in article 1315-1 of the Code Civil (Civil Code): written evidence (deeds, contracts; witness evidence); presumptions; admission, and the oath.[11] Written evidence may include any medium, including the method of transmission, and writing in electronic form is equally admissible as evidence on paper, subject to the additional requirements set out in article 1316-1.[12] In the absence of an express agreement between the parties, it is for the judge to decide the nature of the proof that will be admitted.[13]

---

11. 'Les règles qui concernent la preuve littérale, la preuve testimoniale, les présomptions, l'aveu de la partie et le serment, sont expliquées dans les sections suivantes.' 'The rules regarding literal evidence, testimonial evidence, assumptions, the admissions of the parties and the oath, are explained in the following sections' (Transferred by the provisions of Loi n° 2000-30 du 13 mars 2000 art. 1 Journal Officiel du 14 mars 2000).

12. Article 1316-1 Civil Code: 'L'écrit sous forme électronique est admis en preuve au même titre que l'écrit sur support papier, sous réserve que puisse être dûment identifiée la personne dont il émane et qu'il soit établi et conservé dans des conditions de nature à en garantir l'intégrité.' 'The writing in electronic form shall be admitted into evidence in the same way as writing on paper, provided the person from whom the document originates can be properly identified and it is prepared and preserved under conditions that ensure the integrity of the document.' (Inserted in accordance with the provisions of Loi n° 2000-230 du 13 mars 2000 art. 1 Journal Officiel du 14 mars 2000).

13. 'Lorsque la loi n'a pas fixé d'autres principes, et à défaut de convention valable entre les parties, le juge règle les conflits de preuve littérale en déterminant par tous moyens le titre le plus vraisemblable, quel qu'en soit le support.' 'Where the law does not set other principles, and in the absence of a valid agreement between the parties, it is for the judge to resolve conflicts of evidence by using all the most likely means, whatever the medium.' (Inserted in accordance with the provisions of Loi n° 2000-230 du 13 mars 2000 art. 1 Journal Officiel du 14 mars 2000).

Criminal Proceedings[14]

A judge may admit any form of evidence, and is required to reach a decision based on the evidence adduced during the proceedings, as provided by article 427 of the Code de Procedure Penale (Code of Criminal Procedure):

> Hors les cas où la loi en dispose autrement, les infractions peuvent être établies par tout mode de preuve et le juge décide d'après son intime conviction.
>
> Le juge ne peut fonder sa décision que sur des preuves qui lui sont apportées au cours des débats et contradictoirement discutées devant lui.
>
> Except where the law provides otherwise, offences may be proved by any type of evidence, and the judge will decide according to his innermost conviction.
>
> The judge may only base his decision on evidence submitted during the hearing and discussed before him in an adversarial manner.

The forms of evidence that can be adduced are: admissions; statements, such as official records and reports; the reports of experts; viewing the location of an act; and various other modes of evidence, such as incriminating evidence. There are three levels of evidentiary strength to statements and reports. First, there is the simple information, as set out by article 430 of the Code of Criminal Procedure:

> Sauf dans le cas où la loi en dispose autrement, les procès-verbaux et les rapports constatant les délits ne valent qu'à titre de simples renseignements.
>
> Except where the law provides otherwise, official records and reports noting the existence of crimes only have the value of simple information.

Article 431 of the Code of Criminal Procedure provides a second level of evidentiary strength that is accorded to official records and reports that establish proof of a fact, subject to evidence in rebuttal:

> Dans les cas où les officiers de police judiciaire, les agents de police judiciaire ou les fonctionnaires et agents chargés de certaines fonctions de police judiciaire ont reçu d'une disposition spéciale de la loi le pouvoir de constater des délits par des procès-verbaux ou des rapports, la preuve contraire ne peut être rapportée que par écrit ou par témoins.
>
> In cases where judicial police officers, judicial police agents or the civil servants and agents entrusted with certain judicial police duties have been granted by a specific law of the power to establish misdemeanours through official records or reports, and the proof to the contrary may only be brought in writing or through witnesses.

The third level provides that evidence has an absolute evidentiary strength that cannot be rebutted unless an *inscription en faux* (the inscription is false) has been registered.[15] The registration of an *inscription en faux* is a procedure to verify whether the evidence

---

14. The reader is directed to the detailed treatment of the criminal system in France by Valérie Dervieux 'The French System' in Mireille Delmas-Marty and J. R Spencer, *European Criminal Procedures,* (Cambridge University Press, 2006).

15. 'The inscription is false' in a procedure to verify whether the evidence before the court is a forgery and usually only concerns specific types of evidence, such as official documents written by notaries, judges, or inquirers. If the claim succeeds, the value of the act is invalid.

before the court is a forgery. This kind of claim usually only concerns specific types of evidence, such as official documents written by notaries, judges, or inquirers. If the claim succeeds, the value of the act is invalid. It is rare for the third level to be adduced and to be challenged, and the nature of the evidence tends to comprise an official report of an incident that is signed by a minimum of two officials acting in their official capacity and who witnessed the facts, as provided for in specific statutes.

Electronic Signatures

There are three forms of electronic signature in France: the electronic signature, the secure electronic signature, and the presumed reliable electronic signature. Article 1 of Décret n°2001-272 du 30 mars 2001 Décret pris pour l'application de l'article 1316-4 du code civil et relatif à la signature électronique (Decree n°2001-272 of March 30, 2001 Decree taken for the application of article 1316-4 of the civil code and relating to the electronic signature) provides the following definitions of electronic signatures:

Art. 1er. - Au sens du présent décret, on entend par:

1. «Signature électronique»: une donnée qui résulte de l'usage d'un procédé répondant aux conditions définies à la première phrase du second alinéa de l'article 1316-4 du code civil;

2. «Signature électronique sécurisée»: une signature électronique qui satisfait, en outre, aux exigences suivantes:

- être propre au signataire;

- être créée par des moyens que le signataire puisse garder sous son contrôle exclusif;

- garantir avec l'acte auquel elle s'attache un lien tel que toute modification ultérieure de l'acte soit détectable;

Art. 1er. 1. - For the purposes of this Decree, the following definitions shall apply:

1. "Electronic signature": data resulting from the use of a process meets the conditions defined in the first sentence of the second paragraph of Article 1316-4 of the Civil Code;

2. "Secure electronic signature": an electronic signature that meets, in addition, the following requirements:

- It must be specific to the signatory;

- It is created using means that the signatory can maintain under his sole control;

- It is linked to the data to which it relates in such a manner that any subsequent change of the data is detectable.

Article 2 of Décret n°2001-272 du 30 mars 2001 provides a presumption regarding the advanced electronic signature (the term "advanced electronic signature" is used in the Directive 1999/93/EC of the European Parliament and of the Council of 13 December 1999 on a Community framework for electronic signatures,[16] but it is called the "secure

---

16. OJ L 13, 19.01.2000, p.12.

electronic signature" in the French legislation, and is actually a digital signature, subject to further provisions set out in the Directive)[17] as follows:

> La fiabilité d'un procédé de signature électronique est présumée jusqu'à preuve contraire lorsque ce procédé met en oeuvre une signature électronique sécurisée, établie grâce à un dispositif sécurisé de création de signature électronique et que la vérification de cette signature repose sur l'utilisation d'un certificat électronique qualifié.

> The reliability of the electronic signature process is presumed, until proven otherwise concerning the use of a secure electronic signature, being established by means of a secure electronic signature creation device, and the verification of the signature based on the use a qualified electronic certificate.

Article 1316-4 of the Civil Code provides a number of presumptions relating to the use of an advanced electronic signature for the purposes of private legal transactions, as follows:

> La signature nécessaire à la perfection d'un acte juridique identifie celui qui l'appose. Elle manifeste le consentement des parties aux obligations qui découlent de cet acte. Quand elle est apposée par un officier public, elle confère l'authenticité à l'acte.

> Lorsqu'elle est électronique, elle consiste en l'usage d'un procédé fiable d'identification garantissant son lien avec l'acte auquel elle s'attache. La fiabilité de ce procédé est présumée, jusqu'à preuve contraire, lorsque la signature électronique est créée, l'identité du signataire assurée et l'intégrité de l'acte garantie, dans des conditions fixées par décret en Conseil d'Etat.

> The signature necessary to the execution of a legal transaction identifies the person who affixes it. It makes clear that the parties agree to the obligations which flow from that transaction. When it is affixed by a public officer, it confers authenticity to the document.

> When the signature is electronic, it consists of the use of a reliable process of identification which guarantees its link with the instrument to which it relates. The reliability of that process shall be presumed, until contrary proof; when an electronic signature is created, the identity of the signatory secured and the integrity of the instrument guaranteed, subject to the conditions laid down by decree in Conseil d'État.

Whilst these provisions go beyond that laid down in Directive 1999/93/EC of the European Parliament and of the Council of 13 December 1999 on a Community framework for electronic signatures,[18] nevertheless to a certain extent they provide a degree of certainty about the use of an advanced electronic signature which is lacking in the Directive. Theoretically, the Directive provides for two types of electronic signature: an "electronic signature" and an "advanced electronic signature" (in reality, a digital signature). There is a significant difference between the two types, and one that is not readily imported into a legal framework based on common law. The provisions of article 5 are central to the provisions of the Directive, providing that an electronic signature cannot be denied legal effectiveness or be held inadmissible because it is in electronic form. This

---

17. For a discussion about the confusion over the use of terms, see Stephen Mason, *Electronic Signatures in Law,* 10.4.

18. OJ L 13, 19.01.2000, p.12.

principle applies to all forms of electronic signature, and recital 21 makes it clear that the provisions of the Directive do not touch upon the powers of national courts regarding the rules of evidence. That there might be considered to be more than two types of electronic signature is explained by the concept of the "qualified certificate" (see Annex 1), and the use of "secure signature-creation devices," each of which imports the terms "qualified electronic signature" and "secure electronic signature" into the cannon of the legislation of some of the Member States of the European Union, terms that are predicated upon the use of specific processes and procedures.[19]

Experts

In France, experts are appointed and included on lists maintained by the Courts of Appeal and the Cour de Cassation. An expert will provide evidence on oath and will be subject to cross examination. The report of a digital evidence specialist has no greater value than any other evidence. Normally appointed by a court, nevertheless the parties can brief an expert, although the judge will be required to justify why an expert was not chosen from the list. A judge is not bound by the testimony of an expert, although such a report is almost always indispensable in matters pertaining to digital evidence.

GERMANY[20]

Formal evidence in civil proceedings is governed by a number of fundamental principles of German procedural law. In summary, the parties control the conduct of the proceedings, they also establish which facts are in dispute (*Dispositionsgrundsatz*), which means civil proceedings tend to be the subject of compromise between the parties (*Verhandlungsgrundsatz*), and there are no rules of disclosure and pretrial discovery. Neither party is under an obligation to disclose facts that are not favourable to their case. In criminal proceedings, all facts and evidence that are relevant to the offence charged must be introduced into the proceedings during the oral hearing (*Grundsatz der mündlichen Verhandlung*), and the court and the public attorney are required to investigate the full facts (*Grundsatz der Amtsermittlung*).

Forms of Evidence

There are five forms of formal evidence provided for in German procedural law: witness evidence (*Zeugenbeweis*), expert evidence (*Sachverständigenbeweis*), documentary evidence (*Urkundsbeweis*), the submission of evidence for the judge to inspect (*Augenschein*), and evidence by the examination of a party to the proceedings (*Parteivernehmung*). Each of these forms of evidence are admitted in civil proceedings, whereas in criminal proceedings, the examination of the party is not admitted. It might be usefully mentioned at this point that the parties can mutually agree to divert from this regime in civil proceedings. In the event the parties do so, the court may also consult other

---

19. For an introduction and critique of the Directive, see Stephen Mason, *Electronic Signatures in Law*, Chapter 4.

20. For more detail, see Dr. Alexander Duisberg and Dr. Henriette Picot 'Germany' in Stephen Mason, general editor, *International Electronic Evidence* (British Institute of International and Comparative Law, 2008).

appropriate sources of evidence in accordance with the provisions of section 284 *Zivil-prozessordnung* (Civil Procedural Act) (called the free evidence regime, *Freibeweis*).

Electronic Evidence in Civil Proceedings

Electronic evidence is not recognized as a separate category of evidence in Germany. This means that electronic evidence is introduced within one of the formal types of evidence. Electronic documents are generally submitted as evidence by inspection, in accordance with section 371(1) and (2) of the Civil Procedural Act. By way of example, with the exception of qualified electronic signatures (that is, digital signatures), this applies to evidence of electronic signatures (such as the PIN, "I accept" icon, typing a name at the bottom of an e-mail, an e-mail address, and the biometric measurement of a manuscript signature).

However, where digital evidence includes a qualified electronic signature (*qualifizierte elektronische Signaturen*) in accordance with the provisions of the Gesetz über Rahmenbedingungen für elektronische Signaturen[21] (Signature Act), section 371(a) of the Civil Procedural Act provides the digital evidence with an identical level of reliability that applies to private or public deeds:

§ *371a Beweiskraft elektronischer Dokumente*

(1) Auf private elektronische Dokumente, die mit einer qualifizierten elektronischen Signatur versehen sind, finden die Vorschriften über die Beweiskraft privater Urkunden entsprechende Anwendung. Der Anschein der Echtheit einer in elektronischer Form vorliegenden Erklärung, der sich auf Grund der Prüfung nach dem Signaturgesetz ergibt, kann nur durch Tatsachen erschüttert werden, die ernstliche Zweifel daran begründen, dass die Erklärung vom Signaturschlüssel-Inhaber abgegeben worden ist.

(2) Auf elektronische Dokumente, die von einer öffentlichen Behörde innerhalb der Grenzen ihrer Amtsbefugnisse oder von einer mit öffentlichem Glauben versehenen Person innerhalb des ihr zugewiesenen Geschäftskreises in der vorgeschriebenen Form erstellt worden sind (öffentliche elektronische Dokumente), finden die Vorschriften über die Beweiskraft öffentlicher Urkunden entsprechende Anwendung. 2Ist das Dokument mit einer qualifizierten elektronischen Signatur versehen, gilt § 437 entsprechend.'

§ *371a Evidential value of electronic documents*

(1) With respect to private electronic documents that are provided with a qualified electronic signature, the provisions on the value of private documents shall apply. The appearance of the authenticity of an explanation available in electronic form, which is based on the application of the signature law, its regularity can only be undermined by facts that justify serious doubts about the fact that a declaration was made by the signature key owner.

(2) Where electronic documents are provided by a public authority within the limits of their official powers, or in the form prescribed by a person provided with public faith within it their assigned role in the line of business (public electronic documents), the regulations on the conclusive value of public documents shall apply. If the document is provided with a qualified electronic signature, § 437 shall apply accordingly.

---

21. Signaturgesetz vom 16. Mai 2001 (BGBl. I S. 876), zuletzt geändert durch Artikel 4 des Gesetzes vom 26. Februar 2007 (BGBl. I S. 179).

Although digital evidence signed with a qualified electronic signature is adduced before the court by inspection, it is evaluated in accordance with the rules on the assessment of documentary evidence.

Criminal Proceedings[22]

Evidence gathered during the pretrial investigation is either submitted as documentary evidence (*Urkundsbeweis*) or by the submission of evidence for the judge to inspect (*Augenscheinsbeweis)*. Evidence in digital format is submitted as documentary evidence if the evidence can be read, and may be read out in the court during the main trial. In other cases (for instance, with respect to records of spoken words), the evidence will be submitted by inspection. Digital evidence might also be submitted through expert evidence (*Sachverständigenbeweis)*. An example will be where a person is accused of having abusive images of children in their possession, and they request the search of their computer by a digital evidence specialist to establish whether there is malicious software that could have caused pornographic files to be downloaded without their authority or consent.

Electronic Signatures[23]

Electronic signatures in Germany are governed by the *Gesetz über Rahmenbedingungen für elektronische Signaturen* (Signature Act) and the *Verordnung zur elektronischen Signatur*[24] (Signature Decree). The Signature Decree provides for a secure signature infrastructure and appropriate technical standards. As mentioned briefly above in respect of section 371(a) of the Civil Procedural Act, a digital document signed by a human being with a qualified electronic signature constitutes prima facie evidence that the person is the originator of the document. The evidence can only be rebutted by serious doubts that the person did not sign the document. The other party has the burden of submitting sufficient evidence to support serious doubts that the document was not signed. It must be emphasized that the legislation in Germany is such that the qualified electronic signature (digital signature) is considered to be of far greater value than any other form of electronic signature, and this is illustrated in the case law.[25]

Liability

The European Directive[26] is silent on the liability for an electronic signature, although Article 6 provides for the liability of certification services providers that issue or guarantee qualified certificates, and the Directive does not address what action, if any, a

---

22. The reader is directed to the detailed treatment of the criminal system in Germany by Rodolphe Juy-Birmann, 'The German System' in Mireille Delmas-Marty and J. R Spencer, *European Criminal Procedures,* (Cambridge University Press, 2006).

23. For more detail on electronic signatures in Germany, see Dr Martin Eßer, Chapter 7 'Germany' in Stephen Mason, *Electronic Signatures in Law* (Tottel, 2nd edn, 2007).

24. *Signaturverordnung vom* 16. November 2001 (BGBl. I S. 3074), *zuletzt geändert durch Artikel* 9 Abs. 18 des Gesetzes vom 23. November 2007 (BGBl. I S. 2631).

25. Dr Martin Eßer provides a list of cases at paragraph 7.9 in Stephen Mason, *Electronic Signatures in Law* (Tottel, 2nd edn, 2007).

26. Directive 1999/93/EC of the European Parliament and of the Council of 13 December 1999 on a Community framework for electronic signatures, OJ L 13, 19.01.2000, p.12.

recipient of an advanced electronic signature should take to satisfy themselves that a signature can be relied upon.[27] In Germany, the Signature Act provides for a liability regime in respect of third parties where there are technical or security deficiencies in relation to qualified electronic signatures where a third party relied on the technical authenticity of the signature that has a certificate, as provided by section 11 of the Signature Act:

§ *11 Haftung*

(1) Verletzt ein Zertifizierungsdiensteanbieter die Anforderungen dieses Gesetzes oder der Rechtsverordnung nach § 24 oder versagen seine Produkte für qualifizierte elektronische Signaturen oder sonstige technische Sicherungseinrichtungen, so hat er einem Dritten den Schaden zu ersetzen, den dieser dadurch erleidet, dass er auf die Angaben in einem qualifizierten Zertifikat, einem qualifizierten Zeitstempel oder einer Auskunft nach § 5 Abs. 1 Satz 3 vertraut. Die Ersatzpflicht tritt nicht ein, wenn der Dritte die Fehlerhaftigkeit der Angabe kannte oder kennen musste.

(2) Die Ersatzpflicht tritt nicht ein, wenn der Zertifizierungsdiensteanbieter nicht schuldhaft gehandelt hat.

(3) Wenn ein qualifiziertes Zertifikat die Nutzung des Signaturschlüssels auf bestimmte Anwendungen nach Art oder Umfang beschränkt, tritt die Ersatzpflicht nur im Rahmen dieser Beschränkungen ein.

(4) Der Zertifizierungsdiensteanbieter haftet für beauftragte Dritte nach § 4 Abs. 5 und beim Einstehen für ausländische Zertifikate nach § 23 Abs. 1 Nr. 2 wie für eigenes Handeln. 2§ 831 Abs. 1 Satz 2 des Bürgerlichen Gesetzbuchs findet keine Anwendung.

Section 11: Liability

(1) If a certification-service provider infringes the requirements under this Law and the statutory ordinance under Section 24, or if his products for qualified electronic signatures or other technical security facilities fail, he shall reimburse a third party for any damage suffered from relying on the data in a qualified certificate or a qualified time stamp or on information given in accordance with Section 5(1) Sentence 2. Damages shall not be payable if the third party knew, or must have known, that the data was faulty.

(2) Damages need not be reimbursed if the certification-service provider has incurred no culpability.

(3) If a qualified certificate restricts the use of the signature code to certain applications by type or extent, damages shall be payable only within the limits of these restrictions.

(4) The certification-service provider shall be liable for third parties commissioned under Section 4(5) and when guaranteeing foreign certificates under Section 23(1) No. 2 as for his own actions. Section 831(1) Sentence 2 of the German Civil Code shall not apply.[28]

---

27. Stephen Mason, *Electronic Signatures in Law* (Tottel, 2nd edn, 2007), 4.14 – 4.15.

28. Translation taken from 'Law Governing Framework Conditions for Electronic Signatures and Amending Other Regulations' (unofficial version for industry consultation), available on-line at http://www.bundesnetzagentur .de/media/archive/3612.pdf.

The Bürgerliches Gesetzbuch (German Civil Code) provides for the use of qualified electronic signatures in legal acts in accordance with the provisions of § 126(1) and (3) of the Code:

§ *126 Schriftform*

(1) Ist durch Gesetz schriftliche Form vorgeschrieben, so muss die Urkunde von dem Aussteller eigenhändig durch Namensunterschrift oder mittels notariell beglaubigten Handzeichens unterzeichnet werden.

. . . . .

(3) Die schriftliche Form kann durch die elektronische Form ersetzt werden, wenn sich nicht aus dem Gesetz ein anderes ergibt.

Section 126 Writing

(1) If the written form is prescribed by law, the document must be signed by the issuer with his name in his own hand, or by his notarially certified mark.

. . . . .

(3) The written form may be replaced by the electronic form, unless otherwise provided by statute.

The term "electronic form" is defined in § 126a BGB:

§ *126a Elektronische Form*

(1) Soll die gesetzlich vorgeschriebene schriftliche Form durch die elektronische Form ersetzt werden, so muss der Aussteller der Erklärung dieser seinen Namen hinzufügen und das elektronische Dokument mit einer qualifizierten elektronischen Signatur nach dem Signaturgesetz versehen.

(2) Bei einem Vertrag müssen die Parteien jeweils ein gleichlautendes Dokument in der in Absatz 1 bezeichneten Weise elektronisch signieren.

Section 126a Electronic Form

(1) If the electronic form is to replace the written form prescribed by law, the issuer of the declaration must add his name to it and provide the electronic document with a qualified electronic signature in accordance with the Signature Act.

(2) In the case of a contract, the parties must each provide a counterpart with an electronic signature as designated in paragraph 1.

The written form may be replaced by the digital form, but there are exceptions by which the digital form is excluded and the written form is required.

Weight of Evidence

These rules are particularly important in Germany, because the legislation imposes relatively strict authentication requirements on digital documents that are submitted that do not have a qualified electronic signature. In this respect, judges are required to assess the weight of evidence very carefully. A judge is generally free to decide the weight it attributes to any item of evidence submitted for inspection. In respect of digital evidence, consideration must be given to the authenticity and the integrity of the evidence. Where the authenticity and integrity of an item of digital evidence is not challenged, it will be assumed that both the authenticity and integrity are given. Where a party challenges the authenticity or the integrity of the digital evidence, the party relying on the evidence is required to provide evidence of the authenticity and integrity of the evidence. The weight that will be attributed to the evidence will depend on whether or not the digital evidence includes a qualified electronic signature in accordance with the provisions of the Signature Act.

The weight to be attached to digital evidence is treated differently if it lacks a qualified electronic signature. For instance, where printouts and scanned copies of e-mails do not have a qualified electronic signature, the judge is generally free to assess the weight of the evidence, although judges and legal scholars apparently consider that such "simple" digital evidence cannot be attributed a high weight, a view that is held in regard to e-mail evidence, and is predicated on the ease by which an e-mail can be falsified, which means other sources of reliable proof are required to support the evidence. This view has, not surprisingly, been criticized. Some legal scholars in Germany consider the authenticity and integrity of e-mails should reflect the general life experience and aim at establishing prima facie evidence, but the judges have generally been reluctant to accept this position. However, in practical terms, parties accept the evidence of e-mails and printouts of digital documents, and the judge assumes that facts are not in dispute, and bases their assessment on the undisputed evidence.[29]

Experts

Where a decision on the facts requires specific knowledge, an expert will be appointed by the court. The expert is required to provide a neutral assessment, and they will be selected from a list of certified experts admitted at court (*öffentlich bestellte Sachverständige*). In civil proceedings, the parties are at liberty to agree between them on a named expert to be appointed by the court,[30] although where expert evidence is introduced by one party, it will only be considered as a party assertion. It is for the court to instruct the expert on the scope of the examination and the extent to which the expert may contact and involve the parties. The court will then take the expert opinion into account when reaching a decision, although the expert opinion does not bind the court.

JAPAN[31]

In Japan, the classification of evidence differs between civil and criminal. There are five methods in civil procedure: documentary evidence (*Shosho*), evidence by inspection (*Kensho*), examination of the witness (*Shonin-Jinmon*), expert witness (*Kanteinin*), and examination of the parties concerned (*Tojisha-Jinmon*). There are six methods in criminal procedure: examination of documentary evidence (*Shoko-Shorui*), evidence by

---

29. For further discussion on this, see Dr. Alexander Duisberg and Dr. Henriette Picot 'Germany' in Stephen Mason, general editor, *International Electronic Evidence* (British Institute of International and Comparative Law, 2008).

30. Section 404 and 404(a) Civil Procedural Act.

31. For more detail, see Hironao Kaneko and Hideo Ogura, 'Japan' in Stephen Mason, general editor, *International Electronic Evidence* (British Institute of International and Comparative Law, 2008); also see Kenneth L. Port and Gerald Paul McAlinn, *Comparative Law Law and the Legal Process in Japan* (Carolina Academic Press, 2nd edn, 2003).

inspection (*Shoko-Butsu or Busho*) and examination of persons, the witness (*Shonin*), expert witness (*Kanteinin*), and interpreter (*Tsuyaku*) or translator (*Honyakunin*).

There are no general provisions provided in the Code of Civil Procedure or the Code of Criminal Procedure in relation to the examination of digital evidence. The Code of Civil Procedure was amended in 1996, and article 231 provides for the admission of analogue evidence in the form of audio- and videotapes. Digital data is usually treated differently from analogue evidence because of its characteristics. Hironao Kaneko and Hideo Ogura indicate that there are three principal reasons for the absence of provisions relating to digital evidence: all forms of evidence are admissible in civil proceedings, and they are evaluated on their credibility; in practice, special provisions are not required to examine an digital record—it is thought that a judge can examine the evidence either by examining printouts as documentary evidence (*Shosho*) through an expert witness (*Kantei*), or by inspection (*Kensho*) of the media that stored the information. Hironao Kaneko and Hideo Ogura go on to illustrate the point that account books are categorized as a reliable document, which leads to the suggestion by some commentators that because the information that would normally be added to an account book is now stored in a computer, and can be easily read by a printout in the same way as an account book in documentary form, the media storing the data should be examined as a document. In any event, in criminal proceedings, article 323 of the Code of Criminal Procedure provide that if a document in its class is highly reliable, it is to be considered unconditionally credible.[32]

Admissibility of Evidence and Evidentiary Value

Both the Code of Civil Procedure (article 247) and the Code of Criminal Procedure (article 318) provide for the principle of the free evaluation of evidence (*Jiyu-Shinsho-Shugi*), giving the judge the discretion to determine the veracity of the facts in any given case, although the principle is applied in a different manner in civil procedure and in criminal procedure. There are no limits on the admissibility of evidence in civil proceedings with the exception of illegally obtained evidence. Although evidence obtained illegally is not denied solely on the basis of the illegal way it was obtained, it will not be admitted if the way it was obtained breaches the principle of good faith in such a way that is considered to be serious and overwhelming. In civil proceedings, it is for the judge to determine the facts, taking into account the entire process of the trial (*Koto-Benron-No-Zenshushi*). It should be noted, however, that the principle is not applied to facts that are obvious, or where the parties agree to the facts,[33] or to facts that are not alleged.[34] A judge should not determine facts in an incoherent manner or against experience, because failing to deal properly with the assessment of the evidence is a ground of appeal to the Supreme Court.[35] In criminal proceedings, the principle of the free evaluation of evidence only applies after rules, such as the hearsay rule and other restrictions on the admission of

---

32. For a more detailed discussion of the theoretical and practical analysis of digital evidence, see Hironao Kaneko and Hideo Ogura, 'Japan' in Stephen Mason, general editor, *International Electronic Evidence* (British Institute of International and Comparative Law, 2008).

33. Code of Civil Procedure, article 179.

34. Code of Civil Procedure, article 246.

35. Code of Civil Procedure, article 312(2)(vi).

evidence in law, have acted to limit admissible evidence. Evidence obtained illegally is excluded.

Categories of Evidence

The method by which evidence is examined can be important, because the method chosen will determine whether a party can be coerced into taking part in the examination of evidence. Article 120 of the Code of Civil Procedure requires certain forms of documentary evidence to be produced. Tangible things that are not categorized as documents are examined by inspection. However, it does not follow that a third party is obliged to cooperate with an inspection if they are in possession of a tangible thing that is materially relevant to an inspection. The general interpretation of the provisions of articles 323(2) and 224 of the Code of Civil Procedure (that provide for the consequences of an unreasonable refusal to deliver the documents) suggest that the third party is obliged to cooperate with the inspection, notwithstanding there is no specific rule that requires a third party to cooperate. This is why the choice of the method of examination can be important, because whether a party can be coerced into taking part in an examination of evidence will depend on the method of examination. Apparently the statistics of the Tokyo District Court demonstrate that digital evidence tends to be the subject of inspection, because of the apprehension that the evidence might have been altered. Hironao Kaneko and Hideo Ogura set out the differing views taken when considering the admission of digital evidence: the advocates of examination through inspection (*Kensho-Setu*) suggest that the author's intent can only be determined by inspection, because the digital evidence is not capable of providing visible evidence of the content or the intent of the author; alternatively, it is also suggested that examination of the media as documents (quasi-documentary evidence) (*Shosho-Setu*) is more appropriate, taking into account the function of the storage media, one view of which considers the media as the original document, whilst another considers the media is tantamount to quasi-documentary evidence, and printouts of the content represent a copy of the evidence; yet further, examination by printout (*Shin-Shosho-Setu*) treats a printout of the contents of the storage media as a document that has been generated by the computer, and the media is considered as a support mechanism in order to produce the printout.

Documents are categorized as follows:

a. An original document (*Genpon*).
b. An authenticated copy of the original document (*Seihon*), which is capable of replacing the original, although for a copy to authenticated, it must include the date it was copied, together with a signature or seal.[36]
c. A copy of the document (*Tohon*) and a partial copy of the document (*Shohon*). Copies can be created by physical means or electronically. The relevant code of procedure requires the submission of an authenticated copy or partially authenticated copy.[37] In practice, it is generally sufficient to adduce a copy of any documentary evidence that was the subject of the examination.[38]

---

36. Rule of Civil Procedure, Rule 33.
37. Code of Criminal Procedure article 98, Rule of Criminal Procedure Rule section 57, Code of Civil Procedure article 40.
38. Code of Criminal Procedure article 310 (proviso).

The copy of a document is admissible in the same way as the original if the authenticity of the copy is accepted, but the copy of a document that is not authenticated is called *Utsushi* and is not as admissible as the original. In contrast, the court may admit a copy of a document in criminal proceedings without it being authenticated.[39] An accurate copy, such as a photocopy that is duly authenticated, is admissible, even if the original is lost.[40] The same principle applies for the copy of an electronic file.[41]

Digital Documents and the Presumption of Authenticity

A number of laws were enacted in 2004 to provide for the scanning of images and storing paper documents in electronic format.[42] The Code of Civil Procedure provides that official documents made by a public servant in the course of their duties are presumed to be authentic,[43] and this presumption also applies to official documents created by a foreign government or foreign public offices.[44] Private documents that are signed or sealed by the creator of the document or their agent are also presumed to be authentic,[45] and digital documents with an electronic signature (for a definition, see below) affixed by the creator are also presumed to be authentic.[46] The signature should either show that information on the record refers to the person who affixed the signature, or it must confirm that the information has not been altered.

Electronic Signatures

There is a public policy in Japan that digital signatures have a greater legal effect than that of an electronic signature in any other format. The law provides a presumption that if the user affixed the electronic signature to a document by the provisions of Article 3 of the Law Concerning Electronic Signatures and Certification Services (Law No.102 of 2000), a record is complete when signed by the sender:

> Chapter 2: Presumption of the authenticity of an electro-magnetic record
>
> Article 3:
>
> An electro-magnetic record which is made in order to express information (with the exception of one drawn by a public official in the exercise of his official functions) shall be presumed to be authentic if an electronic signature (limited to those that, if based on the proper control of the codes and objects necessary to perform the signature, only that person can substantially perform) is performed by the principal in relation to information recorded in the electromagnetic record.[47]

---

39. Code of Criminal Procedure article 321 and the following provisions.
40. Supreme Court decision on 1986.3.3, Keishu, Vol.40 No.2 at 175.
41. Mitsunao Ohashi, *Hi-Tech Hanzai Sosa-Nyumon Sosa-Jitsumu-Hen* (Introduction to Investigation of Hi-Technology Crimes on Investigation Practice) (Tokyo-Horei 2005), 74.
42. Law Governing the Use of Information and Communication Technology in the Preservation of Documents that Private Business Perform, and Law Preparing for Its Enforcement (HEISEI 16 HO 149 and 150). A translation into English by the Office of the Prime Minister is available on-line at http://www.kantei.go.jp/foreign/policy/it/051031/law.pdf.
43. Code of Civil Procedure article 228(2).
44. Code of Civil Procedure article 228(5).
45. Code of Civil Procedure article 228(4).
46. Law Concerning Electronic Signatures and Certification Services, Section 3.
47. Taken from the translation available at http://www.meti.go.jp.

That the law refers to a digital signature is made clear in article 2, dealing with the definition of "electronic signature" as follows:

> For the purpose of this law, "electronic signature" shall mean a measure taken with regard to information that can be recorded in an electro-magnetic record (here and hereinafter, any record which is produced by electronic, magnetic, or any other means unrecognizable by natural perceptive function, and is used for data-processing by a computer) and to which both of the following requirements applies:
>
> i. is a measure to indicate that the information was created by the person who performed the measure; and
>
> ii. is a measure that can confirm whether or not any alteration of the information has been performed.

These provisions of the Law Concerning Electronic Signatures and Certification Services are deliberately meant to deal with the formal credibility of documentary evidence (*Keishikiteki Shokoryoku*) in digital format. A document can only be formally credible if the contents are recognized as the expression of the thoughts of the author. When a document is proven to be authentic, it is then considered to be formally credible. The authenticity of a document only needs to be proven by the party adducing it where the other party enters an objection.[48]

Experts

The Code of Civil Procedure was amended in 2003 with the introduction of a specialist (Expert Commissioner, '*Senmon-Iin*') to provide special knowledge, and a person with knowledge of information technology, such as a digital evidence specialist, may become an expert witness in the examination of evidence or the inspection of a digital record, although the provisions governing the procedure to engage such a specialist differs between civil and criminal proceedings.

RUSSIAN FEDERATION

In the Russian Federation, the arbitration court[49] has jurisdiction over disputes that are economic in nature, together with matters relating to entrepreneurial and other economic activities to which the parties are legal entities. At the time of writing, digital documents were generally used in the main by organizations employed in entrepreneurial activity, and Olga I. Kudryavtseva[50] concentrated on providing a discussion of the Arbitration Proceedings Code.[51]

---

48. Code of Civil Procedure article 228(1).

49. For a brief summary in English of the system of arbitration, see http://www.arbitr.ru/eng/ and http://www.supcourt.ru/EN/supreme.htm.

50. For more detail, see Olga I. Kudryavtseva, 'Russia' in Stephen Mason, general editor, *International Electronic Evidence* (British Institute of International and Comparative Law, 2008).

51. In force from 1 September 2002.

Evidence

By way of introduction, evidence presented by the parties to arbitration proceedings is required to be relevant,[52] admissible,[53] reliable,[54] and sufficient.[55] Russian procedural law does not refer to the notion of the relevance of evidence, although evidence is classified into direct and indirect evidence. The general rules on the admissibility of evidence, which are prescriptive in nature, are set out in articles 64 and 68(3), and have two characteristics: First, evidence may only be obtained legally, which in turn is based on the provisions of article 50 of the Constitution of the Russian Federation, which prohibits the use of illegally obtained evidence. Second, some facts can only be verified by certain forms of evidence, such as the forms specified in specific laws. For instance, the provisions of article 2 of the Law on State Registration of Rights to Immovable Property and Transactions (21 July 1997) stipulate that the only evidence of the existence of a registered right is by means of state registration.

Types of Evidence

The Arbitration Proceedings Code provides for the following forms of evidence: written evidence and exhibits, explanations provided by the persons participating in the case, the conclusions of experts, the testimony of the witness, audio and video records, and other documents and materials.[56]

Electronic Documents

The definition of electronic document is contained in article 3 of Federal Law (10 January 2002) N 1-FZ "On Electronic Digital Signature," as follows:

> An electronic document is a document in which information is presented in an electronic digital form.

There is, however, some controversy regarding evidence in digital form. For instance, one of the first sets of rules regulating documents produced by computers as evidence in arbitration proceedings was The Instructive Guide of the State Arbitration of the U.S.S.R. (29 November 1978) No I-1-4. This Guide set out the requirements that documents had to meet to be accepted into evidence when prepared by computers and used in the economic activities of organizations. Subject to a number of procedural requirements, the output of a computer could only be accepted into evidence in the form of an ordinary written document, a position that was reinforced by article 52 of the Arbitration Proceedings Code of 1995, which referred to electronic documents as written evidence. This historic position has now changed, and the current Arbitration Proceedings Code provides for 'other documents and materials' as evidence, and refers to 'documents executed in digital, graphical form or otherwise enabling the authenticity of the document to be ascertained' as written evidence.[57]

---

52. Arbitration Proceedings Code article 67.
53. Arbitration Proceedings Code article 68.
54. Arbitration Proceedings Code article 71(2), (3).
55. Arbitration Proceedings Code article 71(2).
56. Article 64.
57. Article 75(1).

Article 75(3) of the Arbitration Proceedings Code now provides that documents in the form of facsimile transmission, electronic, or any other form of communication, together with documents signed with a digital signature or any other method of appending a manuscript signature are admissible as written evidence in proceedings. The procedural requirements relating to the examination of such documents have yet to be determined, and there remains some uncertainty about the formal procedural mechanism by which digital evidence will be accepted, that is whether such evidence is categorized as a document or an exhibit. In comparison, evidence in analogue form is admissible,[58] such as photographs and film, audio and video records and similar media.

Reliability of Electronic Documents

The Arbitration Proceedings Code provides that the probative value of evidence is determined by its reliability, as set out in article 71(3):

> evidence is acknowledged by a court of arbitration as reliable if its examination shows that the data it contains is trustworthy.

The credibility of evidence is evaluated in terms of the concept of moral certainty, and no evidence has a predetermined strength for a court.[59]

Securing Electronic Evidence Before Trial

It is normal procedure for the parties to proceedings to secure the evidence through the services of a notary before initiating the action. In respect of digital evidence, the parties will approach a notary to secure the evidence as follows: the notary will load the relevant site into their own computer, print out the relevant information from the site, and will then draw up the evidence examination minutes, which the notary will sign and seal. Another option is to secure the evidence by filing a motion.

The procedural problems aside, submitting digital evidence in legal proceedings can be difficult. First, the admission and examination of digital evidence remains a relatively new concept, and procedures are in the process of being developed. Also, judges generally do not understand the concepts very well, and will request additional, supposedly more reliable forms of evidence. This also means that the probative effect of digital evidence can be ignored or misunderstood.

Electronic Signatures

The definition of an electronic signature (called an electronic digital signature in the legislation, but clearly only referring to a digital signature) is specified in Article 3 of the Federal Law No. 1-FZ on Electronic Digital Signature (10 January 2002) as follows:

> an electronic document detail intended for protecting the electronic document against forgery, obtained as the result of cryptographic data transformation through the use of the secret key of the electronic digital signature and allowing identification of the owner of a signature key certificate and also making sure no information distortion has occurred in the electronic document.

---

58. Arbitration Proceedings Code article 64(2) and article 89(2).
59. Arbitration Proceedings Code article 71(1) and (5).

A message signed with a digital signature or other analogue version of a manuscript signature is recognized to be equal to a document signed with manuscript signature, providing that the relevant legislation neither expressly or by implication requires the document to be produced on paper.[60] A manuscript signature is equated to a digital signature, providing it is executed as provided for in Article 4:

1. An electronic digital signature in an electronic document that has the same effect as a handwritten signature in a hard-copy document if the conditions set out below are simultaneously observed:

the signature key certificate relating to the electronic digital signature is not void (is effective) at the time of verification or the time of signing of the electronic document if the time of signing is proven;

the authenticity of the electronic digital signature in the electronic document has been confirmed;

the electronic digital signature is used in compliance with the information specified in the signature key certificate.

2. The participant in an information system may at the same time be an owner of any number of signature key certificates. In such a case an electronic document with an electronic digital signature shall have legal significance in the pursuance of the relations specified in the signature key certificate.

As is the general practice with most legislation across the globe, the obligations that apply to the owner of the digital signature are the least detailed. The owner of the signature key certificate has the duty to keep the private signature key secret, as set out in article 12:

1. The owner of a signature key certificate shall:

not use open and secret electronic digital signature keys for electronic digital signature purposes if he knows that these keys are being used or have been used earlier;

not disclose the secret electronic digital signature key; and

immediately demand that the signature key certificate be suspended if there are reasons to believe that the secret electronic digital signature key has been disclosed.

2. If the provisions of the present article fail to be observed, the owner of signature key certificate shall be liable for damages relating to losses inflicted as the result thereof.

There are no further provisions or guidelines to indicate how the owner should exercise their obligations. It is the owner of the digital signature who determines whether there are sufficient grounds to ask the certification center to suspend the signature key certificate. Whether the private key of a digital signature is compromised or lost and subsequently misused, or used without the authority of the owner, will be the subject of both technical and oral evidence in any dispute.[61] However, it should be noted that

---

60. Article 11(3) of Federal Law No. 149-FZ Information, Information Matters and Protection of Information (27 July 2006).
    61. For a detailed discussion, see Stephen Mason, *Electronic Signatures in Law,* (Tottel, 2nd edn, 2007) Chapter 14 'Evidence'.

regulations may provide a presumption that a digital signature was used by the owner of a digital signature, and, as such, places a greater burden on the holder of the digital signature to provide for its effective security.

Application of Digital Signatures

The digital signature law is limited to the purposes set out in Article 1:

Article 1. The Purpose and Applicability of the Present Federal Law

1. The purpose of the present Federal Law is to create a legal environment for the use of the electronic digital signature in electronic documents that ensures an electronic digital signature affixed to an electronic document is recognised as having the same effect as a handwritten signature on a hard-copy document.

2. The present Federal Law shall extend to relations occurring in the accomplishment of civil legal deals and in other cases as specified by Russian law. The present Federal Law shall not extend to relations occurring when other versions of the autograph signature are used.

Of interest is the Supreme Arbitration Court Information Letter "On Certain Recommendations Adopted during the Consultations on Arbitration Practice" N C1-7/ОП-587 (19 August 1994).[62] This Information Letter considered electronic documents as a means of evidence in arbitration courts and the assessment of the procedure relating to electronic evidence. Part IV of the Letter permits the parties to a contract to adduce evidence prepared with a digital signature in contract disputes, but with a number of caveats:

IV. Can the facts of a case be confirmed by evidence produced and signed by means of computer technology, which used a system of digital signature?

In accordance with the Arbitration Procedural Code of the Russian Federation, each party must prove the circumstances to which they refer as the basis of their claims or objections. Written evidence must be submitted in the original or as a certified copy.

Where the parties have produced and signed the contract with the help of computer technology, which used a system of digital signature, they may submit to the arbitration court other evidence signed with a digital signature in respect of a dispute arising out of the contract.[63]

If a dispute arises between the parties of the very existence of the contract and other documents signed with a digital signature, the arbitration court should request the parties to produce the extract of the contract that sets out the procedure by which disputes are dealt with, demonstrating which party bears the burden of proof of the facts and the credibility of the signature.

The arbitration court examines the credibility of the evidence produced by the parties taking into account the above procedure. If necessary, the arbitration court may appoint an expert on the disputed issue, using the procedure prescribed in the contract.

---

62. Available in Russian on-line at http://www.cryptopro.ru/cryptopro/documentation/pdf/VAS-587.pdf.

63. To make this provision more obvious: the parties are allowed to produce to the court evidence signed with a digital signature *only* where the contract, which is the subject of the dispute, is signed with a digital signature.

Where the contract fails to provide a dispute procedure or a procedure that deals with the credibility of the contract and other documents in relation to the contract, and one of the parties disputes the existence of the signed contract and other documents, the arbitration court may not accept the documents signed with a digital signature as evidence.

The arbitral tribunal, which is called upon to settle a dispute, should evaluate the contract and give full consideration to the provisions and procedures voluntarily included in the contract by the parties for the purpose of dealing with disputes and proof of any facts in dispute, in order to establish the interests of the parties and disagreement on one hand, and with a view to assess the evidence and reach a judgment in the particular dispute.

The tribunal will examine the reliability of the evidence and may even request an expert report, but if the contract fails to provide for the procedure to be adopted, and one of the parties disputes the existence of the contract or any other associated documents, the tribunal may refuse to accept documents signed with a digital signature. Given the guidance set out in the Letter, in practice it is recommended to provide for the signature verification procedure of any documents exchanged between the parties in digital format in a preliminary agreement before concluding a contract.

It is possible for parties to use an electronic signature under the provisions of article 160(2) of the Civil Code, which contains provisions on the use of an electronic signature (as opposed to a digital signature) when performing transactions:

2. The use in effecting the deals of a facsimile reproduction of the signature, made with the assistance of the means of the mechanical or the other kind of copying, of the electronic-numerical signature or of another analogue of the sign manual shall be admitted in the cases and in the order, stipulated by the law and by the other legal acts, or by the agreement of the parties.[64]

Thus a contract can provide authority to the parties to certify the right to dispose of money in a bank account, electronic instrument and other documents with the use of a facsimile reproduction of a manuscript signature, passwords, codes and other means that serve to certify that the order is placed by a person with the relevant authority, as provided in article 847(3) of the Civil Code:

3. The agreement may provide for the certification of rights of disposing of cash placed on the account by the electronic payment facilities and by other documents with the use in them of the analogues of the autograph (Item 2 of Article 160), codes, passwords, and other means confirming that instructions have been given by the person authorized therefor.[65]

Experts

It is normal for arbitration courts to seek the opinion of a digital evidence specialist to examine the reliability of digital evidence. The provisions of article 55(1) of the Arbitration Proceedings Code provide that an expert in arbitration proceedings should be

---

64. Translation available on-line at http://www.russian-civil-code.com/PartI/SectionI/Subsection4/Chapter9.html.

65. Translation from http://www.russian-civil-code.com/PartII/SectionIV/Subsection1/Chapter45.html.

a person that possesses special knowledge in respect of the specific issues of the case before the tribunal. The arbitration court will appoint the expert and request an expert examination, and the court will include in the instructions to the expert, amongst other things, a list of questions for the expert to consider, together with the date the opinion must be submitted to the court. The parties to the proceedings may request an examination on their own initiative, but the resulting opinion is not regarded as admissible evidence, because the procedure for ordering the examination is not valid, not having been ordered by the court.

An expert examination is carried out by state forensic experts under the tutelage of the head of the state forensic expert institutions and by other experts that are deemed to possess the necessary knowledge.[66] Olga I. Kudryavtseva has pointed out that examinations are often ordered when digital evidence forms part of the evidence:[67]

> An examination is often used in cases where digital documents are included as evidence. For instance, in case N КГ-А40/8531-03-П, considered by the Federal Arbitration Court of Moscow Region, the court ordered the examination of the validity of an electronic digital signature. In the dispute, the claimant asserted that the electronic digital signature indicated on the payment order sent from his computer system was counterfeited. However, it followed from the opinion of the digital evidence specialist that the electronic digital signature on the disputed payment order was correct and belonged to the vice general director of the claimant. The examination also indicated that the system in place did not allow the communication session to begin without producing the client's main key. The exact wording of the expert's opinion was ". . . and send documents from the client's computer on behalf of the other client and take into processing documents not signed with duly registered electronic digital signature." This is taken to mean that both keys (the main key and the key of the vice general director) were required, but the expert's opinion is not clear on this point. The claim was dismissed on these grounds.[68]

REQUESTS OF EXPERTS IN NATIONAL LAW

The authors of the chapters summarized in this appendix were requested to cover the following topics, subject to any variations in their own jurisdiction and the limits on their time when preparing their respective chapter:

> a) Types of evidence. Please indicate if your jurisdiction distinguishes between direct and indirect evidence; real evidence; best evidence; primary and secondary evidence. Please indicate how digital evidence (please note, electronic evidence is a general term for two types of evidence: evidence obtained from an analogue device (an example

---

66. Arbitration Proceedings Code article 83(1). In a Resolution of the Plenum of the Supreme Arbitration Court of 20 December 2006, the Supreme Arbitration Court made it clear that where the opinion of an expert has been obtained from an institution other than a state institution, the opinion cannot be challenged on the grounds that a state expert institution ought to have conducted the examination.

67. Olga I. Kudryavtseva, 'Russia' in Stephen Mason, general editor, *International Electronic Evidence* (British Institute of International and Comparative Law, 2008).

68. Resolution of the Federal Arbitration Court of Moscow Region of 5 November 2003 N КГ-А40/8531-03-П.

is a film camera; and digital evidence, that is, any evidence obtained or created by a device that has, at its core, a computer, however small) fits into the evidential schema: it might be worthwhile distinguishing between evidence produced as the result of an analogue device (for instance, a camera), and a digital device (for instance any item of evidence that is produced by a computer or a computer-like device). If your jurisdiction accepts video recorded and tape recorded evidence, please cover this aspect. Admissibility of evidence: please indicate if your jurisdiction has rules about the admissibility of evidence, and if so, how they pertain to digital evidence. Weight of evidence: please indicate if your jurisdiction has rules about the way evidence is assessed or evaluated by the trier of fact, and if so, what guidance is provided by the law and comments by judges in superior courts. Proof: please distinguish between fact and law, and set out the burden and standard of proof. Please elaborate on what is meant by a document, instrument, writing, and record, if any of these terms are relevant; please indicate how these terms are treated in respect of digital evidence. Please provide a brief outline only of the law relating to digital signatures (digital signatures comprise the following: PIN, "I accept" icon, typing a name at the bottom of an e-mail, an e-mail address, biometric measurement of a manuscript signature, digital signature) and authentication of documents—please include reference to all cases in your jurisdiction relating to this topic. Presumptions and inferences: please indicate what, if any, presumptions are made by judges in relation to the reliability or otherwise of digital evidence. Computer-generated animations and simulations: please indicate if computer-generated animations and simulations are accepted in courts: whether civil or criminal or both, and what evidential foundation requirements are considered necessary in order for such simulations or animations to be accepted. Video tape and security camera evidence: please indicate how, if admitted, such evidence is accepted into legal proceedings and what, if any, procedural or authentication requirements are necessary before being adduced into evidence. Data protection: it is only necessary to know what legal requirements have an effect on the exchange of information as between lawyers in litigation proceedings as a result of any relevant legislation relating to data protection. Please include a discussion on the ability of litigants in foreign jurisdictions to obtain witness statements from nationals in your jurisdiction, and if any data protection laws affect the gathering of such evidence. Freedom of Information: please indicate, if relevant, how digital evidence is treated under any freedom of information legislation that might be in place in your jurisdiction, in particular, whether public authorities are required to provide documents that have been deleted, either accidentally or as part of a rolling delete. Role of experts: please outline the role of experts in both criminal and civil cases, what the rules and obligations are and what criteria are used to determine whether somebody can be considered an expert. Digital document management systems (parties and the courts): please provide, in outline only, how courts and parties deal with digital evidence, such as how to get digital evidence to court, including applications and pleadings, and how courts deal with digital evidence in court—for instance, indicate whether the papers are printed out, or if computers are used to show the documents.

b) Civil proceedings. Pre-trial: please outline the rights of parties to obtain urgent search and seizure orders, either before or after proceedings commence; please also include reference to orders requiring the preservation of evidence; please define the discussion in terms of digital evidence, including references to the European Convention on Human Rights (if relevant to your jurisdiction) and how this affects the issuing of such orders. Discovery or disclosure: please provide an outline of the process, scope, extent of duties and obligations of both client and lawyer, and the consequences of non-disclosure; please outline the obligation of the parties to cooperate, if there is such an obligation; please indicate what problems, if any, parties have when disclosing digital evidence—for instance, whether parties complain about the extent and costs of undertaking this task. If so, set out how judges deal with such requests. Please address the duty of the client to preserve documents; set out the duties of the lawyer to ensure the client is aware of their duties; please set out the sanctions available to a court for failing to comply with the retention of documents or the failure to comply with a court order. Confidentiality and privilege: please set out the position with respect to privilege between client and lawyer, and how this is dealt with in digital evidence, including the metadata when documents are exchanged. Costs: please set out the position on costs, and who pays for applications during a trial, and how the costs are dealt with at the end of a trial, please explain, if relevant, how the costs of providing digital documents is dealt with by the courts. Complex litigation: if there are any rules respecting complex litigation, please refer to them, especially with respect to the exchange of digital evidence and how a court deals with these issues

c) Criminal proceedings. Pre-trial: please indicate what powers of search and seizure are available to the relevant authorities; indicate the position as to how warrants are obtained; set out the powers there are with respect to conducing surveillance; how improper interception is dealt with by the courts; what the legal position is with respect to his topic; include references to the European Convention on Human Rights (if relevant to your jurisdiction) and how this affects search, seizure and interception. Disclosure obligations: please set out the obligations of both prosecution and defence respecting disclosure of evidence before trial; include reference to the consequences of non-disclosure; please refer to the European Convention on Human Rights (if applicable) and any other relevant domestic or international requirements pertaining to the rights of the individual to see evidence before trial; please also indicate how disclosure of digital evidence is undertaken is such situations where a person is accused of having child pornography on their computer; please indicate whether the defence has the right to test the computer for malicious software that might have caused the child pornography to be on the computer without owner giving permission or being aware of the pictures. Please set out the position in respect to Human Rights (if applicable) on this issue if the defense does not have such a right. Evidence from other jurisdictions: please cover this aspect in general outline, providing a brief discussion about how evidence can be obtained from other jurisdictions. Human rights issues in relation to the gathering of evidence: please cover this as necessary. Trial: please set out how a defendant may challenge the authenticity of digital evidence; if relevant, please set out the situations by which a judge can refuse to admit evidence.

It follows that the above was a suggested outline with recommended content. Recognizing that the content is organized in line with a common law jurisdiction, it was accepted that not all of the issues listed would necessarily be covered in every jurisdiction. The overview set out in this appendix does not cover every aspect set out above—in fact, the discussion in this appendix is restricted to the concepts and treatment of the following, insofar as they were covered by the respective authors: digital evidence, the forms of evidence, admissibility, electronic signatures, disclosure (mostly called disclosure, not discovery) and the role of experts.

ELECTRONIC EVIDENCE

Analogue Evidence

To a certain extent, the introduction of evidence in analogue format was well within the world view of judges and lawyers for the reason that the concept of a machine that creates an output is relatively easy to follow, whether it is a roll of film from a camera, or a machine for measuring the amount of alcohol in the breath. Analogue systems or products generate evidence in the form of data that is capable of being produced in a permanent form. Consider, for instance, an analogue camera (depending on the type of camera; a camera that produces instant photographs does not have a negative). As the shutter opens and closes, so light is admitted, and the rays of light hit the negative film, and in so doing, the chemicals on the negative will form an image. After the negative film is developed, prints in the form of photographs can then be produced, which are a reverse image of that recorded on the negative film. The negative transparency or plate comprises the primary evidence of the image captured, and arguably is also the best evidence, as well as being real evidence. Any print of an image recorded on the negative is by definition secondary evidence of the original image recorded on the negative, although it is arguable that it might also be considered to be the best evidence of the image. Generally, such an image is admitted into evidence as an exhibit once a person has testified to its production, and there tends to be little discussion of such evidence thereafter. Any number of copies of the primary image can be made, although no printed copy will be an exact copy of the negative or plate, which highlights the point that the photographs as developed from the negative film or plate are only copies of the original image. This is because the processes followed and the mix of chemicals used in transforming the negative into a print will determine how accurately the photograph reflects the image, in particular the degree of contrast (that is, the range of gray tones) captured on the negative. The degree of contrast will affect how bruising is reproduced on the photograph: a high contrast makes the bruising appear darker and more dramatic, whilst a low contrast will lessen the effect of the visual image, making the bruise seem somewhat less consequential. Generally, judges and lawyers are used to dealing with such evidence, and if there is a difference between the parties as to the accuracy of the contract in the photograph, then providing the primary evidence is available (that is, the negative film or plate), then another photograph can be developed with a different mixture of chemicals to achieve a another effect.

There is a significant difference between analogue evidence and digital evidence, mainly because evidence that is the product of an analogue device is only stored on a carrier such as paper or a photographic film, or it may not even be recorded, but it can be a continuous reading, such as early versions of radar. In addition, the machine that caused the output of the evidence to be produced tends not to be considered to be relevant once the output is produced. Thus it is not necessary to exhibit the camera that takes the photographs where a negative film or plate is used, because the image is independent of the device, unlike digital evidence, where the machine will also leave traces of evidence in a digital document. In addition, although the evidence that is recorded by an analogue device is capable of being manipulated, and a well known example was the removal of the image of Davidovich Bronstein (Leon Trotsky) from early photographs that included images of Vladimir Ilyich Ulyanov (Lenin) in Soviet Russia, nevertheless it takes great skill to alter the negative of a photographic film, and most alterations can be detected. In comparison, digital images can be altered with ease.

Digital Evidence

Examples of digital data include anything that has been created or stored on a computer or a computer like device, or is made available by way of the Internet, including CDs, DVDs, MP3s, and digital broadcast radio. The essential point about digital evidence, which is not readily understood by many judges and lawyers, is the complexity of the topic and the nature of the characteristics of digital evidence.[69] By failing to have even a basic knowledge of the subject, lawyers and digital evidence specialists responsible for investigating a case and deciding whether to initiate criminal action against an individual, are in danger of committing grave errors. It is for this reason that judges, lawyers, and legal academics should consider it to be of vital importance that they begin to understand digital evidence.

Definition of Electronic Evidence

The term "electronic evidence" is used widely, but it is commonly used to denote digital evidence, which adds to the confusion. It is suggested that the term "electronic evidence" is a generative term, rather than a specific term, in that it encompasses all forms of data, whether produced by an analogue device, or in digital form, and the following definition is proffered, and comments and criticisms are welcome:[70]

> Electronic evidence: data (comprising the output of analogue devices or data in digital format) that is created, manipulated, stored or communicated by any device, computer or computer system or transmitted over a communication system, that is relevant to the process of adjudication.

The two forms of evidence should not be confused, because different evidential and procedural requirements apply to each form of evidence.

---

69. Stephen Mason, general editor, *Electronic Evidence: Disclosure, Discovery & Admissibility,* Chapter 2 'The characteristics of electronic evidence' for more detail.

70. Stephen Mason, general editor, *Electronic Evidence: Disclosure, Discovery & Admissibility,* paragraph 2.03, which also includes a discussion of the elements of this definition.

The Role of the Vendor and Specialized Software in the Handling of Digital Evidence

Victor Limongelli*

A critical aspect of the handling of digital evidence after a dispute arises is that the same concerns of authenticity—primarily integrity of information—are implicated as before the dispute arose. In addition, given that many forensic and electronic discovery procedures and software systems process information, issues of systems reliability are also present. In this case study, Victor Limongelli, President of Guidance Software, discusses the role of the vendor in such situations.

Digital evidence, unlike physical evidence or documents in paper form, is often collected, processed, and authenticated at trial using hardware and software supplied by vendors. Although traditional physical information records may have been *created* with a vendor-supplied product, such as a typewriter, traditionally they were gathered, handled, and authenticated in court in a manual fashion. Digital informational records, on the other hand, are typically collected, processed, or introduced at trial using tools designed to collect without alteration, preserve, and then translate the 1's and 0's of the digital domain into a format comprehensible to the average juror. Because these forensic tools often play a critical role in how digital evidence is collected, processed, and authenticated in court, the reliability and testability of these products is vitally important.[1]

---

*Victor Limongelli is President and CEO of Guidance Software, Inc. He received his J.D. degree from Columbia University School of Law, where he was a James Kent Scholar, and his undergraduate degree from Dartmouth College.

1. As a preliminary matter, the products most commonly used in *creating* digital information records are rarely, if ever, analyzed during the process of authenticating digital information records. For instance, software programs such as Microsoft Word are commonly used to create digital records, but there is no case on record challenging the reliability of such programs. Everyone—the courts, the litigants, the lawyers, the juries—accepts without challenge that strokes on a keyboard will accurately translate to words in a digital document created in a common word-processing or e-mail program. Challenging the reliability of these types of widely used programs (Microsoft's Office line of products, common e-mail applications such as Outlook and Lotus Notes, etc.) would be futile, because millions or even billions of people, including most jury members, have used them and trust that the products produce accurate results, and, as a consequence, the time and expense involved in challenging their reliability outweighs any likely litigation advantage. The situation might be different if there were thousands of such programs, each with a small cadre of users, but given the standardization that exists, it may fairly be said that these types of products have been thoroughly vetted. That vetting, however, has occurred wholly outside the judicial process, in the realm of popular opinion and use.

259

Indeed, because digital information is easy to manipulate, vendor-supported tools that collect, process, or present digital information records without altering them have become widely used.[2] Although a textual record in digital form can be authenticated by a fact witness, vendors most often play a role when specialized tools (i.e., computer forensics software programs) have been used to collect or process that evidence. In those situations, an expert witness typically opines on the methodology and the tools used to collect, process, and analyze the digital evidence.

Because of the frequent need to use evidence-collection products that themselves process information, a new category of concerns thus arises with digital evidence. How do we know that such processing is not destroying the integrity of the information at issue, or other attributes going to its authenticity? Or, how do we know that the vendor's product is reliably achieving what it purports to do? The vendor product will likely depend on the reading, writing, and analysis functions performed by the program. Is its system reliable? An entire second world of evidentiary concerns awaits us.

THE ROLE OF RULE 901(B)(9)

Courts have allowed digital evidence to be authenticated under Federal Rule of Evidence 901(b)(9), which governs evidence generated by or resulting from a largely automated process or system. For instance, "evidence describing . . . the process of creating X-rays, photographs, tape recordings, computer generated records, radar records, or scientific surveys, when coupled with evidence showing that a particular process or system produces an accurate result when correctly employed and properly operated, and that the process or system was in fact so employed and operated, constitutes sufficient evidence that the result is what it purports to be."[3] As described below, this result is likely because under the Federal Rules of Evidence, proferred evidence can be authenticated if it is reliable; and when certain technical processes become generally accepted, they are deemed reliable. Certain products for the collection, preservation, and analysis of digital evidence have reached the stage of general acceptance, and courts have even begun to take judicial notice of them.[4]

Assuming that the evidence is sought to be authenticated through the testimony of an expert witness, how should such tools and methodologies be measured? In other words, what is the appropriate standard for determining whether the evidence collected or processed with the product is authentic?

BUILT-IN AUTHENTICITY CHECKS

Most vendor-supplied products allow the evidence in a case to be collected and then analyzed. Generally, computer forensics software programs are designed to: (1) create a duplicate set of data, without changing any of the data; (2) authenticate that the dupli-

---

2. For instance, Guidance Software reports that over 25,000 copies of its EnCase computer forensics software have been sold over the last decade.

3. RONALD F. WRIGHT & MARC L. MILLER, FEDERAL PRACTICE AND PROCEDURE (West, 1990) § 6830.

4. Sanders v. State, 191 S.W.3d 272 (Tex. App. 2006) (taking judicial notice of the reliability of EnCase software).

cate data is unchanged from the original; (3) enable detailed analysis of the duplicate data (again, without changing it); and (4) enable the reporting or documentation of the conclusions drawn from the analysis. Thus, computer forensics tools, and their human operators, collect and work with the data that is the evidence in a lawsuit or investigation. And data, after processing by computer forensics tools, is then viewed by the investigator, or by the trier of fact in a legal proceeding.

But how do we know that the data, the evidence, has not been altered? Does it have "integrity"? In other words, are we on a solid digital foundation? And how do we know that all this processing is "reliable," as that term has been used throughout this book?

Clearly, under Federal Rule of Evidence 702, an expert is permitted to testify only if "(1) the testimony is based upon sufficient facts or data; (2) the testimony is the product of reliable principles and methods; and (3) the witness has applied the principles and methods reliably to the facts of the case."[5] The second item, whether the testimony is the product of reliable principles or methods, compels vendors to build into their products functions or processes that backstop reliability, because "[t]he integrity of data may . . . be compromised in the course of discovery by improper search and retrieval techniques, data conversion, or mishandling."[6] In other words, technological processes and functions are built into these systems to ensure that if evidence is altered after collection, such alteration will be evident.

INTEGRITY OF DATA

The typical data-collection effort by a computer forensics examiner provides a good case study. In order to collect digital information records located on a computer drive, a computer forensics examiner can use forensic software to make an exact copy of the data located on computer media, without altering that information in any way. The software contains a built-in authenticity check, by using well-known, established, "industry-standard"[7] mathematical algorithms to confirm that the collected data has remained unaltered from the time that it was collected to the time of the expert's analysis of it. The software does this by utilizing a hash function—the application of an algorithm to the collected data—to create a "digital fingerprint" of the collected data.[8] (See discussion of hash functions in Chapter 4.) If one bit of the collected data is subsequently altered in any way, the application of the mathematical algorithm to the data will cause the hash value to be wildly different.[9] In short, "[h]ash values . . . can be used during discovery of electronic records to create a form of electronic 'Bates stamp' that will help establish the document"[10] for authentication purposes. In addition, certain tools provide additional

---

5. FED. R. EVID. 702.

6. Lorraine v. Markel American Ins. Co., 241 F.R.D. 534, 543–44 n.21 (D. Md. 2007) (*citing* MANUAL FOR COMPLEX LITIGATION at § 11.447).

7. *See* People v. Shinohara, 872 N.E.2d 498, 523 (Ill. App. 1st Dist., 2007) ("forensic software used computer industry standard hashing algorithm to verify that the image taken off the hard drive was accurate").

8. George L. Paul, *The "Authenticity Crisis" in Real Evidence*, THE PRACTICAL LITIGATOR (Nov. 2004.).

9. Under any applicable evidentiary standard (even "beyond a reasonable doubt"), this is true, but it is worth noting that it is not a mathematical impossibility that two different files could have the same hash value. However, using the MD-5 hash algorithm as an example, the odds of two files with different contents having the same hash value is approximately one in ten raised to the 38th power.

10. *Lorraine, supra* note 6, 534, 546–47(D.Md. 2007).

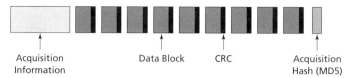

Acquisition Information   Data Block   CRC   Acquisition Hash (MD5)

FIGURE E.1
Stages of Hash of Acquisition Information

authenticity checks, such as generating upon collection a cyclical redundancy checksum (CRC) for every sixty-four sectors (32K) of collected data, as well as data automatically captured concerning the collection (or "acquisition") of the data. By way of example, Figure E.1 shows a representation of an "evidence file" of data collected using a leading computer forensics software:

The CRCs allow the pinpointing of the location of any alteration of a data set (which may be important if other unaltered data segments are sought to be authenticated).

In addition to highlighting any subsequent alteration of collected data, sophisticated data-collection products automatically check and report upon the actual data-collection process, by comparing the hash value generated upon collection with a second hash value generated for verification purposes, as well as reporting on any errors encountered while reading the drive. Immediately upon collection, then, an expert can tell whether the data collection has been properly carried out, as the software automatically captures data about the collection, as shown in Figure E.2.

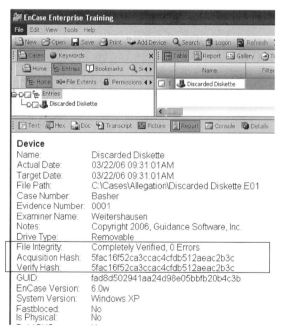

FIGURE E.2
Confirming MD5 Hash Values and Lack of CRC Errors

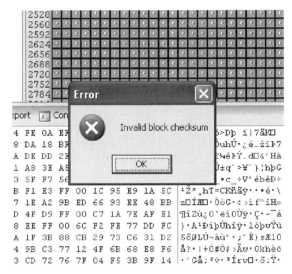

FIGURE E.3
Dialog Box Indicating Error in Data Block

If an error occurs, the software likewise highlights that information by identifying, in the "File Integrity" line, that there were errors, and by displaying that information to the user, as shown in Figure E.3.

In addition to hashing all of the collected data, the user can generate a hash value for individual files (see Figure E.4), and sophisticated data-collection tools can collect

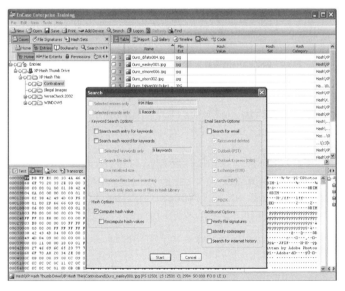

FIGURE E.4
Computing Hash Values for Individual Files

individual files—rather than an entire desktop or server—in order to focus on the relevant data.

Set forth below is an illustration of direct testimony addressing the authentication process:

Q: Please describe the authentication process employed by the software.

A: Specialized software, such as the _____ software I employed, uses a standard mathematical algorithm to produce a value based upon the specific contents of a file or hard drive. When the "Message Digest-5" algorithm is used, the resulting value is known as an MD5 hash value. A hash value is often referred to as a "digital fingerprint." The same software also verifies that this value remains the same from the time it is generated. If one bit of data on the file or hard drive in question is changed—even if a *single character* is altered—the MD5 hash value changes. If the MD5 value has not changed, then it is established that the file has not been altered in any way.

Q: What are the odds of two files with different contents having the same hash value?

A: The odds of two computer files with different contents having the same MD5 hash value is roughly one in 10 to the 38th power (that is, one followed by 38 zeros). By contrast, the number one hundred trillion written out is the number one followed by only 14 zeros.

LOGGING AND THE ISSUE OF WHO DID WHAT WITH THE DATA

The inviolability of the collected data is only one factor, albeit an important one, in establishing the authenticity of a digital informational record. Modern forensic tools for data collection also help establish *who* performed the collection and who performed the processing. Of course, the expert can and should keep a record of what he or she does, and this information can usually be entered into a report or other record prepared by the expert. But layered on top of that kind of manual record keeping, modern tools can build in (and keep track of) "roles" that are then assigned to various identified individuals who are involved in the data collection and review. For example, a particular individual with an assigned role may be limited to collecting data, but not be authorized to review. The inviolability of assigned roles—and restrictions on authenticated users—can be maintained using a public key infrastructure (PKI) scheme to manage users' access and usage rights, or permission types. Figure E.5 shows an example of some of the roles that can be established within a leading network-enabled digital investigation tool (that is, the collection of data occurs across a computer network, but using the same forensics "imaging" code that is used in the old-fashioned off-network computer forensics tool).

Descriptions of some of these permissions include:

- **Acquire Image**—This permission gives the user the ability to acquire full forensic images of computers and other devices attached to the network.
- **Browse File Structure**—This permission displays the file structure and allows the user to navigate through that structure.
- **View File Contents**—This permission gives the user the ability to use the viewer in the View Pane.

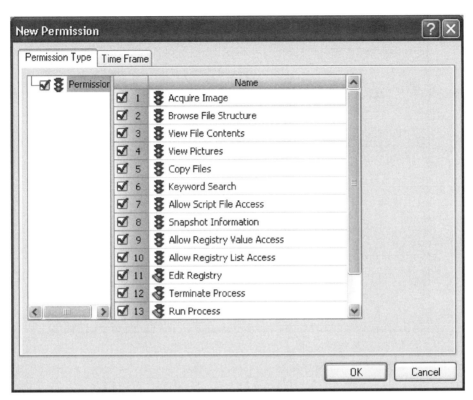

FIGURE E.5
Permissions Assigned to a "Role"

- **View Pictures**—This permission activates the Gallery view in the Table Pane and the Picture view in the View Pane.
- **Copy Files**—This permission gives the user the ability to copy folders as well as to copy/un-erase files. External viewers are also tied to this permission.
- **Keyword Search**—This permission allows the user to only conduct a keyword search. The results will not be displayed if this is the only permission selected.
- **Allow Script Files Access**—This permission allows the use of automated search, collection, and preservation modules to preserve only those files (and associated metadata) that are potentially relevant to a matter.

Likewise, the software can restrict the time frames in which even authorized actions can be taken by an authorized individual, as in Figure E.6.

This allows for fine-grained control over what and when a role can perform any function.

In order to authenticate evidence, it may be necessary to show exactly what actions were taken by the person who performed the collection of the digital informational records. Advanced data-collection tools, and in particular network-enabled tools, incorporate logging functionality. For example, for each role that has been created, the connections and disconnections to network devices (i.e., desktops, laptops, and servers) can

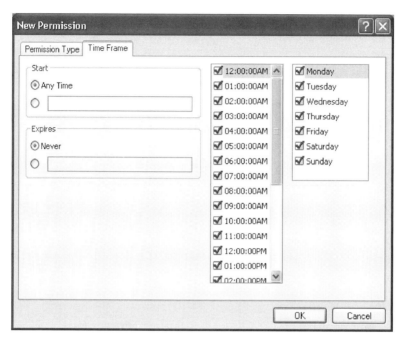

FIGURE E.6
Time Frame Tab for Permissions

be shown. In addition, certain eDiscovery-specific applications[11] enable the creation of logs that record if a file was "identified" and collected as responsive, or if it was rejected, based on the criteria of the search. See Figure E.7, for example.

In other words, this data-collection software can record *every file searched* on *each computer searched* and whether or not each file was responsive to the search criteria used. In addition, the software logs *when* the search was conducted, which can be centrally set by reference to trusted external time sources, for consistency and accuracy. In addition, the user may create a report detailing his or her actions, but this kind of computer-generated data can be crucial in establishing the accuracy of the user's reporting.

Vendors build in these types of capabilities so that when an expert opines that data was collected properly and that the collected data has not been altered since it was collected, he or she can do so, confident that the product contains "a built-in, logical test for authenticity,"[12] or even more than one test. By building in these types of authenticity checks, a vendor makes it easier for an expert to testify, easier for the court to accept that the expert's testimony is the "product of reliable principles and methods," and, ultimately, easier for litigants to have digital information records authenticated. "The authenticity test, allowed by the hash function, allows any electronic informa-

---

11. Such as EnCase eDiscovery.
12. George L. Paul, *supra* note 8.

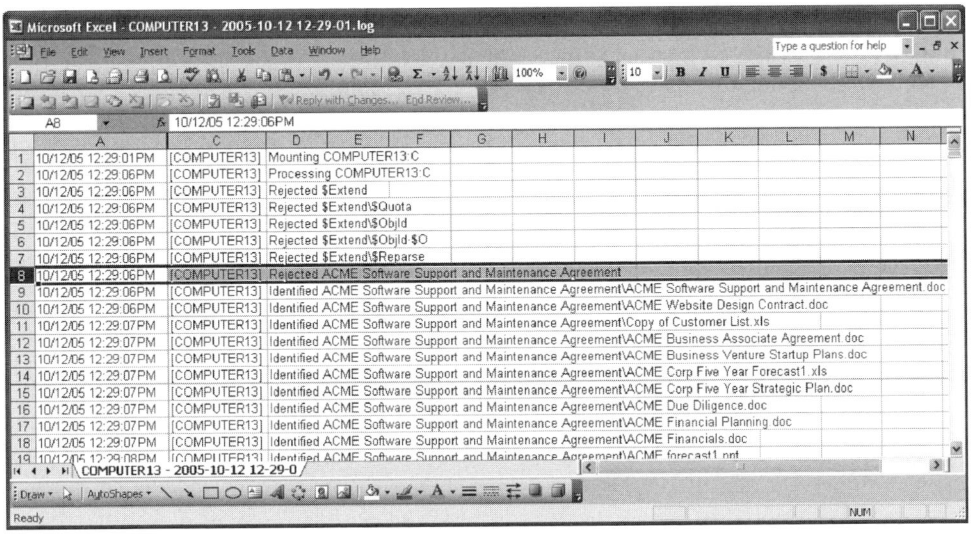

FIGURE E.7
Logfile Identifying Which Files Were Responsive (Identified) or Rejected

tional record to be stored in a provable, frozen state."[13] Conversely, without these types of authenticity checks, every attempt to introduce a digital information record—which, as noted above, is easily altered—can deteriorate into a pitched, chain-of-custody battle. Vendors, by designing their products with these types of built-in authenticity checks, play a crucial role in streamlining the authentication of digital information records.

The Imprecise World of Review Tools for Lawyers

While the ability to authenticate records at the stage of data collection is well established, and the leading products have built-in authenticity checks, the same cannot be said in the area of tools for lawyer review and production. Unique issues are presented when large sets of electronic data are filtered and pared down to reduce the dataset to that which is relevant or not privileged/protected. Additionally, preparation of electronic evidence for production presents unexpected challenges. Those challenges, which present important issues for vendors (particularly service providers) and litigants alike, will be addressed below.

ISSUES REGARDING RELIABILITY OF SPECIALIZED TESTIMONY

Federal Rule of Evidence 702 governs the admission of testimony based on "scientific, *technical, or other specialized knowledge*."[14] Thus, courts considering whether to admit testimony that depends on products used to collect, process, and analyze digital

---

13. *Id.*
14. FED. R. EVID. 702 (emphasis added).

evidence will use the prevailing standards for scientific or technical testimony—either in federal courts and many state courts (the landmark *Daubert* case and its progeny), or in certain state courts (the *Kelly/Frye* standards). In the phrasing of the *Frye* case, when it comes to expert testimony, "the thing from which the deduction is made must be sufficiently established to have gained general acceptance in the particular field in which it belongs."[15]

Many courts still use the "general acceptance" standard today. For instance, in *Commercial Union Insurance Co. v. Boston Edison Co.*, the Court conditioned the admissibility of a customized computer model on a sufficient showing that, among other things, "the program is generally accepted by the appropriate community of scientists."[16] *Daubert*, on the other hand, found that the Federal Rules of Evidence had superseded the *Frye* rule, noting that "a rigid 'general acceptance' requirement would be at odds with the 'liberal thrust' of the Federal Rules."[17] Under *Daubert*, reliability is the watchword: "under the Rules, the trial judge must ensure that any and all scientific testimony or evidence is . . . reliable."[18] Although the *Daubert* Court emphasized that it did not "presume to set out a definitive checklist or test,"[19] it set forth four factors for courts to consider:

1. Is the technique capable of being tested, and whether it has been tested;
2. Whether the technique has been subjected to peer review and publication;
3. What is the known or potential rate of error, and whether there are "standards controlling the technique's operation;" and
4. Is the technique generally accepted within the relevant scientific community?[20]

The *Daubert* Court noted that "[w]idespread acceptance can be an important factor in ruling particular evidence admissible."[21] Although the *Daubert* case addressed scientific evidence explicitly, the Supreme Court extended its reasoning to technical processes in *Kumho Tire Co., Ltd. v. Carmichael*, in which it noted "that *Daubert's* general holding . . . applies not only to testimony based on 'scientific' knowledge, but also to testimony based on 'technical' and 'other specialized' knowledge."[22] As a result, vendors of products designed to collect, preserve, or analyze digital evidence aim to fulfill the *Daubert* factors, with the ultimate goal being widespread acceptance of their products and the underlying techniques.

The role of the digital evidence collection vendors in the authentication of digital evidence surfaces most prominently in five specific areas: (1) education and training of the technical expert who collected or processed the digital evidence, and who testifies about it in court, including formal certification programs for technical experts; (2) tech-

---

15. Frye v. United States, 54 App. D.C. 46, 47, 293 F. 1013, 1014 (1923).

16. 412 Mass. 545, 549, 591 N.E.2d 165 (1992).

17. Daubert v. Merrell Dow Pharmaceuticals, Inc., 509 U.S. 579, 588, 113 S.Ct. 2786, 2794 (1993).

18. *Id.* at 2786, 2795.

19. *Id.* at 2786, 2796.

20. *Id.* at 2786, 2796–97.

21. *Id.* at 2786, 2797.

22. Kumho Tire Co., Ltd. v. Carmichael, 526 U.S. 137, 141, 119 S.Ct. 1167, 1171 (1999).

nological authenticity "checks" or verifications built into the vendor's product; (3) creating and publishing documentation of the functions performed by the vendor's product; (4) encouragement of, and highlighting the results of, peer review and publication; and (5) establishing, over time, general acceptance in the technical community of the vendor's product and the functions it performs.

The first four items all aim toward the fifth item, which is the ultimate goal for a vendor—establishing general acceptance in the relevant technical or scientific community—and which is the standard in courts utilizing the *Kelley/Frye* approach, and is nearly dispositive even under the *Daubert* test. Although general acceptance is not necessary in order to authenticate digital evidence, general acceptance makes things infinitely easier for the vendor, its customers, and the court system, because when a product has achieved widespread acceptance, it is usually not challenged in court (though the skill and training of the user may still be subject to attack, as the use of the product in any particular instance), in much the same way that common e-mail or word-processing programs are not subject to challenge. "[W]ell-established propositions are less likely to be challenged than those that are novel."[23] That makes the authentication of evidence collected, processed, or presented using well-established products faster and less expensive than tools that have not yet been tested in the adversarial process. In other words, there are efficiency gains when the litigation community standardizes on tools for the collection, preservation, and analysis of digital evidence. In fact, when a product becomes very widely accepted, "[j]udicial notice could be a helpful way to . . . facilitate authenticating electronic evidence."[24] Indeed, "once some courts have, through a *Daubert/Kelly* 'gatekeeping' hearing, determined the scientific reliability and validity of a specific methodology . . . other courts may take judicial notice of the reliability (or unreliability) of that particular methodology."[25]

EDUCATION, TRAINING, AND CERTIFICATION OF SERVICE PROVIDERS

While they do not design the authenticity checks or other useful functions in the products themselves, as described briefly under "The Role of the Service Provider" below, providers of forensic examination services provide a key function in the process of presenting digital evidence. These persons must be educated and trained in how these forensic tools function. Vendors support education regarding their products for obvious business reasons, such as making them easier for customers to use, but also to create a group of potential witnesses with sufficient training to qualify as an expert witness, and thus to authenticate the technical process embodied in the vendor's tool. Under Rule 702, a witness qualifies as an expert entitled to give opinion testimony, "by knowledge, skill, experience, training, or education."[26] Set forth below is an illustration of direct

---

23. *Daubert, supra* note 17, at 2786 n 11.

24. *Lorraine, supra* note 6, at 534, 553.

25. *Sanders, supra* note 4, at 272, 278 n.1 (*citing* Hernandez v. State, 116 S.W.3d 26, 28–29 (Tex. Crim. App. 2003)).

26. FED. R. EVID. 702.

testimony establishing the education, training, and certifications of an expert witness in the field of computer investigations:

[After stating name for the record]

Q: Sir, where are you employed?

A: I am a Deputy Sheriff in the Sacramento County Sheriff's Department.

Q: And what is your role as a Sheriff's Deputy?

A: I conduct computer forensics examinations as a member of the Sheriff's Department's computer crimes unit.

Q: Tell us about your educational background.

A: I received a criminal justice degree from CSU Sacramento in 1994.

Q: Did you receive any education in conducting computer crimes investigations while at CSU Sacramento?

A: Not computer investigations, but I did take courses in investigatory techniques generally.

Q: Please tell us about any training that you have taken in the handling and examination of computer evidence.

A: I have taken two courses at Kennesaw State University, "Computer Forensic Introduction," which is eighteen hours of classroom instruction; and "Computer Forensics—Bootcamp," which is a weeklong course. In addition, I have taken three courses from Guidance Software, the maker of EnCase software: (1) EnCase Computer Forensics I; (2) EnCase Computer Forensics II; and (3) EnCase Advanced Computer Forensics. Each of those courses was four days of classroom instruction.

Q: Do you hold any certifications?

A: Yes. I am an EnCase Certified Examiner (EnCE). I also have earned a "Certified Computer Examiner" certification at the Southeast Cybercrime Institute at Kennesaw State University, and I am a Certified Forensic Computer Examiner, which is a certification issued by the International Association of Computer Investigative Specialists.

Q: How do you earn the EnCE certification?

A: In order to qualify to take the certification test, an applicant must have either (1) taken eighty hours of classroom computer forensics training, and have at least eighteen months' experience as an investigator, including at least six months' experience in computer forensics investigations; (2) taken thirty hours of classroom computer forensics training, and have at least two years' experience as an investigator, including at least one year of experience in computer forensics investigations; or (3) taken the EnCase Computer Forensics II course, and have at least eighteen months' experience as an investigator, including at least six months' experience in computer forensics investigations. I qualified under the third option.

Q: If you qualify according to those standards, have you earned the certification?

A: No. Those qualifications entitled you to take a rigorous two-part test. The first part is a computer-based test administered by a third-party testing company known as Prometric. If you receive a score of 80 percent or higher, you are eligible to take the second part, which is a practical test requiring candidates to examine computer evidence sent to them on a CD-ROM. If you score 85 percent or higher on that practical test, you will have earned the EnCE certification.

Q: When did you first earn that certification?

A: In November 2004.

Q: Is your EnCE certification current?

A: Yes. The EnCE certification is valid for two years, and in order to renew it, you must earn sixty-four credit hours of continuing education every two years. I renewed my EnCE certification in October 2006.

[Continue with other certifications.]

As detailed above, a vendor's formal education and certification programs can actually *create* expert witnesses by providing the technician with the training to qualify as an expert witness under Role 702 (although, as highlighted above, there are of course other avenues for such training). In addition, if a certification becomes widely accepted, it becomes a badge of competence and streamlines the qualification of a testifying technical witness as an expert. It is worth noting, as well, that an expert need not be a computer programmer or software engineer. As described by one federal district court:

> Defendants argue that Taylor is not qualified to testify as a computer expert because: (1) none of his degrees are in computer science; (2) he is not fluent in any computer language; (3) he is not a computer programmer; (4) he holds no certificates in computer science; and (5) he possesses no training or special education for Microsoft certification. . . .
>
> The court finds that Taylor qualifies as an expert based on his knowledge, skill, experience, training and education. The field of computer forensics does not require a background in computer programming or reading and writing code. Taylor has been working in the field of computer forensics for five years. During this period, he has completed between 1,600 and 1,700 forensic reports based on his findings, some of which have been accepted by various courts.[27]

CREATING AND PUBLISHING DOCUMENTATION

Much like education and certification programs established by vendors, creating and publishing technical specifications serves the obvious business purpose of making the vendor's products easier for customers to use, but it also serves an evidentiary authentication purpose. The *Daubert* factors include whether the technical tool or process has been subjected to peer review and publication, and whether it has been tested. By publishing documentation regarding its product, and encouraging testing by third parties, a vendor can enable the testing, peer review, and publication that is so important to admissibility of technical evidence under *Daubert* and *Kumho Tire*. With respect to testing, a major advantage of a commercially available product, when compared to custom applications developed in-house by a litigant and not available to the general public,

---

27. Galaxy Computer Services, Inc. v. Baker, 325 B.R. 544, 563 (E.D.Va. 2005).

is that it is easy for customers and other third parties to test the commercially available product:

> Evidence generated through the use of standard, generally available software is easier to admit than evidence generated with custom software. The reason lies in the fact that the capabilities of commercially marketed software packages are well known and cannot normally be manipulated to produce aberrant results. Custom software, on the other hand, must be carefully analyzed by an expert programmer to ensure that the evidence being generated by the computer is in reality what it appears to be.[28]

By providing sufficient documentation, as well as, in certain circumstances, copies of the software to independent third parties to facilitate testing, a vendor can greatly increase the likelihood of peer review and publication. When that occurs, it becomes much easier for a litigant to authenticate digital information records collected, processed, or analyzed with that tool. For example, the U.S. government conducted extensive testing of computer forensics tools, and published its results in June 2003.[29] The testing was conducted as part of the Computer Forensics Tool Testing (CFTT) project, which was a joint effort of the National Institute of Justice, the National Institute of Standards and Technology (NIST), the U.S. Department of Defense, the Technical Support Working Group, and other related agencies. As described on the CFTT website:

> The goal of the Computer Forensic Tool Testing (CFTT) project at the National Institute of Standards and Technology (NIST) is to establish a methodology for testing computer forensic software tools by development of general tool specifications, test procedures, test criteria, test sets, and test hardware. The results provide the information necessary for toolmakers to improve tools, for users to make informed choices about acquiring and using computer forensics tools, and for interested parties to understand the tools capabilities. Our approach for testing computer forensic tools is based on well-recognized international methodologies for conformance testing and quality testing.[30]

Indeed, the project is specifically concerned with court admissibility: "The implementation of testing based on rigorous procedures will provide impetus for vendors to improve their tools *and provide assurance that their results will stand up in court.*"[31] Products that performed well throughout the comprehensive CFTT testing process could (and do) cite the CFTT testing as a stellar example of testing, peer review, and publication, and testifying experts could cite the testing as an external validation of their tool.

Because of the explosion of ESI over the last twenty years, information analysis technologies that had historically not found much use in the legal profession, such as probabilistic models using Bayesian belief networks, have been explored.[32] Vendors of tools utilizing these techniques, however, have been quick to point out that their products are tools for reviewing lawyers to use and do not, in fact, collect any data—rather, they are aimed at reducing the time applied to "document review during large-scale litiga-

---

28. 71 Am. Jur. Trials 111 § 118 (1999).

29. Available at http://www.ncjrs.org/pdffiles1/nij/200031.pdf.

30. Available at http://www.cftt.nist.gov/.

31. http://www.cftt.nist.gov/project_overview.htm (emphasis added).

32. *See* George L. Paul & Jason R. Baron, *Information Inflation: Can the Legal System Adapt?*, 13 Rich. J.L. & Tech. 10, 27 (2007).

tion"[33] by providing "a means for reviewing lawyers to quickly organize, display, search and mark the documents *within a document collection.*"[34] As such, these tools are less directly implicated in evidentiary authentication than products that collect and preserve ESI, although these tools nevertheless *do* handle the evidentiary data, and thus must not alter any data—and such inviolability of the data should be demonstrable and testable.[35] If challenged, such tools ideally would be able to put forth "a scientific showing that the results are accurate, complete, and reliable, [and] the challenging party may argue that the process used by the responding party is essentially an expert technology which has not been validated by subjecting it to peer review, and unbiased empirical testing or analysis."[36] Unlike evidence-collection tools such as computer forensics software, however, which have been through extensive third-party testing, the nascent "data analytics" market has to date had very little published independent testing, and has yet to achieve "general acceptance." Thus, their adoption has been slowed somewhat by the fear of whether a particular method "would withstand a court challenge."[37]

GENERAL ACCEPTANCE

It is obviously helpful for a litigant to use a product that has achieved general acceptance. When that occurs, as noted above, it is far easier for all parties, as well as the court, because the litigation does not get bogged down in questions regarding the reliability of the tools used. Not having general acceptance, on the other hand, can cause the litigant to face difficulty having the evidence authenticated, and may even call into question the litigant's conduct (and, from a vendor's perspective, slows the adoption and use of its tool).

For example, a custom application created by a litigant and used only by it can never, by definition, have general acceptance. As a result, there are advantages to using commercially available products—particularly those that have been on the market for a time, and have undergone the requisite testing and peer review—and there are disadvantages to using self-generated tools. For instance, in the high-profile case of *Coleman (Parent) Holdings, Inc. v. Morgan Stanley & Co.,* which resulted in a $1.4 billion jury verdict (later reversed on other grounds), the court noted that "[a Morgan Stanley employee] reported that . . . she and her team had discovered that a flaw in the software they had written had prevented [Morgan Stanley] from locating all responsive e-mail attachments. [She also] reported that [Morgan Stanley] discovered . . . that the date-range searches for e-mail users who had a Lotus Notes platform were flawed, so there were at least 7,000 additional e-mail messages that appeared to fall within the scope of [existing orders]. . . ."[38] In issuing evidentiary sanctions, the court noted, among other things, that Morgan

---

33. http://www.attenex.com/eDiscovery/corporations/.

34. *See* http://www.dtengine.com/CS_attenexLegal.html.

35. These tools are subject to challenge. *See* The Sedona Conference Best Practices Commentary on the Use of Search & Information Retrieval Methods in E-Discovery, 8 SEDONA CONFERENCE JOURNAL 189 (2007).

36. *Id.*

37. *Id.,* vol. VIII, at 203.

38. Coleman (Parent) Holdings, Inc. v. Morgan Stanley & Co., Inc., 2005 WL 679071 at *4 (Fla. Cir. Ct., Mar. 1, 2005) (emphasis added).

Stanley had "fail[ed] to write software . . . consistent with [existing discovery orders]."[39] Contrast that situation with the operation of commercially available software that is in widespread use, has been tested and subjected to peer review, and has achieved general acceptance in the relevant technical community. It is no wonder that vendors make every effort to ensure that their products achieve general acceptance, as such products are what most litigants are going to seek to use.

THE ROLE OF THE SERVICE PROVIDER

The previous discussion centered on product vendors, and their role in helping to establish the authenticity of digital information records collected, processed, or analyzed using their tools. Vendors of services, however, also play a role. While they cannot design authenticity checks into products themselves, or publish technical specifications for those tools, they can be transparent about their own processes, and participate in standard-setting bodies to establish best practices for services. In addition, if they deploy custom tools that are not available to the general public, they can work to ensure that those tools meet the reliability standards of *Daubert* and its progeny, and undergo extensive testing, peer review, and publication, and formal training for users.

CONCLUSION

Because digital information is subject to manipulation, persons trained to use products and products designed to collect, process, or present digital information records without altering them have become more widely used than would be the case if data were unalterable. Vendors of such products and services play a crucial role in the authentication of digital information records, their analysis, and presentation in court. Software vendors design and test products, publish documentation, establish and obtain certifications, and encourage expert certification and third-party review and testing, all with an eye to establishing general acceptance of the proper use of their product within the relevant technical community. And once that general acceptance of the product and its use has been achieved, the adversarial process can focus its attentions on the merits of the case, rather than the provenance of the tools and methods used to collect, process, or analyze the data. In the end, that is a better, cheaper, and more efficient process for everyone.

---

39. *Id.* at *5.

Will the Real "When" Please Stand Up?

Steven W. Teppler*

In Appendices A, B, and C the reader was provided with examples of eunomic techniques currently being employed to handle digital information. Examples abound, however, where information is not handled pursuant to an ordered scheme. In this chapter, illustrating what can be called dysnomia, Steven W. Teppler, a litigation lawyer in New York and Florida, discusses a real world litigation case study, where a sophisticated corporate defendant was unable to prove the integrity of its information involving the time on its records, or their content.

Evidentiary challenges involving digital time issues are not yet prevalent, but have nevertheless started to appear in some matters, even those where the core disputes do not center around the generation, protection, or authentication of digital information. The following example is excerpted from the real-life case of *Whitney v. JetBlue Airways Corporation,* an action alleging negligence resulting in personal injury and filed in the U.S. District Court for the Eastern District of New York.[1] The case is a good example of a corporation's inability to properly maintain and handle its digital business records, particularly involving proof of the authenticity of its records.

In *JetBlue*, the only provably authentic data (a handwritten report) about an "irregularity" aboard a commercial jet flight was indisputably destroyed by the airline. The party requesting the airline's records of the "Irregularity Report" was first given a scanned version of a paper printout of a computer file, and then a second paper printout that contradicted the first, in that it had a different title and different content. When counsel pressed for the digital evidence, he was given an Microsoft Excel spreadsheet that was alleged to have been created within weeks of the incident. Indeed, the date contained "inside" the content of the spreadsheet supported that assertion. However, the metadata contained in the Excel spreadsheet indicated a creation date that was sixteen months after the incident, and further indicated a different author on the metadata than appeared in the body of the document. The lack of any foundation for the digital records, and the fact that the airliner destroyed the only authentic record, led to the filing of a motion for spoliation and Fed. R. Civ. P. Rule 37 sanctions.

---

*Steven W. Teppler is Senior Counsel to KamberEdelson, LLC, in New York City, and directs the firm's eDiscovery and electronic litigation efforts. Mr. Teppler is also an expert on digital time issues.

1. *See* Whitney v. JetBlue Airways Corp., 07-CV-1397 (E.D.N.Y. 2007).

THE FACTS

Shortly after takeoff from New York's JFK Airport in a JetBlue flight to Tampa, plaintiff Denise Whitney reclined her seat. Soon thereafter, Ms. Whitney noticed wads of paper being thrown at her from the seat behind her. A nearby flight attendant noticed this and asked the paper-throwing passenger seated behind Ms. Whitney to stop. The passenger seated behind Ms. Whitney then started to violently kick the back of Ms. Whitney's seat for an extended period of time, causing the injury alleged in her complaint.[2] Following this event, Ms. Whitney walked to the rear of the plane and reported the incident to the same flight attendant who had earlier warned the passenger to stop throwing paper wads. That flight attendant wrote (by hand, with paper and ink) a report in Ms. Whitney's presence, in part using Ms. Whitney's quoted statements.

In accordance with its Federal Rule of Civil Procedure initial disclosure requirements, JetBlue provided plaintiff a file in PDF format of what appeared to be a scan of a paper computer printout of an "Inflight Irregularity Report," set forth in Figure F.1.

Defendant JetBlue first asserted that this "Inflight Irregularity Report" was *the* report that the flight attendant had prepared in connection with the incident. As can be seen from Figure F.1, this computer-generated document was unsigned and contained no quoted statements from plaintiff Whitney. Further, since this document represented

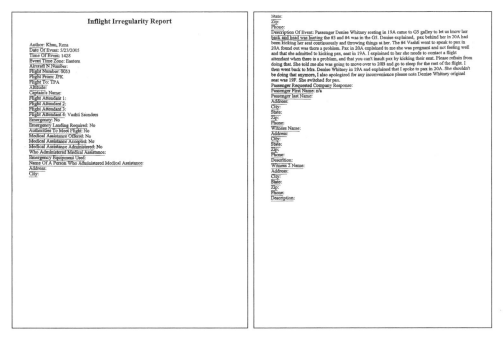

FIGURE F.1
Rule 26 Disclosure: PDF of Inflight Irregularity Report

---

2. Ms. Whitney testified the flight attendant also observed the kicking incident, but failed to either intervene or otherwise take action to ensure her safety. Defendant JetBlue's position was that the flight attendant never observed the kicking incident, and that it was first brought to the flight attendant's attention by plaintiff only afterwards.

a computer file-to-paper-to-computer scan-to-computer file, it was unsearchable for important metadata that could give a circumstantial clue to that document's provenance. The document produced by JetBlue represented a "view of a view of a view of a view" (i.e., a PDF file of a scan of a printout of a computer compilation of some sort), and although the printed content described both a "Date of Event" and a "Time of Event" of May 23, 2005, the disclosure provided no information as to the date or time the record of information was created or input into defendant's information system.

Nearly three months following JetBlue's Rule 26 initial disclosures, and on the day before the deposition of the flight attendant who authored the "Inflight Irregularity Report," JetBlue's counsel e-mailed, what is shown below as Figure F.2, a new PDF file to plaintiff's counsel, which was described by the JetBlue flight attendant as notes prepared in drafting the Inflight Irregularity Report ("Draft IIR": Figure F.3).

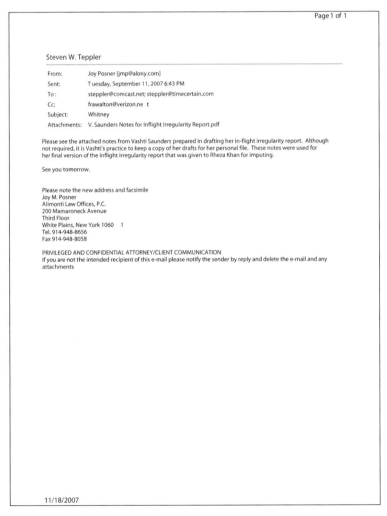

FIGURE F.2
E-mail Transmitting "Notes Prepared in Drafting Inflight Irregularity Report"

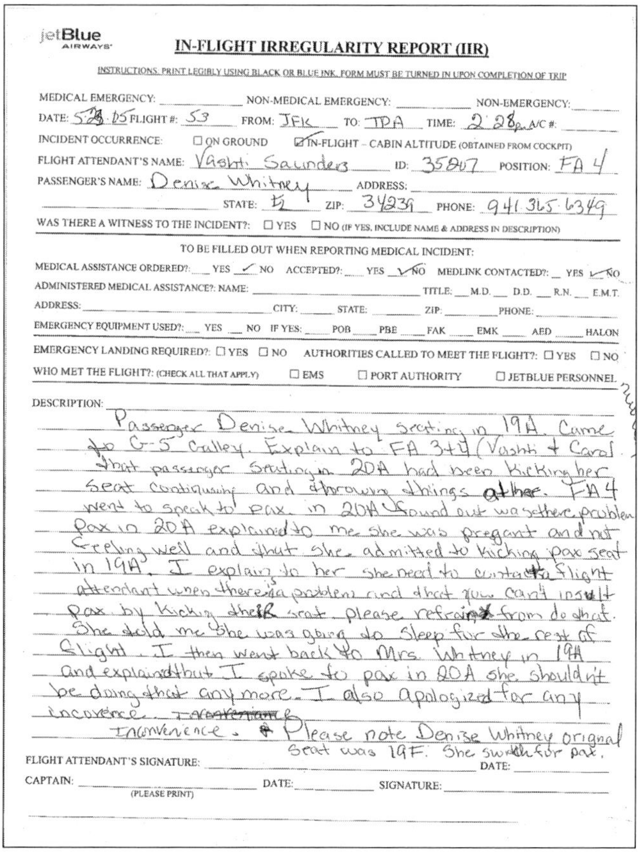

jetBlue AIRWAYS

IN-FLIGHT IRREGULARITY REPORT (IIR)

INSTRUCTIONS: PRINT LEGIBLY USING BLACK OR BLUE INK. FORM MUST BE TURNED IN UPON COMPLETION OF TRIP

MEDICAL EMERGENCY: ______ NON-MEDICAL EMERGENCY: ______ NON-EMERGENCY: ______

DATE: 5-28-05 FLIGHT #: 53 FROM: JFK TO: TPA TIME: 2:28pm A/C #: ______

INCIDENT OCCURRENCE: ☐ ON GROUND ☑ IN-FLIGHT – CABIN ALTITUDE (OBTAINED FROM COCKPIT)

FLIGHT ATTENDANT'S NAME: Vashti Saunders ID: 35807 POSITION: FA 4

PASSENGER'S NAME: Denise Whitney ADDRESS: ______

STATE: FL ZIP: 34239 PHONE: 941 365 6349

WAS THERE A WITNESS TO THE INCIDENT?: ☐ YES ☐ NO (IF YES, INCLUDE NAME & ADDRESS IN DESCRIPTION)

TO BE FILLED OUT WHEN REPORTING MEDICAL INCIDENT:

MEDICAL ASSISTANCE ORDERED?: __ YES ✓ NO ACCEPTED?: __ YES ✓ NO MEDLINK CONTACTED?: __ YES ✓ NO

ADMINISTERED MEDICAL ASSISTANCE?: NAME: ______ TITLE: __ M.D. __ D.D. __ R.N. __ E.M.T.

ADDRESS: ______ CITY: ______ STATE: ______ ZIP: ______ PHONE: ______

EMERGENCY EQUIPMENT USED?: __ YES __ NO IF YES: __ POB __ PBE __ FAK __ EMK __ AED __ HALON

EMERGENCY LANDING REQUIRED?: ☐ YES ☐ NO AUTHORITIES CALLED TO MEET THE FLIGHT?: ☐ YES ☐ NO

WHO MET THE FLIGHT?: (CHECK ALL THAT APPLY) ☐ EMS ☐ PORT AUTHORITY ☐ JETBLUE PERSONNEL

DESCRIPTION:

Passenger Denise Whitney seating in 19A. Came to G-5 Galley. Explain to FA 3+4 (Vashti + Carol that passenger seating in 20A had been kicking her seat continuously and throwing things at her. FA 4 went to speak to pax. in 20A found out was there problem pax in 20A explained to me she was pregant and not feeling well and that she admitted to kicking pax seat in 19A. I explain to her she need to contact a flight attendant when there is a problem and that you can't insult pax by kicking their seat please refrain from do that. She told me she was going to sleep for the rest of flight. I then went back to Mrs. Whitney in 19A and explained that I spoke to pax in 20A she shouldn't be doing that any more. I also apologized for any incovence. ~~Inconvenience~~ Inconvenience. * Please note Denise Whitney orignal seat was 19F. She switch for pax.

FLIGHT ATTENDANT'S SIGNATURE: ______ DATE: ______

CAPTAIN: ______ (PLEASE PRINT) DATE: ______ SIGNATURE: ______

FIGURE F.3
Notes Prepared in Drafting Inflight Irregularity Report

Figure F.3 shows the PDF file consisting of a partially handwritten, partially printed form entitled "Inflight Irregularity Report" and was further described by JetBlue's counsel as notes used by the flight attendant in preparing her "final version" submitted for input into JetBlue's computer database.

With this document, defendant Jet Blue had provided a third-order rendition, or a "view" of a "view" of a "view" of the paper.

As can be seen from Figure F.3, the notes are unsigned, undated, and the handwritten date-of-event appears to have been overwritten at least once, and perhaps numerous times. What appears to be clear from the notes on the form is that the event date occurred sometime in May 2005.

A quick view of the metadata of this PDF document (Figure F.4) shows, however, a "creation" date for that PDF document of September 11, 2007, more than two years after the events in question, and one day prior to the scheduled date for the deposition of that witness.

During the deposition, JetBlue's legal department manager (who attended the depositions but was not deposed) disclosed that JetBlue had "destroyed" the original paper

FIGURE F.4
View of the Metadata of Figure F.3

Inflight Irregularity Report (the "Original IIR"). Jet Blue's trial counsel stated for the record, and one of its Fed. R. Civ. P. 30(b)(6) witnesses provided deposition testimony, that the Original IIR had been destroyed in accordance with JetBlue's document retention policy.

During this same deposition period (and just prior to the flight attendant's deposition) JetBlue's counsel produced yet another paper copy of a PDF of a scan of a computer printout (see Figure F.5), entitled "Inflight Incident Report."

Defendant's counsel stated that this paper document was "the same" as the first PDF document, entitled "Inflight Irregularity Report," (Figure F.1), produced by defendant as part of its Rule 26 initial disclosures, and that the differing title was "just inserted at the top, using the word 'incident' rather than 'irregularity.'"[3] This computer-generated "Inflight Incident Report" had additional content (a statement made by Plaintiff Denise Whitney to the flight attendant about her injury) that did not appear in either the PDF of the Inflight Irregularity Report produced as part of JetBlue's initial disclosure obligations (Figure F.1), or the Notes prepared in drafting the Inflight Irregularity Report (Figure F.3).

---

3. "I believe that when we generated this report it was generated from the database and this title here, which should be taken from the same data as the irregularity report, was just inserted at the top of the document, and using the word incident instead of irregularity. So they should be, it is the same data, just really a—just didn't mirror the exact title on the description on 1-B." Transcript of Statement of Defendant Counsel (Deposition of Vashti Saunders, Whitney v. JetBlue, *supra* note 2, at 44:06-44-15); "To clarify the record, this exhibit was identified by—in the course of Vashti Saunders's deposition as a draft of her in-flight irregularity report that she retained, and later used to complete an actual in-flight irregularity report, so this is not the report that was handed in to be inputted into the system." Statement of Defendant's Counsel (Deposition of Rheza Khan, Whitney v. JetBlue, *supra* note 2, at 16:17-16-24).

At the conclusion of these depositions, there were now:

1. One "destroyed," and thereby unavailable, paper original Inflight Irregularity Report asserted to have actually been used as input into defendant JetBlue's database. This original paper document was asserted to have been so destroyed in accordance with JetBlue's document retention policy.
2. A PDF document of a scan of a computer printout of the "Inflight Irregularity Report" provided by JetBlue as part of its Initial Disclosure obligations (Figure F.1)
3. One unsigned, undated, handwritten "Draft IIR" scanned from paper and generated and produced in PDF format three months after the initial disclosure deadline. The content was stated to "mirror" what was input into defendant's database (Figure F.3).
4. A paper printout of a scan of a computer printout of an "Inflight Incident Report," which was also asserted to mirror the information input from the now-destroyed Original Inflight Irregularity Report, but which differed in both title and content from both the Draft IIR and the computer-generated Inflight Irregularity Report first disclosed by JetBlue (Figure F.5).

A cursory examination of the three documents exposes differences in format, title, *time, and content*. For example, the "Date of Event" in the handwritten notes for Inflight Irregularity Report was overwritten (Figure F.3), and the creation date of the PDF (easily

FIGURE F.5
Inflight Incident Report

obtainable from the PDF document properties)[4] (Figure F.4) from which it was printed shows a creation date of more than two years after the "date" of that draft.

The content among the three documents differs as well. The "Inflight Incident Report," which is asserted to "mirror" the information input into JetBlue's database, contains content missing from the computer-generated Inflight Incident Report provided in satisfaction of JetBlue's Initial Disclosure Obligations. The missing content was relevant:

> She switched, I was sitting in row 19A when after take off, I reclined my seat the lady in 20A started kicking the back of my seat with her feet until she moved my seat forward. I now have a headache and neck(ache). She also threw things at me.[5]

Plaintiff's counsel brought up these discrepancies to JetBlue's counsel, but no explanation acceptable to plaintiff's counsel about the discrepancies was provided.

JetBlue's counsel then e-mailed (Figure F.6) plaintiff's counsel two Excel spreadsheet files ". . . regenerated from the . . . I[nflight] I[rregularity] R[Report]" in order to "further confirm the integrity of data."

FIGURE F.6
October 4, 2005 E-mail Sent to Confirm Integrity of Data

---

4. The Document Properties tab in Adobe Acrobat "reads" the document metadata and renders it into human readable format. Of course, this metadata itself has no reliable time reference or association.

5. Figure F.6.

Both Excel spreadsheet files contained a cell row and column entitled "Date Created" with a date of 6/2/2005. (Refer to Figure F.7.)

Plaintiff's counsel then examined the metadata from these files using two tools. The first tool is contained within the Excel program itself. A few mouse clicks ("File," then

FIGURE F.7
Partial Screenshot of Excel Spreadsheet Showing Creation Date 6/2/2005 at Row 58, Column B

"Properties," then "Statistics") reveal a time of creation of September 6, 2006 (nearly fifteen months later than asserted) and a different author than that stated by JetBlue. (Refer to Figure F.8.)

A second analysis using the "Metadata Assistant" metadata analysis program confirms this information (see Figure F.9).

The original paper record, made by the flight attendant, had been destroyed. In the spoliation briefs, the plaintiff argued it could never be determined whether whatever information that was contained in the now-destroyed Original Inflight Irregularity Report ("Original IIR") was ever truly input into defendant JetBlue's database. There was no "signed and dated" computer information that could be adequately chained back (or connected) to the Original (signed and dated) IIR. JetBlue admitted that the notes on the IIR (Figure F.3) were not used for input into its computer database.

In the briefs, plaintiff argued it was clear that the defendant changed the document asserted to be the same as the now destroyed paper Original IIR by omitting relevant evidence (for example plaintiff's quoted statement) from one electronically generated version, and then added that relevant content in a second version generated more than two years after the incident, and nearly three months after the disclosure of the first version. Plaintiff argued that one cannot assert that two documents are "the same, except

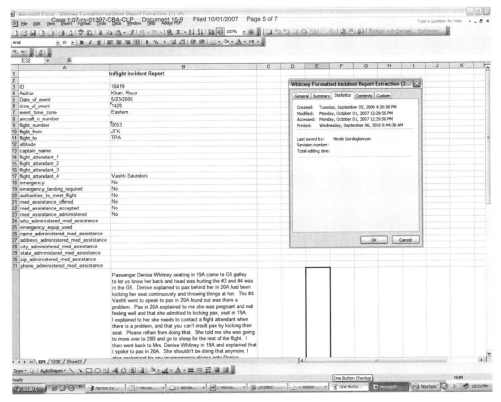

FIGURE F.8
Native Excel Spreadsheet Metadata

Case 1:07-cv-01397-CBA-CLP Document 16-9 Filed 10/01/2007 Page 6 of 7

An alyzing Whitney Formatted Incident Report Extraction (2).xls

Document Name: Whitney Formatted Incident Report Extraction (2).xls
Path: C:\Documents and Settings\Stev en W. Teppler\Local Settings\Temporary Internet Files\OLK AA
Workbook Protection: Unknow n

Built-in file properties:
Built-in properties containing metadata: 7
Author: jkilloch
Last author: Nicole Gurdoglany an
Application name: Microsoft Excel
Last print date: 9/6/2006 9:44:38 AM
Creation date: 9/5/2006 4:38:56 PM
Last save time: 9/19/2007 3:21:42 PM
Company : JetBlue Airw ays

Custom wo rkbook properties:
No custom workbook properties

Cell contents specially fo rmatted to be inv isible:
No cell contents formatted to be invisible

Routing slip:
No routing slip

Shared wo rkbook and tracked changes:
Not a shared workbook

Comments:
No comments

Conv ert to pictures:
No objects to be converted to pictures

Hy perlinks:
No hy perlinks

Defined names:
No defined names

Smart tags:
No smart tags in workbook

Remov e personal information:
Remove Personal Info rmation: [Blank]

Scenarios:
Does not contain scenarios

Font matching background:
No cells or shapes have font matching background

Small font size:
No cells or shapes with small font

Hidden row s:
No hidden row s

Hidden columns:
No hidden columns

Hidden wo rksheet(s):
No hidden sheets

Piv otTable cache:
No PivotT able or PivotTable cache

FIGURE F.9
Metadata Assistant Analysis of Excel Spreadsheet

for" because then they are not "the same." The ease with which these computer files were manipulated begs the question: "What else has been changed or omitted?"

Unfortunately, with the Original IIR now unavailable for examination, plaintiff could never know whether the information contained in JetBlue's database accurately reflected the Original IIR's content, or whether that content truly reflected Flight Attendant Saunders's complete recounting of the events as observed by her, and as fully and completely reported to her by plaintiff.

Plaintiff argued that with the Original IIR destroyed, it would be (and in this case, was) quite simple to undetectably create, modify, alter, or delete any data in the defendant's database to "conform" to the information contained Figure F.3, and then assert that F.3 was nearly identical to the now destroyed Original. The destruction of the paper Original IRR effectively (1) *removes* any impediment to JetBlue's production and assertion of a second, undated and unsigned paper Draft IIR; and (2) permitted the ability to delete, alter, modify, or create digital data into defendant's database to "conform" to that Draft; and (3) renders challenges thereto virtually impossible. Moreover, plaintiff suggested that this clearly proved that a printout of computer-generated data is as easily altered or manipulated as the data from which it is derived. In this case, the alterations included time, document title, and document content.

Plaintiff maintained that the destruction of the Original IIR document by JetBlue resulted in severe prejudice to plaintiff, because plaintiff, the court, and a jury could never thereafter know what information was written on the Original IIR. With the unavailability of the Original IIR, plaintiff argued that she could not know or ascertain whether the Original IIR contents would have corroborated plaintiff's testimony as contemporaneously reported by plaintiff to the JetBlue flight attendant on the date of the incident. Moreover, plaintiff suggested that the court therefore could not ascertain whether JetBlue's database information even remotely mirrored the information set forth in the Original IIR, or for that matter whether the Original IIR content had been further modified or otherwise altered to "conform" to what JetBlue wished plaintiff to receive.

In the briefs, the defendant asserted that plaintiff's counsel harbored "conspiratorial notions."[6] Defendant JetBlue's position was that:

1. The "data" (meaning the Excel spreadsheet cells) showed a creation date of June 2, 2005.[7]
2. A "hard copy" was provided to Plaintiff's counsel to "quell" concerns of improper data manipulation.[8]
3. I . . . extracted data and titled it (somewhat erroneously) as an "Inflight Incident Report."[9]
4. " . . . I supplemented our responses with raw data from defendant's safety database . . ."[10]
5. " . . . [a]ll documents referred hereto or attached hereto are kept in the ordinary course of business. . . ."[11]

JetBlue further maintained in an affidavit provided by defendant's "Safety Analyst" (the author identified in the Excel spreadsheet metadata):

1. "From my perspective, and that of anyone within defendant that would review IIR's the "original" IIR is the computer copy generated by our database upon entry. . . . That is how the data is preserved for future use. To suggest that defendant destroyed an 'original' document is misleading."[12]
2. " . . . There has been no tampering or alteration with its content, which was extracted as entered on that date [presumably June 2, 2005 –*Ed.*]"[13]

The JetBlue Safety Analyst then asserted:

---

6. Defendant's Opposition to Plaintiff's Motion for Spoliation in Whitney v. JetBlue, *supra* note 2, 07-cv-1397 (E.D.N.Y.) at 1.

7. Exhibit 9 to Case Study—Affidavit of Nicole M. Gurdoglanyan in Support of Defendant Opposition to Spoliation Motion, ¶11.

8. *Id.* at ¶12.

9. *Id.* at ¶7.

10. *Id.* at ¶10.

11. *Id.* at ¶2.

12. Exhibit 10 to Case Study—Affidavit of Safety Analyst Donald James Kiloch in Support of Defendant Opposition to Spoliation Motion, ¶8.

13. *Id.* at ¶7.

> As can be seen from [the e-mail], the content of the IIR as originally entered and generated by the database is identical with those provided earlier, *with the exception of the Passenger Comments, which for some reason were not included in some of the reports generated. Exhibit "A" established that these last three sentences were included in the [O]riginal IIR as entered by Ms. Khan.*[14]

One can see that the only proof of integrity or time of the data that associates the computer-generated information with that of the paper Original IIR is the testimonial statement of JetBlue's two Affiants. But these witnesses admitted to altering data, and cannot make the case for data integrity in the records. The defendant's argument relies on the time-honored method of providing human testimony supporting assertions that computer-generated information accurately reflects the paper original from which it is alleged to have been derived.

In sum, the defendant asked the court to "trust testimony" even in light of admitted data alteration, and plaintiff faced the daunting task of convincing a court to see behind the testimony that no time-based data content tampering had occurred. Nonetheless, the current judicial stance is moving inexorably toward a higher standard of scrutiny, and this approach to authenticity is well set out in *In re Vee Vinhnee, supra,* Chapter 8.

The court decided this motion in April 2008, and issued an order sanctioning JetBlue for destruction of the Original IIR under its "inherent power to preserve integrity of the proceedings," and pursuant to Fed. R. Civ. P. Rule 37. It denied the more specific relief requested on account of spoliation of evidence. The court awarded plaintiff fees and costs in connection with the motion.[15]

The court first provided a detailed analysis of the elements required to establish a successful spoliation claim:

> "(1) that the party having control over the evidence had an obligation to preserve it at the time it was destroyed; (2) that the records[16] were destroyed with a culpable state of mind; and (3) that the destroyed evidence was relevant to the parties claim or defense such that a reasonable trier of fact could find that it would support that claim or defense [Citations omitted]"

The court found the plaintiff had established that the destroyed paper Original IIR was relevant; that JetBlue had a duty to preserve that document; and that Jet Blue's destruction of that document was at least negligent (and arguably grossly negligent). The court pointed out, however, that while the paper Original IIR was relevant, plaintiff "ha[d] failed to demonstrate that the destroyed evidence would have been favorable to her." A typical judicial approach, and the one adopted by this Court, is to incorporate the requirement for demonstrating that spoliated evidence would have been favorable to the non-spoliating party into a relevance analysis. Here, the Court acknowledged that the electronic versions of the IIR were different, but not substantially so as to support

---

14. *Id.*

15. A copy of that decision is provided at the end of this case study.

16. In the Second Circuit, the culpability element required for spoliation may be satisfied by a finding of ordinary negligence. See Residential Funding Corporation v DeGeorge et al., 306 F. 3d 99 (2d Cir. 1998); Indemnity Ins. Co. of N. Am. v. Liebert Corp., 96 CV 6675, 1998 WL 363834, at *3 (S.D.N.Y. June 29, 2998).

a finding that the paper Original IIR would have "corroborated plaintiff's version of events," a key element for a finding of spoliation.

The problem engendered with this "corroboration" element is that it requires a non-spoliating party to prove a negative, *i.e.,* prove that what no longer exists would have supported a claim (or refuted the spoliator's claim). When digital evidence is the subject of a spoliation claim, this imposes a well-nigh impossible burden to overcome. This is true because once digital evidence has been deleted, or altered, the likelihood of ascertaining spoliated digital *content* (in addition to ascertaining the event of spoliation) is likely impossible without other fortuitously existing, extrinsic evidence. Fortunately, the "corroboration" requirement is not an absolute, and in his brief, plaintiff's counsel argued that controlling decisional authority permitted circumstantial evidence (*e.g.,* the spoliator's state of mind, or a finding of gross negligence) to be considered in deciding whether spoliated evidence would have supporting a non-spoliating party's allegations.[17] Unfortunately (for plaintiff), the court found that plaintiff had also failed to meet that requirement, in large part because the court chose not to address issues uniquely inherent to digital evidence. First, it is significant that the court chose to downplay whether the paper Original IIR was destroyed in violation of JetBlue's document retention policy ("DRP"), or whether JetBlue's DRP even addressed electronic documents. The language of JetBlue's DRP makes express provision that there was no distinction between paper and electronic versions of identified categories of documents.[18] The DRP also provided that documents maintained in electronic format must retain integrity over time.[19]

That the paper Original IIR and the differing electronic version were not "mere duplicates" was also not addressed by the court. Nevertheless, despite the destruction of a signed paper Original IIR more than one year after the lawsuit had been filed, and despite the production by JetBlue of three unsigned electronic versions differing in time, title, and content, the court "credited [JetBlue's] assertions" and found (1) that plaintiff had not demonstrated that the information contained in the paper Original IIR would have been favorable to her case, and (2) the court "credit[ed] defendant's assertion that under its procedures, the information contained in the destroyed handwritten IIR would have been entered word for word into the complete electronic IIR, which defendant has now shown was generated in full relatively soon after the incident on board."

---

17. Plaintiff counsel argued in his Reply Brief that "[W]here a party seeking an adverse inference adduces evidence that its opponent destroyed potential evidence (or otherwise rendered it unavailable) in bad faith or through gross negligence (satisfying the 'culpable state of mind' factor), that same evidence of the opponent's state of mind will frequently also be sufficient to permit a jury to conclude that the missing evidence is favorable to the party (satisfying the 'relevance' factor)." Residential Funding Corp. v. DeGeorge Fin. Corp., 306 F.3d at 109. *In re* NTL, Inc. Securities Litigation, 2007 WL 241344 at *21.

18. JetBlue's DRP (submitted as a supplemental Exhibit to the Spoliation Motion) provides: "Records: Any documentary material regardless of format (email, electronic, etc.) generated or received by JetBlue in connection with its business."

19. JetBlue's DRP provided that "[I]f a record is maintained in electronic form, it must be done so by a reliable medium that will permit accurate reproduction. The electronic format must be one that will not permit revision or erasure of the Electronic Record." It is perhaps for this reason that the court noted that JetBlue's behavior in providing differing electronic versions of the IIR was arguably "grossly" negligent.

Arguments by plaintiff pointing out the frailty of digital evidence, and its lack of any connection (other than through human testimony) to a paper-based original, were not persuasive to the court. Also to no avail were plaintiff's arguments about the malleability of the digital evidence and its susceptibility to undetectable modification, particularly in light of a showing that (1) a paper original document was destroyed and (2) numerous digital versions differing in time, title, and content were produced. The court here placed more emphasis on the destruction of the paper Original IIR than on the production of differing digital documents,[20] and credited witness testimony over what was clearly manipulated digital evidence.[21]

It is clear from the JetBlue decision that both bench and bar are still at the beginning of the learning curve in addressing issues relating to digital evidence. Future motions should find both attorneys and judges better prepared to grapple with the new terrain. In the meantime, the JetBlue decision nonetheless provides substantial guidance for future motions. A party asserting digital evidence spoliation should always consider providing an expert's declaration in support of any motion (and perhaps testimony at a spoliation hearing) to give meaningful insight about the malleability of digital evidence and the computer-generated environment from which it is produced.[22] An attorney may argue from a vast trove of technological expertise, but will always be constrained by his or her role as advocate in providing the authority explaining the frailty of digital evidence and of the computing environments from which they are generated.

---

20. The Court did note that it was "troubled by the contradictory and confusing information provided" by JetBlue.

21. What is interesting is that the Court tacitly acknowledged that the three proffered versions of the computer-generated IIR, while admittedly differing in time, title and content, nonetheless did not save defendant from a finding of negligent destruction of the paper based Original IIR.

22. Plaintiff's counsel argued this motion without an expert.

Frederick P. Alimonti (FA9651)
Alimonti Law Offices, P.C.
200 Mamaroneck Avenue, Third Floor
White Plains, New York 10601
Phone: 914-948-8044

UNITED STATES DISTRICT COURT
EASTERN DISTRICT OF NEW YORK

Denise Whitney	07 Civ. 1397(CBA) (CLP)
plaintiff,	
	AFFIDAVIT OF
v.	NICOLE L. GURDOGLANYAN
JETBLUE AIRWAYS CORPORATION	
defendant.	

STATE OF NEW YORK)
) SS:
COUNTY OF QUEENS)

NICOLE L. GURDOGLANYAN, being first duly sworn, deposes and says:

1.   I am the Manager, Legal Department, for defendant JetBlue Airways Corporation

(JetBlue). I am not an attorney.

2.   All of the facts referred to herein are based upon my personal knowledge, and all

documents referred to or attached hereto are kept by JetBlue in the ordinary course of

business.

3.   Part of my job function is to assist in the collection of material and information in

response to discovery requests in pending litigation, including the above-captioned claim.

4.   Attached hereto as Exhibit "A" is a "screen print" from JetBlue's database

showing the arrival and departure times for JetBlue Flight 53 on May 23, 2005, plaintiff

Denise Whitney's flight.

5.   The record shows that the aircraft left the gate at 1:35PM, departed JFK at 1:53 PM, arrived in Tampa at 4:10 PM and arrived at the Tampa gate at 4:17 PM. As such, the recorded gate-to-gate flight time was two hours and forty-two minutes.

6.   I note from the police report (Exhibit "J" to Letter of Steven Teppler dated October 1, 2007 (Teppler letter)) that Tampa police received a call relating to this event at approximately 4:33 PM by "Susan." This would be, in all likelihood, Susan C. Everhart, who is also referred to later in the body of the Tampa Airport Police Report and was a JetBlue gate agent at the time.

7.   In assisting to collect information for discovery in this case, I requested a search of JetBlue's Safety Database for all applicable Inflight Irregularity Reports ("IIR's"). I then formatted the extracted data and titled it [somewhat erroneously] as an Inflight Incident Report. The report was nonetheless generated from the same data as the IIR previously provided to plaintiff in hard copy. Exhibit "M" to Teppler letter.

8.   However, it included a recitation of the events as recorded by plaintiff that was not included in the IIR originally provided.

9.   At the time of the incident and thereafter, JetBlue did not have a policy with respect to the retention of the handwritten versions of the IIR's. Rather, the content of these reports was preserved by its storage in our database for the indefinite period.

10.   In order to provide as much information as possible, I supplemented our original responses with raw data from JetBlue's Safety Database on both formatted and unformatted Excel Reports. Hard copies of which are attached as Exhibits "B" and "C" hereto.

2

11. The data provided showed a creation date for the original IIR of June 2, 2005. Exhibits "B" and "C".

12. To further quell any concerns of improper data manipulation, I provided to counsel (who then provided it to plaintiff) a hard copy of an email dating to July 20, 2005 attaching the original IIR dated June 2, 2005, which is identical in content to that provided to plaintiff in our Rule 26 Disclosures. Exhibit "D" hereto.

13. Finally, I arranged for our IT department to pull the original email generated by the database at the time of entry for both the IIR and Station Incident reports. I provided them to counsel on October 3, 2007 and they were immediately forwarded to counsel for plaintiff. Exhibits "E" and "F" hereto. As you would expect, these documents contain the same content previously provided, including the passenger comments contained in the Inflight Incident Report I had previously produced.

14. I also note by way of clarification that John Adams, who is referred to in the JetBlue Investigator's Report (Exhibit "B" to Teppler letter) has never been employed by JetBlue's Legal Department. Rather, he was at the time of the accident, employed in JetBlue's Customer Relations Department. He is currently a member of the Reservations Department.

15. Exhibit "C" to Mr. Teppler's letter of October 1, 2007 includes a true and complete copy of a Station Incident Report, a document maintained by JetBlue in the ordinary course of business. These reports relate to events at a ground station.

16. An Inflight Irregularity Report, as the title suggests, refers to in-flight events.

17.   Not surprisingly, if medical or other services are requested by JetBlue ground personnel, such as a gate agent, they would be reflected on the station report, not the in-flight report.

18.   Exhibit "C" to the Teppler letter is a copy of Ms. Whitney's "Passenger Name Record" ("PNR"), which includes a copy of the Station Incident Report. The date of 22 May 2005 represents the date that Ms. Whitney sought stand-by status for flight 53 ("listed stby").

19.   The notation "Agent: 90422 Date:25 May 2005 Time 7:12a" shows that this Station Incident Report with respect to the incident complained of was appended to the PNR on 25 May 2005 – two days after the incident.

20.   Accordingly, a simple reading of the IIR (Teppler letter Exhibit "G") and the Station Incident Report (Teppler letter Exhibit "C") shows that medical and law enforcement personnel were requested by a JetBlue gate agent. As such, there is no reason why a report prepared by a flight attendant would note this. This is confirmed with respect to law enforcement by the Tampa Airport Police Report, which I have now reviewed. Teppler letter, Exhibit "J".

NICOLE L. GURDOGLANYAN

Sworn to before me this
___ day of October, 2007

Notary Pubic

SAMANTHA WILLIAMS
Notary Public, State of New York
No. 01WI6119979
Qualified in Queens County
Commission Expires December 12, 2008

4

Frederick P. Alimonti (FA9651)
Alimonti Law Offices, P.C.
200 Mamaroneck Avenue, Third Floor
White Plains, New York 10601
Phone: 914-948-8044

UNITED STATES DISTRICT COURT
EASTERN DISTRICT OF NEW YORK

Denise Whitney
 	
                              plaintiff,
 	
                    v.
 	
JETBLUE AIRWAYS CORPORATION
118-29 Queens Boulevard
Forest Hills, NY 11375
 	
                              defendant.
	07 Civ. 1397(CBA) (CLP)
	
	AFFIDAVIT OF
	DONALD JAMES KILLOCH, JR.

STATE OF NEW YORK)
) SS:
COUNTY OF QUEENS)

Donald James Killoch, Jr., being first duly sworn, deposes and says:

1.   I am employed as a Safety Analyst for defendant JetBlue Airways Corporation.

2.   All of the facts herein are based upon my personal knowledge except where noted

to be upon information and belief, in which case I believe them to be true based upon my

review of company records and my understanding of JetBlue's operations and

procedures.

3.   Part of my job function is the oversight of the JetBlue Safety Database.

Specifically, I review the Inflight Irregularity Reports (IIR's) in the database to analyze

trends and safety-of-flight issues that may require corrective action. In performing this

function, I refer only to the Safety Database. I do not use or refer to original handwritten

copies of the IIR.

4.   As noted in the deposition of JetBlue data entry clerk Reza Khan, IIR's are entered into the Safety database as received (Khan depo. at 20:23-21:3). In the course of her employment as a data entry clerk, Reza Khan would have encountered hundreds of IIR's. I am told she testified to having seen 3,000 of them in the two years during which she was a data entry clerk.

5.   Attached as Exhibit "A" is a hard copy of an email generated at the time the report was entered on June 2, 2005. The email was automatically generated on this date at 1:42 PM.

6.   I am advised by our counsel that this email was provided to counsel for plaintiff in the hope of assuaging his concerns as to the integrity of the IIR provided earlier in this litigation.

7.   As can be seen on Exhibit "A", the content of the IIR as originally entered and generated by the database is identical with those provided earlier, with the exception of the Passenger Comments, which for some reason were not included in some of the reports generated. Exhibit "A" establishes that these last three sentences were included in the original IIR as entered by Ms. Khan. There has been no tampering or alteration with its content, which was extracted as entered on that date.

8.   From my perspective and that of anyone within JetBlue that would review IIR's, the "original" IIR is the computer copy generated by our database upon entry. These are the reports used for purposes of review and analysis and for the very safety of the airline's operations. This is how the data is preserved for future use. To suggest that JetBlue destroyed an "original" document is misleading. In fact, the reason the documents are entered into the database is to preserve them.

2

9.   To my knowledge, JetBlue does not use or refer to original hand-written IIR's after they are entered into the safety database.

10.   As reports are generated from data and copied from one computer to another or reformatted (e.g., exported/imported from another database into *Excel*), the "creation date" of a given document will often change. This is by no means an indication of tampering with the document or its content. This is common knowledge for anyone with the most rudimentary of computer experience. Indeed, the sterility of the relevant IIR is demonstrated by Exhibit "A."

DONALD JAMES KILLOCH, JR.

Sworn to before me on this
_____ day of October, 2007

Notary Public

SAMANTHA WILLIAMS
Notary Public, State of New York
No. 01WI6119979
Qualified in Queens County
Commission Expires December 12, 2008

3

UNITED STATES DISTRICT COURT
EASTERN DISTRICT OF NEW YORK
---X
DENISE WHITNEY,

                          Plaintiff,

        - against -

JETBLUE AIRWAYS CORP.,

                          Defendant.
---X

ORDER

07 CV 1397 (CBA)

        By letter dated September 23, 2007, plaintiff Denise Whitney sought permission to file a

motion for sanctions pursuant to Rules 26 and 37 of the Federal Rules of Civil Procedure, based on

the alleged spoliation of a document in the above-captioned case by defendant JetBlue Airways

Corp. ("JetBlue"). Thereafter, pursuant to a status conference held before this Court on September

25, 2007, plaintiff and defendant submitted letter briefing on the spoliation issue, and this Court

held a hearing on January 11, 2008. For the reasons set forth below, the Court denies plaintiff's

motion for spoliation sanctions, but awards plaintiff attorney's fees and costs incurred in

connection with the motion.

FACTUAL BACKGROUND

        In her Complaint, plaintiff Whitney alleges that while on board a JetBlue flight from New

York City to Tampa, Florida on May 23, 2005, the passenger in the seat behind her began to throw

paper wrappers at her shortly after takeoff. (Compl.[1] ¶¶ 4, 12). According to plaintiff, a flight

attendant noticed this activity and warned the passenger seated behind plaintiff to cease throwing

---

[1]Citations to "Compl." refer to plaintiff's Complaint, filed April 3, 2007.

the items. (<u>Id.</u> ¶ 14). Plaintiff further alleges that the passenger behind her proceeded to "violently and repeatedly" kick her seat back, and that although at least one flight attendant witnessed the kicking, no attendant came to plaintiff's aid or took any "step to protect plaintiff from the injuries she sustained" from the kicking. (<u>Id.</u> ¶¶ 15-17). Ms. Whitney asserts that she sustained injuries as a result of the kicking, and subsequently commenced this action against JetBlue, seeking damages for claims of negligent failure to protect and gross negligence. (<u>Id.</u> ¶¶ 34-36, 37-40).

It is undisputed that at some point after the events on board, flight attendant Vashti Saunders completed a handwritten "Inflight Irregularity Report" ("IIR") documenting the incident. JetBlue asserts that the information in the handwritten IIR was "entered into JetBlue's Safety database for posterity." (Def.'s Resp.[2] at 1). A version of the IIR from JetBlue's electronic database was produced to plaintiff in defendant's initial disclosures. (<u>Id.</u> at 2, 5; Pl.'s Mem.[3] at 3-4). In addition, another version of the electronic IIR, containing information not included in the electronic IIR provided in defendant's initial disclosures, was produced by defendant during the depositions of JetBlue's witnesses in September, 2007. (Pl.'s Mem. at 5; Def.'s Resp. at 5).[4] At the same time, defendant produced another document entitled "Inflight Incident Report," which was created over a year after the incident occurred (Pl.'s Mem. at 3, Ex. H), and a "draft" IIR handwritten by Ms. Saunders, which is undated and differs from both versions of the electronic

---

[2]Citations to "Def.'s Resp." refer to the Letter of Defendant JetBlue dated October 9, 2007.

[3]Citations to "Pl.'s Mem." refer to the Letter of Plaintiff Denise Whitney dated October 1, 2007.

[4]The Court notes that this second electronic IIR and the "Inflight Incident Report" contain identical information. (<u>See</u> Affidavit of Nicole Gurdoglanyan, Manager of JetBlue's Legal Department, dated October 9, 2007 ("Gurdoglanyan Aff."), Exs. C, E).

IIR. (Id. at 2, Ex. E).

At the January 11, 2008 hearing before this Court, defendant noted that Ms. Saunders' handwritten IIR had been destroyed in June, 2007 as part of a bulk storage destruction by JetBlue. Counsel for JetBlue acknowledged that all documents related to Ms. Whitney's case should have been retained under a litigation hold, but JetBlue asserts that once the information in the handwritten IIR was entered into the electronic database, the electronic IIR was considered the "original" by JetBlue. (Killoch Aff.[5] ¶ 8).

DISCUSSION

Plaintiff Whitney moves for spoliation sanctions, asserting that JetBlue willfully and admittedly destroyed critical evidence – namely, the handwritten IIR – that was recorded relatively contemporaneously with the events on board and that would have been useful to plaintiff in her claims against defendant. (Pl.'s Mem. at 2). Plaintiff argues that without this document, "there is no way to ascertain that the computer information present in Defendant's database even remotely reflects the information contained in the now destroyed paper-based original," resulting in prejudice to plaintiff, especially in light of Ms. Saunders' inability to recall many of the details surrounding the incident. (Id. at 2, 6). Plaintiff contends that the printouts from defendant's electronic database cannot be trusted because computer data is "ephemeral by design" and can be easily altered, as evidenced in this case by the retitling of the IIR to "Inflight Incident Report" and the differing content of the two electronic versions of the IIR. (Id. at 5-6). It is Ms. Whitney's position that without the handwritten IIR, plaintiff will never know whether the electronic IIR

---

[5]Citations to "Killoch Aff." refer to the Affidavit of Donald James Killoch, Jr., Safety Analyst for JetBlue, dated October 9, 2007.

3

accurately reflects the events observed by flight attendant Saunders and as reported to Ms. Saunders by plaintiff. (<u>Id.</u> at 6). Plaintiff further notes that defendant's employees have stated under oath that JetBlue both did and did not have a formal document retention policy. (Pl.'s Reply[6] at 2 (citing Cook Tr.[7] at 29:9-14; Gurdoglanyan Aff. ¶ 9)). This inconsistency, plaintiff argues, is part of defendant's "pattern of obfuscation" that has revealed itself in the various versions of the report of the incident on board Ms. Whitney's flight. (<u>Id.</u> at 1-2).

In response, defendant argues that plaintiff's allegations about the alteration of the content of the IIR is "speculation, to the point of paranoia." (Def.'s Resp. at 1). Defendant asserts that, contrary to plaintiff's claims, the information in the handwritten IIR was entered into the computer database for the purpose of preserving it, and plaintiff has not demonstrated that the data was manipulated in any way. (<u>Id.</u> at 1-2). JetBlue maintains that its records are consistent and demonstrate that the information in Ms. Saunders' handwritten IIR was accurately and completely entered into the database.[8] As such, defendant argues that the information sought by plaintiff is "cumulative and of minimal relevance" and that plaintiff would be in the same position with or without the handwritten IIR. (Def.'s Resp. at 5, 10).

As for sanctions, plaintiff requests that the Court grant judgment in her favor or that an

---

[6]Citations to "Pl.'s Reply" refer to the Letter of Plaintiff Denise Whitney dated October 12, 2007.

[7]Citations to "Cook Tr." refer to the Deposition Transcript of DeWayne Cook, Manager of Inflight Standards for JetBlue, dated September 13, 2007.

[8]Although defendant does not provide an explanation for why there are two versions of the electronic IIR, it has produced records demonstrating that a complete version was generated shortly after the incident on board. (Gurdoglanyan Aff., Ex. E). In addition, Nicole Gurdoglanyan, the author of the "Inflight Incident Report," explains that she erroneously titled the document after extracting the information from the relevant electronic IIR. (<u>Id.</u> ¶ 7).

4

adverse inference instruction be given to the jury together with the exclusion of defendant's

evidence, and that plaintiff be granted reasonable attorney's fees and costs in connection with this

motion. (Pl.'s Mem. at 1). JetBlue requests leave to apply for attorney's fees and costs in

connection with its opposition to plaintiff's motion. (Def.'s Resp. at 11).

A. Standards for Spoliation

       Rule 37 of the Federal Rules of Civil Procedure authorizes a court to impose various

sanctions when a party "fails to obey an order to provide or permit discovery." Fed. R. Civ. P.

37(b)(2); see also Transatlantic Bulk Shipping Ltd. v. Saudi Chartering, S.A., 112 F.R.D. 185, 189

(S.D.N.Y. 1986) (noting that Rule 37(b) "provides for sanctions where a party fails to honor its

disclosure obligations, especially after court orders"). It is clear that sanctions may be imposed

when a party spoliates evidence in violation of a court order. See, e.g., West v. Goodyear Tire &

Rubber Co. 167 F.3d 776, 779 (2d Cir. 1999) (citing John B. Hull, Inc. v. Waterbury Petroleum

Prods., Inc., 845 F.2d 1172, 1176 (2d Cir. 1988)). Even where there has been no explicit discovery

order issued, the court has the inherent power to preserve the integrity of proceedings by, among

other things, imposing sanctions for the spoliation. See id.; Kronisch v. United States, 150 F.3d

122, 126-27 (2d Cir. 1998); Barsoum v. N.Y.C. Hous. Auth., 202 F.R.D. 396, 399 (S.D.N.Y.

2001).

       The Second Circuit has defined spoliation as "the destruction or significant alteration of

evidence, or the failure to preserve property for another's use as evidence in pending or reasonably

forseeable litigation." West v. Goodyear Tire & Rubber Co., 167 F.3d at 779; accord Byrnie v.

Town of Cromwell, Bd. of Educ., 243 F.3d 93, 107 (2d Cir. 2001). A party has the obligation to preserve evidence when the party is on notice "that the evidence is relevant to litigation or when a party should have known that the evidence may be relevant to future litigation." Fujitsu Ltd. v. Federal Express Corp., 247 F.3d 423, 436 (2d Cir. 2001) (citing Kronisch v. United States, 150 F.3d at 126); Barsoum v. N.Y.C. Hous. Auth., 202 F.R.D. at 400 (holding that a party is under an obligation to retain documents and other evidence that it knows may be relevant to a pending or future litigation). This obligation to preserve relevant documents exists whether or not the documents have been specifically requested in a demand for discovery. Barsoum v. N.Y.C. Hous. Auth., 202 F.R.D. at 400.

Three elements must be established by the party seeking sanctions for spoliation of evidence:

> (1) that the party having control over the evidence had an obligation to preserve it at the time it was destroyed; (2) that the records were destroyed with a culpable state of mind; and (3) that the destroyed evidence was relevant to the party's claim or defense such that a reasonable trier of fact could find that it would support that claim or defense.

Farella v. City of New York, No. 05 CV 5711, 2007 WL 193867, at *2 (S.D.N.Y. Jan. 25, 2007); see also Byrnie v. Town of Cromwell, Bd. of Educ., 243 F.3d at 108-09; Fujitsu Ltd. v. Federal Express Corp., 247 F.3d at 436; Zubulake v. UBS Warburg LLC, 220 F.R.D. 212, 220 (S.D.N.Y. 2003). In analyzing the second prong of this test, it is unclear exactly what degree of culpability is required, with some courts in this Circuit requiring a showing of bad faith, some requiring proof of intentional destruction, and others drawing an inference based on gross negligence. See Byrnie v. Town of Cromwell, Bd. of Educ., 243 F.3d at 107-08 (citing Reilly v. NatWest Mkts. Group Inc., 181 F.3d 253, 267 (2d Cir. 1999), cert. denied, 528 U.S. 1119 (2000)). Thus, the Second Circuit has concluded that "a case by case approach is appropriate." Id. at 108.

6

B. Application

Turning to the first element, although defendant argues that the handwritten IIRs were not considered "originals" and therefore were not covered by JetBlue's document retention policy, there is no question that Ms. Saunders' handwritten IIR should have been retained. Regardless of whether the documents were subject to JetBlue's retention policy, or indeed, regardless of whether such a policy even existed at JetBlue, plaintiff correctly points out that defendant was on notice of Ms. Whitney's claim less than 24 hours after the incident occurred, and certainly in June of 2007, when the handwritten IIR was destroyed. Defendant had a clear obligation, whatever its document retention policy was, to put a litigation hold on any and all documents relating to Ms. Whitney's claim and to maintain them. See, e.g., Fujitsu Ltd. v. Federal Express Corp., 247 F.3d at 436. Defendant also had complete control over the handwritten IIR; indeed, plaintiff notes in her Complaint that although she requested defendant's reports relating to the incident, she never received anything. (Compl. ¶¶ 31-32).

Having determined that JetBlue had an obligation to maintain this document, Ms. Whitney still has the burden to show that the handwritten IIR was destroyed knowingly or negligently, and that it was relevant to her case. See Byrnie v. Town of Cromwell, Bd. of Educ., 243 F.3d at 109. With respect to JetBlue's state of mind at the time of the destruction, the testimony is at odds, with one employee stating that JetBlue had a document retention policy in place (see Cook Tr.[9] at 29:9-14), and another employee stating that no such policy existed. (Gurdoglanyan Aff. ¶ 9). Most recently, defendant indicated at the hearing that the handwritten IIR was destroyed as part of a bulk

---

[9]Citations to "Cook Tr." refer to the Deposition Transcript of DeWayne Cook, Manager of Inflight Standards for JetBlue, dated September 13, 2007.

7

destruction of documents by JetBlue. Although the Court is troubled by the contradictory and confusing information provided by defendant, regardless of whether JetBlue had a formal document retention policy in place, there is no indication that the handwritten IIR was destroyed in bad faith. The Court credits defendant's assertion that the handwritten IIR was included with numerous other similar documents and destroyed en masse.

Although the Court finds that Ms. Whitney has failed to establish that the destruction of these documents was done willfully or in bad faith, sanctions may still be imposed upon a finding of negligence. See Indemnity Ins. Co. of N. Am. v. Liebert Corp., No. 96 CV 6675, 1998 WL 363834, at *3 (S.D.N.Y. June 29, 1998) (holding that sanctions may be awarded for spoliation not just "where the evidence was destroyed willfully or in bad faith, since a party's negligent loss of evidence can be just as fatal to the other party's ability to present a defense") (internal citation omitted); see also Great Northern Ins. Co. v. Power Cooling, Inc., No. 06 CV 874, 2007 WL 2687666, at *9 (E.D.N.Y. Sept. 10, 2007); Smith v. City of New York, 388 F. Supp. 2d 179, 189 (S.D.N.Y. 2005).

Here, the document at issue was obviously relevant to plaintiff's case. Although JetBlue argues that the information in the handwritten IIR was entered completely into its electronic database, the handwritten IIR was nevertheless a more contemporaneous record of the events underlying plaintiff's claim, which plaintiff has the burden to prove. To allow the destruction of this record while the case was ongoing was at best negligent. Indeed, it could be argued that under all of the circumstances of this case, JetBlue was grossly negligent in its responsibility to supervise and ensure retention of this document. See Chan v. Triple 8 Palace, Inc., No. 03 CV 6048, 2005 WL 1925579, at *7 (S.D.N.Y. Aug. 11, 2005) (noting that the "utter failure to establish any form

8

of litigation hold at the outset of litigation is grossly negligent").

As for the relevance prong, JetBlue argues that plaintiff has failed to demonstrate that the destroyed evidence would have been favorable to her. (Def.'s Resp. at 8 (citing De Espana v. Am. Bureau of Shipping, No. 03 CV 3573, 2007 WL 1686327, at *6 (S.D.N.Y. June 6, 2007) (noting that "where the culpable party was negligent, there must be extrinsic evidence to demonstrate that the destroyed evidence was relevant and would have been unfavorable to the destroying party") and Zubulake v. UBS Warburg LLC, 220 F.R.D. at 221 (same))). Indeed, defendant argues that plaintiff has not shown that the information in the electronic IIR is any different from the handwritten IIR or different in substance from Ms. Saunders' draft IIR. (Id.) As such, defendant contends, there is no evidence that the handwritten IIR would support Ms. Whitney's claims. (Id.)

In reply, plaintiff asserts that the handwritten IIR would have corroborated her account of the events on board, namely, that defendant's flight attendants failed to intervene after observing the behavior of the passenger seated behind Ms. Whitney. (Pl.'s Reply at 6). Specifically, plaintiff argues that given that the complete version of the electronic IIR contains plaintiff's "first-person input," it is likely that the handwritten IIR contained more of this type of information, in support of plaintiff's claims. (Id. at 7). Ms. Whitney also contends in the alternative that JetBlue's destruction of the document was in bad faith, and that this alone is sufficient to merit an inference that the handwritten IIR was favorable to her case. (Id. at 6).

The Court has reviewed the disputed documents and finds no substantive difference among them, and nothing to indicate that the handwritten IIR would have corroborated plaintiff's version of events. Both versions of the electronic IIR contain statements or phrases relating to what plaintiff told Ms. Saunders regarding her physical complaints and the fact that the passenger behind

9

her had thrown things at her. (See Pl.'s Mem., Exs. G, M). Although all three versions of the IIR

are slightly different in terms of wording and structure, all recite what plaintiff originally reported

to Ms. Saunders and Ms. Saunders' conversation with the offending passenger after the events had

already occurred. (See id., Exs. E, G, M). There is nothing in any of the reports to indicate that

Ms. Saunders observed the passenger throwing things at Ms. Whitney or kicking her seat, and

plaintiff has not demonstrated that the destroyed handwritten IIR would contain this information.[10]

While there must be "'some showing indicating that the destroyed evidence would have

been relevant to the contested issue,'" Barsoum v. N.Y.C. Hous. Auth., 202 F.R.D. at 400 (quoting

Kronisch v. United States, 150 F.3d at 127), the relevance factor is primarily concerned with

whether there has been prejudice to the party seeking sanctions. Id.; see also Kronisch v. United

States, 150 F.3d at 127; Sovulj v. United States, No 98 CV 5550, 2005 WL 2290495, at *5

(E.D.N.Y. Sept. 20, 2005). Here, although there was a disturbing amount of carelessness on

defendant's part in the retention and production of the IIRs, plaintiff has not demonstrated that the

information in the handwritten IIR would be favorable to her case, or that she has been prejudiced

by its absence. The Court credits defendant's assertion that under its procedures, the information

in the destroyed handwritten IIR would have been entered word for word into the complete

electronic IIR, which defendant has now shown was generated in full relatively soon after the

incident on board. As such, the Court denies plaintiff's request for judgment and for an adverse

inference and exclusion of evidence.

---

[10]Plaintiff also takes issue with the fact that the IIRs indicate that no medical assistance was offered but that defendant's Station Incident Report, relating to the events taking place at the Tampa airport after plaintiff deplaned, document that plaintiff received medical attention. (Id. at 6, Ex. C). However, as defendant notes, this is because the IIRs relate only to events onboard, where no request for medical assistance was made in this case; plaintiff first requested aid at the airport gate. (Def.'s Resp. at 2-4; Gurdoglanyan Aff. ¶¶ 15-17).

The Court finds, however, that plaintiff should be awarded attorney's fees and costs in connection with her motion. Defendant inexplicably destroyed a clearly relevant document in the course of this litigation, when it had been placed on notice of plaintiff's claim shortly after the incident. Furthermore, defendant failed on several instances – in its initial disclosures and in connection with depositions – to provide accurate information to plaintiff. Although plaintiff's claim of spoliation fails, defendant's careless and confusing course of conduct understandably gave plaintiff reason to believe that something improper had occurred.

In accordance with the foregoing, plaintiff's motion for spoliation sanctions is denied, but the Court awards plaintiff reasonable attorney's fees and costs incurred in connection with the motion. Plaintiff is directed to submit an affidavit and supporting time records on or before May 14, 2008 if she wishes to obtain reimbursement for fees. Defendant's request for fees is denied.

SO ORDERED.

Dated: Brooklyn, New York
        April 29 , 2008

Cheryl L. Pollak
United States Magistrate Judge

11

A Day in the Life of the Printed Electronic Document

George L. Paul

In a second example of dysnomia, the author discusses a case study from recent federal court litigation, involving the authenticity of a consulting agreement and the board consent approving the agreement. The evidence at issue constituted printouts of an electronic document. Given the untestability of digital files, and with the available witnesses swearing to authenticity, it was hard if not impossible to test the authenticity of the documents involved. The case study reveals how much one can learn about such files when, as here, a witness suddenly stepped forward to explain how it was created months later than its purported date—indeed after the lawsuit started.

In Chapter 2, we saw that information objects can migrate between the digital and physical realms. This is the cause of a perplexing problem for those trying to determine the authenticity of information. The phenomenon is the "printed electronic document."

This case study examines a typical fact pattern—the falsification of records using the seamless digital editing we have discussed throughout this book, and the consequent printout of the information so as to mimic a paper document signed at an earlier time. It is a classic case in the study of authenticity. Indeed, there are many lawsuits around the country where management of publicly held companies falsifies records, after the fact, in an attempt to gain equity in the company.

The facts are taken from the case of CV06-01291-ROX, which was a shareholder's derivative action filed in U.S. District Court for the District of Arizona. Certain shareholders became suspicious when directors of a public company, Skye, Inc., unexpectedly began acting as if they had consulting agreements. Such agreements had never been disclosed in public filings about the company, and the other insiders appeared to disagree that the interested individuals had authorized consulting agreements.

Shortly after the lawsuit was filed, one of the directors in question, Gregg Johnson, came forward with documents that had never been seen before or disclosed in public filings. In a declaration he filed, Johnson testified obliquely: "In the course of the 2005 audit, I contacted Kreitzer to obtain a copy of my Consulting Agreement, attached hereto as Exhibit A, as well as the Director's Resolution approving the Agreement, attached hereto as Exhibit B. I had not received a final copy of either Exhibit A or Exhibit B before that time."

The testimony in deposition was that his Consulting Agreement had been hidden from him until recently, by management, and that Johnson had only received it shortly after the lawsuit had been filed, and that is why it had not been disclosed before. Mr. Johnson argued that the document was authentic, and had been executed when it purported to have been executed, in August of 2005.

The first page of the Consulting Agreement looked very much like a physical document (see Figure G.1). But studying the document closely, the derivative plaintiffs noticed anomalies. One of the dates appeared not to sync up. For example, in an inconspicuous place, the word "Skye" had been used on the document, when in fact the company was not named Skye at the time of the purported execution, when the company had been named instead "Tankless."

Plaintiffs' counsel spoke to the lawyers on the other side about the anomaly, and suggested the documents recently tendered were not authentic and indeed had been phonied up recently. The opposing lawyers denied any wrongdoing, and vigorously argued possible innocent explanations for any anomalies. They maintained the name "Skye" had actually been used informally by an inner circle of management, for months, before the company had officially been renamed. It was hard to disprove this explanation.

Given the fact that only a "paper document" was in existence, (with all known witnesses unable to locate any electronic files), or so it was asserted by defendants, there was no way to meaningfully test the authenticity of the documents involved with available witnesses. The interested director swore things were authentic in his deposition, and denied he had phonied up anything or been involved in the document's preparation. In summary judgment papers, opposing counsel maintained the document had been created and signed on the date it was purported to have been dated, which was months before the lawsuit had been filed. The only way to defeat the motion for summary judgment was to file a Rule 56 (f) affidavit and request time to do discovery about the genuineness of the document.

By chance, weeks later another witness, who had been incommunicado, agreed to be interviewed. In a fact pattern that is common in this day and age, the witness disclosed that several people had indeed participated in manufacturing the questioned document after the lawsuit started, using editable electronic files and Internet e-mail connectivity—even transmuting Word files into seemingly more-permanent PDF files, which were then printed, and then faxed, and printed by a fax machine. The document indeed appeared to be several months old, except for the anomalies discussed above.

Luckily, this witness had kept the electronic messages involved, with their metadata, that showed dates and times of the transmissions, as well as the two documents as they evolved after the federal court action had started. The director in question had called the witness and told him over the phone that he would be sending him e-mails about the need to create a contract and board consent for his consulting agreement (See Exhibit 4). The director, Gregg Johnson, said in essence that he needed to write "in code," as the auditors of the company were purported to be in the company's offices at that very minute, and might look at Mr. Johnson's computer and discover what people were up to—which was fooling the auditors, according to Johnson, not fooling the plaintiffs in the case.

PERSONAL SERVICES CONSULTING AGREEMENT

THIS AGREEMENT made effective as of the 1st day of August 2005.

BETWEEN:

TANKLESS SYSTEMS WORLDWIDE, INC., a body corporate duly incorporated pursuant to the laws of the State of Nevada, with principal offices in the City of Scottsdale, in the State of Arizona, together with all of its wholly owned subsidiaries from time to time operating (hereinafter, collectively referred to as the "Corporation").

- and -

GREGG C JOHNSON., an individual currently residing in the City of Peoria, AZ (the "Executive").

RECITALS

WHEREAS, the Corporation is engaged in the business of designing, manufacturing and marketing a line of tankless water heaters, as well as a suite of household and commercial health and wellness related appliances and other devices;

AND, WHEREAS, the Corporation wishes to contract for the services of the Executive to serve as the an Officer of the Corporation, and the Executive wishes to be contracted by the Corporation as an Officer;

AND WHEREAS, the Corporation has caused to be issued Seven Hundred & Fifty Thousand restricted common shares of the Corporation to the Executive in consideration for the Executive agreeing to join the Corporation and to act in the capacity as its consultant and Officer;

AND WHEREAS, the Executive has agreed that such shares shall not be eligible for sale, transfer, hypothecation or other disposition except otherwise as in accordance with Schedule "B" attached hereto;

NOW, THEREFORE, THIS AGREEMENT WITNESSETH, that inconsideration of the premises and covenants and agreements hereinafter contained it is agreed by and between the parties as follows:

ARTICLE 1 - CONTRACT

1.1 The Executive will, during the Term (as defined below) or any renewals thereof, perform all of the Duties (as defined below) as the Corporation by action of its Board of Directors shall, from time to time, reasonably assign to the Executive. The Corporation and Executive further agree that any prior

05/24/2006 10:39 4808899998 SKYE INTERNATIONAL PAGE 02/12

FIGURE G.1
Purported Gregg Johnson Consulting Agreement, page 1

Accordingly, even the e-mail record was misleading, as the writers of the emails back and forth knew that one day the emails might be read, so they had to e-mail with a "wink," so to speak. Even humor and "ribbing" were inserted into the e-mails so as to leave a more convincing e-mail trail. For example, one e-mail (See Exhibit 5), written after the author had immediately finished creating a document for the first time, that had obviously never been executed by anyone until May of 2006, says: "Gregg. Here is the original PDF of the contract which was executed on August 1, 2005. I did not have one executed by yourself in the file. I guess we should have not been paying you all these months if you didn't sign it!. . . . " The author had just finished creating the document in Word, transferring it to PDF, and signing it on behalf of the company. In short, the e-mail trail attempted to cover up, and to provide false circumstantial evidence surrounding the post-lawsuit creation of the document for the first time, its backdating, and then its postdated execution.

What happened is that the director sent a Word version of his proposed consulting agreement to the witness, who then circulated it to other defendants to check to see if they agreed. The information was turned into a PDF and backdated by several months, but alas, the wrong seal was affixed (see the second document in Exhibit 5). Unfortunately, the witness had attached the then-current seal—not the seal at the time of the purported events that were to have transpired so long ago.

Everything was accordingly done over again, then printed out in PDF, leaving only tiny date anomalies that were not as glaringly obvious as the wrong seal. People who were not on the public company's Board of Directors then prepared consents approving the backdated agreement, and then backdated the consents. Documents were signed in hard copy. They were then copied and submitted into evidence.

With the witnesses not being forthcoming about the creation of the document, and certainly not volunteering information about its background, and with no electronic copy and only the paper printout to go on, it was impossible to test authenticity without the creator of the document. It is fortuitous this individual was found and decided to tell the truth, and then even more fortuitous that he still had the e-mail trail where all of this unfolded over the Internet. The time marks on the e-mails are not protected by cryptography, but the totality of the many messages make it highly unlikely that all of the messages could have been artfully phonied up by the witness who decided to come forward.

An affidavit (see Figure G.2) about the creation of the document, with exhibits of the e-mails as to its creation, and the various forms the document took along the way, follows to give vivid illustration of the printed electronic document problem.

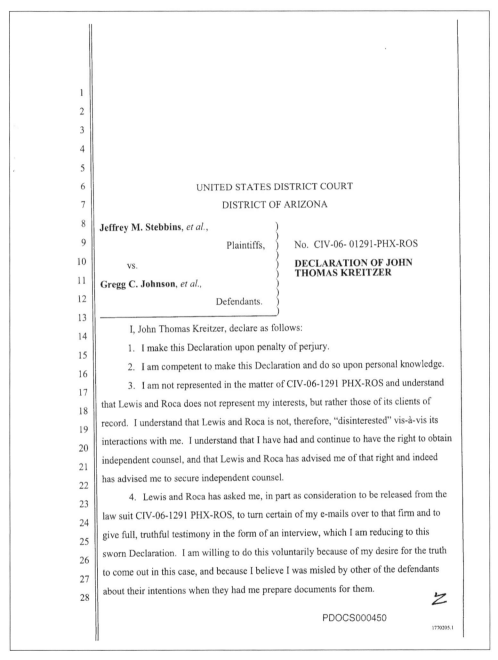

UNITED STATES DISTRICT COURT

DISTRICT OF ARIZONA

Jeffrey M. Stebbins, *et al.*,

          Plaintiffs,   )   No. CIV-06- 01291-PHX-ROS

vs.   )   **DECLARATION OF JOHN**
)   **THOMAS KREITZER**

Gregg C. Johnson, *et al.*,

          Defendants.   )

I, John Thomas Kreitzer, declare as follows:

1. I make this Declaration upon penalty of perjury.

2. I am competent to make this Declaration and do so upon personal knowledge.

3. I am not represented in the matter of CIV-06-1291 PHX-ROS and understand that Lewis and Roca does not represent my interests, but rather those of its clients of record. I understand that Lewis and Roca is not, therefore, "disinterested" vis-à-vis its interactions with me. I understand that I have had and continue to have the right to obtain independent counsel, and that Lewis and Roca has advised me of that right and indeed has advised me to secure independent counsel.

4. Lewis and Roca has asked me, in part as consideration to be released from the law suit CIV-06-1291 PHX-ROS, to turn certain of my e-mails over to that firm and to give full, truthful testimony in the form of an interview, which I am reducing to this sworn Declaration. I am willing to do this voluntarily because of my desire for the truth to come out in this case, and because I believe I was misled by other of the defendants about their intentions when they had me prepare documents for them.

PDOCS000450

1770205.1

FIGURE G.2
Kreitzer Affidavit

1   5. None of the e-mails I am testifying about in this Declaration are attorney client

2   privileged, to my understanding. None of them involve communications with SKYE's

3   counsel, only Dan Campbell and his firm, who were not representing me, my brother, or

4   father, but only Mr. Pinckard and Mr. Johnson, and not SKYE. People made it clear to

5   me that I was not being represented by counsel in the litigation, or elsewhere. Nor did I

6   have any agreement with them that I would keep their communications secret. They

7   emphasized to me that no communications were protected by the attorney client

8   privilege.

9   6. I have reviewed my e-mail records, which have been recorded on my laptop

10   computer, to refresh my recollection about events occurring in May 2006. These have

11   been kept on my laptop computer in the same, authentic form that they have been in since

12   the day they were sent or received. I have also reviewed them and they are accurate,

13   authentic, and they have not been edited or changed. I have also determined the time the

14   e-mails were sent or received from the metadata "Properties" folder for each e-mail. I

15   have printed out the relevant e-mails for the Court's consideration.

16   7. I have also studied the sworn testimony that Gregg Johnson has submitted to

17   the Court about the issues surrounding his purported Consulting Agreement, and the

18   Board minutes that purportedly approved such Consulting Agreement.

19   8. I was in Illinois on May 22, 2006, and was thus unable to know what was

20   going on in the SKYE offices at the time, which are located in Phoenix, Arizona. I

21   understood that the company, and myself and others, had recently been sued.

22   9. At approximately 11:15 a.m. on Monday, May 22, 2006 I resigned from

23   SKYE, where I had been serving as President and CEO. I sent Gregg Johnson, Ken

24   Pinckard, and Larry Ryckman the e-mail marked as Exhibit 1. Gregg Johnson asked me

25   to call him, and in the phone conversation asked me to put the resignation in a more

26   formal form.

27   10. Accordingly, I submitted a letter for resignation from SKYE. I sent it to

28   Gregg Johnson, Ken Pinckard, and Larry Ryckman. They requested that I change the

2   PDOCS000451   1770205.1

1 language slightly, effectively pushing back my resignation date from May 22 to a later

2 date to correspond to the filing of the firm's 10-K. Thereafter, I did this, and transmitted

3 a new version of a PDF file of a signed letter of resignation to Johnson, Pinckard, and

4 Ryckman, sent at approximately 11:39 a.m. This e-mail and attachment is Exhibit 2.

5   11. At approximately 11:40 a.m., I received an e-mail from Gregg Johnson that

6 said "Tom: Thanks for that. You will be missed. Gregg" Exhibit 3.

7   12. After I had resigned, at 11:55 a.m. that same day, May 22, I received an e-mail

8 from Gregg Johnson (Exhibit 4). He sent with the e-mail an attached Word document.

9 His e-mail asserted that he did not have a signed copy of his Consulting Agreement. His

10 e-mail asserted that I had told him that it had been signed in the past, but I had no

11 recollection of his Consulting Agreement ever having been signed. I opened the

12 attachment and looked at it.

13   13. I could not find any signed Consulting Agreement nor did I remember any

14 being signed. Gregg and I then spoke by phone. He acted on the phone as if auditors

15 were in SKYE's office at that moment. He spoke through his teeth in a hushed tone. He

16 acted as if he had to whisper into the phone so as not to reveal that he could not find his

17 Consulting Agreement to show it to the auditors. He also spoke with urgency. He subtly

18 communicated to me that I should make up a new agreement using the Word Document

19 he had sent me, and to sign it, and then to turn it into a PDF document. It was clear to me

20 that in any transmission e-mail to him, I should pretend, for the sake of the auditors who

21 were there, that this document had been executed back in 2005. Playing along with his

22 wishes, and believing it was for the good of the company which was currently being

23 audited, I drafted an e-mail (Exhibit 5). I sent it at 12:40 p.m. on May 22nd. It reads:

24 "Gregg, Here is the original PDF of the contract which was executed on Aug. 1, 2005. I

25 do not have one executed by yourself in my file. I guess we shouldn't have been paying

26 you all of these months if you didn't sign it… J. Thomas." My intent was to get

27 documented what I believed, based on what I was being told to me, were agreements that

28 the company had entered into.

3

1 14. In fact, I did not send Gregg Johnson anything that had been executed in
2 August 2005. I had used his Word document to create a PDF document that hour, and
3 then signed it that hour. I stamped it with a "SKYE" stamp, as is evident on the PDF
4 attachment to the e-mail (Exhibit 5), p. 8.
5 15. Gregg did not tell me anything about proposing that this document be filed in
6 the lawsuit we had just been served with. He said it was for the audit. I sent the newly
7 executed PDF document to Larry Ryckman and Ken Pinckard immediately, at 12:43
8 p.m., with an e-mail (Exhibit 6). It reads: "Ken, Gregg had me deliver this for the
9 auditors. Please be sure it is the right version. Thanks, Thomas." The PDF document I
10 sent to Pinckard and Ryckman had the SKYE corporate seal on it. Looking back, this
11 was significant because our company was not called "SKYE" until several months after
12 August 2005.
13 16. Almost immediately thereafter, Gregg Johnson called me and said he had
14 noticed that the document I sent had the wrong seal on it—the SKYE seal—and that it
15 would not work. It needed a "Tankless" seal on it, because the company was named
16 Tankless at the time the document was purportedly to have been executed. He
17 commented that the company was not yet named SKYE at the relevant time.
18 17. Accordingly, I made up a second document with a "Tankless seal" on it.
19 Before sending it to Gregg Johnson, however, I sent it to Ken Pinckard and Larry
20 Ryckman (Exhibit 7), with an e-mail that said: "Ken, Here is the signed PDF with the
21 correct seal. Gregg does not have this one. He has one with a SKYE seal but it needs a
22 Tankless seal. I won't send him the valid one until I get the ok from you and Larry. He
23 says he needs it today. Thomas." The PDF attachment to that e-mail had a "Tankless"
24 seal on it. I had just executed it that day, using the same Word document that Gregg had
25 sent me earlier in the day.
26 18. I did not hear from Ken Pinckard, which made me anxious, because Gregg had
27 put a lot of emphasis that this had to be done quickly.
28

4

PDOCS000453

1770205.1

1   19. Accordingly, I sought out Ken Pinckard and Larry Ryckman. At about 4:39

2   p.m. on May 22, 2006, I wrote them an e-mail (Exhibit 8), that reads as follows: "What

3   should my response be to Gregg? I emailed that I had signed the one that had the wrong

4   seal so it isn't any good. I now need to respond to his request for one that has the correct

5   seal i.e. the one you got last. Thanks, Thomas P.S. I am going to have to say something.

6   How does this sound: Gregg, After reviewing the signed agreement, that you did not

7   receive, I realize that it was turned over to corporate council and returned to me with

8   some suggested edits which is why it wasn't forwarded to you back in August of 2005.

9   The attached signed agreement has the enclosed edits. Sincerely, Thomas Kreitzer."

10   20. A review of my e-mail records indicates that at 5:12 p.m. on May 22, 2006, I

11   sent Ken Pinckard and Larry Ryckman an e-mail (Exhibit 9), forwarding them the

12   original e-mail that Gregg Johnson had sent me, with his attached Word document. The

13   e-mail says "Document from Gregg."

14   21. Not hearing from either Larry or Ken, I sent them an e-mail at 7:03 p.m. that

15   evening which asked them "Should I just have Gregg call you or Larry?" (Exhibit 10).

16   22. Some time on May 22d, probably in the evening, I had a phone conversation

17   with Ken Pinckard. He seemed angry or agitated that Gregg Johnson had gotten me to

18   sign a document that had never been approved by the company. He seemed happy,

19   however, that at least it had the SKYE seal on it, rather than the Tankless seal on it. He

20   said to hold off on responding to Gregg's request of a document with the Tankless seal on

21   it, until he got back to me on what to do. He said he would send me the agreement that I

22   should send to Gregg. In the meantime, I sent him once again what I had sent Gregg.

23   23. Accordingly, at 7:45 p.m. by e-mail, I sent Ken Pinckard a version of the

24   document that still had the SKYE seal on it (Exhibit 10).

25   24. The next morning, on May 23rd, I checked my e-mail, and I had not received

26   any agreement from Ken Pinckard. I wrote him a follow up e-mail at approximately 8:05

27   a.m. (Exhibit 11).

28

PDOCS000454

1770205.1

25. Ken Pinckard then sent me the document that I understood I was to sign, and to stamp with a Tankless seal. I cannot find that e-mail for whatever reason, perhaps because it was sent to a different computer in the house in Illinois, or was sent to on-line account, or perhaps because I was instructed to delete it -- I simply can't determine why I can't find it. However, I definitely got the document from Ken Pinckard and was instructed to send it to Gregg Johnson. I had no idea what the terms were that Ken Pinckard wanted in the document—only that he would send it to me.

26. Accordingly, at 10:55 a.m on May 23, 2006, I sent an e-mail to Gregg Johnson with a PDF of the document that Ken Pinckard had instructed me to send, this time with a Tankless Seal attached to it (Exhibit 12). The e-mail says: "Gregg, The copy of the contract I forwarded yesterday which I added the Skye Seal to was never released or approved by the Board which is why you never received a copy. Here is a PDF I created from what I had board approval of back then. There was a lot going on back then so just use this one to get through the reporting. Please work with the new Board to get your final version approved and executed. Thanks, Thomas." This e-mail was not an accurate description of what had happened. It was false. We did not have board approval of any specific contract "back then." I was playing along with the pretext, or charade, of what Gregg Johnson and Ken Pinckard were instructing me to do, in my understanding, for the auditors. I knew there was some sort of understanding because we were issuing stock to Gregg and paying him a salary but I was certain that no formal contract had ever been signed.

27. Gregg Johnson then sent me back an e-mail that said "Thank you Thomas. I will pass on the "proposed agreement" as well so the record is complete. Thanks for going through your records." I obviously at the time understood this e-mail to have been a false communication, because, through our phone conversations and e-mails of the previous day, Gregg Johnson, as well as Ken Pinckard and Larry Ryckman, knew that I had no document "in my records." Everyone knew that I had just made up the document, according to Ken Pinckard's specifications, and had just signed it and stamped it with a

PDOCS000455   Ƶ   1770205.1

1   Tankless seal. It was my understanding that everyone involved was leaving a false e-

2   mail trail for the auditors, in case they saw my e-mails, being there with him at the time.

3   28. Shortly thereafter, Gregg Johnson sent me an e-mail (Exhibit 14) pointing out

4   that what I had sent him was different from what he had sent me. It said: "Thomas: The

5   agreements are quite different but I appreciate that the Board did what it believed was in

6   the interests of shareholders. I hope our new Board will adopt the agreement that I

7   thought was executed! Anyhow will you please send me the minutes that approved the

8   Consulting Agreement. Ken thinks that you have these and that it was written in your

9   style of minutes as opposed to a consent as Ken does." I interpreted the comment about

10   minutes as "code" as there were obviously no minutes in existence, but he was asking me

11   to draft some up at the time. It also appeared that Gregg and Ken had been discussing

12   this, as they apparently had decided that I should draft such minutes up, rather than Ken.

13   29. About this time I had a phone conversation with Ken Pinckard about Gregg's

14   e-mail. He confirmed that I needed to immediately draft a form of corporate resolution

15   that appeared as if it had been drafted more than a year ago. My understanding from

16   Pinckard was that he was asking me to draft a corporate resolution. He, like Gregg, told

17   me it was for purposes of an audit. His entire demeanor and conversation implied that

18   this was for an audit. He did not at any time imply that this was for a lawsuit.

19   30. At 1:56 pm on May 23rd, I ran by a proposed, dummied up corporate

20   resolution to Ken Pinckard and Larry Ryckman (Exhibit 15), together with this e-mail:

21   "Ken, does this look right resolution that Gregg is looking for. Let me know."

22   Obviously, I had drafted the resolution in the minutes before sending it. It was not

23   something I found in any file or records. In my mind, this was not improper because I

24   was trying (at least from what I was being told) to document what the company was

25   doing.

26   31. Gregg Johnson kept calling me, asking me for a corporate resolution.

27

28

PDOCS000456

1770205.1

32. Thereafter, on May 24, at 12:13 pm, (Exhibit 16), I sent Ken Pinckard the following e-mail: "Ken, Gregg called again for the Resolution for his contract. Was the one I sent OK? If it is I will send it to him."

33. I thereafter had a phone conversation with Ken Pinckard, where he okayed a form of a back dated corporate resolution to send to Johnson.

34. Having received the okay on the back dated corporate resolution from Pinckard, I sent it to Johnson on May 24 at 1:24 pm. (Exhibit 17), with the following e-mail: "Gregg, Here is the resolution. Let me know if you need anything else." He replied (Exhibit 18) a few minutes later with the following e-mail: "Thank you Thomas. I think we are making real progress in the defense of this case. The audit is going well too. Gregg"

I declare under penalty of perjury that the foregoing is true and correct.

DATED this 19th day of September, 2006.

By _____
John Thomas Kreitzer

PDOCS000457

8

1770205.1

Thomas Kreitzer

From:	Gregg Johnson [gregg.johnson@skye-betterliving.com]
Sent:	Monday, May 22, 2006 11:28 AM
To:	'Thomas Kreitzer'
Subject:	RE: Final Resignation
Follow Up Flag:	Follow up
Flag Status:	Green

Tom:

Please call me 1-877-888-SKYE.

Gregg

From: Thomas Kreitzer [mailto:Thomas@KreitzerBrothers.com]
Sent: Monday, May 22, 2006 11:15 AM
To: Gregg.johnson@skye-betterliving.com
Cc: Ken Pinckard; RyckmanL@AOL.com
Subject: Final Resignation

Gentleman,

It was a pleasure working for Skye. In accordance with our agreement for me to stay on until the 10-K was singed please find attached my final formal resignation.

Should you need anything else signed in relation to the 10-K I have left language in the resignation to cover this.

Once again it has been a pleasure working on this project. Also if you need my assistance or any statements in defense of the shareholder lawsuit please let me know.

Warmest regards,

Thomas

--
No virus found in this outgoing message.
Checked by AVG Free Edition.
Version: 7.1.392 / Virus Database: 268.6.0/342 - Release Date: 5/17/2006

--
No virus found in this incoming message.
Checked by AVG Free Edition.
Version: 7.1.392 / Virus Database: 268.6.0/342 - Release Date: 5/17/2006

PDOCS000459

9/19/2006

EXHIBIT 1

Thomas Kreitzer

From:	Thomas Kreitzer [Thomas@KreitzerBrothers.com]
Sent:	Monday, May 22, 2006 11:39 AM
To:	'Gregg.johnson@skye-betterliving.com'
Cc:	Ken Pinckard (vestnik@aol.com); 'RyckmanL@AOL.com'
Subject:	Revised Resignation Letter
Follow Up Flag:	Follow up
Flag Status:	Green
Attachments:	Resignation Skye Final Rev1.pdf

Gregg,

Per your request here is the final resignation with the wording we discussed.

Thanks,

Thomas

--
No virus found in this outgoing message.
Checked by AVG Free Edition.
Version: 7.1.392 / Virus Database: 268.6.0/342 - Release Date: 5/17/2006

PDOCS000461

9/19/2006

EXHIBIT 2

THOMAS KREITZER
7904 E. Chaparral Road, Bldg. A110 Box 490 • Scottsdale • AZ • 85250
Phone # 602 334-3741• Fax # 602 926-2776
Email: Thomas@KreitzerBrothers.com

Monday, May 22, 2006

Skye International, Inc.
7150 West Erie Street
Chandler, AZ 85226

Dear Sirs:

Please accept this letter as my formal notice of resignation as President and CEO and all other officer positions of Skye International Inc. and its subsidiaries effective upon the final execution of the 2005 10-K. The associations I've made during my employment here will truly be memorable for years to come.

Sincerely,

Thomas Kreitzer

cc : Ken Pinckard

PDOCS000462

Page 1 of 1

Thomas Kreitzer

From:	Gregg Johnson [gregg.johnson@skye-betterliving.com]
Sent:	Monday, May 22, 2006 11:39 AM
To:	'Thomas Kreitzer'
Subject:	RE: Revised Resignation Letter
Follow Up Flag:	Follow up
Flag Status:	Green

Tom:

Thanks for that. You will be missed.

Gregg

From: Thomas Kreitzer [mailto:Thomas@KreitzerBrothers.com]
Sent: Monday, May 22, 2006 11:39 AM
To: Gregg.johnson@skye-betterliving.com
Cc: Ken Pinckard; RyckmanL@AOL.com
Subject: Revised Resignation Letter

Gregg,

Per your request here is the final resignation with the wording we discussed.

Thanks,

Thomas

--
No virus found in this outgoing message.
Checked by AVG Free Edition.
Version: 7.1.392 / Virus Database: 268.6.0/342 - Release Date: 5/17/2006

--
No virus found in this incoming message.
Checked by AVG Free Edition.
Version: 7.1.392 / Virus Database: 268.6.0/342 - Release Date: 5/17/2006

PDOCS000464

9/19/2006

EXHIBIT 3

Thomas Kreitzer

From:	Gregg Johnson [gregg.johnson@skye-betterliving.com]
Sent:	Monday, May 22, 2006 11:55 AM
To:	'Thomas Kreitzer'; thomas_kreitzer@hotmail.com
Subject:	C DOCUME~1 gjohnson LOCALS~1 Temp AttachmentsTemp(5) Consulting Agreement - Gregg Johnson
Follow Up Flag:	Follow up
Flag Status:	Green
Attachments:	C DOCUME~1 gjohnson LOCALS~1 Temp AttachmentsTemp(5) Consulting Agreement - Gregg Johnson.rtf

Tom:

On review of my records I still have not received a signed copy back of this agreement. If you have it will you please PDF and email back to me.

I will countersign once I receive your signed copy.

This is my agreement that dates back to January 1, 2005 and revised to be effective August 1, 2005. I know you have said that it was signed but I have no copy and the auditors want it for their files.

Gregg

--
No virus found in this incoming message.
Checked by AVG Free Edition.
Version: 7.1.392 / Virus Database: 268.6.0/342 - Release Date: 5/17/2006

9/19/2006

EXHIBIT 4

PERSONAL SERVICES CONSULTING AGREEMENT

THIS AGREEMENT made effective as of the 1st day of August 2005.

BETWEEN:

TANKLESS SYSTEMS WORLDWIDE, INC., a body corporate duly incorporated pursuant to the laws of the State of Nevada, with principal offices in the City of Scottsdale, in the State of Arizona, together with all of its wholly owned subsidiaries from time to time operating (hereinafter, collectively referred to as the "Corporation").

- and -

GREGG C JOHNSON., an individual currently residing in the City of Peoria, AZ (the "Executive").

RECITALS

WHEREAS, the Corporation is engaged in the business of designing, manufacturing and marketing a line of tankless water heaters, as well as a suite of household and commercial health and wellness related appliances and other devices;

AND, WHEREAS, the Corporation wishes to contract for the services of the Executive to serve as the President and Chief Executive Officer of the Corporation, and the Executive wishes to be contracted by the Corporation as its President and Chief Executive Officer;

AND WHEREAS, the Corporation has caused to be issued Seven Hundred & Fifty Thousand restricted common shares of the Corporation to the Executive in consideration for the Executive agreeing to join the Corporation and to act in the capacity as its consultant and Chief Executive Officer;

AND WHEREAS, the Executive has agreed that such shares shall not be eligible for sale, transfer, hypothecation or other disposition except otherwise as in accordance with Schedule "B" attached hereto;

AND WHEREAS, the Executive acknowledges that he has been issued Five Hundred Thousand (500,000) options to purchase common shares of the Corporation's securities at $0.50 per share for a period of five (5) years from and after December 24, 2004 as consideration for all stock-based executive incentive compensation for a three (3) year period from the date of issuance thereof; and

NOW, THEREFORE, THIS AGREEMENT WITNESSETH, that inconsideration of the premises and covenants and agreements hereinafter contained it is agreed by and between the parties as follows:

PDOCS000467

ARTICLE 1 - CONTRACT

1.1   The Executive will, during the Term (as defined below) or any renewals thereof, perform all of the Duties (as defined below) as the Corporation by action of its Board of Directors shall, from time to time, reasonably assign to the Executive. The Corporation and Executive further agree that any prior employment and/or consulting agreements entered into between the parties are hereby terminated effective the date of this Agreement.

ARTICLE 2- TERM

2.1   Subject to the prior termination of this Agreement as provided herein, the contracting of the Executive by the Corporation shall commence on August 1, 2005, and end on July 31, 2008 (the "Term').

2.2   Subject to the prior termination of this Agreement as herein provided, upon the expiration of the Term, the Corporation may extend the contract period of the Executive for such period or periods and under such conditions as mutually agreed to by the parties; provided that, any such agreement to extend the contract shall only be binding if made in writing and signed by the parties hereto. For greater certainty, it is understood that Term shall refer to the original term of this Agreement as defined in Article 2.1 herein and to any renewal thereof.

ARTICLE 3 - DUTIES

3.1   The Executive shall, during the Term of this Agreement, perform all of the duties and responsibilities (the "Duties') as the Corporation shall from time to time reasonably assign to the Executive and, without limiting the generality of the foregoing, the Duties shall include those duties set forth in Schedule "A" attached hereto, as from time to time reasonably amended by the Board of Directors of the Corporation. During the Term of this Agreement, the Executive shall devote the majority of the Executive's time and attention to the Duties, and shall do all in the Executives power to promote, develop and extend the business of the Corporation and its subsidiaries and related corporations.

3.2   The Executive shall truly and faithfully account for and deliver to the Corporation all money, securities and things of value belonging to the Corporation which the Executive may from time to time receive for, from or on account of the Corporation.

ARTICLE 4- REMUNERATION

4.1   Subject to Article 4.5 below, the gross annual cash compensation of the Executive shall be the greater of (i) One Hundred Eighty Thousand ($180,000) US Dollars, or (ii) an amount equal to one per cent (1.0%) of the gross sales (the 'Revenue Share") actually achieved by the Corporation during each fiscal year (hereinafter, the "Compensation"). Such Compensation shall be calculated by multiplying the Corporation's actual revenue figure achieved in the month by 0.01. For greater certainty, should such calculation result in an amount of less than Fifteen Thousand ($15,000) US Dollars being paid to the Executive in any monthly period, the Executive shall be entitled to receive the full amount of Fifteen Thousand ($15,000) US Dollars. All Compensation payable hereunder shall be payable on a monthly basis with a mid-month advance of Five Thousand

2

($5,000) US Dollars payable on the 15th of the month with the balance payable on the 5th of the succeeding month. For greater certainty, the Executive acknowledges and confirms that such Compensation methodology is inclusive of any annual bonus or other customary emoluments, perquisites or payments other than those specifically granted under the terms of this Agreement

4.2   Alternate Payment: The Executive agrees that up to 2/3 of such Compensation payable in accordance with Article 4.1 above may, at the discretion of the Board of Directors, be paid in the form of freely-tradable securities of the Corporation representing a value at the time of payment equal to at least the value of such unpaid (cash) Compensation ("Stock Based Payment"). For greater certainty, any securities issued to the Executive in connection with the Stock Based Payment shall be freely-tradable, and shall be priced at the lowest closing bid price of the Corporation's securities over the ten (10) trading days prior to the issuance of securities under such Stock Based Payment mechanism.

4.2   The Executive shall also be entitled to participate, **only if such plans exist**, in the Corporation's group benefit plan, medical and family medical plan, stock savings plan, and disability insurance plan. It is understood that all costs associated with such plans will be borne by the Corporation.

4.3   The Executive will be reimbursed for reasonable business expenses, within such policy guidelines as may be established from time to time, by the Corporation's Board of Directors, provided that such business expenses are incurred in the ordinary course of performing the Duties.

4.4   During the Term hereof the Corporation shall provide the Executive with reimbursement of vehicle operating and insurance costs. For greater certainty the Executive shall NOT be entitled to any other automobile allowance

4.5   The Executive shall NOT be entitled to participate in annual grants of stock options in accordance with the Corporation's Stock Option Plan. The Executive herby confirms that he has received Five Hundred Thousand (500,000) options under that certain Stock Option Agreement, dated December 23, 2004.

ARTICLE 5-BENEFITS AND HOLIDAYS

5.1   The Executive shall be entitled to four (4) weeks paid holidays during each year of the Term. Holidays must be taken at times that are satisfactory to the Corporation, acting reasonably, and must be taken within the year to which the holiday relates and holidays not taken shall be deemed to have been taken and no other compensation shall be payable by the Corporation. For greater clarity it is understood that for the purpose of determining the number of holidays for which the Executive is entitled, each year of the Term will commence on January 1st and end on December 31st.

ARTICLE 6-CONFIDENTIALITY

6.1   The Executive shall not, either during the continuance of the Executive's contract hereunder or at any time after termination of the Executive as consultant to the Corporation, for any reason whatsoever (except in the proper course of carrying out the Duties, or otherwise required by law), divulge to any person whomsoever, and shall use the Executive's best endeavors to prevent the publication or disclosure of:

3

6.1.1   Any confidential information concerning the business or finances of the Corporation or any other corporation, person or entity for which he is directed to perform services hereunder or of any of their dealings, transactions or affairs, including, without limitation, personal and family matters which may come to the Executive's knowledge during or in the course of the Executive's contract: or

6.1.2   Any trade secrets, know-how, inventions, technology, designs, methods, formula, processes, copyrights, trade marks, trade mark applications, patents, patent applications or any other proprietary information and/or data of the Corporation (herein collectively called "Intellectual Property").

ARTICLE 7 - INVENTIONS AND PATENTS

7.1   If the Executive contributes to any invention whether patentable, patented, or not (an "Invention"), any intellectual property, or any improvement or modification to any Invention or intellectual property then the Executive's contribution thereto and the Invention, intellectual property or improvement thereof shall, without the payment of any additional compensation in any form whatsoever, become the exclusive property of the Corporation. The Executive shall execute any and all agreements, assurances or assignments that the Corporation may require and the Executive shall fully cooperate with the Corporation in the filing and prosecution of any patent applications. The Executive hereby reiterates and confirms the application of this Article to all such Inventions, intellectual property and improvements that have been made during the tenancy of that certain consulting position with the Corporation's subsidiaries.

ARTICLE 8- RESTRICTIVE COVENANT

8.1   The Executive will not at any time during the Term, or during any renewal thereof, and for a period of two (2) years following the expiration or termination of the Executive's contract for whatever cause, compete in the United States, directly or indirectly, with any of the businesses carried on by the Corporation, its subsidiaries or affiliates:

8.1.1   As a principal, partner employee;

8.1.2   As an officer, director or similar official of any incorporated or unincorporated entity engaged in any such competing business (the "Other Entity");

8.1,3   As a consultant or advisor to any Other Entity;

8.1.4   As a holder of shares or debt instrument of any kind of any Other Entity;

8.1.5   In any relationship described in subsections 81.1 through 8.1.4 of this section with any incorporated or unincorporated entity which provides services for or necessarily incidental to the business of an Other Entity:

without the prior express written consent of the Corporation, which consent may be withheld by the Corporation for any reason or for no reason.

8.2   Notwithstanding the provisions of Article 8.3 below, the Executive acknowledges and agrees that the time frames for which the aforesaid covenant shall apply have been considered by the Executive who has taken independent legal advice with respect thereto and the restraint and restriction of and on the future activities of the Executive are reasonable in the circumstances.

8.3   The parties agree that if the time frames set out in this Article are found to unenforceable by a court of competent jurisdiction, the time frames will be amended to the time frames as established by a court of competent jurisdiction.

3.4   The Executive acknowledges that any breach of Articles 6, 7 & 8 will cause irreparable harm to the Corporation, for which the Corporation cannot be compensated by damages. The Executive agrees that in the event of a breach of the covenant contained in Articles 6, 7, & 8, the Corporation shall not be restricted to seeking damages only, but shall be entitled to injunctive and other equitable relief.

ARTICLE 9- TERMINATION OF CONTRACT

9.1   The Corporation may terminate this Agreement at any time for cause. The term "for cause" shall include any one or more of the following:

9.1.1   A significant and continuing breach or failure or a continual breaching or failing to observe any of the provisions herein;

9.1.2   An act of dishonesty fundamentally detrimental to the well-being of the Corporation;

9.1.3   Any act of gross negligence relating to completing the Duties;

9.1.4   The commission of a felony offence for which the Executive is convicted, which significantly impairs the Executive's ability to perform the Duties and responsibilities hereunder or which materially adversely affects the reputation enjoyed by the Corporation; or

9.1.5   The failure to comply with reasonable instructions, orders and directions of the Board of Directors of the Corporation in so far as such instructions, orders and directions are not inconsistent with the Duties, or are, in the reasonable opinion of the Executive:

9.1.5.1   In any way demeaning or likely to result in diminution of the value of the Executives services in the future.

9.1.5.2   Likely to result in the conduct of an illegal act.

9.1.5.3   Inconsistent with any court order or other governmental order or directive.

9.1.5.4   Inconsistent with any shareholders' resolution passed at any duly convened meeting of shareholders.

provided that, with respect to each 9.1.1 through 9.1.5 above, the Executive shall be notified within five (5) business days from the date of any such alleged breach and provided a reasonable opportunity to respond thereto. For greater certainty, the Corporation shall not be entitled to utilize any such provision to terminate this Agreement in respect of any action by the Executive that was: (i) not specifically brought to the attention of the Executive within such five (5) day period (ii) specifically required to be performed by direction of the board, directly or indirectly (iii) this dissemination of information required to be reported in the normal course with the Securities and Exchange Commission or any other competent governmental entity having jurisdiction over the Executive or the Corporation, or (iv) honestly and faithfully performed by the Executive for the benefit of the Corporation.

9.2   In the event that the Executive becomes physically or mentally disabled and is unable to perform the Duties for a period of twelve (12) months, as confirmed by a doctor's certificate, the Corporation shall be entitled to terminate this Agreement without further compensation upon sixty (60) days written notice to the Executive. In the case of the death of the Executive, all obligations of the Corporation under this Agreement shall cease immediately; provided that, this provision shall not affect any right, benefit or entitlement accruing to the Executive and/or his estate under any of the Corporation's benefit plans or stock option agreements which arise as a result of the Executive's prior performance hereunder or his death.

9.3   The Executive may terminate this Agreement, and the contract created herein, by giving at least Ninety (90) days prior written notice of such intention to the Corporation. After the expiry of such notice, all obligations, except for the obligations of the Executive under Articles 6, 7 and 8 hereof, which shall continue as provided in those Articles, of the Corporation and the Executive under this Agreement shall cease.

9,4   Notwithstanding anything contained in this Article 9, if there is a Change of Control of the Corporation, as defined in the Change of Control Agreement set out as Schedule "C" attached hereto, the provisions of the Change of Control Agreement shall supersede and take precedence over the termination provisions and covenants contained in this Article 9.

ARTICLE 10-OTHER AGREEMENTS IN RESPECT OF TERMINATION

10.1   In the event of the termination of this Agreement for cause or otherwise howsoever:

    10.1.1   The Executive shall resign as a director and/or officer of the Corporation or any subsidiary or related corporation and the Executive hereby appoints the Corporation as its attorney in fact for the purpose of executing any and all such documents to give effect to the foregoing; and

    10.1.2   The Executive hereby authorizes the Corporation and any subsidiary or related corporation to set off against and deduct from any and all amounts owing to the Executive by way of salary, allowances, accrued leave, long service leave, reimbursements or any other emoluments or benefits owing to the Executive by the Corporation and any subsidiary or related corporation, any reasonable amounts owed by the Executive to the Corporation or any subsidiary or related corporation.

6

10.2   Notwithstanding any termination of this Agreement for any reason whatsoever, whether with or without cause, all of the provisions of Articles 6, 7 and 8 and any other provisions of this Agreement necessary to give efficacy and effect thereto shall continue in full force and effect following the termination of this Agreement.

ARTICLE 11 - GENERAL

11.1   This Agreement, and the Schedules attached hereto, constitute the entire agreement between the parties hereto and cancels, supersedes and replaces all previous written, verbal or implied terms, conditions and representations relating to the Executive's contract.

11.2   The failure of either party at any time to require strict performance by the other party of any provision hereof shall in no way affect the full right to require such performance at any time thereafter. Neither shall the waiver by either party of a breach of any provision hereof be taken or held to be a waiver of any succeeding breach of such provision or as a waiver of the provision itself.

11.3   Each article, paragraph, clause, sub-clause and provision of this Agreement shall be severable from each other and if for any reason any article, paragraph, clause, sub-clause or provision is invalid or unenforceable, such invalidity or unenforceability shall not prejudice or in any way affect the validity or enforceability of any other article, paragraph, clause, sub-clause or provision. This Agreement and each article, paragraph, clause, sub-clause and provision hereof shall be read and construed so as to give thereto the full effect thereof subject only to any contrary provision of the law to the extent that where this Agreement or any article, paragraph, clause, sub- clause or provision hereof would but for the provisions of this paragraph have been read and construed as being void or ineffective, it shall nevertheless be a valid agreement, article, paragraph, clause, sub-clause or provision as the case may be to the full extent to which it is not contrary to any provision of the law.

11.4   The parties hereto submit to the exclusive jurisdiction of the Courts of the State of Arizona in respect of any matter or thing arising out of this Agreement or pursuant thereto.

11.5   All notices to be given by either party hereto shall be delivered or sent by telegram, facsimile or cable to the following address or such other address as may be notified by either party:

11.5.1 If to the Corporation to:

Tankless Systems Worldwide, Inc.
7650 E. Evans Rd. Suite C
Scottsdale, AZ 85260   Attention: Secretary

11.5.2 If to the Executive to:

Gregg C. Johnson
9630 W. Rimrock Dr.
Peoria, AZ 85382

PDOCS000473

11.6   This Agreement shall ensure to the benefit of and be binding upon the parties hereto, their heirs, administrators, successors and legal representatives. This Agreement may be assigned by the Corporation but may not be assigned by the Executive.

IN WITNESS WHEREOF, the parties have duly executed this Agreement.

TANKLESS SYSTEMS WORLDWIDE, INC.

Per: _____

SIGNED, SEALED AND DELIVERED in the)
Presence of:)
)
)   _____
)   **Gregg C. Johnson**
_____)
Witness

8

Schedule A

Duties
(as taken from the SKYE Organizational Manual)

Skye did not yet exist at the purported time

President & Chief Executive Officer
(Chair – Executive Management Team)

Reports to: Board of Directors

Direct Reports: Executive V.P and all Sr. V.P

Liaison: Chairman of Board
                     Chairman of all Board Committees

Job Description: Board of Directors

Review & Comp   Corporate Governance Committee

Accountability: Board of Directors

This position is the leader of the Executive Management Team and is the final responsible party for all business day-to-day planning and operations of the company.

The specific duties include, but are not limited to:

1. Together with the Executive Management Team, directs overall business and organizational policies; develops, recommends and implements through subordinates; recommends annual and long-term company policies and goals to Board of Directors.

2. Responsible for overall company financial, organizational and operational planning activities and growth.

3. Chair of the Executive Management Team, responsible for approving budgetary and operational objectives, overseeing and reporting progress to the Board of Directors.

4. Monitoring performance relative to established objectives and systematically monitor and evaluate operating results.

5. Presents, together with the CFO, Balance sheet, operating and capital expenditure budgets to Board of Directors for approval.

6. Formulates the Corporation's near term and long-range strategic plans and submits them to the Board of Directors for approval.

7. Directs executives in matters concerning the development, production, promotion and sales of the Corporation's products.

8. Promoting positive relations with customers, suppliers and the general public.

9

PDOCS000475

9.   Directs the establishment of fair and appropriate policies for human resource management.

10.   Responsible for the overall strategic management of the Corporation.

11.   Responsible for the daily affairs of the Corporation.

12.   Responsible for ensuring operational compliance with policies and procedures adopted by the Board of Directors.

13.   Primary responsible party for ensuring systemic adherence to Compliance and Ethics mandate.

13.   Together with Board members and the CFO is responsible for all capital fundraising requirements of the company.

14.   Directs, oversees and manages all external contacts with parties involved with funding the capital requirements of the company.

15.   Responsible for making all public representations in connection with investor relations activities.

16.   Together with the Chairman is responsible for all presentations of material to the public.

17.   Any other duty reasonably assigned by the Board of Directors

10

Schedule B

Resale Restrictions

The Executive confirms and acknowledges that there are resale restrictions in respect of those Seven Hundred & Fifty Thousand (750,000) common shares of the Corporation (the "Shares") issued to the Executive in connection with his consultancy to the Corporation and by operation of this Agreement. The resale restrictions imposed under this Agreement and this Schedule are in addition to any other resale restriction that may be applicable by operation of state or federal securities laws.

The Shares shall be subject to a contractual restriction prohibiting the sale, transfer, hypothecation, pledge or other disposition until such shares are eligible for release from this contractual restriction in accordance with the Schedule set forth below.

The Executive shall be entitled to the release of this contractual resale restriction in respect of the Shares by the passing of time and/or active engagement with the Corporation as a consultant or officer thereof. Specifically, the resale restrictions imposed by this Schedule shall be removed in accordance with the following release schedule:

(A)   While employed by or consulting to the Corporation:

1.   On September 1, 2004   250,000 shares

2.   On September 1, 2005   250,000 shares

3.   On September 1, 2006   250,000 shares

(B)   Otherwise:

1.   One Hundred Thousand (100,000) shares for each year from and after September 1, 2004.

For greater certainty, the Executive shall not be entitled to combine the release criteria above so as to result in the accelerated release of such Shares beyond the maximum release schedule specified in category "A" above.

11

PDOCS000477

SCHEDULE C

Change of Control Agreement

CHANGE OF CONTROL AGREEMENT

THIS AGREEMENT made the 1st day of August 2005.

BETWEEN:

> **TANKLESS SYSTEMS WORLDWIDE, INC**., a body corporate duly incorporated pursuant to the laws of the State of Nevada, with principal offices in the City of Scottsdale, in the State of Arizona, together with all of its wholly owned subsidiaries from time to time operating (hereinafter collectively referred to as the "Corporation")..

OF THE FIRST PART

- and -

> **GREGG C JOHNSON**., an individual currently residing in the City of Peoria, AZ (the "Executive").

OF THE SECOND PART

WHEREAS, the Executive entered into that certain Personal Services Consulting Agreement made in writing dated effective August 1, 2005 (the "Consulting Agreement") with the Corporation;

AND, WHEREAS, the Executive and the Corporation agree that it is in the best interests of both parties to enter into this Change of Control Agreement concurrent with the execution of the Consulting Agreement;

AND, WHEREAS, the Company and the Executive are desirous of having certain rights and benefits in the event that the Executive is dismissed or the Executive's consulting relationship with the Corporation is terminated in the manner set out herein;

AND, WHEREAS, the Corporation wishes to retain the benefit of the Executive's services and to ensure that the Executive is able to carry out his responsibilities with the Corporation free from any distractions associated with any change in the ownership of the Corporation or its assets.

NOW, THEREFORE, THIS AGREEMENT WITNESSETH, that in consideration of the premises and the mutual covenants and agreements hereinafter contained, and for good and valuable consideration (the receipt and sufficiency of which is hereby acknowledged by the parties hereto), it is agreed by and between the parties hereto as follows:

ARTICLE 1. - DEFINITIONS

1.1   Terms used in this Agreement but not otherwise defined herein have the meanings as set forth below:

1.1.1   **"Benefit Plans"** means any employee/consultant loan, insurance, long-term disability, medical, dental and other executive and employee consultant benefit plans, including any pension or group 401K plans, IRA contributions, prerequisites and privileges (including use of an automobile and club memberships) as may be provided by the Corporation or any subsidiary of the Corporation to the Executive;

1.1.2   **"Change in Control"** means a transaction or series of transactions whereby directly or indirectly and without express or implied agreement of the Executive and the Board of Directors:

1.1.2.1 Any person or combination of persons obtains a sufficient number of securities of the Corporation to affect materially the control of the Corporation; for the purposes of this Agreement, a person or combination of person holding shares or other securities in excess of the number which, directly or following conversion thereof, would entitled the holders thereof to cast 25% or more of the votes attaching to all shares of the Corporation which may be cast to elect directors of the Corporation, shall be deemed to be in a position to affect materially the control of the Corporation; or

1.1.2.2 The Corporation shall consolidate or merge with or into, amalgamate with, or enter into a statutory arrangement with, any other person (other than a subsidiary of the Corporation) or any other person (other than a subsidiary of the Corporation) shall consolidate or merge with or into, or amalgamate with or enter into a statutory arrangement with, the Corporation, and, in connection therewith, all or part of the outstanding voting shares of the Corporation shall be changed in any way, reclassified or converted into, exchanged or otherwise acquired for share or other securities of any other person or for cash or any other property; or

1.1.2.3 The Corporation shall sell or otherwise transfer, including by way of the grant of a leasehold interest (or one or more of its subsidiaries shall sell or otherwise transfer, including by way of the grant of a leasehold interest) property or assets (a) aggregating more than 50% of the consolidated assets (measured by either book value or fair market value) of the Corporation and its subsidiaries as at the end of the most recently completed financial year of the Corporation or (b) which during the most recently completed financial year of the Corporation generated, or during the then current financial year of the Corporation are expected to generate, more than 50% of the consolidated operating income or cash flow of the Corporation and its subsidiaries, to any other person or persons (other than the Corporation or one or more of its subsidiaries);

1.1.3 **"Expiry Date"** means twelve (12) months after a Change in Control occurs; and

1.1.4 **"Triggering Event"** means any one of the following events which occurs without the express or implied agreement of the Executive:

1.1.4.1 An adverse change in any of the duties, powers, privileges, rights, discretion, salary or benefits of the Executive as they exist at the date of this Agreement; or

1.1.4.2 A diminution of the title of the Executive as it exists at the date of the Agreement; or

1.1.4.3 A change in the person or body to whom the Executive reports at the date of this Agreement, except if such person or body is of equivalent rank or stature or such body, as the case may be, provided that this shall not include a change resulting from a promotion in the normal course of business.

ARTICLE 2- RIGHTS UPON OCCURRENCE OF TRIGGERING EVENT

2.1   If a Change in Control occurs and if, in respect of the Executive, a Triggering Event occurs on or before the Expiry Date, the Executive shall be entitled to elect to terminate his Consulting Agreement with the Corporation and to receive a payment from the Corporation in an amount equal to two times (2x) his highest annual compensation, if any, for the past two (2) years of his consulting relationship with the Corporation (or such shorter period as applicable). This Article 2 shall not be applied if such Triggering Event follows a Change in Control which involves a sale of securities or assets of the Corporation in which the Executive is involved as a purchaser in any manner, whether directly or indirectly (by way of participation in a corporation or partnership as principal, that is a purchaser or by provision of debt, equity or purchase leaseback financing).

2.2   The rights of the Executive created by operation of this Agreement are NOT intended to apply in respect of any Change of Control relative to any arrangement or Change of Control that has been made:

2.2.1   Pursuant to the written consent of the Executive, or

2.2.2   With the active participation of the Executive to execute and complete any such Change of Control, or

14

2.2.3 Pursuant to a lawfully passed resolution of the Board of Directors in connection with a consensual transaction with any third party. For greater certainty this article 2.2.3 shall not relate to any hostile take-over or any other action not fully supported by the then current Board of Directors of the Corporation.

ARTICLE 3-TERMINATION OF RIGHTS CONDITIONAL

3.1   All termination rights of the Executive provided for in Article 2 are conditional upon the Executive electing to exercise such rights by notice given to the Corporation up to six (6) months after Expiry Date and are exercisable only if the Executive does not resign from his consulting with the Corporation for at least sixty (60) days following the date of the Change in Control.

ARTICLE 4- RIGHTS UPON DISMISSAL WITHOUT CAUSE

4.1   The Executive shall be entitled to a payment by the Corporation of the amount calculated as provided for in Article 2 if a Triggering Event does not occur but the Executive is dismissed from his Consulting Agreement with the Corporation without cause, as defined in the Consulting Agreement or otherwise, after a Change in Control and within twelve (12) months after the Change in Control. The Corporation shall not dismiss the Executive for any reason unless such dismissal is specifically approved by the Board of Directors of the Corporation.

ARTICLE 5- PAYMENT UNDER THIS AGREEMENT

5.1   Any payment to be made by the Corporation pursuant to the terms of this Agreement shall be paid by the Corporation in cash in a lump sum within five (5) business days of the giving of notice by the Executive pursuant to Article 3, or within five (5) business days of the dismissal from the Executive's consulting as referred to in Article 4, as the case may be. Any such payment shall be calculated, in the case of Article 2, at the date of giving notice pursuant to Article 3, and, in the case of Article 4, at the date of dismissal.

ARTICLE 6 PAYMENTS IN LIEU OF ALL OTHER DAMAGE CLAIMS, ETC.

6.1   All payments provided for herein shall be in lieu of all other notice or damage claims as regards dismissal or termination of the Executive's consulting with the Corporation or any subsidiary of the Corporation after a Change in Control and the Executive shall be barred from making any claim in that regard.

ARTICLE 7- AGREEMENT SUPPLEMENTAL

7.1   This Agreement shall be supplemental to any other contract, including but not limited to the Consulting Agreement, whether written or oral, that exists between the Corporation or any subsidiary of the Corporation and the Executive, except insofar as any such contract of consulting relates to the termination of the consulting relationship between the Corporation or any subsidiary of the Corporation and the Executive, in which case this Agreement shall supersede the termination provisions of any such contract.

15

ARTICLE 8- BENEFIT PLANS

8.1   In the event that the Executive is entitled to a payment pursuant to Article 2 or 4, the Executive shall be entitled to have all Benefit Plans continued for a period of twelve (12) months after the date of the giving of notice by the Executive pursuant to Article 3, or the dismissal from the Executive's consulting or for any longer period available under any Benefit Plan when coverage is provided from a source other than the Corporation.

8.2   The Corporation shall ensure that all benefits that the Executive may be entitled to receive under any medical and family medical coverage, group disability or life insurance plans Including but not limited to, premiums paid, of the Corporation to which the Executive may be entitled upon termination of the Executive's contract are transferred to the Executive.

ARTICLE 9 - STOCK OPTIONS

9.1   In the event that the Executive is entitled to a payment pursuant to Article 2 or 4 herein, then, subject to Article 3 herein, all unexpired stock options granted to the Executive by the Corporation, or any subsidiary of the Corporation, shall be deemed to be exercised, and the Corporation shall deliver to the Executive that number of common shares for which the Executive is entitled to receive, as a result of the deemed exercise of all the Executive's stock options, without any payment whatsoever required from the Executive to the Corporation for the common shares due to the Executive as a result of the deemed exercise of the options hereunder. The terms of any stock option agreement shall be deemed and are hereby irrevocably amended to reflect the provisions of this Article 9.

ARTICLE 10- DESIGNATION OF BENEFICIARY

10.1   In the even that the Executive dies prior to the satisfaction of all of the Corporation's obligations under the terms of this Agreement, any remaining amounts payable to the Executive by the Corporation shall be paid to the person or persons previously designated by the Executive to the Corporation for such purposes. Any such designation of beneficiaries shall be made in writing, signed by the Executive and dated and filed with the Secretary of the Corporation. In the event that no designation is made, all such remaining amounts shall be paid by the Corporation to the estate of the Executive.

ARTICLE 11 -ASSIGNMENT

11.1   This Agreement shall be assigned by the Corporation to any successor corporation of the Corporation and shall be binding upon such successor corporation. For the purposes of this Article 11, "Successor Corporation" shall include any person referred to in Article 1.1.2. The Corporation shall ensure that the successor corporation shall continue the provisions of this Agreement as if it were the original party in place of the Corporation; provided, however, that the Corporation shall not thereby be relieved of any obligation to the Executive pursuant to this Agreement. In the event of a transaction or series of transactions as described in Article 1.1.2, appropriate arrangements shall be made by the Corporation for the successor corporation to honor this Agreement as If the Executive had exercised his maximum rights hereunder as of the effective date of such transaction.

16

ARTICLE 12- FURTHER ASSURANCES

12.1   Each of the parties hereto agrees to do and execute or cause to be made, done or executed all such further and other things, acts, deeds, documents, assignments and assurances as may be necessary or reasonably required to carry out the intent and purpose of this Agreement fully and effectually. Without limiting the generality of the foregoing, the Corporation shall take all reasonable steps in order to structure the payment or payments provided for in this Agreement in the manner most advantageous to the Executive with respect to the provisions of the Income Tax Act (United States) or similar legislation in place in the jurisdiction of the Executive's residence.

ARTICLE 13 - REVIEW OF AGREEMENT

13.1   In the event of a threatened or pending Change in Control of the Corporation, or following a Change in Control of the Corporation which is not followed within six (6) months by a Triggering Event in respect of the Executive, the Corporation in either case shall enter into a review of the terms of this Agreement and shall implement any amendments hereto which are agreed to by both parties.

ARTICLE 14-GENDER

14.1   Whenever the context of this Agreement so requires or permits, the masculine gender includes the feminine gender.

ARTICLE 15- NOTICE

15.1   Any election or designation to be made by the either party pursuant to the terms of this Agreement shall be by writing and shall be delivered to the either party at the following address

    15.1.1 If to the Corporation to:

        Tankless Systems Worldwide, Inc.
        7650 E. Evans Rd. Suite C
        Scottsdale, AZ 85260   Attention: Secretary

    15.1.2 If to the Executive to:

        Gregg C. Johnson
        9630 W. Rimrock Dr.
        Peoria, AZ 85382

ARTICLE 16-TERM

16.1   This Agreement shall commence as of the date first above written and shall terminate on July 31, 2008 unless extended with the mutual agreement of the parties hereto and approved by the Board of Directors of the Corporation.

ARTICLE 17- GOVERNING LAW

17.1   This Agreement shall be governed by and construed in accordance with the laws of the State of Arizona and the parties specifically attorn to the jurisdiction of the courts of the State of Arizona.

IN WITNESS WHEREOF, the parties have duly executed this Agreement.

TANKLESS SYSTEMS WORLDWIDE, INC.

Per:_____

SIGNED, SEALED AND DELIVERED in the)
Presence of:)
)
)
)   _____
)
)   **Gregg C. Johnson**
)
_____)
Witness

Thomas Kreitzer

From:	Thomas Kreitzer [Thomas@KreitzerBrothers.com]
Sent:	Monday, May 22, 2006 12:40 PM
To:	'Gregg Johnson'
Subject:	Consulting Agreement
Follow Up Flag:	Follow up
Flag Status:	Green
Attachments:	Johnson Consulting Agreement-Skye.pdf

Gregg,

Here is the original PDF of the contract which was executed on Aug 1 2005.

I do not have one executed by yourself in my file. I guess we shouldn't have been paying you

all of these months if you didn't sign it... ☺

Thomas

From: Gregg Johnson [mailto:gregg.johnson@skye-betterliving.com]
Sent: Monday, May 22, 2006 1:55 PM
To: 'Thomas Kreitzer'; thomas_kreitzer@hotmail.com
Subject: C DOCUME~1 gjohnson LOCALS~1 Temp AttachmentsTemp(5) Consulting Agreement - Gregg Johnson

Tom:

On review of my records I still have not received a signed copy back of this agreement. If you have it will you please PDF and email back to me.

I will countersign once I receive your signed copy.

This is my agreement that dates back to January 1, 2005 and revised to be effective August 1, 2005. I know you have said that it was signed but I have no copy and the auditors want it for their files.

Gregg

--
No virus found in this incoming message.
Checked by AVG Free Edition.
Version: 7.1.392 / Virus Database: 268.6.0/342 - Release Date: 5/17/2006

--
No virus found in this outgoing message.
Checked by AVG Free Edition.
Version: 7.1.392 / Virus Database: 268.6.0/342 - Release Date: 5/17/2006

9/19/2006

EXHIBIT 5

PERSONAL SERVICES CONSULTING AGREEMENT

THIS AGREEMENT made effective as of the 1st day of August 2005.

BETWEEN:

> **TANKLESS SYSTEMS WORLDWIDE, INC.**, a body corporate duly incorporated pursuant to the laws of the State of Nevada, with principal offices in the City of Scottsdale, in the State of Arizona, together with all of its wholly owned subsidiaries from time to time operating (hereinafter, collectively referred to as the "Corporation").

> - and -

> **GREGG C JOHNSON.**, an individual currently residing in the City of Peoria, AZ (the "Executive").

RECITALS

WHEREAS, the Corporation is engaged in the business of designing, manufacturing and marketing a line of tankless water heaters, as well as a suite of household and commercial health and wellness related appliances and other devices;

AND, WHEREAS, the Corporation wishes to contract for the services of the Executive to serve as the President and Chief Executive Officer of the Corporation, and the Executive wishes to be contracted by the Corporation as its President and Chief Executive Officer;

AND WHEREAS, the Corporation has caused to be issued Seven Hundred & Fifty Thousand restricted common shares of the Corporation to the Executive in consideration for the Executive agreeing to join the Corporation and to act in the capacity as its consultant and Chief Executive Officer;

AND WHEREAS, the Executive has agreed that such shares shall not be eligible for sale, transfer, hypothecation or other disposition except otherwise as in accordance with Schedule "B" attached hereto;

AND WHEREAS, the Executive acknowledges that he has been issued Five Hundred Thousand (500,000) options to purchase common shares of the Corporation's securities at $0.50 per share for a period of five (5) years from and after December 24, 2004 as consideration for all stock-based executive incentive compensation for a three (3) year period from the date of issuance thereof; and

NOW, THEREFORE, THIS AGREEMENT WITNESSETH, that inconsideration of the premises and covenants and agreements hereinafter contained it is agreed by and between the parties as follows:

PDOCS000487

11.6   This Agreement shall ensure to the benefit of and be binding upon the parties hereto, their heirs, administrators, successors and legal representatives. This Agreement may be assigned by the Corporation but may not be assigned by the Executive.

IN WITNESS WHEREOF, the parties have duly executed this Agreement.

TANKLESS SYSTEMS WORLDWIDE, INC.

Per: _____

Wrong seal used. No such seal at the purported time.

SIGNED, SEALED AND DELIVERED in the)
Presence of:)
)
)
)   **Gregg C. Johnson**
)
)
_____)
Witness

PDOCS000494

ARTICLE 17- GOVERNING LAW

17.1   This Agreement shall be governed by and construed in accordance with the laws of the State of Arizona and the parties specifically attorn to the jurisdiction of the courts of the State of Arizona.

IN WITNESS WHEREOF, the parties have duly executed this Agreement.

No such seal at the time.

TANKLESS SYSTEMS WORLDWIDE, INC.

Per:

SIGNED, SEALED AND DELIVERED in the)
Presence of:)
)
)
)
)   **Gregg C. Johnson**
)
)
_____)
Witness

18

PDOCS000504

Ken,

Gregg had me deliver this for the auditors.

Please be sure it is the right version.

Thanks,

Thomas

From: Gregg Johnson [mailto:gregg.johnson@skye-betterliving.com]
Sent: Monday, May 22, 2006 1:55 PM
To: 'Thomas Kreitzer'; thomas_kreitzer@hotmail.com
Subject: C DOCUME~1 gjohnson LOCALS~1 Temp AttachmentsTemp(5) Consulting Agreement - Gregg Johnson

Tom:

On review of my records I still have not received a signed copy back of this agreement. If you have it will you please PDF and email back to me.

I will countersign once I receive your signed copy.

This is my agreement that dates back to January 1, 2005 and revised to be effective August 1, 2005. I know you have said that it was signed but I have no copy and the auditors want it for their files.

Gregg

--
No virus found in this incoming message.
Checked by AVG Free Edition.
Version: 7.1.392 / Virus Database: 268.6.0/342 - Release Date: 5/17/2006

--
No virus found in this outgoing message.
Checked by AVG Free Edition.
Version: 7.1.392 / Virus Database: 268.6.0/342 - Release Date: 5/17/2006

--
No virus found in this outgoing message.
Checked by AVG Free Edition.
Version: 7.1.392 / Virus Database: 268.6.0/342 - Release Date: 5/17/2006

PDOCS000506

9/19/2006

EXHIBIT 6

SCHEDULE C

Change of Control Agreement

CHANGE OF CONTROL AGREEMENT

THIS AGREEMENT made the 1st day of August 2005.

BETWEEN:

>**TANKLESS SYSTEMS WORLDWIDE, INC.**, a body corporate duly incorporated pursuant to the laws of the State of Nevada, with principal offices in the City of Scottsdale, in the State of Arizona, together with all of its wholly owned subsidiaries from time to time operating (hereinafter collectively referred to as the "Corporation")..

>**OF THE FIRST PART**

>- and -

>**GREGG C JOHNSON**., an individual currently residing in the City of Peoria, AZ (the "Executive").

>**OF THE SECOND PART**

WHEREAS, the Executive entered into that certain Personal Services Consulting Agreement made in writing dated effective August 1, 2005 (the "Consulting Agreement") with the Corporation;

AND, WHEREAS, the Executive and the Corporation agree that it is in the best interests of both parties to enter into this Change of Control Agreement concurrent with the execution of the Consulting Agreement;

AND, WHEREAS, the Company and the Executive are desirous of having certain rights and benefits in the event that the Executive is dismissed or the Executive's consulting relationship with the Corporation is terminated in the manner set out herein;

AND, WHEREAS, the Corporation wishes to retain the benefit of the Executive's services and to ensure that the Executive is able to carry out his responsibilities with the Corporation free from any distractions associated with any change in the ownership of the Corporation or its assets.

12

Thomas Kreitzer

From:	Thomas Kreitzer [Thomas@KreitzerBrothers.com]
Sent:	Monday, May 22, 2006 12:49 PM
To:	'Pinckard@azbar.org'
Cc:	'RyckmanL@AOL.com'
Subject:	FW: Consulting Agreement
Follow Up Flag:	Follow up
Flag Status:	Green
Attachments:	Tankless Agreement- Johnson.pdf

Ken,

Here is the signed PDF with the correct seal. Gregg does not have this one. He has one with Skye Seals but it needs tankless seals. I won't send him the valid one until I get the ok from you and larry.

He says he needs it today.

Thomas

From: Thomas Kreitzer [mailto:Thomas@KreitzerBrothers.com]
Sent: Monday, May 22, 2006 2:43 PM
To: Ken Pinckard (vestnik@aol.com)
Cc: 'RyckmanL@AOL.com'
Subject: FW: Consulting Agreement

Ken,

Gregg had me deliver this for the auditors.

Please be sure it is the right version.

Thanks,

Thomas

From: Gregg Johnson [mailto:gregg.johnson@skye-betterliving.com]
Sent: Monday, May 22, 2006 1:55 PM
To: 'Thomas Kreitzer'; thomas_kreitzer@hotmail.com
Subject: C DOCUME~1 gjohnson LOCALS~1 Temp AttachmentsTemp(5) Consulting Agreement - Gregg Johnson

Tom:

On review of my records I still have not received a signed copy back of this agreement. If you have it will you please PDF and email back to me.

I will countersign once I receive your signed copy.

This is my agreement that dates back to January 1, 2005 and revised to be effective August 1, 2005. I know you have said that it was signed but I have no copy and the auditors want it for their files.

Gregg

PDOCS000526

9/19/2006

EXHIBIT 7

--
No virus found in this incoming message.
Checked by AVG Free Edition.
Version: 7.1.392 / Virus Database: 268.6.0/342 - Release Date: 5/17/2006

--
No virus found in this outgoing message.
Checked by AVG Free Edition.
Version: 7.1.392 / Virus Database: 268.6.0/342 - Release Date: 5/17/2006

--
No virus found in this outgoing message.
Checked by AVG Free Edition.
Version: 7.1.392 / Virus Database: 268.6.0/342 - Release Date: 5/17/2006

--
No virus found in this outgoing message.
Checked by AVG Free Edition.
Version: 7.1.392 / Virus Database: 268.6.0/342 - Release Date: 5/17/2006

9/19/2006

PERSONAL SERVICES CONSULTING AGREEMENT

THIS AGREEMENT made effective as of the 1st day of August 2005.

BETWEEN:

TANKLESS SYSTEMS WORLDWIDE, INC., a body corporate duly incorporated pursuant to the laws of the State of Nevada, with principal offices in the City of Scottsdale, in the State of Arizona, together with all of its wholly owned subsidiaries from time to time operating (hereinafter, collectively referred to as the "Corporation").

- and -

GREGG C JOHNSON., an individual currently residing in the City of Peoria, AZ (the "Executive").

RECITALS

WHEREAS, the Corporation is engaged in the business of designing, manufacturing and marketing a line of tankless water heaters, as well as a suite of household and commercial health and wellness related appliances and other devices;

AND, WHEREAS, the Corporation wishes to contract for the services of the Executive to serve as the President and Chief Executive Officer of the Corporation, and the Executive wishes to be contracted by the Corporation as its President and Chief Executive Officer;

AND WHEREAS, the Corporation has caused to be issued Seven Hundred & Fifty Thousand restricted common shares of the Corporation to the Executive in consideration for the Executive agreeing to join the Corporation and to act in the capacity as its consultant and Chief Executive Officer;

AND WHEREAS, the Executive has agreed that such shares shall not be eligible for sale, transfer, hypothecation or other disposition except otherwise as in accordance with Schedule "B" attached hereto;

AND WHEREAS, the Executive acknowledges that he has been issued Five Hundred Thousand (500,000) options to purchase common shares of the Corporation's securities at $0.50 per share for a period of five (5) years from and after December 24, 2004 as consideration for all stock-based executive incentive compensation for a three (3) year period from the date of issuance thereof; and

NOW, THEREFORE, THIS AGREEMENT WITNESSETH, that inconsideration of the premises and covenants and agreements hereinafter contained it is agreed by and between the parties as follows:

PDOCS000528

11.6   This Agreement shall ensure to the benefit of and be binding upon the parties hereto, their heirs, administrators, successors and legal representatives. This Agreement may be assigned by the Corporation but may not be assigned by the Executive.

IN WITNESS WHEREOF, the parties have duly executed this Agreement.

TANKLESS SYSTEMS WORLDWIDE, INC.

Per: _____

Different seal affixed.

SIGNED, SEALED AND DELIVERED in the)
Presence of:)
)
)   _____
)   **Gregg C. Johnson**
)
_____   )
Witness

8

PDOCS000535

Schedule A

Duties
(as taken from the SKYE Organizational Manual)

Mistake as to use of name, not yet in existence, remains on document.

| President & Chief Executive Officer |
| (Chair – Executive Management Team) |

Reports to:	Board of Directors
Direct Reports:	Executive V.P and all Sr. V.P
Liaison:	Chairman of Board
	Chairman of all Board Committees
Job Description:	Board of Directors
Review & Comp	Corporate Governance Committee
Accountability:	Board of Directors

This position is the leader of the Executive Management Team and is the final responsible party for all business day-to-day planning and operations of the company.

The specific duties include, but are not limited to:

1.   Together with the Executive Management Team, directs overall business and organizational policies; develops, recommends and implements through subordinates; recommends annual and long-term company policies and goals to Board of Directors.

2.   Responsible for overall company financial, organizational and operational planning activities and growth.

3.   Chair of the Executive Management Team, responsible for approving budgetary and operational objectives, overseeing and reporting progress to the Board of Directors.

4.   Monitoring performance relative to established objectives and systematically monitor and evaluate operating results.

5.   Presents, together with the CFO, Balance sheet, operating and capital expenditure budgets to Board of Directors for approval.

6.   Formulates the Corporation's near term and long-range strategic plans and submits them to the Board of Directors for approval.

7.   Directs executives in matters concerning the development, production, promotion and sales of the Corporation's products.

8.   Promoting positive relations with customers, suppliers and the general public.

9

PDOCS000536

9. Directs the establishment of fair and appropriate policies for human resource management.

10. Responsible for the overall strategic management of the Corporation.

11. Responsible for the daily affairs of the Corporation.

12. Responsible for ensuring operational compliance with policies and procedures adopted by the Board of Directors.

13. Primary responsible party for ensuring systemic adherence to Compliance and Ethics mandate.

13. Together with Board members and the CFO is responsible for all capital fundraising requirements of the company.

14. Directs, oversees and manages all external contacts with parties involved with funding the capital requirements of the company.

15. Responsible for making all public representations in connection with investor relations activities.

16. Together with the Chairman is responsible for all presentations of material to the public.

17. Any other duty reasonably assigned by the Board of Directors

10

PDOCS000537

Thomas Kreitzer

From:	Thomas Kreitzer [Thomas@KreitzerBrothers.com]
Sent:	Monday, May 22, 2006 4:39 PM
To:	'Pinckard@azbar.org'
Subject:	Gregg
Follow Up Flag:	Follow up
Flag Status:	Green

What should my response be to Gregg?

I emailed that I had signed the one that had the wrong seal so it isn't any good. I now need to respond to his request for one that has the correct seal i.e. the one you got last.

Thanks,

Thomas

P.S. I am going to have to say something.

How does this sound:

Gregg,

After reviewing the singed agreement, that you did not receive, I realize that it was turned over to corporate council and returned to me with some suggested edits which is why it wasn't forwarded to you back in August of 2005.

The attached signed agreement has the enclosed edits.

Sincerely,

Thomas Kreitzer

(File Attached)

--
No virus found in this outgoing message.
Checked by AVG Free Edition.
Version: 7.1.392 / Virus Database: 268.6.0/342 - Release Date: 5/17/2006

--
No virus found in this outgoing message.
Checked by AVG Free Edition.
Version: 7.1.392 / Virus Database: 268.6.0/342 - Release Date: 5/17/2006

PDOCS000547

9/19/2006

EXHIBIT 8

Thomas Kreitzer

From:	Thomas Kreitzer [Thomas@KreitzerBrothers.com]
Sent:	Monday, May 22, 2006 5:12 PM
To:	'Pinckard@azbar.org'; Ken Pinckard (vestnik@aol.com)
Cc:	'RyckmanL@AOL.com'
Subject:	FW: C DOCUME~1 gjohnson LOCALS~1 Temp AttachmentsTemp(5) Consulting Agreement - Gregg Johnson
Follow Up Flag:	Follow up
Flag Status:	Green
Attachments:	C DOCUME~1 gjohnson LOCALS~1 Temp AttachmentsTemp(5) Consulting Agreement - Gregg Johnson.rtf

Document from Gregg

From: Gregg Johnson [mailto:gregg.johnson@skye-betterliving.com]
Sent: Monday, May 22, 2006 1:55 PM
To: 'Thomas Kreitzer'; thomas_kreitzer@hotmail.com
Subject: C DOCUME~1 gjohnson LOCALS~1 Temp AttachmentsTemp(5) Consulting Agreement - Gregg Johnson

Tom:

On review of my records I still have not received a signed copy back of this agreement. If you have it will you please PDF and email back to me.

I will countersign once I receive your signed copy.

This is my agreement that dates back to January 1, 2005 and revised to be effective August 1, 2005. I know you have said that it was signed but I have no copy and the auditors want it for their files.

Gregg

--
No virus found in this incoming message.
Checked by AVG Free Edition.
Version: 7.1.392 / Virus Database: 268.6.0/342 - Release Date: 5/17/2006

--
No virus found in this outgoing message.
Checked by AVG Free Edition.
Version: 7.1.392 / Virus Database: 268.6.0/342 - Release Date: 5/17/2006

9/19/2006

EXHIBIT 9

Thomas Kreitzer

From:	Thomas Kreitzer [Thomas@KreitzerBrothers.com]
Sent:	Monday, May 22, 2006 7:03 PM
To:	'Pinckard@azbar.org'
Cc:	Ken Pinckard (vestnik@aol.com); 'RyckmanL@AOL.com'
Subject:	Should I just have Gregg Call you or Larry?
Follow Up Flag:	Follow up
Flag Status:	Green

--
No virus found in this outgoing message.
Checked by AVG Free Edition.
Version: 7.1.392 / Virus Database: 268.6.0/342 - Release Date: 5/17/2006

PDOCS000584

9/19/2006

EXHIBIT 10

Thomas Kreitzer

From:	Thomas Kreitzer [Thomas@KreitzerBrothers.com]
Sent:	Monday, May 22, 2006 7:45 PM
To:	'Pinckard@azbar.org'
Subject:	Gregg Contract
Follow Up Flag:	Follow up
Flag Status:	Green
Attachments:	Gregg Doc.rtf

Doc Attached

--
No virus found in this outgoing message.
Checked by AVG Free Edition.
Version: 7.1.392 / Virus Database: 268.6.0/342 - Release Date: 5/17/2006

9/19/2006

PERSONAL SERVICES CONSULTING AGREEMENT

THIS AGREEMENT made effective as of the 1st day of August 2005.

BETWEEN:

TANKLESS SYSTEMS WORLDWIDE, INC., a body corporate duly incorporated pursuant to the laws of the State of Nevada, with principal offices in the City of Scottsdale, in the State of Arizona, together with all of its wholly owned subsidiaries from time to time operating (hereinafter, collectively referred to as the "Corporation").

- and -

GREGG C JOHNSON., an individual currently residing in the City of Peoria, AZ (the "Executive").

RECITALS

WHEREAS, the Corporation is engaged in the business of designing, manufacturing and marketing a line of tankless water heaters, as well as a suite of household and commercial health and wellness related appliances and other devices;

AND, WHEREAS, the Corporation wishes to contract for the services of the Executive to serve as the President and Chief Executive Officer of the Corporation, and the Executive wishes to be contracted by the Corporation as its President and Chief Executive Officer;

AND WHEREAS, the Corporation has caused to be issued Seven Hundred & Fifty Thousand restricted common shares of the Corporation to the Executive in consideration for the Executive agreeing to join the Corporation and to act in the capacity as its consultant and Chief Executive Officer;

AND WHEREAS, the Executive has agreed that such shares shall not be eligible for sale, transfer, hypothecation or other disposition except otherwise as in accordance with Schedule "B" attached hereto;

AND WHEREAS, the Executive acknowledges that he has been issued Five Hundred Thousand (500,000) options to purchase common shares of the Corporation's securities at $0.50 per share for a period of five (5) years from and after December 24, 2004 as consideration for all stock-based executive incentive compensation for a three (3) year period from the date of issuance thereof; and

NOW, THEREFORE, THIS AGREEMENT WITNESSETH, that inconsideration of the premises and covenants and agreements hereinafter contained it is agreed by and between the parties as follows:

PDOCS000586

ARTICLE 1 - CONTRACT

1.1   The Executive will, during the Term (as defined below) or any renewals thereof, perform all of the Duties (as defined below) as the Corporation by action of its Board of Directors shall, from time to time, reasonably assign to the Executive. The Corporation and Executive further agree that any prior employment and/or consulting agreements entered into between the parties are hereby terminated effective the date of this Agreement.

ARTICLE 2- TERM

2.1   Subject to the prior termination of this Agreement as provided herein, the contracting of the Executive by the Corporation shall commence on August 1, 2005, and end on July 31, 2008 (the "Term').

2.2   Subject to the prior termination of this Agreement as herein provided, upon the expiration of the Term, the Corporation may extend the contract period of the Executive for such period or periods and under such conditions as mutually agreed to by the parties; provided that, any such agreement to extend the contract shall only be binding if made in writing and signed by the parties hereto. For greater certainty, it is understood that Term shall refer to the original term of this Agreement as defined in Article 2.1 herein and to any renewal thereof.

ARTICLE 3 - DUTIES

3.1   The Executive shall, during the Term of this Agreement, perform all of the duties and responsibilities (the "Duties') as the Corporation shall from time to time reasonably assign to the Executive and, without limiting the generality of the foregoing, the Duties shall include those duties set forth in Schedule "A" attached hereto, as from time to time reasonably amended by the Board of Directors of the Corporation. During the Term of this Agreement, the Executive shall devote the majority of the Executive's time and attention to the Duties, and shall do all in the Executives power to promote, develop and extend the business of the Corporation and its subsidiaries and related corporations.

3.2   The Executive shall truly and faithfully account for and deliver to the Corporation all money, securities and things of value belonging to the Corporation which the Executive may from time to time receive for, from or on account of the Corporation.

ARTICLE 4- REMUNERATION

4.1   Subject to Article 4.5 below, the gross annual cash compensation of the Executive shall be the greater of (i) One Hundred Eighty Thousand ($180,000) US Dollars, or (ii) an amount equal to one per cent (1.0%) of the gross sales (the 'Revenue Share") actually achieved by the Corporation during each fiscal year (hereinafter, the "Compensation"). Such Compensation shall be calculated by multiplying the Corporation's actual revenue figure achieved in the month by 0.01. For greater certainty, should such calculation result in an amount of less than Fifteen Thousand ($15,000) US Dollars being paid to the Executive in any monthly period, the Executive shall be entitled to receive the full amount of Fifteen Thousand ($15,000) US Dollars. All Compensation payable hereunder shall be payable on a monthly basis with a mid-month advance of Five Thousand

2

($5,000) US Dollars payable on the 15th of the month with the balance payable on the 5th of the succeeding month. For greater certainty, the Executive acknowledges and confirms that such Compensation methodology is inclusive of any annual bonus or other customary emoluments, perquisites or payments other than those specifically granted under the terms of this Agreement

4.2   Alternate Payment: The Executive agrees that up to 2/3 of such Compensation payable in accordance with Article 4.1 above may, at the discretion of the Board of Directors, be paid in the form of freely-tradable securities of the Corporation representing a value at the time of payment equal to at least the value of such unpaid (cash) Compensation ("Stock Based Payment"). For greater certainty, any securities issued to the Executive in connection with the Stock Based Payment shall be freely-tradable, and shall be priced at the lowest closing bid price of the Corporation's securities over the ten (10) trading days prior to the issuance of securities under such Stock Based Payment mechanism.

4.2   The Executive shall also be entitled to participate, **only if such plans exist**, in the Corporation's group benefit plan, medical and family medical plan, stock savings plan, and disability insurance plan. It is understood that all costs associated with such plans will be borne by the Corporation.

4.3   The Executive will be reimbursed for reasonable business expenses, within such policy guidelines as may be established from time to time, by the Corporation's Board of Directors, provided that such business expenses are incurred in the ordinary course of performing the Duties.

4.4   During the Term hereof the Corporation shall provide the Executive with reimbursement of vehicle operating and insurance costs. For greater certainty the Executive shall NOT be entitled to any other automobile allowance

4.5   The Executive shall NOT be entitled to participate in annual grants of stock options in accordance with the Corporation's Stock Option Plan. The Executive herby confirms that he has received Five Hundred Thousand (500,000) options under that certain Stock Option Agreement, dated December 23, 2004.

ARTICLE 5-BENEFITS AND HOLIDAYS

5.1   The Executive shall be entitled to four (4) weeks paid holidays during each year of the Term. Holidays must be taken at times that are satisfactory to the Corporation, acting reasonably, and must be taken within the year to which the holiday relates and holidays not taken shall be deemed to have been taken and no other compensation shall be payable by the Corporation. For greater clarity it is understood that for the purpose of determining the number of holidays for which the Executive is entitled, each year of the Term will commence on January 1st and end on December 31st.

ARTICLE 6-CONFIDENTIALITY

6.1   The Executive shall not, either during the continuance of the Executive's contract hereunder or at any time after termination of the Executive as consultant to the Corporation, for any reason whatsoever (except in the proper course of carrying out the Duties, or otherwise required by law), divulge to any person whomsoever, and shall use the Executive's best endeavors to prevent the publication or disclosure of:

3

6.1.1   Any confidential information concerning the business or finances of the Corporation or any other corporation, person or entity for which he is directed to perform services hereunder or of any of their dealings, transactions or affairs, including, without limitation, personal and family matters which may come to the Executive's knowledge during or in the course of the Executive's contract: or

6.1.2   Any trade secrets, know-how, inventions, technology, designs, methods, formula, processes, copyrights, trade marks, trade mark applications, patents, patent applications or any other proprietary information and/or data of the Corporation (herein collectively called "Intellectual Property").

ARTICLE 7 - INVENTIONS AND PATENTS

7.1   If the Executive contributes to any invention whether patentable, patented, or not (an "Invention"), any intellectual property, or any improvement or modification to any Invention or intellectual property then the Executive's contribution thereto and the Invention, intellectual property or improvement thereof shall, without the payment of any additional compensation in any form whatsoever, become the exclusive property of the Corporation. The Executive shall execute any and all agreements, assurances or assignments that the Corporation may require and the Executive shall fully cooperate with the Corporation in the filing and prosecution of any patent applications. The Executive hereby reiterates and confirms the application of this Article to all such Inventions, intellectual property and improvements that have been made during the tenancy of that certain consulting position with the Corporation's subsidiaries.

ARTICLE 8- RESTRICTIVE COVENANT

8.1   The Executive will not at any time during the Term, or during any renewal thereof, and for a period of two (2) years following the expiration or termination of the Executive's contract for whatever cause, compete in the United States, directly or indirectly, with any of the businesses carried on by the Corporation, its subsidiaries or affiliates:

8.1.1   As a principal, partner employee;

8.1.2   As an officer, director or similar official of any incorporated or unincorporated entity engaged in any such competing business (the "Other Entity");

8.1,3   As a consultant or advisor to any Other Entity;

8.1.4   As a holder of shares or debt instrument of any kind of any Other Entity;

8.1.5   In any relationship described in subsections 81.1 through 8.1.4 of this section with any incorporated or unincorporated entity which provides services for or necessarily incidental to the business of an Other Entity:

without the prior express written consent of the Corporation, which consent may be withheld by the Corporation for any reason or for no reason.

4

8.2   Notwithstanding the provisions of Article 8.3 below, the Executive acknowledges and agrees that the time frames for which the aforesaid covenant shall apply have been considered by the Executive who has taken independent legal advice with respect thereto and the restraint and restriction of and on the future activities of the Executive are reasonable in the circumstances.

8.3   The parties agree that if the time frames set out in this Article are found to be unenforceable by a court of competent jurisdiction, the time frames will be amended to the time frames as established by a court of competent jurisdiction.

3.4   The Executive acknowledges that any breach of Articles 6, 7 & 8 will cause irreparable harm to the Corporation, for which the Corporation cannot be compensated by damages. The Executive agrees that in the event of a breach of the covenant contained in Articles 6, 7, & 8, the Corporation shall not be restricted to seeking damages only, but shall be entitled to injunctive and other equitable relief.

ARTICLE 9- TERMINATION OF CONTRACT

9.1   The Corporation may terminate this Agreement at any time for cause. The term "for cause" shall include any one or more of the following:

9.1.1   A significant and continuing breach or failure or a continual breaching or failing to observe any of the provisions herein;

9.1.2   An act of dishonesty fundamentally detrimental to the well-being of the Corporation;

9.1.3   Any act of gross negligence relating to completing the Duties;

9.1.4   The commission of a felony offence for which the Executive is convicted, which significantly impairs the Executive's ability to perform the Duties and responsibilities hereunder or which materially adversely affects the reputation enjoyed by the Corporation; or

9.1.5   The failure to comply with reasonable instructions, orders and directions of the Board of Directors of the Corporation in so far as such instructions, orders and directions are not inconsistent with the Duties, or are, in the reasonable opinion of the Executive:

9.1.5.1   In any way demeaning or likely to result in diminution of the value of the Executives services in the future.

9.1.5.2   Likely to result in the conduct of an illegal act.

9.1.5.3   Inconsistent with any court order or other governmental order or directive.

9.1.5.4   Inconsistent with any shareholders' resolution passed at any duly convened meeting of shareholders.

provided that, with respect to each 9.1.1 through 9.1.5 above, the Executive shall be notified within five (5) business days from the date of any such alleged breach and provided a reasonable opportunity to respond thereto. For greater certainty,

5

PDOCS000590

the Corporation shall not be entitled to utilize any such provision to terminate this Agreement in respect of any action by the Executive that was: (i) not specifically brought to the attention of the Executive within such five (5) day period (ii) specifically required to be performed by direction of the board, directly or indirectly (iii) this dissemination of information required to be reported in the normal course with the Securities and Exchange Commission or any other competent governmental entity having jurisdiction over the Executive or the Corporation, or (iv) honestly and faithfully performed by the Executive for the benefit of the Corporation.

9.2   In the event that the Executive becomes physically or mentally disabled and is unable to perform the Duties for a period of twelve (12) months, as confirmed by a doctor's certificate, the Corporation shall be entitled to terminate this Agreement without further compensation upon sixty (60) days written notice to the Executive. In the case of the death of the Executive, all obligations of the Corporation under this Agreement shall cease immediately; provided that, this provision shall not affect any right, benefit or entitlement accruing to the Executive and/or his estate under any of the Corporation's benefit plans or stock option agreements which arise as a result of the Executive's prior performance hereunder or his death.

9.3   The Executive may terminate this Agreement, and the contract created herein, by giving at least Ninety (90) days prior written notice of such intention to the Corporation. After the expiry of such notice, all obligations, except for the obligations of the Executive under Articles 6, 7 and 8 hereof, which shall continue as provided in those Articles, of the Corporation and the Executive under this Agreement shall cease.

9,4   Notwithstanding anything contained in this Article 9, if there is a Change of Control of the Corporation, as defined in the Change of Control Agreement set out as Schedule "C" attached hereto, the provisions of the Change of Control Agreement shall supersede and take precedence over the termination provisions and covenants contained in this Article 9.

ARTICLE 10-OTHER AGREEMENTS IN RESPECT OF TERMINATION

10.1   In the event of the termination of this Agreement for cause or otherwise howsoever:

10.1.1 The Executive shall resign as a director and/or officer of the Corporation or any subsidiary or related corporation and the Executive hereby appoints the Corporation as its attorney in fact for the purpose of executing any and all such documents to give effect to the foregoing; and

10.1.2 The Executive hereby authorizes the Corporation and any subsidiary or related corporation to set off against and deduct from any and all amounts owing to the Executive by way of salary, allowances, accrued leave, long service leave, reimbursements or any other emoluments or benefits owing to the Executive by the Corporation and any subsidiary or related corporation, any reasonable amounts owed by the Executive to the Corporation or any subsidiary or related corporation.

6

10.2   Notwithstanding any termination of this Agreement for any reason whatsoever, whether with or without cause, all of the provisions of Articles 6, 7 and 8 and any other provisions of this Agreement necessary to give efficacy and effect thereto shall continue in full force and effect following the termination of this Agreement.

ARTICLE 11 - GENERAL

11.1   This Agreement, and the Schedules attached hereto, constitute the entire agreement between the parties hereto and cancels, supersedes and replaces all previous written, verbal or implied terms, conditions and representations relating to the Executive's contract.

11.2   The failure of either party at any time to require strict performance by the other party of any provision hereof shall in no way affect the full right to require such performance at any time thereafter. Neither shall the waiver by either party of a breach of any provision hereof be taken or held to be a waiver of any succeeding breach of such provision or as a waiver of the provision itself.

11.3   Each article, paragraph, clause, sub-clause and provision of this Agreement shall be severable from each other and if for any reason any article, paragraph, clause, sub-clause or provision is invalid or unenforceable, such invalidity or unenforceability shall not prejudice or in any way affect the validity or enforceability of any other article, paragraph, clause, sub-clause or provision. This Agreement and each article, paragraph, clause, sub-clause and provision hereof shall be read and construed so as to give thereto the full effect thereof subject only to any contrary provision of the law to the extent that where this Agreement or any article, paragraph, clause, sub- clause or provision hereof would but for the provisions of this paragraph have been read and construed as being void or ineffective, it shall nevertheless be a valid agreement, article, paragraph, clause, sub-clause or provision as the case may be to the full extent to which it is not contrary to any provision of the law.

11.4   The parties hereto submit to the exclusive jurisdiction of the Courts of the State of Arizona in respect of any matter or thing arising out of this Agreement or pursuant thereto.

11.5   All notices to be given by either party hereto shall be delivered or sent by telegram, facsimile or cable to the following address or such other address as may be notified by either party:

    11.5.1 If to the Corporation to:

        Tankless Systems Worldwide, Inc.
        7650 E. Evans Rd. Suite C
        Scottsdale, AZ 85260   Attention: Secretary

    11.5.2 If to the Executive to:

        Gregg C. Johnson
        9630 W. Rimrock Dr.
        Peoria, AZ 85382

7

11.6   This Agreement shall ensure to the benefit of and be binding upon the parties hereto, their heirs, administrators, successors and legal representatives. This Agreement may be assigned by the Corporation but may not be assigned by the Executive.

IN WITNESS WHEREOF, the parties have duly executed this Agreement.

TANKLESS SYSTEMS WORLDWIDE, INC.

Per:

SIGNED, SEALED AND DELIVERED in the)
Presence of:)
)
)
)   _____
)   **Gregg C. Johnson**
)
_____)
Witness

8

Schedule A

Duties
(as taken from the SKYE Organizational Manual)

President & Chief Executive Officer (Chair – Executive Management Team)

Reports to:	Board of Directors
Direct Reports:	Executive V.P and all Sr. V.P
Liaison:	Chairman of Board Chairman of all Board Committees
Job Description:	Board of Directors
Review & Comp	Corporate Governance Committee
Accountability:	Board of Directors

This position is the leader of the Executive Management Team and is the final responsible party for all business day-to-day planning and operations of the company.

The specific duties include, but are not limited to:

1. Together with the Executive Management Team, directs overall business and organizational policies; develops, recommends and implements through subordinates; recommends annual and long-term company policies and goals to Board of Directors.

2. Responsible for overall company financial, organizational and operational planning activities and growth.

3. Chair of the Executive Management Team, responsible for approving budgetary and operational objectives, overseeing and reporting progress to the Board of Directors.

4. Monitoring performance relative to established objectives and systematically monitor and evaluate operating results.

5. Presents, together with the CFO, Balance sheet, operating and capital expenditure budgets to Board of Directors for approval.

6. Formulates the Corporation's near term and long-range strategic plans and submits them to the Board of Directors for approval.

7. Directs executives in matters concerning the development, production, promotion and sales of the Corporation's products.

8. Promoting positive relations with customers, suppliers and the general public.

9

PDOCS000594

9.   Directs the establishment of fair and appropriate policies for human resource management.

10.   Responsible for the overall strategic management of the Corporation.

11.   Responsible for the daily affairs of the Corporation.

12.   Responsible for ensuring operational compliance with policies and procedures adopted by the Board of Directors.

13.   Primary responsible party for ensuring systemic adherence to Compliance and Ethics mandate.

13.   Together with Board members and the CFO is responsible for all capital fundraising requirements of the company.

14.   Directs, oversees and manages all external contacts with parties involved with funding the capital requirements of the company.

15.   Responsible for making all public representations in connection with investor relations activities.

16.   Together with the Chairman is responsible for all presentations of material to the public.

17.   Any other duty reasonably assigned by the Board of Directors

10

Schedule B

Resale Restrictions

The Executive confirms and acknowledges that there are resale restrictions in respect of those Seven Hundred & Fifty Thousand (750,000) common shares of the Corporation (the "Shares") issued to the Executive in connection with his consultancy to the Corporation and by operation of this Agreement. The resale restrictions imposed under this Agreement and this Schedule are in addition to any other resale restriction that may be applicable by operation of state or federal securities laws.

The Shares shall be subject to a contractual restriction prohibiting the sale, transfer, hypothecation, pledge or other disposition until such shares are eligible for release from this contractual restriction in accordance with the Schedule set forth below.

The Executive shall be entitled to the release of this contractual resale restriction in respect of the Shares by the passing of time and/or active engagement with the Corporation as a consultant or officer thereof. Specifically, the resale restrictions imposed by this Schedule shall be removed in accordance with the following release schedule:

(A)   While employed by or consulting to the Corporation:

1.   On September 1, 2004   250,000 shares

2.   On September 1, 2005   250,000 shares

3.   On September 1, 2006   250,000 shares

(B)   Otherwise:

1.   One Hundred Thousand (100,000) shares for each year from and after September 1, 2004.

For greater certainty, the Executive shall not be entitled to combine the release criteria above so as to result in the accelerated release of such Shares beyond the maximum release schedule specified in category "A" above.

11

SCHEDULE C

Change of Control Agreement

CHANGE OF CONTROL AGREEMENT

THIS AGREEMENT made the 1st day of August 2005.

BETWEEN:

> **TANKLESS SYSTEMS WORLDWIDE, INC.**, a body corporate duly incorporated pursuant to the laws of the State of Nevada, with principal offices in the City of Scottsdale, in the State of Arizona, together with all of its wholly owned subsidiaries from time to time operating (hereinafter collectively referred to as the "Corporation")..

> **OF THE FIRST PART**

> - and -

> **GREGG C JOHNSON.**, an individual currently residing in the City of Peoria, AZ (the "Executive").

> **OF THE SECOND PART**

WHEREAS, the Executive entered into that certain Personal Services Consulting Agreement made in writing dated effective August 1, 2005 (the "Consulting Agreement") with the Corporation;

AND, WHEREAS, the Executive and the Corporation agree that it is in the best interests of both parties to enter into this Change of Control Agreement concurrent with the execution of the Consulting Agreement;

AND, WHEREAS, the Company and the Executive are desirous of having certain rights and benefits in the event that the Executive is dismissed or the Executive's consulting relationship with the Corporation is terminated in the manner set out herein;

AND, WHEREAS, the Corporation wishes to retain the benefit of the Executive's services and to ensure that the Executive is able to carry out his responsibilities with the Corporation free from any distractions associated with any change in the ownership of the Corporation or its assets.

12

PDOCS000597

NOW, THEREFORE, THIS AGREEMENT WITNESSETH, that in consideration of the premises and the mutual covenants and agreements hereinafter contained, and for good and valuable consideration (the receipt and sufficiency of which is hereby acknowledged by the parties hereto), it is agreed by and between the parties hereto as follows:

ARTICLE 1. - DEFINITIONS

1.1   Terms used in this Agreement but not otherwise defined herein have the meanings as set forth below:

1.1.1   **"Benefit Plans"** means any employee/consultant loan, insurance, long-term disability, medical, dental and other executive and employee consultant benefit plans, including any pension or group 401K plans, IRA contributions, prerequisites and privileges (including use of an automobile and club memberships) as may be provided by the Corporation or any subsidiary of the Corporation to the Executive;

1.1.2   **"Change in Control"** means a transaction or series of transactions whereby directly or indirectly and without express or implied agreement of the Executive and the Board of Directors:

1.1.2.1 Any person or combination of persons obtains a sufficient number of securities of the Corporation to affect materially the control of the Corporation; for the purposes of this Agreement, a person or combination of person holding shares or other securities in excess of the number which, directly or following conversion thereof, would entitled the holders thereof to cast 25% or more of the votes attaching to all shares of the Corporation which may be cast to elect directors of the Corporation, shall be deemed to be in a position to affect materially the control of the Corporation; or

1.1.2.2 The Corporation shall consolidate or merge with or into, amalgamate with, or enter into a statutory arrangement with, any other person (other than a subsidiary of the Corporation) or any other person (other than a subsidiary of the Corporation) shall consolidate or merge with or into, or amalgamate with or enter into a statutory arrangement with, the Corporation, and, in connection therewith, all or part of the outstanding voting shares of the Corporation shall be changed in any way, reclassified or converted into, exchanged or otherwise acquired for share or other securities of any other person or for cash or any other property; or

1.1.2.3 The Corporation shall sell or otherwise transfer, including by way of the grant of a leasehold interest (or one or more of its subsidiaries shall sell or otherwise transfer, including by way of the grant of a leasehold interest) property or assets (a) aggregating more than 50% of the consolidated assets (measured by either book value or fair market value) of the Corporation and its subsidiaries as at the end

13

of the most recently completed financial year of the Corporation or (b) which during the most recently completed financial year of the Corporation generated, or during the then current financial year of the Corporation are expected to generate, more than 50% of the consolidated operating income or cash flow of the Corporation and its subsidiaries, to any other person or persons (other than the Corporation or one or more of its subsidiaries);

1.1.3   **"Expiry Date"** means twelve (12) months after a Change in Control occurs; and

1.1.4   **"Triggering Event"** means any one of the following events which occurs without the express or implied agreement of the Executive:

    1.1.4.1 An adverse change in any of the duties, powers, privileges, rights, discretion, salary or benefits of the Executive as they exist at the date of this Agreement; or

    1.1.4.2 A diminution of the title of the Executive as it exists at the date of the Agreement; or

    1.1.4.3 A change in the person or body to whom the Executive reports at the date of this Agreement, except if such person or body is of equivalent rank or stature or such body, as the case may be, provided that this shall not include a change resulting from a promotion in the normal course of business.

ARTICLE 2- RIGHTS UPON OCCURRENCE OF TRIGGERING EVENT

2.1   If a Change in Control occurs and if, in respect of the Executive, a Triggering Event occurs on or before the Expiry Date, the Executive shall be entitled to elect to terminate his Consulting Agreement with the Corporation and to receive a payment from the Corporation in an amount equal to two times (2x) his highest annual compensation, if any, for the past two (2) years of his consulting relationship with the Corporation (or such shorter period as applicable), This Article 2 shall not be applied if such Triggering Event follows a Change in Control which involves a sale of securities or assets of the Corporation in which the Executive is involved as a purchaser in any manner, whether directly or indirectly (by way of participation in a corporation or partnership as principal, that is a purchaser or by provision of debt, equity or purchase leaseback financing).

2.2   The rights of the Executive created by operation of this Agreement are NOT intended to apply in respect of any Change of Control relative to any arrangement or Change of Control that has been made:

    2.2.1   Pursuant to the written consent of the Executive, or

    2.2.2   With the active participation of the Executive to execute and complete any such Change of Control, or

14

2.2.3   Pursuant to a lawfully passed resolution of the Board of Directors in connection with a consensual transaction with any third party. For greater certainty this article 2.2.3 shall not relate to any hostile take-over or any other action not fully supported by the then current Board of Directors of the Corporation.

ARTICLE 3-TERMINATION OF RIGHTS CONDITIONAL

3.1   All termination rights of the Executive provided for in Article 2 are conditional upon the Executive electing to exercise such rights by notice given to the Corporation up to six (6) months after Expiry Date and are exercisable only if the Executive does not resign from his consulting with the Corporation for at least sixty (60) days following the date of the Change in Control.

ARTICLE 4- RIGHTS UPON DISMISSAL WITHOUT CAUSE

4.1   The Executive shall be entitled to a payment by the Corporation of the amount calculated as provided for in Article 2 if a Triggering Event does not occur but the Executive is dismissed from his Consulting Agreement with the Corporation without cause, as defined in the Consulting Agreement or otherwise, after a Change in Control and within twelve (12) months after the Change in Control. The Corporation shall not dismiss the Executive for any reason unless such dismissal is specifically approved by the Board of Directors of the Corporation.

ARTICLE 5- PAYMENT UNDER THIS AGREEMENT

5.1   Any payment to be made by the Corporation pursuant to the terms of this Agreement shall be paid by the Corporation in cash in a lump sum within five (5) business days of the giving of notice by the Executive pursuant to Article 3, or within five (5) business days of the dismissal from the Executive's consulting as referred to in Article 4, as the case may be. Any such payment shall be calculated, in the case of Article 2, at the date of giving notice pursuant to Article 3, and, in the case of Article 4, at the date of dismissal.

ARTICLE 6 PAYMENTS IN LIEU OF ALL OTHER DAMAGE CLAIMS, ETC.

6.1   All payments provided for herein shall be in lieu of all other notice or damage claims as regards dismissal or termination of the Executive's consulting with the Corporation or any subsidiary of the Corporation after a Change in Control and the Executive shall be barred from making any claim in that regard.

ARTICLE 7- AGREEMENT SUPPLEMENTAL

7.1   This Agreement shall be supplemental to any other contract, including but not limited to the Consulting Agreement, whether written or oral, that exists between the Corporation or any subsidiary of the Corporation and the Executive, except insofar as any such contract of consulting relates to the termination of the consulting relationship between the Corporation or any subsidiary of the Corporation and the Executive, in which case this Agreement shall supersede the termination provisions of any such contract.

15

PDOCS000600

ARTICLE 8- BENEFIT PLANS

8.1   In the event that the Executive is entitled to a payment pursuant to Article 2 or 4, the Executive shall be entitled to have all Benefit Plans continued for a period of twelve (12) months after the date of the giving of notice by the Executive pursuant to Article 3, or the dismissal from the Executive's consulting or for any longer period available under any Benefit Plan when coverage is provided from a source other than the Corporation.

8.2   The Corporation shall ensure that all benefits that the Executive may be entitled to receive under any medical and family medical coverage, group disability or life insurance plans Including but not limited to, premiums paid, of the Corporation to which the Executive may be entitled upon termination of the Executive's contract are transferred to the Executive.

ARTICLE 9 - STOCK OPTIONS

9.1   In the event that the Executive is entitled to a payment pursuant to Article 2 or 4 herein, then, subject to Article 3 herein, all unexpired stock options granted to the Executive by the Corporation, or any subsidiary of the Corporation, shall be deemed to be exercised, and the Corporation shall deliver to the Executive that number of common shares for which the Executive is entitled to receive, as a result of the deemed exercise of all the Executive's stock options, without any payment whatsoever required from the Executive to the Corporation for the common shares due to the Executive as a result of the deemed exercise of the options hereunder. The terms of any stock option agreement shall be deemed and are hereby irrevocably amended to reflect the provisions of this Article 9.

ARTICLE 10- DESIGNATION OF BENEFICIARY

10.1   In the even that the Executive dies prior to the satisfaction of all of the Corporation's obligations under the terms of this Agreement, any remaining amounts payable to the Executive by the Corporation shall be paid to the person or persons previously designated by the Executive to the Corporation for such purposes. Any such designation of beneficiaries shall be made in writing, signed by the Executive and dated and filed with the Secretary of the Corporation. In the event that no designation is made, all such remaining amounts shall be paid by the Corporation to the estate of the Executive.

ARTICLE 11 -ASSIGNMENT

11.1   This Agreement shall be assigned by the Corporation to any successor corporation of the Corporation and shall be binding upon such successor corporation. For the purposes of this Article 11, "Successor Corporation" shall include any person referred to in Article 1.1.2. The Corporation shall ensure that the successor corporation shall continue the provisions of this Agreement as if it were the original party in place of the Corporation; provided, however, that the Corporation shall not thereby be relieved of any obligation to the Executive pursuant to this Agreement. In the event of a transaction or series of transactions as described in Article 1.1.2, appropriate arrangements shall be made by the Corporation for the successor corporation to honor this Agreement as If the Executive had exercised his maximum rights hereunder as of the effective date of such transaction.

16

ARTICLE 12- FURTHER ASSURANCES

12.1   Each of the parties hereto agrees to do and execute or cause to be made, done or executed all such further and other things, acts, deeds, documents, assignments and assurances as may be necessary or reasonably required to carry out the intent and purpose of this Agreement fully and effectually. Without limiting the generality of the foregoing, the Corporation shall take all reasonable steps in order to structure the payment or payments provided for in this Agreement in the manner most advantageous to the Executive with respect to the provisions of the Income Tax Act (United States) or similar legislation in place in the jurisdiction of the Executive's residence.

ARTICLE 13 - REVIEW OF AGREEMENT

13.1   In the event of a threatened or pending Change in Control of the Corporation, or following a Change in Control of the Corporation which is not followed within six (6) months by a Triggering Event in respect of the Executive, the Corporation in either case shall enter into a review of the terms of this Agreement and shall implement any amendments hereto which are agreed to by both parties.

ARTICLE 14-GENDER

14.1   Whenever the context of this Agreement so requires or permits, the masculine gender includes the feminine gender.

ARTICLE 15- NOTICE

15.1   Any election or designation to be made by the either party pursuant to the terms of this Agreement shall be by writing and shall be delivered to the either party at the following address

15.1.1 If to the Corporation to:

Tankless Systems Worldwide, Inc.
7650 E. Evans Rd. Suite C
Scottsdale, AZ 85260   Attention: Secretary

15.1.2 If to the Executive to:

Gregg C. Johnson
9630 W. Rimrock Dr.
Peoria, AZ 85382

ARTICLE 16-TERM

16.1   This Agreement shall commence as of the date first above written and shall terminate on July 31, 2008 unless extended with the mutual agreement of the parties hereto and approved by the Board of Directors of the Corporation.

17

PDOCS000602

ARTICLE 17- GOVERNING LAW

17.1   This Agreement shall be governed by and construed in accordance with the laws of the State of Arizona and the parties specifically attorn to the jurisdiction of the courts of the State of Arizona.

IN WITNESS WHEREOF, the parties have duly executed this Agreement.

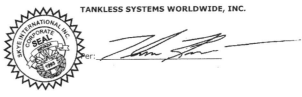

TANKLESS SYSTEMS WORLDWIDE, INC.

Per: _____

SIGNED, SEALED AND DELIVERED in the)
Presence of:)
)
)
)   **Gregg C. Johnson**
)
)
_____)
Witness

18

Thomas Kreitzer

From:	Thomas Kreitzer [Thomas@KreitzerBrothers.com]
Sent:	Tuesday, May 23, 2006 8:05 AM
To:	'Pinckard@azbar.org'
Cc:	Ken Pinckard (vestnik@aol.com)
Subject:	Revised Agreeent
Follow Up Flag: Follow up	
Flag Status:	Green

Ken,

I didn't get the copy of the correct Johnson agreement. Could you resend.

Thanks,

Thomas

--
No virus found in this outgoing message.
Checked by AVG Free Edition.
Version: 7.1.392 / Virus Database: 268.6.0/342 - Release Date: 5/17/2006

PDOCS000605

9/19/2006

EXHIBIT 11

Page 1 of 1

Thomas Kreitzer

From:	Thomas Kreitzer [Thomas@KreitzerBrothers.com]
Sent:	Tuesday, May 23, 2006 10:55 AM
To:	'Gregg Johnson'
Subject:	Signed Consulting Doc for Auditors
Follow Up Flag:	Follow up
Flag Status:	Green
Attachments:	Johnson Agreement - Tankless 08-01-05.pdf

Gregg,

The copy of the contract I forwarded yesterday which I added the Skye Seal to was never released or approved by the Board which is why you never received a copy. Here is a PDF I created from what I had board approval of back then. There was a lot going on back then so just use this one to get through the reporting. Please work with the new Board to get your final version approved and executed.

Thanks,

Thomas

From: Gregg Johnson [mailto:gregg.johnson@skye-betterliving.com]
Sent: Monday, May 22, 2006 1:55 PM
To: 'Thomas Kreitzer'; thomas_kreitzer@hotmail.com
Subject: C DOCUME~1 gjohnson LOCALS~1 Temp AttachmentsTemp(5) Consulting Agreement - Gregg Johnson

Tom:

On review of my records I still have not received a signed copy back of this agreement. If you have it will you please PDF and email back to me.

I will countersign once I receive your signed copy.

This is my agreement that dates back to January 1, 2005 and revised to be effective August 1, 2005. I know you have said that it was signed but I have no copy and the auditors want it for their files.

Gregg

--
No virus found in this incoming message.
Checked by AVG Free Edition.
Version: 7.1.392 / Virus Database: 268.6.0/342 - Release Date: 5/17/2006

--
No virus found in this outgoing message.
Checked by AVG Free Edition.
Version: 7.1.392 / Virus Database: 268.6.0/342 - Release Date: 5/17/2006

PDOCS000607

9/19/2006

Calculated to mislead

EXHIBIT 12

PERSONAL SERVICES CONSULTING AGREEMENT

THIS AGREEMENT made effective as of the 1st day of August 2005.

BETWEEN:

TANKLESS SYSTEMS WORLDWIDE, INC., a body corporate duly incorporated pursuant to the laws of the State of Nevada, with principal offices in the City of Scottsdale, in the State of Arizona, together with all of its wholly owned subsidiaries from time to time operating (hereinafter, collectively referred to as the "Corporation").

- and -

GREGG C JOHNSON., an individual currently residing in the City of Peoria, AZ (the "Executive").

RECITALS

WHEREAS, the Corporation is engaged in the business of designing, manufacturing and marketing a line of tankless water heaters, as well as a suite of household and commercial health and wellness related appliances and other devices;

AND, WHEREAS, the Corporation wishes to contract for the services of the Executive to serve as the an Officer of the Corporation, and the Executive wishes to be contracted by the Corporation as an Officer;

AND WHEREAS, the Corporation has caused to be issued Seven Hundred & Fifty Thousand restricted common shares of the Corporation to the Executive in consideration for the Executive agreeing to join the Corporation and to act in the capacity as its consultant and Officer;

AND WHEREAS, the Executive has agreed that such shares shall not be eligible for sale, transfer, hypothecation or other disposition except otherwise as in accordance with Schedule "B" attached hereto;

NOW, THEREFORE, THIS AGREEMENT WITNESSETH, that inconsideration of the premises and covenants and agreements hereinafter contained it is agreed by and between the parties as follows:

ARTICLE 1 - CONTRACT

1.1   The Executive will, during the Term (as defined below) or any renewals thereof, perform all of the Duties (as defined below) as the Corporation by action of its Board of Directors shall, from time to time, reasonably assign to the Executive. The Corporation and Executive further agree that any prior

PDOCS000608

employment and/or consulting agreements entered into between the parties are hereby terminated effective the date of this Agreement.

ARTICLE 2- TERM

2.1   Subject to the prior termination of this Agreement as provided herein, the contracting of the Executive by the Corporation shall commence on August 1, 2004, and end on July 31, 2007 (the "Term').

2.2   Subject to the prior termination of this Agreement as herein provided, upon the expiration of the Term, the Corporation may extend the contract period of the Executive for such period or periods and under such conditions as mutually agreed to by the parties; provided that, any such agreement to extend the contract shall only be binding if made in writing and signed by the parties hereto. For greater certainty, it is understood that Term shall refer to the original term of this Agreement as defined in Article 2.1 herein and to any renewal thereof.

ARTICLE 3 - DUTIES

3.1   The Executive shall, during the Term of this Agreement, perform all of the duties and responsibilities (the "Duties') as the Corporation shall from time to time reasonably assign to the Executive and, without limiting the generality of the foregoing, the Duties shall include those duties set forth in Schedule "A" attached hereto, as from time to time reasonably amended by the Board of Directors of the Corporation. During the Term of this Agreement, the Executive shall devote the majority of the Executive's time and attention to the Duties, and shall do all in the Executives power to promote, develop and extend the business of the Corporation and its subsidiaries and related corporations.

3.2   The Executive shall truly and faithfully account for and deliver to the Corporation all money, securities and things of value belonging to the Corporation which the Executive may from time to time receive for, from or on account of the Corporation.

ARTICLE 4- REMUNERATION

4.1   Subject to Article 4.5 below, the gross annual cash compensation of the Executive shall be the greater of (i) One Hundred Twenty Thousand ($120,000) US Dollars, or (ii) an amount equal to one per cent (1.0%) of the gross sales (the 'Revenue Share") actually achieved by the Corporation during each fiscal year (hereinafter, the "Compensation"). Such Compensation shall be calculated by multiplying the Corporation's actual revenue figure achieved in the month by 0.01. For greater certainty, should such calculation result in an amount of less than Ten Thousand ($10,000) US Dollars being paid to the Executive in any monthly period, the Executive shall be entitled to receive the full amount of Ten Thousand ($10,000) US Dollars. All Compensation payable hereunder shall be payable on a monthly basis with a mid-month advance of Five Thousand ($5,000) US Dollars payable on the 15th of the month with the balance payable on the 5th of the succeeding month. For greater certainty, the Executive acknowledges and confirms that such Compensation methodology is inclusive of any annual bonus or other customary emoluments, perquisites or payments other than those specifically granted under the terms of this Agreement

2

4.2   <u>Alternate Payment</u>:   The Executive agrees that up to 1/2 of such Compensation payable in accordance with Article 4.1 above may, at the discretion of the Board of Directors, be paid in the form of freely-tradable securities of the Corporation representing a value at the time of payment equal to at least the value of such unpaid (cash) Compensation ("Stock Based Payment"). For greater certainty, any securities issued to the Executive in connection with the Stock Based Payment shall be freely-tradable, and shall be priced at the lowest closing bid price of the Corporation's securities over the ten (10) trading days prior to the issuance of securities under such Stock Based Payment mechanism.

4.2   The Executive shall also be entitled to participate, ***only if such plans exist***, in the Corporation's group benefit plan, medical and family medical plan, stock savings plan, and disability insurance plan. It is understood that all costs associated with such plans will be borne by the Corporation.

4.3   The Executive will be reimbursed for reasonable business expenses, within such policy guidelines as may be established from time to time, by the Corporation's Board of Directors, provided that such business expenses are incurred in the ordinary course of performing the Duties.

4.4   During the Term hereof the Corporation shall provide the Executive with reimbursement of vehicle operating and insurance costs as approved by the Board of Directors from time to time. For greater certainty the Executive shall NOT be entitled to any other automobile allowance

4.5   The Executive shall NOT be entitled to participate in annual grants of stock options in accordance with the Corporation's Stock Option Plan.

ARTICLE 5-BENEFITS AND HOLIDAYS

5.1   The Executive shall be entitled to four (4) weeks paid holidays during each year of the Term. Holidays must be taken at times that are satisfactory to the Corporation, acting reasonably, and must be taken within the year to which the holiday relates and holidays not taken shall be deemed to have been taken and no other compensation shall be payable by the Corporation. For greater clarity it is understood that for the purpose of determining the number of holidays for which the Executive is entitled, each year of the Term will commence on January 1st and end on December 31st.

ARTICLE 6-CONFIDENTIALITY

6.1   The Executive shall not, either during the continuance of the Executive's contract hereunder or at any time after termination of the Executive as consultant to the Corporation, for any reason whatsoever (except in the proper course of carrying out the Duties, or otherwise required by law), divulge to any person whomsoever, and shall use the Executive's best endeavors to prevent the publication or disclosure of:

6.1.1   Any confidential information concerning the business or finances of the Corporation or any other corporation, person or entity for which he is directed to perform services hereunder or of any of their dealings, transactions or affairs, including, without limitation, personal and family matters which may come to the Executive's knowledge during or in the course of the Executive's contract: or

3

PDOCS000610

6.1.2 Any trade secrets, know-how, inventions, technology, designs, methods, formula, processes, copyrights, trade marks, trade mark applications, patents, patent applications or any other proprietary information and/or data of the Corporation (herein collectively called "Intellectual Property").

ARTICLE 7 - INVENTIONS AND PATENTS

7.1   If the Executive contributes to any invention whether patentable, patented, or not (an "Invention"), any intellectual property, or any improvement or modification to any Invention or intellectual property then the Executive's contribution thereto and the Invention, intellectual property or improvement thereof shall, without the payment of any additional compensation in any form whatsoever, become the exclusive property of the Corporation. The Executive shall execute any and all agreements, assurances or assignments that the Corporation may require and the Executive shall fully cooperate with the Corporation in the filing and prosecution of any patent applications. The Executive hereby reiterates and confirms the application of this Article to all such Inventions, intellectual property and improvements that have been made during the tenancy of that certain consulting position with the Corporation's subsidiaries.

ARTICLE 8- RESTRICTIVE COVENANT

8.1   The Executive will not at any time during the Term, or during any renewal thereof, and for a period of two (2) years following the expiration or termination of the Executive's contract for whatever cause, compete in the United States, directly or indirectly, with any of the businesses carried on by the Corporation, its subsidiaries or affiliates:

8.1.1 As a principal, partner employee;

8.1.2 As an officer, director or similar official of any incorporated or unincorporated entity engaged in any such competing business (the "Other Entity");

8.1,3 As a consultant or advisor to any Other Entity;

8.1.4 As a holder of shares or debt instrument of any kind of any Other Entity;

8.1.5 In any relationship described in subsections 81.1 through 8.1.4 of this section with any incorporated or unincorporated entity which provides services for or necessarily incidental to the business of an Other Entity:

without the prior express written consent of the Corporation, which consent may be withheld by the Corporation for any reason or for no reason.

8.2   Notwithstanding the provisions of Article 8.3 below, the Executive acknowledges and agrees that the time frames for which the aforesaid covenant shall apply have been considered by the Executive who has taken independent legal advice with respect thereto and the restraint and restriction of and on the future activities of the Executive are reasonable in the circumstances.

4

PDOCS000611

8.3   The parties agree that if the time frames set out in this Article are found to unenforceable by a court of competent jurisdiction, the time frames will be amended to the time frames as established by a court of competent jurisdiction.

3.4   The Executive acknowledges that any breach of Articles 6, 7 & 8 will cause irreparable harm to the Corporation, for which the Corporation cannot be compensated by damages. The Executive agrees that in the event of a breach of the covenant contained in Articles 6, 7, & 8, the Corporation shall not be restricted to seeking damages only, but shall be entitled to injunctive and other equitable relief.

ARTICLE 9- TERMINATION OF CONTRACT

9.1   The Corporation may terminate this Agreement at any time for cause. The term "for cause" shall include any one or more of the following:

9.1.1   A significant and continuing breach or failure or a continual breaching or failing to observe any of the provisions herein;

9.1.2   An act of dishonesty fundamentally detrimental to the well-being of the Corporation;

9.1.3   Any act of gross negligence relating to completing the Duties;

9.1.4   The commission of a felony offence for which the Executive is convicted, which significantly impairs the Executive's ability to perform the Duties and responsibilities hereunder or which materially adversely affects the reputation enjoyed by the Corporation; or

9.1.5   The failure to comply with reasonable instructions, orders and directions of the Board of Directors of the Corporation in so far as such instructions, orders and directions are not inconsistent with the Duties, or are, in the reasonable opinion of the Executive:

9.1.5.1   In any way demeaning or likely to result in diminution of the value of the Executives services in the future.

9.1.5.2   Likely to result in the conduct of an illegal act.

9.1.5.3   Inconsistent with any court order or other governmental order or directive.

9.1.5.4   Inconsistent with any shareholders' resolution passed at any duly convened meeting of shareholders.

9.1.6   In the event Executive shall be denied entry into the United States by the Immigration authorities of the United States and such inability to be physically present in the offices of the Corporation in Chandler, Arizona shall exist for a period of thirty (30) days or more.

provided that, with respect to each 9.1.1 through 9.1.5 (but not 9.1.6) above, the Executive shall be given written notification of any such alleged breach and provided a reasonable opportunity to respond thereto. For greater certainty, the

5

PDOCS000612

Corporation shall not be entitled to utilize any such provision to terminate this Agreement in respect of any action by the Executive that was: (i) specifically required to be performed by direction of the board, directly or indirectly (ii) the dissemination of information required to be reported in the normal course with the Securities and Exchange Commission or any other competent governmental entity having jurisdiction over the Executive or the Corporation, or (iii) honestly and faithfully performed by the Executive for the benefit of the Corporation.

9.2   In the event that the Executive becomes physically or mentally disabled and is unable to perform the Duties for a period of twelve (12) months, as confirmed by a doctor's certificate, the Corporation shall be entitled to terminate this Agreement without further compensation upon sixty (60) days written notice to the Executive. In the case of the death of the Executive, all obligations of the Corporation under this Agreement shall cease immediately; provided that, this provision shall not affect any right, benefit or entitlement accruing to the Executive and/or his estate under any of the Corporation's benefit plans or stock option agreements which arise as a result of the Executive's prior performance hereunder or his death.

9.3   The Executive may terminate this Agreement, and the contract created herein, by giving at least Ninety (90) days prior written notice of such intention to the Corporation. After the expiry of such notice, all obligations, except for the obligations of the Executive under Articles 6, 7 and 8 hereof, which shall continue as provided in those Articles, of the Corporation and the Executive under this Agreement shall cease.

ARTICLE 10-OTHER AGREEMENTS IN RESPECT OF TERMINATION

10.1   In the event of the termination of this Agreement for cause or otherwise howsoever:

10.1.1 The Executive shall resign as a director and/or officer of the Corporation or any subsidiary or related corporation and the Executive hereby appoints the Corporation as its attorney in fact for the purpose of executing any and all such documents to give effect to the foregoing; and

10.1.2 The Executive hereby authorizes the Corporation and any subsidiary or related corporation to set off against and deduct from any and all amounts owing to the Executive by way of salary, allowances, accrued leave, long service leave, reimbursements or any other emoluments or benefits owing to the Executive by the Corporation and any subsidiary or related corporation, any reasonable amounts owed by the Executive to the Corporation or any subsidiary or related corporation.

10.2   Notwithstanding any termination of this Agreement for any reason whatsoever, whether with or without cause, all of the provisions of Articles 6, 7 and 8 and any other provisions of this Agreement necessary to give efficacy and effect thereto shall continue in full force and effect following the termination of this Agreement.

6

ARTICLE 11 - GENERAL

11.1   This Agreement, and the Schedules attached hereto, constitute the entire agreement between the parties hereto and cancels, supersedes and replaces all previous written, verbal or implied terms, conditions and representations relating to the Executive's contract.

11.2   The failure of either party at any time to require strict performance by the other party of any provision hereof shall in no way affect the full right to require such performance at any time thereafter. Neither shall the waiver by either party of a breach of any provision hereof be taken or held to be a waiver of any succeeding breach of such provision or as a waiver of the provision itself.

11.3   Each article, paragraph, clause, sub-clause and provision of this Agreement shall be severable from each other and if for any reason any article, paragraph, clause, sub-clause or provision is invalid or unenforceable, such invalidity or unenforceability shall not prejudice or in any way affect the validity or enforceability of any other article, paragraph, clause, sub-clause or provision. This Agreement and each article, paragraph, clause, sub-clause and provision hereof shall be read and construed so as to give thereto the full effect thereof subject only to any contrary provision of the law to the extent that where this Agreement or any article, paragraph, clause, sub- clause or provision hereof would but for the provisions of this paragraph have been read and construed as being void or ineffective, it shall nevertheless be a valid agreement, article, paragraph, clause, sub-clause or provision as the case may be to the full extent to which it is not contrary to any provision of the law.

11.4   The parties hereto submit to the exclusive jurisdiction of the Courts of the State of Arizona in respect of any matter or thing arising out of this Agreement or pursuant thereto.

11.5   All notices to be given by either party hereto shall be delivered or sent by telegram, facsimile or cable to the following address or such other address as may be notified by either party:

11.5.1 If to the Corporation to:

Tankless Systems Worldwide, Inc.
7650 E. Evans Rd. Suite C
Scottsdale, AZ 85260   Attention: Secretary

11.5.2 If to the Executive to:

Gregg C. Johnson
9630 W. Rimrock Dr.
Peoria, AZ 85382

11.6   This Agreement shall ensure to the benefit of and be binding upon the parties hereto, their heirs, administrators, successors and legal representatives. This Agreement may be assigned by the Corporation but may not be assigned by the Executive.

IN WITNESS WHEREOF, the parties have duly executed this Agreement.

7

PDOCS000614

TANKLESS SYSTEMS WORLDWIDE, INC.

Per: _____

SIGNED, SEALED AND DELIVERED in the)
Presence of:)
)
)
)   _____
)
)   **Gregg C. Johnson**
)
_____)
Witness

8

PDOCS000615

Schedule A

Duties
(as taken from the SKYE Organizational Manual)

Title:	To Be Determined
Reports to:	President and Chief Executive Officer or such other Officer as the Board of Directors shall determine
Direct Reports:	To Be Determined
Liaison:	Chairman of Board Chairman of all Board Committees
Job Description:	As Determined by the Board of Directors
Review & Comp	Corporate Governance Committee
Accountability:	Board of Directors, President and CE)

This position is as a member of the Executive Management Team and is the final responsible party for all business day-to-day planning and operations of the company.

The specific duties include, but are not limited to:

1. Together with the Executive Management Team, directs overall business and organizational policies; develops, recommends and implements through subordinates; recommends annual and long-term company policies and goals to Board of Directors.

2. Responsible for overall company financial, organizational and operational planning activities and growth.

3. Member of the Management Team, responsible for approving budgetary and operational objectives, overseeing and reporting progress to the Board of Directors.

4. Monitoring performance relative to established objectives and systematically monitor and evaluate operating results.

5. Presents, together with the CFO, Balance sheet, operating and capital expenditure budgets to Board of Directors for approval.

6. Formulates the Corporation's near term and long-range strategic plans and submits them to the Board of Directors for approval.

7. Directs executives in matters concerning the development, production, promotion and sales of the Corporation's products.

8. Promoting positive relations with customers, suppliers and the general public.

9

PDOCS000616

9. Directs the establishment of fair and appropriate policies for human resource management.

10. Responsible for the overall strategic management of the Corporation.

11. Responsible for the daily affairs of the Corporation.

12. Responsible for ensuring operational compliance with policies and procedures adopted by the Board of Directors.

13. Primary responsible party for ensuring systemic adherence to Compliance and Ethics mandate.

13. Together with Board members and the CFO is responsible for all capital fundraising requirements of the company.

14. Directs, oversees and manages all external contacts with parties involved with funding the capital requirements of the company.

15. Responsible for making all public representations in connection with investor relations activities.

16. Together with the Chairman is responsible for all presentations of material to the public.

17. Any other duty reasonably assigned by the Board of Directors

10

Schedule B

Resale Restrictions

The Executive confirms and acknowledges that there are resale restrictions in respect of those Seven Hundred & Fifty Thousand (750,000) common shares of the Corporation (the "Shares") issued to the Executive in connection with his consultancy to the Corporation and by operation of this Agreement. The resale restrictions imposed under this Agreement and this Schedule are in addition to any other resale restriction that may be applicable by operation of state or federal securities laws.

The Shares shall be subject to a contractual restriction prohibiting the sale, transfer, hypothecation, pledge or other disposition until such shares are eligible for release from this contractual restriction in accordance with the Schedule set forth below.

The Executive shall be entitled to the release of this contractual resale restriction in respect of the Shares by the passing of time and/or active engagement with the Corporation as a consultant or officer thereof. Specifically, the resale restrictions imposed by this Schedule shall be removed in accordance with the following release schedule:

(A)   While employed by or consulting to the Corporation:

1.   On September 1, 2004   250,000 shares

2.   On September 1, 2005   250,000 shares

3.   On September 1, 2006   250,000 shares

(B)   Otherwise:

1.   One Hundred Thousand (100,000) shares for each year from and after September 1, 2004.

For greater certainty, the Executive shall not be entitled to combine the release criteria above so as to result in the accelerated release of such Shares beyond the maximum release schedule specified in category "A" above.

11

Thomas Kreitzer

From:	Gregg Johnson [gregg.johnson@skye-betterliving.com]
Sent:	Tuesday, May 23, 2006 9:31 AM
To:	'Thomas Kreitzer'
Subject:	RE: Signed Consulting Doc for Auditors
Follow Up Flag:	Follow up
Flag Status:	Green

Thank you Thomas. I will pass on the "proposed agreement as well so the record is complete. Thanks for going through your records.

Gregg

From: Thomas Kreitzer [mailto:Thomas@KreitzerBrothers.com]
Sent: Tuesday, May 23, 2006 10:55 AM
To: 'Gregg Johnson'
Subject: Signed Consulting Doc for Auditors

Gregg,

The copy of the contract I forwarded yesterday which I added the Skye Seal to was never released or approved by the Board which is why you never received a copy. Here is a PDF I created from what I had board approval of back then. There was a lot going on back then so just use this one to get through the reporting. Please work with the new Board to get your final version approved and executed.

Thanks,

Thomas

From: Gregg Johnson [mailto:gregg.johnson@skye-betterliving.com]
Sent: Monday, May 22, 2006 1:55 PM
To: 'Thomas Kreitzer'; thomas_kreitzer@hotmail.com
Subject: C DOCUME~1 gjohnson LOCALS~1 Temp AttachmentsTemp(5) Consulting Agreement - Gregg Johnson

Tom:

On review of my records I still have not received a signed copy back of this agreement. If you have it will you please PDF and email back to me.

I will countersign once I receive your signed copy.

This is my agreement that dates back to January 1, 2005 and revised to be effective August 1, 2005. I know you have said that it was signed but I have no copy and the auditors want it for their files.

Gregg

--
No virus found in this incoming message.
Checked by AVG Free Edition.
Version: 7.1.392 / Virus Database: 268.6.0/342 - Release Date: 5/17/2006

9/19/2006

PDOCS000620

EXHIBIT 13

--
No virus found in this outgoing message.
Checked by AVG Free Edition.
Version: 7.1.392 / Virus Database: 268.6.0/342 - Release Date: 5/17/2006

--
No virus found in this incoming message.
Checked by AVG Free Edition.
Version: 7.1.392 / Virus Database: 268.6.0/342 - Release Date: 5/17/2006

9/19/2006

Thomas Kreitzer

From:	Gregg Johnson [gregg.johnson@skye-betterliving.com]
Sent:	Tuesday, May 23, 2006 9:49 AM
To:	'Thomas Kreitzer'
Subject:	RE: Signed Consulting Doc for Auditors
Follow Up Flag:	Follow up
Flag Status:	Green

Thomas:

The agreements are quite different but I appreciate that the Board did what it believed was in the interests of shareholders. I hope our new Board will adopt the agreement that I thought was executed!

Anyhow will you please send me the minutes that approved the Consulting Agreement. Ken thinks that you have these and that it was written in your style of minutes as opposed to a consent as Ken does.

Gregg

From: Thomas Kreitzer [mailto:Thomas@KreitzerBrothers.com]
Sent: Tuesday, May 23, 2006 10:55 AM
To: 'Gregg Johnson'
Subject: Signed Consulting Doc for Auditors

Gregg,

The copy of the contract I forwarded yesterday which I added the Skye Seal to was never released or approved by the Board which is why you never received a copy. Here is a PDF I created from what I had board approval of back then. There was a lot going on back then so just use this one to get through the reporting. Please work with the new Board to get your final version approved and executed.

Thanks,

Thomas

From: Gregg Johnson [mailto:gregg.johnson@skye-betterliving.com]
Sent: Monday, May 22, 2006 1:55 PM
To: 'Thomas Kreitzer'; thomas_kreitzer@hotmail.com
Subject: C DOCUME~1 gjohnson LOCALS~1 Temp AttachmentsTemp(5) Consulting Agreement - Gregg Johnson

Tom:

On review of my records I still have not received a signed copy back of this agreement. If you have it will you please PDF and email back to me.

I will countersign once I receive your signed copy.

This is my agreement that dates back to January 1, 2005 and revised to be effective August 1, 2005. I know you have said that it was signed but I have no copy and the auditors want it for their files.

Gregg

--

9/19/2006

PDOCS000623

EXHIBIT 14

No virus found in this incoming message.
Checked by AVG Free Edition.
Version: 7.1.392 / Virus Database: 268.6.0/342 - Release Date: 5/17/2006

--
No virus found in this outgoing message.
Checked by AVG Free Edition.
Version: 7.1.392 / Virus Database: 268.6.0/342 - Release Date: 5/17/2006

--
No virus found in this incoming message.
Checked by AVG Free Edition.
Version: 7.1.392 / Virus Database: 268.6.0/342 - Release Date: 5/17/2006

PDOCS000624

9/19/2006

Thomas Kreitzer

From:	Thomas Kreitzer [Thomas@KreitzerBrothers.com]
Sent:	Tuesday, May 23, 2006 1:56 PM
To:	Ken Pinckard (vestnik@aol.com)
Cc:	'Pinckard@azbar.org'; 'RyckmanL@aol.com'
Subject:	Corporate Resolution
Follow Up Flag:	Follow up
Flag Status:	Green
Attachments:	Tankless Corporate Resolution - Johnson Agreement.pdf; Tankless Corporate Resolution - Johnson Agreement R1.doc

Ken,

Does this look right resolution that Gregg is looking for. Let me know.

Thomas

--
No virus found in this outgoing message.
Checked by AVG Free Edition.
Version: 7.1.392 / Virus Database: 268.6.0/342 - Release Date: 5/17/2006

9/19/2006

PDOCS000626

EXHIBIT 15

CORPORATE RESOLUTION

OF

Tankless Systems Worldwide, Inc.

A special meeting of the Board of Directors of the above corporation was held on August 01, 2004, at the corporation's place of business.

The purpose of the meeting was to reissue 144 shares of the company to a key employee.

  1. **QUORUM.** A quorum was declared present based on the presence of the following directors:

  - David Kreitzer
  - Thomas Kreitzer

The following corporate actions were taken by appropriate motions duly made, seconded, and adopted by the majority vote of the Directors entitled to vote (unless a higher voting approval is stated.

  2. **MEETING APPOINTMENTS** . Thomas Kreitzer was appointed chairperson of the meeting and David Kreitzer was appointed as secretary to prepare a record of the proceedings.

  3. **AUTHORIZATION TO EXECUTE CONSUTLING AGREEMENT.** It was agreed that a consulting Agreement be executed with Gregg Johnson containing the following language:

THIS AGREEMENT made effective as of the 1st day of August 2005.

BETWEEN:

  TANKLESS SYSTEMS WORLDWIDE, INC., a body corporate duly incorporated pursuant to the laws of the State of Nevada, with principal offices in the City of Scottsdale, in the State of Arizona, together with all of its wholly owned subsidiaries from time to time operating (hereinafter, collectively referred to as the "Corporation").

  - and -

  GREGG C JOHNSON., an individual currently residing in the City of Peoria, AZ (the "Executive").

CORPORATE RESOLUTION, 08/01/2004   **PAGE 1**

PDOCS000627

More unseen mistakes in dates.

<u>RECITALS</u>

WHEREAS, the Corporation is engaged in the business of designing, manufacturing and marketing a line of tankless water heaters, as well as a suite of household and commercial health and wellness related appliances and other devices;

AND, WHEREAS, the Corporation wishes to contract for the services of the Executive to serve as the an Officer of the Corporation, and the Executive wishes to be contracted by the Corporation as an Officer;

AND WHEREAS, the Corporation has caused to be issued Seven Hundred & Fifty Thousand restricted common shares of the Corporation to the Executive in consideration for the Executive agreeing to join the Corporation and to act in the capacity as its consultant and Officer;

AND WHEREAS, the Executive has agreed that such shares shall not be eligible for sale, transfer, hypothecation or other disposition except otherwise as in accordance with Schedule "B" attached hereto;

NOW, THEREFORE, THIS AGREEMENT WITNESSETH, that inconsideration of the premises and covenants and agreements hereinafter contained it is agreed by and between the parties as follows:

ARTICLE 1 - CONTRACT

1.1   The Executive will, during the Term (as defined below) or any renewals thereof, perform all of the Duties (as defined below) as the Corporation by action of its Board of Directors shall, from time to time, reasonably assign to the Executive. The Corporation and Executive further agree that any prior employment and/or consulting agreements entered into between the parties are hereby terminated effective the date of this Agreement.

ARTICLE 2- TERM

2.1   Subject to the prior termination of this Agreement as provided herein, the contracting of the Executive by the Corporation shall commence on August 1, 2004, and end on July 31, 2007 (the "Term').

2.2   Subject to the prior termination of this Agreement as herein provided, upon the expiration of the Term, the Corporation may extend the contract period of the Executive for such period or periods and under such conditions as mutually agreed to by the parties; provided that, any such agreement to extend the contract shall only be binding if made in writing and signed by the parties hereto. For greater certainty, it is understood that Term shall refer to the original term of this Agreement as defined in Article 2.1 herein and to any renewal thereof.

ARTICLE 3 - DUTIES

3.1   The Executive shall, during the Term of this Agreement, perform all of the duties and responsibilities (the "Duties') as the Corporation shall from time to time reasonably assign to the Executive and, without limiting the generality of the foregoing, the Duties shall include those duties set forth in Schedule "A" attached hereto, as from time to time reasonably amended by the Board of Directors of the Corporation. During the Term of this Agreement, the Executive shall devote the majority of the Executive's time and attention to the Duties, and shall do all in the Executives power to promote, develop and extend the business of the Corporation and its subsidiaries and related corporations.

3.2   The Executive shall truly and faithfully account for and deliver to the Corporation all money, securities and things of value belonging to the Corporation which the Executive may from time to time receive for, from or on account of the Corporation.

ARTICLE 4- REMUNERATION

4.1   Subject to Article 4.5 below, the gross annual cash compensation of the Executive shall be the greater of (i) One Hundred Twenty Thousand ($120,000) US Dollars, or (ii) an amount equal to one per cent (1.0%) of the gross sales (the 'Revenue Share') actually achieved by the Corporation during each fiscal year (hereinafter, the "Compensation"). Such Compensation shall be calculated by multiplying the Corporation's actual revenue figure achieved in the month by 0.01. For greater certainty, should such calculation result in an amount of less than Ten Thousand ($10,000) US Dollars being paid to the Executive in any monthly period, the Executive shall be entitled to receive the full amount of Ten Thousand ($10,000) US Dollars. All Compensation payable hereunder shall be payable on a monthly basis with a mid-month advance of Five Thousand ($5,000) US Dollars payable on the 15th of the month with the balance payable on the 5th of the succeeding month. For greater certainty, the Executive acknowledges and confirms that such Compensation methodology is inclusive of any annual bonus or other customary emoluments, perquisites or payments other than those specifically granted under the terms of this Agreement

4.2   _Alternate Payment_: The Executive agrees that up to 1/2 of such Compensation payable in accordance with Article 4.1 above may, at the discretion of the Board of Directors, be paid in the form of freely-tradable securities of the Corporation representing a value at the time of payment equal to at least the value of such unpaid (cash) Compensation ("Stock Based Payment").   For greater certainty, any securities issued to the Executive in connection with the Stock Based Payment shall be freely-tradable, and shall be priced at the lowest closing bid price of the Corporation's securities over the ten (10) trading days prior to the issuance of securities under such Stock Based Payment mechanism.

4.2   The Executive shall also be entitled to participate, **only if such plans exist**, in the Corporation's group benefit plan, medical and family medical plan, stock savings plan, and disability insurance plan. It is understood that all costs associated with such plans will be borne by the Corporation.

4.3   The Executive will be reimbursed for reasonable business expenses, within such policy guidelines as may be established from time to time, by the Corporation's Board of Directors, provided that such business expenses are incurred in the ordinary course of performing the Duties.

4.4   During the Term hereof the Corporation shall provide the Executive with reimbursement of vehicle operating and insurance costs as approved by the Board of Directors from time to time. For greater certainty the Executive shall NOT be entitled to any other automobile allowance

4.5   The Executive shall NOT be entitled to participate in annual grants of stock options in accordance with the Corporation's Stock Option Plan.

ARTICLE 5-BENEFITS AND HOLIDAYS

5.1   The Executive shall be entitled to four (4) weeks paid holidays during each year of the Term. Holidays must be taken at times that are satisfactory to the Corporation, acting reasonably, and must be taken within the year to which the holiday relates and holidays not taken shall be deemed to have been taken and no other compensation shall be payable by the Corporation. For greater clarity it is understood that for the purpose of determining the number of holidays for which the Executive is entitled, each year of the Term will commence on January 1st and end on December 31st.

ARTICLE 6-CONFIDENTIALITY

6.1   The Executive shall not, either during the continuance of the Executive's contract hereunder or at any time after termination of the Executive as consultant to the Corporation, for any reason whatsoever (except in the proper course of carrying out the Duties, or otherwise required by law), divulge to any person whomsoever, and shall use the Executive's best endeavors to prevent the publication or disclosure of:

6.1.1   Any confidential information concerning the business or finances of the Corporation or any other corporation, person or entity for which he is directed to perform services hereunder or of any of their dealings, transactions or affairs, including, without limitation, personal and family matters which may come to the Executive's knowledge during or in the course of the Executive's contract: or

6.1.2   Any trade secrets, know-how, inventions, technology, designs, methods, formula, processes, copyrights, trade marks, trade mark applications, patents, patent applications or any other proprietary information and/or data of the Corporation (herein collectively called "Intellectual Property").

ARTICLE 7 - INVENTIONS AND PATENTS

7.1   If the Executive contributes to any invention whether patentable, patented, or not (an "Invention"), any intellectual property, or any improvement or modification to any Invention or intellectual property then the Executive's contribution thereto and the Invention, intellectual property or improvement thereof shall, without the payment of any additional compensation in any form whatsoever, become the exclusive property of the Corporation. The Executive shall execute any and all agreements, assurances or assignments that the Corporation may require and the Executive shall fully cooperate with the Corporation in the filing and prosecution of any patent applications. The Executive hereby reiterates and confirms the application of this Article to all such Inventions, intellectual property and improvements that have been made during the tenancy of that certain consulting position with the Corporation's subsidiaries.

ARTICLE 8- RESTRICTIVE COVENANT

8.1   The Executive will not at any time during the Term, or during any renewal thereof, and for a period of two (2) years following the expiration or termination of the Executive's contract for whatever cause, compete in the United States, directly or indirectly, with any of the businesses carried on by the Corporation, its subsidiaries or affiliates:

8.1.1   As a principal, partner employee;

8.1.2   As an officer, director or similar official of any incorporated or unincorporated entity engaged in any such competing business (the "Other Entity");

8.1,3   As a consultant or advisor to any Other Entity;

8.1.4   As a holder of shares or debt instrument of any kind of any Other Entity;

8.1.5   In any relationship described in subsections 81.1 through 8.1.4 of this section with any incorporated or unincorporated entity which provides services for or necessarily incidental to the business of an Other Entity:

without the prior express written consent of the Corporation, which consent may be withheld by the Corporation for any reason or for no reason.

CORPORATE RESOLUTION, 08/01/2004   PAGE 4

PDOCS000630

8.2   Notwithstanding the provisions of Article 8.3 below, the Executive acknowledges and agrees that the time frames for which the aforesaid covenant shall apply have been considered by the Executive who has taken independent legal advice with respect thereto and the restraint and restriction of and on the future activities of the Executive are reasonable in the circumstances.

8.3   The parties agree that if the time frames set out in this Article are found to unenforceable by a court of competent jurisdiction, the time frames will be amended to the time frames as established by a court of competent jurisdiction.

3.4   The Executive acknowledges that any breach of Articles 6, 7 & 8 will cause irreparable harm to the Corporation, for which the Corporation cannot be compensated by damages. The Executive agrees that in the event of a breach of the covenant contained in Articles 6, 7, & 8, the Corporation shall not be restricted to seeking damages only, but shall be entitled to injunctive and other equitable relief.

ARTICLE 9- TERMINATION OF CONTRACT

9.1   The Corporation may terminate this Agreement at any time for cause. The term "for cause" shall include any one or more of the following:

9.1.1   A significant and continuing breach or failure or a continual breaching or failing to observe any of the provisions herein;

9.1.2   An act of dishonesty fundamentally detrimental to the well-being of the Corporation;

9.1.3   Any act of gross negligence relating to completing the Duties;

9.1.4   The commission of a felony offence for which the Executive is convicted, which significantly impairs the Executive's ability to perform the Duties and responsibilities hereunder or which materially adversely affects the reputation enjoyed by the Corporation; or

9.1.5   The failure to comply with reasonable instructions, orders and directions of the Board of Directors of the Corporation in so far as such instructions, orders and directions are not inconsistent with the Duties, or are, in the reasonable opinion of the Executive:

9.1.5.1   In any way demeaning or likely to result in diminution of the value of the Executives services in the future.

9.1.5.2   Likely to result in the conduct of an illegal act.

9.1.5.3   Inconsistent with any court order or other governmental order or directive.

9.1.5.4   Inconsistent with any shareholders' resolution passed at any duly convened meeting of shareholders.

9.1.6   In the event Executive shall be denied entry into the United States by the Immigration authorities of the United States and such inability to be physically present in the offices of the Corporation in Chandler, Arizona shall exist for a period of thirty (30) days or more.

provided that, with respect to each 9.1.1 through 9.1.5 (but not 9.1.6) above, the Executive shall be given written notification of any such alleged breach and provided a reasonable opportunity to respond thereto. For greater certainty, the Corporation shall not be entitled to utilize any such provision to terminate this Agreement in respect of any action by the Executive that was: (i) specifically required to be performed by direction of the board, directly or indirectly (ii) the dissemination of information required to be reported in the normal course with the Securities and Exchange Commission or any other competent governmental entity having jurisdiction over the Executive or the Corporation, or (iii) honestly and faithfully performed by the Executive for the benefit of the Corporation.

9.2   In the event that the Executive becomes physically or mentally disabled and is unable to perform the Duties for a period of twelve (12) months, as confirmed by a doctor's certificate, the Corporation shall be entitled to terminate this Agreement without further compensation upon sixty (60) days written notice to the Executive. In the case of the death of the Executive, all obligations of the Corporation under this Agreement shall cease immediately; provided that, this provision shall not affect any right, benefit or entitlement accruing to the Executive and/or his estate under any of the Corporation's benefit plans or stock option agreements which arise as a result of the Executive's prior performance hereunder or his death.

9.3   The Executive may terminate this Agreement, and the contract created herein, by giving at least Ninety (90) days prior written notice of such intention to the Corporation. After the expiry of such notice, all obligations, except for the obligations of the Executive under Articles 6, 7 and 8 hereof, which shall continue as provided in those Articles, of the Corporation and the Executive under this Agreement shall cease.

ARTICLE 10-OTHER AGREEMENTS IN RESPECT OF TERMINATION

10.1   In the event of the termination of this Agreement for cause or otherwise howsoever:

10.1.1   The Executive shall resign as a director and/or officer of the Corporation or any subsidiary or related corporation and the Executive hereby appoints the Corporation as its attorney in fact for the purpose of executing any and all such documents to give effect to the foregoing; and

10.1.2   The Executive hereby authorizes the Corporation and any subsidiary or related corporation to set off against and deduct from any and all amounts owing to the Executive by way of salary, allowances, accrued leave, long service leave, reimbursements or any other emoluments or benefits owing to the Executive by the Corporation and any subsidiary or related corporation, any reasonable amounts owed by the Executive to the Corporation or any subsidiary or related corporation.

10.2   Notwithstanding any termination of this Agreement for any reason whatsoever, whether with or without cause, all of the provisions of Articles 6, 7 and 8 and any other provisions of this Agreement necessary to give efficacy and effect thereto shall continue in full force and effect following the termination of this Agreement.

ARTICLE 11 - GENERAL

11.1   This Agreement, and the Schedules attached hereto, constitute the entire agreement between the parties hereto and cancels, supersedes and replaces all previous written, verbal or implied terms, conditions and representations relating to the Executive's contract.

11.2   The failure of either party at any time to require strict performance by the other party of any provision hereof shall in no way affect the full right to require such performance at any time thereafter. Neither shall the waiver by either party of a breach of any provision hereof be taken or held to be a waiver of any succeeding breach of such provision or as a waiver of the provision itself.

CORPORATE RESOLUTION, 08/01/2004   PAGE 6

PDOCS000632

11.3   Each article, paragraph, clause, sub-clause and provision of this Agreement shall be severable from each other and if for any reason any article, paragraph, clause, sub-clause or provision is invalid or unenforceable, such invalidity or unenforceability shall not prejudice or in any way affect the validity or enforceability of any other article, paragraph, clause, sub-clause or provision. This Agreement and each article, paragraph, clause, sub-clause and provision hereof shall be read and construed so as to give thereto the full effect thereof subject only to any contrary provision of the law to the extent that where this Agreement or any article, paragraph, clause, sub-clause or provision hereof would but for the provisions of this paragraph have been read and construed as being void or ineffective, it shall nevertheless be a valid agreement, article, paragraph, clause, sub-clause or provision as the case may be to the full extent to which it is not contrary to any provision of the law.

11.4   The parties hereto submit to the exclusive jurisdiction of the Courts of the State of Arizona in respect of any matter or thing arising out of this Agreement or pursuant thereto.

11.5   All notices to be given by either party hereto shall be delivered or sent by telegram, facsimile or cable to the following address or such other address as may be notified by either party:

11.5.1 If to the Corporation to:

Tankless Systems Worldwide, Inc.
7650 E. Evans Rd. Suite C
Scottsdale, AZ 85260   Attention: Secretary

11.5.2 If to the Executive to:

Gregg C. Johnson
Johnson Address

11.6   This Agreement shall ensure to the benefit of and be binding upon the parties hereto, their heirs, administrators, successors and legal representatives. This Agreement may be assigned by the Corporation but may not be assigned by the Executive.

IN WITNESS WHEREOF, the parties have duly executed this Agreement.

TANKLESS SYSTEMS WORLDWIDE, INC.

Per: _____

SIGNED, SEALED AND DELIVERED in the)
Presence of:)
)
)   _____
)   **Gregg C. Johnson**
)
)
_____   )
Witness

CORPORATE RESOLUTION, 08/01/2004   PAGE 7

PDOCS000633

Schedule A

Duties
(as taken from the SKYE Organizational Manual)

Title:	To Be Determined
Reports to:	President and Chief Executive Officer or such other Officer as the Board of Directors shall determine
Direct Reports:	To Be Determined
Liaison:	Chairman of Board Chairman of all Board Committees
Job Description:	As Determined by the Board of Directors
Review & Comp	Corporate Governance Committee
Accountability:	Board of Directors, President and CE)

This position is as a member of the Executive Management Team and is the final responsible party for all business day-to-day planning and operations of the company.

The specific duties include, but are not limited to:

1. Together with the Executive Management Team, directs overall business and organizational policies; develops, recommends and implements through subordinates; recommends annual and long-term company policies and goals to Board of Directors.

2. Responsible for overall company financial, organizational and operational planning activities and growth.

3. Member of the Management Team, responsible for approving budgetary and operational objectives, overseeing and reporting progress to the Board of Directors.

4. Monitoring performance relative to established objectives and systematically monitor and evaluate operating results.

5. Presents, together with the CFO, Balance sheet, operating and capital expenditure budgets to Board of Directors for approval.

6. Formulates the Corporation's near term and long-range strategic plans and submits them to the Board of Directors for approval.

7. Directs executives in matters concerning the development, production, promotion and sales of the Corporation's products.

8. Promoting positive relations with customers, suppliers and the general public.

9. Directs the establishment of fair and appropriate policies for human resource management.

10. Responsible for the overall strategic management of the Corporation.

11. Responsible for the daily affairs of the Corporation.

12. Responsible for ensuring operational compliance with policies and procedures adopted by the Board of Directors.

13. Primary responsible party for ensuring systemic adherence to Compliance and Ethics mandate.

13. Together with Board members and the CFO is responsible for all capital fundraising requirements of the company.

14. Directs, oversees and manages all external contacts with parties involved with funding the capital requirements of the company.

15. Responsible for making all public representations in connection with investor relations activities.

16. Together with the Chairman is responsible for all presentations of material to the public.

17. Any other duty reasonably assigned by the Board of Directors

Schedule B

Resale Restrictions

The Executive confirms and acknowledges that there are resale restrictions in respect of those Seven Hundred & Fifty Thousand (750,000) common shares of the Corporation (the "Shares") issued to the Executive in connection with his consultancy to the Corporation and by operation of this Agreement. The resale restrictions imposed under this Agreement and this Schedule are in addition to any other resale restriction that may be applicable by operation of state or federal securities laws.

The Shares shall be subject to a contractual restriction prohibiting the sale, transfer, hypothecation, pledge or other disposition until such shares are eligible for release from this contractual restriction in accordance with the Schedule set forth below.

The Executive shall be entitled to the release of this contractual resale restriction in respect of the Shares by the passing of time and/or active engagement with the Corporation as a consultant or officer thereof. Specifically, the resale restrictions imposed by this Schedule shall be removed in accordance with the following release schedule:

(A)   While employed by or consulting to the Corporation:

1. On September 1, 2004   250,000 shares

2. On September 1, 2005   250,000 shares

3. On September 1, 2006   250,000 shares

(B)   Otherwise:

1. One Hundred Thousand (100,000) shares for each year from and after September 1, 2004.

For greater certainty, the Executive shall not be entitled to combine the release criteria above so as to result in the accelerated release of such Shares beyond the maximum release schedule specified in category "A" above.

4. APPROVAL OF ACTIONS SECTION. The actions and undertakings of the directors, officers, employees, and agents of the corporation were approved with respect to:

- All actions herein taken.

5. ADJOURNMENT OF MEETING. The meeting was adjourned at 10:00 AM on, August 01, 2004, at the corporation's place of business.

In accordance with the conditions and requirements of the by-laws of Tankless Systems Worldwide, Inc. I hereby set forth my signature to attest that these are the actions taken by the Board of Directors it Officers and Agents.

_____
Thomas Kreitzer, Secretary

_____
David Kreitzer, Director

CORPORATE RESOLUTION

OF

Tankless Systems Worldwide, Inc.

A special meeting of the Board of Directors of the above corporation was held on August 01, 2004, at the corporation's place of business.

The purpose of the meeting was to reissue 144 shares of the company to a key employee.

1. QUORUM.   A quorum was declared present based on the presence of the following directors:

- David Kreitzer
- Thomas Kreitzer

The following corporate actions were taken by appropriate motions duly made, seconded, and adopted by the majority vote of the Directors entitled to vote (unless a higher voting approval is stated.

2. MEETING APPOINTMENTS .   Thomas Kreitzer was appointed chairperson of the meeting and David Kreitzer was appointed as secretary to prepare a record of the proceedings.

3. AUTHORIZATION TO EXECUTE CONSUTLING AGREEMENT.   It was agreed that a consulting Agreement be executed with Gregg Johnson containing the following language:

THIS AGREEMENT made effective as of the 1st day of August 2005.

BETWEEN:

> **TANKLESS SYSTEMS WORLDWIDE, INC.**, a body corporate duly incorporated pursuant to the laws of the State of Nevada, with principal offices in the City of Scottsdale, in the State of Arizona, together with all of its wholly owned subsidiaries from time to time operating (hereinafter, collectively referred to as the "Corporation").

> - and -

> **GREGG C JOHNSON.**, an individual currently residing in the City of Peoria, AZ (the "Executive").

RECITALS

WHEREAS, the Corporation is engaged in the business of designing, manufacturing and marketing a line of tankless water heaters, as well as a suite of household and commercial health and wellness related appliances and other devices;

AND, WHEREAS, the Corporation wishes to contract for the services of the Executive to serve as the an Officer of the Corporation, and the Executive wishes to be contracted by the Corporation as an Officer;

AND WHEREAS, the Corporation has caused to be issued Seven Hundred & Fifty Thousand restricted common shares of the Corporation to the Executive in consideration for the Executive agreeing to join the Corporation and to act in the capacity as its consultant and Officer;

AND WHEREAS, the Executive has agreed that such shares shall not be eligible for sale, transfer, hypothecation or other disposition except otherwise as in accordance with Schedule "B" attached hereto;

NOW, THEREFORE, THIS AGREEMENT WITNESSETH, that inconsideration of the premises and covenants and agreements hereinafter contained it is agreed by and between the parties as follows:

ARTICLE 1 - CONTRACT

1.1   The Executive will, during the Term (as defined below) or any renewals thereof, perform all of the Duties (as defined below) as the Corporation by action of its Board of Directors shall, from time to time, reasonably assign to the Executive. The Corporation and Executive further agree that any prior employment and/or consulting agreements entered into between the parties are hereby terminated effective the date of this Agreement.

ARTICLE 2- TERM

2.1   Subject to the prior termination of this Agreement as provided herein, the contracting of the Executive by the Corporation shall commence on August 1, 2004, and end on July 31, 2007 (the "Term').

2.2   Subject to the prior termination of this Agreement as herein provided, upon the expiration of the Term, the Corporation may extend the contract period of the Executive for such period or periods and under such conditions as mutually agreed to by the parties; provided that, any such agreement to extend the contract shall only be binding if made in writing and signed by the parties hereto. For greater certainty, it is understood that Term shall refer to the original term of this Agreement as defined in Article 2.1 herein and to any renewal thereof.

ARTICLE 3 - DUTIES

3.1   The Executive shall, during the Term of this Agreement, perform all of the duties and responsibilities (the "Duties') as the Corporation shall from time to time reasonably assign to the Executive and, without limiting the generality of the foregoing, the Duties shall include those duties set forth in Schedule "A" attached hereto, as from time to time reasonably amended by the Board of Directors of the Corporation. During the Term of this Agreement, the Executive shall devote the majority of the Executive's time and attention to the Duties, and shall do all in the Executives power to promote, develop and extend the business of the Corporation and its subsidiaries and related corporations.

3.2   The Executive shall truly and faithfully account for and deliver to the Corporation all money, securities and things of value belonging to the Corporation which the Executive may from time to time receive for, from or on account of the Corporation.

ARTICLE 4- REMUNERATION

4.1   Subject to Article 4.5 below, the gross annual cash compensation of the Executive shall be the greater of (i) One Hundred Twenty Thousand ($120,000) US Dollars, or (ii) an amount equal to one per cent (1.0%) of the gross sales (the 'Revenue Share") actually achieved by the Corporation during each fiscal year (hereinafter, the "Compensation"). Such Compensation shall be calculated by multiplying the Corporation's actual revenue figure achieved in the month by 0.01. For greater certainty, should such calculation result in an amount of less than Ten Thousand ($10,000) US Dollars being paid to the Executive in any monthly period, the Executive shall be entitled to receive the full amount of Ten Thousand ($10,000) US Dollars. All Compensation payable hereunder shall be payable on a monthly basis with a mid-month advance of Five Thousand ($5,000) US Dollars payable on the 15th of the month with the balance payable on the 5th of the succeeding month. For greater certainty, the Executive acknowledges and confirms that such Compensation methodology is inclusive of any annual bonus or other customary emoluments, perquisites or payments other than those specifically granted under the terms of this Agreement

4.2   Alternate Payment: The Executive agrees that up to 1/2 of such Compensation payable in accordance with Article 4.1 above may, at the discretion of the Board of Directors, be paid in the form of freely-tradable securities of the Corporation representing a value at the time of payment equal to at least the value of such unpaid (cash) Compensation ("Stock Based Payment"). For greater certainty, any securities issued to the Executive in connection with the Stock Based Payment shall be freely-tradable, and shall be priced at the lowest closing bid price of the Corporation's securities over the ten (10) trading days prior to the issuance of securities under such Stock Based Payment mechanism.

4.2   The Executive shall also be entitled to participate, *only if such plans exist*, in the Corporation's group benefit plan, medical and family medical plan, stock savings plan, and disability insurance plan. It is understood that all costs associated with such plans will be borne by the Corporation.

4.3   The Executive will be reimbursed for reasonable business expenses, within such policy guidelines as may be established from time to time, by the Corporation's Board of Directors, provided that such business expenses are incurred in the ordinary course of performing the Duties.

4.4   During the Term hereof the Corporation shall provide the Executive with reimbursement of vehicle operating and insurance costs as approved by the Board of Directors from time to time. For greater certainty the Executive shall NOT be entitled to any other automobile allowance

4.5   The Executive shall NOT be entitled to participate in annual grants of stock options in accordance with the Corporation's Stock Option Plan.

ARTICLE 5-BENEFITS AND HOLIDAYS

5.1   The Executive shall be entitled to four (4) weeks paid holidays during each year of the Term. Holidays must be taken at times that are satisfactory to the Corporation, acting reasonably, and must be taken within the year to which the holiday relates and holidays not taken shall be deemed to have been taken and no other compensation shall be payable by the Corporation. For greater clarity it is understood that for the purpose of determining the number of holidays for which the Executive is entitled, each year of the Term will commence on January 1st and end on December 31st.

ARTICLE 6-CONFIDENTIALITY

CORPORATE RESOLUTION, 08/01/2004   PAGE 3

6.1   The Executive shall not, either during the continuance of the Executive's contract hereunder or at any time after termination of the Executive as consultant to the Corporation, for any reason whatsoever (except in the proper course of carrying out the Duties, or otherwise required by law), divulge to any person whomsoever, and shall use the Executive's best endeavors to prevent the publication or disclosure of:

        6.1.1   Any confidential information concerning the business or finances of the Corporation or any other corporation, person or entity for which he is directed to perform services hereunder or of any of their dealings, transactions or affairs, including, without limitation, personal and family matters which may come to the Executive's knowledge during or in the course of the Executive's contract: or

        6.1.2   Any trade secrets, know-how, inventions, technology, designs, methods, formula, processes, copyrights, trade marks, trade mark applications, patents, patent applications or any other proprietary information and/or data of the Corporation (herein collectively called "Intellectual Property").

ARTICLE 7 - INVENTIONS AND PATENTS

7.1   If the Executive contributes to any invention whether patentable, patented, or not (an "Invention"), any intellectual property, or any improvement or modification to any Invention or intellectual property then the Executive's contribution thereto and the Invention, intellectual property or improvement thereof shall, without the payment of any additional compensation in any form whatsoever, become the exclusive property of the Corporation. The Executive shall execute any and all agreements, assurances or assignments that the Corporation may require and the Executive shall fully cooperate with the Corporation in the filing and prosecution of any patent applications. The Executive hereby reiterates and confirms the application of this Article to all such Inventions, intellectual property and improvements that have been made during the tenancy of that certain consulting position with the Corporation's subsidiaries.

ARTICLE 8- RESTRICTIVE COVENANT

8.1   The Executive will not at any time during the Term, or during any renewal thereof, and for a period of two (2) years following the expiration or termination of the Executive's contract for whatever cause, compete in the United States, directly or indirectly, with any of the businesses carried on by the Corporation, its subsidiaries or affiliates:

        8.1.1   As a principal, partner employee;

        8.1.2   As an officer, director or similar official of any incorporated or unincorporated entity engaged in any such competing business (the "Other Entity");

        8.1,3   As a consultant or advisor to any Other Entity;

        8.1.4   As a holder of shares or debt instrument of any kind of any Other Entity;

        8.1.5   In any relationship described in subsections 81.1 through 8.1.4 of this section with any incorporated or unincorporated entity which provides services for or necessarily incidental to the business of an Other Entity:

without the prior express written consent of the Corporation, which consent may be withheld by the Corporation for any reason or for no reason.

8.2   Notwithstanding the provisions of Article 8.3 below, the Executive acknowledges and agrees that the time frames for which the aforesaid covenant shall apply have been considered by the

Executive who has taken independent legal advice with respect thereto and the restraint and restriction of and on the future activities of the Executive are reasonable in the circumstances.

8.3   The parties agree that if the time frames set out in this Article are found to unenforceable by a court of competent jurisdiction, the time frames will be amended to the time frames as established by a court of competent jurisdiction.

3.4   The Executive acknowledges that any breach of Articles 6, 7 & 8 will cause irreparable harm to the Corporation, for which the Corporation cannot be compensated by damages. The Executive agrees that in the event of a breach of the covenant contained in Articles 6, 7, & 8, the Corporation shall not be restricted to seeking damages only, but shall be entitled to injunctive and other equitable relief.

ARTICLE 9- TERMINATION OF CONTRACT

9.1   The Corporation may terminate this Agreement at any time for cause. The term "for cause" shall include any one or more of the following:

  9.1.1   A significant and continuing breach or failure or a continual breaching or failing to observe any of the provisions herein;

  9.1.2   An act of dishonesty fundamentally detrimental to the well-being of the Corporation;

  9.1.3   Any act of gross negligence relating to completing the Duties;

  9.1.4   The commission of a felony offence for which the Executive is convicted, which significantly impairs the Executive's ability to perform the Duties and responsibilities hereunder or which materially adversely affects the reputation enjoyed by the Corporation; or

  9.1.5   The failure to comply with reasonable instructions, orders and directions of the Board of Directors of the Corporation in so far as such instructions, orders and directions are not inconsistent with the Duties, or are, in the reasonable opinion of the Executive:

    9.1.5.1   In any way demeaning or likely to result in diminution of the value of the Executives services in the future.

    9.1.5.2   Likely to result in the conduct of an illegal act.

    9.1.5.3   Inconsistent with any court order or other governmental order or directive.

    9.1.5.4   Inconsistent with any shareholders' resolution passed at any duly convened meeting of shareholders.

  9.1.6   In the event Executive shall be denied entry into the United States by the Immigration authorities of the United States and such inability to be physically present in the offices of the Corporation in Chandler, Arizona shall exist for a period of thirty (30) days or more.

provided that, with respect to each 9.1.1 through 9.1.5 (but not 9.1.6) above, the Executive shall be given written notification of any such alleged breach and provided a reasonable opportunity to respond thereto. For greater certainty, the Corporation shall not be entitled to utilize any such provision to terminate this Agreement in respect of any action by the Executive that was: (i) specifically required to be performed by direction of the board, directly or indirectly (ii) the dissemination of information required to be reported in the normal course with the Securities and Exchange Commission or any other competent governmental entity having jurisdiction over the Executive or the Corporation, or (iii) honestly and faithfully performed by the Executive for the benefit of the Corporation.

9.2   In the event that the Executive becomes physically or mentally disabled and is unable to perform the Duties for a period of twelve (12) months, as confirmed by a doctor's certificate, the Corporation shall be entitled to terminate this Agreement without further compensation upon sixty (60) days written notice to the Executive. In the case of the death of the Executive, all obligations of the Corporation under this Agreement shall cease immediately; provided that, this provision shall not affect any right, benefit or entitlement accruing to the Executive and/or his estate under any of the Corporation's benefit plans or stock option agreements which arise as a result of the Executive's prior performance hereunder or his death.

9.3   The Executive may terminate this Agreement, and the contract created herein, by giving at least Ninety (90) days prior written notice of such intention to the Corporation. After the expiry of such notice, all obligations, except for the obligations of the Executive under Articles 6, 7 and 8 hereof, which shall continue as provided in those Articles, of the Corporation and the Executive under this Agreement shall cease.

ARTICLE 10-OTHER AGREEMENTS IN RESPECT OF TERMINATION

10.1   In the event of the termination of this Agreement for cause or otherwise howsoever:

10.1.1 The Executive shall resign as a director and/or officer of the Corporation or any subsidiary or related corporation and the Executive hereby appoints the Corporation as its attorney in fact for the purpose of executing any and all such documents to give effect to the foregoing; and

10.1.2 The Executive hereby authorizes the Corporation and any subsidiary or related corporation to set off against and deduct from any and all amounts owing to the Executive by way of salary, allowances, accrued leave, long service leave, reimbursements or any other emoluments or benefits owing to the Executive by the Corporation and any subsidiary or related corporation, any reasonable amounts owed by the Executive to the Corporation or any subsidiary or related corporation.

10.2   Notwithstanding any termination of this Agreement for any reason whatsoever, whether with or without cause, all of the provisions of Articles 6, 7 and 8 and any other provisions of this Agreement necessary to give efficacy and effect thereto shall continue in full force and effect following the termination of this Agreement.

ARTICLE 11 - GENERAL

11.1   This Agreement, and the Schedules attached hereto, constitute the entire agreement between the parties hereto and cancels, supersedes and replaces all previous written, verbal or implied terms, conditions and representations relating to the Executive's contract.

11.2   The failure of either party at any time to require strict performance by the other party of any provision hereof shall in no way affect the full right to require such performance at any time thereafter. Neither shall the waiver by either party of a breach of any provision hereof be taken or held to be a waiver of any succeeding breach of such provision or as a waiver of the provision itself.

11.3   Each article, paragraph, clause, sub-clause and provision of this Agreement shall be severable from each other and if for any reason any article, paragraph, clause, sub-clause or provision is invalid or unenforceable, such invalidity or unenforceability shall not prejudice or in any way affect the validity or enforceability of any other article, paragraph, clause, sub-clause or provision. This Agreement and each article, paragraph, clause, sub-clause and provision hereof shall be read and construed so as to give thereto the full effect thereof subject only to any contrary provision of the law to the extent that where this Agreement or any article, paragraph, clause, sub- clause or provision hereof would but for the provisions of this paragraph have been read and construed as being void or ineffective, it shall nevertheless be a valid agreement, article, paragraph, clause, sub-clause or provision as the case may be to the full extent to which it is not contrary to any provision of the law.

11.4   The parties hereto submit to the exclusive jurisdiction of the Courts of the State of Arizona in respect of any matter or thing arising out of this Agreement or pursuant thereto.

11.5   All notices to be given by either party hereto shall be delivered or sent by telegram, facsimile or cable to the following address or such other address as may be notified by either party:

    11.5.1 If to the Corporation to:

        Tankless Systems Worldwide, Inc.
        7650 E. Evans Rd. Suite C
        Scottsdale, AZ 85260   Attention: Secretary

    11.5.2 If to the Executive to:

        Gregg C. Johnson
        Johnson Address

11.6   This Agreement shall ensure to the benefit of and be binding upon the parties hereto, their heirs, administrators, successors and legal representatives. This Agreement may be assigned by the Corporation but may not be assigned by the Executive.

IN WITNESS WHEREOF, the parties have duly executed this Agreement.

TANKLESS SYSTEMS WORLDWIDE, INC.

Per: _____

SIGNED, SEALED AND DELIVERED in the)
Presence of:)
)
) _____
) **Gregg C. Johnson**
)
)
_____)
Witness

Schedule A

Duties
(as taken from the SKYE Organizational Manual)

Title: To Be Determined

Reports to: President and Chief Executive Officer or such other Officer as the Board of

	Directors shall determine
Direct Reports:	To Be Determined
Liaison:	Chairman of Board Chairman of all Board Committees
Job Description:	As Determined by the Board of Directors
Review & Comp	Corporate Governance Committee
Accountability:	Board of Directors, President and CE)

This position is as a member of the Executive Management Team and is the final responsible party for all business day-to-day planning and operations of the company.

The specific duties include, but are not limited to:

1. Together with the Executive Management Team, directs overall business and organizational policies; develops, recommends and implements through subordinates; recommends annual and long-term company policies and goals to Board of Directors.

2. Responsible for overall company financial, organizational and operational planning activities and growth.

3. Member of the Management Team, responsible for approving budgetary and operational objectives, overseeing and reporting progress to the Board of Directors.

4. Monitoring performance relative to established objectives and systematically monitor and evaluate operating results.

5. Presents, together with the CFO, Balance sheet, operating and capital expenditure budgets to Board of Directors for approval.

6. Formulates the Corporation's near term and long-range strategic plans and submits them to the Board of Directors for approval.

7. Directs executives in matters concerning the development, production, promotion and sales of the Corporation's products.

8. Promoting positive relations with customers, suppliers and the general public.

9. Directs the establishment of fair and appropriate policies for human resource management.

10. Responsible for the overall strategic management of the Corporation.

11. Responsible for the daily affairs of the Corporation.

12. Responsible for ensuring operational compliance with policies and procedures adopted by the Board of Directors.

13. Primary responsible party for ensuring systemic adherence to Compliance and Ethics mandate.

13.   Together with Board members and the CFO is responsible for all capital fundraising requirements of the company.

14.   Directs, oversees and manages all external contacts with parties involved with funding the capital requirements of the company.

15.   Responsible for making all public representations in connection with investor relations activities.

16.   Together with the Chairman is responsible for all presentations of material to the public.

17.   Any other duty reasonably assigned by the Board of Directors

Schedule B

Resale Restrictions

The Executive confirms and acknowledges that there are resale restrictions in respect of those Seven Hundred & Fifty Thousand (750,000) common shares of the Corporation (the "Shares") issued to the Executive in connection with his consultancy to the Corporation and by operation of this Agreement. The resale restrictions imposed under this Agreement and this Schedule are in addition to any other resale restriction that may be applicable by operation of state or federal securities laws.

The Shares shall be subject to a contractual restriction prohibiting the sale, transfer, hypothecation, pledge or other disposition until such shares are eligible for release from this contractual restriction in accordance with the Schedule set forth below.

The Executive shall be entitled to the release of this contractual resale restriction in respect of the Shares by the passing of time and/or active engagement with the Corporation as a consultant or officer thereof. Specifically, the resale restrictions imposed by this Schedule shall be removed in accordance with the following release schedule:

(A)   While employed by or consulting to the Corporation:

1.   On September 1, 2004   250,000 shares

2.   On September 1, 2005   250,000 shares

3.   On September 1, 2006   250,000 shares

(B)   Otherwise:

1.   One Hundred Thousand (100,000) shares for each year from and after September 1, 2004.

For greater certainty, the Executive shall not be entitled to combine the release criteria above so as to result in the accelerated release of such Shares beyond the maximum release schedule specified in category "A" above.

4. APPROVAL OF ACTIONS SECTION. The actions and undertakings of the directors, officers, employees, and agents of the corporation were approved with respect to:

- All actions herein taken.

5. ADJOURNMENT OF MEETING. The meeting was adjourned at 10:00 AM on, August 01, 2004, at the corporation's place of business.

In accordance with the conditions and requirements of the by-laws of Tankless Systems Worldwide, Inc. I hereby set forth my signature to attest that these are the actions taken by the Board of Directors it Officers and Agents.

_____
Thomas Kreitzer, Secretary

_____
David Kreitzer, Director

Thomas Kreitzer

From:	Thomas Kreitzer [Thomas@KreitzerBrothers.com]
Sent:	Wednesday, May 24, 2006 12:13 PM
To:	Ken Pinckard (vestnik@aol.com)
Subject:	Board Resolution
Follow Up Flag:	Follow up
Flag Status:	Green

Ken,

Gregg called again for the Resolution for his contract. Was the one I sent OK?

If it is I will send it to him.

Thomas

--
No virus found in this outgoing message.
Checked by AVG Free Edition.
Version: 7.1.392 / Virus Database: 268.6.0/342 - Release Date: 5/17/2006

PDOCS000648

9/19/2006

EXHIBIT 16

Thomas Kreitzer

From:	Thomas Kreitzer [Thomas@KreitzerBrothers.com]
Sent:	Wednesday, May 24, 2006 1:24 PM
To:	'Gregg Johnson'
Subject:	Corporate Resolution Johnson Agreement
Follow Up Flag:	Follow up
Flag Status:	Green
Attachments:	Tankless Corporate Resolution - Johnson Agreement.pdf

Gregg,

Here is the resolution.

Let me know if you need anything else.

Thomas

--
No virus found in this outgoing message.
Checked by AVG Free Edition.
Version: 7.1.392 / Virus Database: 268.6.0/342 - Release Date: 5/17/2006

PDOCS000650

9/19/2006

EXHIBIT 17

CORPORATE RESOLUTION

OF

Tankless Systems Worldwide, Inc.

A NEVADA COMPANY

A special meeting of the Board of Directors of the above corporation was held on August 01, 2004, at the corporation's place of business.

The purpose of the meeting was to approve a consulting agreement and to authorize the President of the company to execute the agreement.

1. **QUORUM.** A quorum was declared present based on the presence of the following directors:

    - David Kreitzer
    - Thomas Kreitzer

The following corporate actions were taken by appropriate motions duly made, seconded, and adopted by the majority vote of the Directors entitled to vote (unless a higher voting approval is stated.

2. **MEETING APPOINTMENTS** .   David Kreitzer was appointed chairperson of the meeting and Thomas Kreitzer was appointed as secretary to prepare a record of the proceedings.

3. **AUTHORIZATION TO EXECUTE CONSUTLING AGREEMENT.** It was agreed that a consulting Agreement (Exhibit A) should be executed with Gregg Johnson and the President of the Corporation was authorized to execute said consulting agreement.

4. **APPROVAL OF ACTIONS SECTION.** The actions and undertakings of the directors, officers, employees, and agents of the corporation were approved with respect to:

- All actions herein taken.

CORPORATE RESOLUTION, 08/01/2004

PAGE 1
PDOCS000651

Mistake in date left in final document.

5. ADJOURNMENT OF MEETING.   The meeting was adjourned at 10:00 AM on, August 01, 2004, at the corporation's place of business.

In accordance with the conditions and requirements of the by-laws of Tankless Systems Worldwide, Inc. I hereby set forth my signature to attest that these are the actions taken Board of Directors it Officers and Agents.

Thomas Kreitzer, Secretary

David Kreitzer, Chairman

EXHIBIT A

THIS AGREEMENT made effective as of _____.

BETWEEN:

> **TANKLESS SYSTEMS WORLDWIDE, INC.**, a body corporate duly incorporated pursuant to the laws of the State of Nevada, with principal offices in the City of Scottsdale, in the State of Arizona, together with all of its wholly owned subsidiaries from time to time operating (hereinafter, collectively referred to as the "Corporation").

> - and -

> **GREGG C JOHNSON**., an individual currently residing in the City of Peoria, AZ (the "Executive").

RECITALS

WHEREAS, the Corporation is engaged in the business of designing, manufacturing and marketing a line of tankless water heaters, as well as a suite of household and commercial health and wellness related appliances and other devices;

AND, WHEREAS, the Corporation wishes to contract for the services of the Executive to serve as the an Officer of the Corporation, and the Executive wishes to be contracted by the Corporation as an Officer;

AND WHEREAS, the Corporation has caused to be issued Seven Hundred & Fifty Thousand restricted common shares of the Corporation to the Executive in consideration for the Executive agreeing to join the Corporation and to act in the capacity as its consultant and Officer;

AND WHEREAS, the Executive has agreed that such shares shall not be eligible for sale, transfer, hypothecation or other disposition except otherwise as in accordance with Schedule "B" attached hereto;

NOW, THEREFORE, THIS AGREEMENT WITNESSETH, that inconsideration of the premises and covenants and agreements hereinafter contained it is agreed by and between the parties as follows:

ARTICLE 1 - CONTRACT

1.1   The Executive will, during the Term (as defined below) or any renewals thereof, perform all of the Duties (as defined below) as the Corporation by action of its Board of Directors shall, from time to time, reasonably assign to the Executive. The Corporation and Executive further agree that any prior employment and/or consulting agreements entered into between the parties are hereby terminated effective the date of this Agreement.

ARTICLE 2- TERM

2.1   Subject to the prior termination of this Agreement as provided herein, the contracting of the Executive by the Corporation shall commence on August 1, 2004, and end on July 31, 2007 (the "Term').

2.2   Subject to the prior termination of this Agreement as herein provided, upon the expiration of the Term, the Corporation may extend the contract period of the Executive for such period or periods and under such conditions as mutually agreed to by the parties; provided that, any such agreement to extend the contract shall only be binding if made in writing and signed by the parties hereto. For greater certainty, it is understood that Term shall refer to the original term of this Agreement as defined in Article 2.1 herein and to any renewal thereof.

ARTICLE 3 - DUTIES

3.1   The Executive shall, during the Term of this Agreement, perform all of the duties and responsibilities (the "Duties') as the Corporation shall from time to time reasonably assign to the Executive and, without limiting the generality of the foregoing, the Duties shall include those duties set forth in Schedule "A" attached hereto, as from time to time reasonably amended by the Board of Directors of the Corporation. During the Term of this Agreement, the Executive shall devote the majority of the Executive's time and attention to the Duties, and shall do all in the Executives power to promote, develop and extend the business of the Corporation and its subsidiaries and related corporations.

3.2   The Executive shall truly and faithfully account for and deliver to the Corporation all money, securities and things of value belonging to the Corporation which the Executive may from time to time receive for, from or on account of the Corporation.

ARTICLE 4- REMUNERATION

4.1   Subject to Article 4.5 below, the gross annual cash compensation of the Executive shall be the greater of (i) One Hundred Twenty Thousand ($120,000) US Dollars, or (ii) an amount equal to one per cent (1.0%) of the gross sales (the 'Revenue Share") actually achieved by the Corporation during each fiscal year (hereinafter, the "Compensation"). Such Compensation shall be calculated by multiplying the Corporation's actual revenue figure achieved in the month by 0.01. For greater certainty, should such calculation result in an amount of less than Ten Thousand ($10,000) US Dollars being paid to the Executive in any monthly period, the Executive shall be entitled to receive the full amount of Ten Thousand ($10,000) US Dollars. All Compensation payable hereunder shall be payable on a monthly basis with a mid-month advance of Five Thousand ($5,000) US Dollars payable on the 15th of the month with the balance payable on the 5th of the succeeding month. For greater certainty, the Executive acknowledges and confirms that such Compensation methodology is inclusive of any annual bonus or other customary emoluments, perquisites or payments other than those specifically granted under the terms of this Agreement

4.2   Alternate Payment: The Executive agrees that up to 1/2 of such Compensation payable in accordance with Article 4.1 above may, at the discretion of the Board of Directors, be paid in the form of freely-tradable securities of the Corporation representing a value at the time of payment equal to at least the value of such unpaid (cash) Compensation ("Stock Based Payment"). For greater certainty, any securities issued to the Executive in connection with the Stock Based Payment shall be freely-tradable, and shall be priced at the lowest closing bid price of the Corporation's securities over the ten (10) trading days prior to the issuance of securities under such Stock Based Payment mechanism.

4.2   The Executive shall also be entitled to participate, **only if such plans exist**, in the Corporation's group benefit plan, medical and family medical plan, stock savings plan, and disability insurance plan. It is understood that all costs associated with such plans will be borne by the Corporation.

4.3   The Executive will be reimbursed for reasonable business expenses, within such policy guidelines as may be established from time to time, by the Corporation's Board of Directors, provided that such business expenses are incurred in the ordinary course of performing the Duties.

4.4   During the Term hereof the Corporation shall provide the Executive with reimbursement of vehicle operating and insurance costs as approved by the Board of Directors from time to time. For greater certainty the Executive shall NOT be entitled to any other automobile allowance

4.5   The Executive shall NOT be entitled to participate in annual grants of stock options in accordance with the Corporation's Stock Option Plan.

ARTICLE 5-BENEFITS AND HOLIDAYS

5.1   The Executive shall be entitled to four (4) weeks paid holidays during each year of the Term. Holidays must be taken at times that are satisfactory to the Corporation, acting reasonably, and must be taken within the year to which the holiday relates and holidays not taken shall be deemed to have been taken and no other compensation shall be payable by the Corporation. For greater clarity it is understood that for the purpose of determining the number of holidays for which the Executive is entitled, each year of the Term will commence on January 1st and end on December 31st.

ARTICLE 6-CONFIDENTIALITY

6.1   The Executive shall not, either during the continuance of the Executive's contract hereunder or at any time after termination of the Executive as consultant to the Corporation, for any reason whatsoever (except in the proper course of carrying out the Duties, or otherwise required by law), divulge to any person whomsoever, and shall use the Executive's best endeavors to prevent the publication or disclosure of:

  6.1.1   Any confidential information concerning the business or finances of the Corporation or any other corporation, person or entity for which he is directed to perform services hereunder or of any of their dealings, transactions or affairs, including, without limitation, personal and family matters which may come to the Executive's knowledge during or in the course of the Executive's contract: or

  6.1.2   Any trade secrets, know-how, inventions, technology, designs, methods, formula, processes, copyrights, trade marks, trade mark applications, patents, patent applications or any other proprietary information and/or data of the Corporation (herein collectively called "Intellectual Property").

ARTICLE 7 - INVENTIONS AND PATENTS

7.1   If the Executive contributes to any invention whether patentable, patented, or not (an "Invention"), any intellectual property, or any improvement or modification to any Invention or intellectual property then the Executive's contribution thereto and the Invention, intellectual property or improvement thereof shall, without the payment of any additional compensation in any form whatsoever, become the exclusive property of the Corporation. The Executive shall execute any and all agreements, assurances or assignments that the Corporation may require and the Executive shall fully cooperate with the Corporation in the filing and prosecution of any patent applications. The Executive hereby reiterates and confirms the application of this Article to all such Inventions, intellectual property and improvements that have been made during the tenancy of that certain consulting position with the Corporation's subsidiaries.

ARTICLE 8- RESTRICTIVE COVENANT

8.1   The Executive will not at any time during the Term, or during any renewal thereof, and for a period of two (2) years following the expiration or termination of the Executive's contract for whatever cause, compete in the United States, directly or indirectly, with any of the businesses carried on by the Corporation, its subsidiaries or affiliates:

CORPORATE RESOLUTION, 08/01/2004

8.1.1 As a principal, partner employee;

8.1.2 As an officer, director or similar official of any incorporated or unincorporated entity engaged in any such competing business (the "Other Entity");

8.1,3 As a consultant or advisor to any Other Entity;

8.1.4 As a holder of shares or debt instrument of any kind of any Other Entity;

8.1.5 In any relationship described in subsections 81.1 through 8.1.4 of this section with any incorporated or unincorporated entity which provides services for or necessarily incidental to the business of an Other Entity:

without the prior express written consent of the Corporation, which consent may be withheld by the Corporation for any reason or for no reason.

8.2   Notwithstanding the provisions of Article 8.3 below, the Executive acknowledges and agrees that the time frames for which the aforesaid covenant shall apply have been considered by the Executive who has taken independent legal advice with respect thereto and the restraint and restriction of and on the future activities of the Executive are reasonable in the circumstances.

8.3   The parties agree that if the time frames set out in this Article are found to unenforceable by a court of competent jurisdiction, the time frames will be amended to the time frames as established by a court of competent jurisdiction.

3.4   The Executive acknowledges that any breach of Articles 6, 7 & 8 will cause irreparable harm to the Corporation, for which the Corporation cannot be compensated by damages. The Executive agrees that in the event of a breach of the covenant contained in Articles 6, 7, & 8, the Corporation shall not be restricted to seeking damages only, but shall be entitled to injunctive and other equitable relief.

ARTICLE 9- TERMINATION OF CONTRACT

9.1   The Corporation may terminate this Agreement at any time for cause. The term "for cause" shall include any one or more of the following:

9.1.1 A significant and continuing breach or failure or a continual breaching or failing to observe any of the provisions herein;

9.1.2 An act of dishonesty fundamentally detrimental to the well-being of the Corporation;

9.1.3 Any act of gross negligence relating to completing the Duties;

9.1.4 The commission of a felony offence for which the Executive is convicted, which significantly impairs the Executive's ability to perform the Duties and responsibilities hereunder or which materially adversely affects the reputation enjoyed by the Corporation; or

9.1.5 The failure to comply with reasonable instructions, orders and directions of the Board of Directors of the Corporation in so far as such instructions, orders and directions are not inconsistent with the Duties, or are, in the reasonable opinion of the Executive:

9.1.5.1   In any way demeaning or likely to result in diminution of the value of the Executives services in the future.

9.1.5.2   Likely to result in the conduct of an illegal act.

9.1.5.3   Inconsistent with any court order or other governmental order or directive.

9.1.5.4   Inconsistent with any shareholders' resolution passed at any duly convened meeting of shareholders.

9.1.6   In the event Executive shall be denied entry into the United States by the Immigration authorities of the United States and such inability to be physically present in the offices of the Corporation in Chandler, Arizona shall exist for a period of thirty (30) days or more.

provided that, with respect to each 9.1.1 through 9.1.5 (but not 9.1.6) above, the Executive shall be given written notification of any such alleged breach and provided a reasonable opportunity to respond thereto. For greater certainty, the Corporation shall not be entitled to utilize any such provision to terminate this Agreement in respect of any action by the Executive that was: (i) specifically required to be performed by direction of the board, directly or indirectly (ii) the dissemination of information required to be reported in the normal course with the Securities and Exchange Commission or any other competent governmental entity having jurisdiction over the Executive or the Corporation, or (iii) honestly and faithfully performed by the Executive for the benefit of the Corporation.

9.2   In the event that the Executive becomes physically or mentally disabled and is unable to perform the Duties for a period of twelve (12) months, as confirmed by a doctor's certificate, the Corporation shall be entitled to terminate this Agreement without further compensation upon sixty (60) days written notice to the Executive. In the case of the death of the Executive, all obligations of the Corporation under this Agreement shall cease immediately; provided that, this provision shall not affect any right, benefit or entitlement accruing to the Executive and/or his estate under any of the Corporation's benefit plans or stock option agreements which arise as a result of the Executive's prior performance hereunder or his death.

9.3   The Executive may terminate this Agreement, and the contract created herein, by giving at least Ninety (90) days prior written notice of such intention to the Corporation. After the expiry of such notice, all obligations, except for the obligations of the Executive under Articles 6, 7 and 8 hereof, which shall continue as provided in those Articles, of the Corporation and the Executive under this Agreement shall cease.

ARTICLE 10-OTHER AGREEMENTS IN RESPECT OF TERMINATION

10.1   In the event of the termination of this Agreement for cause or otherwise howsoever:

10.1.1   The Executive shall resign as a director and/or officer of the Corporation or any subsidiary or related corporation and the Executive hereby appoints the Corporation as its attorney in fact for the purpose of executing any and all such documents to give effect to the foregoing; and

10.1.2   The Executive hereby authorizes the Corporation and any subsidiary or related corporation to set off against and deduct from any and all amounts owing to the Executive by way of salary, allowances, accrued leave, long service leave, reimbursements or any other emoluments or benefits owing to the Executive by the Corporation and any subsidiary or related corporation, any reasonable amounts owed by the Executive to the Corporation or any subsidiary or related corporation.

10.2   Notwithstanding any termination of this Agreement for any reason whatsoever, whether with or without cause, all of the provisions of Articles 6, 7 and 8 and any other provisions of this Agreement necessary to give efficacy and effect thereto shall continue in full force and effect following the termination of this Agreement.

ARTICLE 11 - GENERAL

11.1   This Agreement, and the Schedules attached hereto, constitute the entire agreement between the parties hereto and cancels, supersedes and replaces all previous written, verbal or implied terms, conditions and representations relating to the Executive's contract.

11.2   The failure of either party at any time to require strict performance by the other party of any provision hereof shall in no way affect the full right to require such performance at any time thereafter. Neither shall the waiver by either party of a breach of any provision hereof be taken or held to be a waiver of any succeeding breach of such provision or as a waiver of the provision itself.

11.3   Each article, paragraph, clause, sub-clause and provision of this Agreement shall be severable from each other and if for any reason any article, paragraph, clause, sub-clause or provision is invalid or unenforceable, such invalidity or unenforceability shall not prejudice or in any way affect the validity or enforceability of any other article, paragraph, clause, sub-clause or provision. This Agreement and each article, paragraph, clause, sub-clause and provision hereof shall be read and construed so as to give thereto the full effect thereof subject only to any contrary provision of the law to the extent that where this Agreement or any article, paragraph, clause, sub-clause or provision hereof would but for the provisions of this paragraph have been read and construed as being void or ineffective, it shall nevertheless be a valid agreement, article, paragraph, clause, sub-clause or provision as the case may be to the full extent to which it is not contrary to any provision of the law.

11.4   The parties hereto submit to the exclusive jurisdiction of the Courts of the State of Arizona in respect of any matter or thing arising out of this Agreement or pursuant thereto.

11.5   All notices to be given by either party hereto shall be delivered or sent by telegram, facsimile or cable to the following address or such other address as may be notified by either party:

    11.5.1 If to the Corporation to:

> Tankless Systems Worldwide, Inc.
> 7650 E. Evans Rd. Suite C
> Scottsdale, AZ 85260   Attention: Secretary

    11.5.2 If to the Executive to:

> Gregg C. Johnson
> Johnson Address

11.6   This Agreement shall ensure to the benefit of and be binding upon the parties hereto, their heirs, administrators, successors and legal representatives. This Agreement may be assigned by the Corporation but may not be assigned by the Executive.

IN WITNESS WHEREOF, the parties have duly executed this Agreement.

TANKLESS SYSTEMS WORLDWIDE, INC.

Per: _____

SIGNED, SEALED AND DELIVERED in the)
Presence of:)
)
)   _____
)   **Gregg C. Johnson**
)
)
_____   )
Witness

Schedule A

Duties
(as taken from the SKYE Organizational Manual)

Title:	To Be Determined
Reports to:	President and Chief Executive Officer or such other Officer as the Board of Directors shall determine
Direct Reports:	To Be Determined
Liaison:	Chairman of Board
Chairman of all Board Committees
Job Description:	As Determined by the Board of Directors
Review & Comp	Corporate Governance Committee
Accountability:	Board of Directors, President and CE)

This position is as a member of the Executive Management Team and is the final responsible party for all business day-to-day planning and operations of the company.

The specific duties include, but are not limited to:

1.   Together with the Executive Management Team, directs overall business and organizational policies; develops, recommends and implements through subordinates; recommends annual and long-term company policies and goals to Board of Directors.

CORPORATE RESOLUTION, 08/01/2004   **PAGE 9**

PDOCS000659

2. Responsible for overall company financial, organizational and operational planning activities and growth.

3. Member of the Management Team, responsible for approving budgetary and operational objectives, overseeing and reporting progress to the Board of Directors.

4. Monitoring performance relative to established objectives and systematically monitor and evaluate operating results.

5. Presents, together with the CFO, Balance sheet, operating and capital expenditure budgets to Board of Directors for approval.

6. Formulates the Corporation's near term and long-range strategic plans and submits them to the Board of Directors for approval.

7. Directs executives in matters concerning the development, production, promotion and sales of the Corporation's products.

8. Promoting positive relations with customers, suppliers and the general public.

9. Directs the establishment of fair and appropriate policies for human resource management.

10. Responsible for the overall strategic management of the Corporation.

11. Responsible for the daily affairs of the Corporation.

12. Responsible for ensuring operational compliance with policies and procedures adopted by the Board of Directors.

13. Primary responsible party for ensuring systemic adherence to Compliance and Ethics mandate.

13. Together with Board members and the CFO is responsible for all capital fundraising requirements of the company.

14. Directs, oversees and manages all external contacts with parties involved with funding the capital requirements of the company.

15. Responsible for making all public representations in connection with investor relations activities.

16. Together with the Chairman is responsible for all presentations of material to the public.

17. Any other duty reasonably assigned by the Board of Directors

Schedule B

Resale Restrictions

The Executive confirms and acknowledges that there are resale restrictions in respect of those Seven Hundred & Fifty Thousand (750,000) common shares of the Corporation (the "Shares") issued to the Executive in connection with his consultancy to the Corporation and by operation of this Agreement. The resale restrictions imposed under this Agreement and this Schedule are in addition to any other resale restriction that may be applicable by operation of state or federal securities laws.

The Shares shall be subject to a contractual restriction prohibiting the sale, transfer, hypothecation, pledge or other disposition until such shares are eligible for release from this contractual restriction in accordance with the Schedule set forth below.

The Executive shall be entitled to the release of this contractual resale restriction in respect of the Shares by the passing of time and/or active engagement with the Corporation as a consultant or officer thereof. Specifically, the resale restrictions imposed by this Schedule shall be removed in accordance with the following release schedule:

(A)   While employed by or consulting to the Corporation:

1.   On September 1, 2004   250,000 shares

2.   On September 1, 2005   250,000 shares

3.   On September 1, 2006   250,000 shares

(B)   Otherwise:

11.   One Hundred Thousand (100,000) shares for each year from and after September 1, 2004.

For greater certainty, the Executive shall not be entitled to combine the release criteria above so as to result in the accelerated release of such Shares beyond the maximum release schedule specified in category "A" above.

Thomas Kreitzer

From:	Gregg Johnson [gregg.johnson@skye-betterliving.com]
Sent:	Wednesday, May 24, 2006 1:27 PM
To:	'Thomas Kreitzer'
Subject:	RE: Corporate Resolution Johnson Agreement
Follow Up Flag:	Follow up
Flag Status:	Green

Thank you Thomas. I think we are making real progress in the defense of this case. The audit is going well too.

Gregg

From: Thomas Kreitzer [mailto:Thomas@KreitzerBrothers.com]
Sent: Wednesday, May 24, 2006 1:24 PM
To: 'Gregg Johnson'
Subject: Corporate Resolution Johnson Agreement

Gregg,

Here is the resolution.

Let me know if you need anything else.

Thomas

--
No virus found in this outgoing message.
Checked by AVG Free Edition.
Version: 7.1.392 / Virus Database: 268.6.0/342 - Release Date: 5/17/2006

--
No virus found in this incoming message.
Checked by AVG Free Edition.
Version: 7.1.392 / Virus Database: 268.6.0/342 - Release Date: 5/17/2006

PDOCS000663

9/19/2006

EXHIBIT 18

Bibliography

ARTICLES

A $2.2 Billion Charge at Broadcom, N.Y. TIMES, Jan. 23, 2007.

Bulkeley, William L., *Ex-CA Chief Kumar Agrees To Pay $52 Million in Restitution*, N.Y. TIMES, Apr. 13, 2007.

Bulkeley, William L., *Kumar Is Sentenced to 12 Years For Role in CA Accounting Fraud*, WSJ.COM, Nov. 2, 2006.

Carbine, James E. & Lynn McLain, *Proposed Model Rules Governing the Admissibility of Computer-Generated Evidence*, 15 SANTA CLARA COMPUTER & HIGH TECH. L.J. 1, 15 (1999).

Closen, Michael L., *The Public Official Role of the Notary*, 30 J. MARSHALL L. REV. (1998).

Conviction in Backdating Case, N.Y. TIMES, Dec. 6, 2007: http://www.nytimes.com/2007/12/06/business/06fund.html?ref=business.

Dash, Eric, *Former Chief Will Forfeit $418 Million*, N.Y. TIMES, Dec. 7. 2007: http://www.nytimes.com/2007/12/07/business/07options.html?_r=1&adxnnl=1&oref=slogin&adxnnlx=1197230886-I8TZd9luf//YqsIrd3Q4aQ.

Dash, Eric & Matt Richtel, *Ex-Brocade Chief Convicted in Backdating Case*, N.Y. TIMES, Aug. 8, 2007: http://www.nytimes.com/2007/08/08/business/08brocade.html?adxnnl=1&adxnnlx=1197232159-zaMvjldS47qZ/7e+w/n5AA.

de la Merced, Michael J., *Ex-Leader of Computer Associates Gets 12-Year Sentence and Fine*, N.Y. TIMES, Nov. 3, 2006.

Delivering Mortgages in the Electronic Age: The Case for a Central Electronic Mortgage Note Registration System as a Vehicle for Complying with the UETA and E-SIGN Safe Harbor (Mar. 8, 2002), *available at* http://www.efscouncil.org/frames/Forum%20Members/Fannie_RegistryWhitePaper.doc.

Diffie, Whitfield & Martin Helman, *New Directions in Cryptography*, IEEE TRANSACTIONS ON INFORMATION THEORY IT-22, no. 6 (1976).

Elliott, Karla J., *The Notarial Seal – The Last Vestiges of Notaries Past*, 31 J. MARSHALL L. REV. 903 (1998).

Federal Financial Institutions Examination Council (FFIEC), Authentication in an Internet Banking Environment (Oct. 13, 2005), *available at* http://www.ffiec.gov/ffiecinfobase/resources/info_sec/2006/frb-sr-05-19.pdf.

Fisher, George, *The Jury's Rise of Lie Detector*, 107 YALE L. J. 575 (1997).

Forelle, Charles, *Broadcom Sees Bigger Options Hit,* WALL ST. J., Sept. 9, 2006, at A-3.

Forelle, Charles & James Bandler, *Dating Game—Stock-Options Criminal Charge: Slush Fund and Fake Employees,* WALL ST. J., Aug. 10, 2006, at A-1.

Gallanis, Thomas P., *The Rise of Modern Evidence Law,* 84 IOWA L. REV. 499 (1999).

Gard, Spencer A., *The New Uniform Rules of Evidence,* 2 KAN. L. REV. 333 (1954).

Justice Department's Word on Electronically-Created Evidence, CRIM. PRAC. GUIDE, Mar. 2001.

Kerr, Orin S., U.S. Dept. of Justice, U.S.A. Bull. Vol. 49, No. 2, *Computer Records and the Federal Rules of Evidence* (2001), *available at* http://www.usdoj.gov/criminal/cybercrime/usamarch2001_4.htm.

Stanley A. Kurzban, *Authentication of Computer-Generated Evidence in the United States Federal Courts,* 35 IDEA 437 (1995).

Langbein, John H., *Historical Foundations of the Law of Evidence: A View from the Ryder Sources,* 96 COLUM. L. REV. 1168.

Langbein, John H., *On the Myth of Written Constitutions: The Disappearance of Criminal Jury Trial,* 15 HARV. J. L. & PUB. POL'Y 119 (1992).

Losey, Ralph C., *Hash: The New Bates Stamp,* 12 JOURNAL OF TECHNOLOGY LAW & POLICY (June 2007).

Mason, Stephen, *Electronic Signatures in Practice,* 6 J. HIGH TECH L. 149 (2006).

Michael, Jerome & Mortimer J. Adler, *Real Proof,* 5 VAND. L. REV. 344 (1952).

Nearon, Bruce H. et al., *The Merger of Information Security and Accountability,* 45 JURIMETRICS J.

Nelson, Leonard J., *Garbage In, Garbage Out: The Need for New Approaches to Computer Evidence,* 9 AM. J. TRIAL ADVOC. 411 (1985).

Paul, George L., *The "Authenticity Crisis" in Real Evidence,* 15 PRAC. LITIGATOR No. 6 (2004).

Paul, George L. & Jason R. Baron, *Information Inflation: Can The Legal System Adapt?* 13 RICH J. L & TECH 10 (2007).

Peritz, Rudolph J., *Computer Data and Reliability: A Call for Authentication of Business Records Under the Federal Rules of Evidence,* 80 NW. L. REV. 956 (1986).

Report of Committee on Administration of Justice on Model Code of Evidence, 19 CALIF. ST. B.J. 262 (1944).

Roberts, Jerome, *A Practitioner's Primer on Computer-Generated Evidence,* 41 U. CHI. L. REV. 254 (1973).

Robertson, Jordan, *Brocade Exec Guilty in Stock Option Case,* WIRED.COM, Dec. 6, 2007.

Romano, Leah Voigt, Note, *Electronic Evidence and the Federal Rules,* 38 LOY. L.A. L. REV. 1745 (2005).

The Sedona Conference Best Practices Commentary on the Use of Search & Information Retrieval Methods in E-Discovery, SEDONA CONFERENCE JOURNAL (2007).

Sherry, Keith D., cmt., *Old Treaties Never Die, They Just Lose Their Teeth: Authentication Needs of a Global Community Demand Retirement of the Hague Public Documents Convention,* 31 J. MARSHALL L. REV. 1045 (1998).

Singer, Paula Noyes, *Proposed Changes to the Federal Rules of Evidence as Applied to Computer-Generated Evidence,* 7 RUT. J. COMPUTERS, TECH. & L. 157 (1979–80).

Smedinghoff, Thomas J. & Ruth Hill Bro, *Moving with Change: Electronic Signature Legislation as a Vehicle for Advancing E-Commerce,* 17 J. MARSHALL J. COMPUTER & INFORMATION LAW 723 (1999).

Swift, Eleanor, *One Hundred Years of Evidence Law Reform: Thayer's Triumph,* 88 CALIF. L. REV 2437 (2000).

Wigmore, John Henry, *The American Law Institute Code of Evidence Rules: A Dissent,* 1942, 28 A.B.A.J.

Wigmore, John Henry, *The Spark That Kindled the White Flame of Progress,* 20 J. AM. JUD. SOC'Y 176 (1937).

Adam Wolfson, Note,*"Electronic Fingerprints": Doing Away With the Conception of Computer-Generated Records as Hearsay,* 104 MICH L. REV. 151 (2005).

BOOKS

ABA Subcommittee on eTrust: eNW Whitepaper on eNotarization (American Bar Association, 2006).

American Heritage Science Dictionary (2002).

Benichou, David, & Ariane Zimra, *France, in* STEPHEN MASON, ED., ELECTRONIC EVIDENCE (British Institute of International and Comparative Law, 2008).

BERNERS-LEE, TIM, WEAVING THE WEB: THE ORIGINAL DESIGN AND ULTIMATE DESTINY OF THE WORLD WIDE WEB BY ITS INVENTOR (Harper San Francisco 1990).

BLACK'S LAW DICTIONARY (8th ed. 2004).

BUCKLEY, JEREMIAH S., JOHN P. KROMER, MARGO H. K. TANK & R. DAVID WHITAKER, THE LAW OF ELECTRONIC SIGNATURES AND RECORDS (Glasser LegalWorks 2004).

CAMPBELL-KELLY, MARTIN & WILLIAM ASPRAY, COMPUTER: A HISTORY OF THE INFORMATION MACHINE (1996).

CLEARY, EDWARD W., McCORMACK ON EVIDENCE (3rd ed. 1984).

CLOSEN, MICHAEL L., ET AL., NOTARY LAW & PRACTICE: CASES AND MATERIALS (Nat'l Notary Ass'n 1997).

CORBIN, ARTHUR LINTON, CONTRACTS (one-volume ed. 1952).

Dervieux, Valérie, *The French System, in* MIREILLE DELMAS-MARTY & J. R SPENCER, EUROPEAN CRIMINAL PROCEDURES (Cambridge University Press, 2006).

Diffie, Whitfield, *The First Ten Years of Public Key Cryptology, in* CONTEMPORARY CRYPTOLOGY: THE SCIENCE OF INFORMATION INTEGRITY 136–75 (Gustavus J. Simmons ed., IEEE Press, 1992).

DIGITAL SIGNATURE GUIDELINES (American Bar Association 1996).

DIRINGER, DAVID, THE ALPHABET: A KEY TO THE HISTORY OF MANKIND (3rd ed., rev. 2 vol. 1968).

Duisberg, Dr. Alexander & Dr. Henriette Picot, *Germany, in* STEPHEN MASON, ED., ELECTRONIC EVIDENCE (British Institute of International and Comparative Law, 2008).

DURFEE, WALTER, ALPHABETICS AS A SCIENCE (1956).

Eßer, Dr. Martin, *Germany, in* STEPHEN MASON, ELECTRONIC SIGNATURES IN LAW (Tottel, 2nd edn, 2007).

FAERBER, CHARLES N., 2006–2007 U.S. NOTARY REFERENCE MANUAL (Nat'l Notary Ass'n 2006).

FRIEDMAN, THOMAS L., THE WORLD IS FLAT: A BRIEF HISTORY OF THE TWENTY-FIRST CENTURY (Farrar, Straus, and Giroux 2005).

GAUR, ALBERTINE, A HISTORY OF WRITING (1984).

GILBERT, LORD GEOFFREY, THE LAW OF EVIDENCE (3rd ed. 1769).

GREENWOOD, DANIEL J., ELECTRONIC NOTARIZATION: WHY IT'S NEEDED, HOW IT WORKS, AND HOW IT CAN BE IMPLEMENTED TO ENABLE GREATER TRANSACTIONAL SECURITY (Nat'l Notary Ass'n 2006).

GRÜTBLER, ARNULF, TECHNOLOGY AND GLOBAL CHANGE (Cambridge University Press 1998).

HAFNER, KATIE & MATHEW LYON, WHERE WIZARDS STAY UP LATE: THE ORIGINS OF THE INTERNET (Simon & Schuster 1990).

HANDBOOK FOR MD NOTARIES PUBLIC (MD Sec'y of State 2006).

HARRIS, ROY, THE ORIGIN OF WRITING (1986).

HAZARD, PAUL, LA CRISE DE LA CONSCIENCE EUROPÉENE (Boivin 1935).

HAZARD, PAUL, THE EUROPEAN MIND; THE CRITICAL YEARS (1680–1715) (Yale University Press 1953).

HOYNINGEN-HUENE, PAUL, RECONSTRUCTING SCIENTIFIC REVOLUTIONS: THOMAS S. KUHN'S PHILOSOPHY OF SCIENCE (U. Chicago 1993).

Imwinkelried, Edward, *Evidence Law and Tactics for the Proponents of Scientific Evidence*, in SCIENTIFIC AND EXPERT EVIDENCE (E. Imwinkelried ed. 1981).

Juy-Birmann, Rodolphe, *The German System*, in MIREILLE DELMAS-MARTY & J. R SPENCER, EUROPEAN CRIMINAL PROCEDURES (Cambridge University Press, 2006).

Kaneko, Hironao & Hideo Ogura, *Japan*, in STEPHEN MASON, ED., ELECTRONIC EVIDENCE (British Institute of International and Comparative Law, 2008).

Kudryavtseva, Olga I., *Russia*, in STEPHEN MASON, ED., ELECTRONIC EVIDENCE (British Institute of International and Comparative Law, 2008).

LOCKE, JOHN, AN ESSAY CONCERNING HUMAN UNDERSTANDING (1689).

LOSEY, RALPH C., E-DISCOVERY, CURRENT TRENDS AND CASES (ABA 2008).

MASON, STEPHEN, ED., ELECTRONIC EVIDENCE: DISCLOSURE, DISCOVERY & ADMISSIBILITY (British Institute of International and Comparative Law, 2008).

MASON, STEPHEN, ELECTRONIC SIGNATURES IN LAW (Tottel, 2nd edn, 2007).

MCCORMICK'S HANDBOOK OF THE LAW OF EVIDENCE (2d ed. 1972).

MORGAN, EDMUND M., BASIC PROBLEMS OF EVIDENCE (1962).

Mumford, Lewis, *Technics and the Nature of Man* (1966), *reprinted in* CARL MITCHAM & ROBERT MACKEY (EDS.), PHILOSOPHY AND TECHNOLOGY *at* 77 (The Free Press 1972).

NATIONAL E-NOTARIZATION STANDARDS (Nat'l Ass'n of Secretaries of State 2006).

OHASHI, MITSUNAO, HI-TECH HANZAI SOSA-NYUMON SOSA-JITSUMU-HEN (Introduction to Investigation of Hi-Technology Crimes on Investigation Practice) (Tokyo-Horei 2005).

Pastor-Satorras, Romualdo & Alessandro Vespignani, Evolution and Structure of the Internet: A Statistical Physics Approach (Cambridge University Press 2005).

Paul, George L. & Bruce H. Nearon, The Discovery Revolution: E-Discovery Amendments to the Federal Rules of Civil Procedure (ABA 2006).

Paul, George L. & Jason R. Baron, *Information Inflation: Can the Legal System Adapt?,* 13 Rich. J.L. & Tech. 10 (2007).

Popper, Karl, Conjectures and Refutations: The Growth of Scientific Knowledge (5th ed. 1989).

Port, Kenneth L. & Gerald Paul McAlinn, Comparative Law and the Legal Process in Japan (Carolina Academic Press, 2nd edn, 2003).

Rice, Paul R., Electronic Evidence Law & Practice (American Bar Association 2005).

Rivolta, Dr. Mercedes & Dr. Pablo Fraga, *Argentina, in* Stephen Mason, ed., Electronic Evidence (British Institute of International and Comparative Law, 2008).

Saltzburg et al., Federal Rules of Evidence Manual (6th ed. 1994).

Saltzburg et al., Federal Rules of Evidence Manual (9th ed. 2006).

Spencer, J. R., Jackson's Machinery of Justice (8th ed. 1989).

Starkie, Thomas, Practical Treatise of the Law of Evidence (1824).

Thayer, James Bradley, A Preliminary Treatise on Evidence at the Common Law, 1–2 (Boston, Little Brown 1898).

Weinstein, Jack B. & Margaret A. Berger, Weinstein's Federal Evidence.

Wigmore, John, Evidence (1978).

Winn, Jane K. & Benjamin Wright, The Law of Electronic Commerce (4th ed. Aspen Publishers, Inc. 2007).

Wittgenstein, Ludwig, Philosophical Investigations (1953).

Wright, Charles A. & Kenneth W. Graham, Jr., Federal Practice and Procedure: Evidence (2d ed. 2005).

Wright, Ronald F. & Marc L. Miller, Federal Practice and Procedure (West, 1990).

AVAILABLE ONLINE

Adobe Systems, "PDF Reference, Sixth Edition, version 1.7," Adobe Systems, http://www.adobe.com/devnet/pdf/pdf_reference.html

International Organization for Standardization (ISO). The following standards are available through http://www.iso.org/:

- ISO 15930-1:2001, *Graphic technology—Prepress digital data exchange—Use of PDF—Part 1: Complete exchange using CMYK data (PDF/X-1 and PDF/X-1a)*
- ISO 19005-1. *Document management—Electronic document file format for long-term preservation—Part 1: Use of PDF (PDF/A)*
- ISO/DIS 24517, *Document management—Engineering document format using PDF—Part 1: Use of PDF 1.6 (PDF/E)*

World Wide Web Consortium (W3C). The following publications are available through the W3C Web site at http://www.w3.org/:
- Extensible Markup Language (XML) 1.1 http://www.w3.org/TR/xml11/
- HTML 4.01 Specification http://www.w3.org/TR/html401/

United Nations Commission on International Trade Law, "UNCITRAL Model Law on Electronic Signatures", UNCITRAL, http://www.uncitral.org/uncitral/en/uncitral_texts/electronic_commerce.html

Electronic Signatures In Global and National Commerce Act (ESIGN), http://frwebgate.access.gpo.gov/cgi-bin/getdoc.cgi?dbname=106_cong_public_laws&docid=f:publ229.106

Uniform Electronic Transactions Act (UETA), National Conference of State Legislatures, http://www.ncsl.org/programs/lis/CIP/ueta-statutes.htm

NIST's Special Publication 800-63 Electronic Authentication Guideline, National Institute of Science and Technology, http://csrc.nist.gov/publications/nistpubs/800-63/SP800-63V1_0_2.pdf

EU Directive 1999/93/EC on a Community framework for electronic signatures, http://www.signatur.rtr.at/en/repository/legal-directive-20000119.html

Internet Engineering Task Force (IETF) Requests for Comments (RFC) 3161, Internet X.509 Public Key Infrastructure Time-Stamp Protocol (TSP), http://www.rfc-editor.org

Title 21 Code of Federal Regulations (21 CFR Part 11), http://www.fda.gov/ora/compliance_ref/part11/

Table of Authorities

STATUTES AND RULES

1 Anne. Ch. 9 Section 3 (1702)

Arizona Electronic Act, A.R.S. Section 44-7014

Article IX of the Federal Rules of Evidence

Federal Advisory Committee Note to Subdivision (a) of Rule 901

Federal Advisory Committee Note to Subdivision (a) of Rule 901(b)(1), (b)(2), (b)(3), (b)(4), (b)(5), (b)(6), (b)(7), (b)(8), (b)(10)

Federal Business Records Act, 28 U.S.C. Section 1732.4

In the Matter of Robert C. Guccione, Admin. Proc. File No. 3-11800, Accounting and Auditing Enforcement Release No. 2174 (January 24, 2005)

Model Code of Evidence

Rule 104(a), Federal Rules of Evidence

Rule 702, Federal Rules of Evidence

Rule 803(6), Federal Rules of Evidence

Rule 902, Federal Rules of Evidence

Rule 1001(3), Federal Rules of Evidence

Rule 1001(3) of the Uniform Rules of Evidence

Signatures in Global and National Commerce Act of 2000 ("ESIGN")

The Treason Act of 1696

UCC Section 3-302

UCC Section 3-305(a)(1)

UETA § 12(d); 15 U.S.C.A. § 7001(d)(3)

Uniform Electronic Transactions Act (UETA), National Conference of State Legislatures

Uniform Rules of Evidence

11 U.S.C. Section 523(a)(2)(A)

15 U.S.C. Section 7002(a)(2)(A)(ii)

28 U.S.C. Section 1732(a) (1970)

15 U.S.C.A. § 7001(d)(1)(B)

TECHNICAL STANDARDS AND DEFINITIONS

C. Adams, et al. Internet X.509 Public Key Infrastructure Time Stamp Protocol (TSP) RFC 3161 (2001)

Adobe Systems, "PDF Reference, Sixth Edition, version 1.7," http://www.adobe.com/devnet/pdf/pdf_reference.html

ANSI Standard X9F4 9.95 (Trusted Timestamping)

ANSI Standard for Financial Services, X9.95-2005

Extensible Markup Language (XML) 1.1 at http://www.w3.org/TR/xmlll/

Glossary of the Internet Engineering Task Force's (IETF) at http://www.ietf.org/rfc/rfc2828.txt

HTML 4.01 Specification at http://www.w3.org/TR/html401/

Internet Engineering Task Force RFC 3161 (Trusted Timestamps)

ISO 15930-1:2001, Graphic technology—Prepress digital data exchange—Use of PDF—Part 1: Complete exchange using CMYK data (PDF/X-1 and PDF/X-1a)

ISO 19005-1, Document management—Electronic document file format for long-term preservation—Part 1: Use of PDF (PDF/A)

ISO/DIS 24517, Document management—Engineering document format using PDF—Part 1: Use of PDF 1.6 (PDF/E)

MERS˚ eRegistry, Procedures Manual, version 3.5 (June 4, 2007) ("eRegistry Procedures Manual") and MERS˚ eRegistry, PDF Guidelines (April 15, 2007), both available at http://www.mersinc.org/MersProducts/manuals.aspx?mpid=5

NIST Special Publication 800-12: Part IV Technical Controls, Chapter 16, Identification and Authentication

NIST's Special Publication 800-63 Electronic Authentication Guideline, National Institute of Science and Technology, http://csrc.nist.gov/publications/nistpubs/800-63/SP800-63V1_0_2.pdf

PCI Data Security Standards (DDS)

PCI Security Audit Procedures

World Wide Web Consortium (W3C)

Table of Cases

Index